Oxford A Level
Religious Studies
for OCR

Christianity, Philosophy and Ethics

AS and Year 1

Libby Ahluwalia • Robert Bowie

OXFORD
UNIVERSITY PRESS

OXFORD
UNIVERSITY PRESS

Great Clarendon Street, Oxford, OX2 6DP, United Kingdom

Oxford University Press is a department of the University of Oxford. It furthers the University's objective of excellence in research, scholarship, and education by publishing worldwide. Oxford is a registered trade mark of Oxford University Press in the UK and in certain other countries

British Library Cataloguing in Publication Data Data available

978-0-19-839285-9

10 9 8 7 6 5 4 3

Paper used in the production of this book is a natural, recyclable product made from wood grown in sustainable forests.

The manufacturing process conforms to the environmental regulations of the country of origin.

Printed in India by Manipal Technologies Ltd

Links to third party websites are provided by Oxford in good faith and for information only. Oxford disclaims any responsibility for the materials contained in any third party website referenced in this work.

Thank You

The publishers would like to thank Revd Dr Mark Griffiths and Philip Robinson, RE Adviser to the CES, for their guidance.

This resource is endorsed by OCR for use with specification H173 *AS Level Religious Studies* and H573 *A Level Religious Studies*. In order to gain OCR endorsement, this resource has undergone an independent quality check. Any references to assessment and/or assessment preparation are the publisher's interpretation of the specification requirements and are not endorsed by OCR. OCR recommends that a range of teaching and learning resources are used in preparing learners for assessment. OCR has not paid for the production of this resource, nor does OCR receive any royalties from its sale. For more information about the endorsement process, please visit the OCR website, www.ocr.org.uk.

Contents

Exam support

Introduction

Religious Studies is a fascinating subject at AS and A level. It will give you plenty to think about and help you sharpen up your skills in critical thinking, discussion and persuasive writing – all skills which will be of great benefit to you in later life, whether you choose to go on to further study or move into the world of work. The course should be enjoyed for its own sake. However, you will in all probability be taking exams at the end of it, and while these should not be the main motivation for your study, you will no doubt want to achieve the best grades that you can.

The exams are set and marked by an Awarding Body, so called because it is there to award you for all you have achieved during the course. Exams are not meant to be a punishment, so try not to fear them; they are meant to be an opportunity for you to demonstrate the knowledge you have gained and the skills you have acquired, so that you can be given a grade as an official reward in recognition of your achievements. This award will be something you can show to universities and to employers. A high grade in Religious Studies shows that you have skills which make you very employable, especially in careers which demand attention to detail, empathy with other people's views and the ability to argue fluently. People with qualifications in Religious Studies go on to a wide range of careers, such as law, the police and social services, health care professions, teaching, politics and journalism.

This chapter aims to give you some advice and ideas about ways in which you can work towards getting the best grade of which you are capable.

During the course

How AS and A level essays are assessed

This course can lead to a qualification either at AS level or at A level.

The questions on the exam paper will look similar whether you are studying for an AS or an A level

qualification: the difference between AS and A level standard lies in the way the essays are marked and the importance given to different skills.

Both exams assess your skills in two different areas, called Assessment Objectives (abbreviated to AO). At AS, AO1 and AO2 are equally weighted – in other words, they are each worth 50% of the marks. At A level, there is more weighting given to AO2 than to AO1. AO1 is worth 40% of the total marks, and AO2 is worth 60%.

AO1 tests your knowledge and understanding. To score highly in AO1, you need to have a thorough and accurate knowledge of your material, and you need to be able to demonstrate that you understand it, rather than that you can simply repeat your class notes. Showing you understand it involves things like:

- using it to support an argument

- being able to explain how one view differs from another

- being able to apply your knowledge in relation to a given question or situation

- choosing appropriate examples to support the points you make

- being able to select relevant information from the irrelevant

- being able to show how people arrived at their views

- being able to show how the ideas you are describing have been influential.

Candidates (people sitting exams) who include everything they know about a topic, regardless of the question, give the impression that they do not really understand how it works in different contexts. Being selective in the knowledge you present is a skill.

If you have been successful in AO1 in an essay, when I read it I will feel as if you have taught me the topic so that now I understand it myself. You will not have assumed that I already know what you are referring to, but you will have explained it to me. You will have given me helpful examples to clarify what you are saying, and you will have put the knowledge you present into a context.

AO2 tests your analytical and evaluative skills.
To score highly in AO2, you need to be able to reach a view on different issues and construct an argument in support of your views. Analysis means deconstructing an argument: showing, step-by-step, how a conclusion was reached. Evaluation means weighing up evidence and reasoning: showing why you think one view is more convincing than another. Being critical in your writing does not have to mean being negative. It means weighing up the view and pointing out its strengths and weaknesses, and reaching a reasoned opinion about it.

You need to be able to show that your own view is based on reasons; candidates who present the views of other people uncritically and then write 'I believe X' or 'I agree with Y' in their conclusions do not score highly for AO2 because a simple expression of preference for one perspective is not the same as an argument and does not require much skill.

You could think of this in terms of being asked by a friend to help her choose a dress for a summer wedding. She does not simply want you to point out the options; she can see those for herself. She certainly does not want you to say, 'there are lots of dresses and so there is not one right answer'. She wants your opinion, and your reasons. So you will tell her: the black dress fits well but a black dress isn't really suitable for a wedding; the yellow one doesn't suit your colouring at all; the blue one is a great colour on you but it costs three times your budget and the bridesmaids are wearing that colour; but the green one looks stunning, it's the right length and the neckline is perfect on you, and it's also on sale, so I think you should get the green one.

If you have been successful in AO2 in an essay, when I read it I will understand throughout the essay (not just at the end) what your answer is to the question you were set. If it asks 'How fair is the claim …' I will know whether you think it is entirely fair, only partly fair or not fair at all. If it asks 'Discuss …' I will know which different opinions could be held and, throughout the essay, which one you think is

convincing. I will not only know what you think, but why you think it, because you will have given me reasons to support your view and reasons why I should reject the alternatives.

Supplement your knowledge with further reading

One textbook will not be enough to give you sufficient knowledge and understanding for a very high grade. During the course, aim to read as widely as you can. Of course you will have time constraints when you are also studying other subjects (and want to have a life), but when you do get time, use the Enhance Your Learning feature at the end of each chapter to help you find other ways of extending your knowledge of the topic. If you are hoping to go on to study the subject further, at university level, you will find these suggestions particularly useful in finding things to read to enhance your university application.

Reading widely not only increases your knowledge and helps you to get high marks at AO1, it also gives you the opportunity to understand how people approach issues from different perspectives, when you read different writers who have their own differing opinions. Reading high-quality writing helps to improve your own writing style as you become more familiar with academic ways of expressing ideas. It also establishes good habits for further study, if supplementary reading becomes a normal part of your day.

Constructing an argument

Your skills in argument are essential for high marks in Religious Studies.

Some people struggle with the structure of essays in which they have to present an argument. There are many ways of approaching this, and many different structures which can work well.

Your essay should have an **introduction**. This does not need to be long. It should show you understand the question, put the issue under discussion into context, and establish the direction in which you plan to take the essay. Showing you understand the question in the introduction is very useful because it gives you the chance to pause and think about it, rather than giving in to the temptation to scribble as fast as possible (and sometimes only realise as you get to your conclusion that the question was asking something else). You don't have to state 'I am going to argue X' in your introduction; but it can be a very good idea to do so, as it reassures your examiner that you are going to have an argument, it helps you to have a clear direction in your mind as you begin, and if you do happen to run out of time, at least you did have something in your essay which established your own position.

The **main body of the essay** should be critical throughout. You will need to present different ideas and give them some critical assessment; don't save all your critical comment until the end, but comment on each view or point as you raise it. 'John Hick said … and this is very convincing because…'; 'Aquinas claimed … however, there are weaknesses in his view which …'. Use a new paragraph for each point you make. Your arguments will be more persuasive if you support them with examples.

If you have a firm opinion on an issue, one structure which can be effective is to start with the view you find least convincing. Explain it carefully, being fair to the people who hold that view, and then give your critical comment to say why you think it's wrong. Then move on to the view or views you find more convincing, explaining them carefully too, and show in your critical comment why you find them more persuasive.

If you find all of the different possibilities equally unconvincing, that is a legitimate position to hold and you are entitled to hold it. You still need to say why you find them equally unconvincing. With a question where you think the different ideas are quite equally balanced, you could structure it in such a way that you have 'argument–counterargument–argument–counterargument' all the way through, like a game of tennis.

In the main body of your essay, depending on the question of course, you could consider the implications of taking one view rather than another.

Your **conclusion** should follow naturally from the rest of your argument. It should not be the first time the reader hears about your opinion. It should summarise what you have said, underlining the reasons you have given.

Some people wonder whether it is acceptable to refer to yourself in the first person in an essay, saying 'I think' and 'in my opinion'. There are no rules about this. It can be a very useful way of making clear where you stand on an issue and demonstrating that you personally have engaged with the topic. However, if you prefer to avoid it, you can use expressions such as 'this seems unconvincing because … ' or 'a more persuasive view is …'. Whichever you choose, it won't affect your mark.

Interpreting marking schemes

Marking schemes for past papers become available online once a suitable time has passed. They can be very useful to consider when you are producing your own work, but they do need to be treated with caution. A marking scheme in Religious Studies is not a checklist. The examiner would not have looked through the mark scheme and deducted marks from essays which did not match it, or only awarded marks when a candidate guessed correctly. Instead, the mark schemes show 'indicative content'; they are the sorts of things candidates might have been expected to write in response to that question, but they are not prescriptive. Marking schemes sometimes refer to thinkers or ideas you have not studied. That is not a problem. It doesn't mean your teacher has not taught you well. You will have different examples to use, which will be equally valid.

Examiners' reports are also available online after exams, and these can be useful as they give an indication of the kinds of things examiners decided were good or less good features of candidates' answers. Find out the features they like and try and incorporate them into your own work.

As exams approach

Look after yourself

The first and most important rule for success at this stage in your life is to look after your own physical and mental health. This is even more important than any work you might do. Exam grades are important, but your health is even more important. You can look after your physical health by eating good food regularly, getting enough sleep, getting out in the fresh air every day and getting whatever kind of exercise you enjoy. Staying indoors at a desk and working all through the night while surviving on energy drinks and leftover junk food is not going to help you feel positive and on top of things as exams approach. You can look after your mental health by making sure you take regular breaks from work, have a sensible revision timetable rather than setting yourself impossible goals at the last minute, and spending at least some of your time with people who are not doing exams at the moment, to keep a sense of perspective.

Plan ahead, and try to deal with any health problems as they arise rather than leaving them to get worse because you feel too busy to address them: for example, if you suffer from hay fever every summer, in advance of the exam season try and find a treatment that works for you and doesn't make you drowsy. If you are feeling unwell, see a doctor sooner rather than later. If you are feeling uncomfortably stressed or miserable, talk to someone about it rather than keeping it to yourself.

Revision

This probably is not the first time you have taken exams, and you will already know what works well for you, whether it involves highlighter pens or flashcards or mind maps. As a reminder:

- Allow plenty of time. If you start your revision early, you can keep on top of it. February half-term is a good time to start getting your revision underway.

- Vary your routine. Revision is extremely boring for most people. Try to make it more fun by revising in different places, with friends and without friends, and use a range of techniques.

- Find somewhere quiet. If home life is too noisy for you to concentrate, use a library, a coffee shop or a friend's house.

- Take breaks. Make sure you have a decent break every couple of hours, and get outside if you can. A dog is a great revision aid: most people who

have one are usually very happy to loan them out for walks!

- Treat it like a job. One good technique for revision is to treat it as if you're going to work. Be washed and dressed and at your desk by nine, work through until lunch, with a short tea break. Then do the same in the afternoon, and finish for the day at five. You will be surprised by how much you can achieve.

- Don't try to predict the questions, and ignore those people and websites which pretend to know. You can waste hours on this, and it is a very dangerous gamble. Instead, spend the time learning the material.

- Practise your arguments as well as your factual knowledge. While you are revising, remember to practise articulating your views as well as learning a load of factual material. Try going through past questions and asking yourself of each one, what would I argue? What would my reasons be?

- Practise writing to time. This is a skill which takes practise, like running. The more you do it, the faster you will become.

- Pay attention to your teacher. When you write essays either during the course of the year or as practise for the exams, pay attention to the feedback you are given and remember it for the next time, so that you are always improving.

We wish you the very best of luck.

Studying philosophy of religion

Are there reasonable grounds for holding religious beliefs?

Can religious beliefs and teachings stand up to philosophical investigation?

Why study philosophy of religion?

Philosophy of religion can be quite difficult to define, as people have different views about what philosophy is, and also about what counts as a religion. It is usually understood to be a discipline which applies the methods and tools of philosophical inquiry to the subject matter of religion. These methods include rigorous questioning. A philosopher takes an idea, such as 'justice' or 'existence', holds it up to the light, looks at it closely and asks what it really means. A philosopher will look for any assumptions in the idea, whether obvious or hidden, and question whether it is reasonable to hold those assumptions. A philosopher will try to find counter-arguments and counter-examples to see whether the idea can still stand up, even if faced with criticisms.

Some people find the philosophy of religion quite difficult and challenging: not because the subject matter is academically demanding, but because it calls into question ideas and beliefs that might be very precious and important to them. Someone who has grown up with a firm faith in God might be uncomfortable when asked to justify the grounds for that belief and when presented with alternative, perhaps quite persuasive, arguments supporting an atheist position. People might also feel uncomfortable when they realise that they have been repeating words during worship for a long time but, when they think about it, they are not entirely sure what those words signify. Similarly, people who have been confident of the non-existence of God, or the wrongness of a belief system different from their own, might find it challenging to be presented with a religious belief or idea which makes a lot of sense or which sheds new light on something they had always rejected.

So why study philosophy of religion at all? The answer to this question, perhaps, is that religion deals with many of the most important questions of human existence, and, therefore, trying to find truthful, or at least reasonable, answers to such questions is an extremely valuable quest. Perhaps it is better not to hang on to a belief which does not stand up when challenged, or a belief which makes little coherent sense, however uncomfortable this might be. Perhaps ideas, doctrines and teachings which are alien to our usual ways of thinking should not be too readily dismissed.

What kinds of questions are addressed by the philosophy of religion?

The philosophy of religion looks at all kinds of aspects of religious belief and practice, through a philosophical lens. Probably the most fundamental question for philosophers of religion is the question of whether a God, or gods, exist at all. This also involves the exploration of other, related questions: what does it mean, for a God or gods, to 'exist'? Is it the same kind of existence that we have as humans? Is there, or could there be, any kind of existence beyond the existence of material things?

And then there are questions of what such a God, or gods, might be like: what are the attributes traditionally ascribed to God, and do they make sense, and are they compatible with each other? If we were looking for the existence of a God, or gods, how would we know when we had found what we were looking for? Should we expect a God, or gods, to allow humans and other animals to suffer?

Questions of the place of humanity in the world are also addressed by the philosophy of religion. Are human beings on the earth for any reason? Do human beings have any kind of fundamental value, beyond their importance to their family and friends? Are human beings any more than physical matter? Can human consciousness be satisfactorily explained? Does human suffering have any explanation or purpose? Can humans expect to continue in some way after their own death?

These questions, too, lead to further areas of exploration. Religious experience is a fascinating phenomenon, which invites consideration of the extent to which it has any evidential force, and whether it should be considered equally as reliable or unreliable as other kinds of human experience. The language used to convey religious ideas is also interesting to philosophers of religion, who ask whether it makes any sense to try to describe in ordinary, everyday terms the objects of beliefs in the supernatural and extraordinary.

Can the philosophy of religion provide firm answers to its questions?

Studying philosophy of religion might leave you with more questions and less certainty than you had when you began. Philosophy does not often, if at all, lead people to single, conclusive, firm answers to the questions it raises. However, as a discipline it does develop valuable thinking skills, equipping people with a greater ability to make judgements, to be more precise in their thoughts and the language they use, to be less willing to accept the views of others without challenging them, and to develop their own ideas, which will be more robust and capable of being defended.

Chapter 1.1

Ancient philosophical influences

Who were Plato and Aristotle?

How did Plato and Aristotle understand the nature of reality?

What is the point of thinking philosophically?

How did Christianity come to shape its doctrines using ideas from ancient Greek thought?

Key Terms

Forms: a name Plato gave to ideal concepts

Reason: using logical steps and thought processes in order to reach conclusions

Rationalist: someone who thinks that the primary source of knowledge is reason

Empiricist: someone who thinks that the primary source of knowledge is experience gained through the five senses

Prime Mover: Aristotle's concept of the ultimate cause of movement and change in the universe

Socratic method: the method of philosophical reasoning which involves critical questioning

Analogy: a comparison between one thing and another in an attempt to clarify meaning

Transcendent: being beyond this world and outside the realms of ordinary experience

Dualism: the belief that reality can be divided into two distinct parts, such as good and evil, or physical and non-physical

Aetion: an explanatory factor, a reason or cause for something

Telos: the end, or purpose, of something

Theist: someone who believes in a God or gods

Specification requirements

The philosophical views of Plato in relation to:

- Understanding of reality
- The Forms
- The Analogy of the Cave

The philosophical views of Aristotle in relation to:

- Understanding of reality
- The four causes
- The Prime Mover

Introduction

Plato and Aristotle were philosophers from ancient Greece who have had a profound influence on the development of Christian doctrine, Christian philosophy and Christian ethics, as well as on other world religions and philosophies. They explore ideas about how we can gain true knowledge and about the nature of wisdom. They consider questions about God and about whether there might be another reality beyond the physical world.

Plato was convinced that this world is only an imitation of another, much greater reality. In his view, this world is constantly changing and cannot, therefore, be the object of true knowledge; he thought that there must be another realm where things are eternal and unchanging, a world beyond this one, which he understood to be the realm of the **Forms**. He thought we could gain knowledge of this world primarily through the use of our **reason,** and he is therefore known as a **rationalist**.

Aristotle, in contrast, believed that the physical world around us can give us a great deal of information. He was fascinated by science and thought that sense experience was the primary way to gain knowledge. Aristotle is therefore known as an **empiricist**.

The thinking of Plato and Aristotle was part of the culture and education of those who wrote the New Testament, and so ancient Greek concepts were used to help shape and communicate Christian ideas for the first believers.

How have ancient Greek ideas become influential for the Christian philosophy of religion?

Much of the philosophy of religion as we know it today has come from Western traditions, and because of the culture in which it grew, it has usually concentrated on the beliefs of Christianity. Ideas from Greek philosophy greatly influenced the writers of the New Testament, because the writers were raised in the context of Greek culture, even though they were living in Israel.

For a long time before the birth of Jesus, Israel had been a Jewish nation, worshipping only one God and following (or disobeying) the commandments given to the people by Moses at the time of the Exodus. However, Israel was, and still is, located at a key point for trade routes, forming a land bridge between continents, and throughout its history it has very rarely been at peace. Whenever a nation in the Near East rose to power, its rulers wanted Israel.

Alexander the Great of Greece (356–323BC) was no exception. Alexander was one of the most successful military leaders in the whole of history, and although he probably never visited Jerusalem, the leaders of the city were quick to pay tribute to him when he established his empire. Alexander had been tutored by the great Greek philosopher Aristotle, and raised in Greek culture, so when his armies moved into Israel, Greek culture became predominant. The Jews were allowed to continue practising their own religion and keeping to their own customs as long as they did not cause trouble, and many of them still preferred to speak in their own language, but Greek became the language of the educated classes. Coins were imprinted with bilingual mottos, in both Hebrew and Greek; Greek manners, Greek traditions and Greek ways of thinking spread through the whole of society, and although some Jews held fast to their ancient laws without making many concessions at all to a different way of life, there were others who managed to combine Greek culture with biblical religion, and of course, others who abandoned the Jewish faith altogether in favour of the Greek gods.

The earliest Christians, therefore, were people whose whole way of understanding the world had been shaped by Greek thinking. It was natural that when they embraced the Christian faith and began to establish the first churches, they tried to clarify their understanding of belief in the philosophical terms they had learned from the Greeks. They adopted concepts from Plato and from Aristotle when they conceptualised, expressed and explained ideas about the nature of God, the soul, life after death and morality; but sometimes, these concepts did not quite fit with the ideas and imagery of the Bible.

Those who were trying to work out the main principles of Christian beliefs in the earliest days of the religion had to try and answer some difficult questions.

- Are there reasonable, logical grounds for believing that God exists? Can these beliefs stand up to the sort of philosophical questioning that Socrates was famous for employing?

- If God is eternal, unchanging and outside time (using Plato's understanding of what it means to be perfect), then can God change his mind, respond to prayers and events in this temporal world? Can God come to earth as a human, and if so, what could that mean – could a physical, changeable human person also be perfect?

- Are we, as humans, essentially physical beings, inseparable from the matter from which we are made (as Aristotle might have argued)? Or is there some kind of separate, essential self or soul (as Plato suggested) which is capable of living on after death, perhaps in a different world from this one?

- How far is God involved in this world, and in what ways? Is the God of Christianity like the **Prime Mover** as described by Aristotle, unmoveable and unchangeable and remote? Can the God of the Bible, who 'walks with' people, speaks to them, answers their prayers and becomes incarnate in Jesus, also be this omnipotent creator?

In order to gain a better understanding of the different ways in which Christians and others have tackled such questions, it is necessary to explore some of the key ideas of the ancient Greeks, and in particular, the ideas of Plato and Aristotle. Aristotle was taught by Plato, and Plato in turn was taught by Socrates and, therefore, it makes sense to begin with an introduction to Socratic thinking and methods.

See Chapter 1.2 for more on ideas about the relation between the soul and the body.

Socrates

Socrates (470–399BC) is often considered to be the founder of the kind of philosophy that we have today, because his teaching was the first to encourage a critical questioning of commonly held assumptions. Before Socrates, there were lots of interesting ideas circulating, which offered different ways of understanding the world (from philosophers aptly known as the pre-Socratics), but there seemed to be no way of knowing which, if any, was right. What was needed, Socrates felt, was a critical method of uncovering the truth. People needed to be trained to look beneath surface appearances and learn how to ask questions, how to challenge their own assumptions, how to recognise the difference between knowledge and opinion, and how to form judgements.

One of the key features of Socrates' teaching was his habit of using questions to help find the answer to a problem. He would take a concept, such as 'justice' and try to work out what we actually mean by it, rather

Socrates believed that people needed to be trained to think philosophically and challenge superficial assumptions, if they were to form sound judgements

It has been said that all philosophy since Plato has its roots in the questions he raised

Socrates was put to death with poisonous hemlock after he was found guilty of corrupting the young and not believing in the Greek gods

than assuming that everyone has a common understanding of what justice is about. Having questioned and clarified it, he would then be more able to consider problems such as how a country should be run. Socrates did not assume that he knew all the answers, but thought it was important that people should recognise the limitations of their own knowledge and be prepared to accept that there might not be any final, definitive solutions. He did not only use questions to clarify, but also to challenge. Sometimes, Socrates used questioning as a way of exposing ignorance; his questioning sometimes forced people to admit that they did not really know what they were talking about, or that their views did not make sense. He was known as a 'gadfly' by some: an insect which although small can cause immense irritation to a horse. Eventually Socrates was arrested and put to death, much to Plato's horror.

Plato

Plato is regarded by many as the greatest philosopher who ever lived, and it has been said that all other philosophy is simply 'footnotes to Plato' – people commenting on questions that were originally raised by Plato. Of course, Plato did not cover every topic of philosophical investigation, or give definitive answers to all questions about the meaning of life, but the issues that he raised are issues which still divide thinkers today. His writing is clear, interesting and accessible; many people think that Plato's work is the finest of all surviving Greek literature.

Plato came from an aristocratic Athenian family, whose members were closely involved in politics and who had some quite decided views. Plato was still a relatively young man, probably in his early thirties, when Socrates died, and the death had a profound effect on him.

After Socrates' death, Plato began to write, as a way of keeping the memory of Socrates alive and as a way of defending him against those who tried to spread rumours to discredit his memory. Plato also left Athens for a while on a series of not altogether successful visits to other countries. When he returned to Greece, he used the money he had acquired to found a school called the Academy, where he taught both male and female students until his death at the age of 81.

Plato and the Theory of Forms

One of Plato's best-known ideas is his Theory of Forms. Plato noticed (along with other philosophers before him and since) that the physical world is always changing, and that nothing ever stays the same. Even apparently static, solid objects are changing in ways that might not be immediately visible to our senses. They are growing or decaying, becoming scratched or stained, fading in the sun or darkening with age, getting warmer or cooling down … for Plato, this presented a problem. How could people attain true and certain knowledge, if the objects they wanted to know about were never the same from one moment to the next? As soon as people thought they had understood something, it was different again. Could we never get any further than guesswork and opinion?

Plato came to the conclusion that the things we see around us in the physical world are always in a state of process and change, and therefore they can never be the objects of completely true knowledge. However, he argued that there are also other realities of which we can have certain knowledge, in a different 'world', which are eternal and always stay the same. These realities are concepts, which Plato called 'Forms' or 'Ideas'. We gain true knowledge, according to Plato, through our reason.

In Plato's view, the different things that we see in the physical world around us, and that we learn about through experience by using our five senses, are imitations and examples of their ideal Form. When we see someone doing an act of justice, we recognise it as justice because we know what 'true justice' really is, as a concept. We realise that the human example of justice that we are witnessing is not perfect justice, because in this changing world nothing is ever perfect; but for Plato, the very fact that we realise it is not perfect demonstrates that we have an inner understanding of what 'ideal justice' or 'the Form of justice' might be.

In the same way, we might see examples of circles in the world of mathematics and in the physical world around us. We see things which are circular, such as plates and clocks and wheels, and recognise their circularity. We might be required to draw circles in maths lessons. However, the circles we see in the physical world are never going to be perfect circles. There will always be some little lump or misshapenness which makes it very nearly a circle, but not quite. Our mental concept of the 'Form of a Circle' will be a perfect circle, but whenever it is translated into the physical world, it loses some of that perfection – because, mathematically, the infinite series of points which make up the

Think question

a. The philosopher Heraclitus, who lived before Plato, was known for his wise sayings. He claimed that 'you can never step into the same river twice'.

What do you think he meant? Was he right? Have you ever tried to recreate an experience from the past, for example by rereading a favourite book or revisiting a place you once enjoyed? Was it a success?

Plato believed that all the material things we experience in the world around us are imitations of their perfect Forms

Think question

b. What might 'perfect generosity' involve? Do we all share the same ideas of what it means to be generous and how it might be applied in real life?

circumference of a circle do not take up any physical space, but as soon as we draw one, the line enclosing the circle exists in space.

Plato believed that the physical world in which we live is full of these imperfect imitations. We recognise things for what they are only because of our knowledge of their Forms. So, for example, if we see a tree, we know what it is even when we have not seen that particular tree before, because we understand the concept 'tree'. We recognise it as an example of something which reflects the 'Form of Tree'. We know the concept 'tree' and can see that here we have something which imitates it – although always less than perfectly.

Plato was not simply showing how we apply language to objects. In his view, the physical tree which is available to the senses is inferior to the concept or Form of Tree, because the physical tree is undergoing a process of change. The leaves might be coming into bud, or turning yellow for the autumn, or dropping; the tree might be a little taller than it was last year. Eventually, the tree will die and rot away. However, the Form of Tree is eternal. The idea or Form of the tree, unlike the physical tree, never changes. It does not depend on physical circumstances for its existence. For this reason, the Form of Tree can be the object of true knowledge even though the physical tree cannot.

Plato believed that the unchanging nature of the Forms made them in many ways 'more real' than the ordinary physical objects we can perceive with our senses. Physical, material things are given their reality by the Forms, according to Plato; they 'participate in' the Forms. Plato also thought that we have an understanding of the Forms from birth, even if we do not realise it. We just know, by intuition, what the Form of Beauty is or the Form of Symmetry (or even the Form of Frog), and we make judgements about different qualities of things in the physical world by comparing them with our concepts. Plato decided that, as we seem to have this intuition about the Forms, it must be because at some point, before we were born, we experienced them – and this led him to the conclusion that people must have immortal souls and must have lived in the realm of Forms before being born into the material world as physical human beings.

The Forms, then, are perfect exemplars of different aspects of the world. Material, physical 'stuff' is by nature changing and chaotic, but the Forms exist changelessly. They do not exist within time or space, because they are concepts rather than 'things'.

Sometimes, Plato wrote as though there were Forms only of qualities, such as Beauty or Mercy. However, at other times he seemed to think that there is a Form for each different thing in the world: a Form of Spade, a Form of Earwig, a Form of Rose and so on. Taken to extremes, this can make Plato's theory seem rather ridiculous – are we really supposed to believe that there is an Ideal Form of Computer Mouse or an Ideal Form of Pyjamas? However, this might be seen as missing the point of what Plato was trying to say. For Plato, by far the most important Forms were those of noble qualities, and in particular, the Form of the Good.

Plato thought that the different things we see in the world are given their reality by the Forms

Apply your knowledge

3. Do you think Plato is right in his view that we know goodness or justice or beauty by intuition? If he is wrong, are there other ways instead that we might gain knowledge of such qualities? Or is knowledge of such qualities impossible to achieve? Try to give reasons and examples to support your answer.

The Form of the Good

According to Plato, the different Forms were related to each other, and arranged in a hierarchy. The most important of all of the Forms was the Form of the Good, which illuminates all of the other Forms and gives them their value. Justice, for example, and Wisdom and Courage and even Beauty are all aspects of goodness, so they are the Higher Forms, although not as important as the Form of the Good. Goodness is seen as the purest, most abstract of the Forms, the furthest away from the physical world, and those Forms lower down in the hierarchy are more particular and specific as well as more closely related to material objects, such as the Form of Blueness or the Form of Softness.

As with the other Forms, goodness is something we have never seen perfectly exemplified in this physical world, but nevertheless we have all seen actions and role models we recognise to be 'good'. We recognise their goodness because we understand how they correspond to our intuitive knowledge of the Form of the Good, and we can identify what it is about the actions or the people that is good – we can also recognise the respects in which they fall short of perfection. True knowledge, for Plato, is a knowledge of goodness. A 'philosopher' is someone who loves ('philos') wisdom ('sophia'), and who recognises the nature of true goodness. A lover of wisdom is not going to be someone who simply knows the truth. Love involves action, not passivity. The genuine lover of wisdom, the real 'philosopher', will want to put that wisdom into practice by teaching others and by setting an example, and this, for Plato, was the reason why countries should be ruled by philosopher kings.

Part of Plato's argument was that if someone knows what is good and what is bad, he or she will choose the good. It is only ignorance which causes immorality. People steal or tell lies because they are ignorant of the Form of Honesty. If they became more philosophical and looked for the Form of the Good, they would make better moral decisions.

Plato illustrates how the Form of the Good illuminates all the rest of our knowledge in his **Analogy** of the Cave.

Plato thought that the Form of the Good was the most important of all the Forms and that it illuminated the others

Plato's Demiurge

Plato believed that the world was created by a god he called the Demiurge. The Demiurge made the world by fashioning it out of material that was already there, but which was a shapeless mess before the Demiurge got to work. The name 'Demiurge' itself comes from the Greek word for a craftsman or workman.

In Plato's work *Timaeus* (c.360BC) he describes how the Demiurge is good and desires the best for humanity. The Demiurge tries to make the universe as well as he can, but he is limited by his materials, and so the final result is as good as he can manage; it was never going to be perfect anyway, because it is physical and, therefore, changeable. When Plato applies the word 'good' to the Demiurge, he means that he can be judged in comparison with the Form of the Good. The Demiurge is not in any sense 'Goodness-Itself' or 'the source of all goodness', but is a being which can be measured against the external standards of the Forms.

The Analogy of the Cave

One of Plato's best-known works is *Republic* (c.380BC), which was written when he was about 40. It is undoubtedly one of the finest pieces of philosophical literature ever written. Plato was living in Athens at a time when it was a centre of culture, learning and activity, yet it was also a time when the city was in decline. He was deeply concerned about his fellow citizens and felt that it was his mission to present to people a better, more ethical and more considered way of living.

In *Republic*, Plato illustrates aspects of his philosophy by giving an analogy that has become famous. He asks us to imagine a strange scenario of people being held prisoner in a cave, and then plays out a series of events to clarify and emphasise his points.

When he gives the cave analogy, Plato wants us to understand:

- the relation between the physical, material world and the higher world of the Forms

- the ways in which material, physical concerns can blind people to what is really important

- the ignorance of humanity when people do not engage in philosophy

- the potential for true knowledge that philosophy brings

- that there is another world which we cannot see from the position that we are in, yet which we can reach and which will give us enlightenment

- the initial difficulties of grappling with philosophy

- the hostility that people often feel when faced with philosophical ideas that challenge their previously-held beliefs

- the injustice of the death of Socrates

- that education, if we take the word literally, is a 'leading-out'. It is not stuffing people's minds with information, but a drawing-out of things they already know and an encouragement for them to become new kinds of people.

Plato presents us with a dialogue between Socrates and a man named Glaucon. Socrates asks Glaucon to imagine a scene set in an underground cave. In the cave, there are prisoners, who have been there since childhood; Plato wants us to understand that they have no memory of ever having lived in any different way. The prisoners are chained in such a way that they can only face in one direction, and are unable to move their heads. They all sit facing the back wall of the cave. The only light available to them comes from a fire, which is behind them so that they cannot see it.

All they can see is the light that the fire produces, reflected off the cave wall. Between the fire and the prisoners, still behind them, is a low wall. Plato asks us to think of it as the lower edge of a puppet theatre.

People go along the low wall, carrying a variety of different objects, and as they pass the fire, shadows of the objects are thrown onto the cave wall where the prisoners can see them.

Plato asks us to imagine a strange scene with prisoners in a cave to illustrate his message

66 'And do you see,' I said, 'men passing along the wall carrying all sorts of vessels, and statues and figures of animals made of wood and stone and various materials, which appear over the wall? Some of them are talking, others silent.'
'You have shown me a strange image, and they are strange prisoners.'
'Like ourselves,' I replied, 'and they see only their own shadows, or the shadows of one another, which the fire throws on the opposite wall of the cave?'
'True,' he said, 'how could they see anything but the shadows if they were never allowed to move their heads?'
'And of the objects which are being carried in like manner they would only see the shadows?'
'Yes,' he said. 99

Plato, *Republic,* Book VII, translated by Benjamin Jowett

All the prisoners are able to see, then, is shadows of these different objects, and shadows of each other. They cannot see what the objects are made of, and they have no reason to suppose that some objects are made of one thing and others are made of another. There is no way that they can begin to question the 'essence' of different aspects of their world because as far as they are concerned, they already know the answers. They see only a two-dimensional shadow and not solid objects.

> 66 'And if they were able to converse with one another, would they not suppose that they were naming what was actually before them?'
> 'Very true.'
> 'And suppose further that the prison had an echo which came from the other side, would they not be sure to fancy when one of the passers-by spoke that the voice which they heard came from the passing shadow?'
> 'No question,' he replied.
> 'To them,' I said, 'the truth would be literally nothing but the shadows of the images.'
> 'That is certain'. 99
>
> Plato, *Republic,* Book VII, translated by Benjamin Jowett

In Plato's Analogy of the Cave, he produces a scenario in which the characters are as far removed from reality as he can possibly imagine

Likewise, the only sounds the prisoners are able to hear are voices and echoes. Because of their situation, they are unable to distinguish real voices from the echoes of voices, so they are unable to distinguish between reality and appearance and do not even know that there is any difference. When they name the shadows they see in front of them, they think they are naming real objects.

Plato has set up a scene where people are as far removed from reality as possible. Nothing they perceive with their senses gives them true information. They see and hear only shadowy, flickering images of the ways in which things really are, and they are completely unaware of their own ignorance. As far as they realise, this is the truth. We, Plato's readers and listeners, of course are in the privileged position of knowing exactly what the prisoners are missing. We know that there is a whole world out there, beyond the cave, that they could be enjoying and which would greatly increase their knowledge: just as Socrates knew that there is a whole world of Forms 'out there' that people ignorant of philosophy are missing.

Then Plato asks us to imagine what will happen if the prisoners are released from their chains, and can turn around and see what has been happening. Initially, each prisoner will be completely puzzled and at a loss to understand what it is that he is being shown. If he is shown the actual objects that were making the shadows, he will not at first be able to recognise them, and he will think that the shadows were 'more real' than the solid objects. He will find the whole experience painful because his muscles have been unused for so long, and he will find the glare from the fire hurts his eyes. However, as he gets used to the light, he will gradually become accustomed to it, and his vision will begin to improve.

Plato wants us to understand that when we begin to question the world around us, when we start to wonder what is real and what is illusory, and when we begin to ask ourselves whether we could have been wrong until now, it is a painful experience. Most people only undertake philosophy reluctantly – but it is, nevertheless, a profoundly worthwhile thing to do.

> 66 'And now look again, and see what will naturally follow if the prisoners are released and disabused of their error. At first, when any of them is liberated and compelled suddenly to stand up and turn his neck round and walk and look towards the light, he will suffer sharp pains; the glare will distress him, and he will be unable to see the realities of which in his former state he had seen the shadows; and then conceive someone saying to him, that what he saw before was an illusion, but that now, when he is approaching nearer to being and his eye is turned towards more real existence, he has a clearer vision, what will be his reply? And you may further imagine that his instructor is pointing to the objects as they pass and requiring him to name them, will he not be perplexed? Will he not fancy that the shadows which he formerly saw are truer than the objects which are now shown to him?'
> 'Far truer.'
> 'And if he is compelled to look straight at the light, will he not have a pain in his eyes which will make him turn away to take in the objects of vision which he can see, and which he will conceive to be in reality clearer than the things which are now being shown to him?'
> 'True,' he said. 99

Plato, *Republic,* Book VII, translated by Benjamin Jowett

Once the former prisoner has become more comfortable with looking at the fire, it is time for him to leave the cave and make his way outside. He does not want to go. He has been comfortable with his life of ignorance, and experience already tells him that changing his ideas is a painful challenge. However, he is led up through the mouth of the cave, which is 'steep' and 'rugged' as a metaphor for his struggles. At last, he is out in the light, where the sun, rather than the fire, gives the real world a sharp clarity.

> 66 'He will require to grow accustomed to the sight of the upper world. And first he will see the shadows best, next the reflections of men and other objects in the water, and then the objects themselves; then he will gaze upon the light of the moon and the stars and the spangled heaven; and he will see the sky and the stars by night better than the sun or the light of the sun by day?'
> 'Certainly.' 99

Plato, *Republic,* Book VII, translated by Benjamin Jowett

Think question

Can you think of a time when you have had to reassess your ideas and perhaps change your opinion? What made you do it? Why do we find it so difficult to challenge our own ideas?

Again, the prisoner's initial reaction is one of pain and irritation. His eyes are so dazzled at first that he cannot see anything clearly, but gradually he adjusts. First he understands shadows, and then reflections; he is more comfortable at night than during the day. But later on, as his abilities develop, he is able to see in daylight.

> 'Last of all he will be able to see the sun, and not mere reflections of him in the water, but he will see him in his own proper place, and not in another; and he will contemplate him as he is.'
>
> 'Certainly.'
>
> 'He will then proceed to argue that this is he who gives the season and the years, and is the guardian of all that is in the visible world, and in a certain way the cause of all things which he and his fellows have been accustomed to behold?'
>
> 'Clearly,' he said, 'he would first see the sun and then reason about him.'

Plato, *Republic,* Book VII, translated by Benjamin Jowett

As the former prisoner adjusts to his new life, his wisdom grows. He begins to recognise the importance of the sun in illuminating all of his other knowledge. He realises that the sun gives structure to his life, and that it enables him to see other things as they really are.

With this metaphor, Plato wants us to understand the sun as the Form of the Good. The cave with its shadows is something we experience when we are ignorant of the Form of the Good. When we never ask ourselves about the nature of goodness, we live in a world of illusions, where none of our 'knowledge' is really knowledge at all. It is only when we have an understanding of the Good that everything else falls into place. Knowing what Goodness is allows us to know what Justice is, or Truth, or Patience.

The former prisoner has reached a state of knowledge at last. However, because he has this newly-acquired wisdom, he realises that he has an obligation to help others who are still in ignorance.

Plato asks us to imagine that the prisoners in the cave have made up a simple game to pass the time. As they sit in their chains watching the shadows go past them on the wall opposite, they try and guess what might be coming next. Those who get it right the most often are the winners, and they are prized among the prison community for this special skill – even though it is only guesswork and, therefore, they are getting it right through pure chance, rather than genuine ability.

When the former prisoner goes back into the cave to help his friends to their release, the prisoners are not impressed. The enlightened man finds the darkness a struggle now. He cannot see in the cave as well as he

Apply your knowledge

Look up this short passage in the Bible: 1 Corinthians 13: 8–12.

Here, the writer is talking about the differences between our understanding in the life we have now, and the understanding Christians will achieve in the future.

4. In what way does this passage use ideas which are similar to those of Plato?

used to be able to. Those who are still prisoners look at him and decide that they certainly have no desire to go wherever he has been, because they are better off where they are. In fact, they feel so hostile towards the suggestion that they would be prepared to kill him if he tried to lead them out of the cave.

Plato wants to show, then, that Socrates was well aware of the dangers he faced in trying to bring philosophy to others. He knew that people did not like to have their assumptions, prejudices and superstitions called into question. He knew that, when people start to ask themselves questions about what justice really is, or where the true nature of goodness might be found, they could end up with more questions than answers, and perhaps feel themselves to be less knowledgeable than before. But, in Plato's view, Socrates was willing to take this risk, because for him the human search for the truth was more important than life itself.

At the end of the story, Socrates explains its meaning to Glaucon:

....

66 'This entire allegory,' I said, 'you may now append, dear Glaucon, to the previous argument; the prison-house is the world of sight, the light of the fire is the sun, and you will not misapprehend me if you interpret the journey upwards to be the ascent of the soul into the intellectual world according to my poor belief, which, at your desire, I have expressed whether rightly or wrongly God knows. But, whether true or false, my opinion is that in the world of knowledge the idea of good appears last of all, and is seen only with an effort; and, when seen, is also inferred to be the universal author of all things beautiful and right, parent of light and of the lord of light in this visible world, and the immediate source of reason and truth in the intellectual; and that this is the power upon which he who would act rationally, either in public or private life must have his eye fixed.' 99

Plato, *Republic,* Book VII, translated by Benjamin Jowett

Plato explains that understanding the nature of the Form of the Good comes at the end of the philosophical quest for wisdom

....

66 'I agree,' he said, 'as far as I am able to understand you.'
'Moreover,' I said, 'you must not wonder that those who attain to this beatific vision are unwilling to descend to human affairs; for their souls are ever hastening into the upper world where they desire to dwell; which desire of theirs is very natural, if our allegory may be trusted.'
'Yes, very natural.'
'And is there anything surprising in one who passes from divine contemplations to the evil state of man, misbehaving himself in a ridiculous manner; if, while his eyes are blinking and before he has become accustomed to the surrounding darkness, he is compelled to fight in courts of law, or in other places, about the

images or the shadows of images of justice, and is endeavouring to meet the conceptions of those who have never yet seen absolute justice?'

'Anything but surprising,' he replied.

Plato, *Republic,* Book VII, translated by Benjamin Jowett

Plato's story works on several different levels. His audience would have realised that the prisoner who escaped was meant to be Socrates himself, and that those who had tried and executed Socrates were those ignorant prisoners who had stayed behind and who preferred the comfort of their chains to the challenges of freedom. However, the released prisoner also represents all those who undertake philosophy. Those in the cave are representative of all those who prefer to live an 'unexamined life', and who are content to be impressed with appearances. The ones who are willing to climb the steep slope out of the cave, and to persevere with the journey, are those who recognise their innate ability to perceive the truth behind the illusions presented to our five senses. They recognise that this is not the real world, but that reality is invisible.

An evaluation of Plato's thought

Of course, not everyone has accepted Plato's understanding of the world and of reality. Plato was convinced that there were two realms, one of ideas (Forms) and one of matter (the physical world). However, some people argue that he never gives us any compelling reasons for accepting that this is so – he simply asserts it.

Plato argues that the physical world is not as 'real' as the world of Forms, but this does not convince everyone. Many people argue that the physical world has a very definite reality, saying that if you hit your head on a bookcase, then you have a pretty good indication that the physical world is real. Scientists argue that the physical world is worth studying in its own right and can give us true insights into the nature of reality – and many scientists claim that this physical world is the only reality there is. For some, such as Richard Dawkins, it is nonsense to talk of a **transcendent** 'other world' beyond the physical. This world might be changeable, but we can still study it with all its changes and processes, and gain true and valuable knowledge which benefits us all in our daily lives.

Some people, including Aristotle, criticised Plato's Theory of Forms on the grounds that it becomes ridiculous when pushed to its logical extremes. We might be happy to accept that there are 'ideal concepts' in mathematics, such as the concept of infinity, or the concept of a square root or a prime number. We might even be happy to accept that we have 'ideal concepts' of qualities such as Truth, Justice, Generosity or Goodness. However, it is harder to accept that there might be ideal forms of negative qualities such as Jealousy or Spite, and harder still to accept that every physical thing in the world has an ideal form.

A problem with the Theory of Forms can be seen if we use the example of plants. Is there an Ideal Form of Plant, in general – in which case, what would it be like? Would it have large or small leaves, coloured flowers, soft fruit, nuts, a scent, thorns, branches, catkins? Or is there, perhaps, one Form of Rose, and another Form of Pineapple, and a separate Form of Potato and another Form of Cactus, and so on, for each species? However, if each species has a different Form, the problem still exists, because of the variation within that species. What is the Ideal Form of Rose – a Gertrude Jekyll, maybe, or a Blush Noisette? Is it a climber, a standard, a rambler, a bush? Suppose we decide that the Ideal Form of Rose is a good, red Dublin Bay, and that other kinds of roses are inferior imitations of this ideal Form; we are still left with the problem of whether it is a tall or short specimen, whether it is in flower or not … and if we end up deciding that there must be one Form for those Dublin Bays with 100 leaves, and another for those with 101, then we might as well have a separate Form for each individual rose plant. Our Forms have stopped being universal at all.

It could be argued, however, that this criticism is a misunderstanding of Plato. Plato's thinking concentrated on the Forms of qualities, and there are plenty of philosophers who would agree that we do all have an intuitive knowledge of what goodness is, or of what justice is. Plato's theory might fail if pushed to logical extremes, but there is nothing to compel us to push it so far. Plato himself was ambiguous about whether there is a form for literally everything in the world.

Plato could be criticised for not being entirely clear about the relation between the Forms and the objects of this world – in other words, the relation between concepts and phenomena. He talks about the phenomena 'participating in' their ideal Forms, but is not clear about how this works.

Some dislike Plato's Theory of Forms because in their view it does not have any scientific evidence to support it. We cannot access these 'Forms' in any way, to determine whether or not they exist or what their nature is; there is no way that we could test them, using experiments and experience. For some (such as Aristotle) it makes more sense to focus our efforts on the things we can see around us if we want to understand how the world works and how best to live.

Apply your knowledge

You offer your friends a cup of tea. One asks for a very weak and milky cup with no sugar; another likes a saturated sugar solution of strong tea; another asks for black Earl Grey; and another prefers not to have any tea at all unless it's Fair Trade.

8. Is there any such thing as the Ideal Form of a cup of tea?

9. Do you think we all share the same understanding of what is ideal or perfect? If not, does this make Plato's theory completely useless?

Some have disliked Plato's ideas because his **dualism** has been taken to extremes by those who came after him. As we know, Plato believed that the physical world that the body inhabits is inferior to the transcendent, spiritual world of the Forms available to the soul through reason. This has led later thinkers to the idea that bodily pleasures are bad, and that people should punish their bodies if they want to make spiritual progress. They should, perhaps, avoid all but the simplest food, wear plain clothes, be celibate and avoid pleasure for its own sake. However, this ascetism (the practice of living a very simple life as a means to wisdom) was not Plato's own position. He saw physical pleasures as unimportant in comparison to philosophy, rather than condemning them completely.

Plato believed that knowledge of the Form of the Good was the highest possible kind of knowledge, underpinning everything else. However, this raises difficulties. Some people have argued that it is nonsense to talk as though we all share a concept of goodness and can know what it is. Thinkers such as A.J. Ayer have argued that when we talk of something as being 'good' or 'bad', we are simply expressing our own emotional reaction to it, and not referring to any real knowledge. Some people, such as Aristotle, have argued that there cannot be a single Form of the Good, because goodness always relates to specific actions, situations and people. There cannot be just Goodness Itself, on its own, not in relation to anything. Morality, Aristotle thought, cannot be eternal and changeless with a single 'right answer', because no two situations are the same.

Plato's view of goodness is also challenged because of the way in which he relates it to philosophy. It appears that only those of a certain intellectual calibre are capable of being or doing good; those with learning difficulties, then, could never be good people because they would not understand philosophical issues. This can seem to be an unnecessarily unfair and elitist approach; and not everyone would agree that better philosophers are always more moral people than the less intellectually gifted.

Many would disagree with Plato's view that people only do wrong when they are ignorant of what is right; they argue that people often know perfectly well that something is morally wrong, but they go ahead and do it anyway. Perhaps Plato is overly optimistic in his view of human nature.

Aristotle

In the view of many scholars, Aristotle was an even greater philosopher than Plato. Plato may have asked some vital philosophical questions and suggested some startlingly original approaches to them, but his theories are not ones which everyone is able to accept, and some believe that Plato's arguments in support of his theories are not particularly successful.

Think question

Do you think that people who commit crimes or who are violent or unfaithful only do these things because they are ignorant of what is right? Or do they know their deeds are wrong, but not care? How might Plato's understanding of human motivation affect the way criminals are treated?

Aristotle would have agreed. He was a great admirer of Plato, but he found it difficult to agree with Plato's views. In particular, he did not accept that there is another world, more real than this one, which can be the object of true knowledge. In Aristotle's view, the physical world around us is the key to knowledge, and we can learn about it using our senses.

The painter Raphael illustrated the differences between Platonic and Aristotelian approaches to philosophy in his famous painting *The School of Athens,* painted at the beginning of the sixteenth century (rather a misleading name, which was given to the painting at a later date). Raphael places Plato and Aristotle at the centre of the painting, directly in front of the main source of light, showing them to be the most enlightened and perhaps the most illuminating of all the 60 figures in the painting. Plato, on the left, holds a copy of his book *Timaeus,* while Aristotle holds a copy of his own *Ethics*. Plato's body language expresses his idealism. His hand, and his book, are vertical, pointing upwards to show Plato's belief in another, superior world 'above' this one. Aristotle, in contrast, holds his hand and his book flat to represent the earth, on which both of his feet are squarely planted. This world, he seems to be saying, is where the truth can be found – the physical world under our feet, the world of sense experience and of science.

Detail from Raphael's painting *The School of Athens*. Here, Raphael captured the stark differences of approach between Plato and Aristotle

In spite of their differences, Plato and Aristotle were great admirers of each other. Aristotle was the brightest of Plato's students at the Academy. He came from a well-off Macedonian family, and arrived in Athens at the age of 17 to study as a pupil of Plato. Following in the traditions of Plato and Socrates, Aristotle began to question the beliefs and assumptions he had always held – and also to question the beliefs and assumptions of Plato. In the course of this, he decided against many of Plato's ideas and provided his own alternative ways of looking at the world.

Aristotle rejected the idea that there is a 'world of Forms', separate from this world. He thought that there was nothing to be gained from the dualist approach. Ideas, he thought, can have no real existence just on their own. They have to relate to something, here in the physical world of our own experience. Our journey to knowledge has to start here, where we are, and must be gained through observation of the world around us.

For Aristotle, observation of the natural world was crucial. Aristotle was the founder of many of the sciences we recognise today: physics, biology, psychology, meteorology, astronomy. He had an insatiable desire

Aristotle thought that ideas can have no real existence just on their own. They have to relate to something, here in the physical world of our own experience

to understand the world as it makes itself available to our five senses, and to see if there were universal rules which governed natural processes and which we could understand.

Aristotle's understanding of reality

One question which fascinated Aristotle was the question of cause. Why are things the way that they are – what caused them? What is the 'essence' of this thing or that thing? Why does it exist in the world at all?

Aristotle used the term '**aetion**' when he was thinking and writing about different kinds of explanation. It is usually translated as 'cause', although the words are not exactly the same in meaning, as 'aetion' can include the concept of explanation as well as origin. In other words, 'aetion' can be used to describe what something looks like or what it is made from, as well as what caused it to come into being.

In exploring these aetiological questions, Aristotle recognised that something can have several different explanations for its existence, on different levels. If I ask, for example, what is the 'cause' of my desk, I can answer in a variety of different ways. I could say that it is 'caused' by wood, because it is a wooden desk, so without the wood and the glue and the nails, I would not have a desk. Or, I could say that the desk is caused by the person who made it. Someone has taken this wood and the nails and the glue, and worked to make them into a desk shape – if this person had not bothered, then I would have no desk (or at least, not this one). A third answer I could give is that the desk is 'caused' by having a large and stable flat surface to work on, and sturdy legs that will hold the weight of my computer. If it lacked these characteristics, it would not be my desk. Finally, I could say that the desk exists in order to fulfil a purpose. People need desks so that they don't have to squat on the floor to do their writing. The desk has a function, an ultimate purpose to perform, which is why anyone bothered making one at all.

The four causes

Aristotle, then, thought that 'cause' could be understood in four different ways, to which he gave different names.

1. He called the first the **material cause**. This explains what something is made from. This is a question scientists often try to answer when they are learning about something. They take the thing apart and look at the various kinds of matter of which the object is composed, sometimes through a microscope. So the material 'cause' of a rat would be the blood, the muscles, the fur, the organs, the bones and all the other squishy bits biologists find when they dissect rats. However, the material cause does not explain everything. A heap of bits of rat does not, alone, provide an explanation of the rat itself, although investigating an object's material will help us to understand important aspects of it, and should not be ignored.

2. The second is known as the **formal cause**. This is how Aristotle termed the form, or shape, that something has. The formal cause gives something its shape and allows it to be identified as whatever it is. There are lots of things made by the activity of carpenters, using wood and glue and nails, that are not desks, but my desk is a desk because it is desk-shaped. Within limits, there are other shapes it could be while still being a desk, but there are certain characteristics of form that a desk has to have in order to be recognised as such. The rat is recognisable because of its size and shape and features, such as colour.

3. The third is known as the **efficient cause**. This is the name Aristotle gave to the activity that makes something happen. The rat's efficient cause is the sexual activity of Mummy Rat and Daddy Rat; the efficient cause of my desk is the activity of the carpenter who made it. Aristotle expressed this in terms of the actualising of potential. Wood has the potential to be made into furniture, but it needs the efficient cause of the carpenter's activity to realise this potential. Efficient cause brings about change in something.

Aristotle called the activity which brings something about its 'efficient cause'

4. The fourth, and for Aristotle, the most important cause, is the **final cause**. The final cause of something is its purpose, its reason for existing at all. This can be understood as its '**telos**', which means end (as in 'a means to an end'). The final cause, or purpose, or telos, of a desk is for writing at. The final cause of a mug is for holding drinks; the final cause of fur is to keep the rat warm. This idea of final cause was to be of great significance to Thomas Aquinas when he made use of Aristotelian philosophy in his own theology and ethics.

See Chapters 1.3 and 1.4 for arguments on the existence of God, and Chapter 2.1 for more on natural ethics.

Aristotle used his concept of final cause when he discussed the nature of goodness and the right ways for people to behave. He thought that something was 'good' when it fulfilled its 'telos'. An axe is a good axe if it cuts well; boots are good boots if they keep your feet warm and dry; a person is a good person if … he or she does whatever it is that people are meant to do.

Aristotle's Prime Mover

When Aristotle looked at cause and effect, it made him wonder about the existence of the universe as a whole. He had found a way of understanding, at different levels, the causes of individual objects within the universe but what about the universe itself, in its entirety? The two 'causes' that bothered him the most when applied to the universe were the efficient cause and the final cause. What causes the different objects in the universe to actualise their potential? What is the purpose of the universe as a whole?

Aristotle, like many other philosophers before him, realised that the universe was in a constant state of change and motion. Therefore, he thought, there must be some kind of efficient cause, someone or something performing some kind of action, to make all this change and motion happen. He considered the idea that there might be an endless chain of cause and effect, with each movement being caused by a moving thing, which was being caused by another moving thing and so on for ever, but he rejected this idea. He did not think that endless cause and effect provided a satisfactory solution.

The cause of the universe, Aristotle thought, must be God. God must be the Prime Mover (sometimes called the Unmoved Mover), a cause which actualises the potential in everything else. However, the Prime Mover must be something which causes without being affected (otherwise it would simply be another link in the endless chain). The Prime Mover must be a being with no potential; something which is already everything that it could be, 'pure actuality' with no potential to change or to be acted upon.

Aristotle thought that the Prime Mover caused movement in everything else through attraction. The Prime Mover itself remained unaffected

In Aristotle's view, the Prime Mover was the first of all substances. It causes movement and change in all other things, but it does not do this in a physical way by giving them some kind of push – because, if it did, then the act of 'pushing' would affect the Prime Mover. Instead, the Prime Mover causes change and motion by attracting other things towards itself. It does nothing; but it is the object of everything. The final cause of movement is a desire for God. Everything in the universe is drawn towards God's perfection and wants to imitate it, and so by this great attraction, the Prime Mover causes movement in everything else.

Aristotle worked out the implications of his ideas about the Prime Mover, and came to several conclusions about the nature of God.

1. He believed that God (understood as the Prime Mover) does not depend on anything else for his existence. If he did, then he would have to be capable of change – if, for example, God relied on sunlight

for his existence, then God would change and die if the sun fizzled out. But as God has no potential, which means he has no capacity for change, then he must exist independently, or 'necessarily'.

2. He must also be eternal, because of this lack of potential. If God cannot change, then he cannot cease to be; and if he exists, then he must have always existed.

3. God must be perfectly good, because badness is related to some kind of lacking, an absence of something that ought to be there – and if God is pure actuality, then he must contain everything that ought to be there, so he must be perfect.

4. God must be immaterial, and beyond time and space. All matter is capable of being acted upon, and so God cannot be made of matter. But if God is immaterial, Aristotle thought, then God cannot perform any kind of physical activity – he cannot actually do anything. God must be purely spiritual, pure thought, and not thinking about anything which could cause him to change; which led Aristotle to conclude that God must think only of himself and his own perfect nature.

5. The Prime Mover relates to Aristotle's ideas about causation. The Prime Mover is the final cause of everything that exists in the universe, not only in the sense of being the origin of everything, but also in the sense of being the purpose of everything. The Prime Mover is not the efficient cause; because it cannot do anything, it is incapable of doing the activity which brings things about. Aristotle rather obscurely describes the Prime Mover as the final cause in terms of its being the object of desire and love for the world, drawing everything to itself without itself being affected. The Prime Mover is, therefore, transcendent while, at the same time, being the ultimate reason – telos – for everything else.

In Aristotle's thought there is the picture of God as 'wholly simple'. This is an idea which has had an enormous effect on the shaping of ideas about the nature of God. From Aristotle, Christians inherit the idea that God is changeless. God cannot suffer. He cannot change his mind, and so he cannot be persuaded. God is unrestricted by time and space, so that the future and the past are the same for God. When these ideas are woven into the fabric of Christianity, they create knots which can be difficult to untie.

Although Aristotle was a genius, he did not inherit Plato's Academy. Plato left it to a nephew instead. Maybe it was because of family loyalties on the part of Plato; maybe it was because Aristotle had Macedonian ancestry, which might have led to friction in Athens. But probably, it was because Plato knew that his beliefs and the beliefs of Aristotle were just too different.

An evaluation of Aristotle's thought

Aristotle's work is difficult to evaluate because it often lacks clarity. Although Plato wrote in clear and elegant prose, with plenty of examples

Apply your knowledge

11. Hebrews 13:8 from the New Testament expresses a Christian idea which shows similarities to the Aristotelian idea of the Prime Mover. Look it up and see if you can identify the similarities with Aristotelian thought. What do you think the writer of the letter to the Hebrews might have meant by these words?

Think question

Do you think that we can gain knowledge through other means than the use of our senses or our reason? If so, what methods might these be?

to make sure that others understood him, in contrast Aristotle's work is very difficult to follow. Many scholars believe that the surviving writings of Aristotle were never meant for publication, but are lecture notes. Maybe the notes were made by his students, who jotted down in an abbreviated way the main gist of what they understood. They could have added their own comments and ideas as they went along, giving the impression that Aristotle was contradicting himself or going off at tangents. Whatever the reasons, it remains the case that Aristotle is extremely hard to follow. Some people find this almost impossibly frustrating, while others find it an exciting challenge.

Some, however, criticise Aristotle for his rejection of Plato's belief in another world, more real than this one. Perhaps Aristotle should have been more willing to accept the possibility that we can gain knowledge through other means, as well as through the physical world. Perhaps it also makes sense to talk of 'spiritual knowledge' or 'intuitive knowledge', rather than simply confining ourselves to the scientifically demonstrable.

Aristotle's belief that the universe must have a 'telos' has been criticised by many thinkers, including Russell, Sartre, Dawkins and others. They claim that it makes no sense to talk of a 'purpose' for the universe. It just exists, without any kind of reason or goal. There is nothing that a universe is 'supposed to do'. It is simply the result of chance.

Those who do not believe that the universe requires some kind of explanation are likely to question Aristotle's conclusions about the existence of an Unmoved Prime Mover. Perhaps cause and effect is eternal, in an infinite chain, or perhaps it all began as a result of blind chance. The idea of a Prime Mover to start it all off could seem an unnecessary complication.

Theists often object to the concept of God presented by Aristotle. They argue that Aristotle's God is almost irrelevant to the universe, because he has no interaction with it and is unaffected by it. Theists might claim that the God of their own experience is very different from the one Aristotle arrived at through logic, and that perhaps philosophical logic has its limitations. Perhaps there are other ways in which God can be known, which reveal God's personality as an active being.

How does Plato's Form of the Good compare with Aristotle's Prime Mover?

In some ways, these two different ideas have a considerable amount in common. Both Plato's ideas about the Form of the Good, and Aristotle's ideas about the Prime Mover, have been profoundly influential on the Christian understanding of God. Plato's understanding of the Form of the Good gives Christians the concept of God as a perfect source of goodness, an exemplar of what goodness fundamentally means, with an ultimate reality and existence which is permanent and unchanging, unlike the temporary nature of this physical world and of human goodness. Aristotle's understanding of the Prime Mover gives Christianity an understanding of a God who is the ultimate cause of all that exists but is himself not caused by anything else.

Both the Form of the Good and the Prime Mover ideas give an answer to the question of why anything exists at all. The Form of the Good is seen at the top of a hierarchy, illuminating everything else; physical things are just imitations of the Forms, and so without the Forms nothing would exist. The Prime Mover, too, is seen as the primary cause of existence, the reason why everything is in motion and the first cause of all the causes and effects we see in our dynamic world.

Both the Form of the Good and the Prime Mover, like the God of Christianity, have an independent, 'necessary existence'; they depend on nothing else for their own existence. They were not brought into being by anything outside themselves, and they do not depend on anything else in order to continue their existence.

Also, and unlike the God of Christianity, neither the Form of the Good nor the Prime Mover take an interest in the moral affairs of humanity. The Form of the Good does not have a mind with which to take an interest in anything; the Prime Mover, according to Aristotle, cannot interact with the world (otherwise it would be affected, but in Aristotle's view it is pure cause with no potential for change). Although both are understood as perfect, neither is capable of noticing or caring whether humans behave morally.

The two ideas also have some significant differences. The Form of the Good is not a 'being' with a mind; it has no intentions or emotions. It is the exemplification of a quality, but it does not have any kind of activity. The Prime Mover, in contrast, draws things to itself by attraction, making them move and change. The Prime Mover thinks of itself and its own perfect nature, whereas the Form of the Good does not have a mind with which to think. The Form of the Good is solely goodness, whereas the Prime Mover is more to do with motion, cause and change rather than

> *See Chapter 1.4 for discussion about arguments from reason, and Chapter 1.3 for more about arguments from observation. Both Plato and Aristotle reached the conclusion that there must be things which exist 'necessarily'.*

Apply your knowledge

12. How plausible do you find Plato's concept of the Form of the Good? What aspects of his thinking do you find persuasive or difficult to believe?

13. How plausible do you find Aristotle's concept of the Prime Mover? What aspects of his thinking do you find persuasive or difficult to believe?

14. When comparing the two ideas, do you find either idea more attractive than the other, or are they equally attractive or unattractive? Give reasons for your answer.

15. Some people might argue that Plato's Form of the Good and Aristotle's Prime Mover are actually the same 'being', considered from different perspectives. How far would you agree with this view?

morality. The Form of the Good is something which, possibly, humans might be able to encounter once they have left this physical life, but there is no suggestion that humans could ever gain further knowledge of the Prime Mover after death.

How does Plato's rationalism compare with Aristotle's empiricism?

Plato's rationalism presents us with the view that reason is the ultimate way to gain knowledge. Plato advocates rationalism because, in his view, the physical world of constant change cannot give us the certainty that we need in order to gain knowledge. Reason, such as is found for example in the solving of mathematical problems, gives us answers where there is no room for doubt. We are not going to find a straight line one day which is not the shortest distance between two points, or find two even numbers which add up to make an odd number. Truths arrived at through reason seem to have an unshakeable and enduring quality. For the rationalist, a wise person is someone who has spent time in contemplation, perhaps living in a way which is withdrawn from the everyday world.

Aristotle's empiricism is an example of the view that the primary source of all our knowledge is experience. According to the empiricist, we encounter the world through our senses first, and then we use these sense experiences to form our concepts. We cannot picture in our minds colours we have never seen, and even when we make up imaginary worlds, for example when we play as children, we still use real-life sense experience as a basis for our fantasy worlds. The mind can reach knowledge by reflecting on sense experiences, but, according to the empiricist, sense experience has to come first. For the empiricist, a wise person might be someone who has travelled widely and lived through all kinds of different situations.

Many people will argue that there is no need to choose between using reason and using sense experience to gain knowledge; we can use both together. They might argue that in some areas of knowledge, reason is more important, such as in mathematics and perhaps philosophy, whereas in other areas, sense experience is more important, such as in natural science or the arts; but in all areas of knowledge, we need both rationality and our senses in order to reach understanding. However, this still leaves open the question of which might come first – whether we start with concepts, such as beauty, and then recognise beautiful things when we see them, or whether we see things first, and then follow this with the concept that they are beautiful.

The rationalist might argue that reason is superior to experience because our senses can often mislead us, whereas when we use the logical processes of reason, we can be much more certain of our conclusions. For example, my sense might tell me that when I put my pencil in a glass of water, the pencil is bent. It looks that way. But reason overrides what my eyes are telling me; reason tells me that water cannot bend pencils.

The empiricist might argue that experience is superior to reason, because reason is very limited unless it has sense experiences to provide it with information. I cannot tell, using my reason, whether it's starting to rain on my washing on the line outside; I need to look.

Apply your knowledge

16. In what ways do the subjects you study depend on reason, and in what ways do they depend on sense experience?

17. If you are in a situation where your sense experiences and your reason seem to be in conflict, would you be more inclined to believe your senses, or your reason? For example, if you thought you saw someone walking straight through a wall, would you conclude that you had seen a ghost, or would you conclude that you must be hallucinating? Why would you choose this conclusion?

18. Do you think that morality comes from reason, or sense experience, or a mixture of the two, or somewhere else entirely? Give reasons for your answer.

19. Which do you find more persuasive: Plato's rationalism, or Aristotle's empiricism? How would you support your view?

Learning support

Points to remember

» Remember that Plato and Aristotle lived before Jesus, so avoid writing about them as though they were early Christians.

» During the course, look out for Platonic and Aristotelian ideas being used to shape the thinking of others. You will probably find echoes of Plato in the writings of Paul in the Bible and in the thinking of Augustine. Aquinas depended heavily on the ideas of Aristotle.

» Try to make sure you are thoroughly familiar with the way Aristotle understood cause in four different ways, as it will help your understanding later in the course, especially when you study the ideas of Aquinas.

Enhance your learning

» There is plenty to discover about the cultural background and other writings of Plato and Aristotle, which would make worthwhile further research.

» Plato's Academy and Aristotle's development of different disciplines in science are worth researching for a consideration of the aims of education and the reasons why we classify our knowledge into different 'subjects'. If you want to read Plato's writing in the original: Plato, *Republic*, Book V.476f, Book VII.507b–513e. Plato's ideas are clear and accessible to read.

» Aristotle's writing can be much more difficult to follow than Plato's, it would be a good idea to use a commentary if you want to dip into his original writings: Aristotle, *Physics*, II.3 and *Metaphysics*, V.2.

» Further reading about Plato's background and central ideas will help you to put his thinking into context. You could try Annas, J. (1998) *An Introduction to Plato's Republic*, Chapters 9 and 10.

• *The Stanford Encyclopedia of Philosophy* (2004, rev.2013) is an excellent source for developing your knowledge further. Try the entry on Plato, . http://plato.stanford.edu/entries/plato/

Practice for exams

AS questions and A level questions look identical; the difference between AS and A level assessment is seen in the different proportions of marks awarded for two different skills: the skill of demonstrating knowledge and understanding (Assessment Objective 1, or AO1), and the skill of constructing a critical argument (AO2).

At AS, half the marks (15 marks) are available for knowledge and understanding, and the other half (15 marks) for the quality of your analytical and evaluative argument. You should aim to use your knowledge in order to support the argument you are making throughout the essay, rather than presenting descriptive knowledge in the first half and then an opinion in the second.

At A level, your demonstration of knowledge and understanding is awarded a maximum of 16 marks, and your analytic and evaluative skills are awarded a maximum of 24 marks. You should aim to concentrate on constructing a lucid argument, making use of your knowledge to add weight to the conclusions you draw.

Discuss critically Aristotle's understanding of causation.

For this question, you need to be familiar with Aristotle's ideas about how cause works in four different ways. When a question asks you to 'discuss critically', you need not only to describe but also to make some evaluative comments and give an opinion supported with reasons. You might want to question Aristotle's classification of causes, and perhaps question or support his idea that everything has a 'telos' or final purpose.

Practise your skills for AS level

If you are answering this question for an AS qualification, you need to make sure that you are clear and thorough in the detailed knowledge you present of Aristotle's views, as well as giving a critical assessment. You should explain the 'four causes' and also say what you think of Aristotle's ideas here.

Practise your skills for A level

If you are answering this question for A level, you also need thorough knowledge but should place more emphasis on your critical comment, giving an evaluation of Aristotle's thinking and having a clear line of argument, supported and illustrated by your knowledge.

'Plato's Form of the Good has a lot in common with Aristotle's Prime Mover.' Discuss.

This question is asking you to make a comparison between the ideas of Plato and Aristotle. Try to consider the two ideas together, rather than writing about one and then the other. You might want to consider and compare the reasoning which leads each thinker to his conclusions; you could compare the characteristics of the Form of the Good with the Prime Mover.

Practise your skills for AS level

If you were answering this question at AS level, you would need to make sure that you demonstrated clear knowledge about the two ideas and could describe them with accuracy, as well as considering whether they have much in common.

Practise your skills for A level

For high marks at A level, you would need to establish an opinion about whether these two ideas are similar or not, and support your opinion with clear argument and evidence, while also demonstrating your knowledge and understanding. You are likely to consider that the concepts are similar in some ways but not in others, and you will be able to demonstrate your knowledge and understanding as you explain.

Chapter 1.2

Soul, mind and body

What does it mean to speak of the soul, the mind and the body?

Are the human mind and the human body separate and distinct from each other?

How coherent is the view that the mind is more than just the result of chemical reactions in the brain?

Key Terms

Soul: often, but not always, understood to be the non-physical essence of a person

Consciousness: awareness or perception

Substance: a subject which has different properties attributed to it

Dualism: the belief that reality can be divided into two distinct parts, such as good and evil, or physical and non-physical

Substance dualism: the belief that the mind and the body both exist as two distinct and separate realities

Scepticism: a questioning approach which does not take assumptions for granted

Materialism: the belief that only physical matter exists, and that the mind can be explained in physical terms as chemical activity in the brain

Reductive materialism: otherwise known as identity theory – the view that mental events are identical with physical occurrences in the brain

Category error: a problem of language that arises when things are talked about as if they belong to one category when in fact they belong to another

Specification requirements

- the philosophical language of soul, mind and body in the thinking of Plato and Aristotle
- metaphysics of consciousness, including:
  - substance dualism
  - materialism

Introduction

One of the central questions in philosophy is the question of what it means to be human. This is a metaphysical question. Metaphysics is the branch of philosophy which deals with huge questions about what exists, and the essential nature of things that exist. The existence of God, for example, is a metaphysical issue because it is asking whether God does, or does not, belong in the set of 'things that exist'. The question of what it means to be human is also a metaphysical question, because it addresses issues of the essential nature of human beings as existent things. Are we simply physical, made of material that develops and grows and eventually dies according to the workings of biological processes, and no more? Or do we also have a mind or a **soul**, separate from our physical bodies, which gives us a special kind of essence? These questions are important because our answers to them have significant implications. If everything about us, including our **consciousness**, is nothing more than physical, then it ought to be possible, at least in theory, for us to produce a physical machine which also had consciousness and which could think and feel just as we can. If we are nothing more than physical, then ideas about life after death can be ruled out, as there would be nothing to continue after the death of the body. However, if there is an important part of us which is non-physical, then there are important implications here too. Questions are raised about what exactly that non-physical part is, how it is attached to a particular physical body, whether it is capable of existing separately once the physical body has died and whether it gives human beings some kind of unique status.

In the history of philosophy, there have been thinkers who have argued that the mind and the body are very distinct, separate things. Plato and Descartes are particularly renowned for this view, and it is an idea which has been very influential on Christian thought. However, others such as Ryle and Dawkins have argued that there is nothing 'extra' beyond the physical, and that there is no need to imagine some kind of 'ghost in the machine' in order to understand what it is to be human.

The philosophical language of soul, mind and body

People use the term 'soul' in a range of ways, not always precisely, which can make it difficult for others to grasp exactly what the word means to religious believers. Some people use the terms 'soul' and 'spirit' interchangeably; others talk of the 'body and soul' or 'body and mind' as if the two phrases mean the same thing. However, when people speak of someone having 'a good mind' they mean something very different from when they say someone 'has a good soul'; and to add to the confusion, they talk of people being in 'in good spirits' and mean something different again. This blurring of the use of these terms can often make discussion of the soul, mind and body difficult and confusing.

The soul

Although the word 'soul' can be used with a range of meanings in different contexts, in a philosophical sense it is mainly used as meaning the same thing as 'self', to refer to the subject of mental states and of spiritual experience. If someone says 'I had a panic attack in the supermarket' or 'when I read that poem, I felt God was speaking to me directly', the soul would be the 'I', the essential person who experienced the mental and spiritual events. Philosophers often refer to the 'self' rather than the 'soul', as the soul has religious connotations which the philosopher might not want to include in the discussion. However, 'self' has a wider meaning than 'soul', as the idea of 'self' can include the mind and the body as one coherent person, whereas the term 'soul' is usually used to mean one particular aspect of the self: the part that (according to many religious believers) is capable of having a relationship with God and which carries the possibility of living after death, perhaps without any further need for a physical body. For some thinkers, the soul is the most important part of human nature, given by God to enable people to develop a relationship with him and to exist in the presence of God after this earthly life. For others, the whole idea of a 'soul' makes no sense: the physical, conscious person is simply a sophisticated animal with an impressive range of abilities which disappear at the end of the life of the body.

In the ancient Greek traditions of Plato and Aristotle, there were two very different and distinct understandings of the soul. Plato put forward an idea of a soul which is immortal and which can exist independently of the body, whereas Aristotle's ideas about the soul were completely different.

Plato on the soul

For Plato, the soul and the body were two separate entities. The body is the temporary, physical, material aspect of the person, and the soul is the essential (in the sense of being the essence of the person), immaterial aspect. In Plato's understanding, the soul is temporarily united with a physical body, but can leave the body and move on. To use a modern analogy, the soul might be seen as the driver of a car, who inhabits the car for a while and then gets out and goes off elsewhere.

In his work *Phaedo*, Plato puts into the mouth of Socrates his beliefs about the immortality of the soul. Plato wanted to show that Socrates had not failed in his mission to educate people, even though he had been executed, because his soul would continue to immortality after death. It would be released from the body and able to renew its contemplation of the Form of the Good. Socrates argued that the soul continues to live on in a mode where it still has thought and intelligence. After death, it is undisturbed by the distractions of constant bodily demands so that it can reach its highest state. Socrates also argued that the soul necessarily must continue living, because life is the essence of what a soul is. The soul animates the person by giving it life; so if a soul is a life-giving essence, then it was obvious (to Socrates and Plato) that it must always have life. It would be contradictory for a soul to die.

Plato gives (through the mouthpiece of Socrates) arguments to justify the view that the soul is immortal.

He argues that every quality comes into being from its own opposite, or at least depends on its opposite, to have any existence at all. Something is 'big' because there are smaller things; something else is 'bright' because there are duller things; something else again is 'hot' because there are colder things. Qualities, then, depend on their status relative to each other. Plato uses this notion to draw the conclusion that, therefore, life comes from death, and death comes from life, in an endless chain of birth, death and rebirth.

Plato also uses an argument from knowledge to support his belief in the immortality of the soul. In the dialogue 'Meno', a slave-boy with no education is given a geometry puzzle to solve. Through questioning, the boy is able to work out the answer to the problem, which (to Plato) illustrated that the boy must have been using knowledge he already had, from before birth, because his status in life meant that he could not have had the education necessary to help him solve such problems. Plato thought that our intuitions were evidence of knowledge attained before birth. This, to Plato, showed that our souls had once lived in the world of perfect Forms.

When Plato wrote about the soul, he used the metaphor of a chariot being pulled by two horses. The two horses are 'appetite' and 'emotion', basic needs which pull us along and motivate us; they are controlled by the charioteer 'reason', who holds the reins and makes sure that the appetite and the emotion work together in a rational direction. Without the guiding hand of reason, we can be led astray: for example, if we let our emotions get the better of us, we could say or do something inappropriate, and if we let our appetites take the lead then we can find ourselves over-indulging in pleasures rather than making progress. People who let reason guide the other aspects of their mental lives are wise.

Plato's view of the soul is called a 'tripartite view' as he saw the soul consisting of these three elements, appetite, emotion and reason.

For Plato, because the soul is immortal and the body very clearly is not, the soul and the body had to be two different and distinct things. He did not question the means by which the mind and the body might be joined together and work together in the same person, in the way that Descartes did in the seventeenth century, but he did consider how an immortal soul might become attached to a particular individual person's temporary physical body.

At the end of *Republic*, Plato introduces a story known as the 'Myth of Er', in which he raises some ideas about the immortality of the soul. In the story, told through the mouth of Socrates of course, a soldier called Er died on the battlefield. At least, he appeared to die, but ten days later, when the fighting was over and it was safe for the bodies to be recovered for funerals, there was no sign that Er's body had decomposed at all. On the twelfth day, when Er's body had been placed on the funeral pyre, he

Plato was convinced that people have eternal souls which connect them to the world of the Forms

See Chapter 1.1 for more on role of reason in Plato's thought.

suddenly came back to life, and was able to tell everyone all that he had experienced of the afterlife.

Er told his listeners that, once he had died, he set out on a journey in which he encountered judges who rewarded and punished the souls of those who had died. Those who had lived morally good lives went upward into a place where they were rewarded for all their good deeds; those who had been immoral were punished with pain equal to ten times the amount of pain they had inflicted on earth. Some had committed crimes so bad that they could never be released from underground punishment. Er also witnessed the way in which souls choose for themselves a new life on earth, either animal or human, before being reborn. Sometimes, those who had been rewarded chose new lives of great power and dictatorship, without considering the sorts of deeds they might have to commit in order to achieve such power. Those who had been punished sometimes chose more wisely, having learned from their experiences. Only the philosophical, who understood the importance of choosing a new life of peace and justice, benefited from the cycle of life and death. The others simply ricocheted between happiness and misery, reward and punishment.

According to many scholars, the 'Myth of Er' is meant to demonstrate the necessity of seeking wisdom through philosophy in order for the soul to benefit. They come to understand what makes a good life and leads to reward, and what to avoid. Each person has a conscious choice to make about the next life, and therefore carries all the responsibility for it.

Plato thought that the soul was distinct from the body, a dualist view

Once the souls had chosen their destinies, they were given some special liquid to drink, which made them forget their previous life and their afterlife experiences; except for Er, who was freed to return to his funeral pyre and educate his friends.

Plato, when considering the nature of the soul, was thinking in the context of his dualist understanding of reality. He was trying to work out what was temporary and subject to change, and what was eternal; he was also exploring how humans can relate to the world of the Forms, and how reason can give the best route to certain knowledge and wisdom, as part of his argument that society would be better run by philosopher-kings.

Aristotle on the soul

Aristotle disagreed with Plato. Aristotle was asking himself questions which were rather different; while Plato was interested in the best ways to run society and the importance of philosophical reasoning for the gaining of wisdom, Aristotle was more interested in this physical world and the things that could be learned about it by scientific, empirical observation. When Aristotle considered the nature of the soul, it was in the context of trying to discover the essence of things. What is it, that makes us essentially human? What distinguishes a living person from a dead one?

In Aristotle's view, the soul was a '**substance**', which was a term he used in his own way to mean the 'essence' or 'real thing'. Aristotle saw a problem: how can we say that the newborn baby, the toddler, the child, the adolescent, the adult, and the elderly man are all the 'same person'? His answer to this question, one which has puzzled philosophers for centuries, was that the physical body is in a continual state of change, but the 'substance' remains the same, in terms of the continuing identity. This continuing identity, or 'essence' was what Aristotle understood to be the soul, for which he used the term 'psyche'.

Aristotle is often considered to be the founder of psychology as a science, although the topics he chose to investigate are quite different from those chosen by modern psychologists. Modern psychologists concentrate on consciousness, subconsciousness and various mental states, whereas Aristotle turned his attention to giving an account of the features which distinguish the essence of living things.

Aristotle took a much more materialistic attitude towards the soul than Plato had. He considered it to be not just some kind of invisible part of the person, but include the matter and structure of the body along with its functions and capabilities – its 'form', using the word 'form' in the same sense that he uses it when talking about a 'formal cause'. The soul is that which gives a living thing its essence, so that it is not just matter but has all the capabilities and characteristics that it needs in order to be what it is. His starting point for thinking about the soul is still used in modern biology classes, where students are taught the characteristics of living things: that they feed, move, breathe, grow, excrete, reproduce and are sensitive. Living things are distinguished from non-living things by what they can do, their capabilities, and it is these capabilities that for Aristotle define the 'soul'.

In his treatise *De Anima* ('On the Soul') he began by saying that 'the soul is in some sense the principle of animal life'. His idea of the soul, or 'psyche' was that it is that which distinguishes a living thing from a dead thing.

Aristotle thought that there were various kinds of soul. Plants have a vegetative or 'nutritive' soul, in that they have the capabilities to get nourishment for themselves and to ensure the reproduction of the species, but they have no ability to reason or to make plans. Animals have 'perceptive' souls, because they have senses with which to experience the world around them, and they react to different stimuli. They have enough intelligence to distinguish between pleasure and pain. Humans have a higher degree of soul because they have the ability to reason, and they can tell right from wrong. For Aristotle, then, the soul was not some separate entity, distinct from the body. The soul is the capacities that the body has, to do whatever it is meant to do. In this way, Aristotle's thinking about the soul is linked with his ideas about causality; the soul is that which gives the matter its form, its efficiency and its final purpose (telos).

Aristotle used the analogy of wax with a stamp in it to illustrate his idea that the soul could not be separated from the body

Aristotle believed that the soul was inseparable from the body, and that the soul was that which gives the body its 'essence'

Aristotle tries to explain what he means by giving some examples.

> 66 'Suppose that a tool, e.g., an axe, were a natural body, then being an axe would be its essence, and so its psyche [soul]; if this disappeared from it, it would have ceased to be an axe, except in name …' 99

Aristotle, 'De Anima.'
In *The Cambridge Companion to Aristotle*, ed.
Jonathon Barnes, 1995, p. 172

The soul of an axe, if we can imagine it to be a living thing, then, would be its capacity to chop. A toy axe is not a 'real' axe, because it does not have the capacity to chop wood, so it is just called an axe for the purposes of a child's imagination; it is only an axe in name.

Aristotle also gives the example of an eye, where, if it were an animal, its soul would be its capacity to see. He says that if the eye is unable to see then it is nothing but matter, 'no more than the eye of a statue or painted figure'. He did not think that inanimate objects actually had souls, as he thought that souls distinguished living things from non-living things, but he used non-living examples to clarify what he meant, by asking us to imagine what their souls would be if they were living beings.

For Aristotle, the soul was inseparable from the living body in the same way that the shape stamped into a block of wax is inseparable from the matter of the wax.

The capacity to chop could not have an existence on its own, without the axe, and the capacity to see could not exist without the eye.

Because Aristotle believed that the soul and the body could not be separated, his view did not allow for the idea that the soul could survive

Apply your knowledge

1. What do you think Aristotle would say would be the soul, or psyche, of a pen, or a chair, or a chimney, if we could imagine that they had souls?

2. What do you think is the difference between a living and a non-living thing – how would you explain it?

3. Both Plato and Aristotle would agree that, at the point of death, the soul leaves the body. Explain in your own words the different things that each of them meant by this.

the death of the body in any way. His view was a much more materialist one than Plato's, and has been very influential, especially among non-religious philosophers. However, as his thought developed, Aristotle began to wonder if perhaps the reason might be able to survive even when the body had died; but his thoughts on the nature of human reason and the extent to which the reason requires a physical body are among the most difficult and obscure of his writings. He did not seem to think that the reason could continue in the sense of it still being an individual personality, and it is not likely that Aristotle believed people could live after death in any personal sense.

....

66 To attain any assured knowledge of the soul is one of the most difficult things in the world. **99**

Aristotle, Book 1, *De Anima*

....

Consciousness as a mystery: the mind–body problem

Machines are increasingly sophisticated as technology advances. Not only can they perform some tasks more quickly and efficiently than humans, but they are also becoming more adaptive and responsive. People use cameras with a setting which adjusts automatically to the light levels without the photographer needing to work them out; cars can have parking and reversing sensors to judge the proximity of other objects to help the driver avoid hitting things; ventilators for premature babies can automatically adjust the pressure they use so that the new baby is encouraged to learn to breathe independently. We often use figurative terms that suggest such machines are in some way thoughtful: they 'know' the right light setting, they 'perceive' obstacles, they 'judge' the pressure. However, most people believe that machines are fundamentally different from human beings. People have consciousness whereas machines have nothing more than sophisticated design and programming. The camera might adjust its aperture, but it does not really 'see' the scene around it as a sense perception, and it has no 'mind's eye' where it knows in advance the effect it would like to achieve in the photograph. The reversing sensor might set off a warning noise when the car is approaching a wall but it does not really 'feel' alarmed or anticipate that the car might be damaged and hope to avoid this. The ventilator might regulate its functions but it does not 'know' about the baby to which it is attached, nor care whether the baby survives.

People seem different from machines because we know what it is like to have consciousness. We don't just respond to stimuli in a rudimentary way, as plants do and many non-human animals do; we are also subjective and self-aware. We can talk in terms of 'I have a mind' and 'I have a body', and we mean something by the word 'I'. We even talk about our own thoughts

Most people think that humans are different from machines because humans have consciousness whereas machines do not

Think question

Do you think that machines could ever be developed to a point where they had minds like ours? What reasons would you give to support your opinion?

and feelings as if somehow we are witnesses to them as conscious selves; we don't simply feel happy or feel frightened, but are aware of ourselves feeling emotions and sensations; we know we enjoy feeling happy, and we can remember the last time we felt frightened, and imagine what it might feel like to have an experience we have not yet had. When other people tell us about their 'inner lives', we can relate to the experiences they describe.

The nature of consciousness remains a great mystery to scientists and to philosophers. How, if at all, can we explain our 'inner lives' in scientific terms? Do we all experience consciousness in the same way?

Some people, then, argue that machines differ from humans because machines lack the consciousness that humans have. They might extend this to argue that everything machines can do is capable of being explained in physical terms, whereas in contrast, human beings are more than just physical and there are some aspects of human existence which cannot be explained physically. As well as being made of matter, human beings also possess a faculty known as a 'mind' which enables us to think, to interpret our experiences and to have emotions; in other words, to have an 'inner landscape' which machines could never have because, in this view, the mind is non-physical.

The view, that a human being can be thought of as consisting of two separate things: (1) the physical body; and (2) the non-physical mind, is known as **dualism**. (Dualism is a name given to any belief system which proposes that there are two distinct categories of things. Belief that there are two forces, one of good and one of evil, is a kind of dualism, as is Plato's belief that there is a world of physical things and a separate world of Forms.)

In this dualist view of human nature, the mind and the body are different components of a human person, one a non-physical component and the other a physical component. The physical body, which includes the brain matter, is where physical activity takes place, such as eating, sitting, walking and so on. The mind, in contrast, is the part of the person which is non-physical and which does the thinking and feeling. So although it is my physical body which walks into the kitchen, makes the tea, drinks it and digests it, it is my mind which decides to have a tea break, which chooses the mug I want to use and which enjoys the taste of the tea. This dualist view, although common, is not without its problems.

The mind

Many people understand the mind to be the part of a person which has intelligence and emotions. It enables us to interpret the data we get from our senses so that we experience them; our minds form judgements, make choices and hold memories. However, the question of the nature of the mind is a thorny problem for philosophers, psychologists and scientists. Some argue that the idea of the mind being a 'part of a person' is nonsense; for them, the mind is the activity of physical matter, and not a separate 'part'. It would be like saying that a sneeze is the part of the

Roboy is a robot. While one day his inventors hope he will be able to help humans with daily tasks, he does not have consciousness body that expels irritants from the nasal cavity, when of course a sneeze is something a body does, it is not a part or an aspect of a body.

The body

The human body consists of the physical stuff of which human beings are made. People agree that we all have bodies, but there is even a difference of opinion about the nature of the body in relation to what it means to be human. For materialist philosophers, we are simply our bodies and nothing more; our bodies are not 'the physical part' of us, because there are no other parts. But for others, the body might be understood as a kind of vehicle which the 'self' or 'soul' inhabits for a while but which is in some way less real than the self.

Substance dualism

Substance dualism is the name given to the view that the mind and the body are separate substances which both exist. Philosophers make a distinction between substances and properties. A substance is a subject which has various properties: for example, my mug is a substance, and it has the properties of being patterned, breakable and nonporous. The rug on the floor is a substance and it has the properties of being soft and red. Properties cannot exist on their own, without a substance which has those properties. There is no such thing as the property of being soft, existing separately from soft things.

The question arises, for philosophers of mind, whether the mind is a substance which has properties or whether it is something else. Substance dualists hold the view that the mind is a substance, and that thoughts, intentions, feelings and emotions are properties of the mind. If I am angry, for example, then the substance that is my mind would have the property of anger.

According to substance dualists, the other substance of a human person is the body. The body is also a substance in the same sense of being a subject which has properties. It could have the properties of being tall, or young, or freckled, for example. It has the property which philosophers call 'extension', which means that it takes up space and has measurements. In substance dualism, the mind is not physical and is not extended (does not take up space) but it does have the properties of thought (mental capabilities); and in contrast the physical body does have extension but does not have the properties of thought.

Somehow, according to substance dualism, these two distinct substances are attached to each other and form the human being, a person with both physical and mental capabilities who can have a height, a weight and all other aspects of physicality, while at the same time having an inner, mental life as a 'self' which is quite distinct from anything physical.

This view has had many supporters throughout the history of philosophy. Pythagoras, Socrates and Plato, for example, all held the view that we have an essential non-physical self which could be capable

> ## Apply your knowledge
>
> 4. How would you define the terms 'consciousness', 'mind' and 'self'?
> 5. Which do you find more appealing: the view that we are no more than physical, or the view that there is a part of us that is distinct from the body? Give reasons for your choice.

Substance dualists claim that the mind and the body are two distinct and different substances of existing without the body. Some people also describe having had 'out-of-body experiences' in which they feel as if their 'essential self' somehow left their physical body. The idea that people are made of more than just their physical bodies has been taken up and developed by many different religious world views, mainly because it leaves open the possibility of continuing life after a person's physical, bodily death.

Descartes' dualist understanding of consciousness and the body

Probably the most famous defence of a dualist understanding of human nature comes from René Descartes (1596–1650). Descartes lived in the seventeenth century and was profoundly influential in what was known as the 'Scientific Revolution'. This was a time when the conventional medieval traditions of thought were losing their popularity and were being replaced by experimental methods and more rigorous processes of reasoning. Descartes' background in mathematics made him want philosophy to have the same kinds of certainty and precision as mathematics has; he believed that all human knowledge had the scope to be interconnected in some way. According to many stories of his life, he had a series of visions which showed him how the whole scope of human knowledge, including philosophy, could be reworked into a coherent and unified system of truth, based on mathematics and logical reasoning.

In one of Descartes' earliest works called *Le Monde* (1629–33) (translated as 'the world' or 'the universe') which was about physics and the universe, he suggested that all the matter in the universe was essentially the same kind of thing. There were no 'earthly substances' in contrast with 'heavenly substances' as the medieval thinkers had supposed; and the earth was, in Descartes' view, not uniquely special in its construction, but just one small part of a whole universe which all operated on the same fundamental physical laws of nature. This insight is one which is commonly accepted in modern physics.

Descartes had to be careful with the things he said. In 1633, Galileo Galilei was condemned by the Catholic Church for saying that it was the sun, and not the earth, that was in the centre of the universe – Descartes privately agreed with Galileo and quietly withdrew *Le Monde* from public circulation. He released his next book anonymously in 1637. It was a book primarily about science but it had a preface called 'Discourse on the Method of Rightly Conducting Reason and Reaching the Truth in Sciences' which went on to become one of Descartes' most famous pieces of writing. Commonly known just as 'Discourse', the work discussed, amongst other things, ideas about questions of knowledge, the existence of God, and the relation between the mind and the body.

What were the limits of human knowledge, what could be known for certain and what should be treated with **scepticism**? Could the existence of God be demonstrated through the use of reason? What is the mind, and is it distinct from the body?

Having introduced these ideas and questions in 'Discourse', Descartes went on to explore them in more detail in his masterpiece *Meditations on First Philosophy* (1641), commonly known as *Meditations*. Descartes declared his aim that the book should demonstrate that there is a clear distinction between the 'soul' (or mind) and the body.

Descartes set out on a quest to work out what could be known with certainty. He realised that this was not going to be easy, as our senses can sometimes be mistaken, and so he decided to adopt a method known as 'hyperbolic doubt'. ('Hyperbolic' is used in the sense of being extreme or exaggerated.) He decided to think about all the things he thought could be known, and reject them if there was any doubt at all of their certain truth. By using this method he might be able to establish which beliefs have both endurance and stability.

He started by testing all of his beliefs with sceptical arguments, questioning how he could be sure that his belief was true. Could he trust his sense experiences? Not entirely, because there are times when our senses deceive us and it turns out that the thing we thought we saw or heard was not really there at all. Perhaps all the things he thought he could sense around him were illusions, or perhaps he was dreaming.

Descartes wondered whether he could be certain about the basics of mathematics, such as that a straight line is the shortest distance between two points; but he rejected mathematical axioms too, on the basis that our reasoning could turn out to be wrong, or perhaps God could be deceiving us. From this point, Descartes began to wonder about the possibilities of an evil demon existing, who had the power to deceive us about everything we held to be true. Descartes did not seriously believe in the existence of such a demon, but his point was that we cannot be 100 per cent certain that we are not being deceived about everything.

By the time he had reached this stage of his thinking, Descartes was feeling overwhelmed by the implications of scepticism. However, he then realised that there was one fact, the 'first certainty' which he could not possibly doubt and which could lead him back onto the path of establishing some truths: this was the fact that here he was, thinking sceptically. He could not doubt his own existence as a thinker, because he would have to exist as a thinker in order to be able to do the doubting; and so Descartes arrived at probably the most famous of all his conclusions: 'I think, therefore I am.' (This 'First Certainty' is often referred to in Latin, '*cogito, ergo sum*' or 'the *cogito*' for short.) Later, Descartes revised his 'First Certainty' to 'I am, I exist' because he did not want to sound as though his own existence was a conclusion of an argument but instead he wanted it to sound like a basic fact; but it is 'I think, therefore I am' that has captured people's imaginations and is the phrase that is remembered when they think of Descartes.

Descartes knew for certain that he had a mind, because he could not possibly doubt it without a contradiction; but he could not be certain that

Descartes rejected the idea that sense perception can give us certain knowledge of the world, because our senses can easily be misled

Descartes adopted a system of extreme doubt in an attempt to identify what could be known for certain

Think question

Some films and other works of fiction explore the idea that everything we perceive is an illusion and it is possible that we are being tricked – can you think of any examples of such works?

he had a body (we could, in principle, be deceived into thinking that we had bodies when actually we were some kind of disembodied thinking thing). Therefore, it seemed for Descartes that the mind and the body had to be two distinct substances. The mind has something peculiar about it which means that we cannot doubt its existence, whereas the existence of the body can be cast into doubt.

Descartes followed the thinking of Augustine, in saying that it is possible for us to imagine being without a body, but impossible for us to imagine being without a mind

> 66 I saw … that from the mere fact that I thought of doubting the truth of other things, it followed quite evidently and certainly that I existed; whereas if I had merely ceased thinking, even if everything else that I had ever imagined had been true, I should have had no reason to believe that I existed. From this I knew I was a being whose whole essence or nature is simply to think, and which does not require any place, or depend on any material thing, in order to exist. Accordingly, this 'I' – that is, the soul by which I am what I am – is entirely distinct from the body, and indeed is easier to know than the body, and would not fail to be whatever it is, even if the body did not exist. 99

René Descartes, *Discourse*, 1637, 1:127

For Descartes, therefore, it made sense to speak of a human person as being made of two distinct substances: the physical body, and spiritual mind. He decided that the mind and the body cannot be the same thing, because they have such different properties: thought and extension respectively. There are many other differences too; Descartes was particularly interested in the idea that the body has different parts (the head, the leg, the ribs and so on) whereas, in his view, the mind could not be divided into parts. For Descartes and for other thinkers, it seemed obvious that two things could not be identical if they had different properties.

This left Descartes with some further puzzling questions to address: how are the mind and the body attached to one another and how do they interact so closely?

As well as being interested in mathematics and philosophy, Descartes was also very keen on anatomy. He thought that the pineal gland, which is a very small organ located in the centre of the human brain, had something to do with the connection between the soul and the body. In contrast with the views of modern medicine, and also with quite a lot of the science that was understood by his contemporaries, Descartes thought that the pineal gland contained air-like 'animal spirits' which controlled imagination, sense perception, bodily movement and memory. In a letter of 1640, he put forward the view that the pineal gland was 'the principle seat of the soul' although he was not entirely clear about how this worked. He had come to this conclusion because other parts of the head are 'double': we have two eyes, two ears, two hemispheres of the brain and so on, but just the one pineal gland, which is central. To Descartes, the singularity of the pineal gland strongly suggested that it could be the connecting point between the material person and the immaterial soul.

Property dualism

Many thinkers have not wanted to go quite as far as Descartes in considering that the mind and the body are two completely different and separate substances. They have instead developed different ideas which can be grouped under the heading of 'property dualism'. According to property dualism, there is only one kind of material, physical substance, but there are two distinct kinds of properties: mental properties, and physical properties. The physical matter of the brain has physical properties (such as size and mass and shape) but also has mental properties (such as opinions, emotions and memories).

One popular kind of property dualism is known as 'emergent **materialism**', which is the idea that as physical things become more and more complex, new properties 'emerge' from them, which cannot be reduced simply to the material. The mind, in this view, has its own existence in some sense but is not a completely separate substance from the physical. This is a view which was held by John Stuart Mill, amongst others.

Property dualists hold that the mind and the body have different properties but the same substance

Reductive materialism

Reductive materialism is a theory of mind which has a lot of different names, including 'identity theory' and 'type physicalism'. It is a theory which says that the mind is not distinct from the physical brain but is identical with it.

According to this theory, mental states can be classified into different types, such as memory, pain, happiness, desire and so on, and these different types correspond to activities in different parts of the brain. When chemical reactions are happening in a particular part of the brain, we feel an

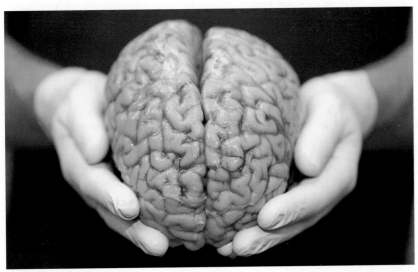

For reductive materialists, mental states are identical with physical events in the brain

emotion or we make a decision or we remember a fact, depending on the type of mental event that corresponds to that part of the brain. As one psychologist with the unfortunate name of Boring asserted, mental events and physical events in the brain are identical; it is not just the case that when X happens in the brain, the consequence is that we feel Y, but it is the case that X and Y are the same thing. Particular reactions in the brain are identical with feeling angry, or with choosing a biscuit from the tin, or having a political opinion. The chemical reactions do not just cause the mental events, but are the mental events. Supporters of reductive materialism recognise that neuroscience does not yet understand exactly how the physical functions of the brain work, but they are convinced that there is nothing more to the human person than physical material.

Reductive materialism, therefore, allows no room for any concept of life after death. There is no way in which the 'self' or consciousness could leave behind the physical body at the point of death, because the consciousness is physical and is nothing more than physical, and therefore when the body dies the consciousness ends.

Gilbert Ryle and the 'ghost in the machine'

Gilbert Ryle (1900–76) made an important contribution to the debate about the relationship between the mind and the body, in his book *The Concept of Mind* (1949). Taking a materialist view, he criticised the notion that the mind is distinct from the body, or that mental states are different from physical states.

In this book, he argued that any talk of a 'self' or 'soul' existing beyond the physical body is a mistake in the way we use language. He used the example of someone watching a cricket match, seeing all the players and the different tactics used during the match but then asking where the 'team spirit' was, as if it is something to be found as an extra to the other observable elements of the game. The 'team spirit' is a term which denotes the way the observable people in the game interact with one another. In the same way, he thought, the mind should not be considered to be something separate and extra, apart from the body. He made fun of the kind of ideas suggested by Descartes, saying that a separate mind and body was like 'the ghost in the machine', as if we were physical machines being operated by some kind of invisible mind.

Ryle argued that treating the mind and body as if they were two things of a similar logical kind was a 'category mistake'

Ryle said that the traditional mind and body distinction was what he called a 'category mistake', because it tries to treat the mind and the body as if they are two different things of a similar logical kind when in fact they are not in the same logical category. He thought that traditionally, people tend to think that the mind and the body are both things that a human being possesses and that they are somehow 'harnessed together' but that they are capable of being separated after death. However, Ryle argues that this view is not at all sound and does not fit with what we know about psychology and neuroscience.

Ryle was not rejecting the idea that people have minds or personalities or consciousness (which some people might call the 'soul' in an Aristotelian sense), but he was rejecting the idea that it was a separate part or aspect of a human being. Just as the team spirit is not found in addition to the team but is a way of describing how the team works, the 'soul' or 'mind' is not an addition to the physical person but a way of describing a person's functions.

Richard Dawkins' materialist views

Modern materialist views, such as those held by Richard Dawkins, assume that there is no part of a person that is non-physical. Following the traditions of Aristotle, materialists believe that the consciousness cannot be separated from the brain, because for the materialist, nothing exists except matter. The materialist view, then, rules out the possibilities of any form of conscious life after death, since consciousness is caused by purely physical phenomena: so once the brain has died, the consciousness must also end.

Richard Dawkins, in his book *The Selfish Gene* (1976) proposes that humans are nothing more than 'survival machines', and he completely discounts the idea that humans have any kind of soul to distinguish them from other species. Humans, like other living creatures, are the vehicles of genes, which are only interested in replicating themselves in order to survive into the next generation. Of course, Dawkins understood that genes do not have the capacity to think and to have intentions in any literal way, so that to speak of what they are 'interested in' or of their 'selfishness' is to use metaphor and analogy; his point was that human beings do not have immortal souls and instead are simply a mixture of chemicals: 'survival machines – robot vehicles blindly programmed to preserve the selfish molecules known as genes' (Dawkins, *The Selfish Gene*, 1976, p. vii).

Dawkins wrote about 'soul one and soul two', by which he meant two different ways of understanding the soul. 'Soul one' is the viewpoint which claims that the soul is a distinctive spiritual supernatural part of a person, capable of knowing God and of surviving death. This is the understanding that Dawkins rejects. 'Soul two' in contrast is a more Aristotelian understanding of the soul, which refers to someone's personality and individuality, to the fact that they have a life and are motivated to make choices. Dawkins accepts 'Soul two', which does not include any notion of the possibility of life after death or any idea that people have some kind of connection with anything divine or supernatural.

In his book *River out of Eden* (1995, p. 18), Dawkins asserts: 'there is no spirit-driven life force, no throbbing, heaving, pullulating, protoplasmic, mystic jelly. Life is just bytes and bytes and bytes of digital information'. For Dawkins, this does not mean that life has nothing awe-inspiring about it. He finds the whole evolutionary process awe-inspiring, as well as the achievements of great men and women. However, he does not believe that we need any additional supernatural 'soul' to explain this, nor any belief in life after death to make sense of what we are as humans.

Dawkins argues, as did Bertrand Russell before him, that religious belief in ideas such as the immortality of the soul have no sound basis. They are beliefs based on wish-fulfilment for those who lack courage, who fear death and who cannot cope with the idea of their own mortality. For the materialist, the consciousness is no more than electro-chemical events within the brain, and therefore the individual person is incapable of surviving brain death.

Discussing soul, mind and body

How might the materialist criticise a dualist approach to questions of consciousness?

With a dualist approach to questions about the nature of consciousness and its relation to the body, the body is seen as a kind of vehicle which the person lives in. When a dualist approach is taken, there are possibilities for belief in life after death, because if the mind and the body are separate, then perhaps they could exist separately, with the mind or soul continuing on after the death of the physical body.

Not all thinkers, however, have agreed about this relationship between the mind and the body.

Descartes' view of substance dualism, in particular, has often been criticised. It could be argued that Descartes has done nothing to demonstrate that the mind is a substance; he has merely asserted it. It could be argued that his views create big difficulties, such as how the mind and body interact in the way that they do.

- We do not just notice that our bodies are damaged, when we hurt ourselves, in the same way that we might notice a dent in the car: we actually feel the pain, and it causes mental consequences such as distress.

- Substance dualism cannot explain how mental thoughts can cause physical responses, such as how my mental decision to go over there can result in walking, or how my feelings of embarrassment can cause me physically to blush.

- Also, substance dualism creates what is known as the 'problem of other minds': if the mind is separate from the body, then we can only perceive that other people have bodies but we have no way of knowing whether they have minds.

In his book *Merely Mortal: Can You Survive Your Own Death?* (2001), Antony Flew argues that talk of life after death, where the soul outlives the body and carries on by itself, is nonsensical. He compares it with the humorous nonsense of which Lewis Carroll was fond, where, in *Alice's Adventures in Wonderland* (1865), the Cheshire cat slowly disappeared until there was nothing left of it but its grin: an idea which appeals to our sense of humour because obviously it would be impossible for there to be a grin on its own, without a face to put it on.

Carroll is playing with the idea that a grin could be a 'thing in itself', a substance. Flew writes:

66 The absurdity here arises from the fact that 'grin' is not a word for a substance. It makes no sense to talk of grins occurring without the faces of which grins constitute one possible kind of configuration. 99

Antony Flew, *Merely Mortal: Can You Survive Your Own Death?*, 2001

Flew uses this analogy, and others, to demonstrate his opinion that to speak of someone's mind, or soul, or personality, as if it were a 'substance' is (in his view) a misuse of the term. For Flew, to refer to a mind or a soul or a personality is to refer to the behaviour of the material, physical person, and no more – so there could not be a survival of the mind or soul or personality after the death of the physical body, because the physical body no longer has any behaviour. This is a very Aristotelian view that is echoed by other philosophers too, such as Daniel Dennett, and by some scientists, such as Richard Dawkins.

People often feel naturally drawn to substance dualism; but this attractiveness on its own does not demonstrate that the theory is true. We talk as though we have minds and bodies as separate things, but this does not prove anything. In their book *The Philosophy of Mind* (1986), Peter Smith and O.R. Jones give examples of how we might talk about somebody's 'sake' or somebody's 'build'. For example, we might say that we were going to have supper later than usual for Jill's sake, as she missed the train; or we might say that Jack needed a shirt with longer sleeves because of his build. However, this does not mean that Jill could be separated from her 'sake' or Jack could go out without his 'build'.

Flew argued that just as a grin is not a substance, neither is a soul without 'it'

The distinction between mental and physical properties is not always as clear as substance dualists suggest. Someone who is skilled at hand–eye coordination, for example, seems to be using both physical and mental capabilities in combination, making mental judgements about the right time and speed and direction to move while simultaneously physically moving. Sometimes emotions can give rise to physical symptoms, for example we can feel sudden physical adrenalin rushes when something frightens us. Dualism does not seem to have a satisfactory answer to questions of how the mind and the body interconnect; how does a decision to greet a friend result in physically smiling and waving, if the mind and the body are so distinct?

If people are going to try and find out whether we have minds which are separate from our bodies, this is a more difficult task than it might first appear, as they are looking for something immaterial and it is not at all clear how they would know when they had found it. Hume raised this difficulty: even when we are personally aware that we are individual thinking beings, this does not help to establish that our thinking nature is separate from our physical nature.

How might the dualist respond to materialist criticisms?

Other thinkers, however, disagree with Flew's materialist view of the soul. Those who believe that the soul is linked with, but not identical to, a person's physical body, maintain that it can make sense to speak of a soul or a personality surviving death and continuing to live in a new mode of existence. Thinkers such as Plato and Descartes, and modern scholars such as Ward and Swinburne, argue that the soul is more than just a word for physical behaviour, and can be capable of independent continued existence after the death of the body.

Some people might argue that we can see a flaw in reductive materialism if we think about the way we use language. We might talk about 'Emily' and also about 'Emily's body' but the terms are not used in exactly the same way. We would not say 'Emily's body went to the theatre' because this would imply that her mind was elsewhere, and if we were told that 'police found Emily's body in her back garden this morning', we would assume that Emily was dead rather than that she was doing the weeding. Perhaps this demonstrates that when we are living, thinking, feeling beings, we are more than simply bodies. However, our use of language does not establish anything more than that we use language sloppily. We might talk as though a living human being is more than just a physical body, but our use of language does not prove anything one way or the other, it shows only our traditional way of thinking.

Perhaps a stronger criticism of materialism comes from Descartes' views about the distinctive properties of the mind and the body. Descartes argues that the mind and the body cannot be identical, because they have such different properties. The mind does not have extension, but the body does. The body does not have thoughts, but the mind does. If two substances are identical, then surely they should have the same properties, not mutually exclusive ones.

It could also be argued that although substance dualism raises questions which we cannot answer, materialism, too, cannot explain how an opinion or a logical chain of reasoning or a strong emotion can be no more than a physical chemical reaction. Neuroscience has a long way to go, and at the moment neither side of the argument can claim to have the total support of science.

The theologians and philosophers Richard Swinburne and Keith Ward both defend, from within the Christian tradition, the idea that human beings have souls which are distinct from physical bodies and which are capable of survival after death. Swinburne, in his book *The Evolution of the Soul* (rev. edn 1997), explains his beliefs that the soul and the body are distinct from each other, so that the soul is capable of surviving even when the body is destroyed. He argues that there are fundamental truths about us as individuals which cannot be explained in purely physical terms, and also that the most important and significant aspects of us which give us our identity are not to be found in our physical bodies. In Swinburne's view, the human soul is unique in that it is capable of logical, ordered and complex thought. The soul is aware of its own freedom to make choices, and also aware of moral obligation. It is because we have souls that we recognise goodness when we see it in other people. It is because of our souls that we have consciences, letting us know when we are right or wrong.

Keith Ward's book *Defending the Soul* (1992) is written as a response to scientists who claim that humans are, in the end, just physical beings:

> 66 Richard Dawkins, Jacques Monod, Desmond Morris and many others have all written popular and influential books, proclaiming that science has now entered the secret citadel of the human soul, and found it empty. Human persons, they say, are not free spiritual agents with a special dignity. They are physical organisms for reproducing genes; and as such, they have no more intrinsic dignity than walking bags of chemical compounds. 99
>
> Keith Ward, *Defending the Soul*, 1992, p. 8

In his book, Ward focuses on the problems he foresees for humanity if belief in the soul is abandoned. He argues that without belief in the soul, morality becomes simply a matter of personal choice and taste, whereas we need the moral claims that the soul recognises as coming from God in order to progress and to achieve that special dignity of being human rather than simply animal. Without the soul, humanity lacks any sense of final purpose.

Ward attacks the materialist position of those who claim that we are nothing more than physical organisms, by returning to the account of the creation of man in Genesis. He writes:

> 66 The Bible puts it supremely well when it says, 'The Lord God took some soil from the ground and formed a man out of it; he breathed life-giving breath into his nostrils, and the man began to live.' Man is made of dust; but he is filled with the spirit of God. He emerges from the simplest material forms, but finds his true kinship in the goal and fulfilment of his existence, the supreme Goodness. 99
>
> Keith Ward, *Defending the Soul*, 1992, p. 147

For Ward, then, it is important that people do not abandon the idea of the soul, because, in his view, if we take the materialist view that we are no more than physical matter, then our moral currency is very much diminished and we no longer think of each other in terms of the sanctity of life.

Brian Hebblethwaite, an Anglican priest, considers the implications for Christianity of developments in the production of artificial intelligence:

> 66 Does it follow that Christian theology is bound to oppose the very idea of artificial intelligence? Not necessarily. Granted, only 'soft', carbon-based, matter has proved itself capable of evolving organisms with brains of sufficient complexity to give rise to consciousness, rationality, and volition [making deliberate choices]. Only through the procreation of human beings have subjects or selves, of whom the language of mind, soul, and spirit can appropriately be used, in fact appeared upon the scene. 'Hard', silicon-based matter, despite the awesome calculating power of digital computers, and despite the possibilities of simulating neural networks through 'sophisticated' feedback mechanisms and built-in randomisers, has shown no signs whatsoever of manifesting even rudimentary forms of awareness, still less affection, imagination, rational thought, or volition. As far as our present knowledge and skill go, artificial 'intelligence' is no more than a metaphor. But if, in the more or less remote future, it were discovered that hard as well as soft matter did, after all, have the capacity to become the vehicle of inner life, including subjectivity, reason, and will, then such artefacts would have acquired selfhood, soul and spirit, and would require to be treated and related to in just the same way as our children. It does not look as if God has made the world that way, but we are not in a position to rule the idea out a priori. 99
>
> Brian Hebblethwaite, 'Soul.'
> In *The Oxford Companion to Christian Thought*, 2000, p. 683

Apply your knowledge

6. Which do you find more convincing: substance dualism, or materialism? How would you defend your choice?

7. What evidence, if any, do you think would be needed to settle the dispute one way or the other?

8. How far would you agree with Keith Ward's claim that our ethics depend on our continuing to believe in the existence of the human soul?

Is the concept of 'soul' better understood metaphorically, or as a reality?

Possibly, problems arise in the distinction between the soul and the body because the idea of a soul is being taken too literally when applied to human persons. We can speak of a 'soul' metaphorically; we might talk of an empty house, with no furniture and no artwork in it, as having no 'soul'; or we might say that someone had put her 'heart and soul' into a project. We would be using the term 'soul' metaphorically, to refer to warmth or to effort. Perhaps, then, the whole concept of soul is better understood as a metaphor, a pictorial way of trying to capture what it means to be human, the special importance of human life and the impressiveness of human endeavours. If talk of the soul is understood as being metaphorical then this could avoid some of the problems that arise when the idea is taken literally, of exactly where the soul is located or how it is attached to the body or where it comes from.

However, if the idea of the soul is understood metaphorically, then this still leaves difficulties. With a metaphor, it can be difficult to know how it is meant to be understood. If it means different things to different people, there is no way of telling whether either is correct, or even whether there is such a things as the 'correct' way to understand. It can obscure understanding rather than enlighten it.

Does discussion of a mind–body distinction always involve category error?

According to Ryle, people who make a distinction between the mind and the body make a '**category error**' because they think that the mind is a thing in the way that the body is a thing. As well as giving the example of team spirit at a cricket match, Ryle also gave the example of someone being shown around the various colleges and faculties of Oxford, and then that person asking 'but where is the university?'; not realising that the University of Oxford was not a separate and distinct thing in itself but was the whole collection of colleges and faculties. Many people would support this view, and say that to think of the mind and the body as distinct things is just the result of taking the metaphor of the 'soul' or 'mind' too literally.

Others, however, would disagree. There is a saying that 'the whole is more than the sum of its parts', and perhaps this is true of the human person. It could be argued that a village is more than just the buildings and the number of individual inhabitants, but that there is also something extra, a community spirit and a history perhaps, which are intangible but nevertheless part of what it means for a village to be a village. Perhaps people who speak of humans being something more than just the physical body are not just making a mistake, but are trying to express something intangible which is, nevertheless, real and important.

Apply your knowledge

9. In what circumstances do people use metaphors rather than literal language? Does this help understanding, or make it more difficult, in your view?

10. Would you argue that the soul is better understood literally, or metaphorically, or neither? How would you support your view?

11. If the soul is understood as a metaphor rather than as a literal substance, what implications might this have for ethical ideas such as the sanctity of life?

Apply your knowledge

12. How far would you agree that talk of a mind–body distinction is just 'category error'?

Learning support

Points to remember

» There are many different opinions about the relation between the mind and the body. Some argue that they are completely distinct (substance dualism), some that they are completely identical (reductive materialism), and many others argue for positions which are somewhere between these two.

» Whether we are just physical beings and no more might have serious implications for our understanding of life after death and of ethics.

» Most people acknowledge that there is a long way to go before scientists understand consciousness, and perhaps they never will; be sceptical about points of view which seem to suggest that the question has been settled.

Enhance your learning

There is a huge amount of literature available on the mind–body problem; this chapter gives just a small selection of possible points of view.

» The substance dualism ideas of Descartes can be found in Descartes' *Principles of Philosophy*, 1.60–65.

» The vocabulary associated with the mind–body problem is often quite daunting, but make an effort to learn the specialist terminology as it will help you to understand the different perspectives you encounter when undertaking wider reading.

» Ideas about artificial intelligence and about the relation between the soul and the body are popular themes for novelists and film-makers. They can be useful, as well as entertaining, ways of developing your own thinking and questioning.

» You could extend your thinking about the nature of consciousness by exploring the ideas of Alan Turing and his 'Turing test' intended to help resolve questions of whether machines can think.

» John Searle's thought experiment commonly known as 'the Chinese Room' would be interesting to research and to think about.

» Chapters 1, 2 and 17 of Susan Blackmore's *Consciousness, An Introduction* (2010) are a useful source of further information on this topic.

» Ryle's ideas about category error can be found in Chapter 1 of Ryle, G. (1949) *The Concept of Mind*.

» The *Stanford Encyclopedia of Philosophy* is an excellent online resource, although often quite demanding. The section on 'Ancient Theories of the Soul' is useful for this topic.

Practice for exams

AS questions and A level questions look identical; the difference between AS and A level assessment is seen in the different proportions of marks awarded for two different skills: the skill of demonstrating knowledge and understanding (Assessment Objective 1, or AO1), and the skill of constructing a critical argument (AO2).

At AS, half the marks (15 marks) are available for knowledge and understanding, and the other half (15 marks) for the quality of your analytical and evaluative argument. You should aim to use your knowledge in order to support the argument you are making throughout the essay, rather than presenting descriptive knowledge in the first half and then an opinion in the second.

At A level, your demonstration of knowledge and understanding is awarded a maximum of 16 marks, and your analytic and evaluative skills are awarded a maximum of 24 marks. You should aim to concentrate on constructing a lucid argument, making use of your knowledge to add weight to the conclusions you draw.

Critically assess the view that human beings have immortal souls.

To tackle this question well, you first need to decide what you think of the view that humans have immortal souls. Do you agree or disagree with the view? You may be undecided, and this is also an acceptable position to take if you support it by saying that neither side is entirely convincing. Notice that the question is asking about 'immortal souls', not just 'souls', so you will need to think about views that say the human soul is immortal.

Practise your skills for AS level

If you are answering this question at AS level, you need to demonstrate knowledge and understanding of different thinkers and their perspectives; you could include Plato, Aristotle, biblical ideas and the views of materialists such as Dawkins. You could include the thinking of Ryle and his ideas about category error. When you present different views, make sure that you comment on them to show your analytical and evaluative skill.

Practise your skills for A level

If you are answering this question at A level, you need to make sure that you have a clear line of critical argument, supported by your knowledge and understanding. Explain where you think the strengths and weaknesses lie in different perspectives, so that the examiner can clearly see that you have dealt with counter-arguments and can see how you reached your conclusion.

Discuss critically the view that the mind and consciousness can be fully explained in terms of physical, material interactions.

For this question, you need to demonstrate a confident understanding of materialist positions in the debate and of contrasting views, and you should be able to justify your opinion by showing its strengths compared with alternative positions.

Practise your skills for AS level

If you are answering this question at AS level, you should be able to explain clearly and accurately different positions on the issue of whether the mind and consciousness are entirely physical. You should be able to give a critical assessment of each position, weighing up their relative strengths and weaknesses and making it clear why you hold your views.

Practise your skills for A level

If you are answering this question at A level, you should start by deciding the position you wish to argue. Do you think that the mind can be explained entirely in physical terms, or do you have a different point of view? You are likely to want to demonstrate your understanding of materialist positions, with careful explanation and reference to thinkers who hold materialist views. Make sure that you include your assessment of their ideas rather than just presenting them in a descriptive uncritical way, and make sure that you have a clear conclusion that follows logically from the arguments you have given.

Chapter 1.3 | Arguments based on observation

Can the existence of God be demonstrated through drawing conclusions from our observations?

Does the natural world provide evidence for the existence of God?

How successful are the traditional teleological and cosmological arguments for the existence of God?

Key Terms

Teleological: looking to the end results (telos) in order to draw a conclusion about what is right or wrong

Cosmological: to do with the universe

Natural theology: drawing conclusions about the nature and activity of God by using reason and observing the world

Contingent: depending on other things

Principle of Sufficient Reason: the principle that everything must have a reason to explain it

Sceptic: someone who will not accept what others say without questioning and challenging

A posteriori arguments: arguments which draw conclusions based on observation through experience

Necessary existence: existence which does not depend on anything else

A priori arguments: arguments which draw conclusions through the use of reason

Logical fallacy: reasoning that has a flaw in its structure

Specification requirements

- The teleological argument
- The cosmological argument
- Challenges to arguments from observations

Introduction

The question of the existence of God is probably one of the most important philosophical questions that there is. However, it is not an easy one to answer through the usual methods of philosophy. Some people believe that the existence of God is not a matter for reasoned argument at all, but a matter for faith; perhaps we need to put away our need for logical steps and for understanding, and try to find God through silence. Others, however, argue that we need to have at least some rational understanding if we are to have beliefs which are at all coherent. We need to have some reasonable basis on which to form our beliefs, and while the traditional arguments for the existence of God might not prove God's existence or non-existence with any degree of certainty, they can at least help to provide some kind of rationale for theism or atheism.

Most arguments for the existence of God are examples of a posteriori reasoning. This means that they depend on experience and observation in order to support their conclusions. They start with something that we can observe, and go from there, using that experience as evidence from which to draw a conclusion. In contrast, there is also a priori reasoning, which relies purely on logic and is independent of experience, for example the kind of reasoning found in mathematics is a priori.

Two examples of a posteriori arguments for the existence of God are **teleological** arguments and **cosmological** arguments.

Teleological arguments attempt to demonstrate the existence of God from the evidence of order and purpose in the world around us. They reason that we would not have complex, purposeful features in the world unless there was a divine intelligence who designed those features.

Cosmological arguments try to demonstrate the existence of God by asking the question 'why is there something rather than nothing?' The existence of the universe, it is claimed, requires an explanation, and the best explanation is the existence of God.

Counter-arguments have been presented to each of these, and so it is left to each individual to decide whether the arguments have sufficient strength to be persuasive.

> ## Think question
>
> Do you think that a reasoned argument, however strong, could result in someone having faith in God? Do we make rational decisions about our religious beliefs, or do they come from somewhere other than our reason?

Natural theology

'**Natural theology**' is the name given to attempts to demonstrate the existence of God and to determine the nature of God using the powers of human reason. It contrasts with 'revealed theology', which is a reflection on the content of what is believed to have been shown to humanity by God.

For most Christians, both natural theology and revealed theology are important and can work in complementary ways. Revealed theology could give people truths that they could never have worked out by themselves, such as truths about life after death or about the saving power of Jesus, but natural theology can also have its role. It can reassure people that their beliefs make sense; it can give them logical reasons to support their faith; it can provide counter-arguments to those who criticise religious belief. It can direct people to evidence of the existence of God in the world around them; for example, in his letter to the Romans, Paul writes to his readers:

> 66 Since what may be known about God is plain to them, because God has made it plain to them. For since the creation of the world God's invisible qualities – his eternal power and divine nature – have been clearly seen, being understood from what has been made, so that people are without excuse. 99
>
> Romans 1:19–20, New International Version

See Chapter 3.3 for more discussion of natural theology.

Natural theology seeks to understand the existence and nature of God through looking at the things we can observe in the world around us

For Paul, it was obvious that we could learn about God just by looking around us. Other Christians have followed this line of thinking and developed natural theology in different directions. We can look at the beauty of the world, and draw conclusions about the creativity of God; we can look at the ways in which different plants and animals have special features which suit their environments, and draw conclusions about an intelligent designer; we can look at vitality and movement in the world, and draw conclusions about a life-giving God; we can look at ourselves, and draw conclusions about the purposes for which God made us.

This approach to theology is not without its difficulties. Not everyone sees a world of beauty, order and purpose; some might look at the suffering and hardships of the world and draw their own conclusions

Is it possible to reach conclusions about God through observing the world around us?

about the nature or existence of God. Some might look for scientific explanations of the workings of the world, rather than assuming that it must have come about through the agency of God. Others believe that we can only learn about God when he chooses to reveal truths to us, and that our powers of reason are not up to the task.

The teleological argument for the existence of God

Teleological arguments for the existence of God are often known as 'design arguments'. The word 'teleological' comes from the Greek 'telos' which means 'tail' or 'end', and teleological arguments are those which look at the end results – the world we can see around us – and use it to draw conclusions, rather like someone might look at a painting and use it to draw conclusions about the artist.

According to teleological arguments, when we look at the world, we see examples of order, beauty, purpose and complexity. The argument claims that these things cannot just arrive as the result of chance: therefore, there must be some being, outside the universe, which designed the world to be this way.

Aquinas' design argument

In the Middle Ages, design arguments were used by Thomas Aquinas (1225–74) in his 'Five Ways' *(Quinque viae)*, which were five ways of demonstrating the existence of God through inductive argument, based on observation and evidence.

Thomas Aquinas is generally accepted to be the greatest of all the medieval philosophers and theologians. He lived at a time when the works of Aristotle had recently been rediscovered by Europeans – they had been forgotten, but preserved by Arabic philosophers, and in Aquinas' time they had only recently come to light because of Christianity's contact with Islam. Aristotle's work was (and still is) immensely impressive, because of its range and its common-sense appeal to logic. It was seen by many medieval church leaders as a threat, because it offered an alternative, and very attractive, way of understanding the world – a way which did not depend at all upon Christian doctrine. Aquinas was among the thinkers who believed that it was necessary to find out where Aristotelian thought and Christian thought could be compatible; he could see the dangers of putting believers in a position where they were forced to choose between Christianity and common sense. A key goal for Aquinas was to show how faith and reason could work alongside each other.

In Aquinas' view, knowledge of God could be reached in two very different ways. One is through revelation, where God chooses to reveal the truth to people, for example through the words of the Bible. The other is through our own human reason (which Aquinas thought was given to us by God for this very purpose). Aquinas thought that if we applied reason

Think question

Do you think it is rational to have scientific explanations for the things we observe in the world and also to conclude that they reveal God?

See Chapter 1.1 for more about Aristotle's philosophy.

Aquinas believed that knowledge of the existence of God could be reached using human reason, in Five Ways

Aquinas believed that faith and reason could be combined in order to reach a better understanding of God

to the evidence that we see around us, we can reach valuable truths. He was a supporter, therefore, of both revealed theology and natural theology.

Aquinas presented 'Five Ways' of showing that God exists, because he was convinced that although the existence of God was not self-evident, it could be demonstrated with logical thought. He wrote about these Five Ways in his book *Summa Theologica* (1265–74), which was written for Christian believers rather than with the intention of persuading others to convert. The book, which was never finished, is over 4000 pages long, and only two of these pages are devoted to the arguments for the existence of God, but these have become some of Aquinas' most famous ideas.

The last of the Five Ways is the one which takes up a version of the design argument for the existence of God. In the Fifth Way, Aquinas said that nature seems to have an order and a purpose to it. We know, he suggested, that nothing inanimate is purposeful without the aid of a 'guiding hand' (he uses the example of an archer shooting an arrow at a target). What he means here is that no non-living thing can have its own purpose; the river cannot decide to flow out to the sea because a river has no mind, and yet it does. The sun cannot decide to rise in the morning and to make each day the right length, and yet it does.

Aquinas used the example of an arrow. If we saw an arrow flying towards a target, he said, we would know that someone must have aimed and fired it, and in the same way, when we look at the world around us and the purposiveness of inanimate objects, we can conclude the guiding hand of God must be behind it. Therefore, everything in nature which is moving but which has no intelligence must be directed to its goal by God.

This is how Aquinas writes it:

Apply your knowledge

1. Can you think of any other examples Aquinas might have used where inanimate aspects of the world seem to have an order and purpose to them?

2. Do you think Aquinas was right when he says that natural objects have a purpose to their movements?

3. Aquinas dismisses the idea that inanimate objects could be 'fulfilling their purpose' by chance. Do you think he was right to dismiss it?

66 The fifth way is taken from the governance of the world. We see that things which lack knowledge, such as natural bodies, act for an end, and this is evident from their acting always, or nearly always, in the same way, so as to obtain the best result. Hence it is plain that they achieve their end, not fortuitously, but designedly. Now whatever lacks knowledge cannot move towards an end, unless it be directed by some being endowed with knowledge and intelligence; as the arrow is directed by the archer. Therefore, some intelligent being exists by whom all natural things are directed to their end; and this being we call God. 99

Thomas Aquinas, *Summa Theologica*, 1265–74

William Paley and the eighteenth-century design argument

It was in the seventeenth and eighteenth centuries that design arguments were at the height of their popularity. These were times of great strides in the fields of science – astronomy, botany, zoology and anatomy were all developing at an exciting pace. Those people who wanted to show that the existence of God could be demonstrated through looking at the world had plenty of material to illustrate their point of view. They could show that scientists were discovering every day how, for example, different plants were suited to their different habitats – some having leaves which allowed maximum water retention in dry countries, while others produced airborne seeds which could be spread by the wind. Different animals were made in different ways so that they could live in different climates and conditions. Physicists were discovering the rules governing forces, motion and gravity, and these rules appeared to work uniformly in all kinds of circumstances, revealing an order in the way inanimate objects operated. The invention of the microscope allowed scientists to observe the intricate structure and function of cells invisible to the naked eye. The more people learned about the world, the clearer it seemed to be that there was an intelligent creator and designer behind it all.

William Paley (1743–1805), who was Archdeacon of Carlisle, put forward what is probably the most famous version of the design argument, in his book *Natural Theology* (1802).

To illustrate his argument, he used the analogy of someone coming across a watch on a heath (this was probably not Paley's own analogy, but one which was popular and which he chose to repeat). Imagine, he said, if someone was out walking on a heath, and looked down and saw a watch lying on the ground. The person finding the watch would notice how well the watch worked in order to tell the time, and would conclude that someone must have made the watch, rather than that the watch had just happened there by chance, or by the random orderings of atoms. Paley said that looking at a watch was similar to looking at the world, or at the human body, and noticing how it all works together – so intricately that one can only infer that there must have been a divine intelligence ordering it. Paley argued that we do not have to have ever seen a watch being made in order to realise that there must have been a maker; the watch does not have to work perfectly for us to realise that it must have been designed. He went on to say that the world itself was even more impressive than a watch in its workings: '… the contrivances of nature surpass the contrivances of art, in the complexity, subtility, [*sic*] and curiosity of the mechanism' (Paley, *Natural Theology*, 1802).

In *Natural Theology*, Paley discusses many different examples of the suitability of the bodily structure of animals to the conditions of their life. He argued that not only is everything clearly designed, but it is designed for a purpose; and it is designed to an infinite degree of care. Even on the smallest scale, there is evidence of craft and skill, and despite the number of different kinds of things in the world, the same care seems to have been taken with the design of each. Paley concluded that this was not only evidence of intelligent design, but of God's care. If God cared enough about each insect to design it with such attention to detail, then surely people can be confident that God will care for them too:

Think question

Some people argue that the theory of evolution shows that God is even more intelligent as a designer than people had imagined. God did not just make the creatures, but he made them with the ability to evolve. What do you think of this argument?

William Paley argued that when we look at the natural world, we can see clear evidence of complex design which cannot have come about by chance

Paley argued that the level of detail we can see in the design of a tiny insect indicates the care God has for his creation.

> ❝ The hinges in the wings of an earwig, and the joints of its antennae, are as highly wrought, as if the Creator had nothing else to finish. We see no signs of diminution of care by multiplicity of objects, or of distraction of thought by variety. We have no reason to fear, therefore, our being forgotten, or overlooked, or neglected. ❞
>
> William Paley, *Natural Theology*, 1802

Paley was not the only eighteenth-century thinker to have produced a teleological argument for the existence of God, but his view became the most famous. Charles Darwin studied Paley's writings as a compulsory part of his university education at Cambridge, and was greatly impressed by them; and many Christian ministers have been trained using the sorts of arguments that Paley put forward.

Apply your knowledge

4. Find some examples of creatures you think are particularly impressive, perhaps because of their beauty or their extraordinary sense perception, their camouflage or a unique way they cope with their environment. Make a few notes, or collect some pictures of them, to use as examples in your writing.

5. Do you think that Paley's analogy of someone finding a watch on a heath is convincing in getting his message across? Explain your answer.

6. Today many people believe that creatures have their distinctive features because of the processes of evolution through natural selection. If the theory of evolution is true, does this mean that Paley was wrong?

The cosmological argument for the existence of God

Cosmological arguments, like the teleological arguments, come from natural theology; they use the world around us to draw conclusions about the existence and nature of God. The cosmological argument uses as its starting point the whole cosmos, or universe, and looks for a reason why the universe should exist.

The basis of the cosmological argument is that the universe cannot account for its own existence. Why do things exist at all – why is there something, rather than nothing? There must be a reason, the argument says, for the existence of the universe, and this reason has to be something which is not part of the physical world of time and space, because the physical world is incapable of being the reason for its own existence.

This argument has a very long history. Plato, in *Timaeus* (c.360BC), argued that everything must have been created by some cause. Aristotle argued that behind the series of cause and effect in the world there must be an Unmoved Mover, and the Kalam argument in Islam is an attempt to show that the universe must have a cause and is not the result of an infinite regress (an endless chain going back for ever).

Two of the best-known cosmological arguments came from Aquinas in the thirteenth century, and Leibniz in the seventeenth. Both drew on the ancient Greeks as inspiration for their explanations of how the existence of the universe provides evidence for the existence of God.

See Chapter 1.1 to compare Aquinas' Unmoved Mover with Aristotle's Prime Movers.

Aquinas and the cosmological argument in the Five Ways

Of Aquinas' Five Ways, the first three are different variants of the cosmological argument. Aquinas based his argument on two assumptions:

1. the universe exists

2. there must be a reason why.

All but the most sceptical would agree with (a); however, not all would agree with (b). Some people, such as Bertrand Russell and Richard Dawkins, are happy to accept that the universe just is, without moving to the conclusion that there should be some reason for it. Aquinas, however, took as a starting point the view that there must be some explanation of why anything exists at all.

First Way – the Unmoved Mover

In his First Way of establishing God's existence, Aquinas concentrated on the existence of change, or motion, in the world. He considered the ways in which objects move, or grow or change in state (for example, become hotter or evaporate). His argument, closely following that of Aristotle, was that everything which is in motion, or changing, has to be put into motion, or changed, by something else. In this way, Aquinas (and Aristotle before him) produced a kind of pre-Newtonian understanding of the physics of motion. Things stay the same unless some force acts upon them to make them change or move. As things are, to our observation, changing and moving, then they must have been set in motion by something; Aquinas thought that this sequence of one thing moving another could not be infinite, but that there must have been an Unmoved Mover to set the whole thing off.

This is how Aquinas writes it:

66 The existence of God can be proved in five ways.

The first and more manifest way is the argument from motion. It is certain, and evident to our senses, that in the world some things are in motion. Now whatever is in motion is put in motion by another, for nothing can be in motion except it is in potentiality to that towards which it is in motion; whereas a thing moves inasmuch as it is in act. For motion is nothing else

Aquinas argued that in the natural world we see motion and change, and from this he drew the conclusion that there must be a First Mover that we call God.

than the reduction of something from potentiality to actuality. But nothing can be reduced from potentiality to actuality, except by something in a state of actuality. Thus that which is actually hot, as fire, makes wood, which is potentially hot, to be actually hot, and thereby moves and changes it …

Therefore, whatever is in motion must be put in motion by another. If that by which it is put in motion be itself put in motion, then this also must needs be put in motion by another, and that by another again. But this cannot go on to infinity, because then there would be no first mover, and, consequently, no other mover; seeing that subsequent movers move only inasmuch as they are put in motion by the first mover; as the staff moves only because it is put in motion by the hand. Therefore, it is necessary to arrive at a first mover, put in motion by no other; and this everyone understands to be God. **99**

Thomas Aquinas, *Summa Theologica*, 1265–74

The emphasis of Aquinas' argument was on dependency, rather than going back in time until a beginning was found; he was using the idea that God sustains the universe, and trying to show that we would not have a universe of change, vitality and motion without a First Mover. The continued changes and movements are because of the continued existence of a mover 'which we call God'.

Second Way – The Uncaused Causer

This argument is very similar, except that it replaces the idea of change and motion with the concept of cause. Every 'effect' has a 'cause', Aquinas argued. Infinite regress (going back and back in time for ever) is impossible, therefore there must be a First Cause 'which we call God'.

Here, Aquinas concentrates on the idea of 'efficient cause', borrowing terminology directly from Aristotle. Aristotle had been very interested in the question of why things exist – not only why they exist in the form that they take, but also why they exist at all – and Aquinas was enthused by the same ideas. When Aristotle had considered the nature of causation, he came to the conclusion that 'cause' works at four different levels, which he named the material cause, the efficient cause, the formal cause and the final cause. By 'efficient cause', Aristotle meant the activity that makes something happen – so, for example, the baker kneading the dough is the efficient cause of the bread, or the musician pulling the bow across the strings is the efficient cause of the music.

Aquinas writes:

> 66 The second way is from the nature of the efficient cause. In the world of sense we find there is an order of efficient causes. There is no case known (neither is it, indeed, possible) in which a thing is found to be the efficient cause of itself; for so it would be prior to itself, which is impossible …
>
> Now to take away the cause is to take away the effect. Therefore, if there be no first cause among efficient causes, there will be no ultimate, nor any intermediate cause …
>
> Therefore, it is necessary to admit a first efficient cause, to which everyone gives the name of God. 99
>
> Thomas Aquinas, *Summa Theologica*, 1265–74

Aquinas took up Aristotle's understanding of causes, to argue that things do not cause themselves in this way – they cannot be their own agents. Therefore, he said, there must be a first efficient cause, and this would be God.

Third Way – contingency

In his Third Way, Aquinas argued that the world consists of **contingent** beings, which are beings that begin and end, and which are dependent on something else for their existence. Everything in the physical world is contingent, depending on external factors for its existence. Things are contingent in two ways: they depend on something having brought them into existence in the first place (for example, volcanic rock depends on there having been the right minerals, sufficient heat and so on to form it), and they also depend on outside factors for the continuation of their existence (for example, plants depend on the light from the sun). Since the time of Aquinas, we have become more aware of the existence of 'eco-systems', and have learned more about how the existence of one species depends very much on the existence of another and on natural resources; some would argue that these discoveries add support to the points Aquinas made.

> *Aquinas depended heavily on Aristotle's understanding of causality in his cosmological argument: see Chapter 1.1.*

> 66 The third way is taken from possibility and necessity, and runs thus. We find in nature things that are possible to be and not to be, since they are found to be generated, and to corrupt, and consequently, they are possible to be and not to be. But it is impossible for these always to exist, for that which is possible not to be at some time is not. Therefore, if everything is possible not to be, then at one time there could have been nothing in existence. Now if this were true, even now there would be nothing in existence, because that which does not exist only begins to exist by something already existing. Therefore, if at one time nothing was in existence, it would have been impossible for anything to have begun to exist; and thus even now nothing would be in existence – which is absurd. Therefore, not all beings are merely possible, but there must exist something the existence of which is necessary. But every necessary thing either has its necessity caused by another, or not. Now it is impossible to go on to infinity in necessary things which have their necessity caused by another, as has been already proved in regard to efficient causes. Therefore we cannot but postulate the existence of some being having of itself its own necessity, and not receiving it from another, but rather causing in others their necessity. This all men speak of as God. 99

Thomas Aquinas, *Summa Theologica*, 1265–74

Aquinas argued that there must be something which is not itself caused or moved, and which does not depend on anything else for its existence, in order to explain the existence of the universe

Aquinas is arguing here that if we agree that everything in the universe is contingent, then we can see that nothing would be here at all. Contingent things need something else to bring them into existence, so nothing would have ever started – there would still be nothing – unless there is some other being, capable of bringing other things into existence but being independent of everything else, or 'necessary'. It would have to be a being that is not caused, and that depends on nothing else to continue to exist – and this, Aquinas thought, would be God.

Gottfried Leibniz

Gottfried Leibniz (1646–1716) was a German philosopher and mathematician, famous in mathematics for the argument he had with Isaac Newton, when both claimed to have invented calculus (it seems likely that each had arrived at the same idea independently). Leibniz's ideas have had a great influence on other thinkers, both in mathematics and in philosophy; one idea which has been particularly influential on the scientists of the twentieth and twenty-first centuries is Leibniz's radical view that the universe is better understood in terms of relationships of space and time than in terms of absolute facts and rules.

Leibniz was a great innovator in logic, both in mathematics and in philosophy

Leibniz raised the question: 'why is there something rather than nothing?' Why does anything exist at all? In order to address his question, Leibniz offered a form of the cosmological argument, which he based on his '**Principle of Sufficient Reason**'. This principle, which is not universally accepted, states that everything which exists must have a reason or a cause for its existence.

According to the Principle of Sufficient Reason:

* if something exists, there must be a reason why that thing exists

* if a statement is true, there must be a reason why that statement is true

* if something happens, there must be a reason why that thing happens.

Whether or not we know the reasons why something exists, or is true, or happens, there still must be a reason, known or unknown.

Leibniz argued that it made no difference whether something was eternal or not – we still need a reason for it. If it exists eternally, we still need a reason for its eternal existence. Leibniz gives the example of the existence of geometry books, to demonstrate that for everything we can think of, whether a book or the entire universe, an explanation is still required:

The Principle of Sufficient Reason states that everything which exists must have a reason or a cause for its existence

66 Suppose that a book on the elements of geometry has always existed, each copy made from an earlier one, with no first copy. We can explain any given copy of the book in terms of the previous book from which it was copied; but this will never lead us to a complete explanation, no matter how far back we go in the series of books. For we can always ask: Why have there always been such books? Why were these books written? Why were they written in the way they were? The different states of the world are like that series of books: each state is in a way copied from the preceding state – though here the 'copying' isn't an exact transcription, but happens in accordance with certain laws of change. And so, with the world as with the books, however far back we might go into earlier and earlier states we'll never find in them a complete explanation for why there is any world at all, and why the world is as it is. … You are welcome to imagine that the world has always existed. But you are assuming only a succession of states, and no reason for the world can be found in any one of them (or in any set of them, however large); so obviously the reason for the world must be found elsewhere. … From this it appears that even if we assume the past eternity of the world, we can't escape the ultimate and out-of-the-world reason for things, namely God. 99

www.earlymoderntexts.com/assets/pdfs/leibniz1697b.pdf, translated by Jonathan Bennett

Apply your knowledge

7. Do you think it is true that everything must have a reason to explain its existence? Could there be things which just exist, or are true, or happen, for no reason at all?

8. Leibniz is arguing that even if the universe is eternal, we still need an explanation for the existence of an eternal universe. Is he right?

9. Are there alternative explanations for the existence of the universe, other than Leibniz's conclusion that it must be God? If so, what are they?

Hume's criticisms of arguments for the existence of God from natural religion

David Hume (1711–76) was a hugely influential Scottish philosopher, who is often referred to as a **sceptic**. He was not willing to accept popularly held beliefs without questioning and challenging them. One of his books, *Dialogues Concerning Natural Religion* (1779), considers the sorts of reasoning put forward by people who attempt to establish the existence of God through natural theology.

Hume wrote this book in the form of a discussion between fictional characters, so that one character, Cleanthes, argues the point of view of the design argument, and another, Philo (who like Hume is a sceptic), argues against it. Demea, another character in the dialogues, defends cosmological arguments. Hume wrote his criticism of design arguments 23 years before Paley gave his famous analogy of the watch; Paley was probably aware of, but not convinced by, the criticisms Hume made. Hume spent a long time writing this book and it was not published until after his death, perhaps because he knew that his criticisms of natural theology would be unpopular.

In his dialogues, Hume made several different criticisms of the idea that design in the world gives strong evidence for the existence of God.

One criticism he made was that the analogy between a watch and the world is weak. Hume said that it cannot be assumed that it is obvious to everyone how the world is like a watch, regularly formed and fit for a purpose. Characteristics of purpose and design might be obvious in a watch, but they are not nearly so obvious in the world. We only make watches because the world is not like a watch; we would only stop and pick up the watch on the heath because it is so unlike the objects which occur in nature. We would conclude that the watch had been designed because we would think it could not have come about naturally, as such design is not seen in nature. It is not right, Hume thought, to draw these comparisons between the world and machines and use them as analogies when there is really very little similarity.

Hume also argued that order in the world does not necessarily mean that someone must have had the idea of the design. Even if we do see order in the world, that does not enable us to leap to the idea of a Divine Orderer. We do not know, for a fact, that all order comes about because of an intelligent idea. The most we can say is, yes, there appears to be some order in the world. The recognition of order, too, has its limitations, because we do not have other worlds to compare with this one, to see if this one is more ordered than another. We have no other standard by which to judge it. Perhaps there are other worlds, a great deal more ordered than this one, which, if we knew about them, would lead us to the conclusion that there is very little order in our own.

Think question

If you saw a queue of people waiting in line at a bus stop, and the people were standing in height order, would you think that someone must have had the idea of lining them up according to size, or would you think that the order must have come about by chance? Do you think it is possible for order to come about by chance, or do you think it is too unlikely to happen in real life?

Order, Hume believed, is a necessary part of the world's existence. If everything were random and nothing suited its purpose, the world would not be here any more. Any world, he thought, will look designed, because if it were chaotic, it would not survive. It is not enough to show that the world is orderly for the conclusion to be drawn that God must have designed it. We also have to be able to prove that this order could not have come about except by God, and this is impossible to show. This self-sustaining order, it is argued, could have come about by chance. This was the kind of idea that Darwin's findings seemed to support, although of course Hume lived 80 years too early to know about Darwinism: the creatures we have around us are suited to their purpose only by chance, because the ones which were not suited (and there were plenty of them) did not survive.

Hume also criticised design arguments because of their assumption that if we look at the effects (the world), we can infer the cause (God). Aquinas had claimed that this was possible – that, in looking at the evidence around us, we can work backwards and see that God must be the cause of it. But Hume attacked this reasoning, saying that cause and effect does not operate as simply as this.

He said that even if we can assume a creator (and he was not sure that we could), there is no reason to suggest that this creator is the Christian God. We have a finite and imperfect world; there is no need to assume that there must be an infinite, perfect God behind it.

Hume used the example of kitchen scales to make his point that we cannot know what caused something when we only have the effect to look at

Hume uses the example of a pair of scales, with one end hidden from view. The end we can see contains a weight that we know – a kilogram, for example – and we can also see that the other end outweighs it, but we have no means of knowing by how much. We cannot infer with any confidence that it must contain a hundred kilograms, or nine, or a tonne; and we certainly could not claim with any authority that it had an infinite weight on it. Similarly, when we look at the world, we have only the effect to look at – the cause is hidden from us. We do not know by looking at the world whether God is clever, or good or loving. He could have been stupid, only copying someone else's ideas, or he could have accidentally stumbled on this design after countless trials and errors. Hume explains:

> 66 But were this world ever so perfect a production, it must still remain uncertain, whether all the excellences of the work can justly be ascribed to the workman. If we survey a ship, what an exalted idea must we form of the ingenuity of the carpenter, who framed so complicated, useful, and beautiful a machine? And what surprise must we feel, when we find him a stupid mechanic, who imitated others, and copied an art, which, through a long succession of ages, after multiplied trials, mistakes, corrections, deliberations, and controversies, had been gradually improving? Many worlds might have been botched and bungled, throughout an eternity, ere this system was struck out: much labour lost: many fruitless trials made: and a slow, but continued improvement carried on during infinite ages in the art of world-making. In such subjects, who can determine, where the truth; nay, who can conjecture where the probability, lies; amidst a great number of hypotheses which may be proposed, and a still greater number which may be imagined?
>
> And what shadow of an argument, continued Philo, can you produce, from your hypothesis, to prove the unity of the Deity? A great number of men join in building a house or ship, in rearing a city, in framing a commonwealth: why may not several Deities combine in contriving and framing a world? This is only so much greater similarity to human affairs. By sharing the work among several, we may so much further limit the attributes of each, and get rid of that extensive power and knowledge, which must be supposed in one deity, and which, according to you, can only serve to weaken the proof of his existence. And if such foolish, such vicious creatures as man can yet often unite in framing and executing one plan; how much more those deities or daemons, whom we may suppose several degrees more perfect? 99

David Hume, *Dialogues Concerning Natural Religion,* 1779

Apply your knowledge

10. Explain in your own words what Hume is saying when he uses the example of a shipbuilder.

11. How convincing do you find Hume's criticisms of natural theology?

12. Do you think Hume has demonstrated that God cannot be the cause or the designer of the world?

Hume argued that if there is order in the world, there are plenty of different possibilities that could be offered to explain it. Order in the world does not demonstrate that it must *have been put there by divine intelligence*

Hume argued that the universe is unique, so we are unable to say what it is like, what it could have been like, or how it must have come into being, because we cannot have experience of any other way that things might have been. We do not know how worlds are usually made, or what degree of order to expect, and so on; and with no other experience, we cannot draw any firm conclusions.

Hume's criticisms of natural theology were based on reason and logic; he argued that you cannot make great leaps and assume that B follows from A as proof, when there could be a variety of other possible explanations.

Hume criticised cosmological arguments by saying that we could not logically move from the idea that everything in the universe has a reason, to say that the universe as a whole must have a reason. Bertrand Russell made a similar point in the twentieth century, by saying that just because every human being has a mother, this does not mean that the human species as a whole has a mother. It is overstepping the rules of logic to move from individual causes of individual things, to the view that the totality has a cause. Hume also argued against the idea that we have to look to God as the cause of the universe; in his book *Dialogues Concerning Natural Religion* (1779), he asks 'Why may not the material universe be the necessarily existent being?' In other words, he was asking why we could not just accept that the universe is eternal and the cause of all the things in it, rather than going one step further and looking for God as an explanation.

Hume also argued that we can imagine something coming into existence without a cause: it is not an incoherent idea. Perhaps the Principle of Sufficient Reason is wrong, and not everything has an explanation. But others have objected that just because you could imagine something existing without a cause, it does not follow that *in reality* it could exist without a cause; the twentieth-century philosopher Elizabeth Anscombe gave the example that we can imagine a rabbit which had no parents and just existed, but obviously this would not be an actual possibility just because we could imagine it.

Discussing arguments based on observation

How persuasive are a posteriori arguments?

A posteriori arguments, because they start from observation of the world, can have an immediate appeal. They draw our attention to something we can see for ourselves: the apparent order in the natural world, for example, or the existence of the universe. The argument then proceeds from a starting point which we are often willing to accept, because we have used our own senses and perceived the things the argument describes, so we might start off in agreement with the premises of the argument.

This does not always work, however. Teleological arguments, for example, start from the observation that the natural world seems orderly and purposive; we are led from this observation to the suggestion that a divine intelligent designer might be the best explanation for the order we observe. However, this argument is only going to start persuading us if we agree with the observation being made. We might think that the natural world seems chaotic and purposeless, in which case the argument is going to do little to persuade us.

A posteriori arguments vary in the extent to which they are persuasive. They involve what is known as 'hypothetical reasoning'; they give us some information based on observation, such as that the world exhibits evidence of order, beauty and complexity, and then they offer an explanation which might account for what has been observed. The persuasiveness of the argument depends on the quality of the explanation, and also on whether it is the best explanation of the observable facts or whether there are other explanations available which might be better.

So, for example, I might observe that the chocolate I bought has gone missing from the cupboard. I might then think of different possibilities, different hypotheses, which might account for this missing chocolate. A persuasive a posteriori argument will offer a hypothesis which seems to give the most plausible explanation to account for the observation. There are all kinds of hypotheses I could consider: perhaps this was a special kind of chocolate which spontaneously evaporated, along with its wrapper, when left in a dark cupboard. Perhaps burglars came in, were not interested in my jewellery or computer or cash but took only the chocolate and then left, cleverly concealing their method of entry. But these are not good enough hypotheses to persuade me. A good piece of hypothetical reasoning is often considered to be one which:

- Introduces the fewest extra assumptions in order to explain the phenomenon. This is known as the principle of 'Ockham's razor'. My hypothesis about the evaporating chocolate involves assuming that such a kind has been invented (raising all kinds of questions about why anyone would do that, and needing other explanations to be found to account for that) and that I unwittingly bought some. My hypothesis about the burglars involves assumptions about an unusual kind of criminal.

- Is plausible; it fits best with what we already know often happens, from previous experience. This criterion is problematic in the context of the cosmological argument, as we do not know how universes are usually caused. My hypotheses about the missing chocolate are implausible, as neither of my suggestions fit with any of my previous experience.

- Matches other evidence we have available. My burglar hypothesis might account for the missing chocolate on its own, but it does not. fit with the untouched jewellery, or the fact that the neighbours saw and heard nothing and that there is no evidence of forced entry.

Probably, then, my missing chocolate is best explained by the hypothesis that another member of the family sneakily ate it. That would introduce few assumptions, as other family members live here and like chocolate; it is plausible, as it often happens that they eat my chocolate, and it matches other evidence such as the discarded wrappers in their rooms.

Can teleological arguments be defended against the challenge of 'chance'?

One of the most common counter-claims made against teleological arguments for the existence of God is that the apparent order or beauty or complexity in the world has occurred by chance. Teleological arguments claim that the best explanation for order, complexity and beauty in the world is the hypothesis that God designed it; that there is an

The principle of Ockham's razor is that the best explanation is usually the simplest, with the fewest extra assumptions required

See Chapter 1.4 for a comparison between a posteriori and a priori reasoning.

Apply your knowledge

13. Do you think the teleological argument for the existence of God presents good hypothetical reasoning? Does it introduce unnecessary assumptions? Does it fit well with what we already know? Does it match other evidence we have available?

14. Similarly, how persuasive do you find the cosmological argument for the existence of God?

intelligent designer who planned and created the universe and intended that it should have these features. Those who disagree often argue that there are better, more plausible explanations for apparent design in the world: these explanations involve the claim that this order, complexity or beauty arose by chance.

Darwin's theory of evolution through natural selection, for example, presents a challenge to teleological arguments for the existence of God. Darwin did not explicitly set out to challenge teleological arguments, but he did present an alternative hypothesis to explain why polar bears have thick fur, why birds have beaks of different shapes appropriate to the food source available to them, why some creatures are well camouflaged to help them hide from predators and so on. The theory of evolution through natural selection suggests that chance mutation of genes accounts for gradual changes in the characteristics of species; a different hypothesis from the one which suggests that species have their characteristics because God designed them that way.

When comparing the hypothesis 'God made it' with the hypothesis 'it happened by chance', the two hypotheses need to be considered to see which is the more persuasive. Perhaps the principle of Ockham's razor leads to the conclusion that 'chance' is a better explanation than 'God'; if we decide that chance can account for apparent order and design, then we do not need to have the assumption of the existence of God, and so maybe the 'chance' hypothesis is simpler. However, we do have to make other assumptions instead. We have to assume that gene mutation could cause something as complex as an eye to develop from basic light-sensitive cells, for example.

We also need to look at which of the two hypotheses is more plausible. Is it more plausible that chance occurrences could account for instances of order and beauty in the world, or is it more plausible that they are here because of intelligent design? Sometimes people who want to defend the existence of God use the example of ink being spilt by chance onto paper. The ink could splash into all kinds of shapes and patterns, by chance. However, if it splashed so that it formed the works of Shakespeare, we might begin to suspect that there was more than chance involved. How much more unlikely (the argument goes) is it that chance could account not only for the works of Shakespeare but for Shakespeare himself, and all the other writers and books and other people and other animals and plants in the world.

A philosopher and theologian called F.R. Tennant was the first to coin the phrase 'the anthropic principle'. By this, he was referring to the way in which the universe seems to be structured so that it was inevitable that life would develop. Physicists have discovered that there are a large number of 'coincidences' inherent in the fundamental laws of nature – and every one of these coincidences and specific relationships between different physical phenomena is necessary for life and for consciousness. If the laws of nature, such as the law of gravity or the laws governing the balance of different gases in the atmosphere, were even slightly different, human life (or any other form of life) could not have happened – and yet, against all the odds, the universe is the way that it is and, therefore, human life exists. For some people, including Tennant, the fact that we are here against all the odds is evidence of the existence of a God who fine-tuned the universe deliberately so that we could exist.

A counter-argument might point out that whatever happens, the odds are always against it. There are so many possible different events that could occur. The odds were against your parents meeting, given that there are billions of people in the world. The odds were against you being born instead of a different sperm meeting that egg at the moment of your conception. Even when people throw dice, the odds are against whichever number comes up. But something has to happen, out of all of the different possibilities, the fact that the odds were against it does not necessarily rule out the possibility of chance.

Whether the existence and apparent design of the universe is the result of chance or of the activity of God is impossible to prove; people have to decide which explanation they find more plausible.

Do cosmological arguments simply jump to the conclusion of a transcendent creator, without sufficient explanation?

Hume's major criticism of cosmological arguments, as well as design arguments, was that they make a jump which is larger than can be justified. His argument is that there are all sorts of different possible explanations for the existence of the universe, and for the apparent design within it. It could have been created by a stupid God who only arrived at the world we have today after countless failed attempts; or it could have been created by a committee of gods, or demons, or by a supernatural being who was only following the instructions given by some other being. Hume did not think that any of these alternative explanations were particularly likely, but he wanted to show that cosmological arguments, and also design arguments, have only demonstrated that God is just one of a large number of possible hypotheses. Demonstrating that 'it could have been God' is not the same as proving that it could not have been anything other than God.

Other people, however, might question whether it is really plausible that anything other than a transcendent God could possibly create and design a universe. Thinkers such as Aristotle and Aquinas draw attention to the need (as they see it) for there to be an Uncaused Causer, an Unmoved Prime Mover, capable of bringing cause and effect and motion into being without being caused or affected. This being would have to have a very special kind of existence, a **'necessary' existence**, where it was not dependent on anything else and was not itself caused but was

Apply your knowledge

15. Which do you find more plausible: that apparent order in the universe has come about by chance, or that it is the result of divine intelligence? What reasons would you give to support your answer?

Apply your knowledge

16. Do you think that other explanations, apart from a transcendent God, for the existence and apparent design of the universe provide an explanation that Leibniz might consider 'sufficient'?

'self-existent'. This being would have to transcend the rest of the universe and exist in a unique, all-powerful way, such that it could only be that 'which we call God' (as Aquinas explains).

Do arguments from observation present logical fallacies which cannot be overcome?

Arguments from observation (a posteriori) are different from arguments which rely entirely on reason (a priori). They do not depend on logic, but on experience, and are about finding an explanation which best fits the experiences we share. People will have different opinions about whether arguments for the existence of God from observation are plausible. They might think that such arguments involve too many assumptions, or that they do not fit well with other evidence or lack of evidence. However, even if an a posteriori argument for the existence of God seems to be flimsy, and other more convincing hypotheses are available, the argument does not fail on the grounds of logic. A posteriori arguments cannot be 'invalid' in the way that **a priori arguments** can, and therefore they do not present **logical fallacies**, only improbabilities.

Apply your knowledge

17. How would you explain the difference between 'improbable' and 'illogical'?

Learning Support

Points to remember

» Teleological arguments and cosmological arguments are both examples of a posteriori reasoning; they start with an observable fact about the world and then use reasoning to try and account for the fact, by claiming that it is best explained by the existence of God.

» Teleological arguments are based on the claim that when we look at the world around us, we see evidence of order, beauty and complexity that, it is argued, suggest the existence of an intelligent designer, which is God.

» Cosmological arguments are based on the claim that there must be a reason and a first cause to account for the existence of the universe. Why does anything exist at all? The cosmological argument claims that the most probable answer to that question is the existence of God.

» When revising the different arguments for the existence of God, make sure that you are clear about which argument is which, otherwise you could lose a lot of marks by writing about the wrong argument entirely.

» When writing a successful essay about the arguments for the existence of God, remember to give your own opinions of the arguments, rather than simply presenting them. You may think that some of the reasoning is weak or unconvincing, in which case, explain why.

Enhance your learning

» A classic formulation of the design argument, accessible and thought-provoking to read: William Paley, *Natural Theology*, Chapters 1 and 2.

» Hume's writing is a pleasure to read for its clarity, good humour and sharp common sense: David Hume, *Dialogues Concerning Natural Religion* Part II.

» Richard Dawkins is a well-known modern writer for the non-specialist intelligent reader; this is one of his best: Dawkins, R. (1991) *The Blind Watchmaker*, Chapter 1.

» A very intelligently written, thorough exploration of the classic arguments for the existence of God: Palmer, M. (2002) *The Question of God*, Chapters 2 and 3.

» Richard Swinburne can be a demanding read but is well worth the effort, especially in conjunction with books by Richard Dawkins: Swinburne, R. (2010) *Is There a God?*

» One of the most popular books for sixth form students as an in-depth, lively and accessible consideration of issues in the philosophy of religion: Vardy, P. (1999) *The Puzzle of God*.

Practice for exams

AS questions and A level questions look identical; the difference between AS and A level assessment is seen in the different proportions of marks awarded for two different skills: the skill of demonstrating knowledge and understanding (Assessment Objective 1, or AO1), and the skill of constructing a critical argument (AO2).

At AS, half the marks (15 marks) are available for knowledge and understanding, and the other half (15 marks) for the quality of your analytical and evaluative argument. You should aim to use your knowledge in order to support the argument you are making throughout the essay, rather than presenting descriptive knowledge in the first half and then an opinion in the second.

At A level, your demonstration of knowledge and understanding is awarded a maximum of 16 marks, and your analytic and evaluative skills are awarded a maximum of 24 marks. You should aim to concentrate on constructing a lucid argument, making use of your knowledge to add weight to the conclusions you draw.

How convincing are teleological arguments for the existence of God?

This question focuses on the teleological (design) arguments for the existence of God, so you need to have a thorough and confident knowledge of what they say. Start by deciding whether you think these arguments are convincing, and your reasons for your opinion. Your essay should present an argument throughout; give examples to support your point of view and consider counter-arguments carefully so that your essay presents a balanced and persuasive case.

Practise your skills for AS level

If you are answering this question at AS level, you should make sure that your knowledge of teleological arguments is detailed and accurate, and that you can distinguish between different versions, for example that from Aquinas and that from Paley. In your argument, make sure you weigh the strengths and weaknesses of the argument rather than simply presenting your own religious or non-religious beliefs as a reason for your opinion.

Practise your skills for A level

If you are answering this question at A level, make sure that you focus on your argument and critical evaluation rather than on giving lengthy descriptions of different points of view. Use the different versions of teleological arguments to support the points you make, as illustrations of the criticisms you give.

'There must be a reason to account for the existence of the universe.' Discuss.

For this question, you need to decide whether or not you agree that the existence of the universe requires a reason. For high marks, you could refer to the views of well-known thinkers such as Aquinas or Leibniz.

Practise your skill for AS level

If you are answering question at AS level, make sure you demonstrate thorough and accurate knowledge of cosmological arguments. Try to use key terms with confidence. Make sure that you give a logical argument to explain your personal perspective.

Practise your skills for A level

If you are answering this question at A level, you should aim to use your knowledge to support your point of view rather than simply presenting it descriptively. You might want to argue that the cosmological argument is reasonable in concluding that there must be a God to account for the universe, or you might argue that the universe is explainable by physics; or you could argue that there is no need for the universe to have an explanation at all.

Chapter 1.4

Arguments based on reason

Can the existence of God be demonstrated through reason and logic?

How successful are traditional ontological arguments in demonstrating the existence of God?

What, if anything, do ontological arguments show about the nature of God?

How do a priori arguments compare with a posteriori arguments?

Key Terms

A posteriori arguments: arguments which draw conclusions based on observation through experience

Ontological: to do with the nature of existence

A priori arguments: arguments which draw conclusions through the use of reason

Contingent: depending on other things

Necessary existence: existence which does not depend on anything else

Predicate: a term which describes a distinctive characteristic of something

Epistemic distance: a distance in knowledge and understanding

Logical fallacy: reasoning that has a flaw in its structure

Specification requirements

* The ontological argument

Introduction

Although most arguments for the existence of God are **a posteriori arguments**, looking to God as an explanation of different aspects of our experience, there is also an argument which claims that God's existence can be demonstrated simply through reasoning. This is the **ontological** argument.

The ontological argument claims that simply by thinking logically about what we understand to be the nature of God and what the implications of that must be, we can deduce that there must be such a God. God has to exist, the argument claims, because it is his nature to exist. It is impossible for God not to exist, as a 'non-existent God' is a contradiction in terms. The ontological argument claims that existence is an aspect of the essence of God, a part of the definition of God.

For example, the word 'giant' carries with it the implication that a 'giant' must be huge; it is impossible, by definition, for a 'giant' to be insignificantly small as hugeness is the defining characteristic of a giant. If it were small, it would not be a giant at all; a giant could not be small. If you think there could be a small giant then you simply have not understood the term 'giant'. Supporters of the ontological argument claim that God exists by definition in the same way; existence is a defining characteristic of God, and God cannot possibly be non-existent. People who think God does not exist, clearly (so the argument says) do not understand the meaning of the term 'God'.

Variations of the ontological argument have been put forward for at least a thousand years, most famously by Anselm in the eleventh century and Descartes in the seventeenth. Discussion of whether the logic of this argument is valid and sound still continues, with some people agreeing that the unique way in which God exists makes his non-existence impossible, while others suggest that there are logical flaws in the reasoning which lead the argument to failure.

Kant, for example, gave a particularly striking counter-argument, claiming that existence is not a characteristic and so cannot be used as a descriptor of God. Many people think that this counter-argument has been fatal to ontological arguments, but there are, nevertheless, other thinkers who continue to defend it against Kant's criticisms.

The ontological argument

Ontology is the branch of philosophy that explores the whole concept of existence. It is important to recognise that there are different kinds of existence. For example, you and I exist in a physical sense – we take up space, we can be seen and heard and bumped into. Prime numbers exist in a different sense, in the realm of mathematical concepts, even though they are not available to the senses and have no physical properties. Forgiveness, boredom and jealousy exist, but in a different sense again as they are not experienced with the five senses but exist on a mental, emotional level. Sometimes scientists have to assume that something exists in reality in the physical world, even if they have never come across an example of it, because a combination of factors indicate that there must be X, even if we have not found it yet, in order to explain other things. Discoveries on the fringes of physics, for example, often work on assumptions that some things exist even before we have any real evidence of them.

The philosophical study of ontology, then, explores what it means for something to exist.

The ontological argument for the existence of God is an **a priori argument**, which means that it is working from first principles, pure conceptual truth and definitions in an attempt to demonstrate the existence of God. It is also a deductive argument, using logic rather than depending on the evidence of sense experience. In this way, then, the ontological argument is different from other attempts to argue for the existence of God. It is not natural theology, but relies entirely on its own internal logic. It is not a posteriori, because the argument depends on no observation or experience but, again, purely on its own internal logic.

God, it is argued by religious believers, is necessary *rather than* contingent

According to the ontological argument, almost everything (with the exception of God) which exists does so in a **contingent** way; it depends upon other factors. We, as individuals, are contingent beings, because we would not exist if our parents had not existed before us, and we would not continue to exist if we had no food or water or oxygen. Absolutely everything else (apart from God) exists contingently too. It exists because of other circumstances, and under some conditions it would cease to exist.

God is not a 'thing'; God has not come about because of anything; there was no time when God did not exist, and there is nothing that could happen which would cause God to cease to exist. God's existence is different from the existence of anything else, in fact some thinkers, most notably the German theologian Paul Tillich, have argued that 'exists' is not the right word to use of God at all.

Anselm and the ontological argument

Anselm (1033–1109) was an Archbishop of Canterbury and a Benedictine monk. He produced an ontological argument from the perspective of 'faith seeking understanding' rather than in an attempt to convert unbelievers; he was not trying to convince people that God really does exist despite their doubts, but was trying to explore, as a Christian, what faith in God is all about.

Anselm starts by defining God as 'that than which nothing greater can be thought'

Anselm set out his argument in his book *Proslogion* (1077–8). It is usually agreed that Anselm gives his argument in two different forms, although some people believe that it is all part of the same train of thought, where Anselm wrote down his ideas and then thought, let me put it another way. In the first form of the argument, Anselm starts by defining God as 'that than which nothing greater can be thought'. We all, he argued, would agree that this is what we mean by God (whether we actually believe in him or not). God is understood to be the highest sum of all perfections, where absolutely nothing could ever surpass God in any way.

Think question

Do you agree with Anselm's definition of God? If there were a God, is this what he would have to be like?

Anselm argued that if we have an idea of a God who is perfect in every way, where nothing could possibly be greater, then this God must exist in reality. This is because a God who just exists merely in our heads, as something we imagined to be great but did not actually exist, would be inferior to a real God – and we have already agreed that God cannot be inferior to anything in any way. So God must exist and be that real God, in order to meet our definition of 'that than which nothing greater can be thought'.

Supporters of Anselm use analogies to make their point. What would be greater, they say – a huge heap of cash that exists in your imagination only, or that same heap of cash on your kitchen table? An imaginary picture in your head of your favourite meal, beautifully cooked and presented, or that same meal actually being in front of you ready to eat? In Anselm's understanding of God, no one could seriously argue that a non-existent God would surpass an existent God in greatness.

Anselm believed that faith was more important than reasoned argument. He presented his ontological argument as 'faith seeking understanding'

1. Anselm's first form of the ontological argument, in summary, follows the line of argument that:

God is that than which nothing greater can be thought.

A real, existent being would be greater than an imaginary, illusory being.

Therefore, the concept of God is surpassed by an actual, existent God.

2. In the second form of his argument, which is closely linked to the first, Anselm argued that it was impossible for God not to exist. The argument goes like this:

God is that than which nothing greater can be thought.

Contingent beings (those which come in and out of existence, and which depend on other things for their existence) are inferior to beings with **necessary existence** (which are eternal and depend on nothing else for their existence, and of which the only example is God).

Because God is unsurpassable in every way, God must have necessary existence.

Therefore God exists – necessarily.

Here, Anselm argued that God must exist, because a necessary being cannot fail to exist – only contingent beings do that. Necessary existence is, in Anselm's view, part of the whole definition of God. It made no sense to Anselm to talk of a God who does not exist, because then he would not be God.

For Anselm, then, the existence of God is not something which needs to be demonstrated by referring to evidence. It is something which we can know simply by considering the concept of 'God', and working out what this means.

Analytic and synthetic propositions

One way of understanding the ontological argument draws a distinction between two different kinds of proposition (a proposition is a statement which 'proposes' something, or says that such-and-such is the case).

See Chapter 2.3 to read more about how Kant used the distinction between analytic and synthetic statements in his ethics.

Anselm argued that 'God exists' is an analytic a priori statement. Existence is part of the definition of God

Apply your knowledge

1. Give some of your own examples of analytic propositions, and some examples of synthetic propositions.

2. Anselm argued (by implication) that 'God exists' is an analytic proposition – that existence is part of the definition of God. Do you agree with him? Explain your reasons.

3. Anselm also argued that the existence of God can be deduced purely from the use of reason. Is he right?

This is a distinction which has been made by many philosophers but is particularly associated with Immanuel Kant.

One kind of proposition is the analytic proposition. An analytic proposition is one which is true by definition: the usual example given is 'bachelors are unmarried men'. There is nothing we need to do to test this proposition – it can be arrived at through deduction. As long as we know what a bachelor is, then we can accept that he is an unmarried man, because the concept of being a bachelor includes the concepts of being unmarried and being male. If he were married, or not a man, then the word 'bachelor' would not apply. Anselm, in his ontological argument, was claiming that the statement 'God exists' is analytic – in other words, that the concept of God includes the concept of existence, and without existence, the term 'God' would not apply.

The other kind of proposition is a synthetic proposition. A synthetic proposition is one which adds something to our understanding, beyond the definition of the word, and we need more than just deduction to know whether or not it is true – we also need experience. So, for example, 'The corner shop sells newspapers' is a synthetic proposition, as the concept of a corner shop does not include the concept of selling newspapers. It might be a florist or a butcher shop – you would have to go to the shop and see if they had any newspapers and if they were prepared to let you buy one, if you wanted to know the truth of the proposition.

Anselm argues that 'God exists' is an analytic a priori statement. The concept of existence is part of the concept of God, he argued. Anselm made reference to Psalm 53:1:

> ❝ The fool says in his heart,
> 'There is no God.'
> They are corrupt, and their ways are vile;
> there is no one who does good. ❞

He found it difficult to understand how anyone could have the concept of God as 'that than which nothing greater can be thought' without also realising that God must exist. As soon as someone understands what God is, then God's existence is surely obvious. Anselm asked:

> ❝ Why, then, did the fool say in his heart 'God is not', since it is so obvious to the rational mind that you exist supremely above all things? Why, because he is a dim-witted fool. … How was the fool able to 'say in his heart' what he was unable to conceive? ❞

John Hick, ed., *Classical and Contemporary Readings in the Philosophy of Religion*, 1990, p. 30

Gaunilo's criticisms of Anselm

Gaunilo was a French monk and a contemporary of Anselm. He was the first to raise objections to Anselm's idea that God exists by definition. Gaunilo, like Anselm, was a Christian and believed in God, but he thought that Anselm's argument was not logical and, therefore, needed to be refuted.

Gaunilo claimed that the flaws in Anselm's logic would be made obvious if we go through the argument again, replacing the idea of God with the idea of an island. In his writings *In Behalf of the Fool* (often translated as *On Behalf of the Fool*) (1078), he explained that we could imagine the most excellent Lost Island; we understand the implications of the phrase 'the most excellent island' and, therefore, this notion exists as a concept in our understanding. We might then, using Anselm's logic, go on to say that for such an island to exist in our minds means that this is inferior to the same island existing in reality. If our island is truly the most excellent, it cannot have the inferiority that comes from it being a concept only – it must, therefore, exist in reality. But clearly, there is no such island in reality. We cannot bring something into existence just by defining it as superlative.

Gaunilo writes:

....

66 It is said that somewhere in the ocean is an island, which, because of the difficulty, or rather the impossibility, of discovering what does not exist, is called the lost island. And they say that this island has an inestimable wealth of all manner of riches and delicacies in greater abundance than is told of the Islands of the Blest; and that having no owner or inhabitant, it is more excellent than all other countries, which are inhabited by mankind, in the abundance with which it is stored.

Gaunilo argued that if we replace 'God' with 'island' in Anselm's argument, we can see how the argument falls down

Apply your knowledge

4. Do you think Gaunilo was successful in pointing out the logical problems with Anselm's argument? Explain your answer.

5. Anselm replied to Gaunilo that the ontological argument works only in the case of God, and not for anything else, as God exists in a different, 'necessary' way, unlike an island. Would you accept Anselm's reasoning here? Explain your views.

Now if some one should tell me that there is such an island, I should easily understand his words, in which there is no difficulty. But suppose that he went on to say, as if by a logical inference: 'You can no longer doubt that this island which is more excellent than all lands exists somewhere, since you have no doubt that it is in your understanding. And since it is more excellent not to be in the understanding alone, but to exist both in the understanding and in reality, for this reason it must exist. For if it does not exist, any land which really exists will be more excellent than it; and so the island already understood by you to be more excellent will not be more excellent.'

If a man should try to prove to me by such reasoning that this island truly exists, and that its existence should no longer be doubted, either I should believe that he was jesting, or I know not which I ought to regard as the greater fool: myself, supposing that I should allow this proof; or him, if he should suppose that he had established with any certainty the existence of this island. For he ought to show first that the hypothetical excellence of this island exists as a real and indubitable fact, and in no wise as any unreal object, or one whose existence is uncertain, in my understanding.

This, in the mean time, is the answer the fool could make to the arguments urged against him. **"**

Cited in John Hick, ed., *Classical and Contemporary readings in the Philosophy of Religion*, 2nd edn, 1970, p. 33

Anselm argued that the ontological argument only works when applied to God, because God exists in a different way from everything else.

See Chapter 1.3 for more information about how Aquinas presented teleological and cosmological arguments to demonstrate the existence of God.

Anselm was impressed with Gaunilo's argument, and included it in later versions of his own book, along with his reply.

Anselm's reply was that, although Gaunilo was right in the case of an island, the same objections did not work when the ontological argument was used of God, because an island has contingent existence, whereas God's existence is necessary. The argument works only when applied to God, because of the uniqueness of God and the unique way in which he exists – which was part of the whole point of the ontological argument.

Aquinas' criticisms of Anselm

Thomas Aquinas (1225–74) also argued against Anselm, even though he was firmly convinced of the existence of God himself. He believed that the existence of God could be demonstrated through a posteriori arguments, but not through a priori reasoning alone.

One of his points was that God's existence cannot be regarded as self-evident. He said that if we take, in contrast, such a statement as 'Truth does not exist', then we can see it is a nonsensical statement, because no one can accept the truth of 'truth does not exist' unless truth actually does exist after all. It is impossible to have a mental concept of the non-existence of truth because it is a contradiction in terms. It is not, however, impossible to have a mental concept of the non-existence of God, because people quite clearly manage it, including Anselm's fool who says in his heart 'There is no God'. If we can imagine a state of godlessness, then it cannot be a contradiction in terms, despite Anselm's claim.

Aquinas also questioned whether everyone would accept Anselm's definition of God as 'that than which nothing greater can be thought'. Aquinas believed that although we can approach an understanding and awareness of God, God will always remain unknowable to the finite human mind. Anselm seemed to start his argument from a confident position of claiming 'we all know what "God" means'; but Aquinas was not sure if this was true. Aquinas, throughout his life and especially at the end of his writings, was very much aware of the limitations of the human mind to comprehend the nature of God and he emphasised that, at least until after death, we have to accept that God is mysterious and beyond human comprehension.

Aquinas also raised doubts about whether this concept of God, even if universally shared, could be sufficient to indicate that such a being existed in reality:

> 66 Perhaps not everyone who hears the name 'God' understands it to signify something than which nothing greater can be thought, seeing that some have believed God to be a body. Yet, granted that everyone understands that by this name 'God' is signified something than which nothing greater can be thought, nevertheless, it does not therefore follow that he understands that what the name signifies exists actually, but only that it exists mentally. 99

Cited in Steve Cahn, ed.
Classics of Western Philosophy, 2013, p. 468

For Aquinas, then, the ontological argument did not work because it assumes we share an understanding of God, which Aquinas did not think was true, and, he thought, it only goes as far as to show that a concept exists in people's minds, not that the same concept applies to something real.

Descartes' version of the ontological argument

Although Aquinas had argued that one reason the ontological argument does not work is that we do not know what God is, René Descartes (1596–1650) disagreed. Descartes reformulated the ontological argument in his work *Meditations* (1641).

Descartes, like Anselm and Plato before him, believed that people were born with some ready-made ideas. In other words, that there are some

Aquinas argued that we do not all share an understanding of what God is, and rejects the premise of Anselm's argument

Think question

Do you think Aquinas' criticisms of Anselm's argument are justified?

See Chapter 1.2 for more about how Descartes presented other ideas about the nature and scope of the human mind and its reasoning, in his discussion of the mind–body problem.

concepts which are innate, imprinted on our minds from birth and which are universally shared by all of humanity. (This is an idea that has been revisited by psychologists such as Jung.) Descartes thought that we understand such concepts as equality, cause, shape and number from birth; and he also believed that we are born with an understanding of what God is. We understand God to be the supremely perfect being, with every perfection as his attributes. By 'perfections', Descartes meant the traditional attributes of God such as omniscience, omnipotence and omnibenevolence.

Descartes explained his understanding of how this innate idea demonstrated the existence of God, by using the analogy of a triangle, and also the analogy of a mountain. Descartes claimed that existence is part of the essence of God, just as three angles adding up to 180 degrees are part of the essence of a triangle, and a valley is part of the essence of a mountain:

> **66** Existence can no more be separated from the essence of God than can its having three angles equal to two right angles be separated from the essence of a triangle, or the idea of a mountain from the idea of a valley… **99**
>
> René Descartes, *Meditations V*, translated by E.S. Haldane, 1911

Descartes recognised that these analogies have their limitations. While we might not be able to think of a mountain without also thinking of a valley, this does not mean that the mountain-and-valley combination in our imaginations actually exists in the real world. God, however, in Descartes' view, is different, because his nature involves not angles or valleys but perfections – and, for Descartes, existence is a perfection.

Because God has all the perfections, and existence is a perfection, God therefore exists, Descartes argues. Descartes goes on to say that as God is perfect, he must be unchanging, and so he must always have existed and will always continue to exist for eternity.

See Chapter 1.1 for more about how Descartes, like Plato, thought that something had to be unchanging in order to be perfect.

Kant's critique of ontological arguments

Many thinkers believe that Kant's criticism of ontological arguments for the existence of God finally demolished such arguments. Kant was arguing against Descartes' version of the ontological argument; it is not clear whether he was familiar with the version put forward by Anselm.

Kant's major criticism of Descartes' argument was that, in his words, 'existence is not a **predicate**'. In other words, existence is not a characteristic or an attribute of something. Predicates of something describe what that thing is like – it might be green, or tall, or round, or sharp. But 'existence', Kant argued, is not the same as a predicate, it does not tell us anything about the object that would help us to identify it in any way. When we say that something 'exists', we are not saying that it has this or that quality or characteristic. What we are saying instead is that this concept, with all its characteristics, has been 'actualised', or 'exemplified'. We are saying that there is at least one example of something with these characteristics in real life.

Kant's point, when applied to ontological arguments, is that when we are thinking of God, whether it is as Anselm's 'that than which nothing greater can be thought' or Descartes' sum of all the perfections, we are thinking of a concept. Whether or not that concept is actualised in the real world, whether there is really such a being that matches our concept, is an issue, but not an issue that can be resolved simply by adding 'existence' to the different predicates we are ascribing to our concept. We can predicate of a triangle that it has three sides, and that its angles add up to 180 degrees, but we would have to investigate to find out whether the triangle we are picturing in our minds has been actualised. We can predicate of a unicorn that it is like a horse and has a single straight horn in the middle of its forehead, but adding 'exists' to our description will not make any difference to whether or not the concept 'unicorn' is actualised so that we could go and find one.

Kant used the example of a hundred Prussian dollars, known as 'thalers', to make his point and illustrate how existence is not a predicate. He argued that adding 'exists' to the idea of God, as a predicate, does not add anything new to what we understand by God; it is, instead, a comment on whether the God we have described really exists. In the same way, an imaginary $100 is not 'added to' if we substitute it for a real $100. We are talking about just the same amount of money whether it is real or imaginary, but when we say 'exists' we are referring to whether it is actual.

Kant's major criticism of the ontological argument was that 'existence is not a predicate'

··

66 Now, if I take the subject (God) with all its predicates (omnipotence being one), and say: God is, or, There is a God, I add no new predicate to the conception of God, I merely posit or affirm the existence of the subject with all its predicates – I posit the object in relation to my conception. The content of both is the same; and there is no addition made to the conception, which expresses merely the possibility of the object, by my cogitating the object – in the expression, it is – as absolutely given or existing. Thus the real contains no more than the possible.

A hundred real dollars contain no more than a hundred possible dollars. For, as the latter indicate the conception, and the former the object, on the supposition that the content of the former was greater than that of the latter, my conception would not be an expression of the whole object, and would consequently be an inadequate conception of it. But in reckoning my wealth there may be said to be more in a hundred real dollars than in a hundred possible dollars – that is, in the mere conception of them. For the real object – the dollars – is not analytically contained in my conception, but forms a synthetical addition to my conception (which is merely a determination of my mental state), although this objective reality – this existence – apart from my conceptions, does not in the least degree increase the aforesaid hundred dollars. ,,

Immanuel Kant, *Critique of Pure Reason*,
Book 2, 1781, Chapter 3

It could be argued, of course, in response to Kant, that God's existence is different from the existence of anything else, because other things exist contingently whereas God exists necessarily. Perhaps necessary existence is a predicate – but it can only be predicated of God. This argument, however, is unlikely to impress the sceptic, who may respond by saying that this makes the ontological argument circular: we have to accept that God exists necessarily, in order to come to the conclusion that God exists necessarily.

Bertrand Russell on the ontological argument

Bertrand Russell criticised the ontological argument by asking us to think of the statement 'The present King of France is bald.' This statement is not true. However, does it mean, therefore, that the statement 'The present King of France is not bald' is a true statement? No; because there is no such thing as the present King of France. Our use of words and the way we apply predicates, such as bald or not bald, is not enough to demonstrate that something exists, and when we start applying predicates to something whose existence is a matter of uncertainty, we cannot expect the normal rules of linguistic logic to apply.

Discussing arguments based on reason

Which is the more persuasive kind of argument for the existence of God: a priori or a posteriori?

A priori ontological arguments for the existence of God can be appealing and persuasive; if their premises are true and the reasoning is sound, then they lead us to a certain truth. Mathematics uses a priori reasoning, and when it is done accurately following logical reasoning, it arrives at conclusions which have a certainty that it is hard to find in other areas of knowledge.

A posteriori arguments, in contrast, can only lead to probabilities. We can offer hypothetical reasoning which best fits the evidence presented to our senses, but there is always the chance that we might come across some new example or piece of evidence which forces us to revisit our conclusions and perhaps modify them. In philosophy the most famous example of this is the knowledge 'all swans are white'. This piece of knowledge was reached through a posteriori reasoning; we see a white swan, and another white swan, and another. Every swan we see is white. However, as soon as someone produced the evidence of a black swan, the knowledge that 'all swans are white' had to be modified.

With a posteriori arguments for the existence of God, the same uncertainty applies. Our experience might tell us 'the world is orderly and works like a human-made machine' – until we encounter the baffling apparent chaos of quantum physics. Our experience might tell us 'the universe exists and the best explanation is God' – until we encounter a plausible explanation from a cosmologist which seems to make sense without any assumption of divine intervention.

Perhaps, then, a priori arguments are more persuasive. However, conceptual reasoning does not appeal to everyone. The ontological argument can seem like an intellectual puzzle made for elite, educated people with little relevance to the average believer or non-believer. People often want more than just logical steps, before they will be prepared to commit themselves to the truth of such an important claim as 'God exists'; they want to see evidence for themselves, using their own senses, rather than rely on the conceptual reasoning of philosophers.

Can existence be treated as a predicate?

For Kant, the biggest objection to the ontological argument is that 'existence is not a predicate'; existence is not a characteristic of something, but is in a different category. Something's existence is not a predicate, in the sense of saying something descriptive about it which characterises it. To say that something exists is to comment on its 'ontological status' – saying something exists is saying that it has the status of being a real thing, a thing which is exemplified in reality. It is not, according to Kant and others, a 'great-making quality' or a quality of any other kind; existence is in a different category from, for example, success or virtue or talent.

Not everyone, however, would agree with Kant's view that existence cannot be a predicate. Some scholars, for example Norman Malcolm (1911–90), argue that perhaps existence in the ordinary, contingent kind might not be a predicate, but that necessary existence, which

Apply your knowledge

6. Would you agree that theoretical mathematics leads to more certain answers than subjects which require experience of the world, such as history or natural science? How would you explain your answer?

7. Which do you find more persuasive (if either) as arguments for the existence of God: the a priori ontological argument, or a posteriori argument, such as the teleological or cosmological? Give reasons for your answer.

8. Which do you find easier to criticise: a priori, or a posteriori arguments? Give reasons for your answer.

Apply your knowledge

9. Do you agree with Kant, that existence is not a predicate?

10. Do you think that Malcolm is right to argue that necessary existence can be a predicate even if contingent existence is not? Give reasons for your answer.

only applies to God, is different. Existence is usually not a characteristic that helps us distinguish between one thing and another, and so it is not usually a predicate; but necessary existence is a characteristic that does draw a distinction between God and everything else; just like God's other characteristics of omnipotence, omnibenevolence, everlastingness and omniscience, which are also predicates. Necessary existence is a distinguishing characteristic which sets God apart, and therefore can be used as a predicate – but only of God – at least according to Malcolm.

Does the ontological argument justify belief in God?

Someone who does not believe in God is not going to change his or her opinion because of the arguments of reason and logic, even if these arguments are sound. Anselm himself did not set out to convert unbelievers to the Christian faith, but claimed to be exploring the nature of his own faith, trying to find understanding of what it meant to believe in the existence of God and to understanding something of the nature of God. He recognised that someone who followed the reasoning of the ontological argument was not going to be persuaded, purely through a priori logic, into a relationship with God. He hoped, however, that someone who already held a belief would be able to gain a deeper understanding of the uniqueness and the greatness of God.

There is more to religious belief than just agreeing to a set of statements: religious belief goes beyond the bounds of reason. This does not mean that it has to be unreasonable; but religious belief consists of more than simple agreement that an argument appears to work. It involves commitment to a whole new way of looking at the world and of behaviour. Comparisons might be made between religious faith and the experience of being in love. A woman might be able to explain to her friends all sorts of good reasons why she is in love with someone, and she could outline many excellent characteristics of this other person. She could show her friends photographs of her beloved, and give examples of his or her acts of kindness, creativity, and so on; but, even if her friends agree with her assessment of the other person completely, they will not be in love with this person themselves simply because of her powers of persuasion. Religious belief, like being in love, is much more than just an intellectual acceptance of certain assertions. It involves emotions, intuitions and commitment. It does not depend solely on the strength of a logical argument, and can sometimes seem to fly in the face of common sense. Just as someone in love might still be in love even when the other person's faults are glaringly obvious, so too the religious believer might continue in complete faith in the existence of God even when obvious flaws in the philosophical arguments have been clearly demonstrated. Whether this faith is therefore misplaced remains debatable.

Faith in God seems to demand an element of uncertainty, and a willingness to take risks in spite of an absence of concrete proof. What would happen if God could be proven beyond all reasonable doubt – if God made himself known in a way that everyone would accept? Many people would argue that God has already done this, through revelation; Christians might argue that the experiences recorded in the Bible, for example, are proof of God's existence, and that the life and resurrection of Jesus was a clear demonstration of God showing people once and for all that he truly exists.

Believers often point out that God must remain partially hidden from the world, in order to maintain **epistemic distance**. By this, they mean that the world should remain 'religiously ambiguous'. It is right that there should be no conclusive evidence for the existence of God, just as there should be no conclusive evidence against God's existence. People should be left with a choice. They should be able to see and explain the world purely in naturalistic terms, or able to see the world as coming from and sustained by God, and have the freedom to decide for themselves which position they wish to take. Only with this epistemic distance, it is argued, is it possible for humans to have a genuinely free will to exercise faith and moral judgements. If God's existence were undeniable, then faith would mean nothing, and people would have no choice but to believe.

Are there logical fallacies in the ontological argument which cannot be overcome?

As the ontological argument depends entirely on logic, the question of whether it works is a question of whether it has logical flaws.

A possible **logical fallacy** in the ontological argument might be one of 'category error'. If, as Kant suggests, existence is not a predicate, then it cannot be ascribed to God as one of his characteristics. Perhaps existence is in a different category, and proponents of the ontological argument are using fallacious reasoning when they treat it as if it were a predicate.

Although many believe that Kant's criticisms of the ontological argument are fatal to it, nevertheless the argument has been revived in the twentieth and twenty-first centuries.

Norman Malcolm accepted that Kant was right to say that ordinary, contingent existence is not a predicate. However, Malcolm believed that the idea of God's necessary existence, from the second formulation of Anselm's argument, could still be used to provide a successful ontological argument.

Malcolm argued that in order to be God, God must have necessary existence; he could not come into existence if he did not exist already, and he could not stop existing if he already exists. If God exists at all,

> **Apply your knowledge**
>
> 11. Do you think that arguments for (or against) the existence of God are likely to change the way people think and believe? Why or why not?
>
> 12. How effective is the ontological argument in justifying a belief in God?

See Chapter 1.2 for more about how another example of a possible category error is the idea that the soul is a substance like the body.

then he exists in this eternal, necessary way. Malcolm's argument takes the following steps:

1. If God does not exist today, then he never can and never will – his existence must be impossible; because a being with the greatness of God is uncaused and has no beginning.

2. If God does exist, then he must exist necessarily, rather than contingently, depending on something else.

3. God's existence is therefore either impossible or necessary, there are no other options.

4. God's existence is not impossible. It is not logically contradictory to have the concept of a God who exists – it is an idea that we can entertain without any logical absurdity.

5. Therefore, given that God's existence is not impossible, it must be necessary, as that is the only other option – so God exists necessarily.

However, Malcolm's argument has not been generally accepted. It might be illogical to say that 'sometimes there is a God, and sometimes there isn't' (if we accept that a God would have to be eternal), but it is not illogical to say 'maybe there is a God, and maybe there isn't'. Malcolm's argument, like other versions of the ontological argument, rests on our acceptance from the start that God's existence is not the same as other kinds of existence. For many critics, this is the same as asking us to believe in God as a premise of the argument, before setting out on the reasons, so that the argument becomes circular and can be reduced to saying, 'God exists necessarily, therefore God exists necessarily.'

Malcolm did concede that his argument would not convince atheists, but felt that it was nevertheless worthwhile because the believer would understand completely the necessity of God's existence, and therefore, the truth of 'God exists' would make perfect sense for the theist. However, perhaps this reduces the ontological argument to the point where it is saying no more than that God is true for those who believe in God – and many theists would want to claim that God exists in reality, whether we believe in him or not.

Learning support

Points to remember

» The ontological argument differs from other arguments because it uses a priori rather than a posteriori reasoning.

» Anselm thought that we share an understanding of God as 'that than which nothing greater can be thought' and that we can use logic to realise that, therefore, God must exist.

» Gaunilo argued that we can see the flaws in Anselm's argument if we replace the idea of God with the idea of a Most Excellent Island.

» Descartes thought that God has all the perfections, including existence.

» Aquinas argued that we do not all share an understanding of what God is.

» Kant argued that existence is not a predicate.

Enhance your learning

» Anselm's classic exposition of the ontological argument, best read once you have got to grips with the argument: Anselm, *Proslogion* 2 and 3.

» Gaunilo's reply to Anselm, a clear and measured response: Gaunilo, *In Behalf of the Fool*.

» Kant is quite difficult to read but is worth a try, especially if tackled after you have an understanding of his argument from secondary sources: Kant, I. *Critique of Pure Reason*, Second Division III.IV.

» Useful for those who wish to explore further the complexities of the ontological argument; it goes beyond the demands of AS and A level: Van Inwagen, P. 'Necessary Being: the Ontological Argument' in Stump, E. and Murray, M. J. (eds) (1999) *Philosophy of Religion: The Big Questions*.

» Plantinga has an interesting modern perspective on the ontological argument, useful for those who want to follow the argument further, perhaps to support a university application: Plantinga, A. (1978) *God, Freedom and Evil*, II.c.

Practice for exams

AS questions and A level questions look identical; the difference between AS and A level assessment is seen in the different proportions of marks awarded for two different skills: the skill of demonstrating knowledge and understanding (Assessment Objective 1, or AO1), and the skill of constructing a critical argument (AO2).

At AS, half the marks (15 marks) are available for knowledge and understanding, and the other half (15 marks) for the quality of your analytical and evaluative argument. You should aim to use your knowledge in order to support the argument you are making throughout the essay, rather than presenting descriptive knowledge in the first half and then an opinion in the second.

At A level, your demonstration of knowledge and understanding is awarded a maximum of 16 marks, and your analytic and evaluative skills are awarded a maximum of 24 marks. You should aim to concentrate on constructing a lucid argument, making use of your knowledge to add weight to the conclusions you draw.

'A priori arguments for the existence of God are more persuasive than a posteriori arguments.' Discuss.

For this question, you need to make a critical comparison between a priori and a posteriori kinds of argument, and therefore you need to be clear about what those are and be able to give examples.

Practise your skills for AS level

For high marks at AS level, you will be able to give clear explanations of the ways in which each kind of argument reaches a conclusion, and you will be able to show that you can confidently use terms such as inductive and deductive reasoning. You need to decide whether you think one kind of argument works better than the other, and have reasons for your view.

Practise your skills for A level

At A level, in order to present a strong line of argument, you will need to decide which kind of argument you think is more persuasive when used in the context of arguing for the existence of God. You might think that neither is persuasive, in which case you can say so. Whatever your point of view, you need to be able to support it with reasoning and give examples to help illustrate your points.

Discuss critically Kant's claim that existence is not a predicate.

This question requires you to be thoroughly familiar with the ontological argument and Kant's criticisms of it. In particular, you need to demonstrate that you understand what he meant when he said that existence is not a quality that can be ascribed to something.

Practise your skills for AS level

If you are answering this question at AS level, you need to have accurate and well-ordered knowledge and understanding of ontological arguments and of Kant's views. You should be able to present an opinion agreeing or disagreeing with Kant, with reasons to support it.

Practise your skills for A level

If you are answering this question at A level, your essay needs to go further than simply describing the argument and Kant's response. You also need to think about whether Kant was right, and whether his criticism can be applied to God in the same way that it can be applied to contingent beings. You might be able to refer to other formulations of the ontological argument in your essay. You should aim for a well-ordered, structured argument leading to a persuasive conclusion.

Religious experience

What defines a religious experience?
Should religious experience be taken seriously?
How can religious experiences be explained?

Key Terms

Mystical experience: experiences of God or of the supernatural which go beyond everyday sense experience

Conversion experience: an experience which produces a radical change in someone's belief system

Corporate religious experience: religious experiences which happen to a group of people 'as a body'

Numinous experience: an indescribable experience which invokes feelings of awe, worship and fascination

Principle of credulity: Swinburne's principle that we should usually believe what our senses tell us we are perceiving

Principle of testimony: Swinburne's principle that we should usually trust that other people are telling us the truth

Naturalistic explanation: an explanation referring to natural rather than supernatural causes

Neurophysiology: an area of science which studies the brain and the nervous system

Specification requirements

- The nature and influence of religious experience, including:
  - mystical experience
  - conversion experience
- Different ways in which individual religious experiences can be understood

Introduction

Religious experience can be difficult to define and it is also difficult to communicate its nature in the language we use every day, because it is so different from everyday experience. Nevertheless, it is an important part of religious life, where people feel their encounters with God shape their beliefs and give their lives a sense of direction.

Different thinkers have tried to capture the essence of religious experience and describe its distinctive characteristics; these thinkers include Friedrich Schleiermacher, Rudolph Otto and William James.

Religious experience has been classified into different types, including **mystical**, **conversion** and **corporate religious**, each of which raises some interesting philosophical questions. Are they no more than internal, emotional events that can be 'explained away' by science, or do they genuinely come from God? Is there any way in which religious experiences could be tested to see whether they are authentic?

What is religious experience?

The term 'religious experience' can mean different things to different people. People sometimes use it to refer to any kind of experience that happens in a religious context, such as attending a service of worship or carrying out daily living with the belief that God is in control. Others claim that 'religious experience' refers to a specific, life-changing event. Religious experience is often solitary and personal, but it can also be corporate (shared by a body of people). Some would argue that whenever a group of Christians share the Eucharist together, or whenever Muslims stand together in pilgrimage on the Hajj, this is religious experience, but others will use the term to refer specifically to particular dramatic events which are totally outside the ordinary.

Religious experience can come in many different forms, such as perceptions of visions and voices, conversion experiences, **numinous experiences** and near-death experiences; and because such experiences are different from natural, everyday life, it can be very difficult, if not impossible, to find words which can adequately describe them to others. All experiences, whether religious or not, have to be understood and expressed through language, and this language is always going to be shaped by the culture from which it comes, with all of its accompanying world-views and belief systems, which makes it difficult to know if people from different times, places and religious backgrounds are describing the same experience. There is also, of course, the issue of whether religious experiences are genuine encounters with something that exists in reality, beyond the subjective, or whether they are simply the result of an overactive imagination, or are hallucinations which are better explained with reference to science.

The influence of religious experience

Despite the issues that religious experience raises, it is nevertheless a central part of many religious traditions. Stories of religious experiences are common throughout the Bible, the Qur'an, and the sacred texts of other religions, such as the Mahabharata in Hinduism. The religious experiences of central figures in religious traditions have had a profoundly influential effect on the shape of those traditions.

Apply your knowledge

1. Use your research skills to investigate stories of the religious experiences of the Prophet Muhammad during the Night of Power. In what ways have these experiences shaped the nature of Islam?

2. Research Sikh beliefs about the religious experiences of Guru Nanak when he was bathing in the river. How did this experience influence the formation of Sikhism?

3. Look at the story of The Transfiguration in the Bible (Matthew 17:1–11). How did this religious experience influence the beliefs of Peter, James and John?

4. When you read these accounts, do you get the impression that the people involved felt they actually saw and heard God, or do you think they were using pictorial language in an attempt to capture a sensation that was hard to describe? Or do you have another interpretation?

On a personal level, some people have changed the whole direction of their lives on the basis of their personal religious experiences, and some people have been willing to sacrifice everything because of their faith in the revelation they believe has been given to others through religious experiences. Collectively, people have drawn on the religious experiences of others in the formation of their doctrines and practices: for example, the Muslim practice of praying five times a day comes from the Prophet Muhammad's personal religious experience in which guidance about prayer was revealed to him, and the style of worship in charismatic Christian Churches is based on the corporate religious experience of the first Christians at Pentecost. The personal religious experience of Francis of Assisi led to the establishment of an order of monks (the Franciscans) who still work today, and the religious experiences of Guru Nanak led to the foundation of the religion of Sikhism.

What makes an experience distinctively religious?

Some thinkers have tried to study religious experience and aimed to identify the features of an experience that make it particularly 'religious', rather than just 'an experience'. Sometimes they have also discussed the place of religious experience in a life of faith or the degree to which accounts of religious experience have any evidential force.

Friedrich Schleiermacher

Friedrich Schleiermacher (1768–1834) was a theologian who claimed that the essence of religion was based in personal experience. For him, it was not enough simply to agree to a set of religious doctrines, or commit oneself to a set of ethical principles. Religious experience, he thought, should be at the heart of faith. Schleiermacher believed that every person has a consciousness of the divine, but that in many people this is obscured by other concerns. Religious people are those who are aware of, and try to develop, this sense of the divine. His most famous book was called *On Religion: Speeches to its Cultured Despisers* (1799).

According to Schleiermacher, religious experience is 'self-authenticating': it requires no other testing to see if it is genuine. He thought that doctrines such as the creed were attempts by individuals to understand their religious experience, which went against the thinking that experience had to be seen within the framework of existing doctrine. In the Catholic tradition, the experiences of mystics had to be tested against the Church's teaching and against Scripture before they were considered to be genuine, whereas in Schleiermacher's view, the experiences should have priority and the statements of belief should be formulated to fit them.

Schleiermacher was reacting against the contemporary view of eighteenth-century Germany, which was that reason was of prime importance. He called religion 'a sense and taste for the infinite' and

> **Think question**
>
> What do you think would be your immediate response if a good friend told you that she had experienced God in a vision? How far do our previously-held beliefs affect our responses to reports of religious experience?

Schleiermacher argued that religious experience is at the core of all religion and is 'self-authenticating' also 'the feeling of absolute dependence', and believed that feeling and experience were all-important. An individual's religious experience was based on the sense of being wholly dependent. In his view, religious experience could take a variety of different forms in different cultures, and the different religions of the world were reflections of this. He believed that Christianity was the highest of the religions, but not the only true one. Christianity was the highest because, in Jesus Christ, there was the only example of someone with complete 'God-consciousness', totally unobscured.

Those who criticised Schleiermacher's view thought that he put too much emphasis on the subjective, reducing religion to emotion and removing the possibility of showing that religious claims are based on fact. Some critics argued that there has to be the possibility of testing experiences against the Bible and the Church. If there were no possibility of testing, then any alleged religious experience could count as valid, even those caused by hallucinations or drugs.

William James

William James (1842–1910) wrote probably the best-known book ever written on the subject of religious experience. *The Varieties of Religious Experience* (1902) was not originally written as a book, but as a series of lectures called the Gifford Lectures, given in Edinburgh in 1901–2, with the sub-title 'A Study in Human Nature'. When the lectures were published as a book, it was immediately successful, not only because its anecdotes of religious experience were fascinating in themselves, but because of the sympathy and intelligence with which James discussed his insights.

In his book, James was not trying to hammer home an evangelical Christian message, and he did not set out to dismiss the importance of religious experience or to prove that it had no basis. His aim was to take as objective a stance as he could, to take personal accounts of religious experience seriously, and to make observations about them which he hoped would lead to some significant insights.

One of the ways in which he did this was to include in his book many first-hand accounts of religious experience, in the words of the people who told him their stories. James considers, for example, what is understood by 'conversion', and gives various accounts of different conversion experiences. His understanding is that the term relates to a process where someone who is 'divided', and conscious of being wrong and unhappy, becomes much more confident about what is right, and much happier, as a 'consequence of a firmer hold on religious realities'. James recognises that this can be a sudden or a gradual process.

James believed that, up to a point at least, the experiences could be tested for validity. In his book he argues that the test of religious experiences was not the dramatic nature of 'super-normal incidents, such as voices and visions and overpowering impressions of the meaning

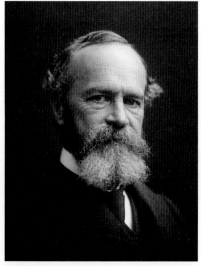

William James studied religious experiences from first-hand accounts and concluded that their validity can be tested by their long-lasting effects

of suddenly presented scripture texts, the melting emotions and tumultuous affections connected with the crisis of change' which 'may all come by way of nature …', but 'the real witness … is to be found only in the disposition of the genuine child of God, the permanently patient heart' (*The Varieties of Religious Experience*, 1902, p. 238). In other words, the worth of a religious experience can be tested by the changes in the subject; they will become less selfish, calmer and more loving. James went on to say that religious experiences from outside Christianity could also be valid, if they produced these same effects in the subject.

For James, then, a religious experience does not have to be marked by dramatic supernatural events, although it can be. The real test of what happened is the long-term change in the person. James is known as a pragmatist; that is, someone who holds that the truth of something can be determined by its practical effects and consequences.

James identified four main qualities of a religious experience:

1. **Ineffability:** by this, he meant that the experience is impossible to express adequately in normal language.

2. **Noetic quality:** the experience gives the person an understanding of important truths, which could not have been reached through the use of reason alone. People who have had religious experiences often speak in terms of having had the truth revealed to them.

3. **Transience:** the experience is over quite soon, lasting no more than a few hours, even though the effect of the experience could last a lifetime.

4. **Passivity:** the person having the experience feels as if the experience is being controlled from outside themselves – they are the recipients of the experience, rather than the instigators of it.

When James gives examples of different experiences, he notes how convincing these experiences are to the person having the experience. He says: 'They are as convincing to those who have them as any direct sensible experiences can be, and they are, as a rule, much more convincing than results established by mere logic ever are' (*The Varieties of Religious Experience,* 1902, p. 72).

James concluded that although religious experience does not give proof of anything, it is reasonable to believe that there is a personal God who is interested in the world and in individuals. He recognised that this was what he called a hypothesis, but said that it was a perfectly reasonable hypothesis, and that it was *not* reasonable for scholars or ordinary people to reject clear evidence of religious experience just because they started from a position of scepticism.

Rudolf Otto

Rudolf Otto (1869–1937) was a Protestant theologian who used his vast knowledge of natural sciences, comparative religion and oriental traditions

William James argued that religious experience could be tested for validity: a valid religious experience brings about a lasting positive effect in the individual

to try to analyse religion. In his book, *The Idea of the Holy* (1917), Otto tried to identify what it was about a religious experience that made it religious, rather than just an experience. He wanted to show that it was fundamental to religion that individuals should have a sense of a personal encounter with natural forces, which he described as 'mysterium tremendum et fascinans' – an awe-inspiring, fascinating mystery. The encounter would bring a sense of awe and mystery, a feeling of strangeness. Otto said that the divine would be recognised as having three main qualities, and he devotes chapters of his book to describing and explaining these different, yet linked, qualities:

1. One is the quality of mystery, a realisation that God is incomprehensible, that God can be met and his work can be seen and yet that God can never be captured, fully understood or described. This idea of Otto's is one that C.S. Lewis takes up in his allegorical Christian fantasy novels, the Narnia series; although the children in the stories love and respect the lion, Aslan, they are sometimes reminded that Aslan is not a pet and not a creature that they can ever expect to understand fully. He is not a tame lion and they need to remember that he can be dangerous and is much stronger than they are.

2. God is recognised as being of ultimate importance.

3. God has a quality that is both attractive and dangerous. Otto tried to explain the feeling that God cannot be controlled, but that at the same time the individual feels a sense of privilege during a religious experience.

Otto made use of the term 'numinous', which he used to describe the feeling of awe-inspiring holiness. He said that ordinary language could not do justice to religious experience, because it is an experience unlike others within normal sense-experience. He argued that religious language is a 'schema', an attempt to find clusters of words which approach the idea being expressed, although the idea in itself is inexpressible (as James had pointed out when he termed it 'ineffable'). All the person who has had the experience can do is to try and describe his or her own feelings during the experience, rather than being able to find any words to define exactly what was giving rise to the feelings.

Otto's book was important because for the first time someone tried to express and to understand the 'otherness' of religious experience, with its distinctive qualities.

Mystical experience

'Mystical experience' is a broad term that encompasses many different kinds of religious experience, including dramatic events where people apparently see visions and hear voices, moments where people feel an overwhelming sense of being in the presence of God, and times where people feel that in some way they have encountered and perhaps been united with God, or whatever they understand ultimate reality to be.

Think question

How would you define 'religious experience'? If someone asked you whether you had ever had a religious experience, what would you think they were asking you?

When people have mystical experiences, they feel that they have reached an understanding of spiritual truth which cannot be accessed through the use of reason and 'normal' sense experience alone.

The term itself, 'mystical experience', is a relatively recent one. Figures within the Christian tradition who are often regarded as 'mystics', such as John of the Cross, Teresa of Avila, Meister Eckhart and Julian of Norwich, would not have understood the term. When they were seeking encounters with God through prayer and when they expressed their inner spiritual experiences through the language and imagery of their times, they would have understood themselves not as 'mystics' but simply as Christians. During the Middle Ages, there was a strong emphasis in Christianity on the power of religious experience, with several striking accounts of events where individuals felt that they had encountered God on a deep personal level, and tried to communicate their experiences to others. These writings often convey a sense of the mystery and otherness of God, feelings of great peace but also a realisation that God will always remain beyond the boundaries of human knowledge.

The term 'mysticism' came about during the late-nineteenth and early-twentieth centuries as part of a movement towards finding common ground between the major world religions. The days of the Victorian missionary, going out amongst savages to convert the heathen, were coming to an end. Some people were becoming less sure that their Christian religion was the only true religion and were beginning to find spiritual comfort and wisdom in some of the other great religious traditions of the world too. There was a growing movement in which people wanted to demonstrate how world religions, although different in practice, came from the same beliefs about the nature of the world and of ultimate reality. They often turned to examples of 'mystical experience' in an attempt to show how, at the most personal level, there is a single truth which God reveals to people, regardless of their religious tradition, in whichever way they will be the most likely to recognise it from their own cultural perspective.

When religious experience is called 'mystical', therefore, it carries connotations of the idea that underneath the different doctrines and practices, perhaps everyone is connecting with the same God, even though this may be in very different ways.

Happold's study of mysticism

F.C. Happold presented a study of mysticism in the 1960s, at a time when people were looking outside the authority of the traditional Christian Church in order to find meaning and truth. It was a time where freedom of thought, speech and behaviour was popular, particularly amongst the young. Happold's book *Mysticism, A Study and Anthology* (1963) reflected this sense that a personal search for truth might involve looking at religious belief systems outside, as well as inside, traditional Christianity. In his book, Happold writes about how he understands mysticism as underlying religion in all its forms, and how it depends on the non-rational, intuitional side of human understanding:

> ❝ Mysticism has its fount in what is the raw material of all religion and is also the inspiration of much of philosophy, poetry, art and music, a consciousness of a *beyond*, of something which, though it is interwoven with it, is not of the external world of material phenomena, of an *unseen* over and above the seen. … In the true mystic there is an extension of normal consciousness, a release of latent powers and a widening of vision, so that aspects of truth unplumbed by the rational intellect are revealed to him. ❞
>
> F.C. Happold, *Mysticism, A Study and Anthology*, 1963, pp. 18–19

Happold argues that, although mysticism is found throughout the world in all different cultural contexts, there are strikingly similar features of it and conclusions drawn from it:

- the mystic understands that this physical, material world is only a part of reality, and that it comes from a 'Divine Ground'

- human nature is such that people can know the 'Divine Ground', not through reason but through intuition

- people have two distinct natures: the ego, which is the part of which we are always conscious, and the spiritual 'eternal self', the 'spark of divinity within him'

- the purpose of humanity is to discover this 'eternal self' and to unite it with the 'Divine Ground'.

Happold's book discusses the nature of mysticism, its relation to scientific truth and the practices of contemplation, before presenting an anthology of mystical writing from a wide range of sources, including Plato, the Hindu Upanishads, Buddhist texts, Sufi mysticism from Islam, and writings from Christianity. He includes some from ancient Christian manuscripts which purport to be a record of the words of Jesus, although they do not appear in the gospels.

Christian mysticism and numinous experience

Visions and voices from God are probably the forms of experience that many people think of when they consider mystical religious experience, and such experiences feature in many of world's religions. In visions, the person having the experience feels that he or she can actually see something supernatural, such as a Hindu Deity Kali, the Virgin Mary, a ladder coming from the sky or something else beyond the realms of normal natural experience. It is not always clear, in reports of such experiences, whether 'sight' is being used as a metaphor, or whether the people believe that they could see their vision in just the same way as they see everything else in their everyday lives.

In the Bible, the vision of Isaiah in the Temple at the point when he was called to be a prophet is a particularly powerful example. Isaiah

Teresa of Avila was a well-known medieval nun who had mystical visions in which an angel pierced her with a lance

'saw God' and afterwards was able to give a detailed description of the different heavenly beings he encountered (see Isaiah 6:1–13). When people hear voices, this can be equally dramatic, and they give reports of exactly what was said to them. In the story of the boy Samuel in the Temple, Samuel is woken from sleep by a voice, and he believes it to be his master Eli because the voice is so vivid, suggesting that this is not meant to be understood metaphorically but as a real sound available to the ears (see 1 Samuel 3:1–18). In many reports, visions and voices are combined, when the person encounters someone who gives a message. For example, Bernadette of Soubirous claimed that she both saw and heard the Virgin Mary at Lourdes. She could describe what Mary had been wearing, and she recorded the words that had been spoken to her.

In Kenneth Grahame's book *The Wind in the Willows*, chapter 7, Rat and Mole have a numinous experience while out on the river

'Numinous experiences' are, by their nature, difficult to define. Some scholars believe that they are a subset of mystical experience, while others put them in a class of their own. According to Otto, numinous experiences are at the heart of all religious experience. Otto describes it as 'the distinctive experience of God, at once ineffably transcendent, remote, yet stirring a recognition that here is the primary source of beauty and love' (*The Idea of the Holy*, 1917, p. 158). These are times when the individual gains a new and deeper understanding of reality, and feels as if he or she has touched on a different dimension, becoming filled with a sense of awe and wonder. It may be triggered by being out in the countryside in the early morning, or while witnessing a scene of beauty or the birth of a baby, but it can just happen out of nowhere in the most ordinary of circumstances. The experience itself may be fleeting, but the effects can be lasting.

The Wind in the Willows (1908) written by Kenneth Grahame, contains a fascinating chapter where two of the characters, Rat and Mole, have something which can only be described as a mystical or numinous experience while they are out on the river looking for the baby otter Portly. They find him, eventually, in the care of the god Pan, and in their encounter with the god they are overcome with awe and humility, conscious that they are in the presence of something far greater than themselves.

> *Numinous experiences are times when the individual gains a new and deeper understanding of reality, and feels as if he or she has touched on a different dimension, becoming filled with a sense of awe and wonder*

Apply your knowledge

5. Find out more about the religious experiences of some of the great mystics of the medieval period. You could research John of the Cross, Teresa of Avila, Francis of Assisi, Meister Eckhart or Julian of Norwich; find out something about their lives and in particular, read about their religious experiences and the ways in which they described them.

6. Some people consider that mystical experiences such as these can be explained in scientific terms; for example, that the subject had been fasting or had a fever and was, therefore, likely to be hallucinating. How far would you agree with a more natural, scientific explanation?

7. Read chapter 7 of *The Wind in the Willows*. How successfully do you think this experience has been conveyed? Why do you think Grahame included this story in his book?

Conversion experience

Conversion experiences can be dramatic, or they can be gentler and slower to develop. The name 'conversion experience' refers to the kind of experience where someone abandons his or her old way of life and belief system, and adopts a new one, based on an inner experience which he or she is convinced comes from God. This kind of religious experience tends to follow a basic pattern.

- The individual is dissatisfied with his or her current 'system of ideas' (a phrase from *Our Experience of God* by H.D. Lewis) – people do not tend to be converted if they are quite content as they are.

- The person searches, at both an intellectual level and an emotional level, for a basis on which to make a decision; for example, they may turn to the Bible, be persuaded to go to an evangelical meeting or a church service, or listen to stories of other conversions.

- There is a point of crisis, which is a time of intense emotion, sometimes with physical symptoms as well as emotions. Often this is described as a sense of the presence of God, a sense of sinfulness and repentance. Sometimes the experience is described in terms of visions, bright light and voices.

- This is followed by a sense of peace and joy, and a loss of worry. There is also a desire to share the new faith with other people, to talk about the experience.

- In the longer term, the convert experiences a change of direction, a new sense of purpose in life, and sometimes a complete change of career.

In *The Varieties of Religious Experience*, William James tried to explain what a conversion experience involves. He writes:

> **66** To say that a man is 'converted' means, in these terms, that religious ideas, previously peripheral in his consciousness, now take a central place, and that religious aims form the habitual centre of his energy. **99**
>
> William James, *The Varieties of Religious Experience*, 1902, p. 196

In other words, a religious conversion experience can change someone's whole outlook on life, so that before the experience they might just have been aware of the existence of religious ideas whereas afterwards, religious ideas are the person's starting-point for his or her interpretation of the world.

James thought that psychology could describe conversion, but it was unable to account for all the factors in any given case, and he asserted that the conversion experience can be tested by its results. If, after a conversion experience, the person is happier, kinder, more loving and more positive, then for James this is enough evidence to suggest that the conversion experience was valid. Christian believers might support James in this opinion; the Bible refers to the 'evidence' of the Holy Spirit as a way for Christians to test their experiences and the claims of others: 'But the fruit of the Spirit is love, joy, peace, forbearance, kindness, goodness, faithfulness, gentleness and self-control' (Galatians 5:22–23, New International Version).

Conversion experiences have been the focus of a number of psychological studies, where psychologists have attempted to determine whether there are particular personality traits or other circumstances which might make some individuals more susceptible to conversion experiences than others.

Conversion experiences can be the subject of controversy. All human behaviour happens within a social context, so it can be difficult to separate internal, spiritual influences from external, social causes, and it can be impossible to tell what a person might have done or how he or she might have felt without those outside influences. Although conversion experiences are often dramatic and life-changing for those who have them, it could be argued that they are the result of social and psychological factors rather than the result of the activity of God.

For a religious believer, however, a conversion experience can be completely and irrevocably transformative. One of the most famous conversion experiences in Christianity comes from the New Testament. Saul (who changed his name to Paul when he became a Christian)

Michelangelo depicts the story of the conversion of Saul from the book of Acts

lived at a time when Christianity was very new and was seen as a threat. Palestine was occupied by the Romans, who allowed the Jews to continue to practise their religion as long as they did not cause trouble and as long as they kept to the Roman laws. Christians were seen as a threat because, allegedly, they had appointed a king of their own – Jesus – and their beliefs were causing dissent among the Jewish community. Saul's job was to seek out Christians and bring them to justice, a job which he undertook with some enthusiasm.

....

66 Meanwhile, Saul was still breathing out murderous threats against the Lord's disciples. He went to the high priest and asked him for letters to the synagogues in Damascus, so that if he found any there who belonged to the Way, whether men or women, he might take them as prisoners to Jerusalem. As he neared Damascus on his journey, suddenly a light from heaven flashed around him. He fell to the ground and heard a voice say to him, 'Saul, Saul, why do you persecute me?'

'Who are you, Lord?' Saul asked.

'I am Jesus, whom you are persecuting,' he replied. 'Now get up and go into the city, and you will be told what you must do.'

The men travelling with Saul stood there speechless; they heard the sound but did not see anyone. Saul got up from the ground, but when he opened his eyes he could see nothing. So they led him by the hand into Damascus. For three days he was blind, and did not eat or drink anything.

In Damascus there was a disciple named Ananias. The Lord called to him in a vision, 'Ananias!'

'Yes, Lord,' he answered.

The Lord told him, 'Go to the house of Judas on Straight Street and ask for a man from Tarsus named Saul, for he is praying. In a vision he has seen a man named Ananias come and place his hands on him to restore his sight.'

'Lord,' Ananias answered, 'I have heard many reports about this man and all the harm he has done to your holy people in Jerusalem. And he has come here with authority from the chief priests to arrest all who call on your name.'

But the Lord said to Ananias, 'Go! This man is my chosen instrument to proclaim my name to the Gentiles and their kings and to the people of Israel. I will show him how much he must suffer for my name.'

Then Ananias went to the house and entered it. Placing his hands on Saul, he said, 'Brother Saul, the Lord – Jesus, who appeared to you on the road as you were coming here – has sent me so that you may see again and be filled with the Holy Spirit.' Immediately, something like scales fell from Saul's eyes, and he could see again. He got up and was baptised, and after taking some food, he regained his strength.

Saul spent several days with the disciples in Damascus. At once he began to preach in the synagogues that Jesus is the Son of God. All those who heard him were astonished and asked, 'Isn't he the man who raised havoc in Jerusalem among those who call on this name? And hasn't he come here to take them as prisoners to the chief priests?' Yet Saul grew more and more powerful and baffled the Jews living in Damascus by proving that Jesus is the Messiah. **99**

Acts 9:1–22, New International Version

Apply your knowledge

8. Some people might account for Saul's religious experience by saying that he must have had some kind of epileptic fit, which the first century writers understood as a religious experience because they had little understanding of epilepsy at the time. Do you think this is a reasonable interpretation of the text?

9. William James might have argued that the conversion of Saul was a valid religious experience because it had the permanent effect of making him into a zealous Christian who eventually gave his life for his faith. Would you agree with James that the effect validates the religious experience? Explain why, or why not.

10. Use any reputable sources you can find to explore the details of other conversion experiences to increase your understanding. You could include conversion experiences in non-Christian religions, such as the conversion of Malcolm X. Make notes about these experiences so that you can illustrate your writing with examples.

Corporate religious experience

Corporate ('as a body') religious experience is where several different people all have the same, or a similar, religious experience at the same time. It is quite unusual. Normally (if 'normally' is the right word) religious experiences occur privately to individuals, but there have been reports of groups of people all sharing the same perceptions and feelings and receiving the same messages.

A biblical example of this might be the story of Pentecost at the beginning of the book of Acts, where everyone (according to the story) felt the same sensation of a rushing mighty wind, and saw the same tongues of fire appearing.

Apply your knowledge

Look up and read the story of the coming of the Holy Spirit at Pentecost in Acts 2.

11. Do you think that someone passing by the building at the time of this event would have seen the tongues of fire and heard the strange languages? Or do you think this is a poetic way of describing an inward spiritual event – or an entirely made-up story? Explain why you hold these views.

12. In the story, the people having this religious experience are given a completely new direction. Do you think that their subsequent behaviour demonstrates that their religious experience was valid (as James would argue)?

Apply your knowledge

13. Research the claims made by those who believe the Virgin Mary did appear to the young people of Medjugorje. How convincing do you find their accounts, and for what reasons?

14. The Catholic Church conducted some investigations into the alleged appearances of the Virgin Mary at Medjugorje. What steps do you think might be taken in such an investigation? What sort of evidence might help to verify the stories, if any?

Another example of corporate religious experience might be those reported in the town of Medjugorje in Bosnia and Herzegovina, where six young teenagers and children allegedly had regular visions of the Virgin Mary, beginning in 1981, and they claimed that they received messages from her. The children said the Virgin Mary appeared to them, giving them secrets and messages of peace, and telling them that the world needed more prayer. The site has become a place of pilgrimage and the six have kept to their original story.

This example is particularly interesting because in some ways it might seem that if six people, rather than just one, report a supernatural event, it might have more evidential force. That most of them were children at the time might also make the story more convincing, as children could be considered less calculating than adults and less able to present a convincing and coherent narrative. However, it might also be the case that the six were encouraging each other to believe that they had seen things; they could have influenced each other's memories of events and, without necessarily meaning to, they could have encouraged each other to believe they saw and heard things that never really happened. The Catholic Church has been sceptical about the claims made about visions at Medjugorje; although it has not explicitly disowned them, it has advised caution, and Pope Francis did not visit the shrine when he was nearby.

The 'Toronto Blessing' is a modern phenomenon in the US and Canada, first documented in the 1990s, where groups of people all worshipping together in a church near the airport in Toronto appeared to have the same ecstatic religious experience. According to reports, worshippers at the church have been overcome by the Holy Spirit, and this causes them to weep or to laugh uncontrollably, to speak in strange 'languages' and to fall to the ground. Some people take this to be a sign of God's blessing, where people can experience the Holy Spirit so intensely that they lose all sense of self in a kind of religious ecstasy. Others, however, argue that this is simply mass hysteria, and reject its genuineness, saying that when the Holy Spirit is genuinely experienced, it leads believers to work for others and to be humble and self-controlled.

How might religious experience be understood?

For some people, religious experience is best understood in terms of a personal encounter with God; for others it can be better explained in other ways which do not involve or necessitate belief in God. Sometimes religious experience is used to support an a posteriori argument for the existence of God: people have these unusual experiences which they take to be encounters with God, and the best explanation (according to the argument) is that they really do come from God, who therefore exists.

Pilgrims visit the shrine at Medjugorje where the Virgin Mary is said to have appeared to six young people

As with other a posteriori arguments, the degree to which religious experience as an argument for the existence of God is persuasive depends on whether the conclusion is the most plausible explanation for the experiences we have, or observe others having. Some argue that other, natural rather than supernatural, explanations are more convincing, while others argue that there are good grounds to support the view that religious experience is evidence of God.

The view that religious experiences are a union with a greater power

Many people believe that religious experiences happen because God chooses to reveal himself to particular individuals, for reasons of his own. They would argue that plenty of people have reported experiences which they believe to have been encounters with God; these reports do not just come from a few unreliable sources, but are a common part of human experience and deserve to be taken at face value.

The philosopher Richard Swinburne (b. 1934) supports the view that religious experience should be taken seriously and also can be taken as evidence for the existence of God. He makes a case that we should treat reports of religious experience in the same way that we treat reports of other, non-religious experiences: unless we have a good reason to be suspicious of these reports, we should believe them and take them at face value. If someone thinks that they can hear someone at the door, then they probably can; and, Swinburne argues, if someone thinks they can hear the voice of God, then they probably can.

Swinburne puts forward his '**principles of credulity** and **testimony**' in his book *Is There a God?* (1979) Swinburne argues that, when people tell us of their experiences, we should accept that the person who has had the experience is in the best position to know what really happened, even if other people subsequently try to put a different interpretation on it.

Apply your knowledge

15. Do you agree with Swinburne's view that religious experiences should be treated with the same degree of acceptance or suspicion as other, more everyday kinds of experience? Why, or why not?

16. Do you think that the view that religious experience comes from God is strengthened if a large number of people have such experiences? Give reasons for your answer.

Swinburne argues that religious experience should be treated with no more scepticism than other kinds of experience

The principle of credulity is very simple: it just says that experience is normally reliable, and the balance of probability says that experience can be trusted. Even if some experiences turn out to be misleading, we should take the more likely view, which is that we can trust experience. Swinburne is not saying that experience is infallible; he is saying that what our senses tell us is more likely to be true than not, and, therefore, we should accept our experiences on balance, unless we have convincing reasons not to. We know that sometimes our senses mislead us, and our experiences can sometimes lead us to draw the wrong conclusions, for example when we think we see someone in the street that we know well and then realise that it is in fact a stranger. But usually, when we think we recognise someone, we need to accept our own instincts, or we will get nowhere. If it appears to our senses that a friend is approaching, it looks like her and sounds like her and is wearing her clothes, then we should not feel the need to be suspicious that perhaps our senses are deceiving us or that it is an imposter. Swinburne argues that the same should apply to religious experiences. He argues that if we think that we are experiencing God, we should be prepared to believe that it really is God, rather than immediately doubting our own perceptions. Our sense perceptions are normally, although not always, reliable.

The principle of testimony works in a similar way. We find that usually, people tell us the truth. Less often, they are mistaken or only joking or being deliberately deceitful, but in most cases, we can believe what we are told. Therefore, we should go with the balance of probability when we are told something, and (according to Swinburne) we should not make different rules for religious experience. Swinburne argues that if someone tells us that they have had a personal encounter with God, we should be prepared to take this seriously rather than immediately assuming that they are wrong or making it up.

A psychological interpretation of religious experience

The German philosopher Ludwig Feuerbach (1804–72) was greatly influential on later thinkers, especially those who prefer a **naturalistic explanation** of religious beliefs and feelings. His ideas included the opinion that religious belief and religious experiences have origins within the human mind rather than coming from God. In his book *The Essence of Christianity* (1841), Feuerbach argued that when people think they are worshipping God or experiencing the presence of God, they are in fact worshipping only their own human nature. People take the best and most admirable aspects of human nature – creativity, hope for the future, heroism, compassion and so on – and, without making a conscious decision to do so, they 'project' these aspects outside themselves and hold them up as something to worship. They imagine themselves to be standing in relation to these ideals, which they call 'God'; but there is no real, objective God existing beyond human nature, Feuerbach thought. People created God in their own image, in order to meet their needs. People want to feel cared for, even if they have insignificant status, and so they invent a God who loves and values them. They want the world to be a fair place, so they invent a God who rewards the good and punishes the wicked.

Sigmund Freud (1856–1939) one of the founders of modern psychology, was strongly influenced by the thinking of Feuerbach. Freud gave an explanation of religion and religious experience which was similarly naturalistic, arguing that people who feel themselves to be in the presence of God are deluding themselves.

One of the reasons for Freud's importance among psychologists is that he was the first to recognise that the human 'psyche', or mind, works on more than one level. He acknowledged that people have unconscious as well as conscious mental processes. Today, this has become generally accepted; we realise that there are thoughts in our minds that we are aware of as we get on with each day, and also that there are other, deeper layers such as memories and associations which can be hidden at deeper levels, but affect who we are. Freud thought that the psyche is made up of three layers:

The ego – this is the layer of the mind which is obvious to us as the conscious self, where we are aware of our opinions and decisions.

The id – this is the unconscious self which is not immediately obvious, containing memories and repressed emotions and desires that we might not want to admit to ourselves.

The super-ego – this could be seen as the equivalent of the conscience, an inner 'moral voice' which tells us that some things are right and others are wrong. In Freud's view, this is created as we grow up, where our parents, siblings and peer group let us know what they find acceptable and unacceptable until it becomes imprinted on our personalities.

Freud's view of religious belief and the religious experiences that might go with it was very similar to Feuerbach's. Freud thought people who think there is a God and who believe that they encounter a God are fooling themselves. He thought that some people are unable to cope with the idea of adult life, and so they invent an imaginary parent-figure who will look after them. They mistake the moral commands of their own super-egos as being the voice of God. They might even believe that this parent-figure talks to them more directly, in personal encounters. However, for Freud, this is an 'infantile neurosis', to use his words, and something that they ought to grow out of in order to live with better mental health.

Freud argued that religious experience was a symptom of an 'infantile neurosis'

Not all psychologists agree with Freud, of course; but he does give a naturalistic explanation of religious experience which some people might find more persuasive than the explanation that there really is a God.

Donald Winnicott (1896–1971) was a paediatrician and psychoanalyst who extended these ideas of Freud's in his highly influential studies of childhood. Winnicott was very interested in the importance of the bond between a child and its mother in early life, and the transitions that needed to be made in order for that child to become a mentally healthy adult.

Winnicott studied playing and its significance in child development. He noticed that many small children develop an attachment to a 'transitional object' such as a teddy bear or a blanket or a toy train, to which the child has a very strong emotional attachment. The child holds it for comfort in unfamiliar situations or at bed time. For the child, the transitional object belongs in a stage between imagination and reality, where the child clings on to the comfort this object brings, imagining that it provides security and taking that illusion very seriously while at the same time knowing that it is just a toy or a blanket. Adults indulge the child with this transitional object and recognise its importance to the child; they might join in with the pretence that teddy is hungry or that Thomas the Tank Engine needs a nap. Playing with the transitional object and living with the illusion that the object is 'real' helps the child to make the step between relying completely on its mother and the self-reliance that comes with growing up.

Winnicott argues that people cannot do without this illusion in their lives, even when they are adults. Those who cannot make the distinction between their illusions and reality are considered to have what he calls the 'hallmarks of madness' (*Playing and Reality*, 1971, p. 3) but illusion is, in his view, an important and natural part of people's mental lives, most often exhibited through creativity such as art and also through religion. We need illusion and imagination in order to make sense of ourselves and our place in the world and to give it significance; this is why we enjoy fiction, films and theatre.

For Winnicott, religious experience is best understood in this context, as illusion; but unlike Freud, he does not argue that people would necessarily be mentally healthier without such an illusion. His argument instead is that illusion of religious experience only becomes 'madness' when the person tries to impose his or her illusions on others and expects them to give it credibility as 'real'.

A physiological interpretation of religious experience

A physiological interpretation of religious experience is one which accounts for religious experience naturalistically in terms of the biology of the human brain.

Neurophysiology is an area of science which studies the brain and the nervous system. It is a rapidly developing discipline where there are still a lot of unknowns. Technological advancement is enabling scientists to be able to map more accurately what happens in different parts of the brain, providing a greater understanding of which parts of the brain are responsible for different aspects of human consciousness such as cognitive thought, memory and emotion. This branch of science has the potential to help people who suffer brain damage, and it is also beginning to shed light on how different stimuli can cause different kinds of mental state, which could possibly aid in the treatment of mental health issues and learning difficulties.

As part of the development of neurophysiology, some scientists have taken an interest in the relationship between what goes on in the brain and the feelings typical of religious experience, such as feelings of being at one with the universe and feelings of standing in the presence of an overwhelming power. One such study took place in the 1980s, led by Michael Persinger. Volunteers wore a helmet-shaped device which transmitted weak magnetic signals through the brain, and a significant proportion of them reported feelings which had striking similarities to those reported by people who claim to have had religious experiences. This study has been criticised for its methodology – for example, some have argued that the participants knew in advance what the investigators were hoping to find, and others who have tried to repeat the experiment have not produced such convincing data – however, it has raised the possibility that religious experiences could be explained by natural, rather than supernatural, causes. It could be that people who are unknowingly in the presence of some kind of magnetic field might think they had encountered God, when in fact it was just the effects of the magnetism.

Other physiological studies have been conducted in order to explore what might be happening in the brain in so-called 'near-death experiences'. Near-death experiences are sometimes reported by people whose hearts may have stopped beating, for example during cardiac arrest, or who are in a coma, and doctors are trying hard to resuscitate them. They describe the sensation of having left their own bodies, being able to look down on the resuscitation scene as if from a height, and feeling that they are in a loving presence. Often these experiences also include the feeling of being able to see a bright light ahead, as if at the end of a dark tunnel. For some, experiences such as these indicate that there is a real hope of life after death in the presence of a loving God. However, physiological studies such as those by Mobbs and Watt (detailed in *Trends in Cognitive Sciences*, 15, 2011, passim) suggest that all the elements of such experiences can be biologically explained through observation of the parietal and prefrontal cortices of the brain, and through measuring the release of emotion-altering hormones in the body at times of stress, such as noradrenaline and dopamine. Some of the medication used to treat patients who are suffering severe trauma could also account for some of the sensations reported in near-death experiences.

It could be, then, that physiology might offer a more plausible explanation of religious experience than the explanation that it comes from God.

Discussing religious experience

Is personal testimony or witness enough to support the validity of religious experience?

Can religious experiences be used as evidence for the existence of God? Many people would say not. The experiences, they argue, cannot be tested by others, and this makes them unsuitable for any kind of 'scientific' study and unsuitable to be used as evidence. Although we have these accounts of experiences, in the person's own words, we have no way of recreating them for ourselves in order to conduct a repeatable experiment. Even if we try to copy the circumstances of other people, for example by fasting or going to a religious meeting or reading the Bible, we cannot make the same experiences happen for ourselves.

The strength of someone's belief that they have encountered God could be considered as evidence that it must have really happened; people who have had religious experiences speak so convincingly of their certainty of the things they heard and saw that their accounts can be very persuasive. However, the sincerity with which an account is given does not necessarily mean that it is true. People can sincerely believe that they have seen or heard something and yet be mistaken in their interpretation.

> **Think question**
>
> Can you think of a time when you have been convinced you saw or heard something, and then later found out that you must have been mistaken?

People disagree about the extent to which personal witness has evidential force. If Swinburne's Principle of Testimony is applied, then we should be prepared to believe someone's report of a private religious experience in just the same way as we might believe a report about a recent holiday. However, not everyone would agree with Swinburne; some thinkers, for example Caroline Franks Davis, in her book *The Evidential Force of Religious Experience* (1989), argues that we should only take someone's word at face value when the issue is relatively trivial. When the issue is of ultimate importance, such as the existence of God, then we need more than someone else's word for it.

William James argued that the evidential force of personal religious experience can be tested for validity by its long-lasting effects. Using the analogy of medicine, he argued that we know a good medicine because it works, and similarly we might know a genuine religious experience from the long-lasting effects such as a greater tendency to kindness and unselfishness.

Biblical writers, too, point out the need to distinguish those who have genuine experience of God from those who are simply attention-seeking or trying falsely to claim that their words are prophecies from God. In Matthew's gospel, people are warned to 'Watch out for false prophets' (Matthew 7:15). The early Christians were well aware that not everyone who claimed to have been given some kind of special revelation from God was telling the truth.

Paul writes, in his letter to the Galatians, that people who are genuine believers exhibit characteristics which can be recognised:

66 But the fruit of the Spirit is love, joy, peace, forbearance, kindness, goodness, faithfulness, gentleness and self-control. 99

Galatians 5:22–23, New International Version

Other thinkers, however, have disagreed with this view. In a radio debate with Frederick Copleston in 1948, Bertrand Russell stated quite firmly his view: 'The fact that a belief has a good moral effect upon a man is no evidence whatsoever in favour of its truth.' Russell argued that it might be possible, for example, for someone to be profoundly affected for the good by a story about a great hero, but this could happen even if the story were a myth and the hero were entirely fictional. The good effects a religious experience might have on someone, according to Russell, would provide no evidence at all that the experience had come from God and did not have a natural explanation.

Can corporate religious experiences be considered more reliable or valid than individual experiences?

Corporate religious experiences can seem to have more evidential force than solitary ones. In science, the more times an experiment can be witnessed by different people, the more weight is added; so perhaps, if several people all share the same religious experience, this might mean that it is more likely to be veridical (relating to something that is objectively real). Rather than the experience being completely private, with only one person to vouch for its truth, several people can give reports which support the account and thereby make it more credible. In a court of law, if evidence is being given by witnesses and several people all claim to have been present and seen and heard the same things, it is likely to be more convincing than the eye-witness account of a solitary person.

The children involved in the reported corporate religious experience at Medjugorje, for example, all described their vision of the Virgin Mary in the same way when they were interviewed separately.

However, it could be argued that the children at Medjugorje would all describe the Virgin Mary in the same way because they had been brought up knowing what statues of her looked like, and thus, they knew what the expectation was.

Others argue that there may be elements of group pressure in corporate religious experiences. Someone might say that they can see and hear something, and others might join in and agree that they can see and hear it too because they want to be included, to the extent that they convince themselves that they really did see and hear the things others are describing. In the case of the Toronto Blessing, for example, many have suggested that the experience was caused by whipped-up hysteria in a heightened emotional atmosphere, rather than caused by the Holy Spirit.

Does religious experience provide a basis for belief in God or a greater power?

In the view of many people, religious experiences are only authoritative for the people who have them. Other people might know you to be

Apply your knowledge

17. If someone were trying to claim that a mental health issue had caused them to commit a crime and that therefore they were not completely to blame, how might a jury decide whether or not this claim was true?

18. Could the same criteria be applied to reports of religious experience? Why, or why not?

Apply your knowledge

19. How far do you think group pressure might be responsible for the corporate religious experiences you have studied?

20. Do you think that reports of corporate religious experience have more evidential force than reports of individual experiences? Give reasons for your answer.

someone who usually tells the truth, who is not prone to exaggeration; they might see that your behaviour changes in some way after the experience that you tell them about, but in the end, only the person who had the experience is going to be totally convinced. Religious experience cannot be tested by others in a way that might be said to provide conclusive proof. Because religious experience is totally individual and unique, it is argued that no one else can look at it and see whether or not it is true. Nevertheless, this is not an opinion which is universally shared. Many claim to have been profoundly influenced by other people's experiences, which they would take to be authoritative. Hindus, for example, might be affected by the story in the Bhagavad Gita of Arjuna's vision of Lord Krishna; Muslims take the religious experiences of the Prophet Muhammad to be supremely authoritative.

People can interpret their experiences in different ways, even if they have exactly the same emotions or visions, even if they hear the same voice telling them the same words. This may be determined by culture and upbringing or a predisposition to believe in God. Someone else who had the same experience might interpret it differently, as hallucination, or coincidence, or give it some other psychological explanation. It could be argued that is impossible to tell conclusively which interpretation is the right one, if indeed there is such an objective thing as the right interpretation.

Critics sometimes point out that members of different faiths encounter God in a way which matches their previously held beliefs; a Catholic might see the Virgin Mary, whereas a Hindu might see Lord Shiva. For some, this undermines the evidential force of religious experience and demonstrates that such experiences are no more than wish-fulfilment. However, in response, it could be argued that surely, if God wants his followers to recognise him when he reveals himself to them, he is going to choose to appear in a form that they will understand.

Those who prefer a naturalistic interpretation of religious experience might point out that Francis of Assisi had religious experiences after severe illness, so perhaps he was hallucinating; and Hildegard of Bingen might have been suffering from a migraine rather than experiencing God; those present at Pentecost who claimed to have been given the Holy Spirit might have been carried away with emotion, given that it was so soon after the death of Jesus, and wanted to believe so much that they imagined they had really seen a vision of tongues of fire.

Others, however, might answer this point by saying that there is no reason why God should not appear to people when they have been taking drugs, or are undergoing experiments, or have been fasting or are grieving. Perhaps, if there is a loving God, then he is likely to want to make himself known to people at times when they are vulnerable and in need of reassurance. Even if scientific experiments with artificially created 'religious experiences' are not caused by God, it does not follow that no religious experience can have come from God.

Apply your knowledge

21. How convincing do you find religious experience as evidence for the existence of God? What reasons would you give to support your position?

Learning support

Points to remember

» Religious experience is reported in all different religions and cultures.

» There are many kinds of religious experience, including mystical experience, conversion experience and near-death experience. Some religious experiences are corporate and others are private, individual experiences.

» Many people have been prepared to change the course of their lives based on their own religious experiences or reports of religious experience from others.

» Naturalistic explanations of religious experience have been presented by psychologists and physiologists, amongst others.

» The argument for the existence of God from religious experience is an a posteriori argument, which means that 'God' as an explanation for the phenomenon of religious experience has to be the most plausible explanation of those available, in order for the argument to be persuasive.

Enhance your learning

» The following passages from the Acts of the Apostles would be useful to read and consider as examples of religious experience: Acts 9:4–8; 22:6–10; 26.

» Rudolf Otto's book *The Idea of the Holy*, Chapters 4 and 5, explores the concept of mysticism and explains Otto's understanding of God as 'mysterious and fascinating'.

» *Autobiography of Saint Teresa of Avila* (2010), edited and translated by E. Allison Peers, gives an insight into the mind and experiences of Teresa of Avila, a brilliant medieval mystic.

» William James' *The Varieties of Religious Experience* provides a wealth of anecdotal evidence of religious experience, as well as some sensitive commentary.

Practice for exams

AS questions and A level questions look identical; the difference between AS and A level assessment is seen in the different proportions of marks awarded for two different skills: the skill of demonstrating knowledge and understanding (Assessment Objective 1, or AO1), and the skill of constructing a critical argument (AO2).

At AS, half the marks (15 marks) are available for knowledge and understanding, and the other half (15 marks) for the quality of your analytical and evaluative argument. You should aim to use your knowledge in order to support the argument you are making throughout the essay, rather than presenting descriptive knowledge in the first half and then an opinion in the second.

At A level, your demonstration of knowledge and understanding is awarded a maximum of 16 marks, and your analytic and evaluative skills are awarded a maximum of 24 marks. You should aim to concentrate on constructing a lucid argument, making use of your knowledge to add weight to the conclusions you draw.

'Corporate religious experiences are more reliable than individual religious experiences.' Discuss.

For this question, you need to compare religious experiences reported by individuals with those reported by groups of people who all claim to have shared the experience (corporate religious experience). You will need to have several examples of both individual and corporate experiences to support your argument.

Practise your skills for AS level

For AS level, you need to demonstrate accurate knowledge of both kinds of religious experience – individual and corporate. You should show that you understand why some people might argue that individual experiences are more reliable, and why others might argue that corporate experiences are more reliable, and you should present a well-reasoned point of view.

Practise your skills for A level

At A level, your essay should not be overly descriptive of the experiences themselves, but should concentrate on forming an argument. You might want to argue that corporate experiences are more reliable, perhaps because different witnesses can all corroborate each other's stories; or you might argue that peer pressure can encourage people to be swept along with the excitement and can distort the truth. Whatever you choose to argue, make sure that you have a consistent and coherent opinion which you support with reasons and examples.

Discuss critically the view that people who claim to have had experience of God should be believed.

This question invites you to consider whether claims to religious experience are credible. You could explore the different possible explanations for religious experience, both natural and supernatural, in your consideration of whether claims to have experienced God are best understood at face value or whether another explanation is more plausible.

Practise your skills for AS level

At AS level, you need to make sure you demonstrate knowledge and understanding of religious experience and the different explanations that have been given for it. You might think that some kinds of religious experience are more credible than others, or that all such experiences are equally believable or unbelievable.

Practise your skills for A level

For A level you should concentrate on presenting a strong line of argument. You might wish to argue that only some such reports should be believed, in which case you will need to identify the circumstances which make a report more or less credible. In your answer, aim to provide a balanced argument, considering both your own view and any counter-arguments with fairness. Supporting your points with examples will help clarify your line of argument.

Chapter 1.6 : The problem of evil

If there is an all-loving, all-powerful God, why is there evil and suffering in the world?

Did God intend that humans and other animals should suffer?

If we have an inclination to do wrong, is that our fault, or the fault of our creator?

Does the existence of evil in the world demonstrate that God does not exist?

Key Terms

Omnipotent: all-powerful

Omniscient: all-knowing

Omnibenevolent: all-good and all-loving

Inconsistent triad: the omnibenevolence and omnipotence of God, and the existence of evil in the world, are said to be mutually incompatible

Theodicy: an attempt to justify God in the face of evil in the world

Natural evil: evil and suffering caused by non-human agencies

Moral evil: the evil done and the suffering caused by deliberate misuse of human free will

Privatio boni: a phrase used by Augustine to mean an absence of goodness

Free will: the ability to make independent choices between real options

Epistemic distance: a distance in knowledge and understanding

Specification requirements

The problem of evil and suffering:
* different presentations
* theodicies that propose some justification or reason for divine action or inaction in the face of evil

Introduction

The problem of evil presents a huge challenge to the monotheistic belief of a God of power and love. If God can prevent evil because of his power, and is perfectly loving and good, why is there evil and suffering in the world? The problem is both one of logic and one of evidence. Logically, it is debatable whether a God of infinite power and love would do nothing to prevent evil; and evidentially, it is debatable whether the world contains sufficient evidence of the power and love of God to make belief tenable, given that there is also evidence of evil and suffering. People have adopted various arguments in order to address the issues:

- Irenaeus argued that God wants us to learn and to grow in spiritual maturity, and therefore gave us challenges and hardships to face out of love for us, so that we could become people who freely choose to have a relationship with him

- Augustine argued that evil came into a world, which God created as perfect, because some of the angels made wrong choices, rebelled against God and fell from heaven. They then corrupted humanity and caused Adam and Eve to sin, which was such a significant event that it corrupted the whole world and threw it into sin

- John Hick followed an Irenaean line of thought with his 'soul-making theodicy'. He argued that the challenges we face in this world are meant to help us reach a free relationship with God, and he also believed that this relationship with God is available and inevitable for everyone, regardless of his or her religious faith.

Different presentations of the problem of evil

The problem of evil as a logical problem

The logical problem of evil says that an omnipotent, omnibenevolent God cannot logically exist if evil exists in the world

The problem of evil presents a powerful logical challenge to belief in the kind of God described by Judaism, Christianity and Islam, and it goes like this: if there is a God who is **omnipotent, omniscient** and **omnibenevolent** then why do evil and suffering exist in the world? Surely, people argue, a wholly good and loving God would want to prevent evil, if he could; and if God can do absolutely anything at all because of his power, then he can both eliminate evil and prevent it from happening. Yet there is clear evidence of evil and suffering in the world. Therefore, the God described by such religions cannot exist.

This logical problem is often attributed to the Greek philosopher Epicurus, although his writings that have survived do not contain it. Nevertheless, David Hume (1711–76) refers to it in relation to Epicurus, in his *Dialogues Concerning Natural Religion* (published after Hume's death, in 1779):

> 66 Epicurus's old questions are yet unanswered. Is he willing to prevent evil, but not able? then is he impotent. Is he able, but not willing? then is he malevolent. Is he both able and willing? whence then is evil? 99

David Hume, *Dialogues Concerning Natural Religion*, 1779

The best-known modern proponent of the logic form of this argument is J. L. Mackie (1917–81).

Mackie writes: 'The problem of evil, in the sense in which I shall be using the phrase, is a problem only for someone who believes that there is a God who is both omnipotent and wholly good. And it is a logical problem, the problem of clarifying and reconciling a number of beliefs: it is not a scientific problem that might be solved by further observations, or a practical problem that might be solved by a decision or an action' (J. L. Mackie, "Evil and Omnipotence." *Mind*, vol. 64 [254], 1955, p. 200).

The problem of evil sometimes makes reference to 'the **inconsistent triad**'. There are three proposals that we are asked to accept:

1. that God is perfectly good

2. that God is all-powerful

3. that evil and suffering exist.

This 'triad' of three ideas is 'inconsistent' because, it is alleged, we cannot believe all of them at the same time without contradiction, and that is where the logical issue lies.

If there is a God who is all powerful, then presumably he could have made any kind of world, or no world at all. He could perhaps have made a world in which there was no pain or illness; perhaps a world where there was no death. Perhaps he could have made people who never chose to do anything but kind and loving acts, or a world where no animal needed to kill another in order to survive. Yet he chose not to, apparently, or was not able to, which is inconsistent with the claim that he is omnibenevolent and omnipotent.

Some people conclude, therefore, that there cannot be an all-loving, all-powerful God if there is evil and suffering in the world, on the grounds of logic alone. They argue that, unless it is false that there is evil in the world, it presents a picture of a self-contradictory God whose attributes are mutually exclusive and therefore such a God cannot exist, in the same way that a square circle cannot exist.

As a logical problem, this argument against the existence of God is a priori. It argues, on the basis of logic alone without the need for experience or evidence, that the existence of an omnipotent, omnibenevolent God is logically inconsistent with the existence of evil.

The logical version of the argument says that the God described by Christianity cannot exist if evil also exists

The problem of evil as an evidential problem

As an evidential problem, the problem of evil is somewhat different. This time the argument is a posteriori. It takes the evidence of our experience: our own suffering, wrongdoing and loss and that which we experience second-hand through news reports and the experiences of people we know. As an a posteriori argument, it asks us to find the best, most plausible explanation for our observation. Is the explanation that there is an omnibenevolent, omnipotent God at work in the world (perhaps with a plan which excuses the evil) a plausible explanation for our experiences? Or are they better explained by some other hypothesis, such as that God does not have the characteristics traditionally attributed to him, or that there is no God at all?

One famous exponent of the evidential argument from the existence of evil is John Stuart Mill. Mill argues that the natural world is full of evidence of evil, and he gives powerful examples of the many ways in which people and other animals suffer. He argues against those who use a posteriori arguments in support of the existence of a good God, saying that in fact, the evidence does not point to an omnibenevolent creator but (if it points to a creator at all) one who is sadistic and who behaves in all the ways that we condemn when we see them in human criminals.

Mill argues that the evidence of nature does not indicate a good and loving creator

....

66 … the order of nature, in so far as unmodified by man, is such as no being, whose attributes are justice and benevolence, would have made with the intention that his rational creatures should follow it as an example …

In sober truth, nearly all the things which men are hanged or imprisoned for doing to one another are nature's every-day performances. Killing, the most criminal act recognised by human laws, Nature does once to every being that lives; and, in a large proportion of cases, after protracted tortures such as only the greatest monsters whom we read of ever purposely inflicted on their living fellow creatures. If, by an arbitrary reservation, we refuse to account anything murder but what abridges a certain term supposed to be allotted to human life, nature also does this to all but a small percentage of lives, and does it in all the modes, violent or insidious, in which the worst human beings take the lives of one another. Nature impales men, breaks them as if on the wheel, casts them to be devoured by wild beasts, burns them to death, crushes them with stones like the first Christian martyr, starves them with hunger, freezes them with cold, poisons them by the quick or slow venom of her exhalations, and has hundreds of other hideous deaths in reserve. … All this Nature does with the most supercilious disregard both of mercy and of justice, emptying her shafts upon the best and noblest indifferently with the meanest and worst; upon those who are engaged in the highest and worthiest enterprises, and often as the direct consequence of the noblest acts; and it might almost be imagined as a punishment for them. She mows down those on whose existence hangs the well-being of a whole people, perhaps the prospect of the human race for generations to come, with as little compunction as those whose death is a relief to themselves, or a blessing to those under their noxious influence. Such are Nature's dealings with life. Even when she does not intend to kill she inflicts the same tortures in apparent wantonness. In the clumsy provision which she has made for that perpetual renewal of animal life, rendered necessary by the prompt termination she puts to it in every individual instance, no human being ever comes into the world but another human being is literally stretched on the rack for hours or days, not unfrequently issuing in death. Next to taking life (equal to it according to a high authority) is taking the means by which we live; and Nature does this too on the largest scale and with the most callous indifference. A single hurricane destroys the hopes of a season; a flight of locusts, or an inundation, desolates a district; a trifling chemical change in an edible root starves a million of people. **"**

John Stuart Mill, *On Nature*, 1904 edn. (1874), pp. 17–18

Mill's argument, then, is that the evidence shows that belief in a loving and all-powerful creator is not supported. He is arguing against supporters of teleological arguments, such as William Paley, who claimed that we only need to look at the world about us to conclude that it must have been made by the power of a God who cares about us. Mill argues that the evidence shows nothing of the kind.

> *See Chapter 1.3. Mill argued that observation of the world does not point to a loving God. His view contrasts with that of Paley.*

Apply your knowledge

1. Read the passage from Mill carefully, and try to summarise the ideas he is putting across in more modern language.

2. When Mill refers, at the end of this passage, to 'a trifling chemical change in an edible root' which 'starves a million of people', he is writing about the Great Famine of Ireland which happened during his own adult life when the potato crop failed due to disease and many starved to death. Find out more about this event. What kinds of questions might it have raised for those with Christian belief?

3. Mill writes of the pains normally associated with childbirth and the not infrequent possibility of maternal and infant death. Perhaps today, with anaesthetics and surgical interventions, the experience of childbirth is less dangerous in the Western world than it was in Mill's time. Do you think the world in general contains less evil and suffering than in the nineteenth century, or is it just different? Are his points equally applicable today?

See Chapter 2.4 for more about utilitarianism. Mill developed a system of ethics which did not involve reference to God: utilitarianism.

A theodicy is an attempt to defend God despite the existence of evil and suffering in the world

Mill uses his evidential argument to support the view that, if there is a God, he does not seem to be at all benevolent. We cannot look to him or to nature as a guide for our own moral behaviour, and we cannot worship him for his goodness.

Responses to the problem of evil: theodicy

An attempt to justify God in the face of evil and suffering is known as a **theodicy.** Someone who presents a theodicy is acting in the way a defence lawyer might act in court, explaining the reasons why an apparent wrong has happened and showing that God does not deserve to be blamed. The word, first used by the philosopher Leibniz, comes from two Greek terms: *theos*, meaning God, and *dikē*, meaning justice. A theodicy, therefore, is an attempt to justify God, and to show that God can still have the character which is claimed by believers despite the evidence of evil and suffering.

Natural and moral evil

Philosophers sometimes draw a distinction between **natural evil** and **moral evil**.

'Natural' evil refers to those parts of existence which cause suffering but which do not result from human wrongdoing. For example, earthquakes, the suffering that other animals inflict on one another, many illnesses and many deaths cause suffering, but are not brought about by human wrongdoing and are not preventable by human action.

'Moral' evil refers to the evil and suffering which results from humanity's choice to do bad rather than good things. The suffering caused by war,

Earthquakes, hurricanes and tsunamis are considered to be examples of natural evil

by bullying, by greed and selfishness, and by violence would be examples of moral evil. Moral evil can also include suffering caused by humanity's failure to do good when the opportunity arises, for example the loneliness felt by many elderly people or the absence of clean drinking water in some countries, even though richer people could afford to provide it.

This distinction between two different kinds of evil has sometimes been helpful in discussion, because, although some people might want to argue that humanity and not God should be blamed for the suffering in the world, it is harder to blame humanity for natural evil and perhaps instances of natural evil require a different explanation.

However, the distinction is not always helpful. It could be argued that all suffering is the result of moral evil, especially if the view is taken that the Fall of Adam and Eve was so significant that it corrupted the whole of the natural order. Or it could be argued that all suffering is natural evil, because we are made in such a way that we can feel mental and physical pain, and if we had been made differently then perhaps we would not have had the capacity for suffering.

For those who reject the idea of God, the problem of evil and the distinction between natural and moral evil is not an issue. People still continue to suffer, whether or not they believe in God, but for the non-theist, there is no conundrum to answer: life simply has its ups and downs, where some people are fortunate and others suffer, through the workings of blind chance.

Augustine's theodicy

Augustine of Hippo (AD354–430) presented one of the most famous Christian theodicies. He disagreed with the thinking of Plato, that everything in the physical world was an imperfect reflection of the Ideal Forms. Because Augustine was a Christian, he did not believe that God could make anything imperfect, especially as the creation stories in the Bible confirmed that 'God saw all that he had made, and it was very good' (Genesis 1:31, New International Version).

In his earlier life, Augustine had been a member of a cult which rivalled Christianity, called Manicheism. The Manichees believed that the universe was held in a cosmic battle between the forces of good and evil (with themselves naturally on the side of good); they believed that people did wrong when the evil forces were winning, and that they could not be held responsible for their own moral actions as they were entirely at the mercy of these supernatural beings. But when Augustine became a Christian, he rejected these beliefs, and could not accept that there was any other power that could possibly rival God.

When Augustine tried to answer the problem of how an omnipotent and perfectly good God could exist given that there is evil in the world, his response had to rule out the possibility that evil is in the world because God made it. Instead, Augustine came to the conclusion that evil is not a real, actual quality in its own right. It is what he called a **privatio boni**,

Natural evil refers to events which cause suffering but are not the fault of humanity. Moral evil refers to suffering caused by human wrongdoing

Think question

Do you think the suffering that results from climate change is a natural evil, a moral evil, both, or neither?

See Chapter 1.1 for Plato's views about imperfection in the world.

See Chapter 3.1 about Augustine's teaching on human nature. Augustine developed an extensive theology exploring the human relationship with God.

a privation (or lack) of the good. In Augustine's view, evil did not have its own separate existence or powerful force, but was a falling away from goodness, just as a shadow falls when one moves further away from a source of light.

According to Augustine, variety is part of the goodness and perfection of the created world. There are so many different plants and animals, and different kinds of people, and above them, angels, in a kind of hierarchy. Each part of creation is good in its own right; even though a tree cannot walk, and a worm cannot sing, for example, this is not 'evil', but a part of the good diversity of creation. It is inevitable that, if the world is to be rich and varied, its constituent parts will be different, but God could still create a tree that was perfect for a tree, or a worm that was perfect for a worm. Difference is a good thing, and the necessary result of difference is that some creatures will be more limited than others.

In Augustine's view, evil first came into the world through the 'Fall' of the angels. He said that the angels were all created perfect, but that some received less grace than others, as a part of the variety of things. By 'grace', Augustine meant that some of the angels received less assistance from God in their attempts to be holy.

The angels then fell away from God as a direct result of their misuse of free will. They chose not to worship God but to rival him. They were trying to become 'lord of their own being' instead of relying on the goodness of God. This was repeated in the Fall of Adam and Eve as representatives of humanity in the Garden of Eden, when they were tempted by Satan, the chief of the fallen angels. All the evil in the world, Augustine thought, has followed on from here, with the kingdom of the angels who remained perfect fighting for the good, while those who are fallen try to pervert the world. In Augustine's own words, in his *Confessions* (AD397–400): 'Free will is the cause of our doing evil

Augustine argued that variety is an aspect of the goodness of creation

… thy just judgement is the cause of our having to suffer the consequences'. Adam and Eve's act of disobedience, mirroring the disobedience of some of the angels, was so terrible that it disrupted the whole world on a cosmic scale for all the generations that followed. It even affected the natural world, causing earthquakes, droughts and plagues; everything wrong with the world could be traced back to the failure of the angels to do their duty in worshipping God.

This theodicy involves some creative interpretation of the story of the Garden of Eden in Genesis 2 and 3. Angels are not mentioned in the Bible story, except as guards of the tree of life once Adam and Eve have been expelled, and the Bible does not say that the serpent was Satan in disguise, it just says that it was a serpent.

The theodicy of Irenaeus

Irenaeus lived earlier than Augustine, from about AD130–202, and was brought up in one of the earliest Christian families. According to many sources, Irenaeus heard the preaching of Polycarp, who knew John, the Gospel writer; so Irenaeus lived at a time when Christianity was still very new, and he helped to form the New Testament with his opinions of which writings genuinely deserved a place in the Bible. The persecution of Christians because of their faith was something that was still at the forefront of people's minds in Irenaeus' time, and so the issue of how a God of love and power could allow such suffering was naturally a topic to which Christian thinkers would turn.

In Augustine's theodicy, the sin of Adam and Eve had cosmic consequences, bringing evil and suffering into a world that God had intended to be perfect

Augustine's theodicy claims that humanity was created perfect, but fell away from God through the misuse of free will. This sin was the cause of suffering throughout the natural world

Irenaeus did not attempt to show that evil and suffering do not really exist, and he admitted that God appears to allow them to continue. His argument was that God allows evil and suffering to have a place in the world, and that the world was deliberately created with a mixture of goodness and evil, so that we can develop and grow as human beings into a mature and free relationship with God.

Irenaeus argued that there had to be evil in the world, for us to be able to appreciate good, just as we might not appreciate warm summer days unless it were cold in the winter, or at least we knew what it was like to feel cold. Many of the good things in life that we take for granted only exist as 'good' because there are other things in the world which are not as good. Good is a qualitative judgement, a comparative, so there have to be other, less good things for goodness to exist at all. All of our most admirable human qualities are relative to other things: some people are generous, or brave, or inspiring or good-tempered, in comparison with other people.

But Irenaeus was not trying to suggest that some people are born with no legs just so that the rest of the population can appreciate being able to walk, for example. He also argued that we have to have evil in the world

Think question

Would there still be such a thing as 'kindness' if everybody were equally kind?

Do you think people would enjoy and appreciate sunny days less if it were sunny all the time?

For Irenaeus, evil and suffering are put in the world by God, for a reason, to enable us to exercise our freedom and develop as humans

in order for us to develop as free individuals who make their own moral decisions and are responsible for them. If everything always went our way, he argued, we would never learn anything. We grow as individuals through tackling problems, making mistakes, persevering and being patient.

According to Irenaeus and others, such as John Hick and Richard Swinburne who have developed their own Irenaean theodicies, when God made people in his own 'image' (Genesis 1:26, New International Version), this had to include giving them **free will**. They had to have, like God, the freedom to make their own choices – whether to be selfish, or whether to care for each other; whether to do something useful with their lives or whether to waste them; whether to develop a loving relationship of obedience to God, or whether to ignore him or try to compete with him. If God had not given people this free will, then they would not have been in his image. They would have been like puppets, only able to do the things that they were made to 'choose'. Perhaps there would have been little point in making them.

Irenaeus argued that our freedom to make real choices between right and wrong is essential if we are to grow into the likeness of God

Irenaeus drew a distinction between God's image and God's likeness. He believed that God made us in his own image, but that we have to grow into his likeness. In God's image, we have the freedom of choice that enables us to be moral agents. As Immanuel Kant was to argue in the eighteenth century, we can only act morally if we have freedom of choice. We cannot be blamed for doing wrong if we were forced to do it, and neither are we admirable for doing good if we had no other option. In order to become the likeness of God, we have to develop and mature, and reach our potential. Irenaeus thought this could only be achieved if we learn to overcome difficulties, cope with our own imperfections and limitations, and resist the temptation to do wrong.

Irenaeus thought that if God simply gave us goodness when we were made, and gave us all the other qualities that go with it, such as patience and compassion and perseverance, then this goodness would not mean anything. Part of being good is an effort of will; looking at the possible courses of action available, and making a conscious choice to opt for the right one and reject the wrong ones. If God stepped in every time someone made a wrong choice, and put right the evil that had been committed or prevented suffering from being the result, then this would be the same as removing the freedom of choice, as well as removing the potential for people to learn from their mistakes.

It might be asked why God did not make us in his own image and likeness, right from the beginning. Irenaeus anticipated this question, and answered it by giving the analogy of a mother feeding a newborn child. The child is not developed enough, right at the start, to be given an adult diet:

> 66 For as it certainly is in the power of a mother to give strong food to her infant (but she does not do so), as the child is not yet able to receive more substantial nourishment; so also it was possible for God Himself to have made man perfect from the first, but man could not receive this (perfection), being as yet an infant. And for this cause our Lord in these last times, when He had summed up all things into Himself, came to us, not as He might have come, but as we were capable of beholding Him. 99
>
> Irenaeus, *Against Heresies*,
> 4: 38:1, c.AD180

Humanity is not capable, in this world, of being in the likeness of God – this only happens after death. It was an essential part of Irenaeus' theodicy that everyone should live after death, and that everyone should eventually complete his or her spiritual development and maturity in order to become the likeness of God. For Irenaeus, as for John Hick sometime later, the afterlife did not bring an immediate end to a person's spiritual journey but allowed him or her to continue to learn and grow on a different spiritual plane.

The Irenaean theodicy, and other theodicies that follow a similar line of argument, are often known as 'free will theodicies' because of their claim that evil is a necessary result of our having the freedom to choose.

John Hick's Irenaean 'soul-making theodicy'

John Hick (1922–2012), a modern philosopher of religion, took a similar approach to that of Irenaeus, arguing that if we never experienced any difficulties or challenges, we would not be able to grow as personalities, we would not learn anything morally.

Apply your knowledge

4. Do you think that Irenaeus' analogy of a mother feeding her newborn child is successful and persuasive in showing why God did not give us his own likeness right from the start? Explain why or why not.

5. Irenaeus argued that free will is essential to help us mature as human beings; how far do you find this convincing?

6. How helpful do you think the Irenaean theodicy might be to someone who is suffering as the victim of a violent crime?

> 66 A world which is to be a person-making environment cannot be a pain-free paradise but must contain challenges and dangers, with real possibilities of many kinds of accident and disaster, and the pain and suffering which they bring. 99

John Hick, *Evil and the God of Love*, 1966, p. 318

Hick describes the world as 'a vale of soul-making' where things happen to us for our own good. He borrowed these words from the poet John Keats (1795–1821), who was a brilliant and sensitive young man with tuberculosis, which he knew would kill him, as indeed it did at the age of 25. Keats, who was trained in medicine and had seen the effects of cholera, yellow fever and smallpox on his patients and also witnessed the death of his mother, imagined the world as a dark valley through which pain and suffering had to be endured in order that the soul should develop and be made fit for meeting God after death – a very Irenaean way of looking at life. Keats nursed his beloved brother Tom through an illness that killed him in 1818. In 1819 Keats wrote to another brother, George, saying:

> 66 I will call the world a School instituted for the purpose of teaching little children to read – I will call the *human heart* the *Book* used in that School – and I will call the *Child able to read, the Soul* made from that *school* and its *book*. Do you not see how necessary a World of Pains and troubles is to school an Intelligence and make it a soul? A Place where the heart must feel and suffer in a thousand diverse ways! 99

John Keats, letter to George Keats, April 1819

Hick took this idea of 'soul-making' and developed Irenaeus' theodicy in a way that he hoped would appeal to the twentieth-century mind. By Hick's lifetime, people had, in general, accepted Darwin's theory of evolution through natural selection and, therefore, many had rejected an Augustinian approach, which necessitated the belief that Adam and Eve were real people and that the Fall was a historical event. Hick, too, rejected the Augustinian theodicy; for him, it was incompatible with a modern scientific view and it created more problems than it solved. Many of Hick's audience had lived through the horrors of the first half of the twentieth century, and had to find a way of understanding why God had allowed these things to happen if they were to retain their belief.

Instead of following Augustine, Hick argued, along with Irenaeus, that evil and suffering in this world are not an unfortunate accident that God failed to anticipate; nor are they problems that God wishes he could resolve for us if only he were capable of helping. According to Hick, God deliberately gave us a world in which we would have the best circumstances under which to choose a free and loving relationship with Him. This includes struggles and hardships, and also includes what is known as '**epistemic distance**'.

'Epistemic distance' means a distance in knowledge. In Hick's view, God deliberately chooses to remain partially hidden from humanity, and does not make his existence absolutely obvious to us but gives us a world which is ambiguous, so that we can make genuinely free choices about whether we want to believe in him or not. If God were to present himself to us so that there could be no possible doubt of his existence, then faith in God would not be a choice. But, Hick argues, God wants us to have that choice, so that if and when we do turn to him, it is because we want to do so and not because we were forced into it. Hick writes:

> 66 For what freedom could finite beings have in an immediate consciousness of the presence of the one who has created them, who knows them through and through, who is limitlessly powerful as well as limitlessly loving and good, and who claims their total obedience? 99
>
> John Hick, *Evil and the God of Love*, 1966 p. 114

The world, then, has to be such that there can be uncertainty about the existence of God: it has to contain both good and evil.

John Hick's approach to theodicy depends on a belief in life after death. Present hardships can only be justified if there is the promise of better things to come after death, if our 'soul-making' experiences are in order to prepare us for some other, better kind of existence ahead.

> The fulfilment of the divine purpose, as it is postulated in the Irenaean type of theodicy, presupposes each person's survival, in some form, of bodily death, and further living and growing towards that end state. Without such an eschatological [everything working out for the best at the end of time] fulfilment, this theodicy would collapse.
>
> John Hick, 'An Iranean Theodicy'. In *Encountering Evil: Live Options in Theodicy,* ed. Stephen Davis, 1981, p. 51

Hick is saying that there has to be life after death for this theodicy to work. If someone dies young after a long and painful illness, or a baby is killed in an accident or dies because of abuse, then it cannot be seen to be 'all for the good' unless in the end it somehow works out for the best – so

John Hick's approach to theodicy depends on a belief in life after death. Present hardships can only be justified if there is the promise of better things to come after death

John Hick's work in multi-faith Birmingham led him to the belief that people of any and every faith will eventually be saved by God

Apply your knowledge

7. Hick writes about his belief that everyone will freely come to God in the end. What do you think of this claim?

8. Hick is writing in a different cultural context from that of Irenaeus. How has he adapted the Irenaean view in order to meet the mindset of twentieth-century people?

there has to be a long-term 'in the end' that goes beyond death in this world. Hick does not use this as an argument for the existence of life after death, but says that the theodicy would not work unless you are prepared to believe in this afterlife. In Hick's view, during the afterlife, people continue with their growth and development towards a relationship with God and, in the end, everyone will be saved. This is an important part of Hick's theodicy – not only will there be salvation for Christians, but for everyone, regardless of their religious beliefs while in this world. Hick came to this view as a result of his work in the 1960s with the multi-faith population of Birmingham, UK. Having lived and worked with people who were genuinely seeking God through their own cultural traditions, he could not accept that an all-loving God would condemn them for eternity, even though his own beliefs were those of an evangelical Christian.

Hick writes:

> If the justification of evil within the creative process lies in the limitless and eternal good of the end state to which it leads, then the completeness of the justification must depend upon the completeness, or universality, of the salvation achieved. Only if it includes the entire human race can it justify the sins and sufferings of the entire human race throughout all history. But, having given human beings cognitive freedom, which in turn makes possible moral freedom, can the Creator bring it about in that the end all His human creatures freely turn to God in love and trust? The issue is a very difficult one; but I believe that it is in fact possible to reconcile a full affirmation of human freedom with a belief in the ultimate universal success of God's creative work. … It can be predicted that sooner or later, in our own time and in our own way, we shall all freely come to God; and universal salvation can be affirmed, not as a logical necessity but as the contingent and predictable outcome of the process of the universe, interpreted theistically.
>
> John Hick, 'An Iranean Theodicy'. In *Encountering Evil: Live Options in Theodicy*, ed. Stephen Davis, 1981, p. 52

Discussing the problem of evil

Is Augustine's view of the origins of moral and natural evil enough to spare God from blame for the evil in the world?

Augustine's theodicy, although it has some strengths, can also be criticised on several grounds. Perhaps its main strength is that it never suggests that God in any way tolerates evil, or wants to have a world with evil in it.

Some of the other theodicies almost seem to suggest that evil is not really that bad because it brings about a good situation in the end; but Augustine never allows the idea that God wants to have anything to do with evil.

However, many people would want to criticise Augustine's theodicy for several reasons. Evil appears to be more serious than a 'privatio boni'. Deliberate cruelty towards a child or animal, for example, seems to be much more powerful and harmful than just a lack of goodness on the part of the tormentor.

A religious group called the Christian Scientists take up this idea of the non-reality of evil. They try to explain evil as some kind of illusion: sin, sickness and death would – according to the philosophy of the founder Mary Baker Eddy – disappear if they were understood to be nothingness and in total contrast to the 'allness' of God. However, it is hard to deny that pain, cruelty and sickness really exist. Even if they are ultimately illusions, the illusion is real enough and has real symptoms (such as the death of the very ill) which cannot be satisfactorily ignored.

Augustine's theodicy gives no explanation for why some of the angels chose evil when they were created to be perfect

Augustine's view gives us no explanation of why God gave some of the angels too little grace, so that they fell into disobedience. Even if we accept Augustine's idea that variety is a good thing, there was no need for that variety to include some angels with so little willpower or goodness that they rebelled against God. The theodicy seems to suggest that God did not think ahead. Also, Augustine's version of events at the creation of the world does not always align with the story in the Bible.

Even if we do accept that evil is no more than a lack of perfection, this does not explain why God allowed this lack of perfection into the world in the first place. Friedrich Schleiermacher, in the nineteenth century, argued coherently against this part of Augustine's theodicy, showing that it is impossible to find a cause or a motive for the angels to sin, unless they were created imperfectly in the first place. Evil would have had to come into the world out of nowhere, unless God made it; and if it did come out of nowhere, this raises some serious issues for the notion of God's omniscience and power.

Augustine's theodicy raises important questions about the nature of God's omniscience; if God knows everything in the sense that he can see into the future and knows what we will do, then why did he create the world, knowing that we would use our free will and freely choose to sin? Even if the choice to sin was wholly ours, God still made the choice to create the world knowing in advance what would happen, and could be blamed for making that choice. Or else, perhaps God did not know what angels or people would do and cannot tell the future. But then we are left

Apply your knowledge

9. How far do you think humanity, rather than God, is to blame for the existence of evil in the world, if we follow Augustine's theodicy?

10. What do you think are the main similarities and differences between the theodicies of Irenaeus and Augustine?

11. Which of these two theodicies do you find more acceptable, if either, and for what reasons?

wondering whether God can really be all-wise if he never guessed that giving his creation the ability to sin was a recipe for disaster.

Can the need to create a 'vale of soul-making' justify the existence or the extent of evils?

Irenaeus' theodicy has been very influential amongst Christians; when faced with suffering, they will often respond by saying that God knows what he is doing and that good will come out of the situation even though it is very difficult to bear at the time. However, there are difficulties with this Irenaean approach.

One argument against an Irenaean view is that some people suffer a lot more than others; does this mean that God wants some people to grow to spiritual maturity, but does not care whether those who lead peaceful and contented lives learn very much? Some people are unable to benefit from suffering but they still experience it. For example, someone with severe learning difficulties might be hurt in a fire, or a tiny premature baby might have a painful infection, and they may not be capable of gaining new insights from their experiences.

Animal suffering, too, is hard to explain using this view, if it is believed that the human soul is special and unique to humans, and that there is no life after death for animals. Perhaps the answer might be that people can learn from the suffering of others, for example a nurse could develop greater compassion and patience from his dealings with children with terminal illnesses, but this does not seem adequate compensation for that child or their parents. In addition, many animals suffer when there are no people around to learn lessons by witnessing it.

Some people seem to be made worse by their suffering, rather than better and stronger. Suffering does not always teach people valuable lessons, but can make them lose their faith or become bitter, or even drive them to mental illness where they can no longer think and act rationally.

John Hick's view of salvation for all has perhaps been the most controversial aspect of his theodicy. Although there are many who welcome this inclusive approach and who see it as a way forward for religious acceptance and diversity, there are others who would argue that it undermines the whole value of Christianity. Why would Christ have died on the cross to save humanity from sin, if there were also lots of other ways to reach God, and if everyone gets to God in the end anyway? The same outcome of salvation for all would have happened without the sacrifice of Jesus, which makes the whole Gospel story appear superfluous and pointless.

In addition, Hick's optimistic view that everyone will eventually freely come to God could be criticised, on the grounds that if this turning to God is inevitable, it cannot also be free. We can only be free to choose if the different options are genuine, but if in the end we all arrive at the same destination, perhaps our choice of different paths is only an apparent choice and not a genuinely free one.

Hick was of the view that human freedom is so important that it is worth paying the price of natural and moral evil in order to have it. However, for some people, even if suffering is worthwhile in terms of the lessons it might teach to people, it would have been better still if God had never made the world. Dostoevsky, in his novel *The Brothers Karamazov* (1880), presented the argument that the price we are expected to pay for our freedom of choice is just too high. In the story, Ivan Karamazov speaks to his brother, Alyosha, who is a novice monk, and points out to him examples of innocent suffering: the cruel treatment of animals, for example, and the torture of a child. Ivan says that it is not God that he doesn't accept, it's just that he 'returns his entrance ticket'; he wants no part in a world where the price is so high. He asks his brother if he would have created a world which was perfect except that it demanded, for its existence, the suffering of just one tiny child, and Alyosha has to admit that, no, he would not have created a world on those terms.

Hick seem to be taking a consequentialist view when presenting his theodicy: the means which God uses might be unpleasant, but they are justified by the ends (which are our freedom of will and our better-shaped souls). However, consequentialist views have been criticised in human ethics, and these criticisms could equally be applied to God. The philosopher Kant, for example, took as a fundamental principle the view that humans should not be used as a means to an end – but if Hick is right, it would appear that God does this when he allows suffering as a means to soul-making, particularly where some people suffer so that others can learn.

D.Z. Phillips, another twentieth-century philosopher, has argued against Hick. In his view, it is not right to suggest that God not only allows evil and suffering, but that he actually planned it to happen, and worked it into his design for the world before the world was even made. He argues that this would be an evil God, if he were prepared to let so many people suffer in order that there should be freedom.

It can be argued, then, that even if the only possible world which could have been created involved suffering as well as freedom, there was still no need for God to have created a world at all. If this world is the only kind of world possible, then God should have left it uncreated.

Which of the logical or evidential aspects of the problem of evil pose the greatest challenge to belief?

To recap, the logical argument from evil to the non-existence of God follows these steps:

- an omnibenevolent God would seek to eliminate evil

- an omnipotent God would have the power to eliminate evil

Consequentialism is discussed in more detail in Chapter 2.4.

Think question

If a world which contains evil and suffering is the best of all possible worlds, then should God have made the world at all?

Apply your knowledge

12. What do you think are the main strengths and weaknesses of Hick's Irenaean theodicy?

13. How far would you agree with the view that we need evil and suffering if we are to develop our true potential?

14. What might be the implications of Hick's Irenaean theodicy for someone who leads a peaceful, healthy and contented life? Should such a person make an effort to suffer more?

- evil exists

- therefore, a God who is both omnibenevolent and omnipotent does not exist.

To discover whether the argument works in providing a real challenge to belief in the existence of God, it is necessary to look at each of the premises more closely.

Premise 1, that an omnibenevolent God would seek to eliminate evil, works on the assumption that it is always better to have no evil than to have evil in the world. This is the assumption which Irenaeus, John Hick and Richard Swinburne challenge. They argue, instead, that there could be good reasons why God does not seek to eliminate evil, and the reasons they suggest are that evil is necessary for us to have free will and for us to mature and develop into a full and free relationship with God. An omnibenevolent God does not eliminate evil, they argue, because it is even more loving of God to provide us with a 'vale of soul-making' than to provide us with a world in which we are bubble-wrapped against all harm and have little real freedom.

Premise 2, that an omnipotent God would have the power to eliminate evil, works on the assumption that an omnipotent God can do absolutely anything at all, and even has the ability to restrict our freedom to choose to do wrong while simultaneously allowing us free will. Some people, including Richard Swinburne, argue that this is a misinterpretation of the idea of omnipotence. God can, he argues, do everything that is possible. However, allowing human freedom while at the same time not allowing evil is not possible, it involves a logical contradiction. Swinburne argues that this is not because God's omnipotence is limited, but because actions that imply logical contradictions are not actions at all. God cannot create a square circle because a square circle is not a thing that can be created; and God cannot remove evil and allow freedom of choice simultaneously because that is illogical too.

Premise 3, that evil exists, might seem self-evident and not in need of further exploration. However, this logical version of the problem of evil does highlight an issue, in that if evil and suffering exist in the world as part of God's loving plan (as Irenaean theodicies argue), then in a way evil and suffering could be considered 'good'. They would, after all, be exactly what God wants, for the benefit and flourishing of his creation, rather like rainfall. If evil is what God wants, and God is omnibenevolent so that everything he wants is necessarily good, then evil becomes good. And if evil becomes good, then the ideas of an all-good God, of human sin and God's requirement of people to keep moral codes make no sense.

The evidential arguments also require further consideration. On the face of it, they do seem very strong. However, their strength rests on the claim that our experience of evil makes the hypothesis of a good, loving God improbable, when compared with allegedly more plausible explanations, such as that good and bad happen by chance.

This gives rise to questions about the notion of probability being used here. If we are saying that our experience of evil makes the God-hypothesis improbable, then we need to know what would make it more probable: we need to know what omnipotent omnibenevolent Gods usually do, and then compare our own experiences with that. For example, if I come home from work and want to know if my son is home, then I can look to see if his shoes are by the door and if the fridge has been raided; I can listen and maybe hear the kind of music he likes, or hear him saying hello. I know what he usually does, and so I can see whether or not he has been doing it, to inform my judgement of the likelihood of him being home.

But we do not know what omnibenevolent, omnipotent Gods 'usually do'. The uniqueness of God, if he exists at all, leaves us without anything on which to base our calculations of probability. We can only guess, using assumptions based on 'what I would do if I were God', and given that we are finite contingent creatures with limited capacities, this could be considered rather a weak position from which to form a judgement.

Is it possible to defend monotheism successfully in the face of evil?

Whether or not monotheism can be successfully defended in the face of evil is a matter for individuals to decide. The traditional Irenaean and Augustinian theodicies have their problems, but nevertheless there are people who do accept them as helpful and comforting explanations of the existence of evil in a world governed by an omnipotent, omnibenevolent God.

There are various different possible positions that could be held.

- Some people might argue that, even if evil does provide strong evidence against the existence of an omnipotent, omnibenevolent God, there is even stronger evidence that such a God does exist. There is not just evil in the world, but also goodness, beauty and love. It could be argued that in total, the good still outweighs the bad and pushes the probability in God's favour.

- It could be argued that even if we do not know a plausible reason for God allowing evil, there could still be such a reason. Our not knowing it does not prove that the reason does not exist.

- It could be argued (and often is) that we should not expect to understand God and the things he does. It should be enough, perhaps, for us to know that there is an all powerful, all loving God who does not make mistakes; we should not require of God that he explains himself to us. It might be argued that theism is about faith in the unknown, and not about the rules of deductive logic or the balance of probabilities.

Apply your knowledge

15. The logical version of the argument from evil aims to demonstrate that an all-loving omnipotent God cannot exist. Because the argument is a priori, if its reasoning is correct and its premises are true, then God with these attributes cannot possibly exist. Do you think the logical version of the argument has succeeded in proving that there is no such God? Give reasons for your answer.

16. The evidential version of the argument aims to demonstrate that experience shows the existence of such a God is improbable, and that there are better hypotheses than the God hypothesis to account for our experience. Do you think this argument has succeeded? Give reasons for your answer.

Apply your knowledge

17. Do you think that there is more evil than good in the world, or more good than evil? Give reasons for your answer.

18. How convincing do you find the argument that we should not expect to understand why God allows evil in the world?

Learning support

Points to remember

» When writing essays on the problem of evil, it is tempting sometimes to launch into a rant about the inequalities and suffering in the world. However, remember that even if you have strong feelings on the subject, you should aim to present different sides of the argument fairly, in a balanced way, and reach your conclusion by using reasoning rather than just emotive language.

» Remember that both Irenaeus and Augustine place emphasis on the importance of human free will in their theodicies – but in different ways.

» Logical and evidential versions of the argument have different approaches; make sure that you understand the distinction.

» Augustine argues that disobedience against God at the time of the Fall is to be blamed for evil and suffering.

» Irenaeus, in contrast, argues that evil and suffering are necessary, to challenge us and help us mature in our relationships with God.

Enhance your learning

» Augustine's ideas about the problem of evil can be read in his book *The City of God* and also in an anthology edited by Brian Davies, *Philosophy of Religion, A Guide and Anthology* (2000), in a chapter called 'What is Evil?'

» John Hick's book *Evil and the God of Love* is fascinating but lengthy; Part IV contains his ideas about a 'vale of soul-making'.

» It is worth being familiar with biblical passages about the Fall of humanity in order to understand Augustine's ideas: Genesis 2:4–25 and 3:1–24. Romans 5:12–13 summarise the Christian idea that the sin of Adam corrupted the world.

» You could develop your thinking about the problem of evil by reading the twentieth-century philosopher Hannah Arendt, who reflects on what she calls the 'banality of evil' in her book *Eichmann in Jerusalem* (1963).

Practice for exams

AS questions and A level questions look identical; the difference between AS and A level assessment is seen in the different proportions of marks awarded for two different skills: the skill of demonstrating knowledge and understanding (Assessment Objective 1, or AO1), and the skill of constructing a critical argument (AO2).

At AS, half the marks (15 marks) are available for knowledge and understanding, and the other half (15 marks) for the quality of your analytical and evaluative argument. You should aim to use your knowledge in order to support the argument you are making throughout the essay, rather than presenting descriptive knowledge in the first half and then an opinion in the second.

At A level, your demonstration of knowledge and understanding is awarded a maximum of 16 marks, and your analytic and evaluative skills are awarded a maximum of 24 marks. You should aim to concentrate on constructing a lucid argument, making use of your knowledge to add weight to the conclusions you draw.

Discuss critically Augustine's view that God cannot be blamed for the existence of moral and natural evil in the world.

For this essay, you need to have a thorough understanding of Augustine's approach to the problem of evil and its grounding in his beliefs about the Fall of Adam and Eve as described in Genesis.

Practise your skills for AS level

For AS level, you need to demonstrate a sound knowledge and understanding of Augustine's teaching on the problem of evil, as well as an understanding of what is meant by natural and moral evil. In your discussion, you should explain the strengths and weaknesses of Augustine's views and you could compare them with other theodicies in order to give your critical assessment.

Practise your skills for A level

At A level, you should not spend a large part of your essay describing the Fall and Augustine's views on it, but should use it to underpin your critical assessment. You need to decide whether Augustine has successfully convinced you that humanity, and not God, can be blamed for evil. You might find his views totally convincing, or totally unconvincing, or find some strengths but also some weaknesses in them. Whatever you choose to argue, you should also consider counter-arguments to reach a well-balanced conclusion.

'Evidence of evil and suffering in the world provides a greater challenge to the existence of God than the logical problem of evil.' Discuss.

This question asks for a comparison between the evidential form of the problem of evil (looking at the probability that a loving God would allow the extent of evil that we observe) and the logical form (looking at the logical problems of the inconsistent triad).

Practise your skills for AS level

For AS level, as well as demonstrating knowledge and understanding of both kinds of argument, you also need to present a point of view, deciding whether one presents a stronger challenge than the other or whether they are both equally challenging (or unchallenging).

Practise your skills for A level

At A level, in answering the question, you should refer to evidential and logical arguments but avoid simply presenting each one at length. Concentrate instead on giving your own argument in answer to the question, explaining why you find one more challenging than the other (or why you think they are equally challenging).

Studying religion and ethics

What is goodness?

What does it mean to be a moral person?

Why study religion and ethics?

Making moral decisions is something every human being does throughout life. How we live has an impact on others. Not just whether we are kind or unpleasant to the people we meet, but also in terms of the sort of relationships we cultivate, the behaviours we adopt or avoid and the principles we choose to live by.

Ethics are often linked to things we believe in, whether that means religious ideas or philosophical principles. For some vegetarians their decision to not eat meat arises from a belief that it is wrong to use animals in that way. For some religious people, charity is not an option but a duty because of features of doctrine, sacred text or religious teaching. Ethics brings responsibilities from beyond our private preferences. It is found in the commitments people make, as well as in their intuitions.

To study ethics we need to examine theories, which are different approaches to making moral decisions that thinkers have proposed. These apply certain principles, rules or ways of thinking about how moral decisions are made. The theories make assumptions about life and how we think, and we can ask whether they are the right assumptions or the right way of thinking. It is important that we don't just take the ideas theories give us for granted, but really look at those ideas to check they seem reasonable.

For some, ethics is a logical, rational thing that, above all, is about some kind of clear thinking, not driven by desire or emotion. For others it is about obedience to a higher authority or power (natural law) or a sense of duty (Kant). Others still see ethical thinking as driven by essential human feelings like love (situation ethics). There are some theories that see ethics as a product of human psychology – our desire for happiness and wish to avoid harm (utilitarianism). Once we understand a theory we can ask what it does to make moral decisions easier and what it misses out that makes moral decisions harder? Does it miss things which seem morally important?

We can explore theories by applying them to particular issues. Do they provide compelling answers to the moral problems of our time, like whether it is right to give people the chance to decide the manner and timing of their own death (euthanasia), or whether certain kinds of business decisions are wrong (business ethics)? Ethics is a practical subject, about making sense of decisions, consequences, human beings and human life.

Sometimes when trying to make sense of ethics we can use hypotheticals or 'what if' scenarios. What if you only had one meal and two people were starving? What if you were with a group of people on a life raft, but there were too many people on board and it was starting to sink? 'What ifs' may be realistic or unrealistic, but they help us to think through ethical ideas and theories. We can also think about historical events and things happening right now and wonder whether the right thing was, or is, being done. Finally, we can think ethical systems through – what sorts of assumptions do they make about the world? Are these assumptions correct?

Is ethics more about the actions or the consequences?

When approaching a moral issue, is it better to focus on the actions or the consequences? For example, consider the boy who steals from the rich tourist. Stealing is the action. One approach to ethics is to refer to rules about actions. So the rule 'do not steal' might be followed, in which case the boy in this example is wrong to do what he does. This is a deontological approach to ethics, one focused on actions. The rightness or wrongness of an action is found inside the act itself – it is intrinsic (within) to the action. Right and wrong is **absolutely** determined by the action itself – there is no question of special circumstances or situations.

Another way of thinking about the issue is to look at the results of the action. In the case of the boy stealing from the rich tourist, the tourist loses money, which seems bad. However, perhaps there is a reason for the theft that should be considered. Maybe the boy needs money to feed his family. Maybe there are no other sources of money, apart from picking the pockets of wealthy and well-insured tourists. Perhaps his family is starving. Ethical thinkers who are interested in consequences might be prepared to set aside the rule 'do not steal' if the outcome is better. If stealing is the only way to survive and if that means a family survives, perhaps stealing in this case is right. This is a **teleological approach**. Rightness or wrongness in this sort of ethic is extrinsic – it places rightness or wrongness outside the action in the consequence/result. Goodness is **relative** to the ends.

The issue here is not to worry too much about the example, but to see that each of these approaches is different. Each leads to different questions being asked about the moral issue. They may reach similar or different conclusions, but perhaps one is better than the other; perhaps one seems more reasonable.

Are morals universal or do they change according to the situation?

Another division between moral theories is between those who think that there are rules or principles that cover all situations, all places, all times and all people – universal laws – and those who think that the best approach to morality is to set aside rules and focus on the situation. Immanuel Kant believed in universal ethics, while Joseph Fletcher thought we should focus on the situation.

Consider this example: after the death of a beloved father, two brothers are sorting through some personal possessions, private letters and documents, as they prepare to say something about their father at the funeral. They know that their father was loving and attentive to their mother, and that she misses him terribly. They discover a stash of letters in the attic and are shocked to realise these record a long-running affair between their father and another person. After considering their options, they place the stash back into its hiding place and write the eulogy for the funeral extolling their father's virtues. They agree to say nothing to their mother.

A universal approach to morality is not going to like this deceit. If honesty is the best policy then it is always the best policy and they should tell their mother. But someone who takes a situational approach might choose a different path. Maybe it is not the most loving thing to do, to reveal such letters. Perhaps it is compassionate not to put their mother through such a trauma. Perhaps keeping secrets can sometimes be good.

What sort of ethics do you want?

1. Do you think ethics should tell us what is right and tell us what to do, or is it more of a guide? Would you prefer clear direction when faced by moral decisions or choice about what to do?

2. Are you the kind of person who uses your head to make decisions, or your heart?

3. Do you believe ethics come from beliefs (religious or philosophical ones) human psychology or something else?

4. Do you think ethics really exist?

How do we live a good life?

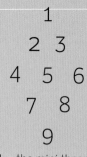

1 = the mini theory you most like;
9 = the mini theory you least like.

There are many ethical theories explored in this book. Consider the mini ethical theories below, which link to the book's chapters. Think about them and arrange them in a diamond nine shape.

A. A moral is a personal opinion, or something linked to a particular culture. People are different and cultures are different, so morals are different. There is no right or wrong answer, only right for you or right for your culture. When in Rome, do as the Romans do! When in Japan, do as the Japanese! Morals are relative.

B. Morals are fixed rules, standing apart from our opinions. They are there to challenge us to live better lives. They are there to protect people from the damage that can be done when lines are crossed.

C. There are some things we should just not do. It is always wrong to rape and abuse children, the poor, the sick, and the elderly. Morals are about understanding that some acts should never be carried out.

D. There are better ways of living and worse ways of living. We need to look at the most important things in life: how precious life is, how important it is to look after each other, how important it is to learn from each other. We need to do things that support the most important things in life, and avoid doing those things which do not support them.

E. The good life is not just about following rules; it is about practicing a way of life. Taking on certain attitudes and behaviours that we can exercise to become good people – honesty, courage, justice, integrity, etc. The attitudes and behaviours which are right, are those which lead to the best overall result. This is something we all do together, not as individuals, so that the behaviours we adopt are shared by our communities.

F. You cannot always predict what the right thing to do is. Sometimes you just have to look at the situation and make a decision at that moment. Rules can get in the way because, in the situation you face, following the rules may do harm. So just try to do the loving thing, and forget about the rules. Being moral is about acting with the most important principles in mind – ultimately you have to decide on a course of action that you think fits these principles.

G. Morals are there to try and get us to think about other people, rather than ourselves all the time. They are there to force us to think about what life is like for people who are not like us, but different from us, maybe even strange to us. It is easy to be nice to people who are like us, but life involves meeting many other people who are not like us. That is when we need morals.

H. We always have to think of the bigger picture. It is easy to rely on rules from the rulebook of life, but life throws up situations where the rules don't seem to help, so we need to think about what happens as a result of what we do. We need to look beyond the moment when we act to the consequence of our actions and ask ourselves – what is the best outcome? Once we have agreed on what that is, we should do whatever it takes to get that outcome, even if that means breaking rules.

I. Human beings are selfish creatures and left to our own devices, society would break down and become a frightening place. We see that in parts of the world where there is no law and order, things become terrible. It could be a dog-eat-dog world if we are not careful. We need a strong moral authority to stop us from tearing each other apart for our own selfish interests.

Chapter 2.1

Natural law

Do all human beings share a common nature or purpose?

Does it matter if we do good for bad motives?

Is morality about reason or emotion?

Key Terms

Deontological: from the Latin for 'duty', ethics focused on the intrinsic rightness and wrongness of actions

Telos: the end, or purpose, of something

Natural law: a deontological theory based on behaviour that accords with given laws or moral rules (e.g. given by God) that exist independently of human societies and systems

Synderesis: to follow the good and avoid the evil, the rule which all precepts follow

Secondary precepts: the laws which follow from primary precepts

Primary precepts: the most important rules in life: to protect life, to reproduce, to live in community, to teach the young and to believe in God

Practical reason: the tool which makes moral decisions

Eudaimonia: living well, as an ultimate end in life which all other actions should lead towards

Specification requirements

Aquinas' natural law, including:

- the telos
- the four tiers of law
- the precepts

Introduction

Greek philosophers explored the idea that morals were based on an eternal dimension, so that justice and law were ultimately universal. Aristotle distinguished between (universal) natural justice and (local) legal justice. St Paul explored the idea that all people could, within themselves, discern a law. It is **deontological**, focused on actions.

> 66 Indeed, when Gentiles, who do not have the [Jewish] law, do by nature things required by the law, they are a law for themselves, even though they do not have the law. They show that the requirements of the law are written on their hearts, their consciences also bearing witness, and their thoughts sometimes accusing them and at other times even defending them. 99
>
> Romans 2:14–15, New International Version

Thomas Aquinas also thought that right and wrong are fixed things. They do not change according to the situation or what might happen as a result. They are linked to some greater idea of a fixed morality in the eternal law of God.

The telos/ultimate end: Aquinas thought moral acts were free acts aimed at achieving an immediate end, and also an ultimate end. Achieving an ultimate end brings ultimate happiness and satisfaction, a thing not found in this world (even love between a couple is tinged ultimately with the sadness of grief). We should pursue this ultimate happiness.

We might, however, act towards an ultimate end for a doubtful reason and we might make a mistake about what is the right thing to do: I must not do bad for good reasons. It is better to do good for good reasons. Motivations matter.

The four tiers of law: Aquinas advocated an approach to ethics based on a universal order that all moral rules were based on. Eternal law was the reason of God, known to human beings through revelation (divine law) and **natural law** (discoverable through the right use of reason). Human law was based on these sources (and if it wasn't, it need not be followed).

The key precept: the synderesis rule: Natural law involves rationality. The order of reason guides our action and must not be ignored. Reason directs us to do good and avoid evil, and all other principles flow from this reason.

Primary precepts and secondary precepts: Aquinas thought that **synderesis** entailed certain primary precepts. Aquinas reflected on the purpose of human beings and concluded that synderesis entailed the need to protect life, reproduce, educate offspring, live in society and love God. **Secondary precepts** are rules that follow a **primary precept** – so, for example, it is right for a doctor to give medicine to a patient to save their life.

Real and apparent goods: Humans do bad things because they are mistaken by apparent goods. Someone who steals a neighbour's new car, has made a mistake about the pleasure gained from acquiring a new car.

The doctrine of double effect: It is possible for some actions to have two effects, one which upholds a precept and another which does not. If the person intends the good effect, then they can be justified in acting in that way. So self-defence is right if I am doing it to preserve life, but not if I am doing it to kill someone. The other effect is foreseen but not intended.

Apply your knowledge

Moral absolutists hold that morals are fixed, unchanging things, set for all time. They are part of the universe and true for all people, places, times and cultures. Moral relativists think this is wrong. How can we see this fixed morality, they ask? Moral relativists think morality changes (is relative) from place to place, time to time, culture to culture and even individual to individual. Moral truth to them is not fixed, or not at all clear.

1. Do you think morals are fixed, unchanging things, that are the same for all?
2. Is it better to have a society based around fixed morals or should morality be flexible depending on (relative to) the situation or individuals?
3. Are morals more about what society thinks or what individual people think? Should morals be the same for everyone or do they differ for person to person?
4. Do you think Aquinas thinks more like a relativist or more like an absolutist? Explain your answer.

What is natural law?

How ought we to live? For some, we should look to whatever social norms suggest (cultural relativism), while others suggest it is determined by whatever you personally believe (subjectivism). Utilitarians prefer living by actions or rules that maximise pleasure for all. Absolutists believe in fixed moral laws such as the transcendental Forms or Ideas of Plato, if we are philosophically smart enough to perceive them. Perhaps we do not need to look to a difficult philosophical journey, human pleasure or our individual desires. Perhaps we should not simply copy what happens around us but instead should try to detect the natural moral way of living: the way that is ordained by cosmic or divine order. Maybe human beings instinctively seek this natural way of living.

See Chapter 1.1, The Forms, and Chapter 2.4, Jeremy Bentham.

Thomas Aquinas (1225–74) was born in the castle of Roccasecca near Naples around 1224–5. As a child he was sent to a Benedictine abbey where he began his studies. He later became a saint in the eyes of the Church and a doctor of the Church – a leading teacher. The importance of his work has meant that, for hundreds of years to the present day, his thinking is a central influence on Catholic moral thought. His major work was *Summa Theologica* (1265–74). His ideas can be linked to universal human rights today.

Natural law thinkers argue there is a human nature, which we should live in accordance with. Aquinas wrote: 'Now a certain order is to be found in those things that are apprehended universally'. Using reason, certain laws are perceived, the first of which is 'good is to be done and

Natural law thinkers argue there is a human nature, which we should live in accordance with

Thomas Aquinas

pursued, and evil is to be avoided'. He continues, 'All other precepts of the natural law are based upon this' (*Summa Theologica*, Benziger Bros. edn, 1947).

This view directly influenced the teachings of the Catholic Church:

> 66 Man participates in the wisdom and goodness of the Creator who gives him mastery over his acts and the ability to govern himself with a view to the true and the good. The natural law expresses the original moral sense which enables man to discern by reason the good and the evil, the truth and the lie: The natural law is written and engraved in the soul of each and every man, because it is human reason ordaining him to do good and forbidding him to sin. … But this command of human reason would not have the force of law if it were not the voice and interpreter of a higher reason to which our spirit and our freedom must be submitted. 99
>
> I. The Natural Moral Law, the *Catechism of the Catholic Church*, www.vatican.va/archive/ccc_css/archive/catechism/ p3s1c3a1.htm, 1954

Hugo Grotius (1583–1645) also developed a theory of natural law as rationally discernible principles for all to follow. Samuel von Pufendorf (1632–94) was also in the natural law tradition. In *Of the Law of Nature and Nations* (1729), Pufendorf suggested that by ourselves we are vulnerable but we live in communities and societies to survive. Other philosophers, such as John Locke, Samuel Clarke, and William Paley, all developed ideas from the natural law tradition.

Where does the idea of natural law come from and what does it mean? The Greek Stoics believed human beings had a divine spark enabling them to discover eternal laws necessary for human happiness. The Stoics considered themselves citizens of the universal law. The Greek philosopher Aristotle also wrote about the natural law:

Man discerns by reason the good and the evil

> 66 The natural is that which everywhere is equally valid, and depends not upon being or not being received … that which is natural is unchangeable, and has the same power everywhere, just as fire burns both here and in Persia. 99
>
> *Nicomachean Ethics*, 350BC, Book V, ch. 7

Aristotle is saying here that natural law is a 'given'. He thought that the purpose of human beings was to live a life of reason: 'Reason is the true self of every man, since it is the supreme and better part' (*Nicomachean Ethics*, Book X, ch. 7).

The Roman lawyer Cicero, in his book *On the Republic*, gives the classic form of natural law.

> 66 True law is right reason in agreement with nature; it is of universal application, unchanging and everlasting; it summons to duty by its commands, and averts from wrongdoing by its prohibitions. ... We cannot be freed from its obligations by senate or people, and we need not look outside ourselves for an expounder or interpreter of it. And there will be not be different laws in Rome and at Athens, or different laws now and in the future, but one eternal and unchangeable law will be valid for all nations and all times, and there will be one master and ruler, that is, God, over us all, for he is the author of this law, its promulgator, and its enforcing judge. 99

Cicero, *On the Republic III*, trans. C.W. Keyes, 1928, xxii

These ideas of universal law, the life of reason, and the law discernable in human hearts come together in Aquinas' theory of natural law. Aquinas writes:

> 66 [T]he first principle of **practical reason** is one founded on the notion of good, viz. that 'good is that which all things seek after.' Hence this is the first precept of law, that '*good is to be done and pursued, and evil is to be avoided.*' All other precepts of the natural law are based upon this: so that whatever the practical reason naturally apprehends as man's good (or evil) belongs to the precepts of the natural law as something to be done or avoided. 99

Thomas Aquinas, *Summa Theologica*, II.I, 94 art. 2, 1265–74, emphasis added

Apply your knowledge

5. What evidence might there be that a universal law exists?

6. Can you give examples of human behaviour that might suggest we can act rationally and are not simply driven by our passions?

7. Do you think moral law is more to do with reason or reasoning than passion and feelings?

The telos/ultimate end

Aquinas begins his own thinking with Aristotle in the *Nicomachean Ethics* (350 BC). Aristotle argues that every agent (every being capable of choosing how to act) acts for an end of some kind, and the human being acts to acquire happiness or **eudaimonia**. Eudaimonia is not pleasure but activity that perfects the highest faculty of a person. Human happiness is the contemplation of these highest objects. For Aristotle something is good if it fulfilled its end. He also thought there was a Prime Mover in the universe responsible for setting it in motion. Aquinas developed this idea, seeing God as the Prime Mover.

For Aquinas, properly moral acts are free acts, which come from a freely acting rational person. We act towards certain specific ends but achieving those ends is not fully satisfying. We are only fully satisfied when we achieve the ultimate end, the universal good. What is this universal good? It is not just physical pleasure because this only satisfies the body, not the whole person. You may have a satisfying breakfast but could still be troubled about the news on the radio, or the troubles in your relationships. The beauty and athleticism of youth is eventually replaced by the wrinkles and infirmity of old age. The thrill of a one-night stand is replaced by the sense of loneliness the next morning because of the absence of a lifelong partner. Even the love of a partner is ultimately replaced by the sadness of their inevitable loss at the end of life. There is no ultimate consolation in these ends.

Aquinas concluded that the ultimate end cannot be found in this world but only in the supreme and infinite God – the ultimate end of all things which rational creatures alone can perceive. He wrote 'Ultimate and perfect beatitude (happiness) can consist only in the vision of the divine essence, which is the very essence of goodness' (*Summa Theologica*, Part II.I, Q4, art. 4). Aquinas believed that the natural light of reason meant that all human beings sought this end. This might mean the pursuit of God, but could also mean the pursuit of the first cause, the purpose for our existence.

Natural law goes beyond human laws to cover all areas of human action because, '… man needs to be directed to his supernatural end in a higher way' (*Summa Theologica*, Part II.I, Q91, art. 4).

Divine help is needed to help direct our motivations as well as our actions. Aquinas is not only concerned about the acts, but the reasons for them – intention matters. You may act in a good way but for a scurrilous reason. You might help someone cross the road, not out of a charitable desire, but to impress your boyfriend. The good exterior act is compromised by a bad interior act. However, we must not do bad for good reasons. It would be wrong to steal money from someone to help a beggar. In addition, your good intentions could lead you astray. You might make a mistake about the good thing to do. You might think that it would be best to help your gran to die because she seems so distressed in her old age and desperate to leave this world, but your emotion might confuse your moral decision-making.

The four tiers of law

Aquinas thinks about morality in terms of law. He says law is 'a certain rule and measure of acts whereby man is induced to act or is restrained from acting' (*Summa Theologica*, Part II.I, Q91, art. 1). There are different kinds of laws that are made known to us in different ways. Aquinas' four main kinds of law are: the eternal (on which all other kinds of law depend), the divine law (revealed to human beings through divine revelation, the Bible), the natural law and the human law.

The eternal law is the absolute and eternal part of natural law. It is part of the mind of God – his unchanging reason. This is the reason God's law is unchanging and universal, for everyone at all times and in all places. Whatever the culture, society, political situation, the eternal law remains the same. It is absolute, and not relative to different people or situations. God plants the eternal law in every person's rational soul. In Aquinas' view the eternal law is in God and not a feature of nature apart from God. Other thinkers give this role to an absolute natural law, without God.

God also sends out information about this eternal law through the second law – **divine law**, which means the commands and teachings of divine revelation that are usually found in the Bible. This include the commandments, the Beatitudes, the Sermon on the Mount, the teachings in the parables, and so on. This sacred scripture, revealed by God, is God teaching human beings how to live.

It is possible for all human beings to perceive God's eternal law, even those who have not read the Bible. This is because of **natural law**. Natural law allows humans to perceive the eternal law through the application of human reason – through reflection on the world. This marks human beings apart from animals and makes God's eternal law accessible to the whole of humanity.

Finally, **human law** is our response to these messages from God in reason and in revelation. Human laws are the customs and practices of society. Look around the world, and many human societies come up with the same kinds of laws – look after the young and vulnerable, protect life, etc. Aquinas is clear that human law is only a proper law if it is good and in accordance with divine and natural law. A practice that is wrong is no law at all and breaking such laws is not immoral. Note that human law does not have to cover all moral wrongs, only the more serious ones. Not all aspects of morality require legislation.

> *God plants the eternal law in every person's rational soul*

Apply your knowledge

On April 12, 1963, Dr Martin Luther King, Jr. was in a jail cell in Birmingham, Alabama. He had coordinated non-violent protests against segregation. Circuit Judge W.A. Jenkins issued an injunction against 'parading, demonstrating, boycotting, trespassing, and picketing'. Dr King disregarded the injunction and marched anyway. He was arrested and thrown in jail, and criticised by a local clergyman for breaking the law. In a letter, he identified a moral responsibility to obey just laws saying, 'one has a moral responsibility to disobey unjust laws'. How to decide whether a law is just or not? King followed Aquinas. He suggested a just law 'squares with the moral law, or the law of God. An unjust law is a code that is out of harmony with the moral law'. Unjust laws are not rooted in the eternal. If the majority group makes a law that applies to a minority group, but the majority do not themselves follow the law, this is unjust. King recalls that much, if not all, of what Hitler did in Germany was legal, while helping Jews in Nazi Germany was illegal. In these cases, the natural equality of the law was being broken.

10. Was Martin Luther King right to break the law? What did King perceive that Aquinas might have suggested was against natural or divine law (nature or the Bible)?

11. Is the thing that makes a law right the fact that it is made by the correct earthly authority, or does rightness come from something behind the legal authority, such as the principle of equality or fairness?

12. On what other grounds might it be right to break a law of the land?

The US civil rights movement sought to change an unjust situation

The precepts

The key precept: the synderesis rule

The key precept is to do good and avoid evil. Reason directs us to do good and avoid evil, and all other principles flow from this reason.

Natural law may appear to be exclusively about following rules but this fails to recognise the role of reason in moral decision-making that Aquinas is concerned about. Natural law is 'law-like' because of its rationality. Aquinas says law is 'an ordinance [order] of reason for the common good … a rule and measure of acts, whereby man is induced to act or is restrained from acting … and the rule of measure of human acts is reason' (*Summa Theologica*, Part II.I, Q90, art. 4 and art. 1). He made strong claims about the importance of reason.

> 66 The natural law is nothing other than the light of understanding placed in us by God; through it we know what we must do and what we must avoid. God has given this light or law at the creation. 99
>
> Thomas Aquinas, 'De praesc. I,' cited in the *Catechism of the Catholic Church*, para 1955

> 66 [The law] is nothing else than an ordinance of reason for the common good, made by him who has care of the community, and promulgated. 99
>
> Thomas Aquinas, *Summa Theologica*, Part II.I, Q90, art. 4

> 66 To scorn the dictate of reason is to scorn the commandment of God. 99
>
> Thomas Aquinas, *Summa Theologica*, Part II.I, Q19, art. 5

> 66 Whatever is contrary to the order of reason is contrary to the nature of human beings as such: what is reasonable is in accordance with human nature as such. The good of the being is being in accord with reason, and human evil is being outside the order of reasonableness … 99
>
> Thomas Aquinas, *Summa Theologica*, Part I.II, Q71, art. 2

Divine reason, the reason of God, is something that exists, though it is impossible for us to fully perceive it. However, with the faculty of human reason we can discern the laws. The moral life is one that is lived by and through reason. Reasoning about the common good leads to certain acts being promoted and other acts being prohibited. If we permit theft, then the common good is undermined – we cannot go to bed at night without fearing we will wake to find our fridges emptied. How could we build a society that permits theft? Because it is act-based, natural law is deontological, although we have already noted there is an ultimate end to which all acts are focused.

Natural laws are universal. Aquinas says natural law is the same for all people. There is a single standard of truth and right for everyone, which is known by everyone. Aquinas writes:

The moral life is one that is lived by and through reason

> 66 [E]very agent acts on account of an end, and to be an end carries the meaning of to be good. Consequently the first principle for the practical reason is based on the meaning of good, namely that it is what all things seek after. And so this is the first command of law, 'that good is to be sought and done, evil to be avoided'; all other commands of natural law are based on this. … As converging on one common primary precept these various precepts of natural law all take on the nature of one natural law. 99
>
> Thomas Aquinas, *Summa Theologica*, Part I.II, Q94, art. 2

This is the synderesis, the key precept from which all other principles flow. It means that we must do that which is proper to our end. If a given action is conducive to this end, then we should do it. If it is not conducive to the end, then we should not do it.

Think question

a. Consider the following examples:

– A field medic working in an Ebola-stricken country is vaccinating his staff and has come down to one last vaccine. He has two nurses left to vaccinate but one is his cousin. What should he do?

– A doctor who suspects her husband is having an affair, receives a new patient who is the possible mistress. The doctor has access to the person's home address and personal details, information that would help her find out the truth. Should she use this information?

– You work in a human resources department of a large company. At an interview selection committee meeting you must decide which candidates to invite to interview and which to reject. You are supposed to use only the information on the application form but recognise one applicant as an old lover who betrayed you. The job requires a trustworthy person. You could easily prevent this former lover from being selected for interview, if you used your personal knowledge. Should you?

b. Is our behaviour governed by reason or passions? What evidence can you suggest to support each example? Give specific examples for each.

c. Suggest how reason and emotion might influence the decision-making processes?

Whatever is a means of preserving human life, and of warding off its obstacles, belongs to the natural law

Think question

d. Is there a common purpose to life that all humans share?

Primary precepts and secondary precepts

Aquinas thought that in all human beings, 'there is first of all an inclination to good' because 'every substance seeks the preservation of its own being'. Therefore, 'whatever is a means of preserving human life, and of warding off its obstacles, belongs to the natural law'. He therefore made preservation of life the first of five primary precepts, things that are good and absolute and describe human flourishing:

1. To worship God: God is the source of eternal law, and God has sent this law to humanity through divine law and natural law.

2. To live in an ordered society: a lawful one where it is possible to follow all of the primary precepts.

3. To reproduce: to ensure that life continues as is God's intention and as is necessary for the continuation of society.

4. To learn: to teach people about God, his eternal law, natural law, divine law and the primary precepts.

5. To defend the innocent: life is most precious.

Because human beings, out of reason, are inclined towards their destiny, to do the good they have 'a natural inclination to know the truth about God, and to live in society'. As a result, humans should, 'shun ignorance, to avoid offending those among whom one has to live, and other such things regarding the above inclination'.

A moral act leads towards the divine or cosmic intention for humanity. These acts fit the purpose humans were made for and are in line with the primary precepts and so are good. Acts which are not in accordance with the primary precepts do not fit the purpose humans were made for and so are bad.

Apply your knowledge

Now a certain order is to be found in those things that are apprehended universally. … the first principle of practical reason is one founded on the notion of good, viz. that 'good is that which all things seek after'. Hence this is the first precept of law, that 'good is to be done and pursued, and evil is to be avoided'. All other precepts of the natural law are based upon this: so that whatever the practical reason naturally apprehends as man's good (or evil) belongs to the precepts of the natural law as something to be done or avoided …

… wherefore according to the order of natural inclinations, is the order of the precepts of the natural law. Because in man there is first of all an inclination to good in accordance with the nature which he has in common with all substances: inasmuch as every substance seeks the preservation of its own being, according to its nature: and by reason of this inclination, whatever is a means of preserving human life, and of warding off its obstacles, belongs to the natural law. Secondly, there is in man an inclination to things that pertain to him more specially, according to that nature which he has in common with other animals: and in virtue of this inclination, those things are said to belong to the natural law, 'which nature has taught to all animals', such as sexual intercourse, education of offspring and so forth. Thirdly, there is in man an inclination to good, according to the nature of his reason, which nature is proper to him: thus man has a natural inclination to know the truth about God, and to live in society: and in this respect, whatever pertains to this inclination belongs to the natural law; for instance, to shun ignorance, to avoid offending those among whom one has to live, and other such things regarding the above inclination.

Thomas Aquinas, *Summa Theologica*, Part II.I, Q94, art. 2

13. Can you suggest morals that all people seem to agree on? What examples of cultural or religious moral behaviours challenge this thought? Decide whether or not you are convinced that there is a common order that most people are able to perceive.

14. Consider the argument that it is more important to act with our minds on the greater principle that our behaviour supports, rather than focus on the situation immediately before us. Find an example where the immediate situation could mislead us into acting in the wrong way, and an example when it might be very important to focus on the particularities of the immediate situation. Explore both thoughts and then decide what you think.

15. Do you think Aquinas is right in his primary precepts: preserve life, reproduce, educate, live in society, worship God. Try to make a convincing argument against one of these and introduce another candidate precept.

16. Should everyone be required to pursue all of the ends of society throughout their life? Aquinas allowed priests to be celibate because of a special role they had in serving God.

Is there a natural order of things?

Secondary precepts are deduced from primary precepts. They are applications of the primary precepts into certain situations. According to natural law and the primary precepts, human beings were made to live, murder and euthanasia end life and so are wrong. Human beings were made to live in society, so antisocial behaviour is wrong. It is possible for secondary precepts to vary as they are based on the application of primary precepts into circumstances that may differ.

> 66 Every act in so far as it has something real about it has something good about it. In so far as it falls short of the full reality that a human act should have, it falls short of goodness, and so it is called bad. 99
>
> Thomas Aquinas, *Summa Theologica*, Part II.I, Q18, art. 1

Natural law leads to some strong conclusions on ethical issues. Euthanasia is prohibited by natural law due to the precept of preserving life. The Catholic Church teaches that suicide is the denial of a natural instinct to live, although people may argue about the nature of life lived (see Chapter 2.5).

Real and apparent goods

Given that Aquinas believed that the nature of every being was basically good, how can we explain evil? If human beings are directed internally towards doing good, they would not pursue evil. A man might feel that to have an affair with the beautiful wife of his neighbour is desirable.

Sometimes we can be distracted from doing the right thing by something else we mistakenly think to be right

Temptation exists. Aquinas thought evil was not desirable. 'No evil can be desirable, either by natural appetite or by conscious will. It is sought indirectly, namely because it is the consequence of some good.' The reason a man lusts after another man's wife is not because he thinks it is good to break up marriages, but because he is mistaken about what he truly desires. The pleasurable desire leads to disaster, and not what he truly wants. 'A fornicator seeks a pleasure which involves him in moral guilt' (*Summa Theologica*, Part 1a, Q19, art. 9).

The man is falling short of the ideal human being that God intended. An immoral act, or sin, is falling short of God's wish for us. That is not in accordance with the purpose for humanity. These tempting goods are apparent, not real. This is an error of reasoning or absence of it. Suppose I love playing Superstrike, an online game where I fight with friends from all over the world. I am tempted to play right now instead of finishing this chapter on natural law. It is good to play Superstrike, it is a lot of fun. But truly, playing Superstrike is an apparent good. I should be working so I can feed my family. I need to use reason correctly to distinguish between the apparent goods that tempt me and the real goods. Human beings want to pursue to the precepts, the natural law, but they make mistakes.

Aquinas, like Aristotle, thought reason identified 'natural' or 'cardinal' virtues: prudence, temperance, fortitude and justice. Some virtues are revealed in sacred scripture: faith, hope and love (1 Corinthians 13:13). We should develop the virtues to help keep the natural law. Aquinas thought this required discipline and practice to become habitual.

It is possible for the very opposite to become habitual if we are not careful. Habits of sinful unnatural activity can develop and overwhelm us.

Apply your knowledge

17. Suggest two examples of desired acts that may not be real goods.

18. To what extent do you think people do wrong things believing them to be right (pursuing a thing they believe is a good when, in fact, it is not good) and to what extent do you think they know their actions are wrong, but do it anyway?

19. How can we tell which goods are real and which are apparent? Suggest an act where it would be difficult to be sure in that moment, whether it was a real or apparent good.

20. Do bad habits lead to worse ones? For example, might watching pornography contribute to poor human relationships? Can you suggest other possible examples?

21. Is it better to be habitually good or does goodness require conscious thought?

22. Do you think there are two effects in using lethal force to defend yourself? Is it just the same effect viewed from a different perspective? Has Aquinas confused different motivations with different outcomes?

23. What happens if a prejudiced and warped racist mindset makes a person view a black man walking down the street towards him at night as a lethal threat. The racist mindset leads to a genuine sense of fear – maybe he is carrying a gun? So the person with the racist mindset draws his own licensed firearm and shoots. He believes he is protecting his life, despite no aggression being shown and no gun being carried. The racist mindset justifies the act with a sense of proportionate behaviour with a feeling of fear born of prejudice and a desire for self-protection. What would Aquinas say about this? Would he be right?

An action may have two effects or ends

The doctrine of double effect

Aquinas introduces a principle of double effect in discussing whether self-defence is permissible (*Summa Theologica*, Part II.II, Q64, art. 7). Let's consider an example to illustrate this: A man attacks a woman walking home one evening and she uses her mace spray to force him away. He stumbles back, trips on the kerb and falls to the ground, hitting his head. As a result of this he dies. If taking life breaks the primary precept then the woman would be wrong for defending herself. Does this mean we could never defend ourselves with strong force? Some (such as Augustine) have argued that indeed this is wrong: 'private self-defence can only proceed from some degree of inordinate self-love'. But Aquinas suggests something different:

> 66 Nothing hinders one act from having two effects, only one of which is intended, while the other is beside the intention. … Accordingly, the act of self-defence may have two effects: one, the saving of one's life; the other, the slaying of the aggressor. … Therefore, this act, since one's intention is to save one's own life, is not unlawful, seeing that it is natural to everything to keep itself in being as far as possible. … And yet, though proceeding from a good intention, an act may be rendered unlawful if it be out of proportion to the end. Wherefore, if a man in self-defence uses more than necessary violence, it will be unlawful, whereas, if he repels force with moderation, his defence will be lawful. 99
>
> Thomas Aquinas, *Summa Theologica*, Part II.II, Q64, art. 7

Aquinas says several things here. Intention matters. Thomas Aquinas was a deontologist – someone interested in actions. Ethical acts are what is important in making moral decisions but he distinguished between interior and exterior acts. Interior acts are about our motivation, our intention behind the act – what we want to happen and why we are acting. Exterior acts are the act that is visible – the act that is actually performed. The best way to act is when both interior and exterior acts are good. I might raise money for charity (a good act) but I may do it to get some attention for the community (a bad intention). Better to do it for selfless reasons (good intentions).

An action may have two effects or ends. If it is good (in this case protecting life) and if the intention in self-defence is to achieve this aim, then self-defence is permissible. However, the force used should be proportionate. So for Aquinas' theory of double effect, the action itself cannot be bad but good or neutral (saving life is good). The bad effect should not be the means by which the good effect is achieved (it is the saving of life that saves life, not the taking of life). The motive should be focused on the good effect (hoping to save life). The good effect should be at least as important as the bad effect (life is in the balance here).

Discussing natural law

Does natural law provide a helpful method of moral decision-making?

Natural law offers a legalistic way of working out what is morally right. We can link the immediate moral dilemma to a bigger general rule. We can identify the general bigger driver (the precepts) that should guide our particular decisions and work out what to do when faced with a choice. It provides moral rules which can be applied to the different situations, dilemmas and circumstances: 'Application of the natural law varies greatly; it can demand reflection that takes account of various conditions of life according to places, times, and circumstances.' It offers clarity and consistency in a world which some think has become relativistic and has lost a sense of moral direction: '… in the diversity of cultures, the natural law remains as a rule that binds men among themselves and imposes on them, beyond the inevitable differences, common principles' (*Catechism of the Catholic Church,* 1957).

However, the primary precepts are inspired by a religious belief in God, which makes them potentially unhelpful for those who do not believe in God. Some might not interpret the world as having a purpose, and order. Some may see it as a more chaotic place, a place of random and unpredictable circumstances with no divine author behind what happens around us.

Natural law comes from reflection on the natural world. We see that children need to be educated; it seems natural to want to protect life. This is straightforward and has proved to make sense to many people. However, others might argue that often things that we observe turn out not to be quite so straightforward after all, and that human reason is capable of coming up with new explanations for observed phenomena that push aside previous observed laws, such as quantum physics for example. Our reflections may not lead to the same conclusions as science teaches us new insights about the scientific world. That would undermine the basis on which natural law generates its precepts and therefore its helpfulness with moral decision-making.

There is also consideration for the importance of conscience; a factor that might offset the legalistic nature of the theory. Natural law provides the kind of system that can be used to frame and inform rules for society. Natural law provides: '… the solid foundation on which man can build the structure of moral rules to guide his choices', '[a] moral foundation for building the human community' as well as 'the basis for the civil law with which it is connected' (*Catechism of the Catholic Church,* 1959).

Critics of natural law say it puts people into boxes where they are defined by their 'ends' – a simplification of human behaviour and

Apply your knowledge

24. Discuss these views:

a. 'Human anatomy does not define the purpose of human life. Natural law simplifies the purpose of living to biological functions and misses emotion.'

b. 'Natural law has a tendency to make existing social practices "normal" by calling them "natural".'

c. 'Natural law keeps ethics close to the reality of human life and the things that really matter in making sure life flourishes.'

d. 'Natural law provides an ordered structure for communities to flourish.'

purpose that suggests our activities are driven towards a single end. Natural law reads morality as a legal operation, missing the more complex nature of moral decision making. Perhaps it unwittingly lends support to established social conventions that are mislabelled as 'natural' like marriage, sex, etc? In making moral decisions, natural law might encourage us to copy socially accepted conventions, when perhaps on some occasions they should be challenged. Social conventions might be read into biological readings of natural law. The sexual act of reproduction is necessary for new life, so same sex unions and reproduction using technology is labelled wrong. But not everyone need participate in each aspect of the act of producing new life. Mothers may die after childbirth – young babies are only at the beginning of the process of producing new adults. Technology makes it possible for same sex couples to reproduce. Definitions of male and female are being challenged by science and social practice. Perhaps the traditions of heterosexuality are being read into natural law, and it is reproducing social norms that one day will be seen as unethical, like the views that once separated blacks from whites and saw mixed race marriages as immoral.

The idea of a universal natural law has an enduring appeal in the world. It is a rationale for universal human rights, providing some basis for the hope that a global system of justice would protect every human being from injustice, the powerful and the wicked. It seeks to ensure that all people may be protected by a system of law that is true and good. Human nature may be more mysterious than was previously supposed, but the demands of universal justice for all will be a prevailing reason why some find natural law more satisfying than alternative moral theories that do not provide such protection.

Does human nature have an orientation towards the good?

Aquinas has a positive view of human nature. He thinks that there is a natural response to do good. The moral laws arise out of this natural response and support the view of a created world where life flourishes. Arguably for a community or society to get along, surely some common morals are needed, especially in an ever more interconnected world with diversity and plurality in populations living together. If we think that we need order in society to try to prevent chaos, or if we think that there is too much freedom in how people should go about living now, then a legalistic morality might appeal. Though society is diverse, perhaps there are enough common features among all people for natural law to make sense. After all, most people are in favour of protecting life, ensuring there are future generations, educating one another and living as a community.

But is this view of the world too rosy? Are human beings more dog-eat-dog than this picture of natural equilibrium? Philosophers like Thomas

Hobbes, who lived through the English civil war that saw Parliament execute the King, and families torn apart by conflict, saw human nature as dangerous and murderous. 'Men from their very birth, and naturally, scramble for everything they covet, and would have all the world, if they could, to fear and obey them' (W. Molesworth, ed., *The English Works of Thomas Hobbes*, 1839, vol. IV, p. 53). To survive, human nature perhaps needs to be limited, as if it was allowed to do what comes naturally, it would become destructive.

Human development is damaging the natural world, through pollution, over-population and the depletion of natural resources. Where is the natural response to do good if the result of mass human activity is the unbalancing of the natural processes that maintain life for countless other species?

The idea that humans have a natural urge towards goodness can be challenged. Perhaps we have a natural urge towards self-preservation, towards furthering our own genetic lines of life (as some geneticists argue), or simply pursing our own pleasure (as utilitarians suggest).

Can a judgement about something being good, bad, right or wrong be based on its success or failure in achieving its telos?

Aristotle's idea of telos has many attractions. The good wheel turns smoothly – the good hammer hammers the nail in well. So we can deduce that a good person is the person who fulfils his or her end or purpose. The problem with this is applying the kind of thinking we use for a tool to a human being. Are humans not different from these fixed ideas around tools? Can moral actions be reduced to a description of the function of actions? Does reason 'sit on top' of actions?

Natural law is a central theory of Catholic moral theology and as such informs the moral thought of the global Catholic Church. It provides an ordered approach to life, a system to weigh moral judgements based on reason and the interpretation of experience, and combines attention to actions as well as the laws of life. It offers stability, and arguably enhances community life, is attentive to wider needs, and beyond individual pleasure or personal opinion.

Catholic teaching prohibits artificial contraception, masturbation and homosexual sex largely on natural law grounds because those acts of sex cannot result in new life. The deliberate use of the sexual faculty, for whatever purpose, outside marriage is contrary to its purpose (its telos) and goes against the 'moral order' (Sacred Congregation for the Doctrine of the Faith, *Persona Humana*, 9 and para. 2352, *Catechism of the Catholic Church*). St Augustine wrote, 'intercourse even with one's legitimate wife is unlawful and wicked where the conception of the

> ## Apply your knowledge
>
> 25. Discuss these two views in relation to natural law:
>
>   a. 'Human beings need rules to remind them who they are and what's best for them, not to tell them what to do.'
>
>   b. 'Human beings are selfish, pleasure seeking and greedy individuals who will always take from life what they can. They need constraining.'

Apply your knowledge

26. Discuss these different points of view in relation to natural law:

a. 'All moral actions have an intention or purpose and this is the thing that should be judged.'

b. 'Morality needs to be judged in the *round*, by its effects and the situation, not just the end.'

c. 'Human beings are too complex and too different to be given simple purposes or ends.'

offspring is prevented. Onan, the son of Judah, did this and the Lord killed him for it' (see Genesis 38:8–10).

Some ethicists believe that this leaves no proper place for human rationality. Rationality does not 'sit on top' of natural acts but guides human process and acts, to bring order and intelligence to the world. Natural law results in a distorted view of the ethical human act which sees it exclusively in terms of the physicality of the act.

Perhaps we need a more historically conscious world view that emphasises the changing, developing, evolving nature of the world, rather than the static view of nature. Art and music show a creativity and complexity in terms of the ends they produce.

Society might have at one time, or in some places, decided that women have a single purpose – that of being a mother and homemaker and this end meant they needed few legal rights, often treated as property. In some parts of the world that are still heavily patriarchal this *order* is seen as *natural* but in many places society has changed, evolved as shown by equal rights, equal pay, the right to vote. In other words, women have more complex ends that are configured by culture and society, not created in a fixed way by God or anything else.

However, the idea of equality, that every human being has equal status, and equal interest or end, is strongly upheld by natural law. Natural law powerfully upholds the idea of universal human rights, rights that recognise the dignity and equality of every human being. Universal human rights are arguably the most significant worldwide example of the benefits of natural law.

Has the universe as a whole been designed with a telos?

Natural law assumes a fixed, immutable, unchanging end for all things that has been created, part of a universe that is intended and designed. However, some do not see the universe and world as something that has an intention or design behind it. There are those who believe in an account of science that has no place for a creator God. There are those who see in the world and wider universe, randomness, chaos, change and dynamism. Perhaps nature is much less ordered and more random than we think. Natural law seems impossible if there is no creator God, or no order to things.

Even those who have some belief in God find the use of telos in natural law difficult. Hans Kung thinks this idea of the natural is 'naive, is static, narrow and completely unhistorical' (*Infallible? An Inquiry*, 1971, p. 35). He thinks that the use of 'natural' is based on a rather arbitrary distinction between natural and artificial as if things like sexuality are simply about biology and not psychology and social attitudes, for example. The idea that we have fixed sexual orientations around polarities (male and female) are increasingly challenged by notions of transgender and changeability. These undermine notions of a single predetermined end. Some think these designations are more to do with society than nature. Kung argues that natural law conceptions of the human nature attach a biological or physical structure to human actions independently of the function of reason.

However, perhaps natural law can still be defended if the order was found to link to the kinds of societies where human beings flourish. If certain societies flourish more than others, maybe there are some points of focus that produce principles, or precepts that can be followed.

Can the doctrine of double effect be used to justify an action, such as killing someone as an act of self-defence?

Natural law can seem quite fixed in its approach to making moral decisions and it seems to protect life and prevent life from being taken. However, the doctrine of double effect brings in more complexity to how it works. It allows a person to intend for one thing to happen, whilst there is also another outcome as well. Supposing I am attacked. I may defend myself in order that I protect life. In doing so I might use force that leads to the attacker themselves being harmed or even killed. My intention is always to protect life but this results in a life taken. I am not motivated out of an intention to act against the natural law, but to uphold it.

This might allow for self-defence, it could justify a defensive war, it might be used to argue in favour of abortion (for example, in some cases a *self-defensive* abortion is medically advisable because of a threat to a mother's life) and might be used to justify feeding one person and leaving another to starve when there is only food for one. How do we agree when an intention is to save life and not take it? If the hand that is intended to save is killing to do so, we might question whether anything is actually different? Can the 'protecting life' act also be a 'taking life' act at the same time? There is an old saying that the road to hell is paved with good intentions. Perhaps our good intentions may lead us astray.

Ultimately, Aquinas is centrally interested in human intention – the extent to which every person, every individual knows their own motivation. Human intention is impossible to judge from the outside, and yet it is fundamental to any moral judgement. We may doubt another person's motives, but we cannot know them. This ethical insight is profound.

The double effect rule can be seen as a helpful method for dealing with difficult decisions, in that the double effect rule can distinguish between intentions and the actions that take place. However, some find these fine distinctions implausible. Deontologists are mostly interested in actions as

Apply your knowledge

27. What sort of societies would help human beings to flourish? What about a society where artificial intelligence (AI) has developed to the point that humans no longer need to work, care for children or the elderly, drive their own cars, produce food, provide healthcare, create entertainment, fight wars – all these jobs being done for them by robots and all daily decisions made for them by AI. Would natural law be helpful for the AI in selecting the right decisions to make for the people it is caring for?

they can be observed. How can an act to save a life that involves taking a life only have one intention, when the life lost is inextricably connected to the life saved. Having a secondary purpose is a way of smuggling something past the prohibition on killing. What this reveals is a weakness in the system – when it faces unpalatable choices natural law seems less convincing. It requires the use of dubious judgements.

Apply your knowledge

28. Discuss the following possible examples with reference to double effect. Do they raise questions about whether natural law adequately addresses the moral issues?

a. Allowing a woman to have an abortion if continuing the pregnancy would inevitably lead to the death of mother and child.

b. Shooting dead a terrorist who is about to trigger a bomb in a crowded place.

c. Ending the life of a dying person who is in agonising pain, such as a wounded soldier on the battlefield or an elderly and terminally ill patient, when they are begging for release from the misery their life has become.

d. Sending children into prostitution to feed the starving family.

Learning support

Points to remember

» Natural law as an ethic bundles together ends (the ultimate end), rules (which should be followed to reach towards those ends) and the specific actions that follow from the rules. Whilst characterised as deontological, act-focused, it has teleology within it.

» Natural law advances a concept of human nature which is a being with a purpose, and intended way of living. This could be understood in religious terms, but it could also be argued from a non-religious standpoint, an account of nature based on evolution, for example. Much in natural law depends on what the human is.

» Aquinas is interested in human intention, not simply following laws for laws' sake. The morality of an action changes according to the human intention – the morality of something is not exclusively about the action, but the motive behind that action.

» It is very important to understand that natural law is not just about following laws which govern 'natural behaviour'. It is also a reason-based ethical system that involves discernment, moral decision-making. Aquinas is interested in our motives as well, and the fact that our intention matters as well as the act itself. This means Aquinas is interested in the moral agent – the human being who has to make decisions. Understanding natural law as ethical legalism does not give adequate respect to the fact that Aquinas thinks human beings should be free in order to act morally.

» It is important to think carefully about how you write about the issues. It might be tempting to criticise Aquinas because of aspects of Catholic morality but you should be careful to distinguish whether it is Aquinas, or how he is used, that you are criticising.

Enhance your learning

» The *Stanford Encyclopedia of Philosophy* (2005, rev. 2011) has an excellent account of Aquinas' Moral, Political and Legal Philosophy, http://plato.stanford.edu/entries/aquinas-moral-political/.

» *Summa Theologica* is the best-known work of Thomas Aquinas. It is an influential classic of Western theology; easily available online.

» Aquinas read Aristotle and this informed his ideas about natural law. For a challenging read look at Aristotle's book *Physics II*, which gives an account of his idea of nature. See part 3 of Chapter II in particular.

» The *Catechism of the Catholic Church* (which is easily available online using any good search engine) has an account of the Natural Moral Law in paragraphs 1954–60.

Practice for exams

AS questions and A level questions look identical; the difference between AS and A level assessment is seen in the different proportions of marks awarded for two different skills: the skill of demonstrating knowledge and understanding (Assessment Objective 1, or AO1), and the skill of constructing a critical argument (AO2).

At AS, half the marks (15 marks) are available for knowledge and understanding, and the other half (15 marks) for the quality of your analytical and evaluative argument. You should aim to use your knowledge in order to support the argument you are making throughout the essay, rather than presenting descriptive knowledge in the first half and then an opinion in the second.

At A level, your demonstration of knowledge and understanding is awarded a maximum of 16 marks, and your analytic and evaluative skills are awarded a maximum of 24 marks. You should aim to concentrate on constructing a lucid argument, making use of your knowledge to add weight to the conclusions you draw.

To what extent does natural law provide a helpful method of moral decision-making?

This is a broad question which requires you to think about the application of natural law as a normative ethical theory in different contexts. You might want to decide what you think a 'helpful' ethical theory ought to do – for example, it might be considered helpful if it gives a clear 'right answer', or if it can be easily understood, or if it is obvious how to apply it in different situations.

Practise your skills for AS level

If you are answering this question at AS level, you need to show good knowledge and understanding of the theory of natural law with its main characteristics and principles. You should show how it might apply in different situations, and give a critical evaluation of whether you think natural law theory is always helpful, sometimes helpful or never helpful.

Practise your skills for A level

At A level you need to make sure that your essay is an argument and not just descriptive. You might think that natural law is always helpful; or perhaps only helpful in some contexts and not so much in others (in which case, explain in which contexts, and why it works better or worse in those); or perhaps not helpful at all. You need to have some sound reasoning to support the line of argument you wish to take. Your essay will be more engaging and your reasoning will be clearer if you can offer some examples to support what you are saying.

Discuss critically when, if at all, the doctrine of double effect should be used to justify an action.

This question asks for a consideration of the doctrine of double effect. You should have a clear and thorough understanding of what this means and of how it might be applied in the context of different ethical dilemmas.

Practise your skills for AS level

At AS level, you should show a thorough knowledge and understanding of the doctrine of double effect and how it works in the context of natural law theory. You might be able to give real or hypothetical examples to demonstrate your understanding. For your evaluation, you are asked to think about whether this doctrine can justify actions. If you think it can, explain under what circumstances, and if you think it can't, then explain why not.

Practise your skills for A level

In order to gain high marks at A level, you need to concentrate on giving critical evaluation; think about the

reasons why some people would support employing the doctrine of double effect, and also the reasons why others might oppose it or prefer a different way of resolving an ethical issue. Try to present a balanced account, giving each position a fair hearing, while at the same time supporting your own point of view with sound reasoning and examples.

Chapter 2.2

Situation ethics

Might doing the right thing involve breaking the rules?
Is love the heart of ethics?
Does the morality of an action depend on the situation?

Key Terms

The following definitions are derived from Joseph Fletcher's theory of situation ethics. They are not universally agreed definitions.

Justice: justice ordinarily refers to notions of fair distribution of benefits for all. Fletcher specifically sees justice as a kind of tough love; love applied to the world

Pragmatism: acting, in moral situations, in a way that is practical, rather than purely ideologically

Relativism: the rejection of absolute moral standards, such as laws or rights. Good and bad are relative to an individual or a community or, in Fletcher's case, to love

Positivism: proposes something as true or good without demonstrating it. Fletcher posits love as good

Personalism: ethics centred on people, rather than laws or objects

Conscience: the term 'conscience' may variously be used to refer to a faculty within us, a process of moral reasoning, insights from God or it may be understood in psychological terms. Fletcher described it as function rather than a faculty

Teleological ethics: moral goodness is determined by the end or result

Legalistic ethics: law-based moral decision-making

Antinomian ethics: antinomian ethics do not recognise the role of law in morality ('nomos' is Greek for 'law')

Situational ethics: another term for situation ethics, ethics focused on the situation, rather than fixed rules

Agape love: unconditional love, the only ethical norm in situationism

Extrinsically good: good defined with reference to the end rather than good in and of itself. Fletcher argued only love was intrinsically good

Specification requirements

Fletcher's situation ethics, including:

- agape
- the six propositions
- the four working principles
- conscience

Introduction

Situation ethics is described by its supporters as a Christian ethic. It is quite different from natural law and legalistic forms of biblical ethics. Its supporters suggest it is consistent with the representation of Jesus in the Gospel. It is viewed, by advocates, as a flexible and practical theory, based on love (agape). Critics think it is unjust, individualistic, unduly demanding of individual conscience and socially destructive. It is viewed by many Churches as controversial and was rejected by the Catholic Church and many conservative Protestant Churches.

Joseph Fletcher (1905–91) argued that love was what morality should serve. He thought that someone making a moral decision should be prepared to set aside rules if it seemed that love would be better served by doing so. 'The situationist follows a moral law or violates it according to love's need' (Fletcher, *Situation Ethics*, 1966, p. 26).

Fletcher developed six fundamental principles that the situationist should apply: (1) 'Only one thing is intrinsically good; namely love: nothing else at all'; (2) 'The ruling norm of Christian decision is love: nothing else'; (3) 'Love and **Justice** are the same, for justice is love distributed; nothing else'; (4) 'Love wills the neighbour's good, whether we like him or not'; (5) 'Only the end justifies the means; nothing else'; and (6) 'Love's decisions are made situationally, not prescriptively.'

Fletcher also developed four working propositions:

- **pragmatism:** being practical rather than always following belief in ideologies or systems

- **relativism:** 'The Situationist avoids words like "never" and "perfect" and "always" and "complete" as he avoids the plague, as he avoids "absolutely"' (Fletcher, *Situation Ethics*, 1966, p.44)

- **positivism:** Love is posited as true or good without demonstrating this is the case. Situation ethics depends on Christians freely choosing faith that God is love, so giving first place to Christian love

- **personalism:** the legalist puts the law first, but the situationist puts people first, the person takes responsibility for the other person. It is person centred.

For the situationist, **conscience** describes the weighing up of the possible action before it's taken, a kind of moral deliberation, rather than a faculty within a human being. The process of moral reasoning, that is conscience, is informed by the situation and love.

This chapter will first outline Fletcher's own account of situation ethics, before engaging with the criticisms laid against it.

A teleological Christian ethic

Religious ethics tend to be thought of in terms of moral rules, which should not be broken, or certain behaviours or virtues that should be practised as part of a 'religious way of life'. It is often seen as deontological, focused on the rightness or wrongness of specific actions. 'Deontology' comes from the Latin word for 'duty'. Religious ethics made up of rules about what you can and cannot do are found in natural law and Protestant approaches to ethics that are based on divine commands.

However, ethics can also be **teleological**, with rightness or wrongness determined by the ends, or consequences instead. Rightness is extrinsic to the action. The idea of a religious form of morality which subverts or breaks rules is quite different from deontological Christian ethics.

Situation ethics identifies its roots in the New Testament references to Jesus setting aside the law or breaking established rules. For Fletcher, situation ethics was a Christian ethic though many Churches disagreed.

Think question

Identify a religious rule that you think is deontological and a religious moral principle that is not deontological.

Fletcher and his three approaches to moral thinking

Joseph Fletcher was an ordained Episcopalian priest and an American academic who taught Christian and medical ethics. For a time, he was President of the Euthanasia Society of America. Fletcher divides moral thinking into three basic kinds: **legalistic**, **antinomian** and **situational ethics**.

Legalistic ethics has a set of predefined rules and regulations which direct how you should behave. Judaism at the time of Jesus had a legalistic character. Pharisaic Judaism had a law-based approach to life, founded on the Halakha, the collective tradition of written and oral law covering all aspects of life. Christianity also shows legalistic features, based on biblical commandments and/or the precepts expounded by Aquinas. Of course Aquinas argued they were discoverable in nature, and not human ordinations.

Fletcher thought this approach led to a legalistic mindset. Due to the complications that life throws up, laws accumulate to cover all eventualities. Once murder has been prohibited, one has to clarify killing in self-defence, killing in war, killing unborn human beings and so on. The legalist must continually add to the law book to cover these eventualities, resulting in a web of laws. To be moral means following the appropriate moral law, or applying the previously determined moral laws. For Fletcher, this mistake is found in both Catholic Christianity through adherence to natural law, and in Protestant Christianity through observance of the sayings of the Bible. Fletcher rejected these legalistic approaches that were based on fixed laws.

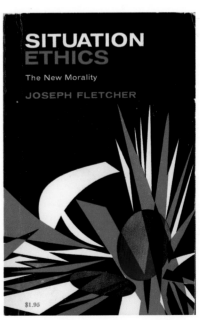

Situation Ethics by Joseph Fletcher

The morality of an action depends on the situation

Antinomian ethics is the reverse of legalistic (law-based) ethics. A person using antinomianism doesn't use any kind of law, rule or principle, or any system of ethics at all. Each attempt at moral decision-making is unique, following no patterns or system. Fletcher was critical of antinomianism: 'it is literally unprincipled, purely ad hoc and casual. They follow no forecastable course from one situation to another. They are, exactly, anarchic – i.e. without a rule' (Fletcher, *Situation Ethics*, 1966, p. 23).

A third approach to ethics is situational. How moral an action is depends on the situation. The situationist enters into the moral dilemma with the ethics, rules and principles of his or her community or tradition. However, the situationist is prepared to set aside those rules in the situation, if love seems better served by doing so. The situationist is more interested in loving people, than loving laws. Situation ethics agrees that reason is the instrument of moral judgements, but disagrees that the good is to be discerned from the nature of things or the love of things. In Fletcher's words, 'The situationist follows a moral law or violates it according to love's need' (*Situation Ethics*, 1966, p. 26). For the situationist, all moral decisions are hypothetical. We may never come to a conclusion about the right thing to do but we need to come to a decision. Moral decisions should depend on what best serves love. The situationist doesn't say that 'giving to charity is a good thing'; they only ever say 'giving to charity is a good thing if in this situation …'. Lying is justified if love better serves the person by lying in this particular situation.

66 Since 'circumstances alter cases', situationism holds that in practice what in some times and places we call right is in other times and places wrong. … For example, lying is ordinarily not in the best interest of interpersonal communication and social integrity, but is justifiable nevertheless in certain situations. 99

Joseph Fletcher, 'Naturalism, Situation Ethics and Value Theory.' In *Ethics at the Crossroads*, by G. McLean and R. Wollak, 1993

Situationism presents itself as a principled approach to ethics which is based on circumstances and love, rather than actions and rules about actions. In his foreword, Joseph Fletcher characterises this approach:

66 Let an anecdote set the tone. A friend of mine arrived in St Louis just as a presidential campaign was ending, and the cab driver, not being above the battle, volunteered his testimony. 'I and my father and grandfather before me, and their fathers, have always been straight-ticket Republicans.' 'Ah,' said my friend, who is himself a Republican, 'I take it that means you will vote for

Senator So-and-So.' 'No,' said the driver, 'there are times when a man has to push his principles aside and do the right thing.' **"**

Joseph Fletcher, *Situation Ethics*, 1966, p.13

Apply your knowledge

1. Choose one moral dilemma and explain how legalists, antinomians and situationists might go about making a moral decision.

Situationism is heavily influenced by Christian theologians who took a different approach to deducing moral guidance from the Bible rather than simply looking for rules or principles. Moral problems are contextually situated answers. The Christian response should be a flexible message of forgiving grace, one founded on love. Fletcher was influenced by the theologians Bultmann, Barth and Bonhoeffer.

Rudolf Bultmann argued against the idea that Jesus sought to establish some new ethical ideology, some set of abstract unwritten immutable legalism or idealism, a law of heaven (Bultmann, *Essays Philosophical and Theological,* 1955, p. 22).

Karl Barth argued that 'God's commanding' can only be this individual, concrete and specific example of commanding, not only a rule (Barth, *Church Dogmatics,* 1957, p. 673). Barth was not opposed to the idea of morally wrong actions. There is an outside chance that it could be right to break a moral law, such as in the case of abortion.

Dietrich Bonhoeffer was also situationist in his ethical thinking. He thought determining the will of God in any concrete situation is based on two things: the need of one's neighbour, and the model of Jesus of Nazareth. 'These are the only rules. The world does not offer moral certainty, and we do not have a God's eye view of good and evil in the world' (Bonhoeffer, *Ethics,* 1964, p. 231). All we can do is act according to these two things and offer our conduct to God's judgement, mercy and grace.

See Chapter 3.6 for more on Dietrich Bonhoeffer's ethical thinking.

Agape love

Whilst utilitarians see the greatest happiness as the highest end, and Kantians look to the *summum bonum*, others look to love, specifically **agape** (pronounced ah-GAH-peh), or unconditional love. Christianity is a religion based on love, a God that is love, and agape love has its origins in the New Testament. It is the love that is referred to in the commandment to love your neighbour (Mark 12:30–31) and such love is held by many Christians as the principle at the heart of moral conduct which demands that enemies are loved, not just friends (e.g. Matthew 5:44) and such love is self-sacrificing, not self-satisfying. This agape love is the love God showed the world when he sent his son to die (John 3:16).

Christianity is a religion based on love, a God that is love

> There is only one ultimate and invariable duty, and its formula is 'Thou shalt love thy neighbour as thyself.' How to do this is another question, but this is the whole of moral duty.

William Temple, *Mens Creatix*, 1917, p. 206

> The law of love is the ultimate law because it is the negation of law; it is absolute because it concerns everything concrete. … The absolutism of love is its power to go into the concrete situation, to discover what is demanded by the predicament of the concrete to which it turns. Therefore, love can never become fanatical in a fight for the absolute, or cynical under the impact of the relative.

Paul Tillich, *Systematic Theology*, Vol.1, 1951, p. 152

Bishop John Robinson wrote, 'there is no one ethical system that can claim to be Christian' and Rudolf Bultmann argued that Jesus had no ethics apart from 'love thy neighbour as thyself', which is the ultimate duty. Joseph Fletcher follows in this tradition. Agape love is the highest end.

In *Situation Ethics*, Joseph Fletcher offers ethical principles that he maintains can accommodate Christian beliefs.

> Christian situation ethics has only one normal principle or law … that is binding and unexceptionable, always good and right regardless of the circumstances. That is 'love' – the *agape* of the summary commandment to love God and neighbor. Everything else without exception, all laws and rules and principles and ideals and norms, are only contingent, only valid *if they happen* to serve with love in any situation. Christian situation ethics is not a system or program of living according to a code, but an effort to relate love to a world of relativity is through a casuistry [clever, but unsound reasoning] obedient to love. It is the strategy of love.

Joseph Fletcher, *Situation Ethics*, 1966, pp. 30–1

Think question

Debate these viewpoints.

- 'Love is all you need but law and order save us from anarchy.'
- 'Sometimes the most moral thing to do is break the law.'

Apply your knowledge

The teaching of Jesus

'The clear teaching of our Lord' is taken to mean that Jesus laid down certain precepts which were universally binding. Certain things were always right, other things were always wrong – for all men everywhere. But this is to treat the Sermon on the Mount as the new Law, and, even if Matthew may have interpreted Jesus that way, there would hardly be a New Testament scholar today who would not say that it was a misinterpretation. The moral precepts of Jesus are not intended to be understood legalistically, as prescribing what all Christians must do, whatever the circumstances, and pronouncing certain courses of action universally right and others universally wrong. They are not legislation laying down what love always demands of every one: they are illustrations of what love may at any particular moment require of anyone …

… Jesus' teaching on marriage, as on everything else, is not a new law prescribing that divorce is always and in every case the greater of two evils (whereas Moses said there were some cases in which it was not). It is saying that love, utterly unconditional love, admits of no accommodation; you cannot define in advance situations in which it can be satisfied with less than complete and unreserved self-giving …

… Jesus never resolves these choices for us: he is content with the knowledge that if we have the heart of the matter in us, if our eye is single, then love will find the way, its own particular way in every individual situation.

… Love alone, because, as it were, it has a built-in moral compass, enabling it to 'home' intuitively upon the deepest need of the other, can allow itself to be directed completely by the situation. It alone can afford to be utterly open to the situation, or rather to the person in the situation, uniquely and for his own sake, without losing its direction or unconditionality. It is able to embrace an ethic of radical responsiveness, meeting every situation on its own merits, with no prescriptive laws.'

John A. T. Robinson,
Honest to God, 1966, pp. 110–15

2. Explain in your own words how Robinson sees Christian moral decision-making, and how it differs from ideas of fixed truths.

3. How might this approach be abused?

The six propositions

Fletcher suggests six propositions that should be kept in mind when seeking a decision.

First proposition: 'Only one thing is intrinsically good; namely love: nothing else at all' (Fletcher, *Situation Ethics*, 1966, p. 56). Only love is good in and of itself. Actions aren't intrinsically good or evil. They always form part of a chain of cause and effect. They are good or evil depending upon whether they promote the most loving result. They are **extrinsically good** or evil, depending on their circumstances and consequences.

> *Actions aren't intrinsically good or evil. They always form part of a chain of cause and effect. They are good or evil depending upon whether they promote the most loving result*

66 Value, worth, ethical quality, goodness or badness, right or wrong – these things are only predicates, they are not properties. They are not given or objectively 'real' or

self-existent. There is only one thing that is always good and right, intrinsically good regardless of the context and that one thing is love … whatever is the most loving thing in the situation is the right and good thing. **"**

Joseph Fletcher, *Situation Ethics*, 1966, p. 60 and p. 65

Love is the only universal, the only thing to oblige us in conscience. Love is substantive in the divine being, God. Human beings may be lovable or loving but only with God is love a property because God is love. Particular acts do not have love in them, they are right or wrong depending on the situation.

Second proposition: 'The ruling norm of Christian decision is love: nothing else' (Fletcher, *Situation Ethics*, 1966, p. 69). Jesus replaced the Torah with the principle of love. Take, for example, his decision to work on the Sabbath day, rejecting the obligations of Sabbath observance (see Mark 2: 27–28), Paul's decision that the food laws need not apply (see 1 Corinthians 10: 23–26). Fletcher argues the Commandments are not absolute. Jesus broke them when love demanded it. Love replaces law. It is not equalled by any other law. Some rules from the Hebrew Scriptures (the Old Testament) are commonly broken within Christianity – images are used in worship, oaths are taken by priests, work is done on Sunday (and Saturday). Situationists hold it as a duty to break these in some circumstances. Immoral killing is immoral, but this points to a possibility of moral killing, such as in self-defence.

Third proposition: 'Love and Justice are the same, for justice is love distributed, nothing else' (Fletcher, *Situation Ethics*, 1966, p. 87). Love and justice cannot be separated. Fletcher writes, 'Justice is Christian love using its head, calculating its duties, obligations, opportunities, resources. … Justice is love coping with situations where distribution is called for' (*Situation Ethics*, 1966, p. 95). Justice is love at work in the whole community, for the whole community. Love takes everything into account, it is not partial. This sometimes means calculating, such as when a doctor has to decide between two patients, and which to give the last unit of blood plasma to, preferring a mother of three over a convicted murderer. This is not sentimental love, but calculating, preferential love.

Fourth proposition: '[L]ove wills the neighbour's good, whether we like him or not' (Fletcher, *Situation Ethics*, 1966, p. 103). The love that Fletcher is concerned about is not a matter of feeling, but of attitude. It isn't sentimental or erotic but, rather, a desire for the good of the other person. This is the New Testament agape love, benevolence, goodwill. Your neighbour is anybody and agape love goes out to everyone; not just those we like, but also those we don't like. Love is in the business of loving the unlikable and the neighbour is anybody, friend or foe. Agape love is unconditional; nothing is required in return.

Think question

a. Is love really the only good in and of itself? What about truth, courage, fortitude?

Think question

b. Should moral action always be calculating and never an instinctive, emotional response?

c. Is there no morality to the idea of friendship, loyalty and family?

The situationist does not have a rule for how to act but must instead keep in mind the proposition when faced with tough choices

Fifth proposition: 'Only the end justifies the means; nothing else' (Fletcher, 1966, p. 120). To consider moral actions without reference to their ends is a haphazard approach. Actions acquire moral status as a means to an end. For Fletcher, the end must be the most loving result. When weighing up a situation, one must consider the desired end, the means available, the motive for acting and the foreseeable consequences. Whether something is lawful or not is irrelevant. Love is the goal or end of the act and that justifies any means to achieve that goal. During the Second World War, the Resistance had to live on lies, forged passports, theft of supplies, even sometimes killing one of their own when in danger of arrest and the whole conspiracy being exposed. These actions broke the rules but served a loving end.

Sixth proposition: '[L]ove's decisions are made situationally, not prescriptively' (Fletcher, *Situation Ethics*, 1966, p. 134). This means that love decides on each situation as it arises, without a set of laws to guide it. Fletcher suggested Jesus reacted against the rule-based approach to life that he saw around him. There were Jewish groups that lived on rule-based moral systems, but Jesus distanced himself from them. Whether something is right or wrong depends on the situation. When we wrestle with moral problems we are in a grey area of uncertainty, facing difficult choices, trying to decide who should get the lifeboat and who must go down with the ship, the area between black and white. We must be free in that moment to make a decision. A morality based on following set codes will be no help here. It becomes repressive. Although Jesus says nothing about sexual ethics, Fletcher feels that Christian legalism pursues sex obsessively with proscribed moral behaviours and rules for family size, 'homosexuality, masturbation, fornication or premarital intercourse, sterilization, artificial insemination, abortion, sex play, petting and courtship. Whether any form of sex (hetero, homo, or auto) is good or evil depends on whether love is fully served' (Fletcher, *Situation Ethics*, 1966, p. 139). Fletcher also strongly supported euthanasia, in

When weighing up a situation, one must consider the desired end, the means available, the motive for acting and the foreseeable consequences

Think question

Does the loving end ultimately come down to counting lives in some moral situations? Or could a loving end ever prioritise the life of one over the lives of many?

breach of traditional Christian rules, believing it could be a loving and compassionate thing to do. In all moral problems, if an action will bring about an end that serves love most, then it is right.

The four working presuppositions

How should the law of love be applied? Different situations are filled with variety and complexity and Fletcher reveals this with some specific examples:

Sacrificial suicide?

> 66 I dropped in on a patient at the hospital who explained that he only had a set time to live. The doctors could give him some pills (that would cost $40 every three days) that would keep him alive for the next three years, but if he didn't take the pills, he'd be dead within six months. Now, he was insured for $100,000 and that was all the insurance he had. But if he took the pills and lived past next October when the insurance was up for renewal, they were bound to refuse the renewal, and his insurance would be cancelled. So he told me that he was thinking that if he didn't take the pills, then his family would get left with some security, and asked my advice on the situation. 99

Joseph Fletcher, *Situation Ethics*, 1966, p. 166

Justifiable mass killing?

> 66 'When the atomic bomb was dropped on Hiroshima, the plane crew were silent. Captain Lewis uttered six words, 'My God, what have we done?' Three days later another one fell on Nagasaki. About 152,000 were killed, many times more were wounded and burned, to die later. The next day Japan sued for peace. When deciding whether to use 'the most terrible weapon ever known' the US President appointed an Interim Committee made up of distinguished and responsible people in the government. Most but not all of its military advisors favoured using it. Top-level scientists said they could find no acceptable alternative to using it, but they were opposed by equally able scientists. After lengthy discussions, the committee decided that the lives saved by ending the war swiftly by using this weapon outweighed the lives destroyed by using it and thought that the best course of action. 99

Joseph Fletcher, *Situation Ethics*, 1966, p. 167

Patriotic prostitution?

> 66 I was reading *Biblical Faith and Social Ethics,* Clinton Gardner's book on a shuttle plane to New York. Next to me sat a young woman of about twenty-eight or so, attractive and well turned out in expensive clothes of good taste. She showed some interest in my book, and I asked if she'd like to look at it. 'No', she said, 'I'd rather talk.' What about? 'Me.' I knew this meant goodbye to the reading. 'I have a problem I'm confused about. You might help me to decide,' she explained. There was a war going on that her government believed could be stopped by some clever use of espionage and blackmail. However, this meant she had to seduce and sleep with an enemy spy in order to lure him into blackmail. Now this went against her morals, but if it brought the war to an end, saving thousands of lives, would it be worth breaking those standards? 99

Joseph Fletcher, *Situation Ethics*, 1966, p. 163

Sacrificial adultery?

> 66 [I]n Ukraine, Mrs Bergmeier learned through a sympathetic commandant that her husband and family were trying to keep together and find her. But the rules allowed them to release her to Germany only if she was pregnant, in which case she would be returned as a liability. She turned things over in her mind and finally asked a friendly Volga German camp guard to impregnate her, which he did. Her condition being medically verified, she was sent back to Berlin and to her family. They welcomed her with open arms, even when she told them how she had managed it. And when the child was born, they all loved him because of what they *[sic]* had done for them. After the christening, they met up with their local pastor and discussed the morality of the situation. 99

Joseph Fletcher, *Situation Ethics*, 1966, p. 166

When faced with difficult moral situations Fletcher thought that what was needed was not moral rules or codes but presuppositions to guide how to think when coming to a solution.

Pragmatism

Pragmatism is based on experience rather than theory. Fletcher doubts strict philosophical systems or ideologies are much help in ethics. Philosophy is preoccupied with the question *what is truth?*, but the situationist follows a pragmatic approach working to answer the question *what works?* Fletcher quotes William James:

Apply your knowledge

Read the four scenarios, and decide in each case:

4. The issue Fletcher is identifying.

5. What you think the right response would be and why.

6. In the four scenarios, try to identify the role of agape love, and the most prominent features from the situationist propositions and presuppositions in these examples.

> 66 A pragmatist turns his back resolutely and once and for all upon a lot of inveterate habits dear to professional philosophers. He turns away from abstraction and insufficiency, from verbal solutions, from bad a priori reasons, from fixed principles, closed systems, and pretended absolutes and origins. He turns towards concreteness and adequacy, towards facts, towards action and towards power. 99
>
> William James, *Writings 1902–1920*, from Lecture II, 1987

Think question

a. Human rights might not be achievable but are the ideals worthwhile? Is it better for ethics to be pragmatic (practical) or idealistic (pointing to something greater)?

b. Are there some actions that are always wrong?

During times of difficulty, sometimes the options available all break one rule or another. During the Bosnian conflict of the 1990s, rape was used as a weapon against civilian women by armies seeking to undermine communities by leaving a generation of children fathered by the invaders. In 1993, in response, the Catholic Church, traditionally opposed to artificial contraception, approved its use as a protective measure. This was a pragmatic decision that set aside ethical ideals.

Relativism

If the strategy of situation ethics is pragmatic, its tactics are relativistic. We live in a contemporary era that is contingent. Europe and the West can no longer presume to be at the centre of the world: 'The Situationist avoids words like "never" and "perfect" and "always" and "complete" as he avoids the plague, as he avoids "absolutely"' (Fletcher, *Situation Ethics*, 1966, p. 44). There are no fixed rules that must always be obeyed. However, nor is it a free for all! There are different degrees of relativism from absolute relativism, in which decisions are random or anarchic, to the situationist approach in which all decisions must be relative to Christian love. Relativism is based on making the absolute laws of Christian ethics relative. Situation ethics 'relativizes the absolute, it does not absolutize the relative' (Fletcher, *Situation Ethics*, 1966, p. 45). Fletcher sees relativism in the behaviour of Jesus in rejecting the fixed rule mentality of the Pharisees and being prepared to break rules in ways that are relative to love. Jesus' followers pick corn on the Sabbath, breaking the rules about work on the Sabbath because 'the Sabbath was made for man, not man for the Sabbath' (Mark 2: 27, New International Version).

Positivism

Religious knowledge or belief can only be approached in one of two ways. With natural positivism reason deduces faith from human experience or natural phenomena. Nature provides the evidence and reason grasps hold of it. Natural law is an example of this approach. The other approach is theological positivism. Faith statements are made and people act in a way that is reasonable in the light of these statements.

Think question

c. Was Jesus relativistic about all rules, moral, social and ritual?

Reason is not the basis for faith, but it works within faith. Thinking is supported by faith. 'Thus Christian ethics "posits" faith in God and *reasons* out what obedience to his commandments to love requires in any situation' (Fletcher, 1966, p. 47). Situation ethics depends on Christians freely choosing faith that God is love, so giving first place to Christian love. It begins with belief in the reality and importance of love. When the situationist approaches a moral dilemma her thinking begins with faith in love, not obedience to rules or trust in human reasoning. The situationist soldier who shoots dead his friend on the battlefield to save the agony of an untreatable injury, acts out of faith in love.

See Chapter 3.5 for more on Christian love.

Personalism

The legalist puts the law first. The situationist puts people first. 'Ethics deals with human relations. Situation ethics puts people at the center of concern, not things. Obligation is to persons, not to things; to subjects, not objects' (Fletcher, *Situation Ethics*, 1966, p. 50). Situationism is people-centred. The situationist asks what to do to help humans best: 'There are no "values" in the sense of inherent goods – value is what happens to something when it happens to be useful to love working for the sake of persons' (Fletcher, *Situation Ethics*, 1966, p. 50). This is not an individualistic creed, however. There is nothing individualistic about personalism.

> 66 Love is of people, by people and for people. Things are to be used; people are to the loved. It is 'immoral' when people are used and things are loved. Loving actions are the only conduct permissible. 99
>
> Joseph Fletcher, *Situation Ethics*, 1966, p. 51

Examples might include how the 'love' of pornography turns human beings into the objects of pleasure for others. The 'love' of buying cheap clothes that are made in sweatshops in developing countries uses the poorly treated workers. The people in these examples are not loved. Instead their objectified body images, or the fruits of their labours are loved. The people are used.

Think question

a. Do you think people need good systems to help guide moral behaviour? Does your school or college use this approach?

b. If pornography is wrong in every situation, because it uses a person for the pleasure of others, should love make some rules about it?

Apply your knowledge

7. Fletcher was accused of using extreme examples, but his response was that these were precisely the occasions when situationism was needed. Do we mainly need ethics to deal with the most difficult problems?

Conscience

Conscience in situation ethics is not a bag of reliable rules and principles to tell you what to do. It in no way guides human action. It is not a part of the human being, like a mind or a soul are suggested by some as being parts of the human being, but something that describes a process. It is not an innate radar, or inspiration from some guardian angel. It is not an internalised value system of the culture and

Apply your knowledge

8. Discuss these two opinions

   a. 'Human beings need to be told what is right and what is wrong. They can't be trusted to work things out for themselves.'

   b. 'When we face moral dilemmas in real life, we do not have moral legal experts on hand to tell us what to do, all we can do is decide for ourselves and hope we are able to act.'

9. Consider the following situations from a situationist perspective – identify which factors would be the ones the situationist would be most interested in:

   a. A young girl learns to pick the pockets of rich Western tourists to save her family from poverty and herself from prostitution.

   b. A doctor helps a patient who wants to end her life due to the incurable illness and terrible pain she is suffering from.

   c. A wife, repeatedly battered and raped by her husband, unable to find help, and too scared to try and escape, resorts to putting rat poison in his curry.

   d. A husband discovers his brother is sleeping with his wife, and in a fit of rage murders his brother.

   e. A woman, startled in the night by a stranger in her house uses a rolling pin and kills him. Switching on the light reveals not a burglar, but her daughter's boyfriend sneaking in.

10. Comment on the suggestion that there are no laws that might not be broken in some situations.

11. Develop the argument that human beings need legislative ethics to guide their behaviour. Think of examples that support this argument. How might a situationist respond?

Conscience is the process of weighing things up, not an inner voice with the answer

society in which you live. The error is in thinking about conscience as a noun instead of a verb. There is no conscience per se. It is a word that describes our attempts to make proper decisions. Fletcher adopts Aquinas' idea that conscience is reason-making moral judgements, though he rejects Aquinas' other moral thoughts (*Situation Ethics*, 1966, p. 53). It does not simply review our actions, but is the process of making the decision.

Discussing situation ethics

Do situation ethics provide a helpful method of moral decision-making?

Christian ethics has been dominated by rules-based, deontological or absolutist approaches to ethics. It has been more likely to repeat the Commandments rather than the example of Jesus challenging the law, for example. Rule-based ethics provide simple answers to difficult questions and offer a sense of assurance – 'don't worry, someone has already worked out what you need to do in this situation'. However, sometimes the situations people actually face seem not to have been considered when rules are formed. Perhaps the point about moral decision-making is that human beings need guidance when the rules do not seem to fit. In these situations, the support that rules provide falls away – there can be no right or good way forward and the person who has to act is in an impossible situation. This is where situation ethics provides something that rules cannot – a guide to the frame of mind, the ideals to keep in focus, when acting in the face of a moral dilemma. Some have argued that Fletcher's examples are unrealistic for everyday decision-making and that may be true, but there are times when the moral situations people are facing are far from everyday, too, and it is for that moment that Fletcher wants to offer something to help people face their own situation with some confidence.

In one sense it is a difficult theory to use: no easy answers; no simple list to follow. It means you have to take responsibility for what you are about to do. You cannot just rely on the advice of others.

Often, more than one person is involved in the moral dilemma. Others are affected. Rules and principles can provide a mechanism for ensuring all interests are considered when deciding what is right, even in circumstances where the interests of others are not obvious. Perhaps situation ethics can consider all other affected parties beyond the most obvious, but that might be a difficult thing to do. Perhaps this is an area where people need more help with such complexities than situation ethics can provide.

An additional question for situation ethics is the definition of 'situation'. What constitutes a situation? What is its possible length, size, location and who is involved? Situation ethics seems to be mainly focused on the immediate situation. Can situations go on for years, like a war might? Does it make sense to talk about the situation of poverty in a country? When viewing ethics at this larger scale it is harder to see how situation ethics could be systematised. It would be difficult to apply the process Fletcher describes on such a scale, which limits its helpfulness.

Can Situation ethics helpfully be described as a Christian ethic? Fletcher himself died a self-professed atheist and many Churches reject his account of Jesus. Fletcher can be accused of conflating Jesus' rejection of the cultic practices and social rules of the time with the moral rules. Most Christian Churches would argue Jesus was a fulfillment of the moral law of the Hebrew Scriptures (Matthew 5:17ff).

Fletcher's approach to justice also raises questions. He advocates personalism, a person-centred approach that pays attention to the needs of the person, and he opposes using people for the pleasures of others. One could therefore ask Fletcher, why should we not make rules after realising the importance of the person, so that the person is not treated so poorly? Arguably, this is what Kant and natural law does one way or another.

On the one hand Fletcher wants us to treat people with love, while at the same time he does not want love to form rules. It is not altogether clear, therefore, how Fletcher's ethics can avoid highly relativistic interpretations. If rules can always be broken, how can any of the principles Fletcher promotes be protected?

Apply your knowledge

12. 'Fletcher's ethics could be likened to learning to ride a bike (in the traditional way with stabilisers). There comes a point where you need to take the stabilisers off and decide which way to peddle your bike.' Explain what you think this means.

13. Should ethical systems only address personal moral circumstances or do social and political issues need to be addressed in the same way? Explain your answer.

Ethical judgement and agape

Can an ethical judgement about something being good, bad, right or wrong be based on the extent to which, in any given situation, agape is best served?

Situation ethics argues that serving agape love is the principal measure for goodness or badness. Agape love is a particular kind of love, conceived in the Christian theological tradition of self-sacrificial love, love for the other person, love that is unconditional, without expectation of any return. It is selfless love. From a Christian perspective this kind of love is at the core of a life of faith. But what does it mean to *serve* love? How is love best served? Many Christians might argue that serving the agape love of the Bible means serving Jesus Christ and that he gave lots of guidance in the form of rules and principles to guide behaviour. Could this not be considered *serving* love? Jesus said, 'If you love me, keep my commandments' (John 14:15). Others might want to argue that different moral ideals matter in measuring goodness or rightness, as well or in addition to serving love, such as maximising the utility. Critics could argue that, in Fletcher's ethics, love is synonymous with utility since the utilitarian calculus demands that we bring about the greatest happiness for the greatest number. If 'agape', as Fletcher defines it, does not mean this, what does it mean? If love means seeking the other person's good, then situation ethics has to require the pursuit of the greatest good for the greatest number of people in a situation where good is different for different people.

When love is served in a given situation, this entails a focus on the person or persons involved but what limit should be set for those affected? How we act in one situation might have repercussions for others not present. The way a hospital treats one patient might have implications for the next patient. Serving love in the first situation cannot easily take account of the future loving needs of the next person, but it might set a precedent which affects the future situation. If serving love in two different situations means doing two different things, perhaps the first action will undermine the second situation. Perhaps ethical judgements need to look beyond the immediate situation. Maybe on some occasions, one person must be sacrificed for others. The utilitarian would worry about the consequences for others. The natural law follower would be focused on natural law and natural rights, which are arguably sacrificed by a situationist approach where no rules (including no rights) can be maintained. Defenders of human rights argue that universal rules are needed to protect people that suffer in situations where rules get broken.

Apply your knowledge

14. Is selfless love, agape love, the only moral consideration? What about truth, justice, lawfulness, the well-being of all? Try to make an argument against selfless love being the highest moral good. This could be from another religious or philosophical perspective.

Does Fletcher's agape mean nothing more than wanting the best for the person involved?

Is Fletcher's understanding of agape really religious or does it mean nothing more than wanting the best for the person involved in a given situation?

Fletcher makes much of the Christian origins of agape love in his moral system. He roots it in the New Testament and argues his ethical system is a reading of Christian ethics, a better one than the rules-based systems of other approaches to Christian morality. By focusing on love, the emphasis is on the virtue of the acting person, the person showing unconditional love. However, it could be argued that the virtue of love is defined by whether or not the person in the moral problem gets a good result for them. For instance, the person can use sexual favours to get what they want. Permitting rule breaking is called loving because someone gets their best result. However, if this is the case, then perhaps it is not really a selfless, loving action. Perhaps it is nothing more than seeking the best result for the person, in which case the link with love and the New Testament is doubtful. Some other ethical systems seek to determine the best result – such as finding the most utility in utilitarianism, or following the best laws.

Many Churches disagree with Fletcher's description of the biblical moral message. Arguably the Bible gives lots of guidance on how to apply love and yet many of the rules seem to be the kind of things that Fletcher wanted to get away from. He used one biblical idea (agape love) as an argument against other biblical ideas (protecting life, sexual purity, being honest, not stealing, etc.). Fletcher also seemed to have forgotten that loving your neighbour is only half of the rule – loving God is also a command of the Bible and to love God you should listen to the whole of his revelation/Goodness, which means taking the rules of the Bible seriously. In short, Fletcher's religious foundation is selective. One response to this accusation might be that the centrality of love is the heart of the Christian message, that God is described as a love and that sacrificial love is the example Jesus sets people.

Does the rejection of absolute rules by situation ethics make moral decision-making entirely individualistic and subjective?

John Macquarrie in his book, *Three Issues in Ethics* (2012) argued that situationism is fundamentally and incurably individualist. It could never be used as the basis of a social morality. If an ethic is to be the basis for a society then it needs to offer solutions for communities, groups of people and societies, but situation ethics is focused on individuals. It does not consider the community or the society. It is not concerned with future scenarios or how it affects groups. But is

Apply your knowledge

15. Discuss these two views

   a. 'If you are lovingly breaking a commandment, then you are not loving and not following Christian ethics. A loving disregard for Christian rules is not a Christian ethical approach.'

   b. 'Love should be at the heart of Christian ethics and Jesus showed this could mean setting rules aside. Situation ethics is a way of dealing with moral issues in the way exemplified by Jesus.'

it not just individualistic: '… as well as suffering from individualism, radical situational ethics suffers from the allied vice of subjectivism. The situationist seems to be compelled by the theories to assume on extraordinary degree of moral sensitivity and perceptiveness in those who are expected to read the demands of the situation' (Macquarrie, *Three Issues in Ethics*, 2012 pp. 33–35).

Situation ethics fails to recognise the subjective perspective that people have when they make their moral decisions, and that human beings are fallible. They fail to consider the interests of others or the weakness of their own conscience. They are concerned with their own interests. In the words of William Barclay, 'If we insist that in every situation every man must make his own decision, then first of all we must make man morally and lovingly fit to take that decision; otherwise we need the compulsion of law to make him do it' (*Ethics in a Permissive Society*, 1972, p. 81).

Perhaps the most contentious aspect of situation ethics is the removal of laws at the heart of ethics and the impact this might have on justice. Universal human rights have come to be relied upon to assure that minorities are protected and to ensure that justice is done. There do seem to be absolutely wrong actions in the world; some would point to the sexual abuse of children, others to the use of nuclear weapons on Hiroshima and Nagasaki during the Second World War. The removal of moral laws seems to leave people vulnerable.

Situation ethics is condemned by many Christian moralists as incurable, individualistic and subjective because it abandons all absolutes. Fletcher would argue that it does not abandon all absolutes – it holds onto love and makes all things relative to love. Situation ethics is arguably the pastoral application of love when the legalistic approach to ethics clumsily crashes through the complexity of moral dilemmas. It is easy to step back from the human experience and make great pronouncements of fixed moral certainty through commandments and prohibitions, but when standing with a person faced with agonising alternatives, situation ethics – in Fletcher's mind – offers a more loving response. Whether it is able to serve the needs of justice is less clear.

Apply your knowledge

16. Discuss the following viewpoints – do you agree or disagree with them?

a. 'People cannot be trusted to make moral judgements because human beings are sinful creatures – they make mistakes. They should be taught what is right and wrong, and taught to follow those rules.'

b. 'Moral dilemmas occur in real situations, and they can sometimes be complicated, permitting few straightforward solutions. What you need in that moment is a clear idea of the principles you should keep in mind when struggling with life, to help make the best choice.

17. 'Rules-based ethics and love-based ethics contradict each other – you have to decide which one to follow.' Evaluate this quote.

Learning support

Points to remember

» It is a mistake to interpret Fletcher's theory as offering a theory to solve moral problems. He did not think ethics worked that way as the modern world is a really uncertain place with very difficult moral decisions to make. Rather, we need to be aware of key principles when we make a moral decision, but we make that decision in the hope that we are right. This contrasts with moral thinkers who believe their moral theories can answer ethical questions definitively.

» Fletcher was accused of using unrealistic or exceptional examples (the ones listed in this chapter [on p. 00] are his examples) which unnaturally stilted his ethical approach. However, he was fully aware of very real difficult decisions, from his work teaching medical ethics. For Fletcher, much of life could be informed by moral rules but there comes a point when the decisions being made are more complex and may simply not offer an option that satisfied those rules. Ethics needs something to draw on in those situations and that's what he proposes situation ethics offers.

» Situation ethics is informed by Christian thought, notably an approach to interpreting the Bible which some Christians would reject (primarily conservative evangelicals and orthodox Catholics). Fletcher drew on theologians who rejected the idea that the Bible was a simple rule book, offering a set of rules for the modern world. Situation ethics may also appeal to those who come from a different worldview, depending on the centrality of love in their worldview.

Enhance your learning

» Fletcher's own book is quite readable and recommended: Fletcher, J. (1963) *Situation Ethics: The New Morality*.

» Chapter 6 of C.S. Lewis's *The Four Loves* (1960 rev.2016) is a classic and thought provoking study of love.

» Chapter 1 of Neil Messer's *SCM Study Guide: Christian Ethics* (2006) provides a good introduction to Christian ethics.

» Roger Crook's Chapter 3 in *An Introduction to Christian Ethics,* sixth edition (2012) locates situation ethics alongside a number of different traditions of Christian ethics and is a helpful introduction for this chapter and for chapters 2.1 Natural Law and 3.5 Christian Moral Principles.

Practice for exams

AS questions and A level questions look identical; the difference between AS and A level assessment is seen in the different proportions of marks awarded for two different skills: the skill of demonstrating knowledge and understanding (Assessment Objective 1, or AO1), and the skill of constructing a critical argument (AO2).

At AS, half the marks (15 marks) are available for knowledge and understanding, and the other half (15 marks) for the quality of your analytical and evaluative argument. You should aim to use your knowledge in order to support the argument you are making throughout the essay, rather than presenting descriptive knowledge in the first half and then an opinion in the second.

At A level, your demonstration of knowledge and understanding is awarded a maximum of 16 marks, and your analytic and evaluative skills are awarded a maximum of 24 marks. You should aim to concentrate on constructing a lucid argument, making use of your knowledge to add weight to the conclusions you draw.

To what extent, if at all, should agape be the guiding principle in moral decision-making?

For this question you need to consider whether situation ethics is right in placing agape as the central guiding principle for ethics, or whether perhaps other principles might be better (such as duty, or the greatest happiness for the greatest number, or dharma, or obedience to the will of God, or any others you have studied). The focus of your essay should be on agape rather than on any other principles.

Practise your skills for AS level

At AS level, for high marks you need to demonstrate a clear understanding of what agape means and how it is used in decision-making, perhaps with some practical examples. You should consider the reasoning of those who agree with the importance of agape, and also the reasoning of those who might disagree, presenting a balanced view alongside giving your own consistently held opinion.

Practise your skills for A level

If answering this question at A level, you need to start by considering whether agape should be the guiding moral principle, in comparison with other possibilities. You should weigh up the strengths of the guiding principle of situation ethics against its weaknesses, such as the difficulties of always knowing what is the most loving course of action. You need to present a clear and consistent line of argument throughout your essay.

'Situation ethics is too subjective to be used for making important moral decisions.' Discuss.

This question raises the suggestion that moral decision-making requires a degree of objectivity, and it invites you consider whether situation ethics has sufficient objectivity to make it an appropriate method for making moral decisions.

Practise your skills for AS level

If you are answering this question at AS level, you should demonstrate knowledge and understanding of the main principles and application of situation ethics in moral decision-making. You should consider what 'too subjective' might mean, and give a reasoned judgement about whether situation ethics is subjective and whether it is 'too' subjective. Think about what could be the advantages and disadvantages of subjectivity in an ethical system.

Practise your skills for A level

At A level, for this question, you have to decide whether or not you agree that situation ethics is too subjective, and your reasons for agreeing or disagreeing. You will want to explain how you understand situation ethics and perhaps also how you understand 'subjective' in this context, but try to avoid making your essay overly descriptive at the expense of argument. You might agree that situation ethics allows different individuals to make different choices in similar situations, and you might think that this is a problem with situation ethics, or you might think that it does give clear direction, or that subjectivity is an asset in a normative ethical system.

Chapter 2.3

Kantian ethics

Should emotions or reason guide moral choices?
Are moral rules universal?
Do people have intrinsic worth?

Key Terms

Moral law: binding moral obligations

Maxims: another word for moral rules, determined by reason

Duty: duties are created by the moral law, to follow it is our duty. The word deontological means duty-based

Summum bonum: the highest, most supreme good

Good will: a person of good will is a person who makes decisions according to the moral law

Categorical imperative: an unconditional moral obligation that is always binding irrespective of a person's inclination or purpose

Hypothetical imperative: a moral obligation that applies only if one desires the implied goal

Kingdom of ends: an imagined future in which all people act in accordance to the moral law, the categorical imperative

Specification requirements

Kantian ethics, including:
- the ethics of duty
- the hypothetical imperative
- the categorical imperative

Immanuel Kant

Introduction

Immanuel Kant (1724–1804) was a German philosopher who lived at a time of great crisis and doubt. He wrote many important works including *Groundwork for the Metaphysics of Morals* (1785), *Critique of Practical Reason* (1788) and *The Metaphysics of Morals* (1797). Developments in science had begun to redefine knowledge with a mechanistic Newtonian understanding of the world, rather than looking to superstition or religion for explanations. What of morality? If moral worth could not be shown to exist then did it exist? Beliefs in the soul, freedom and God came under criticism and Kant's thinking was a response to this crisis. Kant did believe in God and an afterlife but he was suspicious of relying on religious doctrines and dogmas.

Kant thought that how we saw the world and morality were framed by concepts and categories. Knowledge is hung on these concepts and categories, so when we look at a moral problem we make sense of the reality of it using a framework that applies in all situations and at all times.

Kant believed that moral knowledge was known through reason, not experience or emotion. It is first hand, 'a priori', prior to relying on experience and it is synthetic, in that it brings additional information from outside of the experience. It is not hypothetical, dependent on the particular goal we are going for, as it is based on the **moral law**, an objective law that always binds us. This moral knowledge is something we can deduce through reason.

The moral law is something we must categorically follow. It is not something that can be thought of as hypothetical because morals, for Kant, are universal **maxims** – fixed rules that must always apply. Moral laws must treat people as human beings with their own interests, not just to be used for the interests of others, and they must act as if the world is a place where people made and followed universal rules.

For Kant, good people always follow the moral law. They do this because they have a good will and do their duty. This is the good life. The moral life might be a good life, but sometimes, though we do the right thing, bad things happen to us. However, in the ultimate end, possibly beyond this world, we will experience the good life.

Some say you should do what you feel is right – follow your heart. Not so for Immanuel Kant. Kant is a deontological ethical thinker; the rightness or wrongness is determined by the actions in themselves. He believes there is an objective moral law that we can know through reason rather than happiness or pleasure (our feelings – the utilitarian approach), or from revelation (from religion) or from looking at the situation (the situationist). Morals are not connected to those things but are universal.

Moral rules should apply to everyone and moral actions don't change (unlike relativists).

Kant thought that if our morality is driven by desire for pleasure, then we are slaves to animal instinct. Suppose a man desires his neighbours' wife. He can kid himself her husband is not good enough for her and get pleasure from the liaison. Goodness becomes whatever we desire or impulsively want. We act just like the animals. But human beings differ from animals. Rationality frees us to be able to act independently of instinct or desire for pleasure.

Human beings are precious because they have this ability. Human life is beyond price because we act with reason free from desire. We are free to pursue the **summum bonum** – the supreme good where we do good and it brings happiness for all. When we act we must think of what it means for those human beings affected and their future interests. We cannot use people for some good if it sacrifices their own interests.

Kant's approach to his philosophy comes from four basic questions: (1) What can I know?; (2) What should I do?; (3) What may I hope?; (4) What is a human being?

Through his philosophy he provides four basic answers:

1) What can I know? I know the framework of human thought and all that is discoverable within that framework.

2) What should I do? I can act in accordance with the principle of autonomy, which operates under human practical reason and which prevents us from being slaves to desire, and work for the greater human happiness.

3) What may I hope? I hope that it is possible to bring about this greater human happiness.

4) What is a human being? The human is the being that offers us experiences of beauty and organisation and is the source of natural and moral law.

Kant's ethics are complex because there are a number of big ideas that he introduces which connect to one another. The idea of the moral law, the idea of **good will**, duty and the supreme happiness, the **categorical imperative**, a particular understanding of freedom, and a particular understanding of knowledge. To make sense of these ideas, it is important to see how they fit together, then it becomes possible to apply Kantian ethical thinking to moral dilemmas with confidence.

Kant's approach to his philosophy comes from four basic questions: (1) What can I know?; (2) What should I do?; (3) What may I hope?; and (4) What is a human being?

Think question

Which is more important in helping us make a moral decision: our emotions, desires and instincts or our reason and rational thinking?

The moral law, duty and good will

Kant thought our ability to reason freed us from our instincts and distinguished us from animals

Kant thinks there is an objective moral law which is beyond personal opinion, preference or desire. It actually exists and it is knowable through reason.

> 66 Two things fill the mind with ever new and increasing admiration and reverence, the more often and more steadily one reflects on them: the starry heavens above me and the moral law within me. I do not need to search for them and merely conjecture them as though they were veiled in obscurity or in the transcendental region beyond my horizon; I see them before me and connect them immediately with the consciousness of my existence. 99

Immanuel Kant, *Critique of Pure Reason*, [1787] 1964, 5.161

Objective moral law is independent of all individual opinion or preference. It demands all obey it in its own right, not because it promotes individual happiness or helps achieve personal desires. It tells us what we ought to do, irrespective of consequence. Kant is deontological rather than teleological. He is focused on the wrongness or rightness of actions in themselves.

Human beings perceive the moral law through their rational capacity. This makes them beings beyond price. They cannot be used and discarded without concern for themselves. They cannot be bought or sold, used for some other end – such as for the benefit or pleasure of another.

Duty and good will

What is the best motivation we can have for doing good? I might do good because I am fearful of the consequences if I don't, or because it gains me some individual advantage. Kant argues:

> 66 It is impossible to conceive of anything in the world, or indeed out of it, which can be called good without qualification, save only a good will. 99
>
> Immanuel Kant, *Groundwork of the Metaphysics of Morals*, [1785] 1997, G394, p. 59

If I text a charity number to donate without a thought for how it seems to anyone else, because I can help and know I must, then my purity of motive is good in and of itself. It is good irrespective of what it accomplishes. Good will is in accordance with duty but it is not enough to be consistent with duty. Sending the money is the right thing to do, but doing it for a selfish reason to impress someone means I am not virtuous. Good is still done but I get no credit. My action must arise out of duty. The shopkeeper who is honest because he is worried about his reputation is honest in accordance with his duty but is not honest out of his duty. To be honest as a shopkeeper because of your duty is to have good will. You give the right change, not because of what people might otherwise think, but because it is right.

Other motives which have some kind of inclination, such as family loyalty or a feeling of guilt or responsibility, have no moral worth for Kant. This can seem odd. Kant's virtuous person seems quite austere. In fact, he actually thinks that it is important to have an active sympathy for others, and cultivating sympathetic feelings in ourselves. However, we must not be carried away with these emotions. They must not drive our moral thinking.

Kant gives some examples of what our duty is. 'To do good to others, where one can, is a duty', but he also argues that those who do good because they get a sense of inner pleasure by spreading joy are not truly

Apply your knowledge

When visiting my future in-laws, we are all watching TV in the living room. An urgent appeal from charities comes onto the screen. 'Text this number at once ... thousands of children in another country are in need. ... The situation is desperate'. I see these adverts from time to time but I am also aware that my future in-laws believe very strongly in giving to the needy overseas. They are keen to know what kind of son-in-law they might be getting. So I use my new mobile phone to make a donation, in a way that is not too ostentatious but is apparent to everyone in the room.

8. What is the problem with being recognised for the good you do?

9. Is hiding your charitable actions hiding the truth?

Apply your knowledge

10. What is wrong with doing good for selfish motives? Consider these examples:

    a. Two lifeguards. One has heroic fantasies where he imagines himself saving people, and gets great pleasure from telling stories about his escapades, and the adulation this brings about from those he tells. The other saves lives out of a sense of duty and says nothing about it. Both save the same number of lives. Is one better?

    b. Two charitable folk. One keeps her giving to charity a secret. She has a monthly direct debit of 15 per cent of her income, which goes out automatically to her charities without her thinking about it. Another one makes grand gestures of her giving, attending prominent 'donors' dinners' with beautiful party frocks and press coverage. They give the same amount and same proportion of income. Are they morally equal or is one better? Explain your answer.

moral. This does not mean it is wrong, but it conveys no credit on the agent. It is right, but not virtuous.

With this system of developing moral judgements and moral rules, Kant establishes some specific duties to ourselves and others:

- to strive for self-perfection and the well-being of others

- to pursue the greater good, not one's own happiness

- the innate right to freedom

- the duty not to destroy ourselves, to commit suicide (though this act could be considered free, it would end our future freedom and existence)

- the duty not to destroy or limit other human beings (we could sacrifice ourselves for others in battle, as this preserves their future happiness and freedom)

- the duty not to make false promises, as truthfulness is a foundation of human society

- to avoid drunkenness, as this compromises our freedom to act reasonably, or gluttony, as this makes us unhealthy and, therefore, risks our future ability to act freely

- the right to private property and ownership (this cannot include ownership of other people but we can enter into contracts with one another so that, for instance, two people can promise themselves exclusively to each other in marriage, or a person can hire another person to carry out a specific task).

Kant concludes that the state is necessary to makes sure these rights are protected and suitable.

This sounds as though Kant would have a long list of rules to offer but in fact he does not do this. He develops a system for determining whether a moral maxim (rule) meets the criteria for his moral law or not. He is aware that there are challenges in working out what the moral thing to do is.

What should we do? The hypothetical and categorical imperatives

How we perceive the moral law

How do we perceive the moral law? What kind of facts or information are we looking at? What process takes place? The way we decide what is right and what is wrong is linked to how we make sense of the world. It might seem reasonable to look at the situation we find ourselves in – to see what's happening before us. We might want to weigh up the consequences of different courses of actions, or maybe we will trust our gut feeling or our emotional response to give us some kind of answer. What do we desire in this situation? What do we want to get out of it ourselves? Perhaps we can work out what is right by relying on messages from God, through sacred scriptures. For Kant, this is all wrong. Moral knowledge is known through reason not experience or emotion. To understand this approach to morality, we must understand how Kant understood knowledge.

Knowledge arising from sense perception and experience

Kant thinks that we can separate knowledge into two groups. There is the knowledge that we gain through our sense perceptions from the empirical world around us: what we can see and hear, touch and smell and so on. This knowledge comes to us out of experience of particular objects and is a posteriori. It is known as 'post', or after the experience. It arises out of that experience. A posteriori knowledge is quite easy to think about. If I say that woman has a small dog in her handbag, it is pretty clear that I know this because I have seen it. If we say someone's phone is ringing, it is probably because we can hear the ringtone.

Knowledge at first hand, before sense perception and experience

Kant argues that there is a knowledge that is not dependent on experience, it is knowledge we have at first hand, 'a priori', prior to relying on experience. This knowledge is not particular to one physical object, but is a necessary or universal feature of all objects that are a priori. It is independent of experience and even of all impressions of the senses. I can do a sum without having to translate numbers in the objects I have before me. I don't need to have, say, two green apples and two red apples in front of me to work out that $2 + 2 = 4$. Maybe I learnt that way, but I don't need the apples. The knowledge that $2 + 2 = 4$ does not arise out of the experience of playing around with different groups of apples. Mathematical rules do not arise from the experience. We know them in a different way.

I know that it is wrong to be aggressive to people, in the way I saw out of my window in the example of the car crash. I don't know this from seeing the shouting. That might exemplify the problem but the possible assault about to take place is a wrong that is separated from my experience of seeing it that morning. Kant wrote 'though all our knowledge begins with experience, it does not follow that it all arises out of experience' (Kant, *Critique of Pure Reason*, [1787] 1964, B1, p. 41) Moral knowledge comes from within and is a priori, perceivable at first sight.

Apply your knowledge

I hear a screech of brakes and look out of my window, interrupted from writing. A car with an elderly couple has stopped suddenly as a rabbit crosses the road. Moments later an expensive sports car with a couple of young men in it, is forced to brake sharply, but they can't stop in time and hit the back of elderly couple's estate car. The expensive bonnet of the sports car crumples. The young driver gets out. He is screaming and yelling, jumping up and down with frustration. I can hear that he has taken his father's car for a drive. He is yelling aggressively at the couple. I reach for my phone and call the police. Things are turning nasty.

11. In this case, I see the two cars stopping and the argument. Link Kant's thinking about knowledge to this situation.

'I hear a screech of brakes…'

Synthetic and analytic propositions and judgements

As well as knowledge itself, there is also the matter of judgement. The next two terms Kant offers help explain the kind of judgements we make. These are either analytic or synthetic. An analytic judgement is one where the predicate belongs to the subject. Consider this example:

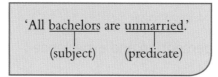

The predicate (unmarried) belongs to the subject (bachelors). Unmarried is to do with the meaning of bachelors. Analytic judgements are *judgements of clarification* as they clarify what is already found in concepts. A road traffic accident involves a vehicle. 'Vehicle' is part of 'road traffic'.

Synthetic propositions are those in which the predicate is outside the subject, and therefore must be made certain with reference to something other than the meanings of terms and laws of logic. For example:

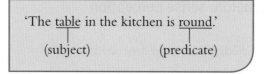

To test whether this is true we need additional information, such as looking at the particular table in the kitchen because tables are not necessarily or universally round. This is a *judgement of amplification* because, when true, it adds new information to the subject. The sports car hit the back of the elderly couple's estate car. Hitting the estate car is new contextual information, not found inherently in sports cars.

We can combine the 'judgement' (analytic or synthetic) with the way we find out this knowledge (a priori or a posteriori). Analytic judgements are a priori because we do not need experience of external objects to know them. They are necessarily true and knowable without experience. We don't need to check every bachelor really is unmarried to know that all bachelors are unmarried. Every motorcar is a vehicle. The vehicle group includes all cars.

Many synthetic propositions can only be known a posteriori. The sports car bumped into the estate car. I needed to see this happen to know the statement is true. We could test this if there are other witnesses or perhaps by judging the skid marks on the road. An a posteriori synthetic statement may be true or false. Perhaps I dreamed the accident after an exhausting morning's writing.

In the case of moral knowledge, looking at what someone does, does not tell you if their behaviour is right or wrong. They might be doing a bad thing that they should not do, or a good thing that they should do. Wrongness cannot be seen in shouting, for instance. We bring something else, our knowledge that to be aggressive towards someone is wrong comes from somewhere else. This is why Kant thinks moral propositions must be synthetic. They bring additional information from outside of the experience. This additional information is the moral law that reason reveals. You have to look at what people ought to do, not just what they actually do. As Kant thinks that moral knowledge comes from reason at first hand, it is a priori *synthetic*.

> ## Think question
>
> **a.** '*Real* knowledge is what I can see, feel touch, hear and so on. Everything else only exists in our head but is not really real.' Discuss.

> ## Apply your knowledge
>
> **12.** Can you think of kinds of knowledge (other than moral or mathematical) that are a priori? What about colours, for instance?
>
> Identify whether the following sentences are analytic or synthetic:
>
> **a.** When it is raining it is not dry.
>
> **b.** Bob is married.
>
> **c.** Bob is writing in his study.
>
> **d.** All libraries have books.
>
> **13.** 'Given that we can't see murder or wrongness in the way we can see whether I am wearing a baseball cap, moral knowledge must be something we find using a different capability.' To what extent do you find this convincing and why?

The hypothetical imperative

The relativist and subjectivist find morals in the customs and practices of people or individuals. Some ethical thinkers believe moral propositions are linked to love (in the case of situationism) or the consequences (in the case of utilitarianism). Maybe what we say to our mother depends upon her psychology and whether or not it really matters what the family thinks. She will feel better if we reinforce her feeling that she is wearing a great outfit, perhaps.

Hypothetical knowledge ('If' statements) are conditional: If it is raining then you may get wet. If I want to learn to hula-hoop, I must practise. Some ethical theories treat moral rules as if they were a matter of hypothetical knowledge. *If* you want to do the loving thing, *then* you should do x. *If* you want to create the greatest happiness, *then* you should do y. In each case the command is conditional on the desired result. You have to follow the command if you pursue the desired result. If you don't pursue that result, then you have not followed the command. The **hypothetical imperative** commands behaviour *for* an end. It only commands us if we have accepted the desired end. If we have not accepted that end, then we need not act.

This is wrong, says Kant. We should look to the moral law which binds us unconditionally.

> ## Think question
>
> **b.** Your mother comes down the stairs wearing a new dress for an important family event. The dress is quite shocking and most unflattering. She says, 'do you like my new dress?' with an expression you know means she thinks it is great. You know it will make her a laughing stock. What should you do?

If the action would be good simply as a means to something else, then the imperative would be hypothetical *but if the action is represented as good in itself in accordance with reason, then the imperative is* categorical

> " All imperatives command either *hypothetically* or *categorically* … if the [commanded] action would be good simply as a means to something else, then the imperative would be *hypothetical* but if the action is represented as good in itself in accordance with reason, then the imperative is *categorical*.' "

Immanuel Kant, *Groundwork of the Metaphysics of Morals*, [1785] 1997, G414, p. 78

The categorical imperative

For Kant, moral knowledge is categorical. If truth telling is morally right, then we should always tell the truth. So in the example of the shocking dress, we should tell the truth about what we think, even if it hurts our mother's feelings. The categorical imperative commands us to exercise our will in a certain way *irrespective* of any end. The moral rules and acts reside in themselves alone (deontological), not in circumstances or whether they bring personal happiness. It doesn't matter if mother is going to get angry with us – the truth must be told. Moral law is categorical in its commanding nature. It tells us what to do, irrespective of our particular objectives, preferences, desires or opinions.

How can we be sure that truth telling is in accordance with the moral law? Kant offers three principles or formulas in the categorical imperative: our actions must be universalisable (good for all people and all situations); we should never treat people only as a means to an end; we should act as if we live in a kingdom of ends. Kant offers these formulas that must inform all laws.

The formula of the universal law of nature

> " Act only according to that maxim by which you can at the same time will that it should become a universal law. "

Immanuel Kant, *Groundwork for the Metaphysics of Morals*, [1785] 1997, p. 44

When we act morally, our action must be something that we could always do and anyone else could always do. It cannot be an exceptional act that only applies in this situation or that culture. Our moral behaviour must be consistent throughout our life and everyone else's.

> 66 Every action is right if it or its maxim allows each person's freedom of choice to coexist with the freedom of everyone in accordance with a universal law. 99
>
> Immanuel Kant, *Groundwork of the Metaphysics of Morals*, [1785] 1998, M230, p. 11

Kant argued that maxims that could not be universalised would be self-defeating.

> 66 I have, for example, made it my maxim to increase my wealth by every safe means. Now I have a deposit in my hands, the owner of which has died and left no record of it. This is, naturally, a case for my maxim. Now I want only to know whether that maxim could also hold as a universal practical law. I therefore apply the maxim to the present case and ask whether it could indeed take the form of a law, and consequently whether I could through my maxim at the same time give such a law as this: that everyone may deny a deposit which no one can prove has been made. I at once become aware that such a principle, as a law, would annihilate itself since it would bring it about that there would be no deposits at all. 99
>
> Immanuel Kant, *Critique of Pure Reason*, [1787] 1964, 5:27

Kant's moral law is a universal law that binds all. Consider the maxim: 'I only lie when it serves my interest.' This maxim could not be universalised for everyone as, inevitably, some interests would conflict. On the other hand, 'I will never break a promise for reasons of self-interest' could be universalised. We must tell the truth because truth telling is the foundation of society – we build relationships on it, do business on it, learn through it, and base our beliefs around it. Undermining truth telling is undermining society.

Is there never a time when it could be right to lie for good motives? Kant's universalisability rule bans all lying. In 1797, the French philosopher Benjamin Constant argued the duty to always tell the truth would make any society impossible. We need to tell white lies or lies for good motives (see 'On a Supposed Right to Lie Because of Altruistic Motives.' In *Critic of Practical Reason and Other Writings in Moral Philosophy*, ed. L. White Beck, 1949, pp. 346–50). Kant had said 'it would be a crime to tell a lie to a murderer who asked whether our friend who is being pursued by the murderer had taken refuge in our house'. Constant replies arguing, 'no one has a right to a truth that harms others'. Kant responds by saying a lie *always* harms someone. 'For a lie always harms another; if

Think question

Universal human rights could be supported by Kant. Explain how.

To be truthful (honest) in all declarations is, therefore, a sacred and unconditionally commanding law of reason that admits of no expediency whatsoever

not some other human being, then it nevertheless does harm to humanity in general, inasmuch as it vitiates [impairs] the very source of right'. Once a lie is told the person is responsible for all the consequences that result.

> " This is because truthfulness is a duty that must be regarded as the basis of all duties founded on contract, and the laws of such duties would be rendered uncertain and useless if even the slightest exception to them were admitted. To be truthful (honest) in all declarations is, therefore, a sacred and unconditionally commanding law of reason that admits of no expediency whatsoever. "

Immanuel Kant, *On a Supposed Right to Lie from Altruistic Motives*, in *Critique of Practical Reason and Other Writings in Moral Philosophy*, 1949, p. 347

Consider eve[...] you have had [...] this week. Every person [...] contract, explicit or implicit, that you made or w[...] in honesty in every exchange you have with a[...] is the foundation of every conversation, ev[...] at the foundation of being, relationships, friendship, the ju[...] the doctor-patient relationship, and so on. Lies undermine e[...] rebounding nature of the defence of this position.

[handwritten note:] Agape — if 'it's about what's best for the person' who decides what's best?

The formula of the end in itself

> " Rational nature exists as an end in itself. … Act in such a way that you always treat humanity, whether in your own person or in the person of any other, never simply as a means, but always at the same time as an end. "

Immanuel Kant, *Groundwork of the Metaphysics of Morals*, [1785] 1997, G429, p. 91

Human beings are rational agents capable of free will and this means that they are beyond price, they cannot be used for some other end. We cannot treat people without regard for their own future life, integrity and ability to make free choices. I cannot use you for my personal pleasure, to the detriment of your own human flourishing. The husband who abuses his wife, takes pleasure in using her sexually for his own gratification without recourse to any consideration for her feelings; the human trafficker who makes profit from the slavery of girls removed from their own countries; the pension fund manager who trades in such a way to maximise his own fee, without long-term concern for the fund, and therefore the interests of all those who have invested their future savings

Apply your knowledge

14. Is it justifiable to lie to a murderer to save a friend?

15. What is the role of trust and honesty in our relationships with people? Are these as important as Kant seems to think? Describe what Kant argues and state whether you agree.

16. Consider some additional cases that make lying appear justified. How could you accept that honesty is a better course of action in these circumstances?

17. Try to develop a maxim that you think could get past Kant's test but would still be wrong. What challenges do you come across?

with him. These actions have no regard for intrinsic quality of the human beings involved and their freedom. The wife feels used and diminished, perhaps losing her self-confidence and capacity to enjoy life. The trafficked women are limited and controlled by the pimps who sell them. The pension fund manager buys a boat with his profits while pensioners who have trusted him find their savings are not what they need to enjoy their retirement. In the case of the unflattering dress, if I lie to my mother I am forgetting to honour her with honesty, falsifying our relationship by telling her only what she wants to hear.

Kant's ethics influenced Catholic moral thought in the twentieth century, especially around the supremacy of human life and the need for universal rules. Before he became John Paul II, Karol Wojtyla wrote in *Love and Responsibility* (1982) about a notion of dignity that seems Kantian:

> 66 Anyone who treats a person as the means to an end does violence to the very essence of the other, to what constitutes its natural rights. … Nobody can use a person as a means towards an end, no human being, nor yet God the Creator. … This elementary truth — that a person, unlike all other objects of action, is therefore an inherent component of the natural moral order. 99
>
> Karol Wojtyla, *Love and Responsibility*, 1982, p. 27

The formula of the kingdom of ends

> 66 In the kingdom of ends everything has either a price or a dignity. If it has a price, something else can be put in its place as an equivalent; if it is exalted above price and so admits no equivalent, then it has a dignity. … Accordingly every rational being must so act as if he were through his maxims always a law-making member in the universal kingdom of ends. 99
>
> Immanuel Kant, *Groundwork of the Metaphysics of Morals*, [1785] 1997, G439, p. 100

We might think we live in a world dominated by the 'law of the jungle' – where no one treats others with consideration for their future freedom or their dignity – everyone seeks selfish ends, using people as a means to their desires. Kant forbids us from making a moral rule that presupposes others will not treat people as ends in themselves. 'I will take all I can as everyone else takes all they can.' It may be that we live in a world where no one is acting morally, no one is treating others as creatures who have worth. We should not base our universal rules on uniform degradation. A universal disregard for people is possible.

Apply your knowledge

18. Consider an army doctor with only one treatment left but two critically wounded soldiers on the battlefield before her. What is the right thing to do? What difficulties could this present to Kant? How might he respond based on what you know so far?

19. Is there *never* an occasion when a person can be used as a means to an end? Consider the following dilemmas – what would Kant do?

   a. You are adrift in a lifeboat on a freezing ocean. But it is too heavily laden with passengers and will sink unless someone is thrown overboard or jumps. No one volunteers to jump. As well as you, the boat contains a pregnant woman, a man with senile dementia, a baby, a teenager with severe learning difficulties, a philosopher, a crew member of the sunken vessel, a fertility doctor and a priest.

   b. A terrorist with explosives strapped to his body is standing in a crowded department store. The terrorist has an innocent civilian in front of him, blocking a headshot. The marksman's rifle is powerful enough to shoot through both heads and kill the terrorist. The terrorist has his hand on the trigger and looks like he is going to detonate.

Apply your knowledge

A father is driving home on a long motorway journey, the traffic slows and he sees there has just been an accident, and a car has overturned. There are children's sunshades in the back windows. The driver has got out and is running round his upturned car. The father still has 200 miles to drive to get to his booked ferry crossing and his own family are in the car with him. If he delays he will probably be late and getting another crossing could be difficult. Anyway, it looks as if another car has already stopped to help.

20. Should he stop and intervene or leave it to others?

Freedom is 'the highest degree of life' and the 'inner worth of the world'

Think question

Do we need to be free to pursue our desires or to be free from our desires?

However, Kant's thinking on the significance of the human person as a rational lawmaker makes this impossible as a moral maxim. The **kingdom of ends** is the world that we must imagine, when we are searching for universal laws.

The three postulates: Freedom, immortality and God

Freedom and the *summum bonum*

The postulate of freedom, sometimes called autonomy, is at the core of Kant's ethics. It means that human beings, human wills, are free, self-directing, autonomous. For Kant, we must postulate freedom – it is 'the highest degree of life' and the 'inner worth of the world' (*Lectures on Ethics*, [1784–5] 1997, 27:344, p. 347). Freedom means freedom to choose the moral law over our instinct or desire. '[I]n morals, the proper and inestimable worth of an absolutely good will consists precisely in the freedom of the principle of action from all influences ...' (*Groundwork for the Metaphysics of Morals*, 1785, pp. 80–7). Rational creatures are free, but they gain this freedom by adopting a formal law of action whereby principles are universalised. We act consistently according to universal rules rather than momentary impulses. Our reason grasps these rules. The father in the car may feel his priority is his family, but the needs of those in the upturned car are probably greater and two helpers would be better than one. The impulse will be to drive on by.

Moral choices are only possible if people are free to make them. We have to be free to do our duty. Autonomy of the will lies at the foundation of Kant's philosophy. If we are restricted and our actions are controlled by another or we simply cannot act, then we do not have moral responsibility.

Immortality

Kantian ethics look towards a perfect future. In a perfect world we would always stop for strangers in need on the road. We would want others to stop to help us. A world in which people always stop would be much better but other people will always be making a pressing journey. Stopping affects our immediate lives and interrupts our plans. It may inconvenience us and our passengers. This is not a future of individual desire fulfilment, but a greater future, a *summum bonum*. There our duty is united with things that give happiness.

To reach this highest good, this perfect world, is not easy. In our present world good people, doing their duty, may not find ultimate happiness in this world and might meet an unhappy end. There might be circumstances where doing the right thing leads to an untimely death. One person may act in a way that sacrifices their own life for others. So we must postulate immortality of the soul to allow for the correct happinesses to be ensured beyond this life.

Some people believe that in the life after this one (heaven) we achieve this ultimate happiness. Kant thought that human beings had the opportunity for endless improvement, or endless striving for improvement beyond death. Human beings were immortal, they lived on beyond this life in heaven and so sacrificial acts of duty are possible.

God

Kant's ethics could be seen as an attempt to step away from a theological starting point. Whereas previous ethical theories sometimes began with a religious understanding (such as natural law and situation ethics), Kant sought to advance an ethical theory which did not begin with God. However, some elements of his ethics seem to imply God – such as the idea of an *eternal* law, the idea that human's are *created* rational creatures, and the idea that sometimes doing the right thing does not lead to the greatest happiness *in this world*. Kant saw that not every virtuous act would lead to happiness in this world. It might be the case that we individually suffer despite doing the right thing. However, he thought we should nevertheless act as if we were in this kind of world. His belief in immortality and heavenly situation would ensure that ultimately happinesses are distributed appropriately in accordance with the moral acts that people have undertaken. God ensured that in the end the world was arranged correctly to ensure the highest good in the end. God recognises the striving that human beings have undertaken.

Kant himself was committed to Lutheran Christianity and Christians today will sometimes draw on Kant, especially his thinking around the preciousness of human life – as beings that have an end and have dignity. However, some Christians think that Kant places too much moral authority on the power of human reason, rather than biblical revelation for instance.

Apply your knowledge

21. Kant is not only interested in moral actions; he is also interested in the development of the human person. Using the information in this section, explain what developments you understand these to be. Write about:
    a. our ability to act as rational creatures
    b. our freedom from impulsive actions
    c. the importance of what motivates our actions.
22. Which of the three things in question 21 do you most value and why?

Apply your knowledge

Is it possible for a person with a misguided conscience to do terrible things but believe they are right and, therefore, be judged virtuous by Kant's thinking? The inquisitor finds and punishes those who hold erroneous beliefs. Let us imagine he has found someone who maintains different beliefs from that of the authorised religion. The inquisitor is concerned for the soul of the 'heretic'; he will go to hell if he does not repent. The inquisitor tortures the man to try and get him to change and in the end burns him to death, the punishment of heresy. While some inquisitors gain pleasure from torture and execution and are evil, this inquisitor is genuinely concerned to save the souls of as many as he can. Is he not a good person in Kant's thinking? No, Kant concludes. Conscience is practical reason, holding a person's duty before them for every trial the inquisitor conducts. The inquisitor has confused his feelings with the moral law.

23. If the inquisitor really believes he is saving souls, should he not do as he is doing in this example?
24. 'You should act according to what you feel is right. Otherwise you will have no integrity.' How does the misguided inquisitor show a problem with this kind of moral thinking? Is there a strong argument you can explore that counters this problem?

Discussing Kantian ethics

Is Kantian ethics a helpful method of moral decision-making?

One way of deciding whether or not Kant's theory is helpful is by testing it. Kant's system of the categorical imperative is supposed to prevent bad moral maxims being made. Suppose we try to make lying a promise with the maxim, 'Whenever I need money, I should make a lying promise while borrowing the money' (L. Pojman, *Ethics: Discovering Right and Wrong*, 2012, p. 143). In universalising this we get, 'Whenever anyone needs money, that person should make a lying promise while borrowing the money' (L. Pojman, *Ethics: Discovering Right and Wrong*, 2012, p.144). However, something is wrong with this – I could will the lie, but if it became a universal law there would be no promises. In making the maxim universal it destroys itself. No one would want to take a promise as a promise unless there was an expectation the promise would be fulfilled. The maxim of the lying promise fails the universalisability test and, therefore, is immoral. Take the alternative maxim, 'Whenever I need money, I should make a sincere promise while borrowing it' (L. Pojman, *Ethics: Discovering Right and Wrong*, 2012, p.147). This can be universalised to become 'Whenever anyone needs money, that person should make a sincere promise while borrowing it' (L. Pojman, *Ethics: Discovering Right and Wrong*, 2012, p.147).

However, Pojman finds that some examples are not so successful. Kant argues his imperative would prohibit suicide as he thinks you cannot universalise: 'Whenever it looks like one will experience more pain than pleasure, one ought to kill oneself', because it contradicts survival, on which the principle is based. But Pojman suggests it would be possible to universalise, 'Whenever the pain of suffering of existence erodes the quality of life in such a way as to make non-existence a preference to suffering existence, one is permitted to commit suicide' (L. Pojman, *Ethics: Discovering Right and Wrong*, 2012, p.148). Pojman concludes that while Kant opposes suicide, his categorical imperative does not.

Kant also gives an example that Pojman questions. Kant suggests that it is not possible to universalise not coming to the aid of others whenever I am secure and independent. He thinks we cannot universalise this because we would not know for sure whether or not we might need the help of others in future. A different maxim is possible that achieves a similar aim – it is possible to universalise I will 'never set myself a goal whose achievement appears to require the cooperation of others' (L. Pojman, *Ethics: Discovering Right and Wrong*, 2012, p.145). This might seem selfish or cruel, Pojman says, but it is not breaking the rules of the categorical imperative.

Kant's attempt at a system for creating moral rules has many advantages. It seeks to raise the status of human beings and to avoid selfish rule-making.

However, it is not clear how successful overall it is in achieving what Kant hoped it would. It might be that we need to build in exceptions and qualifications into the system Kant created but if we introduce conditionals – If this, then that – then the categorical nature of his system seems to be undermined.

Thinking about human beings as having unconditional worth, so they they are never treated as a means to an end but only as an end, is something that seems to match the feeling that many have that life is precious. Rationality does seem to be something of great importance to human life and this thinking seems to connect with the Judeo Christian tradition about the sanctity of life, but also could be upheld by people who have no religious beliefs. However, Pojman questions how should we consider people with different levels of reason or rationality. If it is an intrinsic good, then surely people with more reason are more intrinsically valuable than those with less?

Finally, it may be clear that we should not treat people in terrible ways, abuse them for the the pleasure of others, for instance, but it is not clear how we would response to situations where there was a conflict between helping one person or another. How would we decide how to act then?

Should an ethical judgement about something being good, bad, right or wrong be based on the extent to which duty is served?

Kant's theory has a strong emphasis on what is going on inside the person making a moral decision. They should act out of pure motives, focused on serving duty rather than external pressures, such as the greater good, or internal emotions like love. For Kant this is important because morality is not something that is determined by emotions, and not determined by judgements about the results. Moral behaviour is about human improvement as well as the actions themselves. By striving to act properly we become happier and society becomes happier (and if not in this world in every circumstance, then in the next).

This is a strong and idealised view of moral action and moral motivation, but perhaps it is a little too idealised. It is possible to act for all sorts of reasons that apply in the difficult circumstances life presents. It is not always clear what our duty might be. We may feel torn by different pressures or may have to choose between two undesirable alternatives. Human beings are fallible and prone to all sorts of influences in their inner motivations. Perhaps I desire to appear altruistic. Perhaps my motives are mixed. Kant has little time for these factors, but it may be possible to do things that are still good, even with our fallible, mixed motivations. Perhaps there is a halfway house between self-interest and duty, that allows us those mixed motivations, but can still produce actions which are better.

Apply your knowledge

25. Look at the rules that your school, or another school you know, requires students to follow. To what extent do they comply with Kant's categorical imperative?

26. A person is walking at the end of a seaside pier. There are shouts coming from either side. Two children who were playing on the railings have fallen into the rough sea, one on either side. There is only one safety ring left. The sea looks dangerous and the person on the pier is not a confident swimmer. What solutions might Kant offer for this situation? What problems does this situation pose for Kant's ethical theory?

Apply your knowledge

27. Discuss these views:

a. 'An ethic which does not make people better in the long run is not as good as one that does'

b. 'Human beings will always be motivated by different things, sometimes by things they don't even realise – the purpose of ethics is to make sure what they do is better than it would otherwise be'

c. 'A sense of duty can become a burden – sometimes doing the right thing means abandoning duty and not being held back by it.

We might also question whether the struggle for an individual's inner purity of motivation is as important as the happiness or love that is created. Arguably the most important thing is the result of any inner personal struggle to follow duty. After all, judgements about the morality of behaviour would consider what the behaviour produces. Intention matters, but is it as important as Kant suggests?

Finally, we might question whether it could be our duty to consider the consequences of our actions. Pojman is critical of Kant's attempt to make moral law exceptionless and sacrosanct, and duty something that should always be followed.

Are Kantian ethics too abstract to be applicable to practical moral decision-making?

Kant provides a powerful idealised concept of morality, with attention to the worth of the human person, held high above all other things and with a strong sense of universal rules untainted by human emotion. However, these features of his theory do present some practical challenges. It requires a particular approach to life where a person has learned to separate themselves from their emotions and focus on certain principles when trying to decide what to do. Moral decisions are often made in challenging circumstances when we are under emotional pressure. Kant might be accused of being unrealistic about the expectations he places on people. Human beings are imperfect and the moral law can feel like a constraint.

But Kant requires us to focus on principles. When thinking about a particular individual who may be in acute need, Kant wants us to remember the principle of the universal laws of nature and the kingdom of ends. Kant also wants us to think about treating a person with great respect – as an end and not only a means. This is an idealised view of life. There may be too few emergency relief supplies for the natural disaster hit country. Perhaps you can only save some villages – how to decide? Orders that endanger or even sacrifice soldiers may have to be given in times of war for the greater good. When faced with no win situations, such as the decision to save some lives at the expense of a few, Kant seems unhelpful.

Hospitals have to decide how to use limited resources for the greatest benefit and this can mean deciding to ration treatment or indeed not provide certain kinds of expensive treatments that are only occasionally successful. For instance, some forms of cancer treatment are only effective in a minority of cases. To provide it for everyone would take money away from other treatments that are more reliable. When the resources are fixed you would struggle to use the ideals of Kant to drive your decision-making.

However, systems of ethics based on emotions could easily dissolve into justifications of selfish conduct, so perhaps principles and ideals are what should drive our conduct. They offer flexibility in that rules can be developed from them. Perhaps Kant is offering the system for creating rules that, once disseminated, will guide people. Moral theories that simply provide the rules and not the system for making rules are arguably less useful as new unexpected situations may present themselves. Moral theories that are not interested in the development of the moral person may be less effective at creating a better society. Kant sees ethics as the development of a better world, not just better individual decisions, and that means better people.

Apply your knowledge

The *Westralia* was a 171-metre petrol tanker used to carry fuel for the Australian navy. In 1998, four navy sailors under the age of 30 died in a fire in the engine room when the captain decided to flood the room with carbon dioxide to prevent the spread of the fire, which was endangering the lives of all 90 crew. The fire started when the four crew attempted to fix a broken fuel line. Five sailors tried to rescue them but were injured in the attempt. The fire was threatening to spread when the captain, Commander Stuart Dietrich, abandoned rescue attempts. He had the engine room sealed and flooded with carbon dioxide. Commander Dietrich weighed up the risk to any survivors against the risk to the whole ship when ordering that the engine room be sealed. At the time it was the Australian Navy's worst peacetime disaster since 1964.

28. Was the Captain acting appropriately, thinking about the greater good and his duty to his crew, or was he thinking about the immediate consequences and not considering the inherent dignity of the four sailors in the engine room, and therefore acting inappropriately? Explain your answer carefully.

29. In this situation which is the better rule to follow – the greatest good for the greatest number, or do not kill?

30. What was the right thing to do and why was it right?

Is Kantian ethics so reliant on reason that it unduly rejects the importance of other factors, such as sympathy, empathy and love in moral decision-making?

Emotions are a fundamental part of human experience and emotional connections with loved ones, partners and friends seem to be among the most valuable things in life – the kind of things that get you through the more challenging times. Kant seems a little removed from this emotional importance. When faced with a great threat we might want to save our own child first, but it is not clear from Kant's theory that there would be any moral ground for trying to save those closest to us over and above any other person. Feelings often motivate moral responses – a concern for the poor, a sense of guilt or compassion for someone in distress, or a sense of passion for a cause we feel strongly about. We might find ourselves with impure or mixed motives, such as moral situations involving family members or friends, we may have a sense of loyalty or love for certain individuals. Acting in a rational way that distances ourselves from these things feels quite difficult.

This kind of moral action is not what Kant wants. Kant would question whether emotive actions for others will lead us into immorality. Perhaps we could become corrupt by favouring those we like. Perhaps our feelings for someone could lead us astray. We might pursue selfish self-interested aims – acting to impress or curry favour. If everyone simply followed their emotions, then perhaps the world would become a much worse place – after all, we would all want to be helped when we are strangers in a foreign land and in need. Arguably, morals are most important for their ability to get us to think beyond family and friendship loyalties – they should be focused on other people who are unlike us. If justice was based on emotions, emotional appeal or emotional connection between the judge and jury and the defendant or the accuser, and not a consistent and fair application of the law, we would say that justice was corrupted. Perhaps Kant is right.

Apply your knowledge

In the French film *Amélie* (2001), Amélie is a shy waitress who changes the lives of those around her for the better. One of those people is Mrs Wells, an elderly neighbour whose husband left her many years ago, dying in an accident shortly after leaving her. Mrs Wells talks lovingly of her husband, for whom she has a shrine of photos and mementos. She reads from letters he sent her, but it is clear to Amélie that he was not a good man, that he used and abused his wife. Mrs Wells wants to believe her husband really loved her and seeks for signs of this. Of course, he is dead and so her search is futile. Amélie forges a final conciliatory love letter from the husband, supposedly written shortly before his accidental death and then lost by the French postal service for many years. Mrs Wells is consoled by the letter. She can believe that in the end he really did love her and her years of mourning him and dreaming that she meant more to him than he sometimes implied have not been wasted. It is of course a lie but it helps her find resolution.

31. Telling lies to deceive people about those who they love could not be a moral commandment, but in this case is it justified?

32. Is truth more important than the feelings of Mrs Wells?

33. Does this show the danger of following feelings or sentimentality in moral decisions or the benefit?

34. Is the film dishonest?

Learning support

Points to remember

When writing about ethics, we are linking ideas or concepts to practical examples. Here are some suggestions about how to do this more effectively.

» Make sure you understand the general view that the philosopher has that his or her ethical thought fits into. For Kant this is related to how he understands our perception of knowledge and human value. With other philosophies, such as utilitarianism, this is related to their understanding of the human condition influenced by desiring happiness and avoiding unhappiness. This helps you to make critical observations about the assumptions underpinning the ethical thought, such as whether it is the case that human autonomy is most significant, or whether humans really do pursue happiness.

» Ethical terms and quotes need to be unpacked when you refer to them. This shows you really understand them and can dig a little deeper into the ideas. Don't simply drop the quote or phrase in. Say something about it. So if you are referring to the 'moral law within', don't just say this shows Kant believes in an objective moral law, say more about the significance of how that moral law is perceived, and the fact that human beings are rational creatures who perceive morality.

» It can be easy to dismiss a philosopher by taking one element and then thinking of examples that don't seem to work well. It is much better to really get inside what the philosopher is trying to say and then consider several applications. You might find some moral scenarios where an ethical theory seems to work better than others. This gives your writing a nuanced and balanced feel. Perhaps Kant doesn't work so well when it comes to difficult decisions about which patient to treat in a hospital where funds are tight, but on issues of human rights, his universalistic thinking seems more helpful.

Enhance your learning

» A number of introductions to ethics offer good chapters on Kant: L. Pojman, *Ethics, Discovering Right and Wrong*, 2012, Chapter 8 (or Chapter 7 in some earlier editions); P. Vardy and P. Grosch, *The Puzzle of Ethics*, 1994;

Rachels has a good chapter that focuses on Kant's concept of human dignity, see J. Rachels, *The Elements of Moral Philosophy*, 1993.

» For specific applications of Kant to particular moral problems see O. O'Neill, 'Kantian Approaches to Some Famine Problems.' In *Ethical Theory: An Anthology*, ed. R. Shafer-Landau, 2013; Norman E. Bowie has written 'A Kantian Approach to Business Ethics' which is easily found online in a number of places, and also in *Ethical Issues in Business: A Philosophical Approach*, 7th edn, eds. T. Donaldson, P.H., Werhane and M. Cording, 2002, pp. 61–71. He has given it a thorough treatment in *Business Ethics: A Kantian Perspective*, ed. N.E. Bowie, 1999.

» Reading Kant is an acquired taste but *Groundwork of the Metaphysic of Morals*, Chapter 2, is a good place to start. It is not very long, covers many of the key themes discussed in this chapter and is easy to find memorable quotes from. There are many free versions available online but it is recommended he is read in modern English.

Practice for exams

AS questions and A level questions look identical; the difference between AS and A level assessment is seen in the different proportions of marks awarded for two different skills: the skill of demonstrating knowledge and understanding (Assessment Objective 1, or AO1), and the skill of constructing a critical argument (AO2).

At AS, half the marks (15 marks) are available for knowledge and understanding, and the other half (15 marks) for the quality of your analytical and evaluative argument. You should aim to use your knowledge in order to support the argument you are making throughout the essay, rather than presenting descriptive knowledge in the first half and then an opinion in the second.

At A level, your demonstration of knowledge and understanding is awarded a maximum of 16 marks, and your analytic and evaluative skills are awarded a maximum of 24 marks. You should aim to concentrate on constructing a lucid argument, making use of your knowledge to add weight to the conclusions you draw.

How fair is the criticism that Kantian ethics ignore human emotion and empathy?

This essay invites consideration of a common criticism of Kant, namely that it places too high a value on objective moral duty and fails to take into account individual needs and the possibility of acting with compassion or forgiveness.

Practise your skills for AS level

If you are an AS student, you should be able to demonstrate a detailed and accurate account of Kantian ethics and also present a balanced argument where you consider different points of view while also presenting your own opinions in a persuasive way. You should present your argument so that the examiner is clear about whether you think the criticism is totally fair, partially fair or not fair at all.

Practise your skills for A level

If you are answering the at A level, you need to decide whether it is fair to say that Kantian ethics ignore human emotion and empathy, and also, if they are ignored, whether that is a bad thing. You could consider different hypothetical situations in order to illustrate your argument, and you might want to argue that ethics need to work differently in different contexts.

'Kantian ethics are helpful for moral decision-making in every kind of context.' Discuss.

For this question you need to consider Kantian ethics as a whole system and form a judgement about whether they are always helpful, helpful only in some contexts, or not helpful at all.

Practise your skills for AS level

At AS level you need to show a good level of knowledge and understanding of the main features and principles of Kantian ethics. You also need to give a critical assessment of whether these ethics are helpful in all contexts; for example, you might think that they are more helpful in contexts which affect everyone, such as environmental ethics, and less helpful in personal contexts such as relationships.

Practise your skills for A level

At A level you should concentrate on demonstrating evaluative skill, using your knowledge to support your argument. You might consider issues such as the difficulty of always knowing what one's duty is, and the problems that arise when situations differ or when duties conflict. You might weigh up the helpfulness of Kantian ethics in terms of ease of knowing what to do. For high marks, aim to illustrate the points you make with examples.

Chapter 2.4

Utilitarianism

Do the ends justify the means?
Must an ethical way of life be more than self-interested decision-making?
Is doing good about considering the preferences of everyone equally?

Key Terms

Principle of utility/greatest happiness: the idea that the choice that brings about the greatest good for the greatest number is the right choice

Deontological: from the Latin for 'duty', ethics focused on the intrinsic rightness and wrongness of actions

Teleological: looking to the end results (telos) in order to draw a conclusion about what is right or wrong

Hedonic calculus: the system for calculating the amount of pain or pleasure generated

Consequentialism: ethical theories that see morality as driven by the consequences, rather than actions or character of those concerned

Hedonistic: pleasure-driven

Quantitative: focused on quantity (how many, how big, etc.)

Qualitative: focused on quality (what kind of thing)

Act utilitarian: weighs up what to do at each individual occasion

Rule utilitarian: weighs up what to do in principle in all occasions of a certain kind

Specification requirements

Utilitarianism, including:
*   utility
*   the hedonic calculus
*   act utilitarianism
*   rule utilitarianism

Introduction

Utilitarianism is an ethical theory that looks to create the greatest good for the greatest number. It applies the **principle of utility** to moral problems. This 'utility' refers to the extent to which good and evil is done by a choice. Rather than focusing on rules that should not be broken (**deontological** ethics) it is **teleological**, focused on the results.

Utilitarianism is an ethical theory proposed by Jeremy Bentham and John Stuart Mill. It is also the adopted theory of the Australian ethicist Peter Singer. He introduced utilitarianism in his book *Practical Ethics* (1997) by challenging the idea that ethics is all about sex, rules, religion and what people individually feel is right for them. Ethics is not a 'system of nasty puritanical prohibitions, mainly designed to stop people having fun', he said (p. 1). Ethics, he says, is not about applying some simple rules, like do not kill. This is the view of the deontologists: 'those who think that ethics is a system of rules' (p. 3) Ethics should promote the most happiness, rather than focusing exclusively on particular actions.

For utilitarians, ethics is not about religion. It was Plato who argued that just because God approves an action, this does not make that action right. Ethics is apart from religion for Utilitarians.

Utilitarians also argue that ethics are not codes of the society in which you live. Singer argues that belief and customs influence us, but are set by the powerful. He holds that this is not a principled way to live. Sometimes movements challenge social norms, such as anti-slavery and women's emancipation, for instance. Being ethical is *more than simply self-interest*, it is about the interest of all.

> **66** The notion of ethics carries with it the idea of something bigger than the individual. If I am to defend my conduct on ethical grounds, I cannot point only to the benefits it brings me. I must address myself to a larger audience. **99**
>
> Peter Singer, *Practical Ethics*, 1997, p. 10

If Singer is right and this is not what morality should really be about, then what should it be about? According to utilitarianism, goodness and badness is about the ends, the things sought, rather than how you seek them, the actions. Utilitarianism sets aside religious authority and established rules. This kind of ethics makes decisions about right and wrong that are relative to an end – how much pleasure, happiness or well-being is created and how much pain or unhappiness by any choice. The greatest good is typically the thing that achieves the greatest result (however that is defined) for the greatest number, irrespective of what has to be done to achieve it. Utilitarianism is not trying to list what are the right or wrong

For more about Plato and God, see Chapter 1.1.

actions, but instead claims to provide a practical way of making difficult moral decisions when we are faced with conflicting goods.

Central to utilitarianism is the '**hedonic calculus**', the calculation of the balance between pleasure and pain, and the evil and good that results from any action. When looking at a problem, all of the possible alternative courses of action should be considered and each measured in terms of the hedonic calculus.

Different utilitarian theories emphasise different sorts of ends. Classical utilitarianism, the theories of Bentham and Mill, are common examples of **consequentialism**. This sees goodness as being about happiness, well-being or pleasure, and badness is about the opposite – unhappiness, distress or pain. Classical utilitarianism is **hedonistic**.

Classical utilitarians measure happiness. Jeremy Bentham measures this in **quantitative** terms only, but John Stuart Mill applies **qualitative** pains and pleasures. Mill thinks some kinds of pain and pleasure are worth more than other kinds.

For some utilitarians decisions should be made by individuals at each occasion, each action (**act utilitarians**). For others decisions should be made about general issues and these utilitarian rules should then be followed (**rule utilitarian**).

Utilitarianism is challenged by those who argue that it permits us to break rules and does not provide a basis for fairness and justice. It relies heavily on being able to know the future consequences of actions, and that it assumes shared or common interests or pleasures, when people might be more diverse in their preferences/interests and pleasures.

The principle of utility

Jeremy Bentham's utilitarianism

The first utilitarian was Jeremy Bentham (1748–1832). Bentham wanted a different approach to ethical decision-making than obedience to the Bible, or fixed moral rules. He was concerned about social reform and the situation of the masses. His ethical theory started with an observation of what really mattered to people, and this meant confronting the good and evil in life, the happiness and the trials of living.

Jeremy Bentham wrote:

Jeremy Bentham

....

66 Nature has placed mankind under the governance of two sovereign masters, pain and pleasure. It is for them alone to point out what we ought to do, as well as to determine what we shall do. On the one hand the standard of right and wrong, on the other the chain of causes and effects, are fastened to their throne. They govern us in all we do, in all we say, in all we

think: every effort we can make to throw off our subjection, will serve but to demonstrate and confirm it. In words a man may pretend to abjure [be unaffected by] their empire: but in reality he will remain subject to it all the while. The principle of utility recognises this subjection, and assumes it for the foundation of that system. … Systems which attempt to question it, deal in sounds instead of sense, in caprice instead of reason, in darkness instead of light. **99**

Jeremy Bentham, *An Introduction to the Principles and Morals of Education*, 1781, Chapter 1.1

Bentham describes pain and pleasure as our masters, instead of some divine authority. Wherever possible we instinctively try to avoid pain and seek out pleasure. Bentham comes to his conclusion through observations of human life. We respond to our basic needs. This is the essence of hedonism. The newborn seeks to fill its empty stomach, the toddler recoils from the hot radiator. We pursue hobbies that interest us and we avoid unpleasant people and, if possible, jobs we hate. Is this not the natural course for the hedonistic life?

Bentham argues that we must recognise this basic driver for human life. It is not God, or human reason that motivates us, but the pursuit of happiness. Bentham's moral system is grounded in this world. We might say he starts with human psychology. Bentham is sceptical of the claims people make about their holy lives. They claim that they act according to some divine rule but in truth they don't: that is what Bentham means when he says, 'In words a man may pretend to abjure their empire.' You are pretending when you give money to charity and claim you are altruistic [selfless], you are simply gaining some other kinds of pleasures, perhaps adulation from others for appearing to be generous – perhaps to win the heart of someone who will be impressed by your generosity. Bentham's view of the world is the basis for his principle of utility.

The principle of utility

Given human motivations, a system of law is needed. Bentham developed a principle of utility, or greatest happiness theory, to approve or reject every private action and every action of government. The utility is the extent to which an act produces 'benefit, advantage, pleasure, good, or happiness' or prevents 'the happening of mischief, pain, evil, or unhappiness'. Utility is what moral behaviour should be looking to maximise. The balance between happiness and sadness caused is what should affect our decisions, not any idealised view of moral commandments or rules. The principle of utility uses the human instinct to seek pleasure but applies a democratic principle. It is not enough to talk about the individual when thinking about utility, we

> ### Think question
> If life is driven by desire, then the world is governed by the survival of the fittest. Discuss.

must consider community and the sum of the interest of all the people in the community. In *A Fragment on Government* (1891, first published 1776), Bentham says, 'it is the greatest happiness of the greatest number that is the measure of right and wrong'. Bentham thinks, 'The business of government is to promote the happiness of the society.' The common good is the principle Bentham wants to advance. This is his democratic moral principle.

It is the greatest happiness of the greatest number that is the measure of right and wrong

> 66 The community is a fictitious *body*, composed of the individual persons who are considered as constituting as it were its *members*. The interest of the community then is, what is it? – the sum of the interests of the several members who compose it. 99

Jeremy Bentham, *An Introduction to the Principles and Morals of Education*, 1781, Chapter 1.4

The community is the sum of the individuals. Bentham has no romantic notion of a people united, but simply the sum of all our desires, our attractions and repulsions. Pleasure and the avoidance of pain, seeking to increase the balance of good over evil are the ends that the person and indeed government should consider when deciding what to do. It is the happiness of the community, the aggregation of all individual wants, more than any individual, that matters.

Goodness is relative to the results

Utilitarianism is teleological. Decisions are made relative to the ends, the results of good and evil caused. This means it is a relativist ethical theory. Relative ethical theories do not promote a fixed or absolute set of particular rules (like natural law does). Relativism might be based on personal views of right and wrong or cultural traditions of right or wrong. Utilitarianism offers a different kind of relative ethics. It looks at the situation and decides which actions produce the greatest balance of happiness or well-being over evil or pain. It is a democratic kind of relativism because it wants to maximise the balance of good over evil.

Apply your knowledge

A tram on tracks races down a slope, out of control, towards a family of five who are crossing at that moment. The youngest, a small child, has her foot trapped and they do not see the oncoming trolley. You are by a lever and can switch the tracks to another siding where only one person is on the tracks – a worker. Should you switch? If you were on a footbridge going over the tracks and a heavy man is with you, you could push him over the side and his body would be a cushion for the trolley, ending his life in exchange for the lives of the family.

1. Should you switch tracks? Should you push the man over the side? Is there any difference?

2. What might Bentham think was the right thing to do?

3. What sorts of things might we say with reference to this example to try to argue against Bentham?

The hedonic calculus

Morality does not serve the pleasure of the rich and wealthy few alone, or authorities in a particular cultural system, but the democratic masses. Utilitarianism does not promote a list of rules about which acts are right or wrong, but instead offers a process for weighing up alternatives. The hedonic calculus calculates the balance of pleasure, well-being or goodness, as opposed to pain or evil. There are different dimensions of good and evil. Some goods are momentary, some last a long time. Some affect individuals and some benefit the majority. I may decide I gain great happiness from having many slaves to look after me and do all the work I need to be done, but the majority live in suffering – as slaves. Individual benefit is not enough for utilitarianism. Rules that benefit the minority and leave the majority in pain are not good enough. A number of factors need to be considered to evaluate this balance of good and evil. Bentham suggests the following:

> 1. Its intensity.
>
> 2. Its duration.
>
> 3. Its certainty or uncertainty.
>
> 4. Its propinquity or remoteness.
>
> 5. Its fecundity, the chance it has of being followed by sensations of the same kind: that is, pleasures, if it be a pleasure: pains, if it be a pain.
>
> 6. Its purity, or the chance it has of not being followed by sensations of the opposite kind: that is, pains, if it be a pleasure: pleasures, if it be a pain.
>
> 7. Its extent; that is, the number of persons to whom it extends; or (in other words) who are affected by it.

Jeremy Bentham, *An Introduction to the Principles of Morals and Legislation*, 1781, Chapter 4.4

Think question

Would the hedonic calculus effectively quantify the things that make you happy?

The hedonic calculus measures the quantity of pain and pleasure in any suggested individual act or law. At a time when the wealthy and powerful ruled and the majority were poor, with few rights or legal protections, Bentham argued that laws should be focused on the greatest good of the people.

Calculating the greatest goodness, rather than following moral rules, can have controversial implications. A concern about the quality of life (the well-being or good we seek) could justify euthanasia, abortion, or even in some cases, infanticide, where the child's arrival will lead to greater harm for the many.

In seeking to quantify pleasure or pain there are some difficulties with Bentham. Is pleasure, goodness or well-being the right gauge for morality? Are all pleasures measurable using the same 'toolkit'? Does everyone, or do most people, gain pleasure from similar things? We might question whether the happiness of all or the many is simply a matter of the aggregation of individual wants. Does anything else change when we combine the different individual wants of different people together? Is there anything about the relationships between those different individuals which affects how individual wants transform into communal wants?

Apply your knowledge

4. Is the pursuit of pleasure an appropriate moral gauge? Consider sadism: the teacher who enjoys making a student squirm on the spot with difficult questions in class. Do most people take pleasure in the same things?

5. Can pleasures be compared using the same system? Try to quantify the following: the happiness of the sound of a baby chuckling, the moment when a couple promise themselves to one another in a marriage, the taste of honey, the delight when a favourite team wins the championship, stroking a purring cat on your lap.

6. Why is it important for utilitarians to be confident in what will happen in the future? How far into the future does one have to be able to predict to safely use utilitarianism?

7. Are there any arguments against a democratic notion of the common good? What happens if the majority like to abuse a minority for their own interests? Explain why this is a problem for utilitarianism.

The quality of happiness in the utility principle

John Stuart Mill (1806–73) was Bentham's pupil and he followed utilitarianism.

> 66 The creed which accepts as the foundation of morals, Utility, or the Greatest Happiness Principle, holds that actions are right in proportion as they tend to promote happiness, wrong as they tend to produce the reverse of happiness. By happiness is intended pleasure, and the absence of pain; by unhappiness, pain, and the [de]privation of pleasure. 99
>
> John Stuart Mill, *Utilitarianism*, 1863, p. 60

John Stuart Mill

Mill investigates these pleasures and pains, noting that many people would be disgusted at the suggestion that morality was about base pleasures: 'the accusation supposes human beings to be capable of no pleasures except those of which swine are capable' (*Utilitarianism*, 1863, p. 10). Mill thinks humans are better: 'Human beings have faculties more elevated than the animal appetites, and when once made conscious of them, do not regard anything as happiness which does not include their gratification' (p. 11). These higher pleasures are always better than base pleasures.

The majority might decide to do something really unpleasant to an individual or a minority if they take pleasure from that. Perhaps the crowd will enjoy watching an individual humiliated. Sadists take enjoyment out of pain given to others. This is not the kind of happiness or well-being that Mill thinks utilitarianism has in mind. The utility principle needed to distinguish between quantities of sensual goods and happiness, and more important quality goods and pleasures. The quality of pleasure should also be calculated.

> 66 It is quite compatible with the principle of utility to recognise the fact, that some kinds of pleasure are more desirable and more valuable than others. It would be absurd that while, in estimating all other things, quality is considered as well as quantity, the estimation of pleasures should be supposed to depend on quantity alone. 99
>
> John Stuart Mill, *Utilitarianism*, 1863, p. 11

'It is better to be a human being dissatisfied than a pig satisfied; better to be Socrates dissatisfied than a fool satisfied.' (John Stuart Mill)

Mill distinguished the lower pleasures (drinking, sex, eating, rest) from the higher pleasures (intellectual, aesthetic, social enjoyment, spirituality). The lower pleasures provide powerful gratification but if we overindulge, they bring pain. The distinction Mill made over Bentham was not along any of the axes of the calculus, but in a recognition that there were different sorts of pleasure and pain. He distinguished the higher from the lower by claiming a person would always value the higher over the lower. Higher pleasures are superior to lower pleasures.

> 66 A being of higher faculties requires more to make him happy, is capable probably of more acute suffering, and certainly accessible to it at more points, than one of an inferior type. … It is better to be a human being dissatisfied than a pig satisfied; better to be Socrates dissatisfied than a fool satisfied. 99
>
> John Stuart Mill, *Utilitarianism*, 1863, p. 13

Think question

What would you suggest are higher and lower pleasures?

Mill distinguished that the great and the wise could agree on which aspects of arts and culture gave the greatest pleasures and which gave the more base pleasures. This seems elitist, but on the other hand if we were only to have satisfied our more base pleasures, what kind of life would that be?

Mill argues:

> 66 The happiness which they meant was not a life of rapture; but moments of such, in an existence made up of few and transitory pains, many and various pleasures, with a decided predominance of the active over the passive, and having as the foundation of the whole, not to expect more from life than it is capable of bestowing. 99

John Stuart Mill, *Utilitarianism*, 1863, p. 15

For Mill, utilitarian morality does recognise in human beings the possibility that we can act for the good of others, even renouncing our own interests or happiness in an altruistic way:

> 66 The power of sacrificing their own greatest good for the good of others. It only refuses to admit that the sacrifice is itself a good. A sacrifice which does not increase, or tend to increase, the sum total of happiness, it considers as wasted. The only self-renunciation which it applauds, is devotion to the happiness, or to some of the means of happiness, of others; either of mankind collectively, or of individuals within the limits imposed by the collective interests of mankind. 99

John Stuart Mill, *Utilitarianism*, 1863, p. 19

Apply your knowledge

8. Explain self-sacrifice from a utilitarian perspective
9. Is intellectual happiness greater than sensual happiness? Try to make a case that it is.

When deciding what is right as a utilitarian, should we be thinking about the act in hand or should we be thinking about how all people should act in this kind of situation? When making a decision about the greatest good, should the instance we face be the only thing to think about or should all instances of a similar kind be considered? Should the moral approach we try to forge be about working out a way for people as a whole to act, whenever they face instances of a particular kind, or is morality an individual thing? It might be that in a particular instance we face an exceptional circumstance which is unlike other occasions – so a thing that usually causes happiness, leads to our personal harm. Telling the truth might seem to be something we should do for everyone's happiness, but a person trying to keep a secret or hide a crime, might think differently.

Should you spend your birthday money on an intellectual pleasure or a sensual pleasure?

'intellectual happiness'

'sensual happiness'

Act and rule utilitarianism

The classical utilitarians (Bentham and Mill) were interested in the social benefit of moral decision-making. Utilitarianism could be a system for determining individual moral conduct, or something to guide a community or government policy, but this raises a further question about how utilitarianism is applied in practice. Act utilitarians are driven by the utility (the balance of good and evil done) in each individual situation. Rule utilitarians establish rules for what to do based on the 'calculation' of utility if a given action was chosen in all similar circumstances.

Act utilitarianism

Taking an act utilitarian approach means taking each individual action that any person faces, and making a judgement about the balance of good or evil done in that particular situation. It is individualistic in that the calculation and decision is made by the person presented with the situation. It is responsive to the particular situation, as the person makes the moral decision about what to do, in and for the particular instance facing them. Other moral situations involving different people have no bearing on the immediate situation. There is no duty to adopt a particular approach.

Act utilitarianism has a dynamic and immediate quality. Act utilitarianism could be called extreme or direct utilitarianism. Decisions should be made on a case-by-case basis. The utility (the balance of good and evil done) of a particular option for the moral dilemma faced today, is all that should drive the judgement about what to do. Each moral situation should be taken on its own terms. You should consider the greatest happiness in each given example of a moral dilemma. The power of act utilitarianism is that it always seeks to maximise the greatest utility in every situation. Arguably this means the greatest utility will be created over all. Act utilitarianism also avoids setting up rules. Utilitarianism traditionally sets aside rule-based systems about right and wrong, such as religious rules. These systems may not benefit the people and some claim they benefit other interests. Act utilitarianism takes seriously the human drive towards well-being or goodness and away from evil/harm – this is where Bentham began his thinking with his view that pleasure and pain drive behaviour. Act utilitarianism is arguably closer to this observation about human nature.

An act utilitarian might find it better to lie in some situations, for instance, as it may suit a particular circumstance. This can make act utilitarians appear to be hedonistic – the adulterer hides his liaisons from his wife to maximise his pleasures. However, it also justifies lying to a Nazi about a hidden Jewish family. This undermines the democratic intention of utilitarianism.

Think question

If lying could sometimes be right what might this mean for trust in society?

Apply your knowledge

There might be situations where act utilitarianism concludes that something quite unpalatable is the right thing to do. Discuss the following questions:

10. It may be better to execute an innocent man, whom the majority believe has committed a terrible crime. Justice is not served, but perhaps the crowds will not riot if their hunger for action is satisfied.

11. Act utilitarianism means we can never consider ourselves over another. Does that mean we should never spend money on any luxuries, but always on saving the lives of poor people elsewhere? Surely we have some duty to ourselves?

12. Act utilitarianism finds it difficult to recognise special relationships such as the duties parents have towards children. Children need specific help from their parents but the hedonic calculus does not provide for such special relationships. How should a parent decide whether to spend money on their child's education or helping poor people facing starvation because of a famine in a remote part of the world?

Rule utilitarianism

Rule utilitarians are more focused on establishing the common good. Rule utilitarianism seeks to set up a series of rules that will generally maximise the greatest good for the greatest number: the greatest utility. The general end of an action if it is repeated in different circumstances, is what matters, so there may be occasions when, in a particular instance, more harm is done in that instance, but in the long-run more people will benefit. Rule utilitarians might tell the truth always, as this is generally better for everyone, even if there are particular instances when a lie might be individually desirable. The spouse resists the particular temptation of a one-night stand on a business trip, even though it would never be discovered, as everyone is happier not to be betrayed.

Rule utilitarianism can be thought of in terms of the rules for driving – the Highway Code. There might be a particular situation where no one else is around, and my journey would be far easier if I could quickly use any side of the road as is convenient to me. Assuming I can see there really is no other traffic in the way, I can choose to drive in the way that best meets my needs – this might be the act utilitarian approach. However, rule utilitarians establish that there are rules to the highway that might sometimes cause delays for individuals, but overall there are fewer accidents as a result. So when I set out, I follow the Highway Code which has been set up to generally reduce the harm or evil done by road accidents.

Rule utilitarians might take a qualitative or quantitative approach to measuring well-being. They can seek to deal with the questions of trust, justice and equality if they look to the qualitative measure of happiness that Mill is concerned about. Rule utilitarians may accept that there are circumstances where, for justice to be done, some harm might happen – the crowd may riot against oppression and cause damage, but in the long-term the happiness caused by having got rid of oppressors and brought back a just and fair system benefits more people.

Things like promise-keeping matter for rule utilitarians, so that relationships and business might flourish. Businesses are based on trust,

Apply your knowledge

Consider the following views, giving arguments for and against:

13. 'Utilitarianism seeks to replace obedience of rules with doing what is best for the greater good. Rule utilitarianism creates new rules to obey, undermining the heart of the theory.'

14. 'Act utilitarianism undermines trust, justice and equality and can justify lying and torture for pleasure.'

as they rely on contracts with promises about services, goods or labour. Relationships rely on trust through promises made, friendships and the like. Rule utilitarians can recognise the importance of these things by seeing the long-term well-being or goods generated by them, rather than focusing on the particular benefits of certain circumstances.

Rule utilitarians provide a guide for people to know what to do. They do not need to calculate every individual situation, something that might be rather difficult to do in practice. A set of rules are offered, democratically considered and viewed over the long-term, so moral conduct is more straightforward.

These rules can allow for special circumstances, such as the relationship between parents and children, where children need to be cared for by parents. Special relationships are difficult to justify by act utilitarians, who must always consider everyone equally. But rule utilitarians can accommodate rules for special circumstances, for looking after children, the elderly, the sick, etc. as priority goods that overall need to be recognised alongside other immediate concerns.

Discussing utilitarianism

Does utilitarianism provide a helpful method of moral decision-making?

Bernard Williams (*Morality: An Introduction to Ethics,* 1972) suggests utilitarianism is attractive for four reasons: First, it does not require religious belief of a particular kind and so suggests a rational kind of ethics. This fits a world with competing religious systems and provides a practical way of doing morality that is not obscure. Second, its basic good, happiness, well-being or preferences, seems quite reasonable. Who would not want to be happy in life, who would not want to have their preferences taken into account? Why should we not want to maximise the interests or happiness for as many people as we can? Third, it suggests that moral problems can be solved through a reasonable process, rather than a religious theory, which is not universally agreed, or a conceptual or esoteric approach, which some might find obsure. Fourth, it offers a common currency of moral thought that seems relatively straightforward to apply. The various concerns of different interest groups can be accommodated and weighed against one another. We can look at all the options and take into account all of the different claims. Bentham and Mill were social reformers concerned with the good of the people, they seem to have developed a system of ethics that governments could use when deciding which policies to advance – 'Does the policy produce the best outcome for most people?' This is a question we can ask with the utilitarian system.

There are criticisms of utilitarianism however. It relies on guesses about the future, predictions about what will create the greatest good. Can we be sure such guesses are right? It offers no reason to prohibit any action, but surely some acts can never be justified, like torturing children, genocide, rape? We must need some rules that can never be broken for a convenient result? There also seems to be unfairness towards minorities. Perhaps a community will be much happier if a small migrant group could be forced to leave, but wouldn't something else be lost which is harder to quantify but clear to perceive – something about equality, human rights, justice and fairness? Utilitarianism seems less able to deal with these sorts of ideas and ideals and they seem to matter, morally speaking.

Apply your knowledge

Jim and the Indians

Jim finds himself in the central square of a small South American town. Tied up against the wall are a row of twenty Indians, most terrified, a few defiant, in front of them several armed men in uniform. A heavy man in a sweat-stained khaki shirt turns out to be the captain in charge and, after a good deal of questioning of Jim, which establishes that he got there by accident while on a botanical expedition, explains that the Indians are a random group of the inhabitants who, after recent acts of protest against the government, are just about to be killed to remind other possible protestors of the advantages of not protesting. However, since Jim is an honoured visitor from another land, the captain is happy to offer him a guest's privilege of killing one of the Indians himself. If Jim accepts, then as a special mark of the occasion, the other Indians will be let off.

Of course, if Jim refuses, then there is no special occasion, and Pedro here will do what he was about to do when Jim arrived, and kill them all. Jim, with some desperate recollection of schoolboy fiction, wonders whether if he got hold of a gun, he could hold the captain, Pedro and the rest of the soldiers to threat, but it is quite clear from the set-up that nothing of the sort is going to work: any attempt at that sort of thing will mean that all the Indians will be killed, and himself. The men against the wall, and the other villagers understand the situation, and are obviously begging him to accept. What should he do?

J.J.C. Smart and Bernard Williams, *Utilitarianism: For and Against,* 1973, pp. 98–9

15. What do you think is best way to try and solve this terrible dilemma? By referring to rules about what we must and must not do? By referring to the outcomes, the ends? By thinking about the character of Jim and what any decision he does might do?

16. What do you think Mill and Bentham would say is the right thing to do and why?

Can an ethical judgement about something being good, bad, right or wrong be based on the extent to which, in any given situation, utility is best served?

Ethical judgements are about serving utility, in the view of utilitarians – the judgement weighs goods and evils and works out which option offers the best, or least bad, option. This is a practical benefit for utilitarianism in that there is never a situation where no option is right. If you follow an ethical

The healthy sacrifice

A transplant doctor has five desperate patients. To save them the doctor needs to find a healthy heart, liver, lungs and two kidneys. Time is running out and there are no blood matches. A healthy man comes into the clinic one day for a blood test – he is a perfect match for all five patients. It is their last chance. The doctor considers sacrificing the healthy man to save the lives of the other five.

17. What do you think is the right thing to do from a utilitarian perspective?

18. Is something sacrificed for utility?

Oscar Wilde once said, 'Do not do unto others as you would have them do unto you; they may have different tastes'

system which lists rules and are faced with a dilemma that only presents options which break the rules, then you cannot act morally. Suppose you are halfway across a rope bridge and see a child has slipped off and is hanging on at one end, and and elderly person has slipped and is hanging on at the other end. If you are the only person then you must choose who to run to first and this may mean consigning the other person to a fatal fall. A rule that says 'always save life' does not help, but utilitarianism might nudge you to run to the child on the basis of the future life. The war-time decision to send some troops forward to buy time for the evacuation of a town, places their lives in danger. Weighing the interests of all seems fairer than respecting old rules, rules which may serve the interests of the few, rather than the many – such as the rules of the past that allowed the slave trade.

However, there might be goods other than utility. If an individual can be sacrificed because of the interests of the majority, how can a utilitarian society be just? Alasdair MacIntyre, in his book *A Short History of Ethics* (1966) criticises utilitarianism as possibly justifying horrendous acts for the pleasure of the many. Do minorities have no interests or rights that should be protected? The majority may well take against a minority or single person and may prefer to see them locked away for life, or used for their own happiness (such as people-trafficking for the sex trade) but this would be unfair. If the majority feel safer when someone is locked up and punished for a crime he did not actually commit, how can it be wrong even if the true criminal has long since escaped the town? A utilitarian might have difficulty explaining why this situation is wrong. Justice and fairness, equality and rights are things that seem to matter as well as utility. A society which is prepared to sacrifice aspects of these in certain circumstances might run counter to moral intuitions.

Is it possible to measure good or pleasure and then reach a moral decision?

Utilitarianism relies on measuring happiness or goodness and setting that against sadness or evil. Both Bentham and Mill recognised that these terms (pleasure, goodness, well-being, etc.) gather up lots of different things. There are many quite different sorts of 'goods': the moment of a first kiss, the taste of sugar, the feeling of a job well done, the familiarity of a song from youth, the sensation of pain easing after applying a local anaesthetic, the achievement of a life ambition, and so on. Are joy, happiness, satisfaction, relief, thrill, enjoyment, delight, contentment, enrichment, engagement, all describing the same thing? Perhaps it is not so easy to judge! What happens if we have different views about the goods? Oscar Wilde once said, 'Do not do unto others as you would have them do unto you; they may have different tastes.' If people do not share the same idea of pleasure or share similar ideas about what their interests are then utilitarianism may be more difficult to work through. Alasdair MacIntyre is also suspicious of using notions of happiness: 'that men are happy with their lot never entails that their lot is what it ought to be. For the question can always be raised of how great the price is that is being paid for the happiness' (*A Short History of Ethics*, 1966, p. 239). My happiness may have come at a price others paid.

A second complication is our ability to be confident about the future. Utilitarianism, of every kind, requires some future predictions of how people's interests will be affected by the choices that we make. Is this a straightforward thing to do? Does utilitarianism presume too much foreknowledge?

....

66 For want of a nail the shoe was lost.

For want of a shoe the horse was lost.

For want of a horse the rider was lost.

For want of a rider the message was lost.

For want of a message the battle was lost.

For want of a battle the kingdom was lost.

And all for the want of a horseshoe nail.

99

Traditional

....

Apply your knowledge

19. Which of the following views are the most compelling? Respond to each with arguments for and against:

   a. 'Happiness is not always shared. Sometimes guessing that you will be happy with what I find makes me happy can lead to me imposing on you my values and preferences.'

   b. 'Predicting future happiness is unreliable guesswork. The midwife who delivered baby Adolf for his mother, Mrs Hitler, thought she was doing the right thing.'

   c. 'Weighing happiness/goodness comes down to measuring the worth of human beings. Once we have decided the many are more important than the few then we can do anything we like with the few in the service of the many's happiness, at the sacrifice of the few.'

   d. 'Quantifying happiness is unreliable. How can you compare the joy of spring with being fit and well?'

Learning support

Points to remember

» It is important to be precise about the different ethical thinkers as well as the theories. It is easy to simply refer to a theory without talking about the individuals, but in many cases this can lead to generalisations and mistakes. In the case of utilitarianism, the different forms have different weaknesses and strengths. Act and rule utilitarianism have differences.

» Deontological theories like Kantian ethics, or natural law, bind us to rules about certain acts that are prohibited. Utilitarianism offers a formula to make a judgement about what to do even if there are only two bad options available. Ethical theories linked with religious systems give authority to the religious experts who know the religious laws, the sacred texts or the moral doctrines and how to apply them, whereas utilitarianism is democratic and in the hands of humanity to operate.

» Relativists might be attracted to utilitarianism as it seems unencumbered by rules, although they would be mistaken to think moral judgements should be culturally relative or individually subjective – morality is relative to the results. Absolutists will probably be horrified about the idea that nothing is objectively wrong. Of course absolutists may be absolutist about principles – like the greatest good for the greatest number.

» Utilitarianism seems interested in the development of democracy and a concern for everyone.

» Situationists may feel utilitarianism is close to their thinking. They are concerned with the most loving thing to do, and utilitarians are concerned with pleasure, happiness or preferences. A situationist is prepared to commit an act if, in the circumstances, it is the most loving thing, just as a utilitarian might. Both situationists and utilitarians look towards the ends rather than actions. Both have a system of calculation and both put moral responsibility in the hands of the human being, though situationists are supposed to have some understanding of Christian love. Utilitarians do think there is a right answer, whilst situationists may not.

Enhance your learning

» All of Jeremy Bentham's major works are available online, through an Internet search, and he is quite readable. Look first for Bentham, J. (1789) *An Introduction to the Principles of Morals and Legislation*.

» You can also find John Stuart Mill's work online. It is equally readable. Search for Mill, J.S. (1863) *Utilitarianism*.

» The modern utilitarian, Peter Singer, has written extensively on utilitarianism and is useful both for understanding the theory in general and also because he writes about his own particular form of utilitarianism, preference utilitarianism. See Singer, P. (1993) *Practical Ethics*.

» For a really good chapter on utilitarianism, look at chapter 7 in Pojman, L. (2012) *Discovering Right and Wrong*.

» An older but interesting book which debates classic utilitarianism is Smart, J.J.C. and Williams, B. (1973) *Utilitarianism, For and Against*.

Practice for exams

AS questions and A level questions look identical; the difference between AS and A level assessment is seen in the different proportions of marks awarded for two different skills: the skill of demonstrating knowledge and understanding (Assessment Objective 1, or AO1), and the skill of constructing a critical argument (AO2).

At AS, half the marks (15 marks) are available for knowledge and understanding, and the other half (15 marks) for the quality of your analytical and evaluative argument. You should aim to use your knowledge in order to support the argument you are making throughout the essay, rather than presenting descriptive knowledge in the first half and then an opinion in the second.

At A level, your demonstration of knowledge and understanding is awarded a maximum of 16 marks, and your analytic and evaluative skills are awarded a maximum of

24 marks. You should aim to concentrate on constructing a lucid argument, making use of your knowledge to add weight to the conclusions you draw.

'Rule utilitarianism is an improvement on act utilitarianism.' Discuss.

In this question you are being asked to make a critical evaluation of rule utilitarianism in comparison with act utilitarianism.

Practise your skills for AS level

If you are answering this at AS level, you will need to be able to demonstrate an accurate understanding of both act and rule utilitarianism and the differences between the two. You also need to formulate and justify an opinion about whether rule utilitarianism does improve on act utilitarianism.

Practise your skills for A level

If you are answering this question as an A Level student, you need to combine your knowledge and understanding with a persuasive line of argument. For example, you could consider how practical each is and whether it leads to morally right actions in different contexts. You might think that both are equally valuable or that neither works. Your essay should follow an argument throughout, rather than focusing mainly on a description of different kinds of utilitarianism.

How fair is the claim that there are more important goals for human ethics than the seeking of pleasure over pain?

This question asks you to consider the goal of utilitarianism as the maximising of pleasure and the minimising of pain, and decide whether it is the best possible goal for ethics or whether other goals might be preferable.

Practise your skills for AS level

At AS level, you need to show that you have a thorough understanding of the principle of utility, and you should compare it with other possible goals for ethics, such as the goal of doing one's duty or the goal of living according to the principle of agape. You should aim to give a clear explanation of how fair you think the claim in the question really is.

Practise your skills for A level

At A Level, you should concentrate largely on presenting a persuasive and coherent argument. In your argument, you need to be able to weigh up the justification for different goals for ethics, looking at different possibilities, such as the goal of pleasing God. You should evaluate the strength of the reasoning in support of them and reach your own balanced judgement on which is the most important.

Chapter 2.5

Euthanasia

Should life be preserved at all costs?
Is life ever not worth living?
Does the value of life include the power to choose the manner and time of its end?

Key Terms

Non Treatment Decision: the decision medical professionals make to withhold or withdraw medical treatment or life support that is keeping a person alive because they are not going to get better, or because the person asks them to. Controversially it is also sometimes called passive euthanasia

Active euthanasia: a deliberate action performed by a third party to kill a person, for example by lethal injection. Active euthanasia is illegal in the UK.

Sanctity of life: the idea that life is intrinsically sacred or has such worth that it is not considered within the power of a human being

Quality of life: a way of weighing the extrinsic experience of life, that affects or justifies whether or not it is worth continuing life

Personhood: the quality of human life that makes it worthy – usually linked to certain higher capacities

Autonomy and the right to die: the idea that human freedom should extend to decide the time and manner of death

Voluntary euthanasia: this applies when a person's life is ended painlessly by a third party at their own request

Non-voluntary euthanasia: this applies when a person is unable to express their wish to die but there are reasonable grounds for ending their life painlessly, for example if a person cannot communicate but is in extreme pain

Dignity: the worth or quality of life, which can be linked to sanctity or freedom

Palliative care: end-of-life care to make the person's remaining moments of life as comfortable as possible

Involuntary euthanasia: where a person is killed against their wishes, for example when disabled people were killed by Nazi doctors

Specification requirements

Key ideas, including:

- sanctity of life
- quality of life
- voluntary euthanasia
- non-voluntary euthanasia

The application of natural law and situation ethics to euthanasia

Introduction

There are many ethical questions that can be asked of end-of-life situations. If a person wishes to end their own life because they feel it is not worth living, should they be permitted or stopped? Should they be helped? If they are helped, is there a difference between helping them into a position where they can carry out the final act themselves (such as by giving them lethal pills), and actually doing it for them (such as by administering a lethal injection)? Ethical questions also arise if someone is not in a position to decide for themselves about ending their life because they are in a permanent coma or on a life support machine. Ethical debates about euthanasia are sometimes linked to suicide, but these debates are not the focus of this chapter.

Doctors are often in situations where decisions must be made about withholding or withdrawing medical treatment that is keeping a person alive because they are not going to get better and because the person (or their family) asks for this. Medical professionals call this a **Non Treatment Decision**. A Non Treatment Decision is not against the law in the UK and is not regarded as euthanasia under UK law.

Active euthanasia is where a third party acts deliberately to kill another person. Euthanasia should not be confused with assisted dying or assisted suicide. These involve the person themselves, and not a third party, completing the final action to end their own life. Assisted dying is when the person is terminally ill and dying, and assisted suicide is when the person is seriously ill but not dying.

Euthanasia is illegal in the UK. Some countries, including the Netherlands, Switzerland and Oregon, Vermont and Washington in the United States of America do, however, permit forms of euthanasia, assisted dying and assisted suicide.

The ethical debates around euthanasia typically explore four elements:

- The religious idea of **sanctity of life** is the idea that life has an intrinsic worth that means it should never be ended by human action.

- The secular (non-religious) idea of the **quality of life**, which seeks to establish whether there are occasions when life is not worth living. Quality of life is often explained through discussion of **personhood** and **autonomy and the right to die**.

- **Voluntary euthanasia** – being able to choose the time and nature of one's death because their life is ended painlessly by a third party at their request. Voluntary euthanasia raises questions about autonomy and the quality of life lived.

- **Non-voluntary euthanasia** – deciding to end a person's life when they cannot make that decision for themselves. This tends to be concerned with cases where patients are believed to be brain-dead, or in a persistent vegetative state and doctors, family members or courts are involved in judging whether it is justifiable to remove treatment.

Aquinas' natural law is the subject of Chapter 2.1.

Situation ethics is the subject of Chapter 2.2.

Think question

What makes life so special?

The two ethical theories applied to euthanasia in this chapter are natural law and situation ethics.

Aquinas' natural law approach is deontological. It is based around actions that are in accordance with the purpose of human life, and the key divine laws, the primary precepts which govern human action. The protection of life is central to those laws, and the Catholic Church, which draws heavily on natural law theory, is opposed to euthanasia. Life is a sacred gift from God to be protected. However, burdensome treatment which unnecessarily extends life is not required or even allowed, as there is a natural time to die and the human experience of life is also part of God's purpose.

Fletcher's situation ethics focuses moral decision-making not on legalism, nor on the laws of the land, but on the situation the person is in. It applies unconditional love to the person and makes the decision with love in mind. It does not determine what is right or wrong, but the process for making a good decision, which might involve lovingly helping a person to die. Fletcher also thought that personhood mattered and that on many occasions the person was no longer truly present in situations of euthanasia and, therefore, taking the life could be permitted.

The sanctity of life and its relevance to the modern world

The sanctity of life is an idea based on the supreme and intrinsic specialness of human life in itself. The thinking is as follows: Life is the foundation of all human experience and the protection of life is a basic prerequisite. It is the most precious gift of a human being, affording consciousness, the ability to act, the ability to show compassion and the possibility of change and alternatives. Once life is gone, all other gifts are lost. This may be grounded in religious teachings (human beings are created in the image and likeness of God, or life is God's gift), or in an observation about the qualities of human life (humans are rational free beings), or both.

The religious origins of sanctity of life

In Genesis it is specifically said of human beings, that man and women were created in the image and likeness of God (Genesis 1:27). This image and likeness is not explained in Genesis but is the foundation of some thinking called the 'imago dei'. It is taken to mean that there are both features about human beings which set them apart from other creatures and that in some way are similar to aspects of God, such as the human capacity to love or the level of sentient ability humans have. Perhaps it is these rational and moral features of human life that make them in God's image and likeness.

There is a specialness to humanity. Throughout the Hebrew Scriptures (the Old Testament) God makes covenants with humankind, which gives humans obligations and blessings. They have to be a kingdom of priests and a holy nation. Their rational and moral facilities are joined to a distinctive divine purpose and destiny that God has for them, this means they stand apart from others. In Christian theology, human beings are unique above all other creatures that God has made on earth. The early Christian thinker Lactantius (c.240–320AD) said that God had made humankind as a sacred animal and so humankind has dignity (worth or sanctity). Christian views about God's purpose in creating the world, his purpose in saving humanity by sending Jesus to die on the cross, is all linked to this worth and destiny.

This sanctity means that human life should not be sacrificed. In Genesis 22:2 Abraham is at first ordered to sacrifice his son Isaac but God counters this order and instead instructs that he replace his son with a ram. The practice of offering human sacrifices is not permissible under God as human life has sanctity.

Some Protestant traditions hold that the **dignity**, the image and likeness of God that human beings had at creation was largely lost due to the sin of Adam and Eve (D. Cairns, *The Image of God*, 1973, pp. 127–33). Human beings do have the power of rational thought and will, but it has become corrupted by sinful immorality. However, there is a possibility that this sanctity can be regained through the salvation offered through Christ. In this view, God sent Christ to save everyone, so even if a person lives a sinful life and shows no sense of their own sanctity, there is a possibility of salvation.

The Hebrew Scriptures (the Old Testament) contain examples where the sanctity of life might be questioned; such as God's destruction of Sodom and Gomorrah, the command to Joshua to destroy the inhabitants of the Promised Land because they were evil in God's sight and God's command to Abraham to sacrifice Isaac. However, the Office of the Chief Rabbi issued a memorandum that stated, 'Jewish tradition places at its centre the sanctity of life, viewing life as a precious gift from God, not something we can dispose of at will. Indeed the value of life is absolute and not relative to factors such as age and health' (cited by M. Warnock and E. Macdonald, *Easeful Death*, 2008, p. 69).

The concept that life is sacred is often important to those who are opposed to euthanasia and is often associated with religious beliefs about the prevention of curtailing life before its natural end. Ancient laws ban the taking of life. Life is identified as a gift from God in some traditions, so precious that it falls beyond the things human beings have authority over. Preserving the sanctity of life may be a matter of obedience to religious authority. Philosophers who do not ground their thinking in religion identify features like self-consciousness, rational ability, free will and a capacity for compassion as possible justifications for the higher status of human life granted by the phrase 'sanctity'.

Discussions about the sanctity of life are centred around a number of associated ideas:

- that life taking is an ultimate taboo – it is too precious, untouchable
- that in taking one life other human lives are endangered because the status of life is undermined

Think question

Try to give a secular rationale for the *sanctity* of life.

Apply your knowledge

1. Consider these possible justifying claims for the sanctity of life and any others you can think of: God's creation; humans uniquely have a freedom to act; humans uniquely have the power of reason and rationality; humans uniquely have a moral capacity. Try to reject/ refute each one. Is it possible that there is no special claim for the sanctity of life?

2. Is the sanctity of life ever justifiably set aside for some higher claim? Consider self-sacrifice, self-defence and the greater good.

Think question

Is there ever a point at which life is not worth living and who should decide whether this point has been reached?

Perhaps whether life is worth living is not a question about the inherent or intrinsic qualities of life, but the experience of living it

- that with life there are always unexpected possibilities which end once life is gone

- that once the ending of lives is justifiable, life is undermined in a societal sense – once euthanasia is countenanced, elderly patients may fear hospitals as places where people can choose death for them. It sets a potentially destructive precedent that gives someone else authority to end another person's life.

The link between the claim that life is supremely precious and the ban on it ever being taken can be questioned. There are occasions when taking a life is arguably a moral thing to do, the lesser of two evils, a necessary act to protect a greater number of lives. Sometimes people are required to give up their lives for the good of others – such as soldiers fighting to protect others. The act of self-defence is used to justify breaking the taboo. Self-sacrificial acts, like jumping on a live grenade to save your comrades, might justify breaking the life taboo. Does euthanasia have some equivalent qualifying reasons to justify taking a life (assuming these other examples are justifiable)? A qualifying reason might be regarding the quality of life lived, or the need to show compassion for the suffering individual.

Alternatively, is there an overriding reason why euthanasia is particularly bad, such that there can be no qualifying or justifying reason permitting the breaking of a taboo? Perhaps there is a concern for what this would do to the status of life and what the unintended consequences following from the 'downgrading' of life's status might be?

The quality of life

The Jewish and Christian traditions emphasise the preciousness of human life with the idea of the sanctity of life, the idea that humans are made in the image and likeness of God, and the idea that God has a divine destiny for human lives. Human life is often set above any sense of measurement, in terms of its value to God.

However, other ideas have influenced the debate about euthanasia, particularly those connected with the notion of the quality of life: that human life has to possess certain attributes in order to have value. Closely connected to this are questions of whether a life has personhood or autonomy. Perhaps whether life is worth living is not a question about the inherent or intrinsic qualities of life, but the experience of living it.

There are occasions when a person is in a terrible situation. This may be a deteriorating situation, such as when facing the onset of a disease. It might also be found in the case of severely disabled babies, or when facing a slow and painful death with a terminal condition. Deterioration might include the loss of abilities, leading to muscular degeneration and paralysis. Cognitive abilities may deteriorate affecting the recognition of loved ones or the recollection of memories. As memory disappears the

Although medics told Stephen Hawking in 1963 that he probably had only two more years to live, he has gone on to have a fabulously productive and worthwhile life

personality of a person may change. The body may lose consciousness; the body surviving without self-awareness. A sudden trauma may lead to brain death. In such situations perhaps there is no quality of life – no life worth living. Death could be judged better than life and many secular thinkers argue that religious beliefs about sanctity, or divine punishment are not good justifications for laws against euthanasia.

An alternative to thinking about the sanctity or holiness of life is to consider the quality of life. Human beings should be able to live dignified lives and end life with dignity. This is not simply a matter of pain, but of self-respect. Sometimes it seems that the most compassionate thing to do is give a pet a lethal injection, rather than allow it to live on in a ghastly and confused shadow of a former healthy, active and purposeful life. A life of intolerable pain adds nothing. If there is no hope of recourse, then ending it is arguably the most compassionate thing to do.

The ability to act may be curtailed when individuals are paralysed or suffer degeneration that leaves them unable to perform all but a very limited number of actions. However, individuals such as the world-leading scientist Stephen Hawking, have shown that heavily curtailed physical activity need not prevent a great life from being lived.

The secular (non-religious) origins of the concept of the quality of life

Traditionally, Christianity has opposed euthanasia for the reasons discussed already in this chapter, but there have have always been challenges to this kind of thinking. Plays from Ancient Greece capture the desire for euthanasia. In *Prometheus Bound* by Aeschylus, the character Eos is desperately entrenched in psychological problems. He says, 'It were better

Apply your knowledge

3. What are the different aspects that determine the quality of life? Consider freedom, self-control, having a higher function such as memory and one other of your choice. Identify how these might affect life's quality.

4. Research two examples of lives lived that seem to have meaning despite at first glance having limited quality.

to die once and for all than to drag out my lingering days in anguish' (Aeschylus, 'Prometheus Bound.' In *Aeschylus. Prometheus Bound. The Greeks*, ed. O. Hatzopoulos, 1992, pp. 90–1, lines 760–1). In Sophocles' play the *Women of Trachis*, the character Heracles is suffering from unbearable pain and asks his son Hyllu, to help him die: 'Lay my body thereupon and kindle it with flaming pine-torch. And let no tear of mourning be seen there' (Sophocles, 'Women of Trachis.' In *Sophocles. Women of Trachis. The Greeks*, ed. O. Hatzopoulos, 1992, 136–7, lines 1206–8).

The Greek physician Hippocrates (460–370BC) may have been the originator of the Hippocratic Oath, but he seems to have been in favour of a form of euthanasia in cases of incurable patients. He suggested a doctor should: 'refuse to treat those who are overmastered by their disease realizing that in such cases, medicine is powerless' (S.G. Marketos and P. Skiadas, *Plato: The Most Important Proponent of Euthanasia in Ancient Greece*, 1999/2000, 12, pp. 32–5).

The power of the Church meant that laws opposed euthanasia and suicide in Europe, but euthanasia remained a debated topic.

Over time a number of thinkers began to challenge the domination of the Church on culture and laws and in modern times pressure has grown from organisations seeking to challenge laws developed from Christian thinking. Of course there are Christians who support euthanasia, such as Joseph Fletcher, but a key non-religious argument is that euthanasia has traditionally been prohibited on supernatural grounds related to the afterlife, something about which we can know nothing for certain, and therefore something that people reasonably hold different beliefs about.

One view that expressed this frustration is that of Kevin Smith, a Board member of the Canadian Centre for Inquiry (CFI). This is an organisation that seeks to to provide education and training to the public in the application of sceptical, secular, rational and humanistic inquiry:

66 In our secular society, euthanasia must be a personal decision between the terminally ill and their families, without idle threats of supernatural damnation. It is ethically criminal to toss guilt and shame into a tragic situation. 99

www.patheos.com/blogs/friendlyatheist/2012/01/10/
a-secular-take-on-euthanasia/

Think question

Is an adult chimpanzee more of a person than a newborn human?

Personhood

The extent to which a life has some quality about it is often linked to the extent to which there is personhood. If the human body is living but many or most of the higher functions are missing, should the body continue to be considered a moral person of worth as much as someone

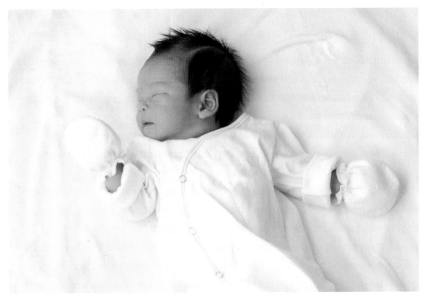

Is a newborn baby only a potential person?

who is healthy? Is euthanasia justified for someone in an irreversible coma, or when the brain is, to all intents and purposes, dead? Perhaps it is possible to distinguish between a living body that has lost its status of worth because it does not have, or has lost, higher functions – the things that truly make us human beings.

The awareness of self, others, the world, and the will and ability to act are the most fundamental features of human life. Once the capacity to be aware of self and the world has been lost, in one sense the person is no longer there. The body may be kept alive through artificial methods and may appear to still be a person but arguably in these cases life should be ended as it is no longer fully human (or fully sacred, in religious terms).

The idea of personhood seeks to distinguish between human bodies which are still living despite the loss of the key defining features of humanity, and human beings which we should preserve because they retain such features. Personhood is usually linked to capacities. At one end of a spectrum there is a conscious human being who controls actions, whilst at the other end is living tissue, such as organs or body tissues which are kept alive (perhaps through transplant) even though there is no conscious being in control of these organs. We do not apply the same moral worth to an organ being transplanted, as we do to a conscious human being, however precious that organ is.

Personhood is usually linked to capacities

The permanent loss of the awareness of self and others and of the world could justify euthanasia. Technology today allows the extraordinary continuation of life but it could be wrong to perpetuate such a life against all odds. Switching off life support machines is not considered euthanasia in most cases today. However, there remains a question around who decides on the definition of personhood and how reliable the

Apply your knowledge

5. Try to identify three reasonable criteria for personhood. Consider the following: free will, rational decision-making, memory, moral awareness or something else of your choice.

6. Consider whether or not the following might not be considered a person using your chosen criteria: a person in an irreversible coma; a sleeping person; a newborn baby; a person declared brain-dead; a child with severe learning difficulties; a sociopath serving a life sentence for multiple murders; a man who is fully paralysed, only capable of moving his eyes and eating; an elderly sufferer of very severe Alzheimer's disease.

Think question

Given that freedom of choice is so important in life, why limit its authority so we cannot apply it to the thing that matters most to us – our own life?

We expect to have control over our bodies in matters of life, and supporters of euthanasia say it should be the same in matters of death

assessment of personhood might be. A wrong decision might lead to the death of someone about to recover.

Definitions of personhood that are based exclusively on their capacities are individualistic and inward looking. Perhaps personhood is about how an individual connects with others. The human person is part of a species and is usually part of a group, a family or community. Others relate to the person. A person may be loved and may still have a purpose in, or for, the lives of others. Another difficulty with personhood is the question of potential. Human beings develop and change over their lifespan, developing different capacities. A newborn baby has few developed features of future ability – are they people, or potential people? Someone may appear to the outside world to have some aspect of humanity missing because of a misinterpretation of their inner experience of life. Autistic children might be interpreted as not having emotion, whilst their internal experience may be of massive emotional overload. Is it reasonable, or possible, for one person to confidently and accurately judge the interior personhood of another?

Autonomy and the right to die

A person facing an incurable deteriorating illness has the option of taking their own life, but to do so they would lose what time they had left with some quality of life. They would rather have that precious time, but once they lost their freedom they would need the help of another person to end their life.

John Stuart Mill argued that in matters that do not concern others, individuals should have full autonomy:

> 66 The only part of the conduct of any one, for which [a citizen] is amenable to society, is that which concerns others. In the part which merely concerns himself, his independence is, of right, absolute. Over himself, over his body and mind, the individual is sovereign. 99
>
> John Stuart Mill, *On Liberty*, 1859, p. 22

We expect to have control over our bodies in matters of life, and supporters of euthanasia say it should be the same in matters of death. Jack Kevorkian, a doctor who has assisted people to take their own lives, said, 'In my view the highest principle in medical ethics – in any kind of ethics – is personal autonomy, self-determination. What counts is what the patient wants and judges to be a benefit or a value in his or her own life. That's primary' (quoted by R.M. Gula. In *Christian Ethics. An Introduction*, ed. B. Hoose, 1998, p. 279). Hans Küng has stated '… as a Christian and a theologian I am convinced that the all-merciful God, who has given men and women freedom and responsibility for their lives, has also left to dying people the responsibility for making a conscientious decision about the manner and time of their deaths' (Voluntary Euthanasia Society, *Factsheet: Religion*, 2001).

Advocates of euthanasia argue that true autonomy is having the right to choose the time and manner of one's own death, and society should permit the giving of help to do this. The loss of freedom and autonomy might lock them into a situation where they can no longer act as they wish, to finish life, deprived of the 'dignity' of their own choice of a good death. To maximise their fully lived life, advocates of euthanasia argue that it should be permissible for a person to get help to die at the time of their choosing, not simply at a time when they are still able to do it themselves. In his article 'Why Physicians Should Aid the Dying' (*Ethics in Practice: An Anthology*, LaFollette, ed., 1977, pp. 22–32), Gregory E. Pence argues that killing humans who don't want to live is not wrong – it is not wrong to help the dying to die, because they are actually dying.

Opponents of euthanasia argue that the autonomous 'right to die' could become an indirect threat to others, especially those with low self-esteem. They might come to see themselves as a burden. The 'right to die' may encourage them, when what they need are other kinds of help. Freedoms come with reasonable limitations and responsibilities; the right to free speech does not permit inciting violence. If a freedom puts others in danger, then it is restricted. The right to die might lead to improper harm for others – it might make it easier for wicked people to get rid of elderly relatives. There are already cases of doctors using their power to end a life against a person's will. Finally, the right to die requires someone to have a responsibility for supporting such a right. This would entail the support of health professionals. Some opponents argue it is wrong to oblige health professionals to be involved in activities or institutions which support the right to die.

Apply your knowledge

7. How might there be tension between individual freedom and the interests of the many if the right to die was permitted?

8. Examine the following views and consider which is most compelling:

   a. 'It is wrong to require some health professionals to assist others in their right to die in the time and manner of their choosing.'

   b. 'The right to die is part of our most basic freedom and a human society should support individual freedom about the things that really matter.'

Voluntary euthanasia

The earliest doctors questioned the ethics of carrying out a *merciful* death. Hippocrates wrote, 'I will not prescribe a deadly drug to please someone, nor give advice that may cause his death.' The Hippocratic oath has informed the ethical code of doctors. Killing a patient seems opposed to what a doctor should do. A doctor should heal and assist people in living a healthy life.

Voluntary euthanasia is when a person's life is ended painlessly by a third party at their own request. Such decisions and requests are a serious matter. Jonathan Glover (*Causing Deaths and Saving Lives*, 1977) suggests several factors that should be considered before deciding what to do when faced with a request.

1. The helper should be convinced the decision is serious: properly thought through and not the result of a temporary state.

2. The helper should think the decision is reasonable. If a person says their life is not worth living but the helper thinks it is, this needs further discussion before a decision is made.

3. The circumstances in which the request comes need considering. Are they liable to change or will unaided suicide never be possible?

Think question

Is there a difference between standing by and allowing someone to commit suicide and actively helping them do so?

Hippocrates of Kos (460–370BC)

Glover says, 'To refuse to provide help is a very serious denial of the person's autonomy over the matter of his own life and death, and is only to be justified by appealing to either the future quality of his life or to side effects' (Glover, *Causing Deaths and Saving Lives*, 1977, p. 184). Glover distinguishes between situations where the person commits the final act themselves (taking pills a helper may have provided) and where another person commits the final act (such as administering a lethal injection to the person who wants to die).

Voluntary euthanasia is often requested in very difficult circumstances. It may also be wished when a person faces progressive paralysis, an inability to control one's bodily functions, or in cases where the ability to communicate or form coherent thoughts are deteriorating. They may be experiencing serious distress when they make the request. Where a person cannot bear to continue – where the quality of life is such that life is considered not worth living, then voluntary euthanasia may be asked for. Glover questions whether we can reliably know how committed a person is to such a request, given their pain. He suggests it may not be possible to ever be really sure what a person truly wants in a neutral sense.

Voluntary euthanasia is often a focus of campaigns for legal change, particularly by those who believe it should be something that people may be assisted with, with some medical support, as an alternative to the more violent and unreliable methods available to a person who commits suicide without access to medical expertise. Campaigners for voluntary euthanasia wish for an option to die in hospital or at home with correct medical supervision and pharmaceutical assistance, instead of having to take chances with other methods.

Another key motivation for voluntary euthanasia is a concern that physical deterioration will at some point make it impossible to easily choose suicide without help, but up until that point a person may want to live. The availability of voluntary euthanasia allows a person to enjoy life up until the point at which they can no longer act autonomously in any meaningful way.

Voluntary euthanasia campaigners are also concerned about the legal repercussions of those who help. Family and friends may face prosecution if they assist a person seeking death, such as taking them to a part of the world where euthanasia is legal and practiced, with the intention to end life.

Voluntary euthanasia is most often carried out through the use of lethal medicines that actively stop life (active euthanasia).

There are three common reasons given for not permitting voluntary euthanasia, which Glover calls side effects:

1. Allowing voluntary euthanasia could lead to **involuntary euthanasia**, as in the situation in Nazi Germany when people were 'euthanatized' (murdered) if they had serious illnesses or disabilities.

2. Allowing voluntary euthanasia would lead to people being discouraged from going to hospital for treatment.

3. Allowing voluntary euthanasia would detrimentally affect end-of-life **palliative care** as the focus would switch to decisions about ending life, not comforting the patient.

Glover rejects all three. He suggests the Nazi policy did not come from a voluntary euthanasia campaign but an evil ideology that devalues certain people's lives. He argues that we do not know how people would behave so cannot assume they would fear going to hospital, and he suggests that it is unlikely that thoughts about ending a life would detract from comforting a person. However, fears about treatment, especially the treatment of the elderly, are a focus of many concerns in the media and, attempts to standardise the process of withdrawing treatment seems in some cases to have led to people not being properly cared for, as in the case of the Liverpool Pathway (discussed later in this chapter).

Glover concludes that while voluntary euthanasia may be morally permissible in principle, this should be subject to the side effects – what actually happens as a result. Any system would have to be carefully devised. The performing of voluntary euthanasia outside any legal process is wrong because it could endanger patients and expose doctors to the risk of being wrongfully accused of murder. Mary Warnock and Elisabeth Macdonald agree, arguing that there may come a time when we need to concede an 'easeful death' to more people than we do currently, and that this would bring compassion into the laws that govern the end of life.

Non-voluntary euthanasia

Non-voluntary euthanasia is euthanasia without request. A person is unable to ask to die and another person acts to end their life on their behalf. Glover distinguishes non-voluntary euthanasia from involuntary euthanasia. With involuntary euthanasia a person is killed against their wishes, such as when disabled people were killed by Nazi doctors – this is regarded as murder. Non-voluntary euthanasia should be in the interest of the person who dies, and not anyone else.

The debate around non-voluntary euthanasia arises from cases where people are in situations where they cannot communicate their wishes but are in a terrible unchangeable state, such as being deprived of their senses, severely brain-damaged or with severe mental deterioration to the extent that they have no higher functions, existing in a state of complete paralysis without the possibility of communication, or brain-dead on life support. Medical science means many of these people can have their physical bodies and physical life sustained, perhaps for the full duration of their natural lives, with no semblance of the person they once were.

Is it compassionate to end these lives? Can love ever justify taking a life? When is it justifiable for doctors to decide a person's life is not worth living and how should that decision become a process of actually ending their life?

Apply your knowledge

Discuss the following points of view:

9. 'Voluntary euthanasia might seem to be a right for the patient, but it becomes a duty for medical staff and turns healers into givers of death. Medical staff should not be required to help people to die. They should be allowed to conscientiously object.'

10. 'Hospitals which allow voluntary euthanasia will frighten the elderly and the sick. They should be places of healing, not places of death.'

11. 'Legalised voluntary euthanasia will encourage mentally distressed people to commit suicide and wicked family members to encourage them.'

12. 'Helping people to die is just another part of helping people to live and is part of a civilised society.'

13. 'Legalising voluntary euthanasia will bring out into the open what probably secretly goes on already, and make it safer.'

Think question

a. What is the ethical distinction between providing ordinary care, such as food and water, and extraordinary care, such as a technology that breathes for the patient?

b. Who should decide when it is right to remove treatment and switch off life support in the case of a persistent vegetative state? Doctors, family members, the courts?

It is common for decisions to be made to withdraw treatment, for example after massive brain damage caused by a stroke in an elderly patient

Some people prepare 'living wills', which advise on their wishes in the event that they suffer an irreparable debilitating injury, leaving them in a state where they have no mental facilities to express their own wishes. This is almost a kind of future intention for conditional voluntary euthanasia in that the person has expressed their will in advance, in the case that certain conditions are met. By definition this precludes any change of mind once the foreseen debilitating circumstances have occurred. However, this could guide doctors and family members in making a decision about ending life-sustaining treatment.

Cases of non-voluntary euthanasia tend to involve cases of brain death, severe brain damage or persistent vegetative state, where there is believed to be no hope of any recovery for a patient left in a condition where no mental thoughts of any sophistication may be formulated or expressed. Obviously a critical issue for non-voluntary euthanasia is the question of who decides that euthanasia should be carried out – family members, doctors or the courts? A second question is whether the state reached is definitely irreversible, or whether there might have been an unexpected or miraculous change in condition where death is not chosen. Some argue that the decision to end a person's life is a decision of defeat which should not be taken.

A distinction is often made between the removal of burdensome treatment which will unnecessarily prolong a painful and unavoidable death, and non-voluntary euthanasia performed by means of lethal injection, for example.

In the UK, the removal of burdensome, extraordinary treatment is permitted and not considered euthanasia. However, a recent attempt to codify this process led to controversy. The Liverpool Care Pathway for the Dying Patient included the use of palliative care options for patients near the end of their lives. It was originally developed to provide quality end-of-life-care but became discredited. Reports suggest patients were casually assessed as terminal, heavily sedated, and denied water with the effect that the diagnosis was self-fulfilling. It was alleged that hospitals were given incentives if they met targets for people who died on the Pathway. It was phased out in 2013/14.

Glover outlines the following options that might frame this moral situation.

Should we:

1. Take all possible steps to preserve life (providing all surgery, medication, food and water possible)?

2. Take all ordinary steps, but not extraordinary steps, to preserve life (limiting surgery and medication but providing food and water)?

3. Not kill, but take no steps to preserve life (not providing surgery or medication, but providing food and water)?

4. Act in a way which does not intend to kill but has death as a foreseen additional effect (for example giving increasingly large doses of morphine, a powerful but ultimately fatal pain reliever and/or removing food and water)?

5. Perform a deliberate act of killing?

(Adapted from J. Glover, *Causing Deaths and Saving Lives*, 1977, p. 195).

This is linked to the doctrine of double effect in natural law, see Chapter 2.1.

Even this range of options is not completely clear-cut. How do we decide precisely what ordinary and extraordinary steps are? Glover suggests that developments in medical technology mean that it is no longer a simple question of whether or not to end a life, but rather whether or not to withdraw a particular treatment option.

Peter Singer describes an example of a case of a woman in the Netherlands in 1984, known as the Alkmaar case (*Rethinking Life and Death*, 1994, pp. 145–6). Mrs B was 95-years-old and on the weekend before her death she was no longer able to eat or drink. She regained consciousness and pleaded with the doctor to help ease her suffering. She pleaded for a mercy killing. The doctor discussed the request with her and her son and agreed life was unbearable. He ended her life and was charged with mercy killing. In court he argued his legal duty not to kill was in conflict with his duty to alleviate suffering. In the end the High Court referred the matter for consideration and the case contributed to the legalisation of voluntary euthanasia in the Netherlands.

Singer argues that the desire for control over how we die marks a turn away from the sanctity of life ethic and that citizens in modern democracies more and more want this control. Increasingly, doctors are willing to break the commandment not to kill, the strongest moral rule that has been taught.

The 'slippery slope' argument comes into discussions about euthanasia. The slippery slope is about unintended consequences that might happen if a course of action is followed. Might voluntary euthanasia lead to undue pressure from the young or the healthy on the elderly or sick? Jonathan Glover (*Causing Death and Saving Lives*, 1977) notes that people who feel they are burdens on their families sometimes commit suicide.

Can we be sure that mistakes will not occur? Suppose that someone chooses death because they have been diagnosed with a fatal, painful and incurable illness. Then, after the person has died, it becomes apparent the diagnosis was incorrect (Brad Hooker, 'Rule Utilitarianism and Euthanasia.' In *Ethics in Practice. An Anthology*, ed., H. LaFollette, 1997, pp. 42–52). Once death has occurred there is no going back. Whilst life remains there are always possibilities.

Slippery slope arguments have a tendency to substitute a worse, future, ethical situation from the immediate one being faced. Focus moves from the actual to the potential. Weighing the fears of future circumstances against the immediate questions of the present is difficult because it requires a future judgement about the consequences.

Whether euthanasia can be distinguished from other actions deemed immoral depends on ethical judgement

Apply your knowledge

14. Explore the issues for each of the following 'interested parties' in considering a case of non-voluntary euthanasia/assisted dying/the removal of life-sustaining treatment and services. List them in order of priority.

   a. Supporting those who have to make the decision on behalf of the patient.

   b. Ensuring the patient's own expressed wishes (for instance through a living will), get them what they want.

   c. Supporting those with the medical responsibility for removing the life-sustaining services.

15. 'For a person who cannot hydrate themselves, withdrawing water is no different from administering a lethal injection. There is no difference between a Non Treatment Decision and active euthanasia in cases of non-voluntary euthanasia'. Discuss.

Think question

Is it ever moral for a person to end their own life or to help someone end their own life?

Euthanasia raises many ethical questions. Is it ever moral for a person to end their own life or to help someone end theirs? Outside war and murderous intention, is it possible that an early death might be the merciful option? Throughout history this has been the issue that has confronted people on battlefields when confronted with a fatally-wounded soldier who will die a lingering death, or perhaps in ancient times by midwives on delivering a baby they believed could not possibly survive. On some occasions the threat of capture was considered worse than death and a defeated side would kill their own, rather than face the consequences. Taking the life of the wounded could be deemed merciful.

Apply your knowledge

A case of non-voluntary euthanasia

Robert Latimer killed his 13-year-old daughter, Tracy, on 24 October 1993. When Tracy was born her oxygen supply was interrupted, leading to cerebral palsy and severe mental and physical disabilities. She had no voluntary control of her muscles, she was unable to walk or talk and was in constant pain. She could not be given painkillers as they caused dangerous seizures. She needed repeated surgery to correct muscular and bone deformities, but attended a special school, and was seen smiling when visited by family. One Sunday, while the rest of the family was at church, Robert Latimer placed his daughter in the trunk of his car and connected a hose to the exhaust. Tracy died of carbon monoxide poisoning. Latimer was

tried for murder and sentenced to life imprisonment with a minimum of 10 years before he would be considered for parole. A retrial found him guilty and sentenced him to two-years imprisonment (Mark Pickup, 'The Murder of Tracy Latimer.' *Human Life Review*, 27, no. 2, 2001, p.74).

16. Which of these rules do you think is the one to follow in this case?

   a. It is always wrong for anyone to kill, because life is sacred.

   b. You can only kill if it results in a better outcome than the alternative.

   c. We must all live in ways that respect life.

   d. You can end life if it is reasonable in the circumstances.

   e. You should never take life, even if the result is bad for you, because killing is wrong in our society.

   f. We must always do the thing that brings about the greatest happiness.

A case of voluntary euthanasia

How to Die: Simon's Choice

Simon Binner was a quick-witted, gregarious, intelligent individual. He was operations director of a business. He was diagnosed with the terminal illness motor neurone disease (MND) and was given six months to live. There is nothing that can be done to slow down such an illness. It progressively removed Simon's ability to speak and, to him, increasingly built a barrier between him and his family members, especially his young son. Simon realised he would no longer see them grow. He could no longer answer the phone. He had to stop driving. Eventually his limbs would stop working until he would be completely paralysed. His breathing would be affected and he would need support for that until his inevitable death. Less than one per cent of patients with MND choose assisted dying. The majority choose palliative care. Most adapt to their increasingly limited circumstances. But for Simon this was too much to consider. Debbie, Simon's wife, was always anti assisted dying. She found the idea of an assisted death horrible and terrifying. In the UK, helping someone to kill themselves is punishable with up to 14 years in prison. Simon's wife found the process of preparing for assisted dying very difficult as did Simon's mother. Simon's mother commented that she did not have the option of being brave, she like the others had to stick it out to the end. On 19 October 2015, Simon Binner died by administration of lethal injection in a clinic in Switzerland. His story was made into a documentary by the BBC called *How to Die: Simon's Choice*.

Apply your knowledge

17. The story presented by the BBC was called 'Simon's Choice'. Who has an 'interest' in Simon's choice? Explain the nature of those 'interests'.

18. The story could have controversially been called 'Debbie's Got No Choice'. Does an individual's right to choose supersede all other interests?

Applying ethical theories to euthanasia

Aquinas's natural law approach

Aquinas' natural law thinking is concerned with morally good actions and the goodness of those actions is determined by the extent to which they accord with the eternal law, a law with a higher authority, and a process of reasoning helps determine what is right and what is wrong. Actions which involve taking one's own life, or that of another, all come under scrutiny. Natural law thinking is concerned not simply with the physical body, but the whole person and their ultimate end, which Aquinas would understand to be linked to God's ultimate plan for that person, and heaven.

Catholic moral thought is informed by natural law. When applying natural law, the primary precepts should be recalled and, in the case of euthanasia, of particular importance is the key precept to do good and avoid evil and the primary precept to preserve life, which upholds the sanctity of life. According to divine law expressed in the Bible, we are created in God's image and knitted together by God in the womb (Psalm 139:13). The purpose of human beings is to live a loving life. The Catholic Church's teachings on euthanasia concludes, therefore, that euthanasia is wrong (*Pastoral Constitution, Gaudium et Spes*, no. 27, 1965) as life is sacred and a gift from God, 'which they are called upon to preserve and make fruitful' (*Declaration on Euthanasia*, 1980). The taking

The Catholic Church's teaching on euthanasia concludes that euthanasia is wrong as life is sacred and a gift from God

of life through euthanasia contravenes divine law. The end of life also ends the possibility of that person bringing love into this world, or love being brought by others in response to that person. It ends the possibility of pursuing any of the other precepts: to educate, live in a community, reproduce, and to worship God. To take a life, according to the Catholic Church, opposes God's love for that person, and rejects the duty of a person to live life according to God's plan. 'Intentionally causing one's own death, or suicide is, therefore, equally as wrong as murder; such an action on the part of a person is to be considered as a rejection of God's sovereignty and loving plan' (*Declaration on Euthanasia*, 1.3, 1980). In addition, the Catholic Church says it is wrong to ask someone to help assist death. No individual can give their consent to such a death: 'For it is a question of the violation of the divine law, an offense against the dignity of the human person, a crime against life, and an attack on humanity' (*Declaration on Euthanasia*, 2, 1980).

Natural law thinking, as interpreted by the Catholic Church, concludes that the act of euthanasia is wrong, and anyone involved in it is committing a wrong act. Euthanasia is an apparent good, that seems to alleviate the suffering of the person, but in fact it is failing to recognise a greater good which is related to the intrinsic nature of life, which in Christian thought is related to that person's place in the mystery of God's greater plan, which includes the people around the person, wider society and life in heaven.

Natural law thinking does not simply lead to conclusions about the taking of an individual life, but also to conclusions about the status of life in general. If it was legal, the practice of euthanasia might scare older people, meaning they may not want to go hospital for fear of being drawn into euthanasia, so they would suffer without the best treatment. Alternatively, it may lead people who would never otherwise have done so to consider euthanasia as an option when they are depressed. This undermines living well together in society as vulnerable people would be harmed, but it also includes some predictions about the 'slippery slope', a future set of circumstances which may or may not actually happen. Euthanasia undermines many of the primary precepts.

The Catholic Church recognises that burdensome treatment should not be offered at the end of a person's natural life. There is a moral obligation not to officiously strive to keep a person alive. A person might feel that they cannot accept treatment because the treatment gives them greater discomfort and makes them less able to live life. For example, cancer patients sometimes decide to stop any further debilitating chemotherapy, although it might extend their life a little, and choose instead to live their remaining life in a way they feel is better and perhaps closer to God's plan for them. Natural law would not prevent them from this kind of choice.

The doctrine of double effect could consider **palliative care** as the principal purpose, even though as a secondary effect, life ends sooner

Aquinas' primary precepts are discussed on pp. 158–60 and the doctrine of double effect on p. 162.

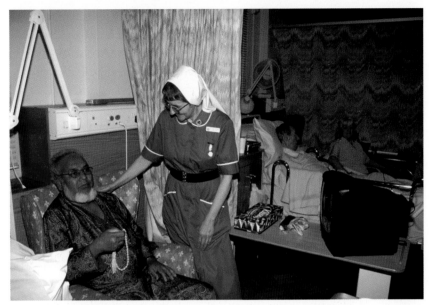

The Catholic Church teaches that people close to the end of their lives should be cared for, but burdensome treatment that undermines the dignity of people in exchange for a little extra time is not appropriate

than otherwise. The intention is not to kill, or to give a person power to end their life, but rather to alleviate pain through reasonable means. This possibility is explicitly recognised in Catholic teaching in the *Catechism of the Catholic Church* and is classified as a Non Treatment Decision in UK medical practice, not euthanasia.

> 66 Discontinuing medical procedures that are burdensome, dangerous, extraordinary, or disproportionate to the expected outcome can be legitimate; it is the refusal of 'over-zealous' treatment. Here one does not will to cause death; one's inability to impede it is merely accepted. The decisions should be made by the patient if he is competent and able or, if not, by those legally entitled to act for the patient, whose reasonable will and legitimate interests must always be respected. 99
>
> *Catechism of the Catholic Church, 2278*

However, there are different circumstances where the human person might not be the sort of person natural law assumes. For example, if the being has none of the higher capacities associated with a human life – decision-making, reasoning and so on; such as in the case of a brain death or permanent coma, then might it be concluded that this body should no longer be considered in the same way? They no longer have the capacity to fulfil their purpose, no longer have the defining characteristics of personhood. This might form the basis of a justification for euthanasia, although there remains the possibility that they could contribute to another person's pursuit of *their* purpose. The physician or

Think question

What is the difference between euthanasia and not using burdensome, life-extending treatment?

Fletcher's situation ethics rejects legalistic approaches to moral decision-making

friend helping to end life might themselves no longer be fulfilling their own purpose in life of showing compassion to another. Also, many of these characteristics are not possessed by young children so using their absence to justify a setting aside of the natural law prohibition of killing seems unlikely.

Fletcher's situation ethics and euthanasia

Fletcher's situation ethics rejects legalistic approaches to moral decision-making. It is grounded in the situation, the experience of the person involved and all those affected in that situation. It is also grounded in love, and more specifically an unconditional (and non-romantic) love that is for, or in the service of others. These are the guiding ideas that are brought to the question of euthanasia. So in the first instance, the question, 'does a situation ethics approach agree with euthanasia?', is always answered, 'it depends on the situation.'

It is the situation of the person that ethics start from according to Fletcher. The person must be listened to attentively and fully understood. Laws about rules and regulations are not brought into the situation, rather the situation must be understood, and the decision made with the full awareness of that situation. It is not that this will decide the right or wrong thing to do, but rather that the moral decision should be made with the information of the situation to hand, along with the guiding principle of unconditional love.

Joseph Fletcher served as president of the Euthanasia Society of America (which was renamed the Society for the Right to Die) from 1974 to 1976 and was seen by some as a chief philosopher of the euthanasia movement. His 1954 book, *Morals and Medicine*, is seen by some as launching the philosophical field of biomedical ethics, where he specifically sets out to argue that there were no absolute moral standards to guide medical treatment, that the ethical thing to do was always guided by the patient's condition and situation. He is attributed to having broken down the barriers to accepting euthanasia. The usual rules about 'do not kill' are not the place to start when making a moral decision, according to Fletcher. You start with the patient, or – in the case of someone in a permanent coma, or in a brain-dead situation – with the physician and/or family members.

Fletcher described euthanasia as death control, like birth control, and saw it as a matter of dignity. He was worried that without death control, or the right to die, as it is called now, people become puppets. Fletcher's approach to euthanasia was based on the notion of patient autonomy. He emphasises the personal dimensions of morality in medical care and rejected naturalism (natural law) as an approach.

For Fletcher (*Situation Ethics*, 1966) the question of the quality of life was more important than the sanctity of life. What was it that made a life valuable, or a life not worth living? He identified positive human criteria, the criteria that might judge whether a being is a human person. They need: a minimal intelligence defined by an IQ of 20 or 40; they needed to have self-awareness and self-control; a sense of the passage of time, the future and the past; concern for others; communication; control of existence; curiosity; the possibility of change and changeability; a balance of rationality and feeling; idiosyncrasy or having an identity; neocortical function (thinking). To be a human being, a person needs these qualities.

It is self-evident, therefore, that situation ethics could support different kinds of euthanasia. It could be considered compassionate to assist a person to end their own life. It could be considered moral to end the life of a being that is not considered a human person. However, it remains the case that Fletcher does not advance a theory that approves euthanasia, but rather that he advances a theory that says the moral decision should be made with the situation in mind, along with love's guiding principle, and without an attachment to legalism.

Discussing euthanasia

Does the religious concept of the sanctity of life have any meaning in twenty-first century medical ethics?

The sanctity of life is an idea that is informed by a particular religious view of the meaning of life — that there is some divine destiny for a person and some purpose to their experience. This is based on a religious belief that God has declared life sacred. However, in an era of democracy and in a time where we recognise there is diversity and plurality of religious belief, should the dogma of the sanctity of life be used to inform law? The absolute ban on taking life that ancient religions have left us precludes the medical science we now have, the ability to know with confidence when life can be saved and when death is inevitable, and the knowledge we have that the human body might continue to survive even when consciousness has gone forever, as when a person is in a persistent vegetative state. Medical science can help us decide when sanctity is no longer a factor as the person no longer exists. Protecting people is one thing, but keeping human bodies alive when the person has gone is another. Arguably, the absolute sanctity of life seems based on outdated knowledge and practices. Now people may live on with a lingering experience of life. Perhaps the religious concept of sanctity fails to accommodate the new medical technologies that enable life to be prolonged.

However, medical science has its limits. Doctors who are experts in palliative care find it difficult to predict when death is inevitable. Death

Think question

Could it be argued that Fletcher's approach to personhood is too prescriptive?

Apply your knowledge

19. Discuss the following claims:

    a. Natural law and character ethics are more interested in society and situation ethics is more interested in the individual.

    b. Situation ethics would justify almost any kind of euthanasia, and is essentially a permissive ethic.

may be extremely likely but there can be considerable uncertainty about time frames. Patients sometimes recover, even if just for a time, when it is least expected.

Perhaps these ideas, while traditionally religious, actually act as social taboos to protect life. There are rational reasons to want to protect and save lives, after all, and it could be argued that modern thought has led us to conclude that all life matters far more than in ancient times. The advent of ideas like democracy and modern notions of dignity and equality, as found in the Universal Declaration of Human Rights, are a concerted attempt to affirm all lives, not just those of the powerful and the rich and not just those that have followed a particular set of beliefs. Sanctity as a concept may have religious origins, but the basic urge to respect all life is one that has currency in many worldviews, religious and non-religious. You do not necessarily need to believe that God has given you a purpose to feel strongly that every life can have meaning and should be respected, recognised and protected from arbitrary decisions.

---

66 Human life is the basis of all goods, and is the necessary source and condition of every human activity and of all society. Most people regard life as something sacred and hold that no one may dispose of it at will, but believers see in life something greater, namely, a gift of God's love, which they are called upon to preserve and make fruitful. And it is this latter consideration that gives rise to the following consequences:

1. No one can make an attempt on the life of an innocent person without opposing God's love for that person, without violating a fundamental right, and therefore without committing a crime of the utmost gravity.

2. Everyone has the duty to lead his or her life in accordance with God's plan. That life is entrusted to the individual as a good that must bear fruit already here on earth, but that finds its full perfection only in eternal life.

3. Intentionally causing one's own death, or suicide, is therefore equally as wrong as murder; such an action on the part of a person is to be considered as a rejection of God's sovereignty and loving plan. **99**

Sacred Congregation for the Doctrine of the Faith: Declaration on Euthanasia, 1980, Vatican: Chapter 1: The Value of Human Life
www.vatican.va/roman_curia/congregations/cfaith/documents/rc_con_cfaith_doc_19800505_euthanasia_en.html

---

Apply your knowledge

20. Discuss the following views:

   a. 'Sanctity refers to religious doctrines that have no place in the modern world of moral decision-making.'

   b. 'The religious tradition that life is sacred, God-given and with some divine purpose, is a way of elevating life's significance.'

   c. 'God gives life and only God has the authority to take life away.'

Should a person have complete autonomy over their own life and the decisions made about it?

Autonomy is an important ethical idea. Philosophers link moral responsibility with our ability to make rational decisions and human beings can be thought of as moral creatures because they can choose when and how to act in life, rather than simply act out of instinct. Advocates of euthanasia argue that our death is a defining aspiration of our life, and a defining feature of human identity. To choose is to be free from enslavement. If autonomy is important throughout life, then it is surely important towards the end of our life.

However, there are a number of questions to consider. In many instances, perhaps most instances, life ends beyond the control of individuals as a result of illness, accident, or the failure of key organs in our body as they reach their natural end. Death comes as a surprise, unexpectedly, and often out of the blue with no time or chance to prepare. To try to hold up autonomy in terms of end-of-life situations flies in the face of the reality that most human beings must face. Our desire to choose this point might be understandable but for the vast majority of people, it is a wish that can never be fulfilled.

Perhaps more difficult is the notion of 'free decision-making' How can we really talk of people being free to choose when presented with their own mortality and their own suffering? Such experiences often overwhelm people emotionally to the degree that the rational decision-making bound up with autonomy is no longer meaningful. Perhaps when advocates of euthanasia talk about choosing the end-of-life circumstances, they really mean allowing desperate people to make desperate decisions, not free ones.

A third question is the extent to which the freedom of some is being given at the expense of the freedom of others. Does my freedom to choose the nature and time of my death oblige other people to facilitate my decision? Does the ability to exercise this kind of right have an impact on others who want a different experience of life, one without hospitals where people are choosing to die, without a culture where death-choice is part of the mix? Will such a culture cause fear among the elderly and vulnerable? Will it create a risk that the processes that permit death will be in danger of abuse or misuse? Rights incur duties on others to enable those rights and the duty to help those who wish for death could be morally difficult to justify, although conscience clauses might work here in the way that they do for issues like abortion. Freedom to choose the manner and time of death of a person raises a number of questions about the nature of freedom and rights. Perhaps one person's freedom becomes another person's duty. Perhaps individual freedom is, in truth, an illusion in that our choices about ourselves have impacts on others.

Apply your knowledge

21. Consider all of the stakeholders who have some 'purchase' on rights around life, death and euthanasia:

    a. The freedom of a sick and elderly person who wants the right to choose the manner and time of their death.

    b. The freedom of medical professionals to refuse death-inducing procedures, and the possible duty of hospitals to provide such services.

    c. The freedom of the sick and elderly to not feel pressured to pursue death under duress and their freedom from the possible abuse or misuse of euthanasia processes.

    d. The freedom or duty of family and friends to help those they care for and love.

Is there a moral difference between medical intervention to end a patient's life and medical non-intervention to end a patient's life?

The medical practice of Non Treatment Decisions is common in the UK. These decisions typically involve withdrawal of, or a decision not to administer, medical or surgical intervention. Ethical behaviour is not just about what you do, it is also about what you do not do. The person who walks on past a drowning person who needs a life ring, is morally responsible for failing to throw it. Inaction, as well as action, has moral consequences. A choice is always made, to act or not to act, and that choosing matters.

What is the difference between allowing someone to die by not doing something and helping them to die by administering a lethal injection? What responsibility do we have for our action and inaction? Are some circumstances more morally justifiable than others?

Some people, when they are suffering from an incurable and debilitating condition, face the possibility that they may need to be resuscitated. Perhaps they are due to have an operation and there is a likelihood they may need to be resuscitated, only then to return to a condition that is arguably even more debilitating than before.

Emphysema in chronic stages is an incredibly debilitating condition, often brought on by smoking. Elderly patients suffering from it face acute difficulties breathing as the linings of the air sacs in the lungs become damaged beyond repair. Air becomes trapped in these spaces of damaged lung tissue causing acute discomfort. Breathing requires painful effort. In this situation it may be necessary to drain the fluid from the damaged areas but for an elderly patient, that operation is very risky. Doctors may decide to ask the patient whether they would wish to be resuscitated should they die during the operation. This is one example where non-intervention would prevent the possibility of a return of life. Another kind of 'non-intervention' is to withdraw the medication that a person needs to stay alive. A third is to withdraw the water and food that a person may be being fed intravenously.

Some would say these cases are different from the introduction of a lethal injection. The lethal injection directly ends a life. It stops the body doing what it naturally seeks to do. It requires a person to act to end life. Perhaps the action has an impact on them. Withdrawing burdensome treatment might make a patient more comfortable as they approach their end. Acting to end life is of a different order: the intention is different; the treatment of life is different. There is a surrender to the natural order of things, rather than a human intervention. Perhaps this difference is subtle, but it is there.

Opponents of euthanasia might argue that the intention of a clinic to bring about the end of life is different from the intention of a medical facility that seeks to save life or, if this is not possible, to make people as comfortable as possible for as long as is not a burden. Opponents of euthanasia always talk about the burdens of treatment but living also brings burdens. A treatment can be legitimately refused if it is painful, debilitating and unlikely to lengthen or improve life significantly; even if such a refusal may lead to an earlier death. This is quite different from the refusal of non-painful, non-debilitating proven treatments (or basic care like feeding, hydrating and keeping warm) in order to bring about death, because life itself is viewed as burdensome and not worth living. It is an important distinction for those opposed to euthanasia.

Apply your knowledge

22. Discuss the differences between these actions/inactions:

a. Not resuscitating a person, with prior consent, because of the likelihood that they would return to an intolerable and worse quality of life.

b. Not undertaking life-sustaining surgery because a person is in a condition that can no longer be improved. The surgery might delay death but not by long and the life experience afterwards would be worse.

c. Removal of medication necessary for life to be sustained when a person says, or has given prior consent, that they no longer wish to be treated once in this state; and when death cannot be delayed for long with the medication and where the life experience is poor.

d. Removal of medication, food and water when a person has had an accident and been placed in a persistent vegetative state with no brain activity.

How important is the presence or absence of prior consent in each example?

Learning support

Points to remember

» Applying Aquinas and Fletcher to euthanasia: these ethical theories show different moral theories in action. Natural law looks at the actions of those involved, while situation ethics seeks to step into the particular context and inform the decision-making, rather than conclude which is right. Examiners will want answers to focus on how the theories address ethical aspects of euthanasia, rather than your personal opinion.

» When applying the theory, note that these thinkers themselves sometimes commented on euthanasia.

» Euthanasia is not about a single moral question, but a set of related moral questions, which go beyond the individual who is experiencing suffering. As is common in moral issues, other people are involved and moral solutions often raise new questions about the impact on others.

Enhance your learning

» Glover's seminal work is excellent reading for this topic. He writes clearly and accessibly: J. Glover, *Causing Death and Saving Life*, 1977, Chapters 14 and 15.

» The Catholic Church's specific response to this question is available online. It is the Declaration on Euthanasia, by the Sacred Congregation for the Doctrine of the Faith (5 May 1980). This is a rich source for quotes on the Catholic teaching on this matter (and its application of natural law to the issue).

» The important contemporary utilitarian philosopher, Peter Singer, has written extensively on this topic, notably in his major work *Rethinking Life and Death: The Collapse of our Traditional Ethics*, 1995; especially Chapter 7, which contains a number of accounts of cases where patients have wanted voluntary euthanasia, and a discussion on the Dutch situation.

» Mary Warnock and Elisabeth Macdonald have written an excellent, readable and short book that looks at more recent cases and focuses on the UK legal situation. *Easeful Death: Is There a Case for Assisted Dying?*,

2008. It is a good development from Glover's and Singer's work.

» British author and euthanasia campaigner, Terry Pratchett, made a moving documentary which is easily found online, called *Choosing to Die*.

Practice for exams

AS questions and A level questions look identical; the difference between AS and A level assessment is seen in the different proportions of marks awarded for two different skills: the skill of demonstrating knowledge and understanding (Assessment Objective 1, or AO1), and the skill of constructing a critical argument (AO2).

At AS, half the marks (15 marks) are available for knowledge and understanding, and the other half (15 marks) for the quality of your analytical and evaluative argument. You should aim to use your knowledge in order to support the argument you are making throughout the essay, rather than presenting descriptive knowledge in the first half and then an opinion in the second.

At A level, your demonstration of knowledge and understanding is awarded a maximum of 16 marks, and your analytic and evaluative skills are awarded a maximum of 24 marks. You should aim to concentrate on constructing a lucid argument, making use of your knowledge to add weight to the conclusions you draw.

'There is a significant moral difference in medicine between not acting to prolong a life and acting to end a life.' Discuss.

This question invites a consideration of whether action to end a life is morally different from a lack of action to prolong a life. If it is different, you need to consider whether the difference is significant.

Practise your skills for AS level

If you are answering this question at AS level, you need to demonstrate understanding of the difference between Non Treatment Decisions and active euthanasia, and the contexts in which each might be a consideration. You are asked to evaluate whether there is a significant moral difference between the two, so you should not concentrate only on what the law says, but also on whether both courses of action are acceptable, whether both are unacceptable, or whether one is more acceptable than the other.

Practise your skills for A level

At A level you could consider different normative ethical approaches in your answer, looking at the extent to which our moral obligations reach, if we have any at all, in the context of the end of life. You might want to argue that some approaches consider that there is a significant moral difference, while others do not; you also need to decide your own opinion on the issue and offer persuasive reasons in support of it.

'In the context of euthanasia, the best way to make moral decisions is to apply the principle of agape.' Discuss.

This question asks you to assess whether issues of euthanasia are best resolved using the approach of situation ethics.

Practise your skills for AS level

At AS level you need to demonstrate a good understanding of the issues of euthanasia and also the main principles of situation ethics, but you should not spend your essay simply describing these. You need to present a coherent line of argument, and decide whether you think agape is a practical and ethical way to guide moral decision-making, and compare this with other approaches to determine which is best.

Practise your skills for A level

At A level, because you are focusing your attention on presenting an argument rather than just description, you should start by considering whether situation ethics is 'best'. This will involve comparing it with other ethical systems, as well as thinking about whether trying to do the most loving thing is practical in the context of decisions about euthanasia.

Chapter 2.6

Business ethics

Do businesses have any responsibilities other than making a profit?
Should businesses base their decisions on ethics?
Can businesses afford to be ethical in a globalised economy?

Key Terms

Capitalism: an economic system based on the private ownership of how things are made and sold, in which businesses compete freely with each other to make profits

Shareholder: a person who has invested money in a business in return for a share of the profits

Corporate social responsibility: a sense that businesses have wider responsibilities than simply to their shareholders, including the communities they live and work in and to the environment

Whistle-blowing: when an employee discloses wrongdoing to the employer or the public

Globalisation: the integration of economies, industries, markets, cultures and policymaking around the world

Stakeholder: a person who is affected by or involved in some form of relationship with a business

Consumerism: a set of social beliefs that put a high value on acquiring material things

Specification requirements

Key ideas, including:

- corporate social responsibility
- whistle-blowing
- good ethics is good business
- globalisation

The application of Kantian ethics and utilitarianism to business ethics

Introduction

What role does ethics have in business? In 1970, the economist Milton Friedman wrote an article in *The New York Times Magazine* titled 'The Social Responsibility of Business is to Increase its Profits'. Friedman was reacting against the idea that businesses have social responsibilities to improve their workers' lives or help the communities they operate in. For Friedman this was socialism, a social system that (he argued) made **capitalism** less effective and restricted the rights of individuals to improve their lives. Friedman was not against the idea that businesses should make everyone better off and improve people's lives, but he thought that the best way to ensure this happened was to let businesses focus on making more profit. Everything that was good would then follow as a result of this principle.

Many businesses today, however, do accept social responsibilities that go beyond what they are required to do by law. Examples could include using materials from sustainable sources, even though non-sustainable resources would be cheaper, choosing not to take sponsorship from companies involved in fossil fuel extraction even though this shuts off access to valuable sources of money, deciding not to test products on animals even though this increases research costs, or investing in local youth sports teams even though this money could be used instead to improve **shareholder** dividend payments. Businesses sometimes choose to offer their staff higher wages than are paid by their competitors, for example by making all staff shareholders in the business. **Corporate social responsibility** describes the concept that corporations (businesses) should be accountable for impacts they have on people and the environment.

Whistle-blowing is when an employee of a business chooses to make public their belief that their employer has acted unethically. Businesses have processes through which employees can report faults or problems so that they can be addressed, but whistle-blowers act when they are convinced that reporting the problem internally will not remedy the situation – nothing will happen, or they will be told to forget what they saw, or they will be punished in some way for making trouble. Whistle-blowers face difficult consequences: colleagues and friends disowning them, allegations being made about their own character and the chance of legal action against them. As a result, whistle-blowers could be seen as individuals with high ethical standards: moral people who are not able to put their own personal comfort and security before doing the right thing. The consequences of whistle-blowing for the business and its employees can be very damaging, and whistle-blowers could themselves be seen as behaving unethically by breaking the contract of trust and confidentiality between themselves and their employer.

The slogan that 'Good ethics is good business' is based on the idea that 'doing the right thing' is a route to business success. Customers prefer to buy from ethical businesses rather than from businesses they suspect are trying to cheat them, exploit others or cause social or environmental damage. The idea that good ethics is good business also extends to business decision-making. This is encapsulated in Google's corporate motto 'Don't be evil', or the less humorously ironic 'Do the right thing' which has replaced it. Not only will customers relate positively to the business if it 'does the right thing', but the business will be more successful if all its decisions are ethical decisions.

However, **globalisation** challenges the ability of companies to 'do the right thing'. Globalisation has created a highly connected global economy that relies on countries removing protection for their own businesses from international competition. The opportunity to move production to low-wage countries and then make enormous profits selling the products in high-wage markets around the world has enabled transnational corporations to dominate international and national economies. Customers in countries like the UK have benefited from much cheaper consumer products, enabling thousands to enjoy a consumer lifestyle. However, working conditions in the producer countries have typically been grim, with little or none of the health and safety protection, minimum wages or limits on excessive working hours, that are standard in Western businesses. Transnational corporations can reduce their production costs, too, by operating in countries with lower environmental controls. Corporations that are wealthier than many countries have used their transnational status to increase profits by channelling revenues through low-tax countries, meaning that only relatively tiny amounts of their massive sales revenues are paid in tax to the governments of the countries they operate in. Exposure of these unethical practices in the media are often damaging to the business, even if they are within the law. If customers start to perceive them negatively, businesses often change what they do. However, if 'good ethics is good business', why were they acting unethically in the first place?

Corporate social responsibility

Business responsibilities

There are many types of business, from sole traders (one person businesses) to the giant transnational corporations (businesses based in many countries). Bigger businesses are set up so that no one person is liable for everything the business does: the business itself becomes its own owner. Investors are able to buy shares in the business and if the business does well, those 'shareholders' are paid dividends. The people managing the business have a duty towards shareholders: it is their responsibility to act in the interest of the shareholders and in many businesses the shareholders are able to have some say about how the business is run. So when Milton Friedman argued that businesses have no other responsibility but to increase their profits, he made the point that it was actually unethical to do anything else: taking money away from making profits to fund corporate social responsibility projects was the equivalent of stealing money from shareholders.

The economics put forward by Friedman convinced politicians like Ronald Reagan in the US and Margaret Thatcher in the UK that if businesses were 'set free' to pursue profit, the benefits of their growth would 'trickle down' to everyone else in the country. To do this government regulation was reduced. This happened in a context of increasing social problems due to rising inequality and increasing awareness of environmental issues. Instead of notions of corporate social responsibility decreasing, more and more businesses accepted responsibilities towards the community and the environment: responsibilities that went beyond their economic responsibility to their shareholders, and beyond their legal responsibilities, towards what Carroll ('The Pyramid of Corporate Social Responsibility: Toward the Moral Management of Organizational Stakeholders', *Business Horizons*, 34(4), 1991, pp. 39–48) termed philanthropic responsibilities (like giving to charity or improving facilities in local communities) and ethical responsibilities, which are the actions society expects the business to take.

Why do businesses take on corporate social responsibilities?

Undoubtedly, businesses do take on social responsibilities because they think these will improve their image with customers, or with a certain type of investor or a certain type of employee. There are many thousands of investors who only want to put their money into 'ethical' businesses – the FTSE4Good Index Series, for example, provides information for investors on businesses that demonstrate 'strong Environmental, Social and Governance practices' (www.ftse.com). The United Nations has also set up voluntary principles for ethically-responsible investment, and as of 2014 investors had put more than $34 trillion into funds committed to these principles. Strong environmental, social and governance practices are measured in many different ways, but would include businesses making efforts to reduce their greenhouse gas emissions and investing in energy efficiency but exclude businesses involved in arms production or selling tobacco products.

Others may take on these responsibilities because they fear that if they do not, they will be viewed negatively by customers. Businesses may improve facilities for employees or offer discounts for employees because they are worried that if they do not, employees will go and work for the competition. Another 'negative' reason for corporate social responsibility is fear that without adopting self-regulation, businesses will face far more restrictive regulation on their activities from government. So, for example, newspaper businesses may agree to restrict their intrusion into the lives of vulnerable celebrities for fear of government legislation being introduced that bans all such intrusion into people's private lives.

Businesses take on corporate social responsibility for many reasons, including to promote themselves with potential customers and in the hope that it will prevent governments from imposing stricter social responsibilities on them

Stakeholders

A related concept to corporate social responsibility is that businesses have much wider responsibilities than just to their shareholders. Business decisions and business processes affect many different groups of people: their employees, their suppliers, their customers, the community in which the business operates, the country as a whole through their contribution to the national economy, and to everyone affected by their impact on the environment. Businesses have a responsibility to everyone who has a stake in their activities – **stakeholders**. Crane and Matten (2004) define stakeholders as follows:

> A stakeholder of a corporation [business] is an individual or group which either:
>
> - is harmed by, or benefits from, the corporation;
>
> *or*
>
> - whose rights can be violated, or have to be respected, by the corporation.

Andrew Crane and Dirk Matten, *Business Ethics: A European Perspective*, 2004, p. 50

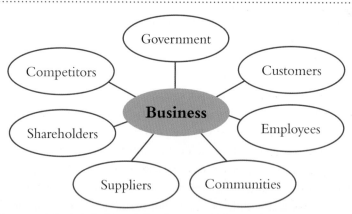

A business and its stakeholders (after Crane and Matten, *Business Ethics*, 2004, p. 51)

While businesses may decide that 'philanthropic' corporate social responsibility offers them good promotional opportunities, stakeholder responsibilities are more likely to be obligations that businesses cannot reject without serious reputational damage. For example, if a transnational corporation wants to shut its UK steel works because global trends in steelmaking have made the UK steel works unprofitable, this is a decision that its shareholders would be likely to back, as otherwise their investments in the transnational corporation will be negatively affected. However, this decision would affect thousands of current UK workers, many UK suppliers, entire communities based around the steelworks and the economy of the

Steelworkers in the UK campaigning against steel industry closures

whole country, since the loss of steelworks would reduce tax payments in to the government and increase unemployment benefits made by the government. As a result, the transnational corporation would be under intense social pressure to consider the interests of all these stakeholders and act to lessen the negative impact of its decision, even if this involved significant loss of profits.

Ethical responsibilities can, therefore, 'oblige corporations [businesses] to do what is right, just and fair even when they are not compelled to do so by the legal framework' (Crane and Matten, *Business Ethics: A European Perspective*, 2004, p. 44). This is particularly the case where business decisions directly affect a large number of stakeholders, or where those stakeholders are perceived as vulnerable, or where businesses have taken on roles previously provided by public (government) services. For example, in the UK businesses have taken on the job of assessing whether people are eligible for disability benefits. In this context, there would be considerable social opposition to the business putting profit first if that was achieved by not giving benefits to disabled people who were legitimately entitled to them, or making the process of applying for benefits so unpleasant that disabled people decided against applying.

Identifying in advance how a business' actions will be perceived by its stakeholders can be very challenging. Stakeholder interests seldom overlap. For example, supermarket businesses compete very intensely for customers and have found the best way to do this is by offering extremely cheap prices on everyday basics such as milk. To achieve these low prices, supermarkets use their purchasing power over their dairy suppliers: if the suppliers want supermarket business then they have to sell milk below the price it costs them to produce it. This makes customers happy but suppliers unhappy. If suppliers campaign to raise awareness of unethical supermarket purchasing practice, customers

Stakeholders can pressure businesses into taking on corporate social responsibilities, even when businesses do not have to do so by law

may become unhappy that 'their' supermarket is behaving unethically and start to move their business somewhere else. Yet if the supermarket increases the price of milk, the customers may move to a competitor that is cheaper.

So although some businesses try always to 'do the right thing', most tend to have a mix of approaches to their social and stakeholder responsibilities. This can include 'philanthropic' corporate social responsibility projects alongside hard-headed business decisions that damage the interests of some stakeholders. The same businesses that champion their environmental credentials, for example, may be forced by public opinion into accepting their social responsibility for the well-being of their suppliers in low-wage countries. Businesses are both choosing to act ethically and being required to face up to their social responsibilities. Perhaps business ethics is best described as a process.

Think question

Is it unethical for a business to take on corporate social responsibilities in the hope of increasing profits?

Apply your knowledge

'Only people have responsibilities. A corporation is an artificial person and in this sense may have artificial responsibilities, but "business" as a whole cannot be said to have responsibilities, even in this vague sense.'

Milton Friedman, 'The Social Responsibility of Business is to Increase its Profits.' *The New York Times Magazine*, 13 September 1970

2. How might business managers who have decided that the business they work for should take on corporate social responsibility argue against this? What might Friedman have argued in response?

Kantian and utilitarian responses to corporate social responsibility

Kant's ethics focused on the need to treat people as ends and not just means for some other purpose because they are beings of dignity – autonomous and rationale. They have worth not because of what they own but because of what they are. This leads to a number of possible applications to the question of business ethics. First there is the quest of trusting in human autonomy and rationality. Companies which control and monitor employees excessively seem to be without respect for the dignity of human beings. Companies that do not ensure safe and fair working conditions and payment for employees would seem to be using them for some end other than the interest of the employee. The balance between the interest of the company and the interest of the employee would be important for a Kantian perspective. This affects how companies treat customers – not fixing a defective product that could cause harm to the consumer, or misleading them with false information about the benefits of the produce (such as health foods which are not so healthy), are all examples of treating people merely as a means to an end.

Utilitarian ethics focuses on the consequences for the greatest good. The greatest good could be interested in terms of the greatest profit.

This might lead to a ruthless attempt to maximise income at all costs. However, utilitarianism has the greater good principle to try to set aside selfish interest for the broader interest of many more people than oneself. This would mean not just acting in the interests of shareholders, but also in the interests of workers and all other stakeholders, including the communities in which the businesses operate, the national economy that it supports and the environmental impacts it might have on a global scale.

Whistle-blowing

Is whistle-blowing ethical?

Whistle-blowing is when an employee discloses wrongdoing to the employer or the public. Whistle-blowing is not generally about a personal complaint or grievance against an employer: whistle-blowers are reporting something that is affecting, or threatens to affect, others. Whistle-blowing may be perceived as an individual moral choice, but in some cases employees would have a legal responsibility to report unethical behaviour because of the likelihood of this behaviour being criminal. Often, a code of conduct for a profession would require a member of that profession to report certain kinds of wrongdoing or potential risks. If, for example, an accountant discovered that the business she was working for was deliberately avoiding paying tax, it would be her legal and professional duty to report this to the relevant authorities. The same would be true if a worker at a chemical plant discovered that a leak had contaminated a nearby stream, or if a teacher discovered that an advance copy of an exam paper had been posted online.

In most cases in the UK, whistle-blowers are protected by law: The Public Interest Disclosure Act (1998). There is an equivalent act in the US: The Sarbanes-Oxley Act (2002), under which business executives who retaliate against whistle-blowers can be jailed for up to 10 years. Whistle-blowers in UK law are treated as witnesses, which means they are not required to provide evidence of what they are reporting. It is also possible for people to whistle-blow anonymously, although this can make investigating the claim more difficult. This is all to encourage whistle-blowing as something that serves the public interest. The government and society see it as good that people are able to pass on information about wrongdoing or risks to safety so that these issues can be put right. Social commentators argue that encouraging whistle-blowing helps convince businesses to take their corporate social responsibilities seriously, as otherwise their unethical practices are likely to be revealed by one of their own employees.

Is whistle-blowing ever unethical?

Legal protection for whistle-blowers does not continue, however, if the person is discovered to be simply making accusations because they have a problem with the business they work for or particular individuals within it. There are also some types of work that are not covered by the

Apply your knowledge

Edward Snowden was accused of spying by the US government and of theft of government documents. Snowden himself said 'I do not want to live in a world where everything I do and say is recorded. ... My sole motive is to inform the public as to that which is done in their name and that which is done against them' (interview, *The Guardian*, 9 June 2013).

3. Was Edward Snowden's whistle-blowing ethical or unethical? Explain your answer.

Although whistle-blowing is encouraged by government because it serves the public good, there are also ethical issues involved for the individual who is thinking about whistle-blowing because of their responsibilities to their employer

Think question

Should loyalty to their employer always make people think twice about whistle-blowing?

Edward Snowden was an employee of the National Security Agency (NSA) in the US, who told American and British newspapers that the NSA was routinely monitoring the communications of millions of ordinary citizens in the US, UK and many other countries, without their consent or knowledge

Public Interest Disclosure Act, and that includes people who work for the armed or intelligence services. This is because whistle-blowing in these areas could risk national security, which could have very negative impacts on the public – or on public trust in those who are supposed to be protecting them from harm.

A business is a group of people who work together on the basis of ethical relationships that they have with one another, for example trust and loyalty. Employees sign a contract with their employer setting out the moral expectations each has of the other. Contracts between employer and employee are the ethical foundation of a business. Norman Bowie states that whistle-blowing violates a '*prima facie* duty of loyalty to one's employer' (Bowie, *Business Ethics*, 1991, p. 140). *Prima facie* means 'from a first impression', which Bowie takes to mean until and unless proven otherwise so whistle-blowing that turned out to serve the public good would be the right thing to do. However, for Bowie, it is more ethical for an employee to make every effort to solve the problem through the business' own complaints procedures first, rather than resorting straight to whistle-blowing.

Kantian and utilitarian responses to whistle-blowing

Kantian ethics emphasises the importance of honesty and promise-keeping through the categorical imperative. A Kantian employee would find it difficult to allow a situation where a company broke the rules in what it did, as in general, companies are expected to follow the rules. This does not sound like universality, something important to Kantians. However, an employer sticking to a contract seems close to the sense that people should keep to their promises they have made in business. Whistle-blowing in a sense involves breaking those promises, going outside the agreed system. But if a company was putting at risk or unfairly exploiting its customers, or some if its employees or even the community it works in (through failing to pay proper taxes, for example) then a Kantian might interpret this as human beings not being treated as ends but only as means for private greed. And there may be a sense that beyond the specifics of a contract, there is a wider sense of duty that must sometimes inspire someone to take a personal risk, even endanger themselves by going to the authorities, where this might be dangerous.

Utilitarians might resist whistle-blowing, depending on how much harm was done by the particular instance of an activity that was unethical or illegal. The utilitarian would have to weigh the balance of good or harm for all those with an interest or stake in the business continuing to do well, and whether this outweighed what was done or put at risk by the infringement. It might be justified for a company to break some rules to succeed in a particular instance, to create greater happiness through the success of the company at that point or on that occasion. Here, rule and act utilitarians might differ. A rule utilitarian might feel that there was a greater good of having companies in general always follow the rules to keep the system of companies ethical, even if in a particular instance it created more happiness to not blow the whistle.

Apply your knowledge

4. Do you think whistle-blowing is wrong, permissible or obligatory? Consider these examples. Should they report the case internally, go to the authorities or the press?

   a. An accountant discovers the company he works for is a front for organised crime/mafia. He knows he will be targeted, and his family too, if he tells the authorities.

   b. The personal assistant of a well-respected company director discovers that the company director has been over-claiming her expenses, but only as the company director is about to retire after 30 years at the same firm.

   c. In order to get contracts in an African country, an employee is told that it is customary to pay bribes, and that everybody does it.

   d. After years of struggling to get a TV role, an actor is chosen for a bit part in a popular TV soap. However, he overhears the director using racist abuse against another actor.

5. A local car tyre maker is an important employer in its community. However, it is being outcompeted on price by a transnational company that uses cheap labour overseas to make its products. In order to reduce its costs, the local business starts to cut corners, increasing the risk that its tyres may become unsafe at high speeds (over the national speed limit). If the company goes bust, then the local people who work there would lose their jobs and the pay given to workers would not be used to buy goods from other local businesses to look after the people in the town. What would a Kantian, an act utilitarian and a rule utilitarian do in this situation?

Good ethics is good business

The idea that good ethics is good business – that good business decisions are good ethical decisions – can be understood in different ways:

- that there is nothing different between business decisions and any other kind of decisions: business decisions are not inherently unethical and so a good business decision like any kind of good decision is likely to also be ethical

- that business decisions are inherently unethical because they are interested only in what benefits the business. This can have negative impacts on the business and such businesses will do better if they make their decision-making based on good ethics

- that most everyday business decisions do not involve ethical choices but that occasionally business decisions do involve a choice between doing the right thing or doing something that might be wrong. At this point those making the decisions would benefit from ethical guidance – perhaps in the form of a policy that sets out what the business must do in such circumstances.

Apply your knowledge

6. Make a case for each of the following being good ethics and good business, or good ethics but bad business.

    a. An environmental law has been passed that requires every retailer to stop giving out plastic bags for free to customers. A family shop facing heavy competition from a nearby supermarket offers to buy plastic bags for 5p for any customer who has forgotten their shopping bags.

    b. A beer company launches a competition to promote its new lager: post a picture of your most outrageous party for a chance to win a crate of beer every week for a term.

    c. A building company decides to boost its reputation for integrity by guaranteeing it will never charge more than the amount it quotes for a job, regardless of circumstances.

    d. A new cafe owner decides to increase her customer base with an online voucher promotion that offers unlimited half-price meals for a month.

    e. A transnational food company sells surplus baby milk powder to developing countries at a heavy discount.

It is difficult for businesses to constantly practise good ethics in a business environment that is based on businesses competing to reduce costs and maximise profits

Because customers like to do business with companies they trust, it seems obvious that good business will also be good ethics. Businesses that act with integrity, honour their agreements, do not cheat their suppliers or act rudely towards their customers should, therefore, have more customers and make more revenue than businesses that do not act in the same way.

However, this is not the experience that most of us have of businesses. If businesses always practised good ethics, then why would it be so much easier to move to a more expensive phone contract than it is to leave a phone company? Why would so many people have been sold expensive insurance products that they were never going to need? When a business acts with complete integrity and offers an honest price for an honest job, why do other businesses immediately pounce and entice their customers away with cheaper deals? Why do the management teams of struggling companies continue to pay themselves eye-watering salaries, or insist on zero-hour contracts for their staff in order to maximise profits? These examples suggest that self-interest leads many businesses away from 'doing the right thing': the self-interest that is driven by the desire to increase profits, and supported by the business' shareholders.

Is good ethics bad business?

Competition is the driving force of our capitalist economy: businesses compete with each other for market share, for talented employees and for investors. If being ethical risks increasing costs and reducing profits, then most businesses will take a 'hard-headed' decision to stay competitive. Is this the fault of businesses? Although customers and some shareholders (and whistle-blowers) have been an important factor in pushing businesses to accept their corporate social responsibilities, it is also consumers and shareholders who demand constant updates, new models, lower prices and faster delivery. Customers and investors have very little loyalty to one business if another one produces something they like more, or sells something at a cheaper price. In a consumer culture, businesses have to do something to stand out. Rather than all businesses becoming ethical businesses, ethics seems a branding choice that some businesses make in a bid to be noticed.

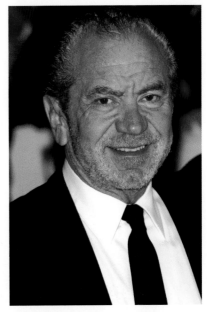

For Lord Sugar, the choice to be ethical is a branding decision

Differentiate yourself from the competition

66 In other words, nail your unique selling point. What are you going to bring to the party? The country's full of mobile phone retailers, recruitment consultancies and estate agents, yet new businesses do appear. And flourish. 'Ask yourself,' says Lord Sugar, 'Am I going to be any different to the 30,000 people already in the marketplace? What are my customers going to get from me that they aren't going to get from someone else?' Are you the cheap one, the one with good service, the ethical or bespoke one? What's your hook? 99

Lord Sugar's rules for first time entrepreneurs
(www.shortlist.com/entertainment/lord-sugars-rules)

> ### Think question
> Is ethics in business anything more than a brand?

Good ethics is sometimes good business

The worldwide recession of 2008 could have been prevented. Although there was nothing illegal about the way international finance went on piling up investments that were inextricably tied into the selling of sub-prime mortgages, it was obviously unethical. This was because the sub-prime mortgages were being sold to people who it was clear did not have the means to repay their debt if they could not keep up with their mortgage payments. However, the money was so good and the process so complicated to understand that no one wanted to stop the party. A credit bubble was created. Even some of those who understood the dangers most clearly then used their understanding to bet on the whole financial system collapsing, making themselves rich in the process. What would have been better, in retrospect, was good ethics, even had that meant lower economic growth, fewer people owning their own homes, lower consumer spending and so fewer jobs.

Because in the long term the cost of this unethical financial dealing was extraordinarily high.

If a permanent commitment to high ethical standards seems unrealistic in our capitalist culture, then perhaps businesses should commit instead to involving ethical expertise when important decisions or choices are being made. Individuals use ethics in this way – not for everyday tasks but for choices with a moral element – and big businesses are vastly more complex than individuals, with many more possible consequences from decision-making because of their wide range of stakeholders. Then good ethics would help business make good choices.

Kantian and utilitarian approaches to the idea that good ethics is good business

Utilitarianism fits well with business decision-making because businesses are used to making 'cost–benefit' decisions:

> 66 Utilitarianism has been very powerful because it puts at the centre of the moral decision a variable which is very commonly used in economics as a parameter which measures the (economic) value of actions: 'utility'. Since one can quantify this variable, the utilitarian analysis is highly compatible with the quantitative, mathematical methodology of economics. So, in analysing two possible actions in a single business decision, we just assign a certain utility to each consequence and each person involved, and the action with the highest aggregate utility is morally correct. Ultimately utilitarianism then comes close to what we know as cost–benefit analysis. 99

Andrew Crane and Dirk Matten, *Business Ethics: A European Perspective*, 2004, p. 84

Although powerful and easy to integrate into existing business practices, the complexity of business operations and the number of variables involved in business decisions could make a utilitarian approach to ethical business too cumbersome for dynamic, fast-paced business environments. It can also be difficult to quantify utility objectively – since businesses are used to putting a number on cost and benefit, businesses might struggle to say how much pleasure or how much pain a decision would cause to each stakeholder involved.

There are also differences between act and rule utilitarians. In a situation where a business is deciding whether or not to move all its employees to zero-hours contracts to give the business a lower cost-base and more flexibility, an act utilitarian might simply conclude that anything is permissible if it increases pleasure for the greatest number, and on balance this would mean their workforce should be moved to zero hours as many more customers would benefit from the cheaper products that could be produced. However, Mill would distinguish between higher and lower pleasures and might consider the exploitation of employees a lower pleasure compared to their good treatment. A rule utilitarian would be concerned about the behaviour of businesses as a whole and be prepared to restrict the conduct of business in some circumstances because of a perceived overall benefit to a wider range of goods, not simply the good of profit. Rule utilitarians might, therefore, agree that zero-hours contracts on principle cause more pain than pleasure, and this would form the basis of their decision-making. A rule-based approach would seem to fit better with a 'good ethics is good business' approach since this is more efficient.

Kantian ethics has similar attractions for business because it enables principles to be developed that apply in every situation. Kantian ethics would fit best for that view of 'good ethics is good business' in which the assumption is that business is naturally unethical because it goes every time for self-interest. The categorical imperative would clarify for a business just what actions are and are not permissible.

The demands of Kantian ethics do not sit very easily with a highly competitive, capitalist business environment, however. The third maxim of the categorical imperative requires that a business acts only in ways that would be seen as acceptable by everyone. This principle fits well with corporate social responsibility, in which society demands certain ethical standards of businesses, but recent history suggests that while one business is trying to act in a fully responsible way, its competitors are rushing to take advantage of the competitive weaknesses that inevitably result from this approach: good ethics but bad business. The second maxim of the categorical imperative says people should not only be treated as means: their own needs and aspirations should always be considered too. This is a principle that fits well with the concept of business stakeholders, but following it could potentially tie a business up in complex considerations of stakeholder outcomes. The first maxim of the categorical imperative demands that any action is only right if it is right for everyone. Businesses that followed this maxim would always tell the truth, because if everyone lied then nothing would work.

Globalisation

Globalisation describes the integration of economies, industries, markets, cultures and policy-making around the world. Transnational corporations have been key to the development of the global economy: mega-businesses that have taken advantage of communication revolutions that allow investment and products to move seamlessly between countries to locate the different functions of their businesses in the most profitable parts of the world. The size of these businesses means the range of their stakeholders extends from national governments to child workers in developing countries.

Apply your knowledge

7. Consider these examples from a Kantian and a utilitarian perspective.

   a. A business is deciding whether to improve profits by making its suppliers accept lower prices and longer notice periods before payment.

   b. A business manager is interviewing candidates for a job vacancy. One candidate is from a rival business. He implies that he would be able to bring a copy of the competitor's business plan for the next five years with him if he were to get the job.

   c. A team of negotiators is close to agreeing a multi-billion-pound deal for a very important client of their business. Just before the deal is done, one negotiator learns of a risk to the project which might mean their client loses a lot of money. If he tells the client, she might pull out of the deal and the business would lose their very valuable commission.

The negative impacts of globalisation are not restricted to developing countries: manufacturing jobs in the West have often been 'lost' to lower-wage countries in the developing world

Moving production from the US and Europe to lower-wage countries such as China and India has rapidly increased economic development and technological know-how in the latter. Although the wages paid by transnational corporations in countries like China are far lower than the wages that the transnational corporation would need to pay in Western countries, they are still much higher than what peasant farmers in China used to earn. This has had enormous economic benefits for stakeholders in these emerging economies.

> 66 Globalisation, more than anything else, has reduced the number of extreme poor in India by two hundred million and in China by three hundred million since 1990. 99

Jeffrey Sachs, *The End of Poverty*, 2005, p. 355

Moving production to low-wage countries has had major impacts on stakeholders in the US and Europe. Consumers have benefited from cheaper products, fuelling a consumer culture. But the shift in manufacturing to low-wage countries has 'hollowed out' manufacturing in the most developed countries – much of that manufacturing has disappeared, along with the jobs it once supported. Transnational corporations that started business in the US have been strongly criticised by the people who used to make their products for them, with those left behind by globalisation feeling abandoned and betrayed.

Whilst global business has the power to bring investment to poorer countries, these countries have often had weak government regulations, allowing unsafe working conditions. On 24 April 2013, a poorly-made Bangladeshi factory collapsed. The factory had supplied Primark and

Globalisation has brought huge changes to rich countries as well as in poorer ones

Can protests against the impacts of globalisation help transnational corporations accept more corporate social responsibility?

other companies, like Wal-Mart and Benetton, with low-cost clothing. Over 1100 people died in the building, called the Rana Plaza, and more than 2500 were injured. The day before the collapse, shops on the ground floor of the eight-storey complex were closed after cracks appeared in the building, but the garment workers were ordered to return to work; some were threatened with being docked a month's pay if they did not go back. An investigation after the disaster showed that the upper factory floors had been built without permits and without any reinforcement for the heavy machines the clothes were made on.

A series of allegations were made. Firstly, that the reason the workers were ordered to go back into a structurally unsafe building was because the factory owners were under pressure to fulfil their contracts with the transnational corporation clothing companies. Secondly, that the Rana Plaza had been converted into a factory and the extra unauthorised floors had been added because the corporations would only give contracts to businesses that could meet large orders for the cheapest prices. And, thirdly, that the transnational corporations had not spent the proper amount of time or money making sure that their suppliers were providing reasonable working conditions, observing health and safety standards or paying workers an appropriate wage.

Against the view that globalisation exports unethical business practices, is the argument that transnational corporations do also sometimes help to improve business ethics in the countries they operate in, and that international reactions to disasters like the Rana Plaza collapse can lead to these corporations being pressured into accepting corporate social responsibility for more of their stakeholders. Although the workers who died at Rana Plaza were not employees of Primark, Benetton or Wal-Mart, public opinion in many different countries was that these corporations shared some responsibility for the disaster for not showing

Globalisation involves the spread of information and ideas, including business ethics, around the world

Think question

If a global company buys products from businesses in developing countries like Bangladesh, does it have responsibility for the ethical standards of those businesses? Does it make any difference that few of those businesses would be in operation, making money and employing thousands of people, if the global company wasn't buying products from them?

concern for the safety and well-being of their stakeholders. A fund was set up to give all the companies who had placed orders at Rana Plaza a chance to contribute to compensation for injured workers and the families of those who had died. There was then a global petition to put pressure on businesses to make a payment into the fund. It took three years, but the fund eventually reached its target of $30 million. Pressure on city authorities in Bangladesh as a result of the disaster, also meant health and safety inspections for all buildings used for manufacturing, with 35 unsafe factories being closed.

Kantian and utilitarian responses to globalisation

For utilitarians, the creation of the greatest good can be understood in global terms. The World Bank has calculated that 800 million Chinese people have been lifted out of poverty since China began to open up its economy in 1978 (www.worldbank.org/en/country/china/overview): predominantly due to globalisation. Then there are all those in developed countries who have benefited from the cheap products and services delivered by globalisation. Supporters of globalisation do indeed argue its benefits in utilitarian terms: the good it does massively outweighs its disadvantages, as proved by the extremely small number of countries that decide to keep trade barriers to block globalisation and protect their own businesses from global competition.

Critics of globalisation argue that this utilitarianism is the self-justification of the rich countries that want poor countries to open their markets to Western goods produced at the lowest possible price by their own workers. Instead of producing the greatest good for the greatest number, such critics would say that globalisation deepens global inequalities. Kantian ethics provide support for such criticisms. Kant argued that everyone should have the same degree of freedom. He accepted that governments would restrict people's freedoms a little but only to ensure that everyone had the same freedom. Without government control, humans would act like other animals – the strongest would dominate and the weakest would lose everything. Kant's views on equality would clash with the inequality generated by globalisation and tolerated by those who benefit from it. Sometimes, the impacts of globalisation on stakeholders do appear to be the strong ruthlessly imposing their will on the weak, or the super-rich on the 'dirt poor'. Transnational corporations *are* often more powerful and wealthier than national governments, and this has inevitably led some corporations into unethical practices.

Bowie (*Business Ethics: A Kantian Perspective*, 1999) suggests Kantian thinking can inform all businesses on how they should organise meaningful work. The Kantian idea of meaningful work means:

• work that is is freely chosen and provides opportunities for the worker to exercise autonomy on the job

- work that supports the autonomy and rationality of human beings; if work reduces autonomy or rationality then it is immoral

- work that should provide a salary sufficient to exercise independent living, and also ensure physical well-being and satisfaction for at least some of the worker's wishes

- work that should not undermine a worker's moral development.

Bowie goes on to suggest some features of a business that Kant would expect. The firm should:

- consider all affected stakeholders when decision-making

- ensure that no one stakeholder automatically takes priority in any decision

- not simply consider the number of stakeholders affected when the interests of one group must be set against another (for instance in deciding that some employees must be made redundant)

- ensure that profit-making has some duty of beneficence (actions done for the good of others)

- ensure that relations with stakeholders should be governed by rules of justice.

Bowie's point about not simply considering the number of stakeholders affected is a clear swipe at utilitarian ethics.

Discussing business ethics

Is corporate social responsibility nothing more than 'hypocritical window-dressing' covering the greed of a business intent on making profits?

Some businesses market themselves as ethical. They do this by arguing that their products are more moral than others, such as environmentally friendly power generation companies, or products that carry the fair trade logo, indicating they give a fairer wage to the producer of the raw materials. Some businesses donate a small amount to charity for every product purchased while others make large and public donations to charities and fundraising. Although some businesses are deeply motivated by social concerns, such as green energy producers, for most, their association with social issues comes from a calculation that this association will help them increase their profits through building up a positive brand image with the customers they want to attract.

Businesses would be acting hypocritically if they pretended to be something they were not, using corporate social responsibility as a cover for their real intentions. There are many cases in which businesses have

Apply your knowledge

8. Look at Norman Bowie's ideas about Kantian work. Which maxims from Kantian ethics have inspired these ideas? What might his reasons be for basing his principles for meaningful work on Kant rather than utilitarianism?

9. What, in your view, would be the best way to persuade transnational corporations to accept more of their corporate social responsibilities with regard to their stakeholders in developing countries like Bangladesh? Consider philanthropic approaches, 'good ethics is good business', whistle-blowing and society's expectations for ethical business in your answer.

Apply your knowledge

10. Examine the mission statements or 'creeds' of some well-known companies, such as the Johnson & Johnson Credo (www.jnj.com/about-jnj/jnj-credo) or Apple's supplier responsibility (www.apple.com/supplier-responsibility/). What do these ethical statements specifically suggest? Which groups are identified and what promises are made? Consider whether you think these are genuine attempts at being ethical or 'window dressing' to attract more customers. Can they be both?

11. Does it matter if we only buy products with moral 'selling points' to satisfy our desire to feel even better when gratifying our desire to accumulate more?

12. If education was fully privatised in the UK, with schools and colleges being run for profit by businesses, then would it be hypocritical of schools and colleges to continue to offer 'high status' subjects that very few students wanted to take, such as A level Latin, but which some stakeholders (Latin teachers, Classics pressure groups, university admissions officers, university Classics departments, some parents) wanted to see provided as options?

promoted a public image that has proven to be at odds with their actual activities: for example, car manufacturers that have promoted their cars as environmentally friendly when in fact the low emissions of the cars involved were obtained by cheating emissions tests. However, the result of this emissions-test cheating being uncovered was that car companies were forced to change their practices. Car producers who had not cheated on emissions saw an increase in sales. Car producers who had cheated suffered a decrease in sales and had to start the long and expensive process of rebuilding public trust in their image. There is an external pressure on businesses to act ethically. If that is the case, can they be accused of acting hypocritically when they are obliged to accept the responsibilities they have to their customers and other stakeholders?

Milton Friedman's argument that 'the social responsibility of business is to increase its profits' was that everyone benefits more if businesses *do* just focus on making money, and that a business is not like an individual: a business cannot accept responsibility. For Friedman, it is hypocritical of society to expect anything else of business than to be intent on making profits. However, much has changed since Friedman's 1970 article (in *The New York Times Magazine*). Environmental concerns mean that it no longer seems appropriate for businesses only to pursue profit without considering the environmental impact. Globalisation means that some transnational businesses can make decisions that impact directly on hundreds of thousands of people, whole communities or even the global economy itself. Privatisation means that many services previously provided by government are now delivered by businesses looking to make a profit. There seems to be a requirement that society holds businesses to account, that people use their power as stakeholders to encourage businesses to act ethically. In other words, we should not expect companies to be genuinely charitable but we can use our choices in the market and through campaigns to persuade companies to 'be good' for sound business reasons.

Can human beings flourish in the context of capitalism and consumerism?

If a key driver in human life is the ever-increasing acquisition of products and services and if this produces greater wealth, then perhaps people flourish best under a successful capitalist economy with good consumers driving progress. **Consumerism** grants individuals the power to make choices and acquire more products, which in turn drives the economy. This drive has been behind many technological developments; it has increasingly enabled people to express their individuality with increasing ownership of private objects. The creation of a mass market for consumer products has revolutionised Western economies.

Capitalism is linked to the Protestant work ethic, the idea that hard work, discipline and frugality are one aspect of a person's salvation in the Christian Protestant faith. Capitalism incentivises human behaviour because there is self-interest in the outcome. If you can make your business better, you gain more of the rewards. The more your activity is controlled by others, so capitalists feel, the less incentive there is for you to try to make business better.

The problem with this approach is that it encourages individuals (and businesses) to pursue wealth and become greedy. They may act irresponsibly in the pursuit of gain. The capitalist system reduces the experience of a human life to that of an essential materialistic consumer, gaining more and more things arguably at the expense of human relationships, morality and spirituality. Capitalism reduces the way we think about the planet to a collection of natural resources to be maximised and acquired, and consumerism encourages a wasteful approach to the products we make. It is not clear that ever-increasing ownership of goods is something that the earth can sustain for everyone, or that everyone will be able to afford. Perhaps the whole capitalist economy just encourages greed, and greed leads to every greater moral corruption.

> 66 An infectious greed seemed to grip much of our business community. ... It is not that humans have become any more greedy than in generations past. It is that the avenues to express greed have grown so enormously. 99
>
> Alan Greenspan, testimony before the US Senate Banking Committee, July 16, 2002, quoted in F. Partnoy, *Infectious Greed: How Deceit and Risk Corrupted the Financial Markets*, 2003, p. 190

Does globalisation encourage or discourage the pursuit of good ethics as the foundation of good business?

Good ethics as the foundation of good business includes the concept that a strong ethical foundation to a business will improve business success, since customers prefer to buy from businesses that 'do the right thing' rather than act unethically. The transnational corporations central to globalisation certainly seem to have embraced this concept in their business slogans and mission statements, as the following brief sample from mission statements and values of some selected top 100 transnational corporations shows:

- General Electric's mission statement includes the desire: 'to build, move, power and cure the world'.

- Toyota's 'global vision': 'Toyota will lead the way to the future of mobility, enriching lives around the world with the safest and most responsible ways of moving people.'

- Exxon Mobil: 'we must continuously achieve superior financial and operating results while simultaneously adhering to high ethical standards.'

Think question

Does consumerism encourage an idea that human beings are what they can accumulate, rather than something related to character, personality or ability? Does consumerism drive an essential materialistic and selfish idea of human nature?

Apply your knowledge

13. Think of your happiest moments. How many of them involve getting new things? Do any of them count as non-consumerist?

14. Winston Churchill said 'Democracy is the worst form of government except for all the others.' Do you agree or disagree with the statement that 'capitalism is the worst economic system to live under, except for all the others?'

15. 'Corporate social responsibility is the best way of reducing our consumerist culture.' How far do you agree with this statement?

- Wal-Mart: 'We save people money so they can live better.'

- Microsoft: 'At Microsoft, our mission is to enable people and businesses throughout the world to realize their full potential.'

In practice, however, there are strong reasons to doubt whether globalisation has encouraged ethical business practices. In the developed West, the industrial revolution of the nineteenth century was notorious for the low wages, poor working conditions, high pollution and dangerous disregard for the health and safety of its businesses. After a century of political struggle, workers in the West succeeded in compelling businesses to accept the necessity of minimum levels of pay, legal limits on working hours, legal requirements on working conditions and on health and safety standards, and structures to ensure all those standards were kept to. Those protections for workers increased business costs, making the opportunity to move production to developing countries where, once again, very few of those protections are yet in force, an unmissable opportunity for any business that could become transnational. Instead of spreading even the most basic foundations of ethical business from the developed world to the developing one, globalisation seems instead to have allowed Western businesses to return to a nineteenth century view of business practice. The same utilitarianism that Charles Dickens railed at in novels like *Hard Times*, where every kind of human misery was excused on the basis that industry was bringing the greatest good to the greatest number, is again the favourite ethic of globalised business. In this view of globalisation, cut-throat competition is engaged in the pursuit of profit and good ethics in the countries of production is most certainly discouraged if it means one penny more on the costs of production. From this perspective, good ethics is, at most, just a promotional front to stop Western customers from thinking too much about the person who made their phone or the clothes they are wearing, and at what cost to that person's dreams and goals.

Perhaps, though, the pursuit of good ethics as the foundation of good business is something that the excesses of globalisation might be encouraging. Some transnational corporations have made sincere efforts to live up to their mission statements. Microsoft, for example, has donated well over $1 billion to charity since 1983, Google is investing $1 billion in providing cheap Internet coverage for developing countries. Not all transnational corporations are Western companies: many of the biggest are now Asian businesses that have operations in countries all over the world, including in Europe and the US. These corporations bring with them the ethical values of their own cultures, and have to deal with the ethical demands of Western society when, for example, they decide to shut down operations in UK plants, risking the unemployment of several thousand people. As societies demand more corporate social responsibility from transnational corporations, perhaps good ethics will become good global business.

Apply your knowledge

16. Discuss these two points of view:

   a. 'You are morally responsible not just for the person who serves you in the shop but also for the conditions in which the worker made the item. Ignorance is no excuse.'

   b. 'Poor countries should be happy to benefit from our purchasing goods that their factories have made.'

17. 'The investment in infrastructure, technology and workforce education and training that transnational corporations have brought to developing countries are not the benefits of globalisation. Western firms have also spread good business ethics around the world.' How far do you agree with this statement? Explain your answer.

Learning support

Points to remember

» Business ethics covers four topics: corporate social responsibility, whistle-blowing, 'good ethics is good business' and globalisation. Each of these involves a range of issues which often seem to overlap. Try to keep a clear idea of the central issues involved in each.

» When considering any question of business ethics, it is important to consider all of the stakeholders involved and all of the different ways they have a stake: employer, employee, investor/shareholder, consumer, communities in which the business operates, natural resources involved, those dependent on the work of the business and those affected in other ways by the work of the business.

» Business ethics often involves particular kinds of ethical considerations: matters of trust, honesty and promises, openness and transparency, (un)reasonable risk taking, the rules for business systems, the role of the state in regulating/managing businesses, the way in which a market operates and may be influenced.

» This chapter has identified Kantian and utilitarianism applications to each of the four topics: while many of the same principles apply to each, avoid just giving the same generalised answers about application of ethics to each of the different topics.

Enhance your learning

» There are many good books on business ethics but one that is kept up to date is Crane, A. and Matten D. *Business Ethics*, 2004 (1st edn), 2016 (4th edn).

» The FTSE4Good Index is designed to measure the performance of companies demonstrating strong environmental, social and governance practices. www.ftse.com/products/downloads/F4G-Index-Inclusion-Rules.pdf

» Milton Friedman's article 'The Social Responsibility of Business is to Increase its Profits' (*The New York Times Magazine*, 13 September 1970) is widely available online and is an excellent piece to refer to in discussions about corporate social responsibility.

» R. Freeman's article on 'A Stakeholder Theory of the Modern Corporation: Kantian Capitalism' (in *Ethical Theory and Business*, 3rd edn, eds. T.L. Beauchamp and N.E. Bowie, 1988, pp. 41–8) covers both stakeholders and Kantian ethics, both central to business ethics. It includes the argument that in order to make sure all stakeholders have a voice in what is going on, businesses should have a stakeholder enabling principle to manage the different interests of stakeholders (employers, financiers, customers, employees and communities).

» Johnson & Johnson's 'credo' (www.jnj.com/about-jnj/jnj-credo) is an excellent example to study for the impact of Kantian ethics on business ethics.

Practice for exams

AS questions and A level questions look identical; the difference between AS and A level assessment is seen in the different proportions of marks awarded for two different skills: the skill of demonstrating knowledge and understanding (Assessment Objective 1, or AO1), and the skill of constructing a critical argument (AO2).

At AS, half the marks (15 marks) are available for knowledge and understanding, and the other half (15 marks) for the quality of your analytical and evaluative argument. You should aim to use your knowledge in order to support the argument you are making throughout the essay, rather than presenting descriptive knowledge in the first half and then an opinion in the second.

At A level, your demonstration of knowledge and understanding is awarded a maximum of 16 marks, and your analytic and evaluative skills are awarded a maximum of 24 marks. You should aim to concentrate on constructing a lucid argument, making use of your knowledge to add weight to the conclusions you draw.

'Corporate social responsibility is nothing more than a hypocritical attempt to make more profit.' Discuss.

This essay asks you to demonstrate an understanding of 'corporate social responsibility' and to assess the motivation behind it.

Practise your skills for AS level

At AS, you should show knowledge and understanding of the concept of corporate social responsibility, and give an assessment of it. You will need to be able to give examples, but should avoid simply giving lots of examples of successful and unsuccessful corporate responsibility without using them to support a line of argument.

Practise your skills for A level

At A level, you should have a sharper focus on evaluative, critical skills. You might think that in some cases, corporate social responsibility is only a part of a company's marketing strategy and does little good; you might think that this is always the case; you might be able to cite examples of where social responsibility is at the heart of a business. You will probably want to consider the criteria by which we can judge whether attempts at social responsibility are genuine.

To what extent do Kantian ethics provide a useful tool in the context of business ethics?

This question invites a consideration of the extent to which Kantian ethics might help businesses to function in an ethical way.

Practise your skills for AS level

If answering this question at AS level, you should be able to show knowledge and understanding of Kantian ethics and the key principles of duty, good will and the *summum bonum*. You need to be able to show how Kantian ethics might be applied in the context of business, choosing examples such as corporate social responsibility, whistle-blowing or responsible marketing. Make sure you have shown how useful you think Kantian ethics are, rather than just describing what a Kantian might do.

Practise your skills for A level

At A level you should focus on an evaluation of the usefulness of Kantian ethics in the context of business, so you will need to consider questions such as whether Kantian ethics are easily applied, whether they give clear direction, whether they help or undermine a business's efforts to make money and whether they are practical. You should show knowledge and understanding of Kantian ethics but your essay should avoid being largely descriptive.

Studying developments in Christian thought

What are the fundamental questions of life?
Why study Christianity in a theological way?

Why study developments in Christian thought?

'Theology at its broadest is thinking about questions raised by and about religions' (D.F. Ford, *Theology, A Very Short Introduction*, 2000, p. 3). At a time when religion is debated and challenged in the world, it seems important to explore question raised by and about religions.

To study theology is to attempt to look at religion from the inside, using the methods, the language and the view of the world from the insider's perspective. It explores the doctrines, dogmas and teachings that Christians live by.

This does not mean there is no debate. From the beginning of Christianity there has been debate, in different attempts to make sense of a Christian life and the fundamental questions that distinguish Christianity: What is the nature and purpose of human life? Is there something unique about a person, and does anything continue of that person beyond death? How is it possible to know anything about these questions? Who is Jesus Christ and what does it mean to live a life of Christian moral principles and actions?

Over time, some have tried to answer these questions, sometimes in strikingly different ways, influenced by the ways of thinking and history of their times, and possibly influenced by something else, something beyond their limitations.

To understand these theological ideas and beliefs it is helpful to cultivate an open mind to the possibility that there might be something meaningful within them. This does not mean surrendering personal belief or opinion, but being disposed to listen to the voices of others, to take seriously their own insights and convictions, and to decide how to stand in relation to this way of understanding meaning and purpose in the world.

The life and the self

Arguably the first question we might ask is what does it mean to be a human being? Is there some purpose to human behaviour or relationships? Is there a development that can happen that might change a human life? The idea that human beings are created, have a purpose and a need to fulfil that purpose is a key aspect of Christian theology. If it is possible to become something more, if it is possible to live a better life than the one already lived, then these questions provoke exploration. What kind of life, what kind of being, can a person become?

Is there something more than the physical, the limited life that a human lives on earth? Is there a future beyond death where something that is meaningfully human continues to exist? These questions are explored through Christian theology on human nature and the purpose of life, life after death and immortality.

Knowledge of God

Religion is a complex aspect of life in today's world. Though religion is declining in some Western countries, religion and belief is becoming more prominent globally. The numbers of people aligning themselves to a religious belief worldwide is greater than ever before.

Given these changes the question of what we can know about God becomes key. What can be known of God, if indeed such a being exists? What is the role of faith? Can such truths be revealed and if so, in what ways?

Jesus

The central figure of Christianity is Jesus. The key doctrines, beliefs and teachings of Christian faith relate in some way to Jesus. The nature of God is interpreted through a sense of the connection between the divine and the human in the possibility that Jesus may be God as well as a man. Whether Jesus was a figure of an ancient world or whether he is encountered in life today, is thought to be crucial to any understanding of a Christian way of life. The question of the identity of Jesus remains a compelling one for people beyond Christian faith. He is a figure who has marked the development of human civilisation like few others.

Christian moral principles and action

Another starting place is to ask what sort of life should a Christian live? What ideals and principles should drive actions in day-to-day life. What would those actions look like?

Christianity is a tradition with a number of moral ideas linked to beliefs about the world – about the place of love and forgiveness, about what it means to live a pure life, a good life. Christianity is not a theoretical system but an applied one. Belief leads to changes in attitudes and behaviour.

At the heart of Christian belief is the idea that there is a communication from God to humanity, a revelation of something that is worth knowing, that contains certain truths which, if followed, make a difference to life.

How to be a theologian

The student of Christianity becomes a theologian. Traditionally theologians were always Christian, and always held Christians beliefs themselves. Theology was an exploration of those beliefs, and this included debate and sometimes argument. However, theology in modern times has developed beyond the confines of Christian belief with some who consider themselves to be outside conventional Christian belief.

Could anyone be a theologian irrespective of belief? Perhaps the student of theology today could be thought of as someone who makes an enquiry from where they stand, looking intently into the mysteries of belief, doctrine and religious life, open to the possibilities that those mysteries might offer people, and with some sense of how they themselves relate to those beliefs, doctrines and approaches to religious life. Perhaps a theologian is an interpreter of religion – one who actively enquires and seeks to comprehend. Taken in this way, the student of Christian theology might be of any belief or religion, or none that is fixed.

In trying to interpret a religion or text there are a number of things you could try to do. These are drawn from scholars of hermeneutics:

- Be attentive to the texts you study. What do they say to you? How do others perceive them?

- Try to spot preconceived ideas affecting how you interpret the sources you are examining. Are you bringing pre-formed decisions and attitudes into your interpretation of what you perceive?

- Be self-critical about your interpretation of the sources. Is it serving your own interests?

- Learn to become aware about how different theological perspectives engage with the different sources and ideas.

- Look out for examples where the sources present something counter-intuitive, or subversive, where something new is provoked. These could be signs that you are making a connection to ideas in those sources, not simply your own preconceptions.

- Try to adopt a charitable approach to interpret the sources and ideas you experience. Try to seek out the meaning that others give before you decide and judge for yourself.

Questions for thought and reflection

A. What is the nature of human life?

B. How, if at all, can human beings learn about the existence and nature of God?

C. How do different beliefs about Jesus influence other beliefs about the Christian faith?

D. What are the implications of Christian beliefs and teachings on ethics?

These are big questions which frame the chapters in this section of the book. Return to them as you explore the different ideas in this section. Give space and time to how you relate to these questions, as well as the ideas presented in this text.

Chapter 3.1 : Augustine's teaching on human nature

What does it mean to be human, according to Christian teaching?

What does Augustine contribute to a Christian understanding of human nature?

Is human nature essentially good, essentially bad, or morally ambiguous?

If people have genuine free will, why do they often choose to do wrong?

Does human life have a purpose?

Key Terms

Will: the part of human nature that makes free choices

Sin: disobeying the will and commands of God

Grace: in theological terms, God's free and undeserved love for humanity, epitomised in the sacrifice of Jesus on the cross

The Fall: the biblical event in which Adam and Eve disobeyed God's command and ate the fruit from the forbidden tree in the Garden of Eden; also used to refer to the imperfect state of humanity

Neoplatonism: philosophical thinking arising from the ideas of Plato

Redeemed: in theological terms, 'saved' from sin by the sacrifice of Christ

Concordia: human friendship

Cupiditas: 'selfish love', a love of worldly things and of selfish desires

Caritas: 'generous love', a love of others and of the virtues; the Latin equivalent of the Greek word agape

Concupiscence: uncontrollable desire for physical pleasures and material things

Ecclesia: heavenly society, in contrast with earthly society

Summum bonum: the highest, most supreme good

Specification requirements

- Human relationships pre- and post-Fall
- Original Sin and its effects on the will and human societies
- God's grace

Introduction

The issue of what it means to be human is one which has concerned philosophers and theologians for centuries, and it is addressed by Christian thinkers too, most notably by Paul (first century) in the Bible and by Augustine (fourth century).

The Bible portrays humanity as made by God for the purposes of ruling over the created world and looking after it as stewards. However, the Genesis stories show that human free **will** gives the capacity to sin and leads people to rebel against obedience to God, and how this rebellion has led to a state of **sin**. According to traditional Christian theology, which was strongly influenced by the thinking of Augustine, the sin of Adam and Eve broke the relationship humanity could have had with God. According to Augustine the Original Sin committed by the first people was passed on through human generations, making it impossible for anyone to live up to the standards of God. The sacrificial death of Jesus on the cross paid the price for sin and allowed the possibility for Christians to be saved through the **grace** of God.

In the Bible Paul explores the question of why Christians continue to sin even after they have accepted the forgiveness of God. Later, Augustine takes up the ideas raised by Paul and, reflecting on his own personal experiences as well as biblical teachings, discusses fallen human nature and the relation between human free will and the grace of God.

Augustine was a very able man and a prolific writer, writing both an autobiographical account of his life experiences and discussions of theological matters. His combination of philosophical thought and honest reflections on his own personal issues made him a popular and influential shaper of Christian thought. His readers could relate to his thinking, even though it contains some demanding ideas, because he never pretended to find the Christian life easy himself. Also, Augustine's views changed in his writings over time, so that the reader can see him revisiting his opinions and refining them as he grew older, which adds to the sense of a man who understood that conversion to Christianity was the beginning of a sometimes difficult journey and not simply a happy ending in itself.

For Augustine, human nature has been fatally damaged by sin as a result of **the Fall**. The only hope of salvation is through the grace of God, made available to humanity in the sacrifice of Christ, for the people whom God chooses.

Augustine's life and influences

In the early fourth century, at around the time Augustine's grandparents would have been alive, Christianity was adopted as the official religion of the Roman Empire by the Emperor Constantine.

Before Constantine, Christianity had been a minority faith and its early followers were persecuted because of their refusal to follow the cult of the Roman emperor; this refusal was considered to be treason and was, therefore, punishable by death. The biblical writers and missionaries Paul and Peter had both been executed in Rome for treason under the reign of Nero. However, when Emperor Constantine adopted the Christian faith for himself in AD312, he gave Christianity a completely different status in the ancient world. He put Christians in positions of power, poured a lot of money into building Christian places of worship, gave special privileges to the Christian ministry and elevated the Christian faith to a state of respectability. Constantine's rule meant that Christianity was decriminalised and that persecution was banned. However, he did not insist that people became Christians, instead he was a promoter of religious tolerance, allowing pagan temples and different philosophical schools to flourish alongside Christianity. The study of non-Christian classical literature was allowed to remain an important part of a good education.

Augustine (AD354–430) was born in North Africa, which was then an important part of the Roman Empire. He grew up in the atmosphere of religious and philosophical pluralism that Constantine had established. Christianity was available as an option but so were many other ways of thinking, including Platonism and philosophical scepticism.

Augustine's mother, Monica, was a devout Christian who was very influential in shaping Augustine's own beliefs, but his father was hostile to Christianity. Augustine's parents were not very well off but they believed in the value of education and recognised that their son's abilities justified the expense of sending him to school. Augustine studied rhetoric (similar to philosophy) and became enthusiastically involved in the excesses of student life, and then as his talents began to attract the attention of wealthy patrons, he moved on to teach in Carthage (in present-day Tunisia), in Rome and then in Milan.

When Augustine was a young man, he followed the thinking of a group called the Manichees, who believed that the world is engaged in a cosmic battle between good and evil. They also believed that people have two different souls, one good and one evil, and that these two souls pull the individual in different directions, creating internal struggles where people are, on the one hand, tempted by wrongdoing, but on the other hand want to do good. They taught that the human soul is naturally a part of the kingdom of light, but it becomes trapped in the kingdom of darkness because of the appetites of the body. According to Manichaean teaching, wisdom and enlightenment involved using human reason to understand

Think question

What do you think are the advantages and disadvantages of growing up in a multi-faith society? How might growing up in a multi-faith society affect someone's religious beliefs?

the causes of evil and wrongdoing. Escape from wrongdoing could be found by following the example of role models, the most important of whom for the Manichees was Jesus. Augustine was very taken with these ideas and for a time became an enthusiastic Manichee missionary, much to his mother's disapproval.

Augustine was also very interested in Plato's ideas, and was heavily influenced by a Neoplatonist philosopher called Plotinus (**Neoplatonism** refers to schools of thought which arose from and developed the thinking of Plato; there are several different strands and they did not all take Plato's thinking in the same direction). Augustine read Plotinus' works with great excitement. He was particularly struck by the way Plotinus seemed almost ashamed of living in a human body, taking to new lengths Plato's ideas that the impermanent physical body and the permanent world of the Forms were in many ways opposites. Plotinus had written about his views on Manichaeism, and disagreed with their assessment of the universe as two distinct realms of good and evil. For Plotinus, there was only the Form of the Good, which people could come to understand through study and self-reflection. Plotinus advocated that people should treat their own characters in the way that sculptors treat the statues they are creating: by looking at it carefully from all angles and chiseling away the parts which are not quite right. Reading this idea gave Augustine a moment of vision: he suddenly understood that evil is 'not a substance', but is non-existent, a turning-away from goodness. The Manichees were wrong.

> *See Chapter 1.6. Augustine believed that evil did not have a power and existence of its own.*

Augustine, despite his absorption in Platonic ideas, found them ultimately unsatisfactory because of their ethics; he did not think that seeking a happy, reasonably virtuous life was quite enough of a goal for human existence. He was also doubtful of Plotinus' assertion that the human intellect was capable of understanding the nature of goodness on its own, because if that were true, then it left no room for Jesus Christ to have an important role. Augustine wanted wisdom and, if it could be found, certain knowledge of truth.

During his search for this truth, Augustine continued engaging with Christians, going to church and studying the Bible, as well as reading non-Christian writings and discussing ideas with thinkers from different backgrounds. Eventually, he went to hear the preaching of the Bishop of Milan, who became known as St Ambrose. Augustine was an excellent speaker himself and wanted to hear Ambrose primarily in order to admire his preaching style, but he was also profoundly affected by the content of the message and renewed his interest in Christianity as a possible answer to the search for certain truth. Reading the letters of Paul, and in particular Paul's letter to the Romans, drew Augustine to the conclusion that humans could not find this truth through their own reason alone, but that they needed the grace of God and needed to turn away from bodily pleasures in order to concentrate on the spiritual life.

Finally, after many years of exploration, Augustine converted to Christianity when he was 32. He later became a priest and then a bishop.

Augustine in the fourth century AD produced and developed some of Christianity's most central doctrines

He was not particularly keen on either role, but in those days, people were appointed to positions of leadership on the spot as a response to the will of the congregation, and so these positions were forced upon him.

Augustine's life as a Christian presented him with theological difficulties, and also with personal ones. Before he became a Christian, he had a mistress with whom he lived and had a child; this was not unusual for young men of his culture. They lived together very much as a family, but once Augustine had been converted, his mother insisted that he give up his mistress and marry someone else, which was very painful for all involved. As a Christian leader, Augustine continued to explore and refine his thinking about spiritual matters, shaping not only his own faith but the way in which Christianity itself was to develop. Although he had enjoyed the freedom to be able to explore different ways of thinking during his own personal spiritual journey, and had also enjoyed the freedoms of fine living and sexual relationships, in later life Augustine became certain that such freedoms were a barrier to spirituality and others should be restricted from them. According to many sources, he did not share Constantine's religious tolerance, instead, once he held a position of influence, he ordered the destruction of non-Christian places of worship. He persecuted as heretics those who had a different understanding of Christianity from his own, both with laws and with pages of written arguments in which he condemned the views of others. Ironically, many of these heresies are remembered today only because Augustine wrote so copiously about them. Augustine especially argued against the views of those who claimed that human reason and human effort could lead an individual to wisdom and moral goodness. For Augustine, the fallen sinful nature of humanity made this impossible without the grace of God.

Augustine's writings encompass 93 formal works as well as many letters and notes for speeches. They include a work called *Soliloquies*, where his own internal voice debates with the personification of Reason; a work called *Divine Providence and the Problem of Evil* and *The 'City of God'*, is Augustine's answer to accusations that Christianity had weakened the Roman Empire; and a remarkable collection of books called *Confessions*, usually published in English under one title, *The Confessions of St Augustine*.

Augustine's *Confessions* are one of the earliest known autobiographical works. They provide a fascinating insight not only into Augustine's own life and thoughts but into the social context in which he lived. In this collection of writings, he details his own development as a thinker and as a Christian, from childhood to early middle age, which is why we know so much about him and about the different influences on his theology. In the books, he reflects on his pre-Christian life and habits, especially on his own moral behaviour, he uses this personal experience as a basis from which to draw conclusions about human nature as a whole. In expressing repentance for past wrongs, reflecting on them and resolving to change through the grace of God, Augustine laid the groundwork for the practice of confession in the Catholic Church (otherwise known as the Sacrament of Reconciliation), where self-examination, acknowledgement of sin and repentance is seen as an important part of Christian life.

Augustine combined his skills in philosophy with reflections on his own personal life in his writings about theological ideas

Augustine's teaching on human nature, the Fall and Original Sin

Some of the most fundamental questions people ask themselves are concerned with what, if anything, is the meaning of human existence. Is there a distinctively human nature? Is there a reason we are here, and if so, what might that reason be? Are we fundamentally good or evil, or morally neutral beings? Do we need to find our own meaning in the world as individuals, or is there a final purpose for which all of humanity was made? These were questions which occupied Augustine throughout his life, and questions to which, he believed, answers could be found in the teachings of the Bible and the Church.

Augustine's ideas about human nature were all about the effects of the Fall on the human relationship with God. For Augustine, the moment when Eve and then Adam chose to disobey God was the turning point for the whole of creation. His views are based around the opening chapters of Genesis and the letter of Paul to the Romans. They are also entwined with Platonic thought and with some of the concepts of Manicheism.

According to Christianity, people are created by God, they have fallen into sin but they can be redeemed

According to Christianity, humanity is to be understood primarily in terms of the human relationship with God. Christianity emphasises three key features of this relationship: (1) people are created by God; (2) they are 'fallen' in nature; and (3) they can be **redeemed**.

Christianity teaches that humanity is deliberately created and planned by God, to occupy a special place in the universe. People are made 'in the image of God' in order to rule (or 'have dominion') over the earth and the other species within it. This comes from the book of Genesis, in which God creates the world with all its different features of day and night, land and sea, plants and animals, and then finally chooses to make humanity.

> 66 Then God said, 'Let us make mankind in our image, in our likeness, so that they may rule over the fish in the sea and the birds in the sky, over the livestock and all the wild animals, and over all the creatures that move along the ground.'
> So God created mankind in his own image,
> in the image of God he created them; male and female he created them. 99
>
> Genesis 1:26–27, New International Version

In the first Genesis creation story, people are made so that they can be stewards of the earth

In Genesis people are made 'in the image of God'; Christians usually interpret this to mean that they have rationality and free will

Think question

Sometimes sceptics suggest that religious believers create God in their own image: they invent a being who is like them but with superpowers. Do you think this is fair?

In this passage, from the first creation story in Genesis, God has a purpose for the creation of humanity, which is one of stewardship. The creation account is written with the sense that everything in the world is made for human purposes; it is all set in place, and then God creates people as the final climax to the story, after which he has completed his work and rests on the seventh day. People are made so that they can be 'stewards' of the earth, in other words caretakers of it, looking after the property of God and keeping it in order. The idea of people being made in the image of God ('imago Dei') is difficult to understand. The Hebrew word used is the same word as would have been used to mean literally that people look like God; but clearly the writer did not have physical resemblance in mind, as God is believed to be non-physical and people do not all look the same.

Christian teaching usually interprets 'imago Dei' to mean that people share something of the nature of God, in that they have rationality, relationality, freedom and a moral nature. People are self-aware and have freedom of choice; they also have the capacity for loving relationships. Perhaps also there is the implicit idea here that all people are, in a fundamental way, equal, because they all share this aspect of being made in God's image.

In the second Genesis creation story, God creates a man from the dust of the ground, showing that although people might have a special place in the universe, they are at the same time part of the natural, physical world and made from the same material as the rest of nature. God animates the man he has made by breathing into his nostrils: not with any kind of detachable soul of the sort that Plato had in mind, but with a life-giving force.

A detail from *The Creation of Adam* by Michelangelo. What do you think Michelangelo was trying to say about the relationship between God and humanity in this image, where God and Adam are almost touching, but not quite?

Once humanity is made, there are rules to follow: be stewards of the earth, be fruitful and multiply, and do not eat from the tree in the middle of the garden. It is clear that the created people have not been programmed like machines to behave in a way that God has fixed in them, but need to be told what is expected. They have the potential to be obedient, but also the potential to disobey: in other words, they have free choices, including moral choice.

From the start of the Bible, the nature and purpose of humanity is clear. People are made 'in the image of God', they are a part of the natural world but also reflect in some ways the nature of God, and are made for the purposes of obeying God's commands with faith. In the Bible, some stories exemplify the need for obedience to God's commands even when they conflict with human reasoning.

Christianity presents humanity as having responsibility because of being the creation of God. They have a duty of obedience to God's commands

Humanity as fallen

In Christian teaching, although all of humanity is made by God, people abuse their freedom of choice by disobeying God's commandments and choosing to do wrong instead. Whether Christians believe that Adam and Eve were real historical people, or whether they believe that the story is a mythical way of explaining the human condition, it is a central belief in Christianity that humanity is inclined to sin.

Christianity teaches that by nature, humans are inclined to disobey God

The creation story of Genesis 2–3 shows how, despite being forbidden to eat the fruit from the tree of the knowledge of good and evil, Adam and Eve went ahead and ate it anyway, in an event known as the Fall. Eve was tempted by the serpent (traditionally understood to be Satan, although the Bible does not say this explicitly) to eat the fruit; the serpent told her that she need not listen to God's warnings, and she made the free decision to listen to the serpent rather than to resist. She encouraged Adam to follow suit, and so both male and female broke the commandment they had been given (Genesis 3:6). This order of events has led to a tradition in which some see women as being more likely to sin than men, because Eve was the first to give in to temptation; and women are sometimes seen as being inclined to lead men into wrongdoing, because of the example of Eve.

Eve was the first to sin, and some Christians argue that this demonstrates women are, by nature, weaker than men

When Adam and Eve have fallen from grace into sin, they are punished. Genesis 3:14–19 presents some familiar features of human life as being the result of the Fall:

66 So the Lord God said to the snake, 'Because you have done this,
'Cursed are you above all livestock
and all wild animals!
You will crawl on your belly
and you will eat dust
all the days of your life.

And I will put enmity
between you and the woman,
and between your offspring and hers;
he will crush your head,
and you will strike his heel.'
To the woman he said,
'I will make your pains in childbearing very severe;
with painful labour you will give birth to children.
Your desire will be for your husband,
and he will rule over you.'
To Adam he said, 'Because you listened to your wife and ate fruit from the tree about which I commanded you, "You must not eat from it,"
'Cursed is the ground because of you;
through painful toil you will eat food from it
all the days of your life.
It will produce thorns and thistles for you,
and you will eat the plants of the field.
By the sweat of your brow
you will eat your food
until you return to the ground,
since from it you were taken;
for dust you are
and to dust you will return.'

Genesis 3:14–19, New International Version

For the writers of the book of Genesis, then, the enmity between humans and snakes, the difficulties of childbirth, the need to work hard to make a living, and the inevitability of death can all be accounted for by the Fall: they are all the consequences of disobedience to the will of God.

Before the Fall, when Adam and Eve lived in the Garden of Eden, they seem to have lived in close proximity with God. Once they have eaten the fruit, they hear God 'walking in the garden in the cool of the day' (Genesis 3:8, New International Version) and this is presented as a normal state of affairs, where God was clearly apparent to them and a companion of theirs; an aspect of the 'state of perfection' of creation before the introduction of sin. However, when their disobedience comes to light, they are banished, sent out from the garden into the harsh reality of the rest of the world, where they can no longer see God readily and where there is a barrier between them and God, guarded by angels with swords. The barrier is one humanity has made for itself, by sinning.

Although Genesis itself does not say very much about what humans were like before the Fall, Augustine had some ideas about how he thought they must have been, using the Bible to draw his conclusions.

In the Genesis account, people are punished for sin by being sent out into the harsh reality of the world

Human nature and will before and after the Fall

Before the Fall, Augustine thought, Adam and Eve must have lived in a spirit of loving friendship, friends both with each other as partners and with God. They would have lived in harmony with other living creatures, co-operating fully. God had made them exactly the way he wanted to, and so in Augustine's view they must have been in a 'state of perfection', living without sin in the way that God planned people should live.

God had commanded them to 'Be fruitful and multiply', so they would have enjoyed a sexual relationship, but it would not have been a relationship governed by lust, because lust was part of the punishment God gave to Eve following the Fall, so clearly it had not been present beforehand. When Adam and Eve sin in the Genesis story, they immediately realise that they are naked: so before the Fall, they must have lived quite comfortably with their bodies, with no suggestion that there was anything wrong with being naked. Augustine was a great believer in the value of human friendship, which was a recurrent theme in his writings. In *Confessions* he writes about being surrounded by, and living alongside, groups of friends with whom he could discuss his ideas, sometimes sitting out on the grass under the trees. He wrote that there are two things that are essential for humans: a healthy life, and friendship. We are, he thought, naturally social creatures, and friendship is the highest form of that sociable nature. He wrote of how friends can increase each other's happiness and lessen each other's sadness, of how friends love each other for their own sakes and not for any ulterior motive, and how

The story of the Fall of Adam and Eve in the book of Genesis was central for the thinking of Augustine

we accept the strengths and weaknesses of our friends as they accept ours. When Augustine writes of friendship, the expression he uses is '**concordia**', to mean the easy, comfortable and understanding relationships that good friends have with one another. In writing about Adam and Eve living in a spirit of friendship, then, he did not mean that they were 'just friends' in any sense of having less meaningful, casual feelings towards one another; he meant that they were living in what he thought was the best of all possible human relationships.

Augustine held a firm belief that human beings have free will, given to them by God, and this is one of the chief characteristics of being made in the image of God. However, he also was convinced that people are in the grip of sin, and that we are born into sin ('Original Sin') because we are descendants of Adam and, therefore, in Augustine's view, inherit Adam's sin and guilt. There is nothing we can do by ourselves, he thought, to become free from sin; we can only be saved by the grace of God.

The problem of evil was of special interest to Augustine: he had difficulty with the existence of evil in the world when he also believed that God is perfectly good, like Plato's Form of the Good. Augustine's response to the problem of evil was focused on the idea that humans are rational creatures, and that they were originally given free will, which he made the subject of a book, *On Free Will*. In this book, he tried to argue against the Manichee idea that the world has two powers in it, good and evil: for Augustine, there was only one power, God.

> *See Chapter 1.6. Augustine thought that the existence of evil in the world is entirely the fault of humanity.*

When God made Adam in his own image, he made him with freedom of choice, without which Adam would not have been free to choose to obey God's commands. However, this same freedom also made it possible for Adam to sin, as if he was going to have the capability of freely choosing what was good, there had to be other options too. For Augustine, evil in the world was entirely due to the human misuse of free will, and could not possibly be the fault of God. The human will could, and should, choose to obey the changeless goodness of God, but people instead were attracted by the changeable world of material goods because they had become tainted with sin through Adam and Eve.

Augustine saw the human will as capable of being pulled in different directions

Augustine saw the human will as being driven by love, which (after the Fall) could pull the person in the right direction or in the wrong one although fallen human nature inevitably led people to do wrong. He outlined two different kinds of love, one wrong and one right:

1. **Cupiditas** – this is the love of impermanent, changeable earthly things, and love of self and selfish needs; it is an 'error of will' to follow cupiditas, and choosing this path is entirely the individual's own responsibility and own fault. People who choose this path are ignorant and often unhappy because they have subjected themselves to the laws of the world which are the human laws of social life.

2. **Caritas** (the Latin equivalent of the Greek work agape) – this is a generous love of others, an expression of the will of God as eternal law, and is displayed through the virtues, which Augustine lists as prudence, fortitude,

temperance and justice. Choosing to exercise one's will according to the principles of caritas leads to happiness, not necessarily worldly happiness in terms of good fortune, but spiritual happiness that is the result of being obedient to the will of God. This choice originally given by God, however, Augustine saw as having been removed by sin, putting people in the position of being unable to do right except by the grace of God.

In Book 2 of Augustine's *On Free Will*, he emphasised his belief that all good things, including the free human will, come from God. However, not all human actions come from God, because sometimes people clearly choose sin. Augustine could not explain why Adam and Eve chose to sin, although he supposed that it had to have been due to some kind of pride, of the sort where people imagine themselves to be better than they are; but this still leaves unanswered the question of where this pride came from.

Original Sin and its effects on the will and human societies

Augustine thought we could explain humanity's sinful nature after the Fall by looking at the state of ignorance which is the inevitable consequence of choosing a path of cupiditas, the path of lust, selfishness and attachment to impermanent material goods. Adam and Eve chose this path and passed on the tendency to sin to future generations through sexual intercourse, as 'Original Sin', where people inherit the flawed human nature of their parents through the generations.

Original Sin is the term used to denote the belief that all human beings are sinful by nature, and are born that way, because they have inherited this nature from Adam. The inherited sin of Adam means that people are unable to live morally pure lives, however hard they try. Augustine argued in his writings with a thinker called Pelagius. Pelagius held the view that people could, if they tried hard, live morally. Adam had set a bad example, but it is not one which everyone has to follow. Augustine disagreed passionately. In his view, the sin of Adam corrupted everything, including human freedom to be good and follow God's will. People are beyond rescue by their own efforts, and can only be saved from sin by God's grace through Christ. One of Augustine's arguments against Pelagius' view was that, if people could achieve goodness through their own efforts, then this made Jesus' sacrifice unnecessary.

He saw human will, after the Fall, as being 'divided'; people still have the God-given ability to reason and to recognise right from wrong, but they have corrupted this will, so that they are always inclined to do wrong and to be selfish and lustful. They end up arguing with themselves, wanting to do right but also wanting to do wrong. Augustine could very much relate to Paul's thinking in Romans 7, where Paul describes struggling between his spiritual inclinations and his selfish and physical desires. Paul writes:

66 We know that the law is spiritual; but I am unspiritual, sold as a slave to sin. I do not understand what I do. For what I want to do I do

Apply your knowledge

4. 'Prudence', 'fortitude' and 'temperance' are not used in general conversation very much, find out and make a note of what these words mean.

5. Do you think Augustine's four virtues are the best characteristics for a person to cultivate? Would you add any to the list, or remove any? Give reasons for your answer.

6. 'Caritas' has been chosen as the name for an aid organisation. Find out something about its origins and aims. Why do you think the organisation chose this name?

In Augustine's thinking, cupiditas is the path of self-love, lust and love for material things; caritas is the path of generous, unselfish love for others not do, but what I hate I do. And if I do what I do not want to do, I agree that the law is good. As it is, it is no longer I myself who do it, but it is sin living in me. For I know that good itself does not dwell in me, that is, in my sinful nature. For I have the desire to do what is good, but I cannot carry it out. For I do not do the good I want to do, but the evil I do not want to do – this I keep on doing. Now if I do what I do not want to do, it is no longer I who do it, but it is sin living in me that does it.

So I find this law at work: although I want to do good, evil is right there with me. For in my inner being I delight in God's law; but I see another law at work in me, waging war against the law of my mind and making me a prisoner of the law of sin at work within me. What a wretched man I am! Who will rescue me from this body that is subject to death? Thanks be to God, who delivers me through Jesus Christ our Lord!

So then, I myself in my mind am a slave to God's law, but in my sinful nature a slave to the law of sin. **"**

Romans 7:14–25, New International Version

There has been discussion amongst biblical scholars about whether Paul is speaking about his own current nature, after he became a Christian, or whether he is trying to describe and sum up his experiences before his conversion, or whether he is using 'I' when he means to refer to unsaved humanity in general. Most, although not all, have understood the passage to be about Paul's attempts to live his life as a Christian and his recognition that although he has been saved he still has to face all the temptations to sin and the weaknesses that come with being human and a descendant of Adam.

In the passage, Paul describes how he longs to be free from sin, but that he feels chained to it, pulled in different directions. He contrasts the 'spiritual' nature of God's law with his own 'fleshly' nature. He describes the helplessness he feels when he recognises and wants to do the right thing and yet does not seem to be able to do it, falling back into sinful ways through weakness. He is clear that the law of God is not itself to blame, because God's law is good; and yet it can also lead to sin because it gives human nature something to rebel against. Once we know that something is wrong, it makes doing it all the more desirable.

Paul writes almost as though sin has a life of its own and lives within him, overriding his freedom of choice; it almost seems as though he is claiming not to be to blame for the things he does, but then he uses 'I' and returns to taking full responsibility for his own thoughts and actions. His will to do good is powerless because he is sinful by his very human nature. He suggests that there will never be a time, until perhaps after death when he no longer has the same physical body, when he will be free from the chains of sin.

Paul emphasises that Christians are 'forgiven sinners'; they have not stopped sinning, but they are now forgiven for their sins because of their faith. This has often been felt to reflect the experience of Christian living, and it explains why Christians carry on behaving badly just as they did before they accepted their salvation. Paul goes on to ask rhetorically whether there can be any release from the torment of continuing to sin despite knowing that it is wrong, and he implies that the release will come after death when his soul can leave the physical body that gives in so easily to temptation.

For many Christians, this short passage has been a source of comfort and some relief to know that even someone with Paul's strength of faith had the same difficulties with sin that they themselves face. It gives, perhaps, an insight into the psychology of the man Paul and of Christian life. It has given rise to contrasting interpretations, however. Some point out that the apparent admission of weakness here is in stark contrast to other writings of Paul where he seems very confident about his transformation as a Christian, his abilities to lead and his own character as a potential role model for others, and are troubled by the idea that Paul had to put up such a fight against sin within himself.

Augustine studied this piece of Paul's writings carefully and could relate it to his own inner life. He remembered a time when, as a child, he had stolen a pear from someone else's garden – even though he was not hungry and had plenty of good food in his own home. He stole it simply for the pleasure of stealing. (Whether Augustine really did steal the pear, or whether he was embroidering his autobiography in order to draw a parallel with the forbidden fruit of the Garden of Eden, is not clear.) For Augustine this demonstrated that sin has become a part of human nature, something that is displayed even by children because they are born with it.

Augustine on men, women and sexuality

For Augustine, as he explains candidly in *Confessions*, a particularly difficult issue was celibacy and sexuality. His own history with his mistress and then with his wife gave him a great deal of food for thought; he believed that ideally, he should be able to control his own sexual desire, but at the same time he knew he found this impossible. Augustine thought that sinful humanity is particularly at the mercy of '**concupiscence**', by which he meant primarily sexual desire but also other kinds of appetites and lusts for things in the material world. He included the strong emotions of affection and jealousy that occur in human friendships as examples of concupiscence, as these can absorb a person's emotional energy and be a distraction from loving and obeying God. Even feeling hungry and then enjoying a good meal can lead people into concupiscence.

In his writings Augustine does not seem to have an entirely consistent view. He seemed to think that sexual desire was evidence of sinful cupiditas and often encouraged the idea that married men and women should take a vow of celibacy once they had enough children; he also suggested that people should try to live as plain and simple a lifestyle as they could, in order to devote themselves to God. But then he wrote to a woman called Edicia and

Augustine thought that people, in their sinful nature, were driven by concupiscence, an uncontrollable urge for material and physical pleasures

Although more sympathetic to women than other writers of his time, Augustine had some inconsistent and sometimes unrealistic ideas about the evils of human sexuality

told her off because she had decided to stop having sex with her husband, and as a result the husband had committed adultery. Edicia had also given away the family jewellery and her expensive clothes in order to be more spiritual, and her husband was annoyed. Augustine told her that she should have waited until her husband agreed with her desire to renounce physical pleasures rather than going ahead on her own.

His own life, as Bishop of Hippo (modern-day Annaba, in Algeria), was said to be simple and adequate, not going to extremes of poverty (he always enjoyed a good dinner with his friends) but also not over-indulgent. He tried hard to make sure that his conversation was steered well away from gossip, and in order to keep himself chaste and maintain the 'purity of will' that he so much wanted, he did not allow women to visit his home, not even his own sister.

However, Augustine is usually lot more sympathetic to women than other writers and thinkers of his time. Perhaps because of his premarital relationship, he rejected the view of many of his contemporaries that women were more evil than men, or weaker, because of the sin of Eve. Augustine thought that because men and women are both created in the image of God, they both share equally in this image as they both have a rational nature capable of forming a loving relationship with God. A woman is not inferior to a man, but she is (according to Augustine) more passive, and therefore should take the passive roles in the home and allow the man to be the main decision-maker.

Augustine on Original Sin and human society

Augustine believed that before the Fall, people were capable of living together harmoniously without the need for any kind of repressive political authority. He thought that if people had not been rebellious against God, they would still have needed some kind of leadership, but he saw this in terms of a kind of fatherly authority, similar to the way a Roman head of the family would have looked after his wife and children.

People with Original Sin, however, needed a forceful political authority, according to Augustine, otherwise they would behave according to their sinful natures of greed, violence and lust, and society would not be able to function. Aquinas, much later than Augustine, understood contribution to the common good of society as a virtue, but Augustine did not see it that way. In his work *City of God*, he expressed the view that in the Bible, people are told to rule over other species when they are created (and he quotes Genesis 1:26), but they are not told to rule over each other and to make some people subject to the rules of others. Augustine said that before the Fall, the leaders of society were shepherds rather than kings, guiding and protecting other people rather than enforcing restrictions on them. Augustine pointed to the practice of slavery, in particular, as evidence of sin at a societal level, something that would never have occurred before the Fall.

See Chapter 2.1 on Aquinas and Natural Law. Aquinas thought contribution to a well-ordered society was a virtue, but Augustine saw it as an unfortunate necessity resulting from sin.

Augustine argued that even if good people are subject to the authority of bad people, they should submit to this and use it as a learning opportunity in which to practice humility. However, he did not think that 'earthly peace', the kind that societies usually try to achieve, was a great ideal. He saw it in contrast to 'heavenly peace'. 'Earthly peace', Augustine said, was just a compromise made between sinful human wills, where everyone comes to an uneasy truce in order to make sure that the members of a society have access to material goods. People only aim for earthly peace because they have 'mortal interests'; in other words, their aim in living in a peaceful society is just for their own material well-being, and not a spiritual aim.

People in their sinful state are by nature greedy and violent, wanting more for themselves in comparison with others. Augustine thought that earthly peace can only be achieved with repressive political structures which control sinful natures by force, and earthly peace is always precarious. The best sort of life that sinful people can hope for is earthly peace, but even that, like the individual human will, is corrupted. Augustine points out that some of the so-called virtues necessary for people to live together in earthly peace, such as self-control and physical courage, are only necessary because of Original Sin. If Adam and Eve had never sinned, then there would have been no need for such qualities.

Attachment to the common good, then, was not seen as a moral virtue by Augustine, but as a consequence of sinful human nature. He gave the metaphor of 'a pilgrim in a foreign land' to explain how the Christian should behave in relation to the advantages of human society. The Christian has to, by necessity, live in an earthly society and therefore needs to live as earthly people do, but the Christian should keep his or her eyes on the destination, which is the 'City of God', until the time comes when he or she can enter heavenly society and heavenly peace.

This heavenly society, or '**ecclesia**' is the perfect way to live. Earthly society is only a very partial, corrupted, poor reflection of heavenly society, which people will only come to know fully after death and through the grace of God.

Augustine's teaching about grace

Augustine was certain that people cannot be reconciled with God through their own efforts. He taught that the only way in which humanity and God could be restored to harmonious living was through the grace of God: in other words, through the generous giving of God's love to people, despite the fact that they can never deserve it. The sacrifice of Jesus on the cross, for Augustine, provided the only way forward, where the price for the sin of Adam and Eve was paid by Jesus' death. Augustine's teaching has earned him the nickname 'the Doctor of Grace' because of the way in which he prescribed the grace of God as a cure for the sinfulness of the human condition.

Augustine taught that people could only be saved from sin through the grace of God and not through their own efforts

Along with Paul, Augustine realised that people would continue to sin even after they had accepted the grace of God, but (according to Augustine) God would nevertheless elect some people for eternal life in heaven. For Augustine, this was indicative of God's goodness; everyone is tainted by Original Sin, but nevertheless, God is prepared to allow some of them to go to heaven after death, and God will choose which people those are. When Paul asked, in Romans, 'Who will rescue me from this body that is subject to death?' Augustine realised that the only answer was the grace of God.

For Augustine, grace is understood as:

- The love and mercy of God

- A quality of God that is capable of reaching the heart and will of a person

- A quality which can give moral guidance to the lives of Christians

- Something which no human person can deserve on their own merit

- That which encourages the soul to recognise when it has offended God

- That which encourages the soul to praise God

- That which transforms the will so that it is capable of obedience to God

- That which can overcome human pride

- That which calms the soul with forgiveness and hope

- That which can be seen in the sacrifice of Christ and in the gift of the Holy Spirit working in the Church.

Augustine believed that the grace of God is the only thing that can save people from eternal punishment for their sinful nature. He rejected the idea that human reason can lead people to enlightenment, or that performing acts of kindness and charity could be a way of earning a place in heaven. For him, the grace of God found in Christ was the only way to overcome the damage done by Adam and Eve in their act of disobedience.

Augustine, like many other thinkers, wrote about the ***summum bonum*** or the highest, most supreme good. He considered Plato's understanding of the Form of the Good as being in many ways similar to the goodness of the God of Christianity. Augustine argued that the highest good is only available for those who set their hearts on God and whom God chooses through his grace. In this earthly life, although there are times when we can be very happy, it is always only temporary, and we know even while we are happy that we will not feel this way for ever. In contrast, the *summum bonum* is a state of eternal happiness which comes from being in the presence of God and is the highest goal that humans can hope to achieve, but it can only be achieved through God's grace and cannot be earned. Augustine also writes of the *summum bonum* as an aspect of God, especially when he is writing about evil and the way in which it is a 'lack of goodness', a distance away from the supreme goodness of God.

> ## Apply your knowledge
>
> 7. How do you think Augustine would respond to someone who was trying to lead a good life and follow the will of God, but in the context of a religion other than Christianity?

Discussing Augustine's teaching on human nature

How convincing are Augustine's teachings on the historical Fall and Original Sin?

Augustine's theology has been very influential on Christian thought, especially his understanding of human nature and sin and the ways in which people find themselves wanting to do right and yet constantly being tempted to choose material pleasures. His views, however, can be criticised.

It could be argued that the whole of Augustine's thought is based on the Genesis story of the Fall, but many people (including many Christians) believe that this is not a literal, historical account. If the Genesis stories are instead understood to be a mythical, pictorial way of expressing truths about humanity, then it might make less sense to talk about 'before the Fall' and 'after the Fall', even if the ideas connected with the human inclination to disobey God still have value.

Many people in the twenty-first century accept the view that humanity evolved over a long time, through the process of natural selection. This could make it difficult to accept that there is something special about the human will and rationality which sets people apart from other animals. It begs the question of when exactly in human evolution did humanity become 'in the image of God' in this way, and it calls into doubt the idea that Adam and Eve were real historical people and that the Fall was an actual event in history.

The idea of Original Sin, where people are born already condemned because of the actions of other people long ago, can be seen as unattractive, unjust and difficult to reconcile with the notion of a loving and forgiving God. Even if there is the possibility of salvation (for the chosen) through the grace of God, it does not fit easily with our sense of justice that people of one generation could be held responsible, and even eternally punished, for the sins of another.

Augustine's willingness to engage with the human experience of seeking the truth, and his recognition of his own weaknesses, make his ideas very recognisable even to people in the twenty-first century. This is a thinker who involves the reader in his own struggles, and who does not present himself as someone who is in a position to cast judgement on others from on high. Although some of his ideas, from the context of the fourth century, do not sit comfortably with modern ways of thinking, he describes personal challenges and failures that are just as much a part of the human condition today as they were for Augustine, and therefore on an emotional level they can be seen as convincing because of their sincerity.

Although some of Augustine's ideas might be considered unpalatable for modern people, it could be argued that this has little bearing on their truth. We might not like the idea that we are inherently sinful and corrupt, but whether we like it or not, it could nevertheless be true. We might be used to thinking that we can get anything we want if we set our minds to it and work hard, but this might not be true either; perhaps Augustine is right in saying that humanity can never approach the perfection of God unless people accept God's help.

Is Augustine right that human sin means that humans can never be morally good?

Augustine is adamant that everyone is tainted with Original Sin and therefore falls short of the standards of morality that God requires.

However, some people might argue that even if people cannot reach a state of total perfection, nevertheless they can still aspire to be good people as far as it is possible, as much of the time as is possible. Augustine's views could lead people to the idea that there is little point in trying at all as the damage has already been done; but most people, including most Christians, would argue that there is every point in continuing to aim for high standards in personal morality.

It could be argued, however, as a counter to this criticism, that Augustine's recognition of human imperfection is actually more likely to lead to moral progress. Reliance on human effort alone, such as Pelagius promoted, is always doomed to failure as, since the Fall, we simply do not have the capacity for moral perfection; and so rather than being naively optimistic and setting out on an impossible quest, it would be wiser to listen to Augustine and realise that we have to rely on the grace of God from the outset. By doing so, we might have a genuine hope rather than a false one.

It could be argued that Augustine's emphasis on the sordid nature of humanity calls God's mercy and wisdom, love and justice into question. God's mercy is called into question if he expects of us standards that we

---

Apply your knowledge

8. How far do you think Augustine's ideas about Original Sin fit with the view that people can exercise free will?

9. Do you think that people can be held responsible for wrongdoing committed by their ancestors? For example, should modern Westerners apologise to modern members of indigenous cultures, for the wrongdoings of their ancestors? Explain why or why not.

cannot possibly hope to meet; and his wisdom is questioned if he did not know that we would sin when he made us, and if he did not give Adam and Eve enough moral strength to resist the temptation to do wrong. It raises questions about God's omnibenevolence, if God allows the disobedience of Adam and Eve to condemn the whole of humanity as a species rather than forgiving them or using his omnipotence to undo the damage that was done.

Many people find Augustine's equation of sexual desire with sin to be repressive and potentially damaging; they might argue that sexual desire is a healthy part of being human and not something which needs to be suppressed. His influence has been such that it puts Christianity at odds with other religious belief systems. Judaism, for example, encourages and celebrates sexual relationships in the context of marriage, as does Hinduism, whereas Augustine's influence on the shaping of Christian sexual ethics leads to views that there is something impure or shameful about sexuality. However, it could be argued that all societies put some restrictions on sexual behaviour, because it needs to be controlled for everyone's good. Perhaps Augustine's views are rather extreme, but maybe he is right in drawing attention to the dangers of uncontrolled sexual behaviour and the powerfully corrupting effects it can have on society and on relationships, leading to jealous passions, abuse and treating others merely as objects of lust.

Some people argue that Augustine is wrong in his understanding of human nature as fundamentally corrupt. Other, later thinkers have agreed with him in this respect; the philosopher Thomas Hobbes, for example, argued that people are by nature selfish and that they work together only because they know it is in their own interests. But others disagree. Jean-Jacques Rousseau, for example, thought that people are by nature good and in general want to defend the weak and work for a society that is fairer for everyone. Whether people are good or bad by nature is a difficult thing to establish scientifically, but there are studies in psychology in which people's instinctive reactions to others in trouble are measured, with varying conclusions. Augustine, however, would not have been persuaded by any such study, however reliable its data, because for him, even our best efforts towards moral perfection are hopelessly spoilt and damaged by the sin of Adam and Eve.

Augustine's views about Original Sin and inherited guilt became less popular during the Enlightenment (which was a surge in the popularity of reason in philosophy during the eighteenth century in Europe). Thinkers such as Jean-Jacques Rousseau and John Locke tended towards the view that people are born with a 'blank slate', known in Latin as a 'tabula rasa'. In this view, babies are neither good nor evil, but born with a fresh start ready to make free choices and learn and become whatever they become. Today, many modern Christian theologians write of 'original blessing' and of a 'benevolent' universe, emphasising the goodness and love of God in his dealings with humanity, and many steer away from Augustine's focus on sin, guilt and condemnation.'

Apply your knowledge

10. Should people have moral goals which are within their grasp, or should they strive for moral perfection even if it is impossible? Give reasons for your answer.

11. Would you agree with Augustine's views that human nature is fundamentally corrupt?

12. Find out more about psychological studies of altruism. Do you think the evidence suggests that people are by nature good or bad?

Is Augustine's view of human nature optimistic or pessimistic?

Augustine is often considered to have a pessimistic view of human nature. It seems that even from the moment we are born, we are already in the wrong and there is no escape from it except by the grace of God. Other thinkers take radically different views which might seem more attractive. In the Quaker movement (properly called the Religious Society of Friends), for example, there is an emphasis on each person carrying the divine light of God, and on seeking moral purity in thoughts and action. Outside the Christian religion, humanists celebrate the achievements and potential of humanity. Existentialist thinkers, such as Jean-Paul Sartre, take the view that we have the freedom to create our own natures and our own destinies, and that we start out in total freedom rather than already condemned.

Augustine's view of human free will became more pessimistic as he grew older. In his earlier writings, he had talked about the possibilities of virtuous living and how wrongdoing was an 'absence of goodness' rather than a real evil force. However, later in his writings he came to the opinion that there is no escaping our fallen nature through our own efforts. We are completely at the mercy of our sinful desires and our inability to be truthful even to ourselves. Augustine's doctrine of election can make his ideas seem even more gloomy, if our future fates in the afterlife are already decided. This seems to remove much of our responsibility for our moral actions, if we have no real freedom, and also removes much of the incentive to try to be a better person.

It could be argued, however, that Augustine's thinking is profoundly optimistic. He did put a great deal of time into writing about all the things that are wrong with humanity. However, he did not just make a diagnosis of the human condition, but also offered a cure: the saving grace of God through Jesus Christ, even though we do not deserve it. If he gave only the diagnosis but no cure, it could be called pessimistic, but he did see a way out of sin for humanity, and pointed people towards this door to freedom.

Is there a distinctive human nature?

Augustine clearly believed that there is such a thing as human nature, and he had plenty to say on the subject. He believed that there was the ideal human nature which God intended for people, as seen in Adam and Eve before the Fall. The human nature which God had intended was innocent, with people able to live in friendship with one another, untainted by greed and lust and capable of having a society which did not require repression or harsh authority. After the Fall, once sin came into the world, human nature became dominated by cupiditas, with everyone having a desire for material pleasures and for 'earthly peace', desires which could never lead anyone to the *summum bonum*.

Many other philosophers, too, have presented different views on what they see as the distinctive character of humanity, in which there are not

Apply your knowledge

13. Do you consider Augustine's view of human nature to be optimistic, pessimistic (or perhaps just realistic)? Give reasons for your answer.

just individuals who have their own character traits, but the species as a whole is seen to have character traits too. Some thinkers have gone further and suggested that there is a 'male nature' which is distinctive from 'female nature' and they have ascribed different qualities to each.

In Buddhism, for example, there is a distinctive human nature which is characterised by impermanence and suffering (dukkha) brought about through attachment and desires. For modern evolutionary biologists, there is a distinctive human nature which is fundamentally driven by the survival instinct, where we are genetically programmed to pursue whatever is in our best interests as individuals and as a society. Followers of Confucius disagreed over whether Confucius thought human nature was basically good, or basically bad – but they all thought that there was such a thing as 'human nature', whatever conclusions they reached about its essence.

Other thinkers, however, have doubts about the whole concept of 'human nature'. One example is Jean-Paul Sartre (1905–80) who was an influential existentialist of the twentieth century. He believed that we do not come into this world already determined by a 'nature' or by culture or by anything else, but that we are free as individuals to decide who we are and what we want to become; a freedom which could be frightening as well as liberating.

Apply your knowledge

14. Do you agree that there is a distinctive human nature, in terms of character traits that we (for the most part) share?

15. How far do you think that people are free to choose what sort of a person they want to be? What kinds of constraints might be on them to prevent them from having total freedom of choice?

Learning support

Points to remember

» Augustine believed that the Fall of Adam and Eve had totally corrupted human nature in a way that could only be redeemed through the grace of God in Christ.

» Augustine thought that since the Fall, everyone is born with Original Sin and can only be saved by the grace of God.

» Try to make sure you are familiar with the key theological terms used in this chapter so that you can use them confidently and accurately in your writing.

» Whether or not you share the beliefs of Paul or Augustine, try to present their views as fairly as possible, and try to find reasons for your opinions about them rather than simply asserting that this is what you believe.

Enhance your learning

» The *Catechism of the Catholic Church*, paragraphs 385–409 are useful background reading to support an understanding of the ideas raised in this chapter.

» McGrath's *Christian Theology* (2010), pages 348–55 and 371–2 are very helpful and accessible.

» Augustine is challenging to read but worth the effort; try reading some of his books, *Confessions* and *City of God*, both of which are accessible on the Internet.

» The story of the Fall of Adam and Eve is a popular choice for Christian art. Try researching paintings of the story by different artists to see how they have chosen to depict the symbolism of the story.

» If you have the chance to study Milton's *Paradise Lost* (1667), see if you can spot where Milton has made use of the thinking of Augustine in the way he tells the story.

Practice for exams

AS questions and A level questions look identical; the difference between AS and A level assessment is seen in the different proportions of marks awarded for two different skills: the skill of demonstrating knowledge and understanding (Assessment Objective 1, or AO1), and the skill of constructing a critical argument (AO2).

At AS, half the marks (15 marks) are available for knowledge and understanding, and the other half (15 marks) for the quality of your analytical and evaluative argument. You should aim to use your knowledge in order to support the argument you are making throughout the essay, rather than presenting descriptive knowledge in the first half and then an opinion in the second.

At A level, your demonstration of knowledge and understanding is awarded a maximum of 16 marks, and your analytic and evaluative skills are awarded a maximum of 24 marks. You should aim to concentrate on constructing a lucid argument, making use of your knowledge to add weight to the conclusions you draw.

How convincing is Augustine's teaching about the Fall and Original Sin?

This question asks for a clear understanding of Augustine's theology of the Fall, and a critical assessment of its persuasiveness as an understanding of the human condition.

Practise your skills for AS level

If answering this question at AS level, you need to demonstrate a good accurate knowledge of Augustine's teaching about the Fall and what Augustine believed its consequences for humanity to be. You need to develop a line of argument in assessment of his theology, in order to answer the question of how convincing his views are, by explaining what you think the strengths and weaknesses are and whether, on balance, you find them convincing.

Practise your skills for A level

If you are an A level candidate your focus should be on giving a reasoned assessment of how convincing Augustine's theology is, rather than simply on describing it. There are several different ways of considering this: for example, you could consider whether it is convincing as an account of human nature, whether it is convincing as a way of interpreting the Bible, and whether it holds together convincingly as a coherent theological position. Simply asserting that you do or don't hold the same beliefs as Augustine is not enough to earn you high marks for critical analysis.

**'Augustine's view of human nature is deeply pessimistic.'
Discuss.**

Here you are asked to give an assessment of whether
Augustine's view of human nature is accurate, optimistic or
pessimistic.

Practise your skills for AS level

As an AS student, you should show that you have a
thorough knowledge of Augustine's understanding of
human nature as fallen and irretrievable except by the
grace of God, and you should be able to explain how he
arrived at this position. In your evaluation, you might want
to argue that Augustine is simply being truthful about how
things are and thereby giving hope to people by offering
them a genuine way forward; you might think he is being
pessimistic by overlooking human altruism and courage, for
example; or you might argue that he is optimistic because of
his teachings about the grace of God.

Practise your skills for A level

As an A level student, you should concentrate on your
argument rather than on giving lengthy descriptions of
Augustine's theology. Your knowledge and understanding
of Augustine will be demonstrated as you explain and give
examples to support your opinions. You might want to select
different aspects of Augustine's thinking and argue that it is
pessimistic in some respects but not in others.

Chapter 3.2

Death and the afterlife

How do Christians understand the afterlife?
Are 'heaven' and 'hell' places, or should they
be understood in some other way?
What do Christians believe about judgement
after death?

Key Terms

Disembodied existence: existing without a physical body

Resurrection: living on after death in a glorified physical form in a new realm

Beatific vision: a face-to-face encounter with God

Purgatory: a place where people go, temporarily, after death to be cleansed of sin before they are fit to live with God

Election (in a theological sense): predestination, chosen by God for heaven or hell

Limited election: the view that God chooses only a small number of people for heaven

Original Sin: a state of wrongdoing in which people are born (according to some Christians) because of the sin of Adam and Eve

Unlimited election: the view that all people are called to salvation but only a few will be saved

Universalism: the view that all people will be saved

Parable: a story told to highlight a moral message

Particular judgement: judgement for each person at the point of death

Parousia: used in Christianity to refer to the Second Coming of Christ

Specification requirements

Christian teaching on

- heaven
- hell
- purgatory
- election

Introduction

One of the prime concerns of religious belief is the nature of the human person and in particular, what happens to us when we die. When we lose someone we love, those questions become particularly pressing: will that person live on after death, and if so, in what form? Will we see him or her again one day in a way we can recognise? Can we hope for an afterlife ourselves, and if so, what form might it take?

Christianity teaches that people have souls which are capable of surviving the death of the body. They believe that after death, people are resurrected, and live on in a new dimension, some with God in heaven. All of these ideas are mysterious and have a range of interpretations, and many of them also raise philosophical difficulties. What is meant by the 'soul' and can it survive the death of the body? What are 'heaven' and 'hell', and how is belief in them to be understood?

Although the Bible does present teaching about life after death, it is not always clear how this teaching is to be interpreted. Perhaps it should be understood literally, in which case we might expect our physical bodies to be brought back to life in the same sense that we use the word 'life' to talk about our present existence. Perhaps the teaching should be understood metaphorically, as a pictorial way of expressing ideas which cannot be expressed in everyday language, in which case there is a need to try and understand what the metaphors might mean.

Christian teaching about life after death also needs to be considered in conjunction with other Christian beliefs. For example, although the Bible makes reference to hell and to eternal punishment, this could be seen as incompatible with the notion of a God of infinite love and forgiveness, and so some consideration must be given to what ideas of hell could mean. Although the Bible implies that we have free will to choose our moral actions and our religious beliefs and behaviour, there is also the idea of an omniscient God who knows even before we are born which choices we will make and which choices he has made for us. This raises questions about how God's control over who goes to heaven might operate.

These questions and issues have been addressed in different ways by Christian thinkers and by philosophers, giving rise to divergent beliefs within the Christian tradition.

The way people understand life after death depends on the way they understand the relation between the soul and the body. See Chapter 1.2.

Christian teaching about the afterlife

According to Christianity, there is life after death, not in this world but in a new kind of existence. Christians reject the idea that a human soul can leave one physical body at the point of death and be reborn into a new physical body in this same world (reincarnation). They also reject Plato's idea that the soul and the body could part company, with the body decomposing while the soul moves on by itself (**disembodied existence**). Instead, Christian teaching is that life after death will take the form of **resurrection**, where the person will be given a renewed spiritual body in which to continue his or her journey into the next life. It is important to Christians that Jesus' tomb was empty when people went to visit his body; they found that it had gone, because he had been resurrected from death to eternal life.

There are two sources for this view: the idea of the resurrection of the body was around in Judaism by New Testament times (the Pharisees believed it) and it was clearly an idea that Jesus also believed. The other source is from the ancient Greeks, although they had a range of quite different and sometimes opposing views about the afterlife.

Life after death is by no means a prominent theme in the Jewish scriptures (the Old Testament, to Christians), but there are references to the possibility of it. For example, in the book of Genesis, the death of Abraham is recorded.

> 66 Then Abraham breathed his last and died at a good old age, an old man and full of years; and he was gathered to his people. 99

Genesis 25:8, New International Version

This is interesting because not only does the verse emphasise three times that Abraham had lived out the full extent of a human life ('a good old age', 'an old man', 'full of years') but also it contains the intriguing phrase 'he was gathered to his people'. The same phrase 'gathered to his people' is used of other prominent men of the Old Testament, too. Accounts of the deaths of Ishmael, Isaac, Jacob, Moses and his brother Aaron all include the phrase 'he was gathered to his people'. What does this expression mean? It does not refer to the body being returned to family land or a family grave, as in several of these cases, the deceased was buried far away from the land of his birth. Who were these 'people', and what was it that was gathered? The Bible does not tell us, but there are certainly hints that something of the original man was going to continue and going to join others with whom he was familiar, perhaps loved ones or perhaps people of the same culture or religious beliefs.

There are also other biblical passages about future hope and the 'Last Days', in which there is clear reference to resurrection. For example, in the apocalyptic Book of Daniel, there is a prophecy about the end of time where the writer says:

> 66 Multitudes who sleep in the dust of the earth will awake: some to everlasting life, others to shame and everlasting contempt. 99

Daniel 12:2, New International Version

Apply your knowledge

Look up and read 2 Kings 2, in the Old Testament, which is the story of the end of the life of the prophet Elijah.

1. What do you think this story might imply about the possibility of life after death?

2. Do you think this story is meant to be taken literally, as an actual historical event which happened and could have been seen by any passer-by, or might it be a mythological or symbolic way of expressing ideas about the death of Elijah? Give reasons for your answer.

3. Find out a little about the importance of the following people in the Old Testament story: Abraham, Ishmael, Isaac, Jacob, Moses and Aaron.

The book of Daniel is one of the last books of Jewish scriptures, probably written in about 165BC as a way of encouraging Jews who were being persecuted for their faith. It may have been the case that the Jews began to develop their ideas about life after death as a way of coping with their circumstances. During religious persecution, those who remained the most faithful and obedient to God's commands seemed to be the ones who came off worst, whereas those who wanted to survive at all costs and abandoned Judaism for pragmatic reasons sometimes escaped. Life after death may have seemed to the Jews the obvious solution to the problem of God's apparent injustice in this earthly life. In this life, people suffer, sometimes because of their faithfulness to God. Therefore, a God of love and justice must make it possible for those people to be rewarded after death.

By the time of Jesus, in first-century Palestine, debates about life after death divided opinion amongst the Jewish population. The Pharisees were distinctive in their belief in resurrection while the Sadducees taught that there was no life after death. Later in Judaism, the idea developed that dead people would be resurrected from their graves in order to begin a new kind of life, once the Messiah has come to liberate people and at a time of God's choosing.

The ancient Greeks also had a considerable influence on Christian ideas about life after death. Plato's dualist ideas about the body and the soul influenced the Christian view that although we are physical beings, we also have a spiritual soul which is non-physical and which is capable of surviving after the death of the body to return to contemplating the perfect Form of Goodness.

In Christianity, ideas about life after death became much clearer and more certain than the ideas of Judaism, because of the conviction that Jesus' death by crucifixion was not the end of the story. Christians believe that after Jesus died on the cross he was resurrected, and they also believe that this is evidence to show that the same will happen to the rest of us. This does not seem to be a belief which has crept into the written gospel accounts later, once Christianity was developing a system of doctrine, but is a central belief which can be traced back to the very earliest New Testament writings (the letters to new Churches) when people were still alive who had lived during Jesus' lifetime.

According to the Bible, after Jesus died, his body was placed in a tomb – but on the third day after his death, when some of his female followers went to the grave to anoint the body, they discovered that the grave was empty, even though the entrance had been guarded and covered with a heavy stone. The stone had been rolled away.

In the gospel accounts, Jesus was then seen as a physical person, walking around. There is no hint that this might be a pictorial way of saying something else, such as that Jesus lived on in people's memories. The accounts make it clear that Jesus was physically present, after his death, in a way that could be experienced by the senses of those who were there. Jesus could

In the Bible, ideas about life after death become more prominent in the New Testament

> Plato's dualism (see Chapter 1.1) had a strong influence on Christian ideas about life after death.

How has the artist tried to convey that Jesus is resurrected from the dead in this painting?

be heard and touched, although even the people who had been his closest friends did not always recognise him immediately, suggesting that his appearance had changed in some way. After Jesus had spent some time on earth in physical form, he 'ascended into heaven'; it is not clear whether he discarded the resurrected physical body at this point and lived on in some kind of spiritual form, or whether he continued in the resurrected body for eternity. Most Christians believe that Jesus continued to live in the transformed spiritual body.

Apply your knowledge

4. Look up and read the different accounts of Jesus' Resurrection in the gospels. What are the common features of the stories?

5. How do the gospel accounts differ?

6. Why do think there might be differences in the stories?

7. Do you think the writers are trying to describe what they believed to be a literal, historical event, where anyone walking past would have been able to see this, too? Or do you think they are trying to write symbolically about a kind of inner spiritual renewal, rather than saying that Jesus literally survived death? How would you support your view?

Belief in the physical resurrection of the body is central to Christian doctrine but it raises some logical difficulties

Although these gospel stories provide the basis for Christian belief about the afterlife, they still leave many questions unanswered. Was Jesus' Resurrection an experience unique to Jesus, or is it something that everyone can expect, or only those who are believing Christians? Will the resurrection of the dead take place for each individual immediately once they have died, or will it be an event at the end of time? Is there some kind of temporary way of existing before the end of time, for those who have died, something that will come to completion at the end of time? Will people require some kind of body after death, and if so, what will it be like and in what sense will they be the same person as they were before death? Where will these physical bodies go, how will they get there and how will they live?

The passage which addresses some of these issues most directly, although still obscurely, is in 1 Corinthians 15, where Paul is trying to answer new Christians in the early Church who had similar questions. Paul was adamant that Christ had risen from the dead, and took this to be the central fact of Christian faith. He was also quite clear that the Resurrection of Christ was a promise for all Christians that they too would be resurrected and was not unique to Jesus. Paul uses the metaphor of a seed in an attempt to explain how life after death can be understood:

66 But someone will ask, 'How are the dead raised? With what kind of body will they come?' How foolish! What you sow does not come to life unless it dies. When you sow, you do not plant the body that will be, but just a seed, perhaps of wheat or of something else. But God gives it a body as he has determined, and to each kind of seed he gives its own body.

...

So will it be with the resurrection of the dead. The body that is sown is perishable, it is raised imperishable; it is sown in dishonour, it is raised in glory; it is sown in weakness, it is raised in power; it is sown a natural body, it is raised a spiritual body. **"**

1 Corinthians 15:35–39, 42–44, New International Version

This metaphor still leaves some puzzles. What is a 'spiritual body'? Is it made of material stuff, and if so is it the same kind of material that our bodies are made of before death? Paul's suggestion here, with the idea of the seed, is that the body will be transformed and radically changed, although it is not clear how.

In 2 Corinthians 5, two other metaphors are used:

66 For we know that if the earthly tent we live in is destroyed, we have a building from God, an eternal house in heaven, not built by human hands. Meanwhile we groan, longing to be clothed instead with our heavenly dwelling, because when we are clothed, we will not be found naked. **"**

2 Corinthians 5:1–3, New International Version

Paul's use of the idea of a tent being replaced by a more solid house suggests an idea that at the moment we 'live in' the bodies that we have now but they are not truly us, and that we will be given a more substantial and eternal home in the afterlife. The metaphor of the tent carries with it the idea of impermanence in contrast to the house. Paul seems to be echoing a Platonic way of understanding this physical life on this earth as temporary and fragile, in contrast with the permanent solid certainty of life in another realm.

He writes at first of the more solid house 'clothing' or covering us, and this takes him into his second metaphor, where we will be clothed in heaven rather than naked. The suggestion here is an echo of the Genesis story of the Fall of Adam and Eve, where as soon as the people have committed sin, they realise they are naked and run away to hide from God because they are ashamed. Paul seems to be saying that in this life, we are aware of our own sin and have to be ashamed of who we are, but in the afterlife, God will transform us so that we are not in a state of sin any more.

Although there are different variations within the Christian understanding of life after death, there are some ideas which are central:

1. Christians believe that resurrection will involve a bodily life of some form, not just a disembodied spiritual existence. Resurrected bodies will be 'spiritual' and 'glorified' (whatever that means) and no longer capable of being corrupted or destroyed. Some Christian theologians have written about a kind of disembodied existence in an interim

> **Think question**
> In what ways, if at all, is a fully-grown plant 'the same as' the seed which was planted?

Paul uses metaphors in an attempt to explain life after death for Christians.

period between death and resurrection, but they are all agreed that in the end, people will have resurrected bodies.

2. Christians also believe that the resurrected person will be the same person as the one who died. People will continue in their resurrected state as individuals; they will not merge with God in some way or with each other, but will share an identity with the particular individual who died. They will not just be similar to that person, but will be the same person.

3. Thirdly, Christians believe that life after death will be a miracle given by God, and not just a natural process. The person is resurrected through the gift and the grace of God, not just because resurrection is something that souls naturally do.

Aquinas on the afterlife

Aquinas (1225–74) had some tensions to resolve in his thinking about the afterlife. On the one hand, he was a passionate admirer of Aristotle and included many of Aristotle's ideas in his own thinking; but on the other hand he held a more Platonic view in which there was the possibility of the soul surviving the death of the body and being capable of 'the **beatific vision**', or coming face-to-face with God. He had to find some kind of middle ground between these two opposing views.

> *See Chapter 1.1 for an understanding of Aristotle's 'formal cause'*

Following Aristotle, Aquinas taught that the soul was a 'life principle' and also the 'form' or distinctive character of living things. In Aquinas' view, all living things had souls in the sense that they all had essential characteristics; for example, animals had 'sensitive souls' and plants had 'vegetative souls'. These ideas put forward by Aquinas came straight from Aristotle's work, *De Anima* (*On the Soul*). But in Aquinas' view, human beings have souls which are strikingly different from the souls of other creatures. Other life forms have souls which die when the body dies, but human beings have a special kind of soul, a 'rational soul', which enables life after death as a possibility.

Aquinas thought that the ability to reason and to think with intelligence, to philosophise and to form chains of logical thought, could not come from any physical, bodily organ but had to be non-physical.

For Aquinas, as for Aristotle, the soul was that which gave a living creature its ability to do whatever it does. But because Aquinas was writing as a Christian, his understanding was that the soul is that which gives humans the ability to accomplish their purposes and reach the potential for which they were made: in particular, to reason and to make a free choice to love God, with the final goal and reward of living eternally in the presence of God.

Aquinas reasoned that in this life, although we can have plenty of times when we are happy, it is never perfect happiness because we know that it is only temporary because it is often brought about by material circumstances, which change. Perfect happiness, he thought, could only be achieved after death, by living eternally, outside time, in a state of perfect bliss. This, for Aquinas, meant being in the presence of God, where faith in God would be replaced by knowledge of God. With faith, people have to decide that they are going to believe in God even though they have some doubts and even though there might be some evidence against, as well as evidence for, God's existence. But in the beatific vision, all doubt would be gone and the believer would see God face-to-face. Aquinas used the thinking of Paul to explain his understanding of the afterlife:

> 66 For now we see only a reflection as in a mirror; then we shall see face to face. Now I know in part; then I shall know fully, even as I am fully known. 99
>
> 1 Corinthians 13:12, New International Version

Because Aquinas believed that the afterlife would be beyond space and time, his view of the beatific vision does not have some of the problems that the more Protestant understanding of heaven might encounter. If the beatific vision is eternally timeless in the sense of a being a single 'simultaneity' rather than a timeline, then there is no need to wonder what the people in heaven would be doing all the time and how they would fill their endless days without getting bored, because there would be no 'all the time' and no more 'endless days'. There would just be one eternal moment of being in the presence of God.

However, the concept of the beatific vision does have other issues. If the soul is timeless in the presence of God, it is difficult to understand how this could be 'the same person' as the one who had the physical body while on earth and went about a physical daily life. Many of the characteristics which make us the people we are involve a relationship with linear time. For example, we think in sequences, first thinking of this, and then that follows: we respond to circumstances in our own individual ways, so that when this happens, I usually respond like that; there are activities we enjoy which happen in time. The difference between a person living in time, and a timeless soul, is perhaps so great that it is impossible to assert that this person experiencing the beatific vision is really the same person as before death.

Aquinas believed that after death, Christians would be able to see God face-to-face in a 'beatific vision'

Traditional Christian teaching on purgatory, heaven and hell

Belief in heaven and hell is characteristic of Christianity and Islam, and to some extent Judaism. For some people, both of these ideas raise such difficult philosophical questions that it makes them impossible to believe; others however are content to accept that we cannot have a clear idea of the afterlife until we actually get there; and some believe that the teaching of holy scripture gives us plenty of information about what the afterlife will be like.

Most Christians believe that life after death will involve some kind of judgement.

The story of the rich man and Lazarus in Luke's gospel, for example, gives a clear message that there will be a separation after death between some kinds of people and others. The rich man who has been too interested in material possessions and has ignored the poor man at his gate, is sent into eternal punishment, while Lazarus is united with Abraham in heaven. In this story, the inhabitants of heaven and hell are aware of each other, but are unable to do anything about their position:

66 The time came when the beggar died and the angels carried him to Abraham's side. The rich man also died and was buried. In Hades, where he was in torment, he looked up and saw Abraham far away, with Lazarus by his side. So he called to him, 'Father Abraham, have pity on me and send Lazarus to dip the tip of his finger in water and cool my tongue, because I am in agony in this fire.'

But Abraham replied, 'Son, remember that in your lifetime you received your good things, while Lazarus received bad things, but now he is comforted here and you are in agony. And besides all this, between us and you a great chasm has been fixed, so that those who want to go from here to you cannot, nor can anyone cross over from there to us.' **99**

Luke 16:22–26, New International Version

Christians believe that heaven and hell will involve some kind of physical existence for the people there; it may not be the same kind of physical existence that we are used to, but nevertheless the belief is that we will continue as whole people, comprised of souls and bodies, into the next life.

Heaven

Traditionally Christianity teaches that after death, the faithful will go to heaven. Heaven, because it is in a different dimension from this world, has to be described figuratively, with different metaphors and symbols to point the believer in the right direction while still recognising that the afterlife is a mystery. Heaven is understood, for example, as the place where God lives, seated on his throne and surrounded by his angels. Christians do not believe that God has an address at which he lives, but that God is in all places and at all times; nevertheless, the metaphor of a mighty ruler seated on a throne in charge of his kingdom is one which people have found helpful.

The metaphor of God the Father is also used in the context of heaven, where heaven is seen in terms of the family home, the place where an adult might return to stay with his or her father. The Lord's Prayer, for example, which was taught by Jesus and is a central prayer in Christianity, begins 'Our Father, who art in heaven …'. In John's gospel, Jesus tells his disciples: 'My Father's house has many rooms; if that were not so, would I have told you that I am going there to prepare a place for you?' (John 14:2, New International Version). This metaphor conveys ideas of comfort, return and familiarity under the authority of unconditional love.

Another metaphor used is one of plenty, where, according to the book of Revelation, 'the great street of the city was of gold, as pure as transparent glass' (Revelation 21:21, New International Version), signifying that there will be so much 'wealth' around that people can even afford to walk on it; no one will go without. Heaven is also described as somewhere where there will be no more suffering, no pain, and no death, where sin will be washed away and people will be purified and live in peace.

The Catholic tradition has usually expressed its understanding of heaven in terms of the beatific vision described by Thomas Aquinas. Protestants have tended to understand heaven as an everlasting existence, where people would live in the presence of God, reunited with their loved ones and able to worship God every day.

Both of these ideas, however, raise issues which some philosophers have questioned. The moral philosopher Bernard Williams, for example, wondered whether an eternity in heaven would really be desirable – surely however pleasurable heaven was at the beginning when we first arrived, it would become boring after a while? We would have literally all the time in the world, and so we would be able to do and achieve everything we wanted, especially if we had perfected bodies so that we were not hindered by physical limitations. Every target that we set for ourselves would be achievable, even if it took a long time to get there. If we wanted to learn to play an instrument, we would have forever to master it; in fact, we would have time to master them all and to invent new ones – and then what? Whatever we wanted to do, we would be able to do it, and perhaps the excitement of anticipation would disappear. Williams argued that part of the pleasure of living is making choices about what we will do with our limited lifespans, and setting ourselves challenging objectives which we might or might not be able to achieve, so that if and when we do achieve them, we feel a sense of pride. However, if we have time to choose absolutely everything, and have infinite time so that eventually everything is achieved, the pleasure is gone. He describes a possible scenario in which a woman is experiencing eternal life and hating it:

....

❝ EM was 342; because for 300 years she had been 42. … Her problem lay in having been at it for too long. Her trouble was, as it seems, boredom: a boredom connected with the fact that

Bernard Williams argued that eternal life in heaven would become boring and undesirable

everything that could have happened and make sense to one particular human being of 42 had already happened to her.

Bernard Williams, *Problems of the Self: Philosophical Papers*, 1973, p. 90

Think question

Can you think of any kind of food that you would want to eat endlessly, if miraculously you never became over-full? Or any kind of music that you would want to hear endlessly? Is Bernard Williams right in his view that heaven would be boring, or is he interpreting the idea too literally?

Some respond to these objections by saying that in heaven, God would make sure that this did not happen; perhaps we might miraculously never be bored, just as we would never be sad and never suffer. However, if our minds and emotions are going to be controlled and programmed like this, we would lose our free will. It also raises the question of why God did not make us like this in the first place, so that we were never bored or sad or suffering in this life either. Perhaps coming to understand the wonders of God could never get boring, especially if these are infinite wonders where it is never possible to run out of things to learn. Interestingly, the Catholic theologian Karl Rahner made the same point as Bernard Williams, arguing that the limited span of our earthly lives gives them their meaning, and used it as a reason to support the view of a timeless afterlife.

There is also the issue of personal identity. It is difficult to see how we could still be the same person, in a life after death, if we were incapable of feeling pain and incapable of negative emotions and wrong doing, especially if we also had bodies which are very different from the physical, imperfect, changing bodies we have in this world.

Hell

In contrast with the idea of heaven, Christian teaching has also presented the notion of hell, in which after death a person is separated from God for eternity. Sometimes this is seen as a place of eternal pain and punishment, often depicted in art as a place in which people are tortured by demons and with fire. In the Bible, hell is sometimes described figuratively as a rubbish dump, where the useless people are thrown; sometimes a metaphor from agriculture is used, where the good wheat is kept but the leftover husks and weeds are burned to get rid of them. In the book of Revelation, the writer has a vision in which the bad people are thrown into a lake of fiery sulphur (Revelation 21:8). Hell is seen figuratively as being downwards, below the physical world.

The concept of hell raises a difficult issue. Can the existence of hell, with eternal punishment that can never be escaped, be compatible with the existence of a perfectly loving and perfectly just God? It might be hard to think of any sin that we could commit where eternal pain with no chance of parole would be a fair punishment. David Hume raised this problem, suggesting that the whole idea of hell calls God's justice into question because (in his view) a finite sin can never deserve an infinite punishment.

Some argue that whenever we do wrong, we wrong God, and that every kind of wrong deserves eternal punishment because wronging God is eternally bad; but this would mean that pain for all eternity would be

What images and symbols does the painter use to convey his beliefs about hell?

a fair punishment for relatively minor offences, such as pretending that your friend looks great in the jeans she is trying on, just because you are bored with shopping and want to go home. It is hard to imagine a perfectly loving God allowing his creatures to suffer for all eternity. When a loving parent punishes a child, even if severely, the punishment does not go on for ever, but just for long enough to teach the child a lesson – so surely a loving God would not allow eternal punishment in hell?

Eternal punishment might be, in the end, as boring as eternal pleasure. We might become immune to pain and suffering and stop feeling it any more. And what would eternal punishment achieve, if there were no possibility of redemption and if the good were too far away to need protection from the bad?

John Hick rejects the traditional doctrine of an eternal hell, because in his view, it is incompatible with belief in a God of love. He argues that this belief was developed as a form of social control, encouraging people to be fearful of disobeying the teachings of those in religious authority, but that it is not conceivable that a God of infinite love and mercy would consign his creatures to a punishment from which they had no hope of escaping.

One view which is gaining in popularity is that Hell refers to a second death for the person who has not gained entry into heaven. The body dies, at the point of physical death, and then the soul dies. The view is developed from a verse in the Bible: 'But the cowardly, the unbelieving, the vile, the murderers, the sexually immoral, those who practise magic arts, the idolaters and all liars – they will be consigned to the fiery lake of burning sulphur. This is the second death' (Revelation 21:8, New International Version). In this view, the soul is not eternal in the way that God is eternal, but can be brought to an end if this is the will of God. This view avoids the problems created by the idea of eternal pain and suffering, which are seen not as literal but as metaphorical.

The concept of hell seems to some people to be incompatible with the notion of an all-loving God

John Hick believed that a God of love would ensure that no one goes to hell for eternity. See Chapter 1.6.

Purgatory

The doctrine of **purgatory** is a Catholic teaching which was developed by early Christian thinkers such as Origen and Augustine. Pope Gregory in the sixth century developed this idea. He wanted to explain contemporary practices of praying for the dead and he based his ideas on a passage from Matthew's gospel, where Jesus is recorded as saying:

66 Whoever is not with me is against me, and whoever does not gather with me scatters. And so I tell you, every kind of sin and slander can be forgiven, but blasphemy against the Spirit will not be forgiven. Anyone who speaks a word against the Son of Man will be forgiven, but anyone who speaks against the Holy Spirit will not be forgiven, either in this age or in the age to come. 99

Matthew 12:30–32, New International Version

Pope Gregory saw that this passage refers to the possibility of forgiveness, not only in this age but also 'in the age to come'. He understood this to mean that forgiveness does not only happen during a person's earthly life but is also a possibility after death, and so, building on the thinking of other Christians before him, he reasoned that there must, therefore, be a kind of temporary state after death in which people have the opportunity to rid themselves of sin and be forgiven. The point of death does not have to mark an individual's last chance to put things right.

Purgatory, as the name suggests, is a place or state in which after the death the soul is 'purged'. In other words, it is made clean or purified, before the person is ready to enter heaven. It is not an individual's final destination, but an interim state between the moment of death and life in heaven. According to Catholic teaching, some souls are not in a sufficient state of grace to warrant being sent straight to heaven. There is, therefore, a need for a cleansing process that brings healing. There is also, for some, a need for punishment – not eternal punishment, but punishment with an end result – which is understood as being more painful than anything that can be experienced on this earth. The imagery of fire is often used, as it is in descriptions of hell. Catholic teaching is that the prayers of the living can contribute to this cleansing process, helping the dead soul to get through the purgatory and become ready to enter the presence of God. Catholics also teach that the process of purging sin can be started in this earthly life, where people can voluntarily decide to purge themselves of sin by going to confession and repenting, and by putting right the things they have done wrong as far as they can, for example by being generous to those in need and by working hard to become more virtuous in their daily lives.

Purgatory is seen as a time of cleansing for the soul, in the Catholic tradition

What do you think the artist Douglas Stratton is trying to convey in giving this image the title *Purgatory*?

The Catholic theologian Karl Rahner developed the doctrine of purgatory in a way that many saw as more attractive for twentieth-century minds, arguing that purgatory should be understood not as a horrible place of pain, but as a metaphor for the soul's greater awareness of the consequences of sin, especially the individual's own sin, in the time between death and the Last Judgement. The pain of purgatory is, therefore, a self-inflicted personal pain, as the individual comes to terms with the full meaning of repentance and grace.

Although purgatory is an accepted doctrine in Catholic Christianity, Protestant Christians tend to reject it, partly because they do not see that it is supported by the Bible, and partly because they think it is contradictory to biblical teaching about salvation. In the Protestant view, ideas of purgatory are wrong because they suggest that Jesus did not complete the final act of salvation on the cross.

How do Christian teachings about the afterlife affect moral behaviour?

Beliefs about the afterlife have often been used in an attempt to influence moral behaviour, with promises of heaven for those who are obedient and threats of hell for those who appear to be behaving in a way which contradicts Christian teaching.

In Christianity, since its earliest days, there has been a tension between 'faith' and 'good works' as necessary for entry into heaven. Most Christians will argue that both are required; the person who claims to accept that Jesus was the Son of God and who goes to church every Sunday but does nothing for anyone else is not going to get to heaven, and neither is the person who raises a lot of money for charity and looks after others but has no Christian faith. This is not a universal Christian view, however; some will argue that a deathbed conversion where there is no time left to do any deeds, good or otherwise, will be sufficient for entry to heaven; and some will argue that a God of love would not give eternal punishment to people who have spent their lives caring for others, whatever their beliefs. Others, also, might argue that if someone is devoted to helping those in need, he or she is an 'anonymous Christian', living a Christian life without explicitly recognising it.

Some critics argue that desire for heaven and fear of hell should not be used as the motivation for moral behaviour. If someone looks after people in need only because he wants to be rewarded in heaven, perhaps it is not moral behaviour after all but thinly-disguised selfishness. Immanuel Kant, for example, argued that the only right motivation for doing good is because it is the right thing to do, there should not be any other motivation at all.

For the individual, then, a belief in heaven and hell will affect moral behaviour, because the individual will have an expectation of standing before God in judgement as a sole agent, personally responsible for his or her own choices. It might mean that the individual would sometimes make moral choices which are in opposition to the view of the majority within the Church; for example, a Christian might decide that it would be right to refuse to fight in a war, even if the Church were promoting loyalty to the country, or a Christian might decide to go on a demonstration against gay rights despite the Church accepting equal marriage laws. The person could reason that in judgement after death, it would not be sufficient excuse to claim that he or she just went along with everyone else despite having misgivings.

Different ways of understanding ideas about the afterlife

Christian teachings about the afterlife are open to a variety of interpretations. Some thinkers from the evangelical tradition of Christianity take the ideas quite literally, with the view that heaven, hell and perhaps purgatory are actual physical places on a different plane from this world. In supporting this view, they argue that the Bible teaches that Jesus had a physical body after his Resurrection, and this physical body went up into heaven; therefore, it must have gone to a physical place. Biblical depictions of heaven describe a physical place, full of angels, and hell as full of fire.

Others, however, prefer to understand teachings about the afterlife in terms of metaphor. Heaven, hell and purgatory are understood as spiritual states rather than places in a physical sense. Someone might 'go to heaven' after death in the sense of becoming fully aware of having shed the physical body and being eternally in the presence of God. They might be 'in purgatory' after death as they recognise their earthly sins and the ways in which they have fallen short of God's standards, and might work to repent and make themselves fit for God's presence. They might be 'in hell' when they realise that they have separated themselves from the love of God by rejecting him. All of these ideas about heaven and hell being spiritual states rely on the view that people will have conscious thoughts and wishes after death; this depends on a view of the relation between the mind and the body in which the mind is capable of surviving the death of the body. We experience emotional states of happiness, guilt and despair in this earthly life, so perhaps ideas of the afterlife in the Bible are metaphors referring to similar states after death. If we are essentially the same people after death, then perhaps we continue to experience the same kinds of thoughts and emotions.

It could also be argued that heaven, hell and purgatory are symbols of a person's moral and spiritual life as experienced on this earth, rather than after death. People sometimes talk in terms of heaven when they are blissfully happy, of purgatory when they are going through testing times and of hell when they suffer bereavement or mental health problems. This interpretation of heaven, hell and purgatory does not assume the existence of an afterlife, and so, in many ways, it avoids the

See Chapter 1.2 for more on ideas about the afterlife presupposing that the mind or soul is capable of existing without a physical body

Apply your knowledge

10. Look up the Apostles' Creed, which is a statement of Christian belief. What do you think are the ideas about life after death supported by this statement? Do you think they are meant literally, or metaphorically? Give reasons for your answer.

philosophical problems that these ideas raise. However, in order to make this interpretation, many biblical teachings about heaven and hell have to be discarded as they often refer to heaven and hell in the context of life after the physical death of the body. Alternatively, it could be that such experiences in our earthly moral and spiritual lives are glimpses of states which will be understood much more fully after death.

Christian teaching about election

'**Election**' or 'predestination' is one of the most controversial ideas in Christian theology. The idea is most often associated with John Calvin (1509–64), but he was not the first to defend it; Augustine, in the fourth century, made a firm case for election and it was also a popularly-held belief in the Middle Ages.

To believe in election, in Christian theological terms, is to believe that God chooses the eternal destiny of each human person. God knows, even before we are born, who will be damned to the fires of hell and who will rise to glory in heaven. This doctrine arises from belief that God's omniscience (all-knowingness) means literally that nothing is unknown for God. God does not have to wait and see what happens, because he is outside time and space. In some versions of Christian teaching about election, God does not just know who will be saved and who will be damned, but chooses it himself.

Within Christianity there are divergent views about election. Some, like Augustine, have held that only a few Christians will be saved so there will be only **limited election**. Others hold that all people are called to salvation, in an unlimited way, but not everyone responds to that call and so only some are saved; and others such as John Hick hold a universalist belief in which all people will be saved.

Belief in election means belief that God chooses who is destined for heaven and who is destined for hell

Augustine, living in the early days of Christianity when doctrine was still being formed, had some views on the idea of election, in which election was limited to a few. When Augustine was alive, there was a popular view called Pelagianism, which proposed that people were born with a blank slate, neither good or evil, and could earn a place in heaven. Augustine, however, disagreed. He thought that people were born with '**Original Sin**': because of the sin of Adam and Eve when they disobeyed God in the Garden of Eden (the Fall), every subsequent human being to be born was already sinful right from the start. No one, thought Augustine, could earn salvation, because that would be the same thing as telling God 'I deserve reward in heaven', and this did not fit with Augustine's firm belief that everyone shares in the sin of Adam and cannot possibly reach God's standards through his or her own efforts, but only by the grace of God.

Augustine's ideas about election were linked with his other ideas about Original Sin and the Fall.

Augustine at first concluded that people were predestined for heaven or hell because of God's 'foreknowledge': that is, because God knows everything with certainty, God would therefore already know people's destinies before they were born. Although God would know this, God's knowledge would be of what people would freely choose to do. However, as Augustine got older, his views changed. He moved towards the belief that God did not only know who would be saved, but chose those people, deciding who was going to receive his saving grace and who was not going to be saved from Original Sin. Augustine based his thinking on passages from the Bible:

> 66 And we know that in all things God works for the good of those who love him, who have been called according to his purpose. For those God foreknew he also predestined to be conformed to the image of his Son, that he might be the firstborn among many brothers and sisters. And those he predestined, he also called; those he called, he also justified; those he justified, he also glorified. 99
>
> Romans 8:28–30,
> New International Version

Praise be to the God and Father of our Lord Jesus Christ, who has blessed us in the heavenly realms with every spiritual blessing in Christ. For he chose us in him before the creation of the world to be holy and blameless in his sight. In love he predestined us for adoption to sonship through Jesus Christ, in accordance with his pleasure and will – to the praise of his glorious grace, which he has freely given us in the One he loves. In him we have redemption through his blood, the forgiveness of sins, in accordance with the riches of God's grace that he lavished on us. With all wisdom and understanding, he made known to us the mystery of his will according to his good pleasure, which he purposed in Christ, to be put into effect when the times reach their fulfilment – to bring unity to all things in heaven and on earth under Christ. In him we were also chosen, having been predestined according to the plan of him who works out everything in conformity with the purpose of his will, in order that we, who were the first to put our hope in Christ, might be for the praise of his glory.

Ephesians 1:3–12, New International Version

Augustine and Calvin taught a doctrine of limited election, where only a few were chosen for salvation

Augustine could see that some people might find the idea harsh and uncompromising, but for him, election was a sign of the grace of God. All people, he thought, are born with Original Sin, and so no one deserves eternal life with God. It is, therefore, evidence of God's great love and mercy that he allows anyone at all to be saved.

John Calvin, in the sixteenth century, also taught this same idea that God had predestined some people to eternal punishment and others to eternal life with God. Calvin's ideas, taken from Augustine, were based on his belief in the unshakeable sovereignty of God: God is in absolute control over everything that happens. Therefore, it would not be possible for anything to happen that was beyond God's control or outside God's knowledge; no one could come to Christian faith and surprise God by doing so, and no one could reject God when God had expected otherwise. No one, in fact, could make any choice at all that God did not have under control. Therefore, it had to be the case that God already knew who would be saved and who would not; and this could not be a situation that God knew about but had no control over, so therefore God would have to have chosen the destiny of each human life before it began.

Calvin wrote:

> 66 All are not created on equal terms, but some are preordained to eternal life, others to eternal damnation; and, accordingly, as each has been created for one or other of these ends, we say that he has been predestinated to life or to death. 99
>
> John Calvin, *Institutes of the Christian Religion*, 1536

The idea of limited election, although a very influential one particularly in the Protestant tradition, has not been universally accepted by Christians. Many argue that it gives such a controlling picture of God that it does not leave any room for human freedom of choice. If God already knows and controls everything we do, then there might seem little point in us making any effort to act morally, or making any effort to worship God – whatever we do, God will control it anyway so that we have no other choice than to behave in the way God has chosen. If we are predestined for heaven or for hell, then perhaps we can behave however we like, as we cannot change anything about the end result.

Other Christians, therefore, have argued that the message of Christianity is that the love of God and the possibility of salvation that it brings is for all people, not just a few. This is a doctrine of **unlimited election**, which was developed by the theologian Karl Barth (1886–1968) in the twentieth century. Barth argued, in his famous work *Church Dogmatics*, that Jesus Christ brought salvation for the whole world. Barth saw election in terms of choice, and wrote about election as the choice that God made to send Jesus, the elected man, into the world. God made this choice timelessly for the purposes of saving sinful humanity. In this way, Barth tried to combine the idea that people are only saved if God chooses, and not through their own efforts, with the

Many Christians object to the doctrine of election on the grounds that it gives no place to human free will

Think question

If you knew that your exam results had already been decided and the grades fixed, and there was no possibility of that grade changing, what would be the point, if any, of continuing with your education and turning up to the exam?

Apply your knowledge

11. Look up the following passages:

    John 3:16–17

    1 John 2:2

    1 Timothy 2:3–6

    How far do you think these passages support the theology of Karl Barth?

Karl Barth taught a doctrine of unlimited election, where everyone has the possibility of being saved

Hick believed in universal salvation, where everyone is saved and no one is elected above anyone else

idea that a loving God would not choose only a few for salvation. Barth writes that Jesus is 'both the electing God and elected man in One' (*Church Dogmatics*, 2004, p. 3). The election of individuals is bound up with the election of Jesus as their representative, and Jesus is elected so that everyone can have the possibility of eternal life.

The theologian John Hick (1922–2012) took a different view from Karl Barth. Barth taught that salvation was available for everyone who has faith in Jesus, but Hick went further and argued that God will save all people, whatever their beliefs. Hick was an evangelical Christian who spent some time working in multicultural Birmingham, and through his contact with good people who had firm beliefs in religions other than Christianity, he came to the view that a God of love would not reject everyone except Christians. Hick's is a **universalist** position. In his books, *God and the Universe of Faiths* (1973) and *Death and Eternal Life* (1976), he argues that everyone will reach God in the end, after death. Hick believed that the afterlife will provide further opportunities for people to develop their faith in God and to grow towards making a choice for God. In his view, different religions are different expressions of the same universal human desire for God, so that there are not 'right' and 'wrong' religions but simply different traditions of doctrine and practice which stem from cultural differences.

Hick's view has its critics. Cardinal Ratzinger, who went on to become Pope Benedict XVI, for example, argued that Hick's view made Christ's death on the cross seem pointless. If everyone is going to be saved regardless of whether or not they accept the teachings of Christianity, then the sacrificial death of Jesus becomes just one of the many possible ways to heaven rather than a once and for all cosmic event.

A study of Matthew 25:31–46

In Matthew's gospel, the teachings of Jesus are collected and arranged in groups, often thematically. This passage for study follows immediately from 'The **Parable** of the Ten Virgins', which is about the need to be watchful in case of the sudden return of Christ at the end of time. The whole section is about the judgement of God and the separation of the faithful from the unfaithful. It is part of the 'Olivet Discourse', or in other words, the teaching Jesus is said to have given on the Mount of Olives. Jesus had been asked by his followers to tell them more about the end of time and the signs they should look for.

Matthew 25: 31–46 is usually known as 'The Sheep and the Goats'. In this parable, Jesus writes about the time when the 'Son of Man' comes and separates people according to their deeds.

6 6 When the Son of Man comes in his glory, and all the angels with him, he will sit on his glorious throne. All the nations will be gathered before him, and he will separate the people

one from another as a shepherd separates the sheep from the goats. He will put the sheep on his right and the goats on his left. Then the King will say to those on his right, 'Come, you who are blessed by my Father; take your inheritance, the kingdom prepared for you since the creation of the world. For I was hungry and you gave me something to eat, I was thirsty and you gave me something to drink, I was a stranger and you invited me in, I needed clothes and you clothed me, I was ill and you looked after me, I was in prison and you came to visit me.' Then the righteous will answer him, 'Lord, when did we see you hungry and feed you, or thirsty and give you something to drink? When did we see you a stranger and invite you in, or needing clothes and clothe you? When did we see you ill or in prison and go to visit you?' The King will reply, 'Truly, I tell you, whatever you did for one of the least of these brothers and sisters of mine, you did for me.'

Then he will say to those on his left, 'Depart from me, you who are cursed, into the eternal fire prepared for the devil and his angels. For I was hungry and you gave me nothing to eat, I was thirsty and you gave me nothing to drink, I was a stranger and you did not invite me in, I needed clothes and you did not clothe me, I was ill and in prison and you did not look after me.' They also will answer, 'Lord, when did we see you hungry or thirsty or a stranger or needing clothes or ill or in prison, and did not help you?' He will reply, 'Truly, I tell you, whatever you did not do for one of the least of these, you did not do for me.' Then they will go away to eternal punishment, but the righteous to eternal life." **"**

Matthew 25:34–46, New International Version

Key ideas from the parable

This parable is, on the surface, relatively easy to understand, although it does raise some issues and questions. Firstly, there is the theological issue of the title used by Jesus, 'Son of Man'. The various different titles used of and by Jesus are a huge topic for exploration and it is not possible to treat them in any depth here, but one interesting puzzle to consider is whether, when in telling this parable, Jesus meant to refer to himself, or whether he did not understand himself to be the long-awaited Messiah but was referring to some other figure.

The parable makes a sharp division between two groups of people, the 'sheep' and the 'goats'. There is no middle ground. Those who are rewarded with the promise of eternal life with God are those who have taken care of other people in need. They have given food to the hungry and clothes to the naked, they have cared for the sick and visited people in prison. There is nothing here about their beliefs: no mention of the need for them to be Christians or even of the need for them to believe in God at all.

> *The question of who Jesus was is central in Christian theology, and is explored in Chapter 3.4*

Think question

Do you think that ignoring people in need when you could have helped them is morally equivalent to doing deliberate harm?

Apply your knowledge

12. John Hick argued that a God of love would not send people to eternal punishment. What do you think this parable is teaching about eternal punishment? Is it consistent with ideas about an omnibenevolent God? Give reasons for your answer.

13. What do you think this parable is teaching, if anything, about those who care for people in need some of the time, but not as much as they could?

14. Do you think it is practically possible for anyone to care for those in need to the extent that this parable suggests – is it setting an impossibly high standard for people? Give reasons for your answer.

However, many Christian interpretations of the text argue that the reason the 'sheep' behave in the way that they do is a result of, rather than a cause of, their salvation. God has 'prepared a place for them' from eternity and because of their faith in God (it is argued), they are displaying the characteristics of Christian love that follow from having been given the Holy Spirit. Faith is, therefore, seen as inextricably linked with 'good works'.

The 'goats' in the parable face a harsh and eternal punishment, and similarly, at first it is difficult to see what they have done that is so wrong. However, the answer is not that they have done something bad, but that they have failed to take the opportunities they could have taken to do good to others. The parable is saying that when people have an opportunity to do good to those in need, but ignore it, they are ignoring Christ.

Doom Paintings such as this were popular in the Middle Ages, showing the righteous being separated from the unrighteous

Discussing death and the afterlife

Does God's judgement take place immediately after death or at the end of time?

There is considerable confusion in Christianity about whether God judges each person immediately after death, or whether judgement happens at the end of time for everyone together. Both views can be supported by biblical texts, which has led some thinkers to the view that there is both judgement immediately after each death and a final judgement at the end of time.

Some of the early Christian writers, such as Irenaeus, believed that most Christians do not enter heaven until the final Day of Judgement, which is when God's whole plan for the universe comes to its conclusion and time comes to an end. Before this time, but after death, they live in peaceful happiness while they wait for their final reward of heaven. Some exceptional people, such as prophets, saints and martyrs, might be admitted on a fast-track to heaven without having to wait. This has become a popular Christian view, especially because it fits in with some passages from the Bible. This is a view where what is known as known as '**particular judgement**' is distinct from '**final judgement**'. Calvin supported this view, arguing that the dead are not sleeping while they wait for the Last Judgement, but are conscious, either in peaceful bliss or in pain depending on whatever God has chosen for them.

The view contrasts with 'final judgement' or 'general judgement' which is usually used to mean the same as the Last Judgement. This is believed to be when whole nations are judged as well as every person, in a final conclusion to all of creation.

An alternative Christian view is that people go straight to heaven or hell as soon as they die. The parable of the rich man and Lazarus in Luke's gospel (Luke 16:19–31) seems to suggest that Lazarus was taken straight to heaven after his death, although the parable is clearly meant to be an illustrative story rather than a literal account and therefore it could be unwise to read too much into it. Many Christian prayers refer to deceased Christians as though they are already in heaven.

Jesus' words on the cross in Luke's gospel have added to the puzzle of whether or not people go straight to heaven after death. When Jesus was crucified, according to Luke's gospel one of the criminals crucified alongside him recognised Jesus' innocence, and then spoke to Jesus:

> 66 Then he said, 'Jesus, remember me when you come into your kingdom.'
>
> Jesus answered him, 'Truly I tell you, today you will be with me in paradise.' 99
>
> Luke 23:42–43, New International Version

This passage seems to show that Jesus was promising the criminal that he would be going to heaven right away, as soon as he had died. However, although this English translation introduces a comma into Jesus' words, in the Greek language of the original gospel text, there is no punctuation and Jesus is recorded as saying 'I tell you today you will be with me in

Apply your knowledge

15. Look up Matthew 7:13–23, Matthew 13:40–43 and Revelation 20:11–12

    What do these passages seem to teach about God's judgement?

16. What understanding of heaven can be found in 1 Thessalonians 4:13–18?

17. What do you think might account for ambiguities in biblical teaching about life after death?

paradise'. Was Jesus saying, 'You will be in paradise with me today' or 'Today I tell you, you will be with me in paradise'?

Are heaven and hell eternal?

Christian thinkers agree that heaven is eternal, although they do not all agree on what this means. For many, the eternity of heaven is to be understood in the same way as the eternity of God, as timeless. In Aquinas' view, for example, the beatific vision of God is an eternal, timeless moment, rather than a length of time which stretches on into infinity. This view allows an escape from the idea of heaven as boring, because there would not be time to fill or any sense of repetition, as there would be no 'before' and 'after'.

However, for others the eternity of heaven is seen in terms of an endless, everlasting length of time, because this seems the most compatible with teachings of the Bible which refer to activities in heaven, such as singing God's praises or learning about God. Singing and learning are examples of activities which happen in time, where first one note is sung and then the next, or a new piece of knowledge is added to knowledge that was there before. It also seems more compatible with the idea that we will in some way continue to be ourselves in heaven. Given that we exist in time, and everything we do happens in sequence, perhaps an eternal heaven makes more sense alongside the view that we continue to be the same people.

Whether hell is eternal begs the questions of whether a God of love would send his creatures to a punishment from which there is no escape. Some, Hick for example, find the idea of hell to be totally in contradiction to the Christian concept of God, while others argue that the perfect goodness and justice of God inevitably requires that those who reject him are distanced from him. It also raises questions of whether any human sin could be so bad that it deserves eternal punishment; some argue that we all deserve it because we have all failed to live in God's image and likeness. Augustine famously took this view and argued that we all deserve eternal punishment in hell, but others have a more optimistic understanding of human nature.

Is heaven the transformation and perfection of the whole of creation?

The Book of Revelation, at the end of the Bible, describe visions of the end of time, in a dreamlike, highly symbolic way. The writer records his religious experiences in which the end of the world is revealed to him by God. He writes: 'Then I saw "a new heaven and a new earth," for the first heaven and the first earth had passed away, and there was no longer any sea' (Revelation 21:1, New International Version). Other passages also leave open the possibility that heaven might refer to a 'new earth', transformed back to the state of perfection God intended when he made the Garden of Eden. The Messiah would come back and people willingly would live under God's rule.

Apply your knowledge

18. Which view do you find more plausible, if either: the view that life after death is timeless, or the view that it lasts forever in an endless line of days? Give reasons for your answer.

19. Which view do you find more attractive, if either? Give reasons for your answer.

This idea was popular in the early days of Christianity and is also popular among some Christians today. The term '**Parousia**' is used to describe it; a term which comes from the Greek and was used to denote a state visit by a king. In Christianity, the Parousia is usually taken to mean the Second Coming of Christ: an event in which Christ will return to the earth to complete the whole plan for creation, to judge people and to take up his rule.

As with other beliefs about the future, different Christians have different views. Some take the ideas of the Bible literally where they refer to a second coming of Christ, and look forward to this time; others, such as Karl Barth, interpret it to mean events such as the Resurrection of Christ and the giving of the Holy Spirit at Pentecost. Some believe that it will be a single and final event, while others believe that the transformation and perfection of creation is underway and is the role of Christians in the world today.

Is purgatory a state through which everyone goes?

Ideas about the existence of purgatory have remained a part of Catholic doctrine. However, it is not generally popular in the Protestant tradition; Protestants tend to see it as an unnecessary doctrine, and reject it on the grounds that Jesus' sacrifice on the cross was total in its defeat of sin, enabling people to go straight into the presence of God if they accepted Jesus' saving power. Ideas about purgatory and the possibilities of the living helping the dead to pass through purgatory more quickly gave rise to the selling of 'indulgences' in the Middle Ages. Indulgences were understood to be a way of reducing the suffering of a loved one in purgatory; it can be difficult to be clear about exactly how the idea was employed because so many of the records of the time are shaped by anti-Catholic feelings. A living person could perform an act of pilgrimage, say some prayers, fast or, allegedly, buy from the Church some kind of token which would (so the purchaser was told) reduce the sufferings of the dead person. Inevitably this put grieving people under immense pressure to buy such tokens by paying money to the Church when often they could not afford it. This abuse of the doctrine of purgatory was one of the key catalysts for the beginning of the Protestant movement. The Protestant reformer Martin Luther in the sixteenth century was vehement in his rejection of the selling of indulgences, and gradually also rejected teachings about purgatory, arguing that there was no biblical support for the idea. Luther believed that the doctrine of purgatory undermined biblical teaching about God's saving grace through faith.

The Catholic tradition, however, takes the view that purgatory is necessary for souls to be purified sufficiently to enter the holy presence of God. Some people might spend only a very short time in purgatory ('time' being used figuratively, as life after death is said to be timeless), especially if they are saints or have been martyred for their faith, but nevertheless they would argue that purgatory is a state through which everyone goes before moving on either to heaven or to hell.

Apply your knowledge

20. Look up Titus 2:13 and 1 Corinthians 1:7–8. Do you think the writers of these passages meant to refer to a single final event, or might they have meant to give a metaphor of an ongoing process? Give reasons for your answer.

21. Look back at the parable of the Sheep and the Goats from Matthew 25. What do you think Jesus meant when he said 'When the Son of Man comes in all his glory'?

Apply your knowledge

Some people might argue that purgatory is not literally a place but a spiritual state of mind, where after death people come into the presence of God and immediately realise they are sinful.

22. Look up these passages and consider whether they support the view that people should go through purgatory before they are fit to stand in the presence of God.

    1 Samuel 6:20

    Isaiah 6:1–6

    Luke 5:8

    Matthew 5:48

    2 Corinthians 7:1

23. How convincing do you find the view that purgatory is a metaphor for a spiritual state of mind? Give reasons for your answer.

Learning support

Points to remember

» Belief in resurrection after death is central for Christians.

» Christians have different ideas about precisely what happens after death, but most believe that God will judge people and that there is a heaven for those who believe in Jesus.

» Ideas about election propose the view that God chooses which people will enter heaven, even before they are created.

» In your writing, remember that Christians often use metaphor to convey ideas about the soul and the afterlife; avoid writing as though all Christians take these metaphors literally.

» Try to recognise and refer to common and divergent views in your essays.

» Although most people find it impossible to have a clear and firm opinion about life after death, it nevertheless ought to be possible to make an evaluation of the relative coherence of different ideas. Perhaps one possibility seems to make no sense at all, while another might be more coherent, even if you cannot reach a definite conclusion.

» Try to give a fair hearing to opinions which are different from your own. Even if you feel strongly that a view makes no sense or has too many flaws to be plausible, make sure that you nevertheless explain it accurately and adequately before pointing out its shortcomings.

Enhance your learning

» You might want to extend your thinking about the issue of predestination by finding out about the thinking of Søren Kierkegaard, a Christian existentialist who wrote about the centrality of personal choice and commitment in Christian faith. His view is completely different from that of Augustine and Calvin.

» Christian ideas about the Parousia (Second Coming of Christ) and the development of such ideas over time make a fascinating area for study and could be worth exploring.

» The 'Matthew effect' is an interesting line of thinking in sociology and economics, and parallels are drawn with the parable of the sheep and the goats; it could be a thought-provoking concept to research.

» The *Catechism of the Catholic Church* paragraphs 422–478 sets out key Catholic doctrines and would make a useful point of reference when you are explaining your ideas.

» Brian Davies' *An Introduction to the Philosophy of Religion* (1982), Chapter 11, is a very accessible and thought-provoking read about life after death.

» John Hick's *Death and Eternal Life* (1985), Part III is a large book and quite demanding to read, but useful for gaining a deeper understanding of Hick's views.

» Alister McGrath's *Theology, the Basics* (2011), Chapter 8, is very clear and straightforward, without being too basic.

Practice for exams

AS questions and A level questions look identical; the difference between AS and A level assessment is seen in the different proportions of marks awarded for two different skills: the skill of demonstrating knowledge and understanding (Assessment Objective 1, or AO1), and the skill of constructing a critical argument (AO2).

At AS, half the marks (15 marks) are available for knowledge and understanding, and the other half (15 marks) for the quality of your analytical and evaluative argument. You should aim to use your knowledge in order to support the argument you are making throughout the essay, rather than presenting descriptive knowledge in the first half and then an opinion in the second.

At A level, your demonstration of knowledge and understanding is awarded a maximum of 16 marks, and your analytic and evaluative skills are awarded a maximum of 24 marks. You should aim to concentrate on constructing a lucid argument, making use of your knowledge to add weight to the conclusions you draw.

To what extent can belief in the existence of purgatory be justified?

This question invites you to consider teachings about the nature of purgatory and to explore the reasons for holding such beliefs.

Practise your skills for AS level

If you are an AS student you should demonstrate good accurate knowledge and understanding of what it means to believe in the existence of purgatory. For high marks, you will show awareness that there are different interpretations of this idea. You need to give an argument to support your opinions of belief in purgatory, with reasons – a simple statement of your own belief is not the same as a critical argument.

Practise your skills for A level

If you are an A level student, you should first think about what you plan to argue. You need to consider different views about purgatory, for example the traditional Catholic view about a place of cleansing, perhaps also Rahner's view of purgatory as a spiritual state, and perhaps Luther's view that the doctrine of purgatory is wrong. You might also want to consider ideas about the soul, mind and body and consider the views of materialists who argue that there is no life after death. When you are considering views, you need to do more than simply present them in a descriptive way. Decide whether you think the idea is coherent (whether it fits together without contradiction) and whether it is plausible, and assess its strengths and weaknesses as a viewpoint, in order to arrive at a well-justified conclusion.

'Heaven is not a place but a state of mind.' Discuss.

This question invites a consideration of different understandings of the concept of heaven, and asks for a critical evaluation of whether the idea of heaven as a state of mind is the most helpful.

Practise your skills for AS level

If you are an AS student, start by considering what you think is the best understanding of the idea of 'heaven'. You might agree with one of the perspectives you have studied, or you might think that several of them are right in different ways, or perhaps you disagree with all of them. Aim to support your view with reasoning, rather than simply asserting that this is what you believe.

Practise your skills for A level

If you are an A level student your focus should be on the quality of your argument. Rather than simply presenting different ideas about heaven, one after the other, and then saying which is your favourite at the end, you should aim to argue persuasively all the way through. In your essay, you should explore the different possibilities: that heaven is a place, or that it is a perfection of this world, or that it is a state of mind both before and after death, and decide which you find the most convincing.

Chapter 3.3 | Knowledge of God's existence

What do Christians believe about the ways people can gain knowledge of God?

Can truths about God be worked out, using human reason?

Can truths about God be observed in the natural world?

Does God reveal himself to humanity, and if so, in what ways?

Are some ways of gaining knowledge about God better than others?

Key Terms

Faith: voluntary commitment to a belief without the need for complete evidence to support it

Empiricism: a way of knowing that depends on the five senses

Natural theology: drawing conclusions about the nature and activity of God by using reason and observing the world

Protestantism: a form of Christianity which rejects the authority of the Catholic Church and places greater emphasis on the Bible and on personal faith

Revelation: 'uncovering'. In theological terms, this is when God chooses to let himself be known

Immediate revelation: where someone is given direct knowledge of God

Mediate revelation: where someone gains knowledge of God in a secondary, non-direct way.

Grace of God: God's unconditional and undeserved gifts

Wisdom literature: a genre of writing from the ancient world, teaching about wisdom and virtue. In the Bible, books such as Proverbs and Job are classified as wisdom literature

Introduction

The nature of knowledge has presented philosophers with puzzling questions for thousands of years. It is clear that we gain knowledge as individuals, but how does this happen, and how can we know when we have reached a point at which we can be certain that what we know is true? Many different answers have been suggested.

In ancient Greece, the puzzle was seen in terms of the difficulty of gaining certain and true knowledge of a world which is in a constant state of motion and change. How could we know about something if, as soon as we thought we understood it, it was different again? For Plato, this question was addressed by his Theory of Forms, where true knowledge is gained by the soul in a permanent, eternal world beyond this physical one. He thought we already have knowledge when we are born, and that when we think we are gaining knowledge we are in fact recognising things that we knew when we lived in the world of the Forms.

Aristotle, in contrast, thought that we can only learn anything meaningful through science, by looking at the physical world around us and conducting repeatable experiments. He thought that our knowledge develops the more that we experience things, through our senses. This has led some people to the conclusion that the physical world contains all that is worth knowing about, and even all that *can* be known.

As well as the possibility of being born with knowledge, and learning through sense experience, we can also learn through reason and logic, taking deductive steps such as those in mathematics to work out what is true. We also learn from sources of authority, such as teachers, parents, books and experts, where we have to have a degree of **faith** that what they are telling us is true.

Some people argue that the only kinds of knowledge that are genuine and worth pursuing are those which come either from reason or from sense experience. Religious believers, however, argue that these methods are limited because they only give people knowledge of the physical world. They do not help people to gain knowledge of spiritual, supernatural truths, or ethical truths about how we ought to live and what sort of

Plato thought that we already have knowledge before we are born. See Chapter 1.1 for more on this.

Apply your knowledge

1. Make a list of five things you feel you know for certain. How did you gain that knowledge? (For example, did you learn it through your senses? Were you taught it by a reliable authority? Did you work it out for yourself?)

2. Do you think some ways of gaining knowledge are more reliable than others? If so, which and why?

3. Do you think that different ways of knowing are suited to different purposes, or, for example, should everything be examined scientifically? How would you justify your response?

people we should aim to become; but some will argue in return that there are no such things as 'supernatural truths' or absolute 'ethical truths' and might also argue that this material physical world is all that exists.

If there are supernatural truths, and if there is a God, how is knowledge of God to be gained? In Christianity this question has been approached in a variety of ways. There is discussion of the extent to which people can learn about God through their own efforts, for example through contemplation and meditation, through observation of the natural physical world and through the logical powers of human reason. There is also discussion of the extent to which people are limited in their abilities to understand through their own efforts, and need to have truths about God revealed to them.

How can God be known, according to Christianity?

The question of how, if at all, God can be known is an interesting one. In many world religions, including Christianity, God is understood to be unavailable to the five senses because God is not physical. For people who believe that the only real knowledge is that which can be discovered through empirical experience (experience gained through the five senses), this means that God cannot be known at all, perhaps even does not exist at all, and questions about God could be seen as meaningless questions. If people believe that knowledge can be gained through reason and logic, this too could mean that God cannot be known at all, as he is said to be beyond the realms of the rational and beyond the capabilities of the human mind. Christians and many other religious believers, however, do not accept that empirical experience and logical reasoning are the only methods of gaining knowledge available to humanity.

Bonaventura, a Franciscan monk from the thirteenth century, considered the question of how God can be known in his work *The Mind's Road to God*. He believed that the human mind has at least three different ways of knowing, to which he referred using the analogy of an eye to represent different ways of 'seeing'. We have, he suggested:

- the 'eye of the flesh', which is the way of knowing that incorporates sense perception: the **empiricism** of science. This 'eye' is the means by which we gain knowledge about the physical world

- the 'eye of reason', which is the way of knowing that lets us work out mathematical and philosophical truths through the use of logic

- the 'eye of contemplation', which is a way of knowing which allows us to come to a knowledge of God by going beyond the scope of both sense experience and reason and gaining knowledge of God through faith.

The idea that the way we can know God is different from the way we can know other things has been popular throughout Christian history and is still used by modern writers. John Polkinghorne, for example, a Cambridge physicist and also an ordained Anglican priest, also used Bonaventura's metaphor of different eyes. Polkinghorne often writes about what he calls 'binocular vision', or looking through two different eyes. He sees science through one 'eye', which shows him the physical world and the laws and processes behind it; and he understands spiritual truths about God through the other 'eye' which shows him purposefulness and the world in the context of the creation of God. Polkinghorne argues that both eyes need to work together to give a complete picture in all its dimensions. He argues that it is foolish of some religious people to ignore the discoveries of science, and equally foolish of some scientists to close one eye and refuse to engage with the possibilities of God.

John Polkinghorne used the metaphor of binoculars to explain how knowledge of God and knowledge of the physical world can be gained simultaneously through different 'eyes'

For religious believers, God can be known not only in the way that we know facts, but also known in the way that we know other people. 'Knowing' that the prime minister exists is different from 'knowing' the prime minister personally; religious believers argue that God can be known, not just in the sense of knowing of his existence and his attributes, but also known personally in a relationship.

A distinction has been made in Christian thought between 'natural' and 'revealed' theology, where **natural theology** is about gaining knowledge of God through the powers of human reason and observation, while revealed theology is about God choosing to reveal himself to humans directly, for example through religious experience and through scripture. Many Christians believe that both of these can help people to understand religious truths; however, there are some who argue that revealed theology is the only way that we can gain reliable knowledge of God and that natural theology should be rejected.

Natural theology is about gaining knowledge of God through human observation and reason, whereas revealed theology is about gaining knowledge of God through scripture and religious experience

When science began to develop rapidly, in the seventeenth and eighteenth centuries, a metaphor for understanding how God can be known became popular: this was the metaphor of 'God's two books'. Robert Boyle, familiar for his work in science as well as for his theology, wrote in terms of 'two great books', the natural world and the Bible, which were both created by the same 'author'. The words of the Bible and the discoveries of science were seen as complementary, each enhancing the other as means by which people could deepen their understanding and knowledge of God.

Apply your knowledge

Although the discoveries of science were understood to support the teachings of the Bible in the seventeenth century, in the modern world people often argue that science has 'disproved' religion.

4. What might have caused this change of attitude towards the relation between science and religion?

5. Do you think that science and religion are two complementary ways of looking at the evidence to gain a fuller picture, or do you think science and religion give contradictory pictures – or do you have another view? Give reasons for your answer.

Natural theology

Natural theology is the name given to attempts to discover truths about the existence and the nature of God by using human experience and human reason. For most Christian thinkers, natural theology has played an important part in forming and supporting belief. Looking at the beauty of the world leads many to the conclusion that there must be a creator God, for example. William Paley, who famously gave a design argument to demonstrate the existence of God, titled his work: *Natural Theology or Evidences of the Existence and Attributes of the Deity* (1802). For Paley, the natural world presented clear evidence of God.

The Bible, too, offers the view that the natural world demonstrates truths about God. In the book of Psalms, for example, the writer looks up at the night sky and sees clear evidence of the existence of God and of God's relationship with humanity:

> **66** When I consider your heavens,
> the work of your fingers,
> the moon and the stars,
> which you have set in place,
> what is mankind that you are mindful of them,
> human beings that you care for them?
>
> You have made them a little lower than the angels
> and crowned them with glory and honor.
> You made them rulers over the works of your hands;
> you put everything under their feet:
> all flocks and herds,
> and the animals of the wild,
> the birds in the sky,
> and the fish in the sea,
> all that swim the paths of the seas.
>
> Lord, our Lord,
> how majestic is your name in all the earth! **99**

Psalm 8:3–9, New International Version

The wonders of the world, in this passage, are presented as evidence. Humanity simply has to look at the natural world in order to realise the power and the unfathomable wisdom of God, and to see that people have a responsibility towards God in a duty to take care of and rule over other species.

Paul, in his letter to the Romans, expressed the view that human experience and human reason easily lead to knowledge of God. In this

Paley was a strong supporter of natural theology. Chapter 1.3 has more on this.

passage, Paul argues that people have made God angry because they have ignored the obvious fact of God's existence and instead lead godless lives of immorality:

> ❝ The wrath of God is being revealed from heaven against all the godlessness and wickedness of people, who suppress the truth by their wickedness, since what may be known about God is plain to them, because God has made it plain to them. For since the creation of the world God's invisible qualities – his eternal power and divine nature – have been clearly seen, being understood from what has been made, so that people are without excuse.
>
> For although they knew God, they neither glorified him as God nor gave thanks to him, but their thinking became futile and their foolish hearts were darkened. ❞
>
> Romans 1:18–21, New International Version

In Paul's view, God's attributes of eternity, omnipotence and holiness are 'plain' to everyone

For Thomas Aquinas in the thirteenth century, natural theology was important in demonstrating that Christian belief was reasonable. The discovery of the work of Aristotle had made some of Aquinas' contemporaries question whether Christian belief could be replaced by scientific 'common sense' thinking. Aquinas was keen to show that Christianity was not in opposition to reasonable common sense, but that reason and observation could be employed in support of Christian belief.

For example, from seeing that the world is in a constant state of change due to cause and effect, we can work out that there must be

Apply your knowledge

6. Paul writes that God's eternal power and divine nature are made obvious to humanity. What might he have thought was the 'plain' evidence of the existence of an eternal and omnipotent God?

7. What might evidence for the existence of God, or evidence of the absence of God, look like?

Natural knowledge of God is the knowledge of God that can be gained through sense perception and reason

For arguments for the existence of God based on the idea that we can use our reason to discover God's existence, see Chapter 1.4

Natural theology involves using human reason to uncover truths about God

Apply your knowledge

8. Religious belief seems to be a common feature of the vast majority of human cultures. Is 'people must therefore have an innate sense for God' the best explanation of this phenomenon?

9. If people do have an innate sense of God, does this demonstrate that, therefore, God must exist? Give reasons for your answer.

an Uncaused Causer of the world; and from observing that everything in the world depends on something else for its existence, we can work out that there must be some being which depends on nothing at all but which exists necessarily. Aquinas thought there are some general observations, such as that there is motion and cause, which anyone would accept and from which any intelligent person can reason for the existence of God.

Modern supporters of the traditional arguments for the existence of God, such as Richard Swinburne, also put forward the view that our human reason and powers of observation provide us with solid grounds for supporting the probability that there is a God. Swinburne argues, for example, that we have good reason to think that the world shows signs of order, regularity and purpose; reason therefore (he argues), leads us to conclude that there is probably an intelligent being who is the author of the universe, which we call God.

Natural theology as arising from an innate human sense of the divine

Some thinkers argue that a sense of the divine is an intrinsic part of human nature. One common argument for the probability of God's existence, made by the Roman philosopher Cicero and many others since, notes that in all cultures and all times in history, people have had a sense that there is an infinite being who is in control of the universe. Cultures which cannot possibly have known anything about each other's existence nevertheless often develop religious beliefs which are remarkably similar, looking to an invisible, powerful spiritual being which they worship with rituals. Perhaps, then, we are all born with a sense for God, a recognition of the existence of this infinite being.

There are places in the Bible which seem to support the idea that people are born with a sense for God. In the account of the creation of humanity in Genesis, God makes people in his own image (Genesis 1:27), and breathes into Adam with his own breath (Genesis 2:7), suggesting that there might be a 'spark' of divinity in each human life, which could in turn be interpreted to mean that there is something in human beings which is designed to seek and respond to God.

John Calvin, the sixteenth century **Protestant** theologian, claimed in his writings known as 'Institutes' that we have a 'sensus divinitas' which could be translated as a 'seed of divinity' or an innate sense of God; he wrote: 'There is within the human mind, and indeed by natural instinct, an awareness of divinity.'

He used this to argue that, therefore, people have no excuse if they fail to worship God and dedicate their lives to his service. Calvin did not think that this 'sensus divinitas' was restricted to Christians, but believed that it is universal to all human beings. Anyone, therefore, who can reflect on the natural world, its beauty and order, should be able to understand without difficulty the existence and character of God. Calvin writes that knowledge of God through this inbuilt sense of the divine is not just available to the intelligent and educated, who will be confronted with God's works as they study 'astronomy, medicine and all of natural science', but it is so straightforward that it can be gained by anyone 'even the most unlearned and ignorant people' (John Calvin, *Institutes of the Christian Religion*, 1536, 1.1.3).

Calvin argued that the created world is a 'mirror' or a 'theatre' for God, who sometimes increases the human capacity for awareness of his presence so that no one can have any excuse for pretending that he or she was unaware of God's existence. For Calvin, the 'sensus divinitas' means that everyone, universally, is aware of God (although not everyone uses this sense in the right way, and some turn to idolatry in following religions other than Christianity). Everyone, therefore, has a sense of his or her own sinful nature and the need to live in fear of God's punishment. Any lack of clarity about God in the natural world comes about because of human sin, which clouds people's understanding of God and prevents us from having a full awareness of his nature and purposes.

Other writers talk about the 'epistemic distance' between people and God, by which they mean the distance in knowledge and our inability to grasp and comprehend the nature of God. Usually, this epistemic distance is attributed to God himself, deliberately making himself obscure to people in order to preserve their free will and allow them to choose whether or not to have a relationship with him. However, for Calvin, the epistemic distance is created by human beings. God has made it impossible for people to ignore him and his will unless they quite deliberately choose to do so, and if they are unable to recognise God in the world then this is their own fault.

The idea that people are made 'in the image of God' has led supporters of natural theology to the view that we are made in such a way that we can appreciate and understand beauty and goodness in the world, and can recognise them as manifestations of God's creativity and goodness.

Similarly, supporters of natural theology argue that we have an innate sense of morality, which we can also tell, using our reason, must come from God. Moral arguments for the existence of God take our experience of conscience as evidence that God exists. Thinkers such as Joseph Butler, John Henry Newman and C.S. Lewis claim that we all have feelings of guilt when we do something wrong, even if no one sees us, and we all feel satisfied when we know we have done the right thing. They argue that this 'inner voice' of conscience is evidence not only of the existence of God but of a God who makes moral demands of his people and wants them to follow his commandments.

Calvin thought that we are born with a sense for the divine

See Chapter 1.6: Calvin thought that epistemic distance is the fault of sinful humanity.

Supporters of natural theology claim that we can find evidence for God by looking at our own human nature

Natural theology as arising from the order of creation

As well as the view that people naturally have an instinct for God, there is also the view that God can be clearly seen in the order and beauty of creation.

The pre-Christian writer Cicero, in his dialogue *On the Nature of the Gods* (c.45BC), has one of his characters present this view: 'for what can be clearer and more obvious, when we have lifted our eyes to the sky, and have gazed upon the heavenly bodies, than that there exists some divine power of exalted intelligence by which these are ruled?' (translated by F. Brookes, 1896).

It is argued that we naturally recognise and understand that beauty comes from God. John Calvin took the view that the beauty of the world is clear evidence of the existence of God, not only the beauty in the detail of small plants and animals but also the beauty of the whole system of planets, of natural forces and of the laws of physics. Calvin writes about the natural beauty of the universe as a 'sort of mirror' of God, using a metaphor from the Bible. The creation reflects the nature of God in its beauty and orderliness. Calvin is careful to show that God is not nature itself, but that nature is a means by which people can learn something about God. They can understand God's power and eternity, and God's care for humanity, his justice and mercy, through observing the natural world with their senses and contemplating it with their reason.

> 66 This skillful ordering of the universe is for us a sort of mirror in which we can contemplate God, who is otherwise invisible. 99
>
> John Calvin, *Institutes of the Christian Religion*, 1536, 1.5.1

Calvin put forward the view that the natural world is a mirror of God's nature

Revealed knowledge of God

Revealed theology is the name given by Christians to ideas about God which (they believe) God has decided to show to people. They are not ideas which people could have worked out by themselves, but ones which have been shown to people at a time and in a manner chosen by God.

This distinction between natural and revealed theology began to be made in the Middle Ages. It was thought that natural theology could show the existence of God, the existence of the human soul, and the existence of human free will; even people who believed in religions other than Christianity had managed to work out these truths. But revealed theology was special. It did not rely on people having particularly strong intellectual gifts, but was available for everyone through faith. It confirmed the findings of natural theology, but also uncovered further truths which were unavailable to reason alone, such as the doctrine of the Trinity, the truth about Jesus as the Christ and Son of God, and ideas about life after death. These were not truths which people could ever have worked out simply by using their reason and observation of the world around them; they could only be known because God chose to reveal them.

Christians believe that the fundamental, distinctive teachings of their faith have been given to them by God as **revelation**. The English word 'revelation' comes from the Latin word 'revelatio', which is turn is a translation of the original Greek of the New Testament, where the word is 'apocalypsis'. These words mean 'unveiling', 'uncovering' or 'making clear something that was hidden'.

Immediate and mediate revelation

Sometimes theologians make a distinction between 'immediate' and 'mediate' revelation. 'Immediate' revelation is understood as that in which God makes himself directly known to people. The prophets are said to have had **immediate revelation** of God, when God gave them the exact words that they were to speak to their listeners. Adam and Eve had immediate revelation of God before the Fall, when God walked with them in the Garden of Eden; Abraham had immediate revelation of God when God told him to sacrifice his son Isaac and promised a land to his descendants; Moses had immediate revelation of God when God spoke to him out of the burning bush in Exodus. Everyone who met Jesus had immediate revelation of God, and this is what gave the apostles their authority after Jesus' death.

'Mediate' revelation is when people learn about God and gain knowledge about him less directly. Those who listened to Moses and trusted him to take them out of slavery into the Promised Land had **mediate revelation** of God passed on to them by Moses. Those who heard the words of the prophets had mediate revelation, and so did those who learned about Jesus from those who had met him. The Bible is considered to be mediate revelation of God by most Christians, where the words of those who had immediate revelation are preserved and interpreted and read by others. For some Christians, however, the Bible is immediate revelation, where every word comes directly from God dictating to those who wrote it down.

Revelation through faith and God's grace

In Christian belief, as humans are sinful and have finite minds, natural theology is not sufficient to gain full knowledge of God. Some knowledge of God is possible through experience and reason, but it is not complete. A much fuller knowledge of God can be gained by revelation through faith and by God's grace in giving knowledge of himself through the Holy Spirit. These are theological terms which need some explanation.

Faith is usually considered to be a type of belief which is held in spite of a lack of conclusive evidence, or even sometimes held in opposition

Revealed theology involves truths disclosed to people by God, without the need for human reason

Immediate revelation is understood as a direct encounter with God whereas mediate revelation involves learning about God from others

to evidence or reason. It is considered to bridge the gap when sense experience and reason cannot give an answer to a question and yet the person wants some kind of certainty; a 'leap of faith' makes a commitment to a particular way of thinking even without sufficient evidential or reasonable support. The lack of evidence and lack of reasonable support for a belief is compensated for by an effort of will, where the person chooses to commit to the belief on trust.

In the thirteenth century, Thomas Aquinas wrote about the nature of faith and the ways in which it both complements and differs from other kinds of knowledge. In *Summa Theologica*, he explores how empirical and logical knowledge, which he called 'scientia', is certain because we can see the evidence in front of us, either through our senses or by using our reason. Faith, in contrast, does not have this firm self-evident certainty, and, therefore, it is a voluntary choice, which Aquinas calls 'an act of the intellect assenting to the truth at the command of the will'. Aquinas argued that we cannot have faith and scientific knowledge about the same thing, because faith is about those things where certainty is not readily available whereas science is about the things we can test and confirm for ourselves.

Faith differs from opinion, too, in Aquinas' view, because opinion does not have the certainty that faith does. Like faith, opinion is a matter of choice, where the evidence is not clear in supporting one view or another; but opinion is open to change, where people might be persuaded to change their opinions, whereas faith has a certain and solid commitment that does not have elements of doubt.

For people without religious belief, faith can be seen as a barrier to knowledge and something that should be abandoned or disregarded in favour of trying to get more empirical evidence. However, in Christianity, faith is seen as a virtue. Christianity does not see faith and reason as standing in contradiction to each other, but sees faith as a leap that can be taken once sense experience and reason have gone as far as they can. The Catholic Church, for example, teaches that faith and reason should work together as both are given to humanity as gifts from God. Christian thinkers argue that it is impossible to have faith without knowledge first, as we need knowledge and understanding of something before we can choose to put our faith in it.

The gospel of John comments on the relation between faith and knowledge. John's gospel has some significant differences from the other three gospels of the Bible, especially in the style of writing. One of the distinctive features of John's gospel is the way in which he presents Jesus as a revealer of secret knowledge; the writer also draws attention to the decisions people make about whether or not to put faith in Jesus. In this short passage, presented after miracle stories where Jesus fed five thousand people with a few loaves and fishes and then miraculously walked on water, some of Jesus' followers began to lose interest and wandered off. Simon Peter (one of Jesus' closest friends) and others are asked whether they plan to leave too, and Simon Peter answers on their behalf:

Think question

Do you agree with Aquinas' distinctions between scientific knowledge, faith and opinion? Do you think it is possible to have certainty through faith?

Apply your knowledge

The letter to the Hebrews in the New Testament contains a chapter about faith. Read Hebrews 11.

12. What does the first verse of this chapter say faith is?

13. What is it that the people listed in this chapter have in common?

14. Find out more about the biblical characters listed here; follow up the stories about them in the Old Testament.

> 66 Simon Peter answered him, 'Lord, to whom shall we go? You have the words of eternal life. We have come to believe and to know that you are the Holy One of God.' 99
>
> John 6:68–69, New International Version

The writer makes a distinction between 'believe' and 'know', but also puts them together showing that it is possible to believe and to know both at the same time. Later in the gospel, the writer states his purpose in writing the gospel, which is that readers and listeners should choose to have faith:

> 66 Jesus performed many other signs in the presence of his disciples, which are not recorded in this book. But these are written that you may believe that Jesus is the Messiah, the Son of God, and that by believing you may have life in his name. 99
>
> John 20:30–31, New International Version

Christianity emphasises faith as a means to have knowledge of God, and it does so in the context of the **grace of God**, or God's unconditional giving to humanity. According to Christian teaching, people are able to have knowledge of God through faith because of God's grace: God gives them the gift of faith, and also sustains this faith and strengthens it through his Holy Spirit. Christians believe that God can be understood as a Trinity – three in one – where God is simultaneously the Father, the Son and the Holy Spirit. God the Father is the creative, omnipotent aspect of God; God the Son is the person of Jesus; and God the Holy Spirit is the activity of God in the world, often symbolised in terms of a mighty wind or as fire, or as a dove of peace.

The grace of God is an important part of the Christian understanding of knowledge of God, because it is believed that people can only have full knowledge of God when God graciously chooses to give it. God as the Holy Spirit is believed to:

- give the prophets of the Old Testament the right words to say at the right time

- guide the writers of scripture so that they produce the word of God, with God-given authority

- give people wisdom by which to understand what has been revealed to them

- give people faith with which to believe the Christian message

- give people the confidence to share the Christian faith, even in times of danger

- enable people to live a Christian life on a personal level
- strengthen the Church as a community of believers
- bring people to salvation.

How revelation is understood in the Bible

The Bible itself shows many different ways in which people can gain knowledge of God, and does not make a distinction between natural and revealed theology but takes for granted that God will want to communicate with his people in a whole range of ways. For example:

- **Through the beauty of the world** – according to the Bible, the existence, creativity and wisdom of God is obvious everywhere we look. In Psalm 19, the writer describes how, when looking up at the sky, we can see the work of God:

> 66 The heavens declare the glory of God;
> the skies proclaim the work of his hands. 99
>
> Psalm 19:1, New International Version

- **Through the events of history** – in Christianity, and especially in Judaism, there is the belief that people can gain insight into the purposes of God by looking at the past. The events of history are seen as the work of God, and so by recalling the past, people can gain a greater understanding of what God wants from them and what displeases God. In the book of Jeremiah, for example, the prophet summarises how the people of Israel have ignored the things God has done for them through history and so brought punishment on themselves:

> 66 You brought your people Israel out of Egypt with signs and wonders, by a mighty hand and an outstretched arm and with great terror. You gave them this land you had sworn to give their ancestors, a land flowing with milk and honey. They came in and took possession of it, but they did not obey you or follow your law; they did not do what you commanded them to do. So you brought all this disaster on them. 99
>
> Jeremiah 32:21–23, New International Version

- **Through traditional wisdom** – in the Bible, especially in the books known as '**wisdom literature**', there is the idea that God can be revealed through the insights of wise people. Those who have many years of experience of trying to live a moral life gain an understanding of God which is revealed in their sayings and writings for anyone who is willing to listen, for example:

> **"** Trust in the Lord with all your heart
> and lean not on your own understanding;
> in all your ways submit to him,
> and he will make your paths straight. **"**

Proverbs 3:5–6, New International Version

- **Through the words of the prophets** – the biblical prophets are seen as messengers of God, people who were chosen and commissioned to reveal God's words to the people. In the books of prophecy in the Bible, the prophets often made it plain that they were not just giving their own opinions about people's moral behaviour or about future judgement, but were speaking 'the very words of the Lord'. This short passage from the book of Isaiah describes how, after seeing a vision of God seated on a throne in the Temple, Isaiah was called to be a messenger from God to reveal his words to the people:

> **"** Then one of the seraphim flew to me with a live coal in his hand, which he had taken with tongs from the altar. With it he touched my mouth and said, 'See, this has touched your lips; your guilt is taken away and your sin atoned for.'
>
> Then I heard the voice of the Lord saying, 'Whom shall I send? And who will go for us?'
>
> And I said, 'Here am I. Send me!' **"**

Isaiah 6:6–8, New International Version

- **Through religious experiences and visions** – in the Bible, as well as throughout Christian history, God is understood to reveal himself to people through personal religious experiences. Sometimes God is said to appear to people in dreams to give them messages and warnings; sometimes God is presented to them in visions or as a voice; sometimes God's words are transmitted to them by angels. For example, in the book of Genesis, Jacob has a dream in which land is promised to his descendants:

> **"** He had a dream in which he saw a stairway resting on the earth, with its top reaching to heaven, and the angels of God were ascending and descending on it. There above it stood the Lord, and he said: 'I am the Lord, the God of your father Abraham and the God of Isaac. I will give you and your descendants the land on which you are lying. **"**

Genesis 28:12–13, New International Version

- **Through the natural laws and design of the material world** – the Bible takes it for granted that the natural laws of physics which can easily be experienced demonstrate the existence and nature of God. In this passage from the letter to the Romans, Paul says that people have no excuse for saying they did not know about God's power or God's eternal nature, because it is obvious in everything God has made:

> 66 … since what may be known about God is plain to them, because God has made it plain to them. For since the creation of the world God's invisible qualities – his eternal power and divine nature – have been clearly seen, being understood from what has been made, so that people are without excuse. 99
>
> Romans 1: 19–20, New International Version

- **Through the person of Jesus** – in Christianity, Jesus is understood as being the incarnation of God: God in human form. Christians, therefore, believe that God is revealed through Jesus as the 'Christ' ('anointed one') who came into the world for the purpose of revealing God fully and finally to humanity. God came into the world as a man, according to Christianity, so that people could understand God at their own level, because the infinite power and love of God is impossible for limited, finite human minds to comprehend.

In Christian belief and according to John's gospel, Jesus was the 'Word made flesh'; in other words, he was the eternal creative wisdom and power of God, born into the world as a man. Jesus' words are believed to be the very words of God, and his actions and sacrifice on the cross are believed to be the actions and sacrifice of God, revealing the extent of God's love for humanity. Jesus' miracles, according to Christian belief, reveal the nature of God in different ways: for example, Jesus calming the storm reveals God's omnipotence over the laws of nature; Jesus' healing of people from leprosy, blindness, bleeding and paralysis reveals God's grace in restoring people; the miracle of the feeding of the multitude shows God is giver of everything people need for their lives, and miracles such as the raising of Lazarus reveal God as the giver of life after death.

> 66 The Word became flesh and made his dwelling among us. We have seen his glory, the glory of the one and only Son, who came from the Father, full of grace and truth. 99
>
> John 1:14, New International Version

For Christians, Jesus was not only a role model and a prophet, but also the final revelation of God made complete, so that there was no need for any other prophets to come after him. In the New Testament, those who become followers of Jesus are those who recognise him for who he is.

See Chapter 3.4 on the person of Christ

- **The Bible itself** – for Christians, the Bible reveals truths about God. Christians have different views about how the Bible is to be read and understood, but whether it is considered to be the literal word of God or whether it is seen as a collection of ancient teachings and stories full of mythology, Christians believe that the Bible is a source through which God can be known. Some passages in the Bible refer to the importance of holy scripture as a means by which God is revealed, for example:

> " … from infancy you have known the Holy Scriptures, which are able to make you wise for salvation through faith in Christ Jesus. All Scripture is God-breathed and is useful for teaching, rebuking, correcting and training in righteousness, so that the servant of God may be thoroughly equipped for every good work. "
>
> 2 Timothy 3:15–17, New International Version

The Bible, according to Christianity, reveals knowledge which people could not have gained in other ways. For example, it reveals knowledge about the creation of the world, and about the disobedience of humanity and the Fall of Adam and Eve. It reveals stories about founders of the Jewish and Christian religions, such as stories of Noah, Abraham and Moses. It records the words of God as spoken to the prophets. Most importantly for Christians, it reveals the purposes of God in the person of Christ, recording his words and actions, his sacrificial death on the cross and his Resurrection.

The Bible also contains 'wisdom literature', in the Psalms, Proverbs and elsewhere. This is understood to be collections of revealed wise insights, passed on through generations, about all kinds of subjects of concern to humanity, such as the extent to which someone should desire wealth, the characteristics of a good wife, how to distinguish between wise and foolish people and the right ways to treat others.

Treating the Bible as a source of revealed truth does create issues. It is difficult to know whether the writers somehow knew exactly which words to write, given to them by God in some mysterious way, or whether they used their own feelings, insights and religious experiences to record their ideas in their own ways. Some people point out what they see as inconsistencies in the Bible, or factual errors, and argue that the Bible cannot be considered as an infallible source of revealed truth but has to be interpreted and sometimes treated as myth.

- **The life of the Church** – in the Catholic tradition, the tradition and the scriptures communicate the truths already (and finally) revealed, whereas in the Protestant tradition the Bible is seen as a superior source of truth.

Apply your knowledge

In Judaism at the time of Jesus, part of the Temple was screened off from the general public by a heavy curtain. Only the High Priest was allowed into this special, secret and holiest part of the Temple.

Look up Matthew 27:51.

15. What happened to the Temple curtain at the time of Jesus' death, according to the gospel?

16. What do you think the writer was trying to convey by including this detail in the narrative?

Think question

Do you think that any of these ways of knowing about God are reliable? Are some more reliable than others? If so, which and why? If you think they are all unreliable, what reasons would you give to support your view?

In Christian belief, the Church is made up of the people of God, who follow on in continuity from Israel in the Old Testament. God chose Israel to be his special nation and kingdom of priests at the time of Moses, according to the Bible, and Christians believe that the Church exists to continue this role as God's representative, with a mission to spread the Christian message and to set an example of holiness. The Church is seen as 'the body of Christ', continuing the work done by Jesus when he lived on the earth; so the Church can reveal God's working through the Holy Spirit. Sometimes Christians refer to the Church in terms of Jesus' 'hands'. They see it as their responsibility to work in the world in the ways that Jesus taught, by caring for the poor, visiting people in prison or when they are ill, providing shelter for the homeless and advocating justice.

The Church as a centre for Christian worship is seen to have a revelatory function, especially in the celebration of the Eucharist (holy communion). In this sacrament, Christians share bread and wine in remembrance of Jesus at the last supper before his Crucifixion, and this is understood to reveal the nature of Jesus' sacrifice on the cross to Christians who take part in the service together.

The Church is also considered to have the responsibility for safeguarding the word of God in the Bible, so it is up to the Church to make sure that people study the Bible and interpret it correctly. In the Catholic tradition, the Church is seen as an important authority in understanding the teachings of the Bible and showing how they are to be applied in Christian life. Protestants, however, take the view that God can be revealed directly to people through the reading of the Bible guided by the Holy Spirit, and so they give more prominence to the Bible than to the teachings of the Church.

A study of Acts 17:16–34

This passage from the New Testament is interesting to study in the context of questions about natural and revealed theology, because it combines elements of both.

....

Christians accept that there are many different means by which people can come to know God; different groups within Christianity emphasise some more than others

66 While Paul was waiting for them in Athens, he was greatly distressed to see that the city was full of idols. So he reasoned in the synagogue with both Jews and God-fearing Greeks, as well as in the market-place day by day with those who happened to be there. A group of Epicurean and Stoic philosophers began to debate with him. Some of them asked, 'What is this babbler trying to say?' Others remarked, 'He seems to be advocating foreign gods.' They said this because Paul was preaching the good news about Jesus and the resurrection. Then they took him and brought him to a meeting of the

Areopagus, where they said to him, 'May we know what this new teaching is that you are presenting? You are bringing some strange ideas to our ears, and we would like to know what they mean.' (All the Athenians and the foreigners who lived there spent their time doing nothing but talking about and listening to the latest ideas.)

Paul then stood up in the meeting of the Areopagus and said: 'People of Athens! I see that in every way you are very religious. For as I walked around and looked carefully at your objects of worship, I even found an altar with this inscription: TO AN UNKNOWN GOD. So you are ignorant of the very thing you worship – and this is what I am going to proclaim to you.

'The God who made the world and everything in it is the Lord of heaven and earth and does not live in temples built by human hands. And he is not served by human hands, as if he needed anything. Rather, he himself gives everyone life and breath and everything else. From one man he made all the nations, that they should inhabit the whole earth; and he marked out their appointed times in history and the boundaries of their lands. God did this so that they would seek him and perhaps reach out for him and find him, though he is not far from any one of us. "For in him we live and move and have our being." As some of your own poets have said, "We are his offspring".'

'Therefore since we are God's offspring, we should not think that the divine being is like gold or silver or stone – an image made by human design and skill. In the past God overlooked such ignorance, but now he commands all people everywhere to repent. For he has set a day when he will judge the world with justice by the man he has appointed. He has given proof of this to everyone by raising him from the dead.'

When they heard about the resurrection of the dead, some of them sneered, but others said, 'We want to hear you again on this subject.' At that, Paul left the Council. Some of the people became followers of Paul and believed. Among them was Dionysius, a member of the Areopagus, also a woman named Damaris, and a number of others.'

Acts 17:16–34, New International Version

This passage comes from the book of the Acts of the Apostles in the Bible, which tells how the first followers of Jesus worked to spread the Christian message after Jesus' death. The book describes the difficulties the apostles encountered and how the Holy Spirit helped them to overcome challenges, bring people to faith and establish the earliest Christian communities.

Paul's audience of philosophers in Athens led him to use reason as well as revelation in his speech

In this extract, the apostle Paul has gone to Athens, which was not as politically powerful as it had once been, but was still a centre of culture, philosophical discussion and university education. It was also a place where there were many idols to different gods. Paul was used to debating in the synagogues with the Jewish teachers on his missionary journeys, but this was the first time that he had attempted to present the message of Christianity to an audience with a philosophical background, people who were used to reasoning and debate as methods of uncovering the truth.

Paul engages people in conversation and preaches in the market places about Christianity. He makes a point of going to the synagogue, where he can talk with Jews about how Jesus was the Messiah foretold by the Old Testament prophets. The writer of Acts (who was probably Luke the gospel writer) says that Paul 'debated' or 'reasoned' with them. Paul would have been showing points of similarity between the prophecies and the life and death of Jesus. Through human reason, Paul hopes that his listeners will gain new knowledge of God.

Some of his listeners call him a 'babbler' – the literal translation of the Greek word is 'seed-picker', which was an insult accusing Paul of just picking up little bits of knowledge here and there without having any real idea what he was talking about. Others are interested in the novelty of his ideas and want to know more, and so they invite Paul to speak at a meeting at the Areopagus, an official meeting-place where the leading thinkers of the city would be able to hear what he had to say. When Paul usually spoke to people about the Christian message, he used the writings of the Old Testament in order to make his points, but this time

Paul made reference to both natural theology and revealed theology in his speech to the people of Athens

the crowd were interested in Greek philosophy rather than having a background in Judaism. Paul takes as his starting point a statue he has seen with the inscription 'To an unknown god'; an attempt by the Athenian people to insure against the possibilities of failing to worship one of the gods because they were unaware of his existence. It is in this context that Paul explains to them how the real God does not remain unknown, but reveals himself and his purposes to people so that they can know of him.

Paul accuses his audience of superstition. They are 'very religious' but their worship of unknown gods shows that they do not know what they are worshipping or why their gods might be worthy of worship. They simply build temples and statues out of fear rather than through knowledge. Paul claims, using reasoned argument, that they are wrong. There is only one God who is much bigger than the little idols the Athenians were worshipping. Instead of looking for mysterious unknown gods, they should understand that the true God is the ground of the whole of existence and that humanity is created by God as his 'offspring'. This was not an unusual idea to the Greek audience, whose philosophical background had already introduced them to ideas about a cause for everything in existence.

Paul tells them they can use their reason to discern from this that such a God, if he is so powerful as to be capable of creating the world and creating all the different nations with their boundaries and populations, does not, therefore, need to have temples built so that he can live in them. He is not dependent on humans giving things to him, but rather humans are dependent on God. Reason can also demonstrate that such a God cannot have his likeness captured by humans, in statues made of physical material. Using natural theology, they can work out some of the attributes of such a God. Paul moves on to talk about the grace of God in giving people everything that they have. Paul's speech in Athens seems to have had only limited success in converting his listeners to Christianity, and in subsequent speeches to different audiences on his missionary journeys, he changed the way he delivered his message.

Calvin refers to this passage in his own writings, *Institutes of the Christian Religion* (1536), where he uses it to argue that everyone has the capacity and the disposition to believe in God, although not everyone recognises God or chooses the Christian life. Nevertheless, as the passage from Acts points out, all people exist only because God is sustaining their existence; their life comes from God and everything they do is only possible because of God, and therefore people are 'living in God', whether they realise it or not. Calvin also refers to the argument that the sheer number of people who believe in God suggests that an awareness of God is a natural part of what it means to be human.

> **Think question**
>
> How, if at all, might religion be distinguished from superstition?

Discussing knowledge of God's existence

Can the existence of God be known through reason alone?

One of the best-known objectors to the idea that human reason can give knowledge of God came from the Protestant theologian Karl Barth. For many other Christians, natural theology and revealed theology work well together and support each other. Christians can use their powers of observation and their reason to make some discoveries about God; they can use revealed theology to gain knowledge of truths that are not available to observation and reason. Natural theology provides people with a sound and rational basis for faith, and revealed theology supplies the details of that faith. Also, natural theology provides an opportunity for people to share discussion about God, whatever their personal beliefs about what has been revealed; everyone is human and everyone has access to the natural world, to the conscience and to the fact of our existence and is able to consider and draw conclusions from this. Natural theology can thereby provide a starting point for dialogue between people of different faiths, or between theists, atheists and agnostics.

For some, however, natural and revealed theology are not seen as mutually supportive, but revealed theology is understood to be the only means by which God can be known and, therefore, only those who believe in that revelation consider themselves to have any knowledge of God. Christians might argue that God can only be known through Christianity. In the mid-twentieth century, Karl Barth took a strong position in declaring that natural theology was almost a kind of idolatry, where people made up and worshipped false ideas, believing that they were so clever they could access absolute and eternal truths. Barth believed that it was a form of arrogance to imagine that fallible human reason could lead people into any knowledge of God. Perhaps the fact that Barth was witnessing the rise of Nazism in Germany influenced his views that human reason alone can lead people into completely wrong directions; it reinforced his Protestant conviction that human nature was hopelessly flawed and could not be relied upon.

Barth believed that people could only know God when God chose to disclose himself to them. Revelation, he thought, only happens when God decides. People are clearly incapable of working out right and wrong by themselves, and need God's commandments as revealed in the Bible. Barth believed that God was ultimately revealed in Christ, and, therefore, for Barth there was no truth to be found in other world religions, except where they happened to be saying the same things as Christianity. Only Christ could break through the barrier of human sin to reveal God, and so any attempt to understand God without Christ was bound to be corrupt and wrong.

Defenders of natural theology, however, argue that Barth's view is too extreme. If human reason is given no part to play in the knowledge of

Think question

What might be the strengths and weaknesses of the view that Christianity is the only means of learning truths about God?

God, then people have no way of judging between true and false beliefs. One person might claim that God had disclosed a truth to him, and another might make a similar claim, but the two 'revealed truths' might be contradictory: how would it be possible to know whether either was right or wrong unless human reason were allowed a role?

One of the problems of natural theology, then, is that human reason is too limited to reach an understanding of God. But a further problem comes from an understanding of the nature of God as being beyond reason – not irrational, but non-rational. Whatever rational justifications can be given for concluding that God must be like this or like that, the difficulty still remains that God is not something that can be grasped and understood through logical reasoning. Arguments for the existence of God based on reason are not able to lead people to certain knowledge of God.

Is faith sufficient reason for belief in God's existence?

> 66 Faith is the great cop-out, the great excuse to evade the need to think and evaluate evidence. Faith is belief in spite of, even perhaps because of, the lack of evidence. 99
>
> Richard Dawkins, Untitled Lecture,
> Edinburgh Science Festival, 1992

According to Richard Dawkins and many other atheist thinkers, faith does not just provide insufficient reason for belief, but is actually harmful, encouraging people to be lazy in their thinking and avoid trying to reach any kind of certainty. Dawkins is a scientist who is particularly concerned with what he sees as religion's tendency to avoid dealing with gaps in human knowledge by describing them as a mystery, things which can be dismissed by saying 'God did it' and claiming faith is all that is required while evidence is unnecessary.

Faith, for Dawkins, is an insufficient reason for believing anything. In his view it is equivalent to saying 'I have just decided to believe this on the basis of very little evidence, and now that I have decided, I refuse to think about it further.' Dawkins likens belief in God to belief in the tooth fairy or belief that there is a teapot orbiting Mars – these beliefs cannot be conclusively disproved but there is no evidence to support them, and therefore no good reason to commit to them.

David Hume, in the eighteenth century, claimed 'A wise man … proportions his belief to the evidence' (*An Enquiry Concerning Human Understanding*, 1739–40). Hume made this claim in the context of his discussion on miracles; his argument was that rather than allowing faith or superstition or anything else to cloud our judgement, we should look at the evidence before us and decide on that basis what would be appropriate to believe.

Others argue, however, that sufficient reason for believing something does not have to depend solely on the kind of evidence that is available to sense experience and to rational argument. There are many aspects of life where we have insufficient empirical or rational evidence on which to base our decisions. We cannot know with any certainty whether we are free to make our own decisions or whether we are entirely determined by external factors; we cannot know whether the world we think we inhabit is 'real' or whether it is all illusory. We cannot guarantee that the sun will rise tomorrow morning. The balance of probability, based on our past experiences, leads us to carry on our daily lives without being in a permanent state of doubt. However, our faith that the future will resemble the past and that our past experiences act as some kind of guarantee is not supported by firm evidence.

Most Christians would argue that faith is essential for belief in God, but they might question the idea that it is 'sufficient', in other words they might question the view that faith is all that is necessary. A Christian would argue that faith is not held in a vacuum, but builds on knowledge. The 'fact' that we exist at all, that we live in a beautiful and ordered world, that we experience love, that we have moral awareness, that we have a desire to discover truth, would be used by a Christian to underpin faith. Belief in the claims of Christianity, they would argue, is not like belief in a teapot orbiting Mars, because there is no knowledge to support belief in the teapot and yet there is plenty of knowledge which could support belief in God. The knowledge that can be gained through sense experience and reason does not provide conclusive evidence, which is why faith is necessary.

It could also be argued that sense experience and reason are not the only ways in which beliefs can be justified. We base some of our beliefs on emotion: people buy houses because they 'feel right'. Some of our beliefs are based on memory, or on intuition. Perhaps faith is also an appropriate basis for taking a position, especially on those questions which cannot be answered through science and logic.

Apply your knowledge

19. Do you think people working in areas such as science, history and economics sometimes have to make 'leaps of faith' in order to reach conclusions? Give reasons for your answer.

20. Are there some areas of knowledge where a leap of faith is justifiable, and others where it is not? Explain your answer.

21. What sort of evidence might you use to make a decision about whether to commit to another person as a life partner? Would you base your decision solely on logical reasoning and solid empirical evidence? Give reasons for your answer.

22. Would you agree or disagree with Dawkins' claim that faith is damaging? How would you support your position?

23. Do you think we arrive at our ethical judgements through sense experience and reasoning – can we tell, with our senses, whether something is right or wrong, or work it out through logic? If not, how do we form our ethical judgements? Give reasons for your answer.

Might the Fall have completely removed all natural human knowledge of God?

For some thinkers, such as Augustine, the Fall of Adam and Eve when they disobeyed God in the Garden of Eden was so catastrophic as to place an insurmountable barrier between God and humanity. Augustine argued that Original Sin prevented people from being able to know God because they had become corrupt in their will and could never be holy enough to approach God through their own efforts.

Karl Barth, the Swiss Protestant theologian of the twentieth century, argued in a similar way that God reveals himself to us as and when he wants to, and that all our attempts to attain knowledge of God on our own will fail. We have finite capacities to form concepts and to understand, and we have a sinful nature, so without the help of God we are never going to reach knowledge through our own efforts, we will simply create distorted and misleading ideas about God. Barth also argued that attempts at natural theology are unnecessary as God has revealed himself perfectly and finally in Jesus. There is no need to try and work out God for ourselves when we have already been given the truth.

Other thinkers however, such as Thomas Aquinas, have argued that God gave us the ability to use our senses and our reason for a purpose, as well as giving us revealed knowledge of God, and that both can be used. We should use revealed knowledge to guide us when we use our reason to work out natural knowledge of God, but both can be used together to complement each other. Aquinas' Five Ways of discovering the existence of God through reason have become an important part of Christian arguments for the existence of God.

It could also be argued, against Barth, that the Bible does suggest that humans can gain natural knowledge of God. If the Bible is revealed by God, and that revelation from God suggests we can learn truths naturally, then perhaps both natural and revealed theology are helpful.

Towards the end of his life, Aquinas gave up writing about God, commenting that all he had written seemed 'like straw' to him. He was not saying that his writings were worthless, but that they were like the most basic of building materials. He came to the point where he decided that knowledge of God in this world could only reach the most basic level and that God is essentially unknowable.

Is natural knowledge of God the same as revealed knowledge of God?

Although the distinction between natural knowledge of God and revealed knowledge of God has been discussed, it could be argued that on some levels they are the same, on the grounds that everything that exists does so because God has chosen that it should. If God is the source of all that exists, the source of all knowledge, and nothing happens except that

Augustine thought that sin had a devastating effect on human knowledge: see Chapter 3.1

See Chapters 1.3 and 1.4 for more on arguments on reason and arguments based on experience

Apply your knowledge

24. How far would you agree with Barth's view that natural theology is incapable of giving any knowledge of God? Give reasons for your answer.

25. Look at Chapter 2.1. How does Aquinas combine natural and revealed theology in his understanding of human ethics?

Apply your knowledge

26. Explain in your own words why Barth made a sharp distinction between natural and revealed knowledge of God, and what he thought were the implications of this distinction.

27. Explain in your own words what Aquinas thought could be learned about God through reason.

God chooses it should happen, then perhaps it is not possible for people to know anything apart from what God has revealed simply because there is nothing that God has not revealed.

Natural knowledge of God has been distinguished from revealed knowledge of God in terms of the ways in which people have arrived at such knowledge. Natural knowledge is reached through reason, and revealed knowledge is reached through faith. Nevertheless, if it is argued (as Aquinas did) that God can reveal truths to us through our reason, and that our reason was given to us so that we might learn more about God, then the distinction between the two becomes blurred.

Many Christians would still argue that there is a difference between the kinds of knowledge that can be gained through reason and through revelation. They argue that beliefs about the beginning of the world and the creation of humanity could not have been worked out with reason or known about through sense experience: similarly, beliefs about the nature of Christ, the Trinity of God and life after death had to be revealed and are not available to natural knowledge.

Is belief in God's existence sufficient to put one's trust in him?

At first sight, it seems obvious that belief in God's existence is not the same as putting trust in God. After all, we can believe that all kinds of things and people exist, but that does not mean we trust them or want to commit ourselves to a relationship of any kind with them. Some people who believe there is 'something out there' do not lead any kind of religious life. They might agree that probability makes it likely there is a God, or they might claim to have some kind of spiritual feelings which they ascribe to the existence of God, but this assent to the likely existence of God does not have much effect on the way they conduct their lives. Agreeing that a reasoned argument for the existence of God is a strong argument and sounds plausible is not the same as faith.

Some people might argue that they believe in God but that their experience of evil and suffering in the world leads them to conclude that God is not to be trusted. They might argue that God seems to have favourites, or that although they believe in God, because some tragic event has happened, they do not want to trust him or have a relationship with him.

It could also be argued, however, that those who believe in the likely existence of God, and those who believe there is a God but not one they wish to worship, have misunderstood the nature of God. Anselm, in his ontological argument, expressed the view that God exists necessarily. God is not like a contingent thing, which might or might not exist, where there could be degrees of probability about its existence. There is (for Anselm) no 'might not exist' about God, because God exists in such a way that 'might' and 'might not' do not apply. If, therefore, someone believes on the basis of reason that there is probably a God, then that person has missed the point, and is believing in something contingent rather than in God. Similarly, Anselm might argue, if someone believes in 'something out there' but also does not believe that such a being is worthy of worship or is worthy of complete trust, then that person has not understood that God is 'that than which no greater can be conceived' but is instead imagining a much lesser being and then rejecting this fiction instead.

Belief in the existence of God, in a rational way, requires the addition of a 'leap of faith' in order to place trust in God; however, if Anselm is right, then if a person understands what God is, belief in God cannot lead anywhere other than trust in him.

Anselm thought God's existence is necessary, not just probable: see Chapter 1.4

Apply your knowledge

28. How would you distinguish between belief and faith?

29. When you put faith in something in your own life, what is it that makes you do so?

30. Do you think it is possible to believe in God and yet not have a religious faith?

Learning support

Points to remember

» Natural knowledge of God is knowledge which could be gained through the use of human reason, whereas revealed knowledge of God is that which can only be gained through faith.

» Theologians have different views about the extent to which God can be known through human reason and sense experience.

» Try to make links between the ideas of Christian theology and other ideas from the philosophy of religion and ethics. In this chapter, there are links between natural theology and design arguments for the existence of God, as well as links with natural law as a system of ethics.

Enhance your learning

» There is a huge amount of literature available to enhance your understanding of the Reformation in Europe and the roles played by different characters such as Calvin, which helps to explain some of the differences between Catholic and Protestant thought.

» It would be worth doing some further research to develop your understanding of key differences between Protestant and Catholic thought.

Practice for exams

AS questions and A level questions look identical; the difference between AS and A level assessment is seen in the different proportions of marks awarded for two different skills: the skill of demonstrating knowledge and understanding (Assessment Objective 1, or AO1), and the skill of constructing a critical argument (AO2).

At AS, half the marks (15 marks) are available for knowledge and understanding, and the other half (15 marks) for the quality of your analytical and evaluative argument. You should aim to use your knowledge in order to support the argument you are making throughout the essay, rather than presenting descriptive knowledge in the first half and then an opinion in the second.

At A level, your demonstration of knowledge and understanding is awarded a maximum of 16 marks, and your analytic and evaluative skills are awarded a maximum of 24 marks. You should aim to concentrate on constructing a lucid argument, making use of your knowledge to add weight to the conclusions you draw.

Discuss critically the view that Christians can discover truths about God using human reason.

This question invites a discussion of natural theology, and will require an exploration of the extent to which reason can lead Christians to knowledge of God, if at all. You will need to consider the views of those who support natural theology as well as those who disagree with it.

Practise your skills for AS level

At AS level, you could demonstrate your knowledge and understanding by giving good examples of thinkers who have different points of view on this issue. Make sure that your own opinion is clear and well supported with reasoning as you offer critical comment on the different views you present.

Practise your skills for A level

At A level, make sure that you start with a clear sense of your own views on this issue and decide how you are going to support them with reasons and examples. Try to avoid your essay simply becoming a list of who said what, instead, try to make it persuasive.

'Faith is all that is necessary to gain knowledge of God.' Discuss.

For this question you need to explore the nature of faith and its role in knowledge of God; you also need to consider the idea that it is 'all that is necessary' for knowledge of God.

Practise your skills for AS level

If you are an AS student, you should show your knowledge and understanding by clearly explaining how 'faith' is understood, and showing awareness of the different ways in which people might believe that knowledge of God can be gained. You need to form an opinion on the importance of faith. If you think that faith is unhelpful in gaining knowledge then it is quite legitimate to say so, as long as you give reasons.

Practise your skills for A level

If you are an A level student, you need to develop a strong line of argument and use your knowledge to support it. You could draw a comparison between those who argue that faith is absolutely necessary for knowledge of God with those who argue that it leads people away from reasoned truth. Consider whether other things might also be necessary, such as church teaching or the Bible, and how these interact with faith.

Chapter 3.4 | The person of Jesus Christ

Was Jesus the son of God?
Was Jesus a teacher of wisdom?
Was Jesus a revolutionary?

Key Terms

Son of God: a term for Jesus that emphasises he is God incarnate, one of the three persons of the Trinity

Liberator: a general term for someone who frees a people or group

Rabbi: a Jewish teacher, often associated with having followers

Hypostatic union: the belief that Christ is both fully God and fully human, indivisible, two natures united in one person

Homoousios: of the same substance or of the same being

Word: from the Greek logos, another name for the second person of the Trinity, used at the beginning of John's Gospel to describe the incarnation which existed from the beginning, of one substance with and equal to God the Father

Redemption: the action of saving or being saved from sin, error, or evil

Incarnation: God born as a human being, in Jesus Christ

Zealot: a member of the Jewish political/military movement that fought against Rome in the first century AD

Messiah: in Christianity, the word is associated with Jesus Christ, who is believed to be the Son of God and the Saviour. In Judaism the word is associated with individuals who rose up against oppression, the people of Israel

Specification requirements

Jesus Christ's authority as:

*   the Son of God
*   a teacher of wisdom
*   a liberator

Introduction

Jesus lived and died in an obscure corner of the Roman Empire. He led no army. He held no political office and he died owning little or nothing. Yet he is arguably the most controversial figure of history and faith, and perhaps the most well know human being who has ever lived.

There can be little doubt that a man named Jesus existed. He is mentioned by the Roman historians Suetonius (c. AD69–122) and Tacitus (c. AD56–117), and the writer Pliny the Younger (c. AD61–113), as well as the Jewish scholar Josephus (c. AD37–97). Jesus of Nazareth really existed. But who was he? This question lies at the heart of what distinguishes Christianity from other religions.

Jesus the Son of God

'Son of God' is a title used for Jesus in the New Testament and in the early Church. Key events in the New Testament (for example Jesus' baptism and transfiguration) emphasise Jesus as Son of God. This doesn't just mean Jesus was related to God. The idea links to the Christian doctrine of the Trinity (God as three-in-one: Father, Son and Holy Spirit) and the doctrine of incarnation (God becomes human), as well as to the debates within the Church about how Jesus could be both human and divine. For Christians today, being the Son of God is central to Jesus' authority.

Jesus the teacher of wisdom

There is something in what Jesus said and did that has created a wisdom that some have felt vital to hand down across the centuries.

- Jesus' teachings and moral example have an enduring appeal to Christians and others. He is believed by many to be a good and holy man who lived a life close to God and advocated repentance, forgiveness and spiritual purity. His life is an example for others.

- His teachings focused on loving others, forgiveness, healing the sick and looking out for the outcasts, the vulnerable and the dispossessed. He saw wealth and power as problems.

- Jesus' wisdom also contained a message of good news: salvation from sin and death and being reborn to eternal life.

Jesus the liberator

Some see Jesus as a religious revolutionary, someone who challenged the established religious authorities, institutions and rules with a radically different spiritual message that sought to break down the division between God and people. Jesus challenged religious institutions and initiated a new order. To some he was a reformer seeking political revolution: the liberation of the people of Israel from the Romans, as a Messiah. Perhaps he wanted to overturn the traditional approaches to religion. Maybe he wanted to overturn the social structures in society.

Think question

a. What is your reaction to the idea of Jesus as a revolutionary?

b. What moral messages do you know from the life and work of Jesus that stand out, irrespective of anything else about him?

Jesus is referred to as the Son of the Father and is often depicted as such in Christian art

Jesus the Son of God

Early Christians identified Jesus with God. The New Testament applies the term 'God' to Jesus (John 1:1,18; 20:28; Hebrews 1:8-9, see also Romans 9:5; Titus 2:13; 2 Peter 1:1; 1 John 5:20). Paul speaks of Jesus as God's 'own Son' (Romans 8:32, see also John 1:14). The New Testament says Jesus is God's 'only' son or 'own' son, implying something unique. Jesus seems uniquely close to God as shown in the Baptism of Jesus (Matthew 3:13–17; Mark 1:9–11; Luke 3:21–23) and the Transfiguration (described in Matthew 17:1–9, Mark 9:2–8, Luke 9:28–36, and 2 Peter 1:16–18).

Jesus' knowledge of God

The relationship between Jesus and God-the-father is mysterious. Jesus calls God 'Abba' (Greek for 'father' or 'dad') and a heavenly voice declares Jesus 'my son' (the Baptism of Jesus, Mark 1:9–11; The Transfiguration, Matthew 17), but Jesus does not use the term 'son' himself. The Gospels say Jesus comes into this world through the intervention of the Holy Spirit and Mary (Matthew 1:18). The ancient world contained myths of gods producing demi-god/hero offspring with humans: these offspring were not gods themselves but had God-like powers. But Christians do not see Jesus as a figure like the ancient heroes of Greeks and Romans. Instead, Jesus is directly associated with God by the text and is believed to be so by Christians:

- St John writes of Jesus as **Word**, and that the 'Word was God' (John 1:1)

- (Doubting) Thomas refers to Jesus as 'my Lord and my God' (John 20:28)

- in the letter to the Hebrews a psalm is addressed to Jesus as God (see Hebrews 1:8)

- God's spirit will come again in Jesus' name (see John 14:16, 26)

- Jesus has a saving God-like power (see Matthew 1:21; and Luke 2:11)

- Jesus is worshipped, something done to a God (see Romans 1:23; and 1 Corinthians 1:2).

How Jesus 'knows' God is an ancient puzzle. In the fourth and fifth centuries there were many debates about the identity of Jesus and his closeness to God. If Jesus is God and human, does that mean he had two beings inhabiting one body with one in power over the other? While this explains how Jesus could know God, it would mean Jesus is both God and a separate human being. This was rejected in the early Church at the Council of Chalcedon:

> 66 We, then, following the holy Fathers, all with one consent, teach men to confess one and the same Son, our Lord Jesus Christ, the same perfect in Godhead and also perfect in manhood; truly God and truly man, of a reasonable [rational] soul and body; consubstantial [coessential] with the Father according to the Godhead, and consubstantial with us according to the Manhood; in all things like unto us, without sin; begotten before all ages of the Father according to the Godhead, and in these latter days, for us and for our salvation, born of the Virgin Mary, the Mother of God, according to the Manhood; one and the same Christ, Son, Lord, Only-begotten, to be acknowledged in two natures, inconfusedly, unchangeably, indivisibly, inseparably; [...]. 99
>
> Philip Schaff, *Creeds of Christendom, with a History and Critical notes, Volume II, The History of Creeds*, 1876, p. 62

This belief in the 'perfect conjunction' of Jesus' two natures was termed a **hypostatic union** by the early Church. But there were still difficulties.

How human was Jesus?

In order to save humanity from sin, Jesus had to be divine as only God has that redemptive power. However, if Jesus was God, does that mean he didn't really suffer on the Cross – as how can a God suffer? If Jesus did not feel pain and did not actually die from crucifixion, that would mean his Resurrection was not real, the cross is false and Jesus wasn't a real human being. He had to be God, as only God can save. He had to be a human being, as only humans needed saving. If he wasn't God he couldn't overcome the forces of evil; if he wasn't human he couldn't overcome those forces for humanity. If he's not God, he can't reveal the Father; if he isn't human, he can't reveal the Father to us. Or as Gregory of Nazianzen put it, 'what he has not assumed he has not healed'.

If Jesus was fully human as well as divine, then that also creates problems. Paul wrote that humans have a sinful, corrupting nature (Romans 7:18–19), so if Jesus became human, wouldn't he become corrupted?

Think question

- 'I like to think of Jesus as a person like me, someone who understands me, someone who can relate to me.'
- 'Jesus is my saviour, so much greater than me, and he is able to save me, take away all my sin.'

Discuss how these two views link with the debate described above.

Chalcedon established a key principle that as long as it is acknowledged that Jesus Christ is both truly divine and truly human, how this is possible is not a question of central importance

Think question

'Christians have no problem accepting Christ as holy, as God. But they always have problems accepting him also as a human being at the same time.

Franco Zeffirelli, film director and Italian State Senator, b.1923

Do you think Zeffirelli is right? Why/why not?

Bishop Apollinaris of Laodicea worried that 'a human mind – that is a changeable mind … is enslaved to filthy thoughts', so suggested the Word *replaced* the human mind and soul with a divine one, without taking on fallible human nature. But how could humanity be fully redeemed if not all of human nature was saved? Gregory of Nazianzen (AD329–390) rejected Apollinaris' suggestion because it constituted a 'half salvation'. Apollinarianism was rejected as heresy.

How the Churches resolved the question of Jesus' humanity and divinity

Most Christian Churches today, including the Eastern Orthodox, Catholic, and most Protestant Churches, follow the agreement established by the major ecumenical councils. The First Council of Nicea in AD325 resolved that Jesus was of the same substance as the Father, or of one being – **homoousios**. The Council of Chalcedon in AD451 affirmed that Christ is acknowledged in two natures, which come together into one person and one hypostasis. Jesus was not a mix or a blend.

The Council of Chalcedon's definition is not recognised by any Oriental Orthodox Church and, as a result, these Churches may be classified as non-Chalcedonian.

The following extract from the Council's agreement, gives an insight into both the nature of Jesus, as Christians believe today, and how this links to salvation.

> Following, then, the holy Fathers, we all unanimously teach that our Lord Jesus Christ is to us One and the same Son, the Self-same Perfect in Godhead, the Self-same Perfect in Manhood; truly God and truly Man; the Self-same of a rational soul and body; co-essential with the Father according to the Godhead, the Self-same co-essential with us according to the Manhood; like us in all things, sin apart; before the ages begotten of the Father as to the Godhead, but in the last days, the Self-same, for us and for our salvation (born) of Mary the Virgin Theotokos as to the Manhood; One and the Same Christ, Son, Lord, Only-begotten; acknowledged in Two Natures unconfusedly, unchangeably, indivisibly, inseparably; the difference of the Natures being in no way removed because of the Union, but rather the properties of each Nature being preserved, and (both) concurring into One Person and One Hypostasis; not as though He were parted or divided into Two Persons, but One and the Self-same Son and Only-begotten God, Word, Lord, Jesus Christ; even as from the beginning the prophets have taught concerning Him, and as the Lord Jesus Christ Himself hath taught us, and as the Symbol of the Fathers hath handed down to us.

Thomas Herbert Bindley, *The Oecumenical Documents of the Faith*, 1899, p. 297

What was the extent of Jesus' self knowledge?

The question of whether Jesus had two centres of consciousness or not is still debated. Was he free to choose what he did? Is freedom is a basic part of being human? Was his knowledge a human knowledge or did he look onto the world as the creator looks onto its creation? To what extent did he have knowledge of his divine reality? Did he wander around being the Son of God, without realising it? Did he know he was the saviour of all?

If Jesus had divine knowledge what do his expressions of emotions mean? Was his anxiety in the Garden of Gethsemane and his tears at the death of Lazarus just fake? Did he feign ignorance when he asked who touched him (Mark 5:30)? Medieval theology responded with three kinds of knowledge that Jesus might have:

- knowledge of the divine reality of God, face-to-face, and all the created realities (scientia visionis)

- an infused knowledge (scientia infusa)

- knowledge of life in the normal way of human life (scientia experientiae).

Theologian Karl Rahner suggests a genuinely human consciousness must have an unknown future in front of it. Our life is conditioned by our uncertainty. If Jesus was conscious of God the Father's awareness all the time, then his view of life can hardly be called a human one. Rahner's solution is to think of an onion, with its many layers of skin. Psychologists sometimes describe human self-awareness as layered, like an onion. We have deep within us better understandings of our self which are not always on the surface of our consciousness. The expression of fear in Gethsemane or uncertainty in the desert or on the cross makes sense if Jesus' human self-consciousness was close to the surface but his divine self-consciousness was deep within.

Apply your knowledge

1. Does it really matter if Jesus only pretended to have human emotions?

2. Rahner implies that if Jesus was fully conscious of his divine nature all the time he lived, he wouldn't be like a real human because real humans live with uncertainty. Do you agree? Discuss this idea.

3. How convincing is Rahner's 'onion' solution?

Rahner suggested that Jesus' consciousness could have had many layers, like an onion

Gerald O'Collins (*Interpreting Jesus*, 1993, pp. 184–5) challenges the possibility of answering these kinds of questions.

1. It is very difficult to undertake any study of the inner world of any being, alive or dead, so trying to make sense of the kind of inner experience of life that Jesus might have is very challenging, particularly as he left no writings of his own.

2. Before anyone can say 'yes, Jesus knew he was the saviour' a person must first show an appreciation of the complexity of knowledge, the multi-layered structure of how we experience reality, with memory, emotion, experience, intuition, instinct, identity and many other factors playing a part. Know thyself is easier said than done.

3. Consciousness is not the same as knowledge of a separate object. Knowledge of a separate object takes place without reflection, but consciousness always involves a degree of reflection.

O'Collins concludes that one answer is possible given all of these caveats:

> 66 What did Jesus know about himself and his mission? … He knew that he stood in a unique relationship to the Father and that as Son he had a mission of salvation for others. These were not discoveries to be made, by primordial facts of his consciousness. His basic awareness of his Sonship did not mean observing the presence of God, as if Jesus were facing an object out there. It was rather a self consciousness and self-presence in which he was intuitively aware of his divine reality. 99
>
> Gerald O'Collins, *Interpreting Jesus*, 1993 p. 185

Think question

Is there a difference between knowing something and being conscious of it?

Miracles

In the New Testament, Jesus is shown as being a 'miracle worker', healing the sick and driving out demons (Mark 7:37; Acts 10:38). There is no doubt that these miracle stories have been and remain important to Christians today, but they are controversial. By being able to work miracles, Jesus confounded the mechanical orderliness of the universe with his authority and the power of God.

Jesus' power to walk on water, his power to drive out demons, to recreate sight, speech and even life, are things that only God can do, reinforcing the message that Jesus is God's Son. Many Christians believe that miracles occur today too and are evidence of the Holy Spirit's continued presence. Some Christians believe that they have witnessed healing miracles. Some Christians go to holy sites like Lourdes in France in the hope of healing.

One miracle healing story is Mark 6:47–52 when Jesus' disciples were in a fishing boat struggling in a storm. Jesus, who was on the land, 'saw the disciples straining at the oars, because the wind was against them […] he went out to them, walking on the lake.' Fearful and seeing Jesus, the disciples cried out and Jesus said, 'Take courage! It is I. Don't be afraid.' Jesus climbed into the boat and the wind died down. Referring to an earlier miracle, the text continues: 'They were completely amazed, for they had not understood about the loaves; their hearts were hardened.'

How might these accounts be interpreted?

Hume's *Essay on Miracles* (1748) argued that because we have no present day, direct experience of miracles ourselves, it is not possible to trust the accounts of Jesus walking on the water, or any other miracle given by New Testament writers, even if they did believe in them completely. People do not truly walk on water today. Either the Gospel account must be taken on trust or rejected. If accepted it points to Jesus' amazing power over nature.

Edward Schillebeeckx identified a second way in which Jesus' miracles can be interpreted: as having a spiritual or metaphorical meaning for today, rather than (just) a literal one about a past remarkable event. Perhaps Jesus is the source of calm in daily life, and perhaps people need to allow him to step into their lives and not live in fear of the troubles they face. This is not necessarily scientifically any easier to comprehend. Just how Jesus steps into and calms the life of people is still quite a mysterious idea.

Perhaps it is more important to ask what we think the Gospel writers are doing in reporting the miracles. N.T. Wright (*Jesus and the Victory of God*, 1996) discusses this in terms of Jesus' healings. Jesus not only cures a lot of people, but he cures people from groups that have become excluded from society. Jesus is reuniting socially excluded, ritually unclean, separated groups back into a relationship with God: the blind, deaf and dumb, lepers, the woman with an issue of blood, tax collectors, sinners and so on. Wright might suggest we need to think about ordinary people, like fishermen, who experience turmoil in their life.

In Wright's interpretation, Jesus' miracles show a greater authority than simply a power to alter the way the universe usually works. Jesus is able to gather the community of *all* Israel for the renewed covenant and the forgiveness of sins, and the reach of this gathering goes far beyond the categories of people who were socially accepted at the time. Jesus is inaugurating God's Kingdom on Earth which is more than the world was before (see the fig tree that bears no fruit, Luke 13:6–9; Mark 11:12–25). In the case of Jesus walking on the water, he steps into the boat and joins them and brings calm, a foretaste of his Kingdom.

John 9:1–41 contains an account of a miracle that is then discussed. Jesus heals a man who has been blind from birth. It is possible that this action could be read as a sign of Jesus' power, or as having a message for the sick today, that Jesus can heal them. However, the discussion around the action is about sin. Jesus is asked what possible sin could have led to

Miracle stories may be interpreted as a rupture with nature, a spiritual consolation or as a sign of a renewal of the people of God

The more important question to ask first is what we think the Gospel writers are doing in reporting the wonders performed by Jesus

Think question

Are miracles great deeds of power or the weakest link of Christianity?

the blindness, touching on the ancient idea that sin caused illness but also asking the more ultimate question about whether any sin could justify someone being born blind. In this case, there is a focus on those whose circumstances cannot be caused by their own action.

John records Jesus himself making a link with who he is – 'this happened so the works of God might be displayed in him. […] While I am in the world, I am the light of the world.' Jesus himself identifies his action as a pointer to the power of God working in him. The miracle is not automatically accepted and there is considerable discussion about the person and whether he only looks like the person who was (and perhaps truly is) blind. Pharisees investigate seeking to find out whether this healing has really happened and questioning whether someone like Jesus could do this, someone they consider a sinner for having worked on the Sabbath. The investigation reveals the man was truly blind and can now see but the Pharisees reject the testimony they are hearing and throw the (formerly blind) man out.

Later, Jesus speaks with the man again and he expresses his belief in Jesus. Jesus says, 'For judgment I have come into this world, so that the blind will see and those who see will become blind.' The action is linked to the wider purpose of Jesus' mission, perhaps suggesting that Wright's thinking could be correct. The treatment of blindness in the New Testament is controversial as present day thinking would link blindness with disability, not faithlessness. What is clear is this discussion seems more focused on how the action of healing is linked to the wider purpose of Jesus and his identity, than simply on an incredible miracle.

Resurrection

> 66 The Easter mystery throws a new and final light on the whole story of Jesus and his mission. 99

Gerald O'Collins, *Christology*, 1995, p. 97

Paul says that 'we have testified about God that he raised Christ from the dead. But he did not raise him if in fact the dead are not raised' (1 Corinthians 15:15). For Paul, if Jesus was not resurrected then all preaching would be in vain, sins would not be washed clean, and at death all would perish. A Christian faith without resurrection is impossible for Paul.

The Resurrection distinguishes the life of Jesus from that of other preachers at the time. E.P. Sanders (*The Historical Figure of Jesus*, 1995) asks, 'Without the Resurrection, would [Jesus'] disciples have endured longer than did John the Baptist's? We can only guess, but I would guess not.' N.T. Wright suggests that the belief that Jesus had been raised from the dead was the reason why Jesus' disciples regrouped and rapidly

'And if Christ has not been raised, our preaching is useless and so is your faith' (1 Corinthians 15:14, New International Version)

changed their traditional worship practices to focus on Jesus. The disciples had been shattered by Jesus' crucifixion and without this belief in his Resurrection, the Christian Church would not have developed.

Resurrection became fundamental to what Christians believe about God: in the same way that God raised Jesus from the dead, God will raise everyone from the dead (1 Corinthians 6:14). And salvation is dependent on believing that Jesus was resurrected: 'If you declare with your mouth, "Jesus is Lord," and believe in your heart that God raised him from the dead, you will be saved' (Romans 10:9).

The Resurrection and the authority and divinity of Jesus

Christians find many meanings in the Resurrection and it relates to a range of different theologies including those that relate to salvation, **redemption** and God's activity in the world. It also has specific meanings for the authority and divinity of Jesus.

Belief in Jesus' Resurrection began with the discovery that his tomb was empty

- **More than the greatest miracle?** It is certainly a great miracle, perhaps the greatest that is performed – such a great demonstration of power underlines Jesus' status. On the other hand, Jesus himself raised Lazarus and Jairus' daughter from the dead.

- **The Resurrection of Jesus discloses God in a new and startling way,** through a focus on suffering, new life and unconditional love (O'Collins, *Christology*, 1995, p. 102). McGrath suggests that the Resurrection of Jesus plays a key role in Christian theology:

....

66 It establishes and undergirds the Christian Hope… it enables the death of Christ upon the cross to be interpreted in terms of God's victory over death [and] it gives both foundation and substance to the Christian hope of eternal life. 99

Alister McGrath, 1996, p. 335

....

- **The Resurrection vindicates his certainty in the future Kingdom of God:** O'Collins (Christology, 1995) argues that Jesus' rising from the dead vindicates his certainty in the future Kingdom of God (Mark 14:25). The preaching and miracles of Jesus had met with apparent defeat but its power is demonstrated through the Resurrection and justifies Jesus' personal authority. Luke emphasises vindication in the Acts of the Apostles (Acts 2:36, 3:14–15, 4:10).

- **The Resurrection is the full and final revelation of Jesus:** It fully and finally reveals and seals the meaning and truth of Jesus' life, person, work and death. Paul emphasises revelation (Galatians 1:12, 1:16) in his reading of the Resurrection, and the New Testament presents the Resurrection in a very different way from any other miracle. It is described as the beginning of the end of all things.

- **The Resurrection reveals the glorified transformed being:** It reveals Jesus in a new and finally transfigured way. It is the fulfillment of the promise Jesus made to the Sanhedrin, 'And you will see the Son of Man sitting at the right hand of the Mighty One and coming on the clouds of heaven' (Mark 14:62, New International Version), and this is visualised through his ascension into heavenly glory (Luke 24:51; Acts 1:9–11 and John 20:17).

- **Realisation that the weak can mediate God's revelation:** In the Resurrection there is the realisation that 'the weak, the despised, and the suffering – those who become fools for God's sake – can serve as special mediators of revelation (and salvation)' (O' Collins, *Christology*, 1995, p. 107). Jesus shows God's self-giving, divine love, even to the extent of an appalling death: 'But God demonstrates his own love for us in this: While we were still sinners, Christ died for us' (Romans 5:8, New International Version).

'For God so loved the world that he gave his one and only Son, that whoever believes in him shall not perish but have eternal life' (John 3:16, New International Version).

Apply your knowledge

Explanations of the Resurrection

The Resurrection did not happen – because resurrection doesn't happen today we can be sure it didn't happen for Jesus. We should not be required to accept the testimony of others (the witnesses of the risen Christ).

A subjective experience in the minds of the disciples – clearly Christians came to believe in the Resurrection even though it could not have happened, and so the dead Jesus transformed into an imaginary risen Christ.

An event beyond enquiry – the significance of the Resurrection is not found by trying to explain some extraordinary event from the Bible; the Resurrection calls for a decision of faith, not a historical report. The Resurrection cannot be studied.

An event open to critical enquiry – it is unreasonable to believe only in events you have witnessed yourself, disregarding the testimony of actual witnesses. Who knows what future technologies might discover about death and the possibility of resurrection?

An event that left the disciples sure it had happened and inspired them profoundly – differences in the accounts of the Gospel writers about the Resurrection make it impossible to reconstruct what happened. They may suggest the writers could not comprehend what happened, or they may be down to different writing styles. Whatever actually happened, the disciples were sure Jesus was risen.

6. Order these accounts from least to most convincing. Give a rationale for your decision.

7. Explain the implications of each account for the idea that Jesus was the Son of God.

Jesus the teacher of wisdom

66 Jesus was a great moral teacher. 99

Richard Dawkins, Interview in *The Guardian* in 2011 (www.theguardian.com/science/video/2011/ oct/24/richard-dawkins-video-interview)

A rabbi with a special message

Jesus was a teacher, providing guidance and advice on the application of law to moral problems. Jesus is sometimes described as a 'Rabbi' (see Mark 9:5, 11:21, 14:45; John 1:39, 1:49, 3:2, 4:31, 6:25, 9:2, 11:8; Matthew 23:7, 26:25, 26:49). Rabbi was a term of respect but could also be used for educated teachers who interpreted the law, surrounded by followers.

> 66 In discussing with other scribes, gathering disciples around him, teaching in synagogue worship and answering the theological enquiries of lay people, Jesus, the former disciple of the rabbi John, corresponded to the contemporary notions of a rabbi. 99
>
> Gerd Theissen and Annette Merz, *The Historical Jesus*, 1998 p. 355

Jesus clearly could read (see Mark 2:25 and Matthew 22:31, 12:5) and he spent time teaching in synagogues (see Mark 1:39 and Luke 4:16), with some listeners being surprised at his level of education (see John 7:15).

Jesus spoke on moral issues and ideas: the importance of love, self-sacrifice, concern for the poor and the dispossessed, the importance of honesty, justice, peace. He used moral education techniques with controversial or surprising stories. These took unexpected turns and seemed designed to get his listeners to think again about preconceptions (such as calling the gentile pious and the religious impious in the parable of the Good Samaritan).

Perhaps Jesus is best understood as a teacher of wisdom, with the 'message' Jesus has for people today being a moral message that has carried far beyond the time and setting in which it first occurred. Jesus had a moral wisdom from valuable insights in the Hebrew tradition which he applied for life for everyone.

> ## Think question
>
> Which moral messages stand out most from what you know about Jesus? Choose two and explain what you think is their significance.

Jesus' moral teaching

The teaching and actions of Jesus carry profound moral messages that remain striking. Jesus' wisdom is a message of repentance and forgiveness – repent and believe the good news. He continually speaks of the forgiveness of sins (Mark 2:1–12; Matthew 9:2–8; Luke 5:17–26, 7:36–50) and much of his work involved healing the sick (see Mark 7:37) and spending time with groups of people who were rejected, or outcasts, such as tax collectors and sinners (see Mark 2:16). There is hope for those who have been thrown out by society – sins may be forgiven (see Luke 7:47). Jesus brings an abiding message of forgiveness and hope to those cast aside by society. His vision is a universal one of healing, bringing God and all of humanity back together. This is the wisdom of his Good News.

The direct moral messages of Jesus' teachings are extensively concerned with love, love of each other (see John 13:34), love of neighbours

An illustration of Jesus' sermon on the mount

(see Matthew 22:37–40), love of enemies (see Matthew 5:43–48 and Luke 6:35) and love of God. There is an 'other-centred' quality of Jesus' teachings about love, and this ranges far beyond family or particular social groups. The focus on love was to heavily influence key passages in Paul (see 1 Corinthians 13:4–7). This love is self-giving, sacrificial and overwhelming of all other things. People should act out of pure love for one another, not because of their status, their family or social connections.

Jesus was an advocate of moral purity and identified a moral purpose in life. Love, forgiveness and the orientation towards those most in need seem to be the basis of the Beatitudes (see Matthew 5:3–12) in the Sermon on the Mount which extend blessings to the poor, those who mourn, the meek, the hungry, the merciful, the pure at heart, the peacemakers, those that search for justice or who are persecuted. They also found in Matthew 24, in the judgement of nations, where Jesus says whatsoever you do for the least of his brothers are done to him. He commands that the hungry be fed, the naked clothed, the stranger welcomed, the sick healed.

The wisdom of Jesus is that goodness goes beyond the external actions we perform but reach inside to the motivations that drive us. The purity that we should seek, is not measured by externalities, but by the inner intention. This contrasted with contemporary ideas of moral purity linked to rituals and certain practices. The moral purity that Jesus talked about was an inner purity. It is what comes out of your mouth that makes you unclean, not what you put in (Mathew 15:11). Those that are pure at heart will see God (Matthew 8:9). Doing the right thing, being morally pure, was more important than maintaining ritual purity (Mark 5:21; Luke 10:25).

Jesus' wisdom entailed overturning social norms. His involvement with women is striking. He has women as followers and women are mentioned many times in the Gospels. Jesus heals women through touch, something scandalous at the time (see Luke 13:13; Matthew 8:14–15, 9:18; Mark. 1:30–31; Luke 4:38–39). This suggests he had an inclusive attitude towards women, in contrast to the patriarchal times he was living in.

His moral teaching extended to insights about power and wealth. He warns followers not to lord power over others and in answering the question of who is the greatest, he points to the little children (see Mark 9:33–37). He identifies wealth as an obstacle to closeness with God

(Matthew 19:22), saying that it is easier for a camel to pass through the eye of a needle than it is for a rich man to enter heaven (see Matthew 19:24). Jesus' moral teaching is disruptive, overturning social norms.

One of many inspiring holy people

In 1977, John Hick published a series of essays under the title *The Myth of God Incarnate*, in which scholars examined, challenged and reinterpreted a number of Christian doctrines. In this, Hick notes that the way in which Jesus is aware of God's will and God's willingness to act is not unique to Jesus but is found in Moses, Jeremiah, the Isaiahs, Muhammed, Guru Nanak, St Francis, Kabir, Ramakrishna and many others. In this interpretation, Jesus is not a unique figure with a unique role in salvation.

Hick's conclusion is that Christianity without the **incarnation** becomes one of many religions that each perceive God in different ways. Each help a person to change and transform from self-centeredness to other-centredness and love-centredness. This transformation is the real meaning of salvation, and such a salvation would liberate the world, if every human being made such a change. Jesus is a model for the kind of transformation suggested, a moral man, in touch with God, who lived an exemplary life and continues to influence many people today.

Adopting a metaphorical understanding of incarnation, rather than a literal one, means setting aside the traditional Christian doctrine that Jesus had a divine nature. However, it is possible to retain a great significance around the life and work of Jesus, the historical figure, as a divinely-inspired moral teacher, a wise and holy man. Jesus as a metaphorical incarnation, in Hick's words, remains close to God and inspiring for the world today as an example of how to live a moral life.

Jesus without the incarnation can still be seen as a moral guide to how we should live

Think question

What is the difficulty in maintaining that Jesus is unique in the salvation of the world, as incarnation, in a universe which may have many worlds with intelligent life, that might never visit one another due to the distances? How might traditional Christians respond to this?

Apply your knowledge

The myth of God incarnate is the story of the pre-existent divine Son descending into human life, dying to atone for the sins of the world, thereby revealing the divine nature, and returning into the eternal life of the Trinity. The mythic story expresses the significance of a point in history where we can see human life lived in faithful response to God and see God's nature reflected in that human response. … To the extent that a man or a woman is to God what one's own hand is to oneself, to that extent God is 'incarnate' in that human life. The idea of the incarnation of God in the life of Jesus, so understood, is thus not a metaphysical claim about Jesus having two natures, but a metaphorical statement of the significance of a life through which God was acting on earth. In Jesus we see a man living in a startling degree of awareness of God and of response to God's presence.'

John Hick, *The Metaphor of God Incarnate*, 2012, pp. 105–6

8. What kind of meaning is Hick in favour of and what kind does he propose?

9. How are the two meanings different (the traditional and the one Hick advocates)?

10. How would you describe the kind of interpretation that Hick gives of Jesus?

Think question

- 'Salvation is about redemption, escape from sin and death and eternal life with God or it's not worth bothering about.'
- 'Salvation is about becoming the most loving human being you can be for others, it's not about saving yourself.'

Discuss these two statements. What are the implications of them both for how Jesus is to be understood?

Responses

Hick's understanding of Jesus can be seen as an attempt to keep Jesus and Christianity while removing the beliefs about Jesus that he sees as contentious. As such, Hick tries to provide a universally acceptable understanding of Jesus which retains the ethical message of Christianity.

However, Hick's solution creates some new problems. His other-centred/love-centred version of religion has a distinctively Christian flavour and differs from religions that emphasise detachment, like Buddhism for example. Hick interprets salvation as personal change, but this is quite different from salvation from sin *and death* and seems to lack the Gospel's message of political and social change. Phrases like 'eternal life' have less meaning in Hick's version.

Christians reject the idea that Jesus' moral guidance can be separated from his divine nature. C.S. Lewis (author of the *Narnia* series and many books on Christian belief) criticised those who accepted Jesus as a teacher of moral wisdom but not as the Son of God:

> 66 I am trying here to prevent anyone saying the really foolish thing that people often say about Him: 'I'm ready to accept Jesus as a great moral teacher, but I don't accept His claim to be God.' That is the one thing we must not say. A man who was merely a man and said the sort of things Jesus said would not be a great moral teacher. He would either be a lunatic – on a level with the man who says he is a poached egg – or else he would be the Devil of Hell. You must make your choice. Either this man was, and is, the son of God: or else a madman or something worse. You can shut Him up for a fool, you can spit at Him and kill Him as a demon; or you can fall at His feet and call Him Lord and God. But let us not come up with any patronizing nonsense about His being a great human teacher. He has not left that open to us. He did not intend to. 99

C.S. Lewis, *Mere Christianity*, 1952, pp. 55–56

Bonhoeffer links the incarnation to both human salvation and an understanding that we meet God in human beings. This has strong links to the idea that we encounter God in the oppressed, the struggle for justice, and so on. Without the incarnation, a connection is lost with the idea of encountering God in human life and human lives, their seriousness and significance. Bonhoeffer writes:

Without the incarnation a connection is lost with the idea of encountering God in human life and human lives, their seriousness and significance

> 66 When God's Son took on flesh, he truly and bodily, out of pure grace, took on our being, our nature, ourselves. … Now we are in him. Wherever he is, he bears our flesh, he bears us. And where he is, there we are too – in the incarnation, on the cross,

and in his Resurrection. We belong to him because we are in him. That is why the scriptures call us the body of Christ. **99**

Dietrich Bonhoeffer, *Life Together,* 1954, p. 33

Some prominent atheists are also highly critical of the argument that Jesus was a wise moral teacher. Christopher Hitchens, a critic of Christianity, argued against several of Jesus' teachings. For instance, he wrote 'if only the non-sinners have the right to punish, then how could an imperfect society ever determine how to prosecute offenders?' (*God Is Not Great*, 2011, p. 121).

> ## Think question
>
> What more is added to the moral teaching of Jesus by the idea that God becomes human so that humanity can become divine?

Apply your knowledge

'I am the first and the last – the self-existing One. Do you need your sins forgiven? I can do it. Do you want to know how to live? I am the light of the world – whoever follows me will never walk in darkness, but will have the light of life. Do you want to know whom you can trust? All authority in heaven and on earth has been given to me. Do you have any worries or requests? Pray in my name. If you remain in me and my words remain in you, ask whatever you wish, and it will be given you. Do you need access to God the Father? No one comes to the Father except through me. The Father and I are one.' What would you think about your neighbor if he seriously said those things? You certainly wouldn't say, 'Gee, I think he's a great moral teacher!' No, you'd say this guy is nuts, because he's definitely claiming to be God.

Norm Geisler and Frank Turek, *I Don't Have Enough Faith to be an Atheist*, 2004, quoted in http://apologistpankaj. blogspot.co.uk/2009/03/self- understanding-of-jesus.html

11. What is the most convincing thing Geisler and Turek say that might convince someone that the moral teacher picture of Jesus is just not enough?
12. 'People who define Jesus in terms of his oral teaching, fail to understand the significance of what he did.' Discuss.
13. On the subject of the incarnation, what would Bonhoeffer say to Hick and how might Hick respond?

Jesus the liberator

Jesus is commonly interpreted as a liberator, someone who wanted to free people from social convention, religious restriction, political domination and someone who wanted to liberate people from sin and death. Jesus was a figure of controversy and conflict with authorities. There are many examples where he was involved in arguments with Pharisees and Scribes over matters of religious law. He was arrested by the Sanhedrin, the Jewish council, and then handed over to Pontius Pilate, the political authority, to be executed. He was a figure of political, religious and social challenge.

Jesus and the challenge to political authority

At the time of Jesus, the Jewish people lived under Roman occupation, through a client king in the north and the Roman Procurator, Pontius Pilate, in the south. There were unpopular Roman taxes and mixed

Jesus the revolutionary?

MEEK MILD AS IF
Discover the real Jesus

feelings amongst the people about their government. Some collaborated with the system and even benefited from it, whilst others suffered in poverty. The situation deteriorated with assassinations, murders, and a series of open military rebellions. The final great revolt led to tens of thousands of people being enslaved, over a million deaths, and the Jerusalem Temple being burned down in AD73. One of the groups involved in leading open conflict against the Roman occupation was called the **Zealots**. Zealots were probably not an organised group at the time of Jesus but there must have been similar people calling for violent revolution during his lifetime.

Jews have often faced oppression through their long history. The story of the Exodus, when God delivered the Jewish people from slavery in Egypt through the leadership of Moses, is retold and re-enacted at the feast of Passover. In Jesus' time, when the Jews were again under the oppressive leadership of foreigners, the story of Exodus gave the Jews hope that God might again send them a deliverer, as prophesised in Isaiah 11:

> 66 A shoot will come up. … The Spirit of the Lord will rest on him, the Spirit of wisdom and of understanding, the Spirit of counsel and of might, the Spirit of the knowledge and fear of the Lord – and he will delight in the fear of the Lord. … He will strike the earth with the rod of his mouth; with the breath of his lips he will slay the wicked. 99
>
> Isaiah 11:1–4, New International Version

In Jesus' time many Jews hoped God would send a military **Messiah** to lead a rebellion against Roman rule. This concept of a Messiah has overtones of military revolution – a victor over the enemies of the Jews, a restorer of Israel. The people looked to a warrior king and a bringer of God's justice. Could Jesus have seen himself as this warrior king, coming to save God's people from Rome? In a recent book, *Zealot: The Life and Times of Jesus of Nazareth* (2013), Reza Aslan argues that Jesus was involved in a much more confrontational resistance than is presented in the New Testament.

A political revolutionary?

Suggesting Jesus was a political revolutionary might seem to clash with his usual depiction as a loving and caring person. However, it is possible the way Jesus was understood by his followers changed over time. When confronted with the death of Jesus, perhaps some of his followers reinterpreted his whole teaching as a spiritual message. Perhaps the Early Church tried to hide Jesus' revolutionary tendencies in an effort to evade persecution by the authorities.

Jesus may have seen himself as this warrior king, coming to save God's people from Rome

Think question

In popular culture, especially movies, the idea of one who will come to free the people remains a powerful idea that seems to capture the imagination. Identify some movies where you see this idea. Why do you think it is such a powerful idea?

There are links between Jesus and the Zealots' cause. Jesus did suggest a coming revolution or conflict: 'I did not come to bring peace, but a sword' (Matthew, 10:34, New International Version). Jesus' followers had weapons which they used to defend themselves in Gethsemane against the arresting authorities. Jesus' followers have 'suspicious' names. For example, there was another Simon (not Simon Peter) called Simon the Zealot. Judas, who handed Jesus over to the authorities, was called Judas Iscariot, and Iscarii – 'dagger men' – was another name for Zealots.

Catniss Everdeen, from *The Hunger Games*, takes on a 'messiah like' role fighting against an oppressive dictator, but she is manipulated by the resistance and represented by them in distorting ways

In the Bible Jesus' titles link him to revolution, and a bringing of God's justice: the Son of David title captures this sense (Daniel 7:13; Matthew 24:30). Jesus was hailed as coming in the name of the Lord (Matthew 23:39). When Jesus was arrested he was labelled King of the Jews and put to death for some civic crime, not a religious one (John 19:19). The Romans may have executed him as a possible revolutionary.

Jesus was Jewish and held the Passover festival as important, with its link to the Exodus narrative of liberation from slavery. He went to Jerusalem with his friends to celebrate it. He was coming to the city at a time when violent revolution was in the air, as the population of the city swelled with religious pilgrims coming to celebrate Passover. The Romans doubled their troops in the city in the expectation of trouble. In choosing to come to Jerusalem at that time, Jesus chose confrontation with Rome.

Aslan identifies Jesus' entrance into Jerusalem as a key moment signifying much about him. It is AD30 and Jesus enters Jerusalem riding a donkey and flanked by a crowd who are singing and shouting, 'Hosanna! Blessed is he who comes in the name of the Lord! Blessed be the coming kingdom of our father David!' Some spread cloaks on the road, as the Israelites did for Jehu when he was declared king (see 2 Kings 9:12–13). Others wave palm branches in remembrance of the Maccabees who liberated Israel two centuries earlier (see 1 Maccabees 13:49–53). Aslan claims this was meticulously orchestrated by Jesus and his followers to fulfil Zechariah's prophecy: 'Rejoice greatly, Daughter Zion! Shout, Daughter Jerusalem! See, your king comes to you, righteous and victorious, lowly and riding on a donkey, on a colt, the foal of a donkey' (Zechariah 9:9, New International Version). Aslan believes the event was deliberately set up to send a message that the long-awaited Messiah and King of the Jews had arrived to free Israel from bondage.

Some scholars interpret the entry into Jerusalem as a political act

Think question

If Aslan is right, why might later Church authorities have wanted to hide this radical aspect of Jesus?

Evaluating the political challenge claims

Aslan's book, *Zealot: The Life and Times of Jesus of Nazareth (2014)*, is controversial. Some argue it is both selective and misrepresentative. There are certainly many instances in the Gospel where Jesus seems to have rejected violent revolution:

- he stops his disciples from defending him with violence (see John 18:10 and Matthew 26:51)

- he is ambivalent about the traditional messianic titles, not confirming the 'King of the Jews' title that Pilate accuses him of (see Mark 15:2)

- if Judas was linked to violent revolutionaries, then his decision to hand Jesus over might be because Jesus was simply not politically radical enough

- when asked about his views about Roman rule, Jesus sidestepped the question (see Mark 12:17)

- Jesus emphasised peace: 'Blessed are the peacemakers' (Matthew 5:9, New International Version)

- Jesus spoke of a kingdom that was not of this world. He seemed less interested in political and military change in this world (see John 18:36).

Aslan's argument also assumes Jesus was poor, but he was described as a 'carpenter' which means a small builder: not a poor class of person. Jesus was frequently called rabbi, suggesting an educated teacher, not a poor, simple farm worker. Jesus' disciples were not poor men. Fishermen are better characterised as small businessmen.

A social revolutionary?

Jesus is also seen as social revolutionary by some New Testament scholars. Robert Webb suggests at the time of Jesus there was a movement of 'social banditry' which sought to free the poor peasants from their life of poverty. Richard Horsley describes social banditry as Robin Hood-style resistance. Rome was holding the people of Israel in servitude through their military occupation and heavy taxation. Social banditry was the first step in a spiral of violence to overthrow the overseas power that held people in servitude and oppression.

Although Jesus referred to banditry in a negative light – the Good Samaritan story begins with bandits doing wrong to an innocent traveller (see Luke 10:25–37) – there is biblical evidence for Jesus' active engagement in challenging negative impacts of the oppression. He spent time both with those who were oppressed (the poor, the sick and the outcasts) and also the tax collectors who maintained the system (see Luke 7:34, 19,1). He was prepared to act confrontationally with authorities (in disputing the Temple of Jerusalem by turning over the money changers' tables). He was executed alongside bandits on the cross (see Mark 15:27), so perhaps the Romans considered him one too!

The idea that Jesus was a social revolutionary has influenced some twentieth-century Christian movements including the social justice movement, and the Liberation Theology movement but most Churches reject the depiction. As with views that Jesus was purely a moral teacher, the spiritual purpose behind Jesus' life and the redemption and salvation it brings is lost if he was purely a revolutionary figure who lived and died, having failed to lead an uprising against Rome.

Nevertheless, it remains a compelling idea. Revisionist historians remain willing to argue that the early Church has tidied the image of Jesus and downplayed his revolutionary tendencies, and he was executed for crimes against Rome, alongside others judged as criminals by agents of the occupying powers.

Jesus and the challenge to religious authority

To what extent was Jesus' religious message a break or challenge to the religion of the time? There are plenty of examples that suggest Jesus was on good terms with leading religious' figures, such as when he was entertained by a leading Pharisee (Luke 7:36, 11:37, 14:1). However, the Pharisees sought to transform Israel through a drive for religious purity. What Jesus says about handwashing (Mark 7:3, 7:5), tithing (Luke 18:12 and Matthew 23:23), the Sabbath (Mark 3:1–5) and an approach to rules that perverted divine will (Mark 7:8) went against the religious purity demanded by the Pharisees.

The Temple was a major point of focus in the Jewish religion, although the Pharisees were opposed to those who ran the Temple, the Sadducees. Jesus made criticisms of the Temple and its cult, expressing the idea that it would be replaced by something better (Mark 14:57 and Acts 16:13). He challenged the role of the money changers at the Temple because of their practice of making money out of the ritual obligation that required people to buy suitable animals for sacrifice at the Temple. In a time of hardship and heavy Roman taxation, these obligations added to the economic challenge facing poorer people.

Jesus' opposition led to conflict with the Sanhedrin, the supreme court of justice in Jerusalem, which was made up of chief priests, lay elders and the scribes and scholars (often Pharisees or Sadducees). Mark sees all three groups as being in conflict with Jesus (Mark 8:31). The rules and systems that were used by religious leaders to keep a holy separation of people from God, seem to be at the heart of the critical challenges that Jesus made. O'Collins writes:

> 66 … in general there was much in Jesus' activity to provoke them [the religious authorities]: his initiatives towards sinners, reinterpretation of the Sabbath obligations, claims to unique religious authority, and promise of salvation to the gentiles. 99

Gerald O'Collins, *Interpreting Jesus*, 1995, p. 76

The Churches reject the depiction of Jesus as a Zealot, a military revolutionary or a social bandit

Apply your knowledge

14. Consider the case that Jesus may have been a political and/or social revolutionary. Set out a table showing the evidence that Jesus might have been a leader of political revolution planning a military overthrow of the Roman occupation and evidence that he was involved in 'social banditry': helping the poor with a message of resistance against their oppression. You can use the Bible quotes and arguments from this section, and any other biblical texts you are familiar with.

At the heart of Jesus' conflict with religious authority was a message that sought to reconnect with God those people the authorities had excluded because they were tainted or ritually impure

Jesus the revolutionary Jew?

In the first century, as scripture was being collected, the early Jewish Christian movement was separating from Judaism in an acrimonious 'divorce'. Paul and others are recorded as being driven out, stoned, or arrested in many places, often due to Jewish reactions to their preaching (see Acts 13:44–51, 14:5–6, 14:19–20, 17:1–15). This division may have influenced how the Gospels were written, downplaying Jesus' Jewishness and up-playing his conflict with Judaism – for example, John's Gospel repeatedly uses the phrase 'the Jews' – something the early Jewish Christians would not have been able to make sense of as everyone was Jewish.

New Testament scholar E.P. Sanders (*The Historical Figure of Jesus,* 1993) and the Jewish scholar Geza Vermes (*Jesus the Jew,* 1973, and *The Religion of Jesus the Jew,* 1993) think Jesus was more Jewish than Christian tradition admits. Their views include concerns that:

- the Gospel writers added in stories to suggest tension between Jesus and Judaism, e.g. Sanders doubts there really were Pharisees waiting to surprise the disciples picking corn in the grain fields on the Sabbath

- Jesus lived his life as a Jew with Jews. References to non-Jews like Samaritans could be later additions

- Jesus did not reject or replace the Jewish law: 'It is easier for heaven and earth to disappear than for the least stroke of a pen to drop out of the Law' (Luke 16:17, New International Version). Jesus sometimes disagreed with its application but did not seriously break Jewish Law

- Jesus rejected becoming the 'Messiah' that his disciples wanted. They wanted to resist his arrest by force; he forbade this

- Jesus never described himself as the Son of God.

Instead of seeing Jesus' life as beginning the split with Judaism, these writers instead see Jesus leading a Jewish renewal movement, concerned with rethinking the Jewish religion through repentance and forgiveness; the imitation of God: being merciful as God is merciful.

....

66 I am not saying … that Jesus rejected his own religious culture. I am saying that Jesus offered a fresh interpretation of the scriptural tradition which he shared with his Jewish contemporaries. His was a critique from within. 99

N.T. Wright, *Jesus and the Victory of God,* 1996, p. 380

....

Jesus' old and new messages

The Jewish Jesus theory is compelling, but there are some issues: though the first disciples were Jewish, they formed a Jewish-Christian movement which eventually became a separate religion. Something in what Jesus did and said triggered a change: there is some continuity between Jesus and the eventual separation of Christians from Jews.

Apply your knowledge

- 'Jesus sought to free people from the Jewish religion of his time.'
- 'Jesus sought to free people from the Jewish authorities of his time.'
- 15. Discuss these two views with reference to the ideas, authors and biblical texts mentioned in this section. Develop a mind map that links together the different views of Jesus' challenge to religious authority, examples from the Bible and the theologians and scholars mentioned.

Apply your Knowledge

- Did Jesus' actions lead to conflict with religious authorities?
- Did Jesus continue with, modify or supersede the religious traditions of the past?

A critical reinterpretation of the role of the Temple?

16. Compare what Jesus says to the Samaritan woman about worship and the Temple (John 4:1–26) with what he does with the money changers (Mark 11:15–19; Matthew 21:12–17; Luke 19:45–48; and/or John 2:13–16).

A critical reinterpretation of the Law?

17. Compare what Jesus says about maintaining the law (Matthew 22:37–40), fulfilling the law (Matthew 5:17–20), and ensuring the law serves man (Matthew 12:1–13 and Mark 2:23–28).

A critical reinterpretation of attitudes to those who traditionally were excluded?

18. Examine how Jesus acts towards women (Matthew 9:20–22; Mark 5:25–34; Luke 8:43–48), the sick (Matthew 9:18–23; Mark 1:40–45; Luke 17:11–19), the 'immoral' (Luke 7:36–50; Luke 19:1–10; Matthew 9:10).

19. Examine how his actions and teaching might be differently interpreted as showing *continuation* (in line with the traditional religious understanding), *modification* (adapting to a new understanding but retaining the importance of traditional religious understandings) or *supersession* (replacing previous religious understandings).

Discussing the person of Jesus Christ

Was Jesus only a teacher of wisdom?

Jesus clearly had an important moral message for Christians communicated through what he said and what he did. He came from the Jewish tradition and some of that wisdom is found within the Hebrew Scriptures (the Old Testament). What if anything did Jesus add that was new? Did he simply communicate it in a new way for a wider group, beyond the local Jewish population? Perhaps this is his key contribution – that he in some way encapsulates a wisdom of life that many people find compelling and perhaps this is his enduring legacy?

Nevertheless, there are those who dispute his wisdom, who criticise some of his moral teachings. Perhaps Jesus is not all that wise! A further question is whether his wisdom is just about morality? What of the spiritual messages, forgiveness of sins and the salvation from death? Arguably his message is more than a moral one. His message, for some, is himself, who he is. The good news of his message is not just what he said but who he was and what he did. It was this that changed his followers and empowered them to go out spread the message. For the first Christians the reality of the Resurrection was crucial in understanding the good news message of Jesus. There have been many wise people throughout history but, for Christians, the impact of Jesus goes beyond all other human beings. Perhaps there was something uniquely different about him, that went beyond the rational message but is encapsulated in a mystical and spiritual reality.

Was Jesus more than a political liberator?

Jesus' message was one of freedom – freedom for the poorest, the outcasts, the most needy. He associated with groups of people who were excluded

Apply your knowledge

20. Discuss the following views:

   a. 'We should forget the fanciful stories of miracles and magic from the stories of Jesus, but keep the moral wisdom.'

   b. 'The wisdom Jesus brings is not new and it's not moral.'

   c. 'Jesus has affected the world more than any other human being, including all the leaders or armies, all the great emperors, philosophers and scientists. A carpenter from Nazareth brought wisdom that changed the world.'

from society and was criticised for these associations. He appealed to the poor and the sick, to women, sinners tax collectors, and this brought him into conflict with the more respectable classes. He clearly had a socially radical message that confounded existing norms and generated considerable conflict with the ruling religious and social classes.

Some scholars have gone further to suggest he was interested in political liberation as well – that he associated with disciples linked to Zealots, or other movements interested in political change. Some have argued he wanted to lead or join a revolutionary movement against Roman oppression.

Others see his liberating message as something that should encourage radical change today – he has inspired social reformers throughout history, including those who have advocated black liberation in modern times, for example. His message is not one of conformity and conservation, but one that brings changes to the established order. Indeed, some are critical when Christianity seems too closely linked to the established ruling classes. The threat Jesus posed to the political establishment may have led to his execution by the political authority, Pontius Pilate.

However, the Bible speaks of liberation from sin and death, as well as social and political liberation. This is a different kind of liberation – something that reaches beyond the physical world and touches people in a different way. There have been many political liberator figures but Jesus' message has a spiritual reality that, for Christians, makes him much more than a figure of history.

Was Jesus' relationship with God very special or truly unique?

At the heart of traditional Christian thought is the idea that Jesus is a unique figure, not simply a political revolutionary or a teacher of wisdom, but a unique being connected to God in a unique way. The Bible suggests Jesus had a closeness to God that goes beyond the messages of the Prophets or the Patriarchs of the Hebrew Scriptures. He was spoken to by God and seemed to hear what God said to him on a number of occasions that seem critical to his life (his baptism, the transfiguration and in the Garden of Gethsemane).

There was clearly some concern about Jesus' association with God in that he did some of the things traditionally reserved for God in terms of the forgiveness of sins and also in his reinterpretation of the religious laws, which he would set aside in some instances. This brought him into conflict with official guardians of the Jewish law and contributed to the accusations of blasphemy that were laid against him at his trial.

In John's Gospel and in the new Testament Letters and Acts, the association of Jesus with God is made much more explicit. These texts suggest the earliest followers of Jesus saw him as having a unique and close relationship to God, that he was God made man and the son of God, and this debate was important in the early centuries of the Church.

Apply your knowledge

21. 'Christianity has tamed the real message of Jesus to make him acceptable to polite society but his real message would entail revolution, violence and the liberation of the poor and the oppressed.'

Consider this view. What evidence might support it? What arguments could be brought against it?

Did Jesus think he was divine?

Jesus' self-understanding is a complex question because answers given can lead to new problems. If Jesus was clearly aware of his divine nature all the time, then how could he have been a normal human being? His childhood would not have been human in any sense we would recognise. He would have been aware of adult aspects of life. As an adult he would have known what was going to happen, he would have been able to see inside people's minds and would have had a clear sense of his own place and purpose in the universe.

If this is the case, then what are we to make of Jesus' moments of questioning and the appearance of an ordinary man that he conveyed? Was this a pretence? Did he really have the emotions he presented, such as fear or mourning, or were these put on for show? This would be a problem if it suggests there is something deceitful about Jesus. It also undermines the sense in which his experience of life could have been remotely comparable to ours and, therefore, for him to be considered human.

However, if he was not aware of his divinity then how could he have said the things he did without a sense of their true significance? How could he have taught about death and sin, and forgiveness and God's love with reliable authority? To what extent is it meaningful for God to have been fully in Jesus if God did not provide Jesus with access to his divine consciousness (and what do these words mean anyway?).

Modern psychology suggests that the kind of self-knowing that human beings have is complex. We have layers of awareness of self consciousness that can change. Human self awareness is a complex mystery and debates about Jesus' self understanding are simplistic even by human terms. Human beings can deceive themselves and only be aware of surface thoughts, and have personal insights later that they did not realise earlier. Jesus may have understood himself through these layers as well.

Learning Support

Points to remember

» Jesus is described as the son of God, a figure with a unique, close relationship to God. He is seen as someone who is in in close contact with God, who seems to know the mind of God, and seems to be in a special relationship with God, using an intimate word for father (Abba, or dad), to address God. This is exemplified in moments when Jesus sought God (in the desert) or experienced closeness to God (such as in Garden of Gethsemane), as well as his teaching. This places him in a unique position, someone who is both human and divine, someone who crosses the threshold from the 'beyond' to the immediate.

» Jesus is described as a teacher of wisdom, a rabbi, a figure who has special insight, an understanding of God's message and in particular the changes God wants for how people live with each other. Some dispute whether his moral message was all that moral. Others suggest this wisdom is in fact all he brings, that he does not have the divine qualities mentioned before. He is (only) a wise moral teacher, much like other morally inspiriting figures. His wisdom is the only good news he brings. It is not about a greater sense of salvation.

» Jesus is described as a liberator, a figure who brings a liberating message, or seeks to start a liberation. That liberation can be understood in different ways. It can be of a social kind that changes the circumstances of the poor and disposed, a political kind that ignites an actual liberation from the current political forces, specifically Rome, or a religious kind that sets aside purity laws, religious institutions and approaches to law for a closer and more direct connection with God. Liberation is linked to a sense of being saved and the idea that salvation is more than a change with our relationship with God, but includes a change in the situation on earth.

Enhance your learning

» Alister McGrath's chapter 4 in *Theology: The Basics* (2011), is a good introduction to theology, and McGrath writes clearly and in a balanced theological way.

» Gerd Theissen's *The Shadow of the Galilean* (2010), brings alive the life and times of Jesus – dramatic and terrific.

» Read paragraphs 422–78 of Geoffrey Chapman's *Catechism of the Catholic Church* (1994) – this is also available online.

» Two other good accounts exploring the classic account of theology and history of Jesus are Gerald O'Collins' *Interpreting Jesus* (1985) and E.P. Sanders' *The Historical Figure of Jesus* (1993).

» To explore the case that Jesus was more Jewish than many think, read Geza Vermes' *Jesus the Jew* (1973).

» A recent book which thinks Jesus was a revolutionary is Reza Aslan's *Zealot: The Life and Times of Jesus of Nazareth* (2014).

» A book that develops the idea that Jesus is spiritually important but not the incarnation is John Hick's *The Metaphor of God Incarnate* (revised edition 2012).

Practice for exams

AS questions and A level questions look identical; the difference between AS and A level assessment is seen in the different proportions of marks awarded for two different skills: the skill of demonstrating knowledge and understanding (Assessment Objective 1, or AO1), and the skill of constructing a critical argument (AO2).

At AS, half the marks (15 marks) are available for knowledge and understanding, and the other half (15 marks) for the quality of your analytical and evaluative argument. You should aim to use your knowledge in order to support the argument you are making throughout the essay, rather than presenting descriptive knowledge in the first half and then an opinion in the second.

At A level, your demonstration of knowledge and understanding is awarded a maximum of 16 marks, and your analytic and evaluative skills are awarded a maximum of 24 marks. You should aim to concentrate on constructing a lucid argument, making use of your knowledge to add weight to the conclusions you draw.

'There is no evidence to suggest that Jesus thought of himself as divine.' Discuss.

In this question, you are asked to consider whether Jesus thought of himself as being divine or whether perhaps this was an interpretation that developed later.

Practise your skills for AS level

If you are answering this question for AS level, you need to show that you have a thorough understanding of what Christians believe about the divinity of Christ, as well as giving an evaluation of whether there is any reliable evidence that Jesus thought of himself as divine.

Practise your skills for A level

If you are answering this question for A level, you might want to consider what counts as evidence in helping to reach a conclusion. The question claims that there is 'no' evidence, so you might want to agree, or say that there is a little, or a substantial amount. You will need to give examples to support your view.

To what extent can Jesus be regarded as no more than a teacher of wisdom?

This question asks you to consider Jesus' role, and assess whether you think it was primarily as a teacher of wisdom, or whether he also had some other role and perhaps, if so, whether that was more important.

Practise your skills for AS level

If you are answering this question for AS level, you will need to demonstrate a good understanding of Jesus as a teacher of wisdom, giving examples and showing how Jesus compared with the role of a rabbi in the first century. You need to consider whether he was 'no more than' a teacher of wisdom, looking perhaps at Jesus' sayings and accounts of his miracles to support your reasoning.

Practise your skills for A level

If you are answering this question for A level, you will need to develop a line of argument in which you consider whether 'teacher of wisdom' was all that Jesus was, or whether he had other roles such as 'miracle worker', 'political leader' or even 'Son of God'. Your own personal beliefs are obviously important, but you need to be able to justify your argument here with reasoning and examples rather than just assertions of faith or absence of faith.

Chapter 3.5

Christian moral principles

Should Christians obey the rules of the Bible?
Should Christians obey the morals of Church and Tradition?
Should Christians put aside rules and follow the Law of Love?

Key Terms

Bible/Scripture: the collection or canon of books in the Bible which contain the revelation of God

Church tradition: the traditions of how Christian life in community works, in worship, practical moral life and prayer, and the teaching and reflection of the Church handed down across time

Sacred Tradition: the idea that the revelation of Jesus Christ is communicated in two ways. In addition to Scripture, it is communicated through the apostolic and authoritative teaching of the Church councils and the Pope

Agape love: unconditional love, the only ethical norm in situationism

Specification requirements

The diversity of Christian moral reasoning and practices and sources of ethics, including:

- the Bible as the only authority for Christian ethical practices
- the Bible, Church and reason as the sources of Christian ethical practices
- love (agape) as the only Christian ethical principle which governs Christian practices

Introduction

How do we decide what to trust as a guide for moral action? Should we read about the approaches taken by those of the past who are considered wise? Should we follow the practices of the community in which we live? Should we trust in a single ideal of principles that we make sense of ourselves?

Christians take different approaches to moral decision-making. They might draw on the **Bible** as the exclusive repository of the commands of God, to be followed and obeyed. They might rely on their **Church tradition** and reason to guide how they understand the Bible and moral rules of God. These are both deontological approaches. They might follow the guide of love, rather than a list of traditional or biblical rules. This might be more situational in approach.

For all Christians the Bible is an important moral source, but they read it in different ways when making moral decisions. The Bible contains rules, principles, symbols as well as the whole paradigm of the human condition and the nature of God. There are questions about which texts to draw on, how they are interpreted and whether the Bible as a whole should be used or specific parts should be given greater weighting.

For some Christians, the Bible alone is the source of the ethical commands to be followed – sola scriptura. Bible-believing Christians, those that take the Bible as a literal word of God, see it as containing commands from God – what should be done and what should not be done. For these Christians, Bible-based morality is about obedience to its commands which can be plainly read and understood.

For many Christians, how Church tradition makes sense of the Bible, and how they make sense of both the tradition of the Church and the Bible, is all part of moral decision-making. For such Christians, the Bible takes its authority from the Church, whose authority determined its shape, size and content. Within the Protestant tradition there is a view that sees Bible (Scripture), Church (tradition) and reason as all having a part to play in interpreting the moral messages of Jesus in today's world. Reason is needed to make sense of scripture and tradition.

Within the Catholic tradition there is a sense that **Sacred Tradition** is a separate stream of moral guidance, the oral tradition that Jesus passed to his followers by word of mouth and by living with them. This is passed down through the generations under the authority of the Apostles (including the Popes). Reason, for Catholics, can also offer direct access to the God's moral teachings. There is one source and one revelation, and the two streams cannot be in conflict with one another but must be mutually interpreting and connecting.

A key difference between Catholic and Protestant Christianity is around the order of priority to Church tradition, the Bible and reason. The Catholic Church puts tradition first, then the Bible, followed by magisterium and then reason. Protestant Churches put the Bible first and then some emphasise tradition and then reason.

Some Christians see morality as centred on unconditional love (agape). This is understood in different ways. If love is an ultimate law that informs moral decisions this might lead to a more flexible approach to morals (as with situation ethics), although it might also inspire a fervent wish for a more just and loving world that does not abandon moral rules.

Think question

Are Christians seen more as Bible followers, Church tradition followers or love followers when it comes to morality?

Different approaches to a Christian moral reading of the Bible

How do Christians use the Bible in making moral decisions? Whenever a Christian uses the Bible to make a moral decision, a number of factors might affect how that process works. To reveal these factors Richard B. Hays (*The Moral Vision of the New Testament*, 1996, p. 209 and p. 212) thinks we should ask the following questions.

1. How accurate is the account of what the texts used mean? (I might deliberately take texts out of context or use poor translations to try to get them to mean whatever I want them to mean)

2. What range of texts are used? (Is the whole decision based on one single quote in an unusual passage with no other similar references made elsewhere?)

3. Does a particular selection of passages tend to be used rather than the Bible as a whole – is there a Bible within the Bible? (Is it all about Paul and never from the Gospels or vice versa? Do the Hebrew Scriptures [the Old Testament] have any role to play?)

4. How are different texts managed? (For example how might the reference to peace in the beatitudes [Matthew 5:9] be managed with the later text that says Jesus has not come to bring peace [Matthew 10:34]?)

5. Are particular focal images used (the loving Jesus or the Jesus of righteous anger?)

Hays then asks if there are some further hermeneutical (interpreting) questions which draw out how the Christian has appealed to the text.

1. Has she focused on the rules, the direct commandments of the Bible (for instance the rule of divorce in Mark 10:2–12)?

2. Has she focused on the principles of the Bible (for instance in the double commandment of love of Mark 12:28–31 and its basis of Deuteronomy 6:4–5 with Leviticus 19:18)?

3. Has she focused on the paradigms of the Bible, the stories or summary accounts of characters who are examples of positive or negative conduct (for example a paradigm mode is shown in the parable of the Good Samaritan answering the question 'Who is my neighbour' with a story [Luke 10:29–37])?

4. Has she focused on the symbolic world of the Bible – what it says about the human condition or God? (for example what it says about how humans live as part of a fallen world [Romans 1:19–32] or what it says about God – who makes the sun rise on the good and bad and sends rain on the just and the unjust [Matthew 5:43–48])?

Apply your knowledge

1. Read the following statements, which could be said by different Christians, and decide which of the different approaches listed you can identify.

2. Choose one statement and develop it using two approaches from the list and your knowledge of Christian belief.

'I have read what it says in Leviticus about homosexuals. It clearly condemns men lying with men so I think gay sex is wrong. It doesn't fit with Genesis either.'

'I think God is at the heart of the Bible and God is a God of love so love has goodness in it, and it is not for me to say whether one person's love is better than another's.'

'People are very angry with these banking financiers and traders who caused so much damage to our economies. Their greed and selfishness has harmed many people's standard of living. Like all human beings they are sinners in a sinful world.'

'The Bible is clear that it is wrong to kill. That's why I think euthanasia is wrong.'

Apply your knowledge

3. Use the Internet to find out the key teachings on love from the Bible (love of God, neighbours, enemies).

4. What other ideas in the Bible might have important moral implications? Consider 'The Kingdom' (Matthew 5:20, 6:31–33, 7:13–14, 13, 19:13–14, 19:16–26 and Mark 9:35–37) or Obedience (Matthew 28:18 and Luke 22:42).

5. 'Do unto others as they would do unto you' is a powerful principle in the Bible and other sacred and philosophical texts. What kind of ethical approach is it suggesting?

6. Look at the Beatitudes. What sorts of virtues/dispositions do these encourage? How might they influence moral decision-making?

Propositional and non-propositional revelation

Knowledge comes in different forms. Propositional knowledge refers to knowing or accepting that something is so. Examples include knowing when your birthday is, knowing who wrote *Great Expectations*, knowing Boyle's Law or knowing the French for 'please'. Propositional knowledge has a 'truth value' – it can be true or false, or somewhere in between. It is conveyed through language, where statements and claims are made.

Propositional faith and revelation is faith as acceptance of truths revealed by God, as propositions to be accepted. God speaks to people in words, passing information to his listeners. Such truths might be the words of scripture, the Creeds, Church doctrines or the Confessions of the Reformers. This information is about how God will save them from sin, and information about the events in the life of Jesus, and about the moral standards demanded by God, and about life after death. It is not accessible through reason, or through experience of the world.

Non-propositional knowledge refers to other kinds of knowledge: knowing how to do something and gain skills through the procedures of experience ('procedural knowledge'). For example, knowing how to ride a bicycle, or whistle. My knowledge of such things will increase the more I practise them.

Non-propositional faith and revelation is belief or faith in God. This is the faith of a personal encounter, gaining knowledge of God through experience, by experiencing a sense of God's presence and guidance, for example. Some may experience God through nature, or by meeting the risen Christ in human experience. God reveals Himself and the person has faith in that self-revelation.

These two different kinds of knowledge often work together in everyday life. We combine factual knowledge with experience to achieve what we need to do. The two different ways of explaining how God reveals truths are not incompatible or mutually exclusive – most Christians would say they learn about God through the words of the Bible and also see the hand of God in nature and in their relationships with others. In reading the Bible some knowledge of linguistics and history is necessary to make sense of the words used and how they may accurately be interpreted to capture their sense.

Propositional and non-propositional approaches to the Bible

A propositional approach accepts as truth that the words of the Bible are messages from God. God is revealed directly to the reader through the words on the page. This approach leads some Christians to view the Commandments and Beatitudes as fixed moral principles to be transmitted, the life and work of Jesus as actual events to know about, and the parables as having fixed meanings.

A non-propositional approach is different. When God revealed himself in Jesus he didn't write a book or a set of propositions but lived a human life and died a human death. This can be seen as a more personal and experiential approach to the Bible. Many Christians understand the story of Jesus' life, death and resurrection as speaking to their whole life, and their experiences in life: hope, love, denial, being handed over or abandoned, facing the fear of death. The Bible is a gateway into encountering the living God.

You might think of the difference between propositional and non-propositional approaches as the difference between getting to know someone through reading their CV and getting to know someone by having dinner with them.

The Bible as the only source of authority for Christians

It is clear that the Bible is a key source of authority for Christians and that they can draw on it in a number of ways, but for some Christians it is seen as revealing God's will directly, making it the only authority for Christian ethics. 'Sola scriptura' means 'by scripture alone', and it stands for the doctrine that the Bible is the supreme authority in all matters of doctrine and practice: God's biblical ethical commands that should be followed (such as the commandments, Exodus 20:1–17). Behind this belief is the idea that scripture is self-authenticating – any rational reader can clearly see the meaning which presents itself. It is its own interpreter ('Scripture interprets Scripture'); we do not need any other interpreter as the meaning is obvious and clear from the text. The Bible offers propositional revelation and that revelation includes clear teachings on morality.

Some Christians consider the Bible to be the literal word of God. It is almost as if it was dictated by God to the writers, word by word, punctuation mark by punctuation mark – the writers are not authors, but scribes, recording what God writes or says (amanuensis). The Bible is considered to have authority for Christians because it was 'inspired by God'. They find basis for this view in the words of the Bible itself:

> 66 Above all, you must understand that no prophecy of Scripture came about by the prophet's own interpretation of things. For prophecy never had its origin in the human will, but prophets, though human, spoke from God as they were carried along by the Holy Spirit. 99
>
> 2 Peter 1:20–21, New International Version

> 66 Then the Lord reached out his hand and touched my mouth and said to me, 'I have put my words in your mouth'. 99
>
> Jeremiah 1:9, New International Version

This way of understanding the authority and inspiration of scripture has been especially popular in more evangelical, Protestant Christian Churches.

Inspiration is taken to mean different things within the Christian tradition. It is not commonly taken to mean dictation, or some form of God taking control of the minds of the writers. On the other hand, inspiration does not just mean inspired in the way that other great literature is – in terms of its literary quality. Divine inspiration in biblical literature usually refers to its character as divine revelation in writing, but such divine revelation does not take away the character of the human authors, such as Paul in his letters. Divine revelation comes through the words of human authors who have their own personalities and cultural dimensions.

There are some advantages in holding the belief that the entire Bible is inspired directly and without mistake from God, particularly with regards to moral matters, as it makes the Bible an infallible source of information. Believers will know that they can trust it and rely on what it says. It gives the right answer whenever it provides ethical guidance, and whenever it gives advice about how to organise family life and religious life. This view of the Bible means that it has no errors, no mistakes – the *inerrancy of Scripture*. This 'Bible-believing' Christian view sees any other sources with suspicion as they could be the product of evil.

Richard Mouw makes a case for the role of biblical imperatives:

> 66 If the command to love is the only biblical command which has normative relevance to moral decision making, then much of the substance of Christian ethics can be established without reference to the Scripture. But if the Bible does offer other commands and considerations which bear on our decision making, then the task will be one of finding correlations between biblical revelation and moral issues at many different points. 99
>
> Richard Mouw, 'Biblical Imperatives.' In *From Christ to the World: Introductory Readings in Christian Ethics*, eds. Boulton et al., 1994, pp. 31–3

Mouw specifically rejects those who take a situational approach or those who focus on love exclusively. Just because there is one biblical commandment, a law of love, does not rule out the possibility of other biblical commandments on other issues which also matter although Mouw notes not all biblical commandments are about morality today (for example, God told Abraham to leave his home to find the promised land, but arguably this was a specific command for Abraham at that time, rather than one that Christians should follow today). Also, it would be wrong to see the whole Bible in terms of a long list of commands. There is much in the Bible that is not a command – in the histories and the poems, for example. Mouw concludes:

> 66 … the writer of Ecclesiastes suggests our whole duty consists in obeying God's commandments … he is telling us … that we must conform to whatever God requires of us, to all that the Creator instructs us to do – whether that guidance is transmitted through parables, accounts of divine dealings with nations and individuals, or sentences which embody commands. 99
>
> Richard Mouw, 'Biblical Imperatives.' In *From Christ to the World: Introductory Readings in Christian Ethics*, eds. Boulton et al., 1994, pp. 31–3

For Christians using the Bible in this way, their approach to life is framed by the commandments and teachings (such as the Sermon on the Mount). Decisions about taking life will be informed by the commandment not to

Just because there is one biblical commandment, a law of love, does not rule out the possibility of other biblical commandments on other matters

kill and the teachings of Jesus on life. Attitudes to homosexuality will be influenced by passages in the Hebrew Scriptures (Old Testament) or Paul's letters which are often linked to that question. Behaviour in marriage or decisions about marriage might be linked to quotes about the purpose of men and women in Genesis and the Bible's treatment of divorce. Issues which are not directly mentioned in the Bible (such as a genetic ethics or business ethics) may be approached with references to the virtues implied by the teaching of Jesus. Truthfulness, an important quality in the Sermon on the Mount, might be used to inform business ethics, for instance. Of course, as Neil Messer discusses in the *SCM Study Guide to Christian Ethic* (2006, p. 6), there are different ways in which you can draw on the Bible and there are different kinds of scripture – history, saga (epic narratives), law, biography, instruction and warnings. History or saga may not be as easy to draw on as the direct teachings of Jesus, although there might be parallels between the history recorded in the Bible and present issues, such as conflicts or questions of good government.

Criticisms

This way of understanding the Bible is popular, especially among conservative and evangelical Christians, but it is not without its problems. Critics argue that it is impossible to read the Bible 'straight' without making any interpretation of it, saying that we are bound to read subjectively, in relation to our own experiences and with our own interpretations, because we are all human individuals with our own lives and thoughts and contexts, and we cannot separate ourselves from that. That means to read the Bible and try to understand it literally is a subjective choice as much as any other.

There are some general difficulties in taking a literal view of the Bible. If God really did dictate every word of the Bible then why does the Bible contain such different styles of writing? For example, John's Gospel has a more mystical, theological style, suggesting different influences from the other Gospels. Matthew's Gospel contains allusions to Jewish culture and scriptures, giving the impression he was Jewish and expected his readers to be Jewish, too. But Luke, in his Gospel, pauses in his narrative to explain aspects of Judaism as if his readers were unfamiliar with them. In contrast to the other Gospel writers who write in fluent, excellent Greek, Mark's Greek is not very accomplished. These differences have made it difficult for some to accept that God dictated his words directly to the Gospel writers.

Arguably the biggest problems are related to conflicts within the Bible. For example, Jesus' teaching in Matthew 5, the Sermon on the Mount, contradicts some earlier teachings in the Hebrew Scriptures (the Old Testament). If God wrote every word, why would he not be consistent? Secondly, there are rules in the Hebrew Scriptures that Christians do not follow, including extensive passages of rules in the Book of Leviticus that don't seem to refer to morality or be applicable to a moral issue. For

Apply your knowledge

Savi Hensman in the article *Thinking Theologically: Bible, Tradition, Reason and Experience* (www.ekklesia. co.uk/node/13404) illustrates a criticism of claiming no interpretation is necessary of the Bible:

Imagine that you find yourself on a plane and the passenger next to you looks familiar. You realise with a shock that you have seen him on the news, a notorious warlord known for kidnapping children and sending them into battle, and seizing girls to serve as sex-slaves to his troops.

He notices your reactions with some amusement, and starts to talk to you. He explains that he is a devout Christian, and was inspired to recruit child-soldiers after reading the story of David and Goliath (1 Samuel 17:1–54). Similarly, his massacres in the villages he conquered were prompted by the punishment of the Amalekites (1 Samuel 15:1) and the inhabitants of Jericho (Joshua 6:21) in what Christians call the Old Testament.

According to him, girls are taken from their homes to service his soldiers because, in Deuteronomy 22:28, it states that if a virgin not pledged in marriage is raped, her rapist is required to marry her and never send her back to her family … he is supremely confident that he is doing God's will, in accord with the 'plain meaning' of the Bible, which indeed he frequently quotes. Though some think him harsh, he sees himself as a 'soldier of Christ' (2 Timothy 2:3) in a time of turmoil, sent to rule with a rod of iron, as when earthen pots are broken in pieces (Revelation 2:27). How likely are you to be able to persuade him to rethink his views if this would mean re-examining his life, giving up the power he wields and coming to terms with the harm he has caused?

7. How might a literal Bible-believing Christian respond to this challenge?
8. What is the role of using the whole of the Bible?
9. Is it possible to avoid the role of interpretation given this example?

For some, the argument that Scripture has authority does not settle the question of how that authority functions, how it actually works

example Leviticus 19:27 prohibits cutting head hair and facial hair in a particular way, something many Christians do. Leviticus 11:6–8 prohibits touching pig skin, but many Christians wear pig leather products. Leviticus 19:19 prohibits planting two crops in the same field, but Christian farmers wouldn't usually feel constrained by such a teaching. If the whole Bible is believed to be literally true, then explanations are needed to deal with internal contradictions and why many rules in the Hebrew Scriptures are ignored.

Bible, Church and reason as sources of Christian ethics

Church tradition and the Bible

Catholic Christians believe the Bible grew out of the Church, on the grounds that the Church formed the canon of scripture (the Bible). Some Protestants seek to exclusively follow the Bible (sola scriptura), whilst others hold that the early Church grew out from the Bible and this makes Church tradition a living expression of the Good News and a living source of access to God's revelation. The Bible is the principal source of authority (prima scriptura), but it is understood through and with the Church traditions and human reason. Arguably, whenever a person reads the Bible (scripture) they do so, influenced by prior traditions, prior ways of thinking. William Spohn and Richard Hays explain this approach, and in so doing explicitly reject those who proclaim the Bible is the sole source of moral inspiration:

> 66 No matter how seriously the Church may take the authority of the Bible, the slogan of sola Scriptura is both conceptually and practically untenable, because the interpretation of Scripture can never occur in a vacuum. The New Testament is always read by interpreters under the formative influence of some particular tradition, using the light of reason and experience and attempting to relate the Bible to a particular situation. 99

Richard Hays, *The Moral Vision of the New Testament*, 1996, p. 209

> 66 Some ... view their work as strictly descriptive, providing no path from what a text meant to what it might mean for believers today. They are concerned that drawing inferences from a biblical text for life today usually wrenches the text from its unique historical context and ignores contradictory voices within Scripture. 99

William Spohn, 'Scripture.' In *The Oxford Handbook of Theological Ethics*, eds. Meilaender and Werpehowski, 2005, pp. 93–4

The interpretation of Scripture can never occur in a vacuum

These scholars argue you cannot examine scripture without reference to the Church communities and traditions in which it functions. Thus the focus should not be on what individual scholars make of a text when trying to decide what to do. It is wrong to start with the question 'how should I "use" this text?' but rather 'how do we as Christians, as part of a living Christian community and tradition, interpret this text?'

> 66 Biblical ethics is unyieldingly diverse. The Bible contains many books and more tradition, each addressed once to a particular community in a specific cultural and social context facing concrete questions of moral conduct and character. Biblical ethics does not provide an autonomous and timeless and coherent set of rules; it provides an account of the work and will and way of one God and evokes the creative and faithful response of those who would be God's people. 99

Allen Verhey, 'Biblical Ethics.' In *From Christ to the World: Introductory Readings in Christian Ethics*, eds. Boulton et al., 1994, p. 17

Think question

'It is impossible to read the Bible from no point of view. We always interpret, whether we know it or not. Therefore, interpretation is much better done in groups than alone, to reduce the risk of bias and narrowness.' Discuss each part of this quote.

Church communities and traditions are shaped by scripture, and these communities express the stories, symbols and moral convictions that shape the character of their members. The Church community of faith is the central community to which an individual Christian belongs and that community has a claim over the individual Christian.

The Christian Church has a concept of synod, meaning council or assembly, convened to discuss and agree together on issues of teaching, doctrine or administration. This can be understood in terms of the governing body of a church, a council of the Bishops of the church, a diocesan council or the local church group of elders or council members. In some traditions, it means a regional area of a church. Key in all these notions is some sense of decision-making and discernment together.

Anglican tradition

The common Anglican conception of Church tradition refers both to the early traditions (practices and beliefs) of the first Christians and the current traditions of the Church. For these Christians, the Bible comes first (prima scriptura), but is not the only source of understanding: tradition is an interpretation of scripture that should be listened to and practised. Some non-conformist Protestant Churches, such as the Methodist Church, also refer to tradition as the connection between the current Christian community and the first Christian community. The key idea here is that these influences are combined when decisions are made about moral questions.

Hays defines Church tradition as the time-honoured practices of worship, service and critical reflection. Messer describes it as 'a shared understanding within the Christian community about the kind of community it is, where it has come from, what it exists for and, in the light of that, how it and its members ought to live their lives' (Messer, *SCM Study Guide to Christian Ethics*, 2006, p. 6). The life of prayer

A debate at the Anglican Synod

and worship, the organisation of Church, the common preaching and teachings of that Church all make up 'tradition'. Tradition should not be thought of as a fixed thing but a healthy debate as the living Church has sought, throughout ages to make sense of the times and situations it experiences. Tradition is not separate from scripture, and this link can be understood in different ways.

- Church tradition is how the community of the Church worships and prays using scripture.

- The Bible starts tradition because it records the life of the first Christians in the New Testament letters and the Acts of the Apostles. The Bible gives an account of how early Christians began to discuss what the teachings and works of Jesus meant to them in their lives.

- The Bible has already been interpreted by tradition – the Church chose which texts were to be part of the Bible and some texts were excluded because they were judged unreliable.

The Gospels themselves were written at a time when the early Church had already formed and some argue that the interpretation of the works and life of Jesus by the first Christians was affected by the difficult times they were living through. For example, some New Testament scholars think that the references to the destruction of the Temple (Mark 13.2, 15:29, 14:57; John 2:19; Matthew 26:61) and the miracle of the calming of the storm (Mark 4:35–41 and Matthew 8:23–27) reflect the tumultuous experience of uncertainty and danger that the early Church experienced, which they read into the words and actions of Jesus.

Catholic Sacred Tradition

The Catholic tradition is quite different. The canon of sacred scripture, the authoritatively recognised selection of texts considered, was determined by the Church. This involved a process from the first disciples (and the Hebrew Scriptures which were already treated as sacred) and the early writings of the followers of Jesus, and ultimately through the early Church councils an agreement was made about the canon, about what was in the Bible. It was the authority of the Church that decided what the Bible was — tradition precedes the Bible.

Sacred Tradition is an equal means of coming to know the revelation of Jesus alongside the Bible

The common Catholic conception of Sacred Tradition is different from the conception of tradition in churches such as the Anglican Church. Sacred Tradition is an equal means of coming to know the revelation of Jesus alongside the Bible because it is the oral tradition handed down by Jesus to his disciples and then on to the first Christian leaders and down through history to the present through the Apostolic succession, the line of Bishops and Priests from the first Apostles.

Sacred Tradition in the Catholic Church, therefore, has equal authority to the Bible because the Church teaches it comes from Jesus. Tradition is how the Holy Spirit makes the Risen Lord present.

A gathering of cardinals of the Catholic Church

> ❝ Sacred tradition and Sacred Scripture form one sacred deposit of the word of God, committed to the Church. [...] But the task of authentically interpreting the word of God, whether written or handed on, has been entrusted exclusively to the living teaching office of the Church [the magisterium], whose authority is exercised in the name of Jesus Christ. This teaching office is not above the word of God, but serves it, teaching only what has been handed on, listening to it devoutly, guarding it scrupulously and explaining it faithfully in accord with a divine commission and with the help of the Holy Spirit, it draws from this one deposit of faith everything which it presents for belief as divinely revealed.
>
> It is clear, therefore, that sacred tradition, Sacred Scripture and the teaching authority of the Church [the magisterium], in accord with God's most wise design, are so linked and joined together that one cannot stand without the others, and that all together and each in its own way under the action of the one Holy Spirit contribute effectively to the salvation of souls. ❞

Vatican II Council, Dei Verbum,
'Dogmatic Constitution on Divine Revelation,' par. 10.
In *Vatican Council II: The Conciliar Documents*, ed. Flannery, 1975

This process of handing down is referred to in the New Testament:

> ❝ So then, brothers and sisters, stand firm and hold fast to the teachings we passed on to you, whether by word of mouth or by letter. ❞

2 Thessalonians 2:15, see also 1 Corinthians 11:23,
15:3 and 2 Timothy 2:1–2

Catholic Sacred Tradition is summarised in the *Catechism of the Catholic Church* (CCC). It summarises many of the decrees and declarations of the Church councils on various moral issues such as abortion (CCC 2270) and euthanasia (CCC 2276-79), nuclear weapons (CCC 2316), workers' rights (CCC 1939–42) and so on, framed around biblical references, in particular the commandments (the whole of part 3, section 2 of the CCC is framed in this way). The Catechism is a summary of how a church integrates tradition and scripture together through a process of reasoning. The Catholic Church draws on Natural Law for that reasoning (CCC 1950ff).

The Catholic Church has a strong sense of the magisterium – the teaching authority of the Church expressed in the Pope, the Bishops and the

Church Councils. This authority allows clear decisions on moral teaching across a range of areas. The Catechism resolves to provide an unambiguous answer to many moral problems Christians face today, also suggesting a way of thinking about difficult moral dilemmas. It still recognises the importance of individual conscience in moral decision-making (CCC 1776ff) – moral action is not simply obedience to authority but should include conscientious action and prayer (CCC 1785).

This approach reflects the importance of Sacred Tradition as a binding authority and source of guidance in moral life. The Sacred Tradition of the Church connects the Christian community today with that of the early Church and with the authority of the first Apostles and Jesus. Some Church denominations do not express binding official teachings that must be followed, but provide teaching as guidance for the individual to reflect on and use to make an informed choice. This is a reflection of the different sense of authority that tradition has.

The Anglican tradition can be expressed as scripture, tradition and reason. The Catholic tradition can be expressed as tradition, scripture, magisterium and then reason.

The Sacred Tradition of the Catholic Church connects the Christian community today with that of the early Church and with the authority of the first Apostles and Jesus

Reason

Any decision-making requires the operation of reason. Reason is needed to make sense of experience and respond to it, to process and reflect on the Bible and tradition and apply the guidance obtained from those sources to the problem.

Philosophers from the enlightenment onwards thought that reason was in some way objective or neutral, but in the later twentieth century many rejected this idea. Rather than being objective, the rules and principles used for reasoning are just as influenced by our contemporary culture as anything else.

....

66 [R]ationality itself, whether theoretical or practical, is a concept with a history: indeed, since there are a diversity of traditions on enquiry, with histories, there are, so it will turn out, rationalities, rather than rationality … 99

Alasdair MacIntyre, *Whose Justice? Which Rationality?*, 1988, p. 9

....

Hays agrees:

....

66 … reason itself is always culturally influenced. … Rationality is a contingent aspect of particular symbolic worlds. Consequently, when we ask about the relation between Scripture and 'reason'

as sources of authority, we are in effect seeking the best way to coordinate the cultural logic of the New Testament writings with the cultural logic of our own historical setting. **"**

Richard B. Hays, *The Moral Vision of the New Testament*, 1996, p. 210

In other words, Christians need to negotiate between the world of the New Testament and their particular world in the present to find a way of making moral decisions. It might be that in this negotiation or interpretation some factors of the difference between the two worlds become important or prioritised. For example, modern views of the place of men and women in leadership are different from those expressed in some comments about women made by St Paul (1 Corinthians 14:33–35).

So reason can produce different interpretations of the Bible and result in differing Church traditions and different responses to ethical decision-making. For example, for the Catholic Church the idea of just war comes through a process of reason, and this is used to inform the Church's position that war can sometimes be justified. However, there is also a pacifist tradition within the Christian Church, found especially among non-conformist denominations, including Quakers. The tradition of pacifism is something that has come from a different interpretation of the Bible. The Quakers and others were persecuted in the past for not fighting in the army, and this experience has further influenced their Church tradition. There are different Christian traditions in response to the ethics of using violence for self-defence and the defence of the faith. Some Christians have fought in wars against ideologies they believe are evil, including both of the World Wars of the twentieth century.

When confronted with a moral question, Christians who draw on the Bible, Church tradition and reason will consult a number of sources. They might turn to the teachings or rules of their Church on that issue, using a catechism or other guidance document. Many Churches provide information about issues and their teachings on those issues. For many Churches specific advice on issues like sexual ethics, contraception, divorce and euthanasia can be found. These teachings are developed by leaders of the Churches using the Bible and reason to come to specific conclusions. Some stress the importance in following the rules of the Church and these deliberations. Other Churches encourage their members to reach their own conclusions, perhaps through a process of reasoning and prayer, alone or in groups, with previous teachings in mind. There may be a question of how best to interpret the Bible, and whether knowledge of the ancient languages and the ancient world in which the Bible was written can help make sense of what it might mean for moral questions now. Churches may engage in deliberate focused prayer around a particular difficult decision before reaching a

Apply your knowledge

Many Churches publish moral advice on different issues.

10. Use the Internet to review the text of the Catholic Catechism and look at two examples from: abortion (CCC 2270), euthanasia (CCC 2276–79), nuclear weapons (CCC 2316) and workers' rights (CCC 1939–42). Summarise the teaching and try to describe the tone of the language. What kind of message is it giving? How might different Christians, including Catholics, respond to the moral language? Might it seem authoritative and trustworthy or overly commanding?

11. Now compare this information with the teaching on another church's website of your choice. Does it provide similar sorts of guidance and does it come to the same sorts of conclusions or different ones?

conclusion and sometimes a Church will call a Council to try to decide what to do about a question, following the tradition of the early Church – a tradition which, in turn, helps councils to make decisions about teachings.

Differences

There are important differences between the Catholic and Protestant views of how Bible, Church and reason work in moral questions. For Catholic Christians, relying on Sacred Tradition is a matter of trust in the authority of the Church. Church teachings on moral questions are to be trusted as much as if they were written in the Bible and should be obeyed, although not unthinkingly so as conscience plays a part. For Protestant Churches which recognise Church tradition, tradition is a way of interpreting the Bible, which may change with time as practice and meanings are seen in the light of the present. However ultimately, moral authority always rests with the Bible.

For Catholics, reason provides another source of direct access to revelation, through the moral laws implicit in the created world. This is the basis for Natural Law. Within the Catholic Church, the Bible (Sacred Scripture), Sacred Tradition and Reason each access the one source of revelation in different ways. For Protestant Christians, reason is the process of making sense of Bible and Church tradition. Within some Protestant traditions reason operates to make sense of the Bible and how it has been interpreted through the practices from the early Church to the present.

Church tradition is a way of interpreting the Bible

Criticisms of the 'Bible, Church and Reason' approaches

- **Protestant concerns about 'Sacred Tradition'.** For many Protestants the Catholic view that tradition is equal to the Bible as a distinctive way of knowing the one source of revelation is problematic. This concern comes from the Reformation itself, when Martin Luther and others became critical of practices of the Church that were sanctioned by its authority but which reformers thought were in conflict with the Bible. Some Christians communities today are sceptical about the role of tradition. Non-conformist Protestant Churches see the traditions of Catholicism and Anglicanism as something apart from the rule of God. Perhaps this process of following traditions is a distraction from the moral commands found in the Bible.

- **Jesus' attitude to tradition.** Philip Turner notes that *paradosis* (translated as traditions) are sometimes criticised by Jesus. Usually these are to do with the traditions of the Jewish elders 'that Jesus contrasts unfavourably with the "word" or "commandment" of God' see, for example, Matthew 15:2–3, 15:6; Mark 7:3, 7:5, 7:8–9,

7:13; Galatians 1:14 (Philip Turner, 'Tradition in the Church.' In *The Oxford Handbook of Theological Ethics*, eds. Meilaender and Werpehowski, 2005, p. 131). Jesus condemns the tradition or teaching of the Pharisees and the Scribes because their traditions represent the rules of men rather than the commandment of God (Matthew 15:2–9 and Mark 7:3–13) and Paul criticises the traditions of his Jewish tradition and continues by contrasting how he used to be devoted to their traditions but now is devoted to God's Son (Galatians 1:13–17). Turner suggests that these references to traditions in fact mean interpretations of the law, rather than the law itself. However, Turner continues noting that there are positive references to tradition as well, in terms of Christian traditions that are handed over by Paul to others to follow (1 Corinthians 11:2 and 2 Thessalonians 2:15, 3:6), and which he has received 'from the Lord' (1 Corinthians 11:23).

- **Concerns about the exclusion of women's perspectives.** The feminist theologian Rosemary Radford Ruether is critical of the power of Church tradition and its starting point, scripture, for a different reason ('Feminst Interpretation: A Method of Correlation.' In *From Christ to the World: Introductory Readings in Christian Ethics*, eds. Boulton et al., 1994, pp. 88–91). She argues that both tradition and the Bible are shaped almost exclusively by male experiences of life, which means the universality and authority of tradition can be questioned because it excludes women's experiences. The current tradition and interpretation of the Bible is one sided, partial and incomplete.

- **Concerns about reason being set against faith.** Reason is sometimes viewed suspiciously by Christians as an attempt to create some distance from the sources of the Bible and tradition. It can be linked to the rise of reason in the Enlightenment, as science developed systems of thought separate from any biblical basis. Christians who rely on the Bible alone are sceptical of such sources.

Apply your knowledge

'I trust in the moral guidance of the Church.'

'I trust in the moral authority of the Bible.'

'I trust in my ability to make sense of moral dilemmas myself.'

'The Bible is always interpreted.'

'Tradition expresses cultural norms which might be immoral.'

'Human sources of moral advice cannot be trusted.'

12. Explain how Christians might respond to these quotes differently.

Love (agape) as the only Christian ethical principle

For many Christians the fundamental New Testament principle of love (**agape**) is an essential guide throughout their lives. The principle of love is at the root of all of Jesus' teachings and actions and the New Testament is littered with prominent quotes about love. These emphasise its challenge, its unconditional, self-sacrificial nature and its moral supremacy:

66 One of the teachers of the law came and heard them debating. Noticing that Jesus had given them a good answer, he asked him,

'Of all the commandments, which is the most important?' 'The most important one,' answered Jesus, 'is this: "Hear, O Israel: The Lord our God, the Lord is one. Love the Lord your God with all your heart and with all your soul and with all your mind and with all your strength." The second is this: "Love your neighbour as yourself." There is no commandment greater than these.' 99

Mark 12:28–31, New International Version,
see also Matthew 22:37–39

66 But love your enemies, do good to them, and lend to them without expecting to get anything back. Then your reward will be great, and you will be children of the Most High, because he is kind to the ungrateful and wicked. 99

Luke 6:35, New International Version

66 Love is patient, love is kind. It does not envy, it does not boast, it is not proud. It does not dishonour others, it is not self-seeking, it is not easily angered, it keeps no record of wrongs. Love does not delight in evil but rejoices with the truth. It always protects, always trusts, always hopes, always perseveres. Love never fails. But where there are prophecies, they will cease; where there are tongues, they will be stilled; where there is knowledge, it will pass away. 99

1 Corinthians 13:4–8, New International Version

66 And now these three remain: faith, hope and love. But the greatest of these is love. 99

1 Corinthians 13:13, New International Version

66 Whoever does not love does not know God, because God is love. 99

1 John 4:8, New International Version

JESUS ♥ ATHEISTS

Some scholars argue that ultimately Jesus' only command was to love, and it is for human reason to decide how to apply that command, rather than follow a list of rules. Reinhold Niebuhr (1892–1971), American theologian, ethicist and public intellectual, wrote about prophetic Christianity and orthodox Christianity.

- Orthodox Christianity tended to become one of two contrasting types of religion, one that denies the relevance of love in ordinary moral matters, and another which tries to reduce moral behaviour to conformity of tradition and the common sense of generations.

- On the other hand, a prophetic tradition in Christianity insists on the relevance of the ideal of love to the moral experience of mankind on every conceivable level. The ultimate law of life is love, Niebuhr wrote, and this is the basis of all moral standards.

The ultimate law of life is love

For Rudolf Bultmann, the challenge of Christian moral behaviour is to move beyond laws and judgements to forgiveness based on love: 'The statement "God is love" does not express an idea, a notion of the imagination, but rather it has a wholly concrete content: God forgives sin' (Sermon on December 19, 1924 in *Das verkündigte Wort*, 1984, pp. 211–12).

Paul Tillich and justice, love and wisdom

Paul Tillich (1886–1965), a German-American Christian existentialist philosopher and Lutheran theologian, suggested three ethical norms, or rules, should work together for Christians: justice, love and wisdom. Most important of these, for Tillich, is love, which he saw as being guided by wisdom and having justice as its 'backbone'.

Tillich argues that agape love includes all the dimensions of love: *eros*, the love of the true the good and the beautiful; *philia*, the love of friendship and trust; and *libido*, sexual love. Tillich describes love as a continuous desire to break through the isolation which is connected to every person.

In 'Ethical Principles of Moral Action' (1994), Paul Tillich is critical of the kind of Christian moral decision-making which follows fixed rules. He calls this moral Puritanism which promotes principles 'which identify the Christian message with the prohibition of eating this or that, of drinking this or that, or of acting in sexual relations in this or that way' (p. 250). Instead agape love is a person-centred moral principle, binding us to the other person and their particular situation. Love needs to act in the immediate, concrete moral situation facing the person, not a hypothetical situation. Tillich thought each particular situation has its own voice which cries out to us and which we can hear if we are driven by love.

Think question

a. Is love more about forgiveness than justice?

Think question

b. 'The Bible and tradition just stop people doing the right thing, and sometimes encourage the wrong thing, but love will set us free to do good.' Discuss.

However, Tillich identified a problem for people trying to respond to this voice:

> 66 But there is something between love and the situation, and these are the laws of religions, the laws of nations, and the laws of society. They are embodied in the traditional laws which we read and learn. How can we judge them? 99
>
> Paul Tillich, 'Ethical Principles of Moral Action'. In *From Christ to the World: Introductory Readings in Christian Ethics*, eds. Boulton et al., 1994, p. 250

Tillich sees these traditional laws as the wisdom of the past, including the commands of the Bible, but he does not think they were meant to operate as abstract technical forces telling us what to do in every situation. This would be against the situation-centred principle of love. Therefore, for Tillich, 'nobody should feel compelled – religiously and morally – to follow [laws] unconditionally' (p. 250): slavishly following the laws of religions, societies and nations is no good.

Tillich recognises that it can be difficult to know how and when to bend or break a commandment for love, but sees that difficulty as being part of moral life. Tillich concludes:

> 66 … a moral action is an action in which we actualize ourselves as persons within person-to-person encounters. Its principles are the love whose backbone is justice, the love which, though unconditional itself, listens to the concrete situation and its changes, and is guided by the wisdom of the past. 99
>
> Paul Tillich, 'Ethical Principles of Moral Action'. In *From Christ to the World: Introductory Readings in Christians Ethics*, eds., Boulton et al., 1994, p. 251

> **Think question**
> 'Nobody should feel compelled – religiously and morally – to follow commandments unconditionally or slavishly.' Discuss.

> *Tillich's thinking influenced Joseph Fletcher's Situation Ethics (Chapter 2.2)*

The way Tillich thinks love influences Christian ethics is radically different from those who seek to find and observe all of the biblical commands and allow them to act as principles that tell us what to do. It is also different from those who think that the Bible and Church tradition should guide and inform our deliberations. Tillich gives ultimate authority to the individual Christian's own deliberation of what to do according to the particular situation she faces, not just what previous rules suggest. Tillich is not saying the rules have no bearing at all but that they must always be interpreted through love in accordance with the particular people involved and the moral dilemma they face.

Tillich himself balanced this loving principle with the wisdom of the moral rules, as a corrective to the subjective perspective of the moment.

Think question

G.K. Chesterton wrote, 'Tradition means giving a vote to most obscure of all classes, our ancestors. It is the democracy of the dead.' Should we listen to the voice of love over the inherited laws of the people of the past?

Apply your knowledge

Discuss the following statements with reference to this section on love and either the section on Church tradition or the Bible.

13. A Christian should set aside the biblical texts that refer to same sex issues and focus on the loving couple and their situation.

14. A Christian should set aside the teachings of peace in the case of a just war.

15. A Christian doctor should respond to the moral needs of a dying person by lovingly helping to end their pain and letting them die if that is their wish.

Enhance you answers by using the Internet to find examples of Christian organisations or groups which support euthanasia, war or same sex relationships.

However, taking the love principle to its furthest application could mean setting aside those rules and justifying actions on the grounds of the person, the situation and hearing love's voice. Perhaps the biblical teachings on same sex relationships can be set aside for the loving couple and their situation? Perhaps the teachings of peace can be set aside for the need to fight just wars? Perhaps the moral needs of a dying person justify a doctor ending their pain and letting them die in the way they wish?

Pope Francis and Love

Pope Francis has not changed Catholic moral teaching but he has altered the approach taken when applying moral teaching to different situations and issues. In the *Joy of Love* ([*Amoris Laetitia*], 2016, Post-Synodal Exhortation, Vatican, [https://w2.vatican.va/content/dam/francesco/pdf/apost_exhortations/documents/papa-francesco_esortazione-ap_20160319_amoris-laetitia_en.pdf]) he writes about the many different crises that beset people in the Bible from the first page onwards (2016, p. 7, p. 16). On the moral difficulties families face he says, 'Nor it is [*sic*] helpful to try to impose rules by sheer authority' (paragraph 35). He has advocated a more compassionate approach, questioning attempts to control people using rules. His thinks the Bible contains both wisdom about the rules of marriage and family life and also is realistic in the stories of family and marriage difficulties. His approach is a compassionate one to these problems. He writes, 'We have long thought that simply by stressing doctrinal, bioethical and moral issues, without encouraging openness to grace, we were providing sufficient support to families, strengthening the marriage bond and giving meaning to marital life' (paragraph 37). Francis is advocating moral guidance grounded in love, recognising the rules of the Christian tradition but also the challenges of modern life and the difficulties of human relationships. This is a distinctive combination of different ethical approaches discussed in this chapter, and also in Chapters 2.1 and 2.2.

In a word, love means fulfilling the last two commandments of God's Law:

> 66 You shall not covet your neighbour's house; you shall not covet your neighbour's wife, or his male or female servant, his ox or donkey, or anything that belongs to your neighbour. 99
>
> Exodus 20:17, New International Version

> 66 Love inspires a sincere esteem for every human being and the recognition of his or her own right to happiness. 99
>
> Pope Francis, *The Joy of love: Amoris Laetitia*, Post-Synodal Apostolic Exhortation of Love, paragraph 96

Discussing Christian moral principles

Are Christian ethics distinctive?

Some Christians take a deontological approach, following the rules of the community. Many people might say this was sensible approach to making moral decisions, especially when we need to get along together. Other Christians respond in the moment to the particular situation and needs of the person they face. This is similar to a pragmatic approach to ethics which encourages a freer approach to moral problems. The Bible is a distinctive text which perhaps marks Christians apart from others, and whether the Bible is considered a source of God's commands or an inspiration for Love, of the Church tradition, it is always part of the mix in moral decision-making.

This sets Christian moral action apart from Utilitarian approaches to morality, which begins with human desire. Kantian ethics also has no place for the Bible, although there is a place for moral law and the power of reason to discern morality. This is also true for Natural Law, which acknowledges the Bible but does not require it to interpret the moral messages available through reasoned reflection on creation. Some Christians will see ethics as strongly linked to Natural Law and perhaps also Kantian ethics, but others will see these as external to the Bible, and therefore untrustworthy.

To be comprehensive, any answer to the question 'are Christian ethics distinctive?' needs to delve deep into the different approaches Christians take.

Are Christian ethics personal or communal?

Should Christian moral decision-making be a matter of individuals deciding what they should individually do or a matter for communities co-operating together and deciding as a group what everyone inside the community should do?

Some scholars argue you cannot examine scripture without reference to the communities and traditions in which it functions. In other words, whenever a person interprets the Bible they do so through a particular tradition. At the same time, communities and traditions are shaped by the Bible, and these communities express the stories, symbols and moral convictions that shape the character of their members. The community of faith is the central community to which an individual Christian belongs and that community has a claim over the individual Christian.

Communities are structured by rules, be they the rules of tradition or arguably the rules of the Bible. Perhaps the Bible is the guide book of

> ## Apply your knowledge
>
> 16. What kind of ethics are Christian ethics? Explain why each of the following possible answers might be the best answer
>   a. Following God's rules (deontological)
>   b. Following the principle of love (situational)
>   c. Following reason.

Apply your knowledge

17. Did Jesus give an individualist message or a community one? Consider the following factors: he had a close group of friends who he lived and worked with; he had many disputes with community leaders (e.g. Pharisees); he broke the laws of communities when he thought they were wrong; his followers established a community, the Church, after he left them; his teaching comes from the holy book of the people of God; his movement eventually broke away from the Jewish community.

18. Discuss these two views 'Religious fanatics who break away from conventions are dangerous', 'Sometimes we need prophets who can imagine a different and better world than the one we live in and inspire the change needed.'

the Christian community. However, others might point to Jesus' own arguments within his community – his debates with Pharisees and his willingness to break rules for the needs of people and out of love. Perhaps if Jesus is a model for Christians, they as individuals must be willing to read the situation they are in, look to those who need care and love and respond in a loving way, rather than in a prescriptive or legalistic way.

However, the foundation narrative of Christianity is found in the Bible. Arguably it is this book that should guide action and this book is a book of the people of God, not the individuals of God.

Is the principle of love sufficient to live a good life?

Agape love is a powerful ethical principle, challengingly self-sacrificial and almost frightening in the demands it might place on people. It is hard to imagine a good life without love, and love seems to underpin many different ethical ideas in the Christian life and the moral life in general. However, even Tillich felt that love needs careful explanation. It is not *just* love but love with a 'backbone' of justice as well as the love of compassion and forgiveness. Love is, in fact, a complex idea with many different parts; it seems to link to fairness and reliability, honesty and selflessness. In short, perhaps to reduce all of these things to love simplifies unreasonably what love really means. Perhaps the good life needs a more comprehensive description.

Also, the loves of many individuals have to somehow be negotiated with one another. If we are to live together then how do I negotiate *my* thoughts about love with *everyone else's*? The solution to this that communities have traditionally offered is to co-operate around agreed rules. Co-operating means doing things in tandem with one another, making sure everyone gets heard and making sure decisions are made communally and perhaps democratically. These notions of co-operation, community and democracy seem to be important in how ethics are worked out in practice. Perhaps this is where the Church or community traditions come in – to help ensure everyone has a voice.

Another question about love is the extent to which it could motivate people to be individualistic and selfish. Is there a dangerous precedent in allowing rules to be broken for loving reasons? How would I know I was not allowing myself to be tempted by sin when I used love to justify an illicit relationship, or doing something that traditionally Christian Churches have opposed?

A final question about love is the one Mouw raised at the start of this chapter. Just because there is one biblical commandment, a law of love, does not rule out the possibility of other biblical commandments on other matters. If the law of love is right because it is a command of the Bible, what about the other commands in the Bible?

Is the Bible a comprehensive moral guide?

The Bible contains a vast array of different kinds of books with poems, histories, narratives, letters and laws capturing the experiences of many communities over a long period of time. This breadth of experience makes it an extraordinarily unique collection, one that has spoken to peoples across the ages. As a source it is possible to find many examples of how the people of God responded to different moral dilemmas and how God spoke to them in those situations. This is one reason why it seems to have been so comprehensively popular down the ages. Another is found in the belief that the Bible is the word of God and, therefore, it is a revelation of the living God who made and created all things. Reading it provides access to the teaching of God and so it can speak to a whole host of situations.

However, the Bible is, at the same time, the sacred book of one particular cultural community from a small corner of the Middle East. It does not capture the thought and experiences of East Asia, the Americas, or sub-Saharan Africa, for instance. It shows how a people of a particular culture responded to some universal moral situations, but through the limitations of their own time – a time with views about the place of women, for example, which are not comprehensively shared today. It does not contain reflections on present day challenges brought about in the modern world. It has not benefitted from modern insights, understandings and experiences. This is where tradition can help in the interpretation of the Bible for the world we now live in.

Learning support

Points to remember

» For some Christians the Bible is the sole source of authority. This offers authority and certainty in moral questions that are explicitly addressed in the Bible. Being moral for these Christians is about obedience to the laws of God set out in the Bible.

» The teaching of the Church, or Church tradition, has different meanings. For some it combines the ways of Church communities today with the Bible and uses reason to interpret the two experiences – life today and sacred revelation. The Bible and tradition are both sources, but tradition grows out from the Bible. In the Catholic Church, Sacred Tradition refers to the authoritative teaching handed down through the disciples and apostles.

» Agape love is a central Christian idea and many Christian moral thinkers argue that a love-centred approach should set aside legalistic approaches to ethics. This does not make Christian morality soft, as justice is part of love, but a love-centred approach is a person-centred approach to moral issues.

Enhance your learning

» The Commandments, also known as the Decalogue, can be found in two places: in Exodus 20:1–17 and also in Deuteronomy 5:4–21. They include instructions to worship only God, to honour parents, and to keep the Sabbath. They prohibit idolatry, blasphemy, murder, adultery, theft, dishonesty, and coveting. The commandments are widely interpreted in different ways.

» St Paul's poetic and profound treatise on love can be found in 1 Corinthians 13:1–7; it is also popular in wedding ceremonies.

» Excellent introductions to Christian ethics include: Neil Messer's *SCM Study Guide to Christian Ethics* (2006) and Roger Crook's *An Introduction to Christian Ethics* (sixth edition, 2012).

» A good collection, edited by Bernard Hoose, is *Christian Ethics: An Introduction* (1998).

Practice for exams

AS questions and A level questions look identical; the difference between AS and A level assessment is seen in the different proportions of marks awarded for two different skills: the skill of demonstrating knowledge and understanding (Assessment Objective 1, or AO1), and the skill of constructing a critical argument (AO2).

At AS, half the marks (15 marks) are available for knowledge and understanding, and the other half (15 marks) for the quality of your analytical and evaluative argument. You should aim to use your knowledge in order to support the argument you are making throughout the essay, rather than presenting descriptive knowledge in the first half and then an opinion in the second.

At A level, your demonstration of knowledge and understanding is awarded a maximum of 16 marks, and your analytic and evaluative skills are awarded a maximum of 24 marks. You should aim to concentrate on constructing a lucid argument, making use of your knowledge to add weight to the conclusions you draw.

How fair is the claim that there is nothing distinctive about Christian ethics?

This question is asking about the 'distinctiveness' of Christian ethics, so you need to think about whether Christian ethics have features which make it different from other ways of doing ethics or whether it is very similar to, or the same as, non-Christian ethics.

Practise your skills for AS level

If you are answering this question for AS level, you will need to show a good knowledge and understanding of the key principles of Christian ethics; you might want to argue that Christian ethics are very similar to secular ethics (perhaps especially in post-Christian societies) or you might want to argue that Christian ethics have distinctive features which set them apart.

Practise your skills for A level

If you are answering this question for A level, you need to start by deciding what you want to argue and then use this to structure your essay, presenting reasoning and dealing with counter-arguments. You might think there are elements of Christianity that are distinctive, perhaps considering agape or the principle of following the example of Christ, or you might consider that these or other features are also found in other ethical systems. Whatever you choose to argue, you should support it with sound reasoning and examples leading to a persuasive conclusion.

'The Bible is all that is needed as a moral guide for Christian behaviour.' Discuss.

For this question you need to consider whether the Bible is totally sufficient as a guide for Christians or whether it needs to be supplemented or even overruled by other sources of moral authority.

Practise your skills for AS level

If you are answering this question for AS level, you could demonstrate knowledge and understanding by showing how the Bible is used in Christian life and especially in moral decision-making. You could demonstrate your critical evaluative skill in your assessment of whether this is all that Christians need or whether it needs to be supplemented in some way in order to address the demands of modern living.

Practise your skills for A level

If you are answering this question for A level, you should aim to give a balanced answer, considering the kind of moral guidance given by the Bible, and other possible sources of moral guidance for Christians, such as the conscience and the teachings of the church. You might want to reflect on some possible inconsistencies in biblical teaching as well as the potential for difficulties when people are faced with moral dilemmas which relate very much to the modern world. In your answer you should aim for a consistent line of argument supported with plenty of examples.

Chapter 3.6

Christian moral action

Should a Christian ever attack their state?
*What is the role of the Church community
in wider life?*
*Is Christian discipleship essentially a life
of suffering and sacrifice?*

Key Terms

Discipleship: following the life, example and teaching of Jesus

Cheap grace: grace that is offered freely, but is received without any change in the recipient, and ultimately is false as it does not save

Costly grace: grace followed by obedience to God's command and discipleship

Passion: Jesus' sufferings at the end of his life

Solidarity: an altruistic commitment to stand alongside and be with those less fortunate, the oppressed, those who suffer

Specification requirements

The teaching and example of Dietrich Bonhoeffer on
- duty to God and duty to the State
- Church as community and source of spiritual discipline
- the cost of discipleship

Introduction

Christians have often been in conflict with governments. From the very beginnings of Christianity, Christians were threatened by the State. In the twentieth century both fascist and communist states sought to control or remove Christianity because of its challenge to the authority of the State. These totalitarian states wanted total control over their people, and the Church could threaten this.

What should a Christian do, when a key part of their faith is, as they see it, undermined by a law they are required to follow? This was the situation faced by the German Lutheran pastor Dietrich Bonhoeffer when he lived in the National Socialist (Nazi) State headed by Adolf Hitler. Bonhoeffer's response to the situation has had a profound effect on modern Christian thought.

Bonhoeffer was a key founding member of the Confessing Church, a breakaway church that rejected the way much of the German Christian establishment had accepted Nazi ideology, including its anti-Semitism. He went on to found his own religious community at Finkenwalde. Bonhoeffer valued the Church community as a support for living as a Christian, and also as a source for spiritual discipline of life. For Bonhoeffer Christian ethics was an ethic of responsibility for others.

Christian life can often come across as a comfortable, 'nice Christianity' culture – the cozy local community focus, with flower festivals, Sunday School, community gatherings and celebrations of special foods and festivals. However, many Christians experience their faith as a struggle with persecution, personal loss and challenge. Bonhoeffer's experience of life and faith led him to a profound sense of the cost of **discipleship**, and the sacrifice and suffering that it entails. For Christians today this might both inspire and challenge them in their understanding of what being Christian entails.

Dietrich Bonhoeffer (1906–45)

> **Think question**
>
> What is wrong with 'comfortable' Christianity?

Duty to God and duty to the State

The Church and State

Bonhoeffer lived in Germany at a time when German Christians were divided by the rise of Hitler and the Nazi Party. Some joined the Party, and incorporated the ideology of Nazism into their belief or 'creed'. This led to a split in the German Protestant Churches in 1934 between the Christians in the Nazi-controlled German Church, and a Confessing Church which sought to be authentically Christian, separate from political ideology. It was a time where Nazi politics merged into religion, as Hitler tried to crush any possible source of opposition to his control over the German people. A spokesperson for the 'German Christians' declared that:

> 66 … the time is fulfilled for the German people in Hitler. It is because of Hitler that Christ, God the helper and redeemer, has become effective among us. Therefore National Socialism is positive Christianity in action. … Hitler is the way of the Spirit and the will of God for the German people to enter the Church of Christ. 99

> Hermann Grüner, quoted in Geffrey B. Kelly et al., *Dietrich Bonhoeffer: The Life of a Modern Martyr (Christianity Today Essentials)*, 2012

Nazi ideology gained strong influence and control over the Church. Some leaders of the German Christians began to wear brown uniforms, linking themselves to National Socialism. They promoted the Nazi Aryan Clause, which prohibited ministers who had Jewish ancestry from working for the Church. Some campaigned for the removal of the Old Testament from the Bible, because it was Jewish. Hitler was seen as the leader of Christianity, alongside Jesus.

Nazi influence and control over the Church

Bonhoeffer was ordained in 1931 and with a group of 'young reformers' tried to change what was happening to Christianity in Germany. He saw the situation as a conflict between German*ism* (the Nazi ideology about the pure Aryan race) and true Christianity – he accused the German Christians of not confessing their faith, not being true to their discipleship and the commands of God. He spoke against the Nazi persecution of Jews. A new Confessing Church was formed of those Christians who rejected the anti-Jewish rules and the Nazi influence over the German churches. Bonhoeffer's criticism of Nazism and the Nazi influence over churches brought him into conflict with the Nazi State.

Obedience, leadership and doing God's will

For Bonhoeffer the call to discipleship is a call to obedience to the leadership of Jesus and the will of God. The first disciples responded to the call not with a profession of faith, or a rational account of the theology that they believed in, but an act of obedience. Often religion is defined and described as essentially a set of beliefs, but Bonhoeffer is clear, the encounter with Jesus is:

66 … a testimony to the the absolute, direct and unaccountable authority of Jesus. There is no need for any preliminaries, and no other consequence but obedience to the call … there is no road to faith or discipleship, no other road – only obedience to the call of Jesus. 99

Dietrich Bonhoeffer, *The Cost of Discipleship*, 1959, p.48, p. 49

Religion is often presented as a question of what you need to believe. But according to Bonhoeffer, Christian discipleship is fundamentally about something you do; which leader you obey:

> 66 The disciple simply burns his boats and goes ahead. He is called out, and has to forsake his old life in order that he may 'exist' in the strictest sense of the word. The old life is left behind, and completely surrendered. The disciple is dragged out of his relative security and safety into a life of absolute insecurity. ... It is nothing else than bondage to Jesus Christ alone, completely breaking through every programme, every ideal, every set of laws. No other significance is possible, since Jesus is the only significance. Beside Jesus nothing has any significance. He alone matters. 99
>
> Dietrich Bonhoeffer, *The Cost of Discipleship*, 1959, p. 48

Bonhoeffer believed that obedience should be to the leadership of God alone

Discipleship entails the exclusive obedience to the leadership of God and all other legal ties are burnt. This is controversial as it places discipleship above the law and any human leadership, above the responsibilities of citizenship.

Bonhoeffer quotes Luke 9:57–62 where Jesus speaks of the Son of Man having no place to rest. One man who Jesus calls says he must first bury his dead father, following the legal responsibility he has, but Jesus says the the dead should be left to bury the dead. Even the law cannot stand in the way of the call of Jesus.

Doing God's will means that we cannot take on the call on our own terms, fitting it in around our life in a way that is convenient. Obedience to God entails cutting ourselves off from the previous existence. It produces a new situation, one in which the disciple walks with the Son of God. For Bonhoeffer, the road to faith passes through obedience to the call of Jesus and the severing of all earthly ties. 'Only he who believes is obedient, and only he who is obedient believes' (Bonhoeffer, *The Cost of Discipleship*, 1959, p. 54).

Bonhoeffer believes that such an act of obedience is the only real faith. God's call of a person to discipleship demands that they act in response. There is no time to think things through, or make a declaration of your belief, you simply have to act:

> 66 Every moment and every situation challenges us to action and obedience. We have literally no time to sit down and ask ourselves whether so-and-so is our neighbour or not. We must get into action and obey – we must behave like a neighbour to

Think question

'Christians who followed Bonhoeffer's ideas today would be viewed as radical, extreme and dangerous.' Do you agree?

him. But perhaps this shocks you. Perhaps you still think you ought to think out beforehand and know what you ought to do. To that there is only one answer. You can only know and think about it by actually doing it. You can only learn what obedience is by obeying. It is no use asking questions; for it is only through obedience that you come to learn the truth. "

Dietrich Bonhoeffer, *The Cost of Discipleship*, 1959, pp. 67–8

'Single-minded obedience' is what Bonhoeffer called for. Jesus called Peter to risk his life and walk on the sea. Reason, conscience, responsibility and piety are all things that stand in the way of single-minded obedience. By responding to the call into obedience faith becomes possible. Putting aside single-minded obedience (perhaps replacing it with freedom, individual preferences, choice, etc.) replaces the justification of God with self-justification. Obedience to Jesus is not something that lies in human power. Like the rich young man (Matthew 19:24–26), we may never be able to give away all of our possessions – we may be enslaved to them. It is Jesus' offer to us that makes it possible to respond, to step away from at attachments of life, and into the space where faith is possible.

" We do not walk under our self-made laws and burdens, but under the yoke of him who knows us and whole walks under the yoke with us. "

Dietrich Bonhoeffer, *The Cost of Discipleship*, 1959, p. 82

Civil disobedience

These beliefs about discipleship meant that Bonhoeffer saw duty to God as far outweighing duty to the State. In his work, *Ethics*, he wrote that there was a need to break with the Lutheran teaching that a Christian should obey the civil authority and its laws. Bonhoeffer wrote in a letter to Reinhold Niebuhr:

" Christians in Germany will face the terrible alternative of either willing the defeat of their nation in order that Christian civilization may survive, or willing the victory of their nation and thereby destroying our civilization. I know which of these alternatives I must choose; but I cannot make that choice in security. "

Dietrich Bonhoeffer, 'No Rusty Swords: Letters, Lectures and Notes, 1928–1936.' In *The Collected Works of Dietrich Bonhoeffer,* vol. 1, ed. E.H. Robertson, 1965, pp. 479–80

He also said, 'There is no standing amid the ruins of one's native town in the consciousness that at least one has not oneself incurred guilt' (Bonhoeffer, *Ethics* 2012, p. 304) – i.e. that one was just as guilty of the town's destruction for doing nothing as for being amongst those who burnt it down. Love required injustice to be actively challenged, and resisted.

Bonhoeffer was not content to accept the law of Germany's new state. He spoke out against Nazi ideas in the university where he worked and lost his job for it. He spoke against the Nazis at public lectures and was banned. He criticised the Confessing Church when it faltered under pressure from Hitler to conform. He participated in an illegal seminary. He spoke openly about praying for the defeat of his country and was adamant that Hitler was anti-Christ and 'therefore we must go on with our work and eliminate him whether he is successful or not' (Kenny *et al., Dietrich Bonhoeffer: The Life of a Modern Martyr [Christianity Today Essentials]*, 2012). It is possible that he joined the plot to assassinate Hitler in 1945.

Bonhoeffer was made a member of German military intelligence by his brother to protect him from arrest after the Gestapo had banned him from public speaking. Bonhoeffer became a double agent, using the links the new role gave him to work with the Resistance and the Allies. He passed on information to the Allies through ecumenical meetings and used information to smuggle Jews into Switzerland and to safety as supposed agents of military intelligence. It was this that led to his eventual arrest by the Gestapo.

Church as community and source of spiritual discipline

In the Sermon on the Mount, Bonhoeffer sees the requirement that the followers of Jesus must be salt and light. This is a metaphor for the presence of Christians amongst other people in the community: just as salt adds flavour to food, so Christians must act as moral people, just as a light held high lights up a whole room (Matthew 5:13–16). Here Bonhoeffer is writing about what he calls the 'visible community' of the Church which must follow in its mission and be a sign for others. Bonhoeffer is adamant that without 'salt and light', the Church is lost.

66 The followers are a visible community; their discipleship visible in action which lifts them out of the world – otherwise it would not be discipleship. And of course the following is as visible to the world as a light in the darkness or a mountain rising from a plain. 99

Dietrich Bonhoeffer, *The Cost of Discipleship*, 1959, p. 106

Apply your knowledge

'Bonhoeffer's words are radical, extreme and cultish by today's standards. Students should not be allowed to read Bonhoeffer in schools as it encourages acts against the State. Followers of Bonhoeffer should be reported to the authorities on account of their disloyalty or public rejection of the law, and their irrational obedience to their God.'

'Bonhoeffer did place loyalty to the word of God above all else, but the conflict he had with the German State came about because of the immoral rules it professed under a dictatorship. In a democracy which promotes human rights for the weak someone like Bonhoeffer could influence things without needing to take such extreme measures and he would be likely to see those human rights as an expression of Christian solidarity.'

1. Discuss these two viewpoints in relation to Bonhoeffer's thoughts. Is either account reasonable, and if so, which one and why? If not, why not?

The followers are a visible community; their discipleship visible in action which lifts them out of the world

The light should shine for all men and women. Bonhoeffer notes the Bible does not say you *have* the salt but you *are* salt. In other words, it is about the being of the disciples, not the sense that they have special information. It is about what they do that matters – good works.

> 66 It is in this light that the good works of the disciples are meant to be seen. … The good works are poverty, peregrination [making long journeys], meekness, peaceableness, and finally persecution and rejection. All these good works are a bearing of the cross of Jesus Christ. 99

Dietrich Bonhoeffer, *The Cost of Discipleship*, 1959, p. 107

Bonhoeffer's role in the Confessing Church and his religious community at Finkenwalde

> 66 We publicly declare before all evangelical Churches in Germany that what they hold in common in this Confession is grievously imperiled, and with it the unity of the German Evangelical Church. It is threatened by the teaching methods and actions of the ruling Church party of the 'German Christians' … the theological basis, in which the German Evangelical Church is united, has been continually and systematically thwarted and rendered ineffective by alien principles, on the part of the leaders and spokesmen of the 'German Christians'. … In view of the errors of the 'German Christians' of the present Reich Church government which are devastating the Church and also therefore breaking up the unity of the German Evangelical Church, we confess the following evangelical truths: … 99

From the *Theological Declaration of Barmen*, written by Karl Barth and the Confessing Church in Nazi Germany in response to Hitler's national church (www.sacred-texts.com/chr/barmen.htm)

The declaration confessed a number of evangelical truths. It asserted the centrality of Jesus Christ as the only way to God and rejected other worldly leaders, such as Hitler. It asserted Jesus' authority over the whole of a person's life and rejected the idea that another authority (National Socialism) could have authority over part of a person's life, rather than God.

The Confessing Church was the breakaway church that in 1934 rejected the Nazi ideology of Aryan supremacy, the anti-Jewish laws, and the identification of Hitler as a figure who fulfilled the Christian vision. As Hitler's power strengthened, the leaders of the Confessing Church came under increased pressure to support his plans. A key issue was the taking of the civil oath to Hitler, which was something Bonhoeffer opposed.

In 1935, the leaders of the Confessing Church asked Bonhoeffer to lead and direct a secret and illegal seminary – a place that trained new pastors. The main universities were applying the Aryan law restrictions, and by establishing an independent seminary, those restrictions could be evaded. It was funded by donations and would enable the Confessing Church to train ministers free from the Nazi ideology that was now part of the German Churches. The new seminary eventually moved to a disused private school in Finkenwalde.

The days in the seminary were a time of peace and reflection, in contrast to the political debates raging in the wider Church. They were marked by prayer, working together, Bible study and reflection. The prayer would include reading the Psalms, the prayer book of the Bible as it is called, and also the singing of black spirituals, which Bonhoeffer had heard when he spent time in America. Bonhoeffer's teaching at the seminary gave rise to his book, *The Cost of Discipleship*.

Bonhoeffer's decision to become involved in the seminary at a time of growing political unrest may seem difficult to understand. Why turn to focus on the development of ministers at such a time? The answer might be found in Luke 10:38–42, when Jesus is staying with Mary and Martha and he rebukes Martha for getting angry about Mary and the preparations of the house while Mary sits at his feet and listens, 'you are worried and upset about many things, but few things are needed – or indeed only one. Mary has chosen what is better, and it will not be taken away from her' (Luke 10:41–42). Perhaps his work in the seminary reflected Mary's decision to focus on the one thing that mattered.

The seminary was closed in 1937 by the Gestapo. Bonhoeffer described his time at the seminary as an experiment in community in a book called *Life Together* (1939), and he argued that it was essential to challenge the nationalist ideology with the experience of Christian community. The Church community and congregation must not be closed in on itself, he argued. It must be a source of renewal for all those spiritually damaged or drained and it should be a refuge for the persecuted. It is a source of spiritual discipline, offering the life of prayer and the caring service of the Church

The religious community at Finkenwalde

Bonhoeffer would frequently quote Psalm 31:8 at Synod: 'Who will speak up for those who are voiceless?'

Apply your knowledge

2. What do you think Bonhoeffer found so positive about his experience of being part of the Finkenwalde community?

3. What beliefs led Bonhoeffer to first support the Confessing Church and then to criticise it?

as a sign and expression of Christ being present in the community. This, Bonhoeffer came to see, was what it meant to live under the Word of God.

After the closure of the Finkenwalde seminary, Bonhoeffer became concerned that the Confessing Church was not prepared to voice criticism against the treatment of the Jews and the collapse of civil rights in Germany, but was preoccupied with concerns about its own situation. Bonhoeffer became bitter about the bishops' failure to stand up to the tyranny. He would frequently quote Psalm 31:8 at Synod 'Who will speak up for those who are voiceless?' and he would often ask 'Where is Abel your brother' when Synod meetings were avoiding the difficult topics of the Jews or other persecuted groups. Geoffrey Kelly says a key turning point came when Dr Friedrich Werner, state commissar for the Prussian Church, threatened to expel any pastor refusing to take Hitler's civil oath. The Synod did not stand up for the freedom of pastors but instead made the issue a matter for local leaders to decide. Bonhoeffer thought they were avoiding their responsibility as leaders and accused them of killing the spirit of free conscience (see Kelly, 'The Life and Death of a Modern Martyr.' In Kenny et al., *Dietrich Bonhoeffer: The Life of a Modern Martyr [Christianity Today Essentials]*, 2012.

The cost of discipleship

'When Christ calls a man, he bids him come and die. … Suffering then, is the badge of true discipleship' (Bonhoeffer, *The Cost of Discipleship*, 1959, p. 79, p. 80).

Cheap grace

Grace is a key theological idea meaning God's love and mercy, given freely to people, which includes the forgiveness of sins and the offer of eternal life. Grace is not offered as a reward for action – in other words it is not earned by human actions but a freely given gift. It comes from God's desire to save all sinners.

In his book *The Cost of Discipleship* (1959) Dietrich Bonhoeffer begins with a strong statement about **'cheap' grace** as opposed to **'costly' grace**.

Cheap Grace is the deadly enemy of our Church. We are fighting today for costly grace. Cheap grace means grace sold on the market like cheapjack's wares.

66 Cheap Grace is the deadly enemy of our Church. We are fighting today for costly grace. Cheap grace means grace sold on the market like cheapjack's wares. The sacraments, the forgiveness of sin, and the consolations of religion are thrown away at cut prices. Grace is represented as the Church's inexhaustible treasury, from which she showers blessings with generous hands, without asking questions or fixing limits. Grace without price; grace without cost … the account has been paid in advance; and because it has been paid, everything can be had for nothing. 99

Dietrich Bonhoeffer, *The Cost of Discipleship*, 1959, p. 35

This is a powerful and troubling opening remark. It attacks churches that do not place any expectations that people should struggle to be a good Christians. It criticises the idea that Christian living is an easy, comfortable experience, full of rewards without any effort, struggle or price.

This is troubling because of an idea within Christianity that Jesus Christ has saved everyone from their sins and death. Bonhoeffer is concerned that people think because Christ paid the price for grace, the Church can keep on giving it out for free – making the good news a happy message that everything is going to be all right and you can carry on doing what you were doing before without bothering to make any changes. God loves everyone so much that they do not even have to notice him. Bonhoeffer writes 'the world finds a cheap covering for its sins; no contrition is required, still less any real desire to be delivered from sin' (*The Cost of Discipleship*, 1959, p. 35). You can preach forgiveness without requiring repentance, offer baptism with no expectation of living a disciplined life, offer communion without requiring a person to make a confession. Grace is offered without discipleship or the cross. For Bonhoeffer ultimately this means without Jesus, because part of being a Christian means 'picking up your cross' just as Jesus did. It seems as though Bonhoeffer thought the knowledge of being forgiven could mislead people into thinking they did not have to make any changes to their lives.

What is wrong with such a generous and loving message? Bonhoeffer is clear that this is an unpicking of the heart of Christianity. 'Cheap grace therefore amounts to a denial of the living Word of God, in fact, a denial of the Incarnation of the Word of God' (*The Cost of Discipleship*, 1959, p. 35) Cheap grace is effectively a lie, it is not the grace of God but a self-congratulating grace we give ourselves. Easy Christianity, or Christianity-lite, is actually no Christianity at all. If cheap grace is a deception, is there another kind of grace?

Costly grace

Bonhoeffer's answer is costly grace. Costly grace is the grace that is the 'treasure hidden in a field' that a person would gladly sell everything to obtain (Matthew 13:44). In other words, it is something that is worth sacrificing everything for to get. It is the kingly rule of Christ 'for whose sake a man will pluck out the eye which causes him to stumble, it is the call of Jesus Christ at which the disciple leaves his nets and follows him' (*The Cost of Discipleship*, 1959, p. 36; see also Mark 9:47 and Matthew 4:19–20). In other words, the rule of Christ does mean taking seriously his commands and treating him as a King or Lord. Grace is costly because it calls us to follow Jesus and that means making changes to our lives and our decisions.

> **Think question**
>
> a. Has religion become too easy?

> **Think question**
>
> b. Is there anything wrong with liberating people from the worry that their sins may condemn them?

Costly grace binds people to the yoke of Christ, it places an expectation on people that they live a certain way, it requires people to acknowledge who Christ is

> " It is costly because it costs a man his life, and it is grace because it gives a man the only true life. It is costly because it condemns sin, and grace because because it justifies the sinner. Above all it is costly because it costs God the life of his Son. … Above all it is grace because God did not reckon his Son too dear a price to pay for our life, but delivered him up for us. Costly grace is the Incarnation of God. "

Dietrich Bonhoeffer, *The Cost of Discipleship*, 1959, p. 37

Bonhoeffer is worried that the Church has become secularised and has lost this sense of costly grace. Perhaps there has been a pressure to take on the values of the modern world, the priorities and principles of modern life. The early Church became integrated into the Roman empire and the business of government. The monastic movement, where the religious lived apart from ordinary life, created a sense in which a select few, the saints, had to be disciples, whilst the many did not need to follow that way. Bonhoeffer thought Luther had seen this and sought to take up the costly grace:

> " Luther did not hear the word: 'Of course you have sinned, but now everything is forgiven, so you can stay as you are and enjoy the consolations of forgiveness.' No. Luther had to leave the cloister and go back to the world, not because the world in itself was good and holy, but because even the cloister was only part of the world. "

Dietrich Bonhoeffer, *The Cost of Discipleship*, 1959, p. 40

Luther proclaimed that grace alone is needed for salvation but Bonhoeffer thought some have misinterpreted this as meaning the commands of Jesus can be disobeyed. Receiving grace means you become subject to absolute obedience to God. Bonhoeffer was concerned that his Lutheran Church in Germany had made the mistakes he spoke of. He thought the result was a nation that had become Christian and Lutheran, but at a cost of true discipleship. For Bonhoeffer, the consequence of this is terrible, amounting to, in his words, millions of spiritual corpses.

Apply your knowledge

4. Consider the following statements:

   a. I believe the Church should adapt to the modern world and update its moral messages to make them more relevant to people living today.

   b. I believe that the Church should be a challenge to modern ways of life which seem to reject the commands of Jesus Christ.

   What examples might each view-holder use to illustrate their argument (consider attitudes to euthanasia, sexual issues, diverse lifestyles, etc.)?

Sacrifice, suffering and the cross

The fourth chapter of *The Cost of Discipleship*, begins with Mark 8:31–38, the account of the suffering of the Son of Man, and these famous words about Christian discipleship:

The disciple is a disciple only in so far as he shares Jesus' suffering and rejection and crucifixion.

> 66 Whoever wants to be my disciple must deny themselves and take up their cross and follow me. For whoever wants to save their life will lose it, but whoever loses their life for me and for the gospel will save it. 99
>
> Mark 8:34–35, New International Version

Bonhoeffer says the call to discipleship is clearly linked to the **passion** of the death of Jesus, his suffering and rejection – death without honour, without the admiration and sympathy of the world. 'To die on the cross means to die despised and rejected of men' (Bonhoeffer, *The Cost of Discipleship*, 1959, p. 76). For disciples to try to resist this is to be tempted by the words of Satan: 'Get behind me, Satan! …You do not have in mind the concerns of God, but merely human concerns' (Mark 8:33, New International Version). Suffering and sacrifice are inherent to discipleship for anyone who follows Jesus because they must pick up his cross and follow the path of suffering that Jesus walks.

> 66 Jesus must therefore make it clear beyond all doubt that the 'must' of suffering applies to his disciples no less than to himself. Jesus as Christ is Christ only in virtue of his suffering and rejection, as the disciple is a disciple only in so far as he shares his Lord's suffering and rejection and crucifixion. Discipleship means adherence to the person of Jesus and therefore submission to the law of Christ which is the law of the cross. 99
>
> Dietrich Bonhoeffer, *The Cost of Discipleship*, 1959, p. 77

Think question

Many Christians emphasise that the Good News of the Gospel should be a joyful and happy message – why might Bonhoeffer think they are not quite right?

To Bonhoeffer discipleship and costly grace entails self-denial and endurance of the cross. However, this is not some terrible tragedy. In his thinking, allegiance to Jesus Christ involves suffering not like the suffering of human life in general terms, the pains of life which all people face (loss, illness, disappointment, etc.), but a specific suffering that is essential to Christian life. It is suffering and rejection, and rejection not for a cause that we may have, but rejection for the sake of Christ. If Christian life looks no different from ordinary life, because *being Christian* has simply become a phrase for being normal, or being British (or in Bonhoeffer's case, German or Lutheran) then it is not truly Christian. The life of a Christian is a life of suffering for Christ.

Apply your knowledge

5. 'The Church should be a joyful place because Jesus has saved us from sin and death.' Discuss this view from the perspective of Bonhoeffer.

6. Discuss the following examples of Christians who experience suffering in the light of Bonhoeffer's thinking on suffering, sacrifice and the cross. What issues do they raise?

   a. The man who has converted to Christianity and is executed by a government which sees conversion as a crime punishable by death.

   b. The woman who endures the violent behaviour of her husband because of her belief in the Christian sanctity and permanence of marriage.

   c. The successful businessman who abandons his work, becomes a missionary and dies of an illness within a year of his arrival with little obvious sign of having made any impact at all.

> The cross is laid on every Christian. The first Christ-suffering which every man must experience is the call to abandon the attachments of this world. It is that dying of the old man [the person's old self] which is the result of his encounter with Christ. As we embark upon discipleship we surrender ourselves to Christ in union with his death – we give over our lives to death. Thus it begins; the cross is not the terrible end to an otherwise god-fearing and happy life, but it meets us at the beginning of our communion with Christ. When Christ calls a man, he bids him come and die. … In fact every command of Jesus is a call to die, with all our affections and lusts.

Dietrich Bonhoeffer, *The Cost of Discipleship*, 1959, p. 79

The burden of Christian life also involves temptation and the burden of forgiving others, which is a kind of bearing of the burden of the sins of others, rather than seeking out revenge for acts done against them. This is the kind of cross that Jesus refers to and bearing it is the only way of triumphing over the suffering. Jesus prays in the Garden of Gethsemane 'let this cup pass me by' but the way in which he leaves suffering behind is by drinking the cup. This is the path to victory. Through the fellowship of Jesus' suffering the way is open to come into communion with God.

> Suffering has to be endured in order that it may pass away. … Under his yoke we are certain of his nearness and communion. It is he whom the disciple finds as he lifts up his cross.

Dietrich Bonhoeffer, *The Cost of Discipleship*, 1959, p. 81, p. 82

Solidarity

Bonhoeffer's thoughts around suffering are linked to the idea of **solidarity** of 'existence for others'. In one of his letters from prison he said:

> We have for once learned to see the great events of history from below, from the perspective of the outcast, the suspects, the maltreated, the powerless, the oppressed, the reviled – in short, from the perspective of those who suffer.

Bonhoeffer, *Letters and Papers From Prison, Dietrich Bonhoeffer Works, Vol 8*, 2010 ed. J.W. DeGruchy, p. 52

Bonhoeffer felt he had to live through the experience of suffering that his people were enduring, rather than waiting in safety and security. He could have stayed away from Germany but chose to return and accept the risk. In prison he reflected on his own suffering and the suffering of Jesus Christ. Bonhoeffer saw Christ as a man for others. For Bonhoeffer, we encounter the transcendental God in the middle of life when we are there for our neighbours, when we are within reach of their situation. Being there for others is what makes a Christian. The purpose of Christian life is not to be 'religious' but rather to be in a relationship with God through living an existence for others. In a letter to his friend Eberhard Bethge, he wrote:

> 66 Our relation to God is not a 'religious' relationship to the highest, most powerful, and best Being imaginable – that is not authentic transcendence – but our relation to God is a new life in 'existence for others,' through participation in the being of Jesus. 99

Bonhoeffer, *Dietrich Bonhoeffer: Letters and Papers From Prison*, ed. E. Bethge, 1971, p. 381

The goal of the Christian life is not to become 'religious' but to be there for others. Being there with others is an experience of transcendence. As he became available to humanity, Jesus' transcendence was found in his 'existence for others'. Christian faith and Christian discipleship is participation with this 'existence for others' and this is what the Christian Church should do. Geoffrey B. Kelly (*The Cambridge Companion to Dietrich Bonhoeffer*, 1999, pp. 246–68) argues that this is not a glib answer, explanation or reason for suffering. God makes a bond of suffering with humanity, such as the suffering caused by the monstrous acts of dictators of the twentieth century, like Hitler.

For Bonhoeffer, this conviction of being with and for others led him to the decision, only 21 days after arriving in America (and safety), to return to Berlin. He was determined to share in the time of suffering with the German people. That sharing of suffering included his decision to get involved with the Resistance. Some see it as a shift from his work in matters of the Church and religion, towards social action. David H. Jensen, in his article, 'Religionless Christianity and Vulnerable Discipleship: The Interfaith Promise of Bonhoeffer's Theology' (*Journal of Ecumenical Studies* 38, no. 3, 2001, pp. 151–67), explores the idea that solidarity, for Bonhoeffer, became a subversive act. It was against the State and for the sake of human relationships with each other (the thing that the Nazi State was damaging). It would fit with the idea that Christians were called to live responsibly in the world, and that in a sense, Christianity should be religionless and the Church should be interpreted into a language that was meaningful for people.

The goal of the Christian life is not to become 'religious' but to be there for others

'In the resistance against dictatorship and terror their lives have been given for freedom and human rights'

Discussing the work and life of Bonhoeffer and Christian moral action

Does Bonhoeffer put too much emphasis on suffering?

Bonhoeffer lived at a time of very great suffering and danger, when extreme ideologies led countries in Europe and it could be argued that his experience of suffering in Nazi Germany influenced his writing so much that it led to an overemphasis on suffering as a concept of discipleship. Not all Christian communities experience such times. Perhaps it is not possible to live a Christian life according to Bonhoeffer's ideas in times of peace and justice, or maybe there is always a need for such a struggle. Arguably Bonhoeffer's notion of discipleship and Church depends upon the existence of injustice and the suffering this causes. How else could discipleship be shown?

Nevertheless, all experience suffering in their life, be it the result of injustice, illness, betrayal or bereavement. Bonhoeffer's message does not only dwell on suffering but solidarity, being with those who experience the most suffering, and those who receive the company of friendship at difficult times may find this a consolation and a relief.

Some may argue his thinking might seem to downplay the joy and hope of the message of the Resurrection – the Good News. Jesus' Passion includes suffering, but reaches beyond it. Perhaps Bonhoeffer's thinking is too closely 'stuck' to the cross, rather than the empty tomb and the hope of Resurrection and the defeat of sin and death. Bonhoeffer would argue you have to pass through the cross, and the real danger he wrote about was in trying to avoid that passage altogether, as to avoid the sacrifice and the suffering would mean to fail to follow the call of Jesus.

Should Christians practise civil disobedience?

Paul's letter to the Romans includes a passage about submission to governing authorities. Paul writes, 'Let everyone be subject to the governing authorities, for there is no authority except that which God has established. The authorities that exist have been established by God. Consequently, whoever rebels against the authority is rebelling against what God has instituted, and those who do so will bring judgment on themselves (Romans 13:1–2).

A plain reading of this text suggests that Christians should not challenge authority. But Bonhoeffer did. Was Bonhoeffer being unchristian given Paul's writing on the matter? One question to ask is whether this injunction of St Paul is a message that has universal significance for all time, or was only of significance in terms of the early Christian community in Rome, and the civil authority of Rome?

Bonhoeffer advocated opposition to the Nazi State. He actively sought to evade the State's attempts to silence him. He was involved in an illegal seminary. He became involved in activities which sought to undermine the Nazi Government through working with the Allies and the Resistance. Should a Christian take from this that civil disobedience is acceptable? The Bible contains different messages about civil disobedience. The prophets often spoke out against rulers who they said were failing in their responsibilities to the people. The New Testament is more complex. Jesus does not openly challenge the rule of Pontius Pilate and he does not encourage people to refuse to pay taxes (Mark 12:17), but he often spoke out against the status quo in society and challenged local religious authorities.

Arguably, Bonhoeffer justifies civil disobedience because of his emphasis on obedience to God, over everything else. But in an age of terrorism and extremism this feels like a dangerous idea. How would we view those who choose to disobey the British Government because its laws go against the holy law of their religion? Should we support those Christians who disobey the law in their actions against abortion?

Bonhoeffer's civil disobedience was in the context of a totalitarian state, where democracy had ended and where the laws were rapidly becoming increasingly oppressive of many groups of civilians, including Jews, Roma Gypsies, the disabled, lesbians and gays, Jehovah's Witnesses, as well as the Nazis' political opponents. Bonhoeffer's ethics are ethics of action but in a democracy his speech and public teaching roles would have been opportunities to argue for change and his commitment to shared living is clear from the seminary he led. For Bonhoeffer, civil disobedience became a necessity because of the extreme injustice of the State, which utterly undermined the moral teachings of Christianity with devastating effects for German society. Perhaps whether civil disobedience is justified or not should be linked to the nature of the civic authorities and what they are doing.

Apply your knowledge

11. Should Christians get involved in civil disobedience? What might be Bonhoeffer's response to the following situations?

    a. A government legalises euthanasia. A group meet to start to plan to disrupt the process by targeting doctors undertaking the work. They plan to send threatening letters, throw bricks through windows and try to stop the doctors at the doors of the hospital. What might Bonhoeffer's advice be to Christians approached to join the group? What would be the right thing for a Christian to do?

    b. A government launches an all out war against a country to remove a dictator. There is strong opposition to the war among the population and a group decide to start organising violent demonstrations. What might Bonhoeffer's advice be to Christians approached to join the group? What would be the right thing for a Christian to do?

    c. A government decides to sell some warplanes to another government who is suspected of involvement in oppressing people in a third country and using its military to do so. A group decides to plan to break into the base to cause some damage to the planes so they cannot be sold. What might Bonhoeffer's advice be to Christians approached to join the group? What would be the right thing for a Christian to do?

    d. A government puts up taxes to fund a new nuclear weapon system. Taxes are compulsory, but a group of Christians are planning to stop paying their taxes. What might Bonhoeffer's advice be? Would you agree?

Apply your knowledge

12. What might have led Bonhoeffer to change from focusing on his work for the Church to direct social and political action for people suffering the oppression of the Nazis?

13. Why might an individual Christian hearing a call to 'direct action' be viewed as controversial? Consider the following:

    a. The nature of the 'direct action'.

    b. What difference it makes if the Church in general is supporting the action or opposing it.

    c. Whether the individual Christian is a trained minster or not.

Is it possible always to know God's will?

Bonhoeffer placed great importance on obedience to God's commands even to the extent of being prepared to go against legal authorities. His book, *The Cost of Discipleship* (1959), includes many interpretations of passages from the Bible. However, his interpretations might not be the only reasonable interpretations. His account of God's will might be mistaken in some places. Perhaps it is not so clear how God wants us to act in a given situation. If we find it difficult to interpret God's will then how can we act confidently in the way Bonhoeffer thought true disciples should?

Bonhoeffer could be seen as dangerously encouraging individuals with distorted views of God's will. Arguably, his becoming involved in an assassination attempt might encourage acts of violence. This could be a consequence of uncertainty about the will of God. (It is not certain, but some claim Bonhoeffer was involved in the attempt to kill Hitler. He was arrested in relation to the attempt and executed, but so were many people who had nothing to do with it.)

However, Bonhoeffer advocated a life in community, based on shared reflection and readings of scripture. This was the approach taken in the seminary he led. This shared experience of common life and living and working together with the Bible should provide a good basis for really understanding all of the Bible, not just the parts we might want to read (Bonhoeffer insisted on his students reading through the Psalms in order, so that they would be confronted by each psalm in turn, rather than simply picking and choosing the bits they thought meaningful or relevant to them). A common life together could reduce any risk of a peculiar or distorted meaning.

In fact, most Christians today would have strong sympathy with Bonhoeffer's account of what was wrong with the German Christian movement and also the Confessing Church towards the later period as it kowtowed to Hitler. We may not know the will of God, but from the perspective of the present, Bonhoeffer's judgement about true Christianity seems more accurate than the kind of Christianity advocated by the German Christians.

Bonhoeffer spent part of his life as a parish priest and worked to train new ministers at the seminary. The latter part of his life involved direct social and political action for people suffering the oppression of the Nazi Government. These two different kinds of activity suggest at some point he felt called to change his work.

Is Bonhoeffer's theology relevant for today?

Many aspects of Bonhoeffer theology could be seen as relevant for today. First it is arguable that in Western societies there is an obsession with material benefit and self-interest which, in countries like the UK, is held alongside a deep sense of unhappiness. Bonhoeffer's powerful challenge to abandon self-interest and the trappings of an easy life might lead people to a more meaningful life. Second, there are many examples of people who are suffering in the world and Bonhoeffer's message of solidarity with the poor, the lonely, the unjustly dealt with and so on, seems relevant. Bonhoeffer seems to have suggested something that runs counter to the ideology of capitalism and consumerism.

There are many pressures on Christianity to modernise, to adapt to be more inclusive and adopt the values of the modern age, perhaps updating some of the moral messages. Bonhoeffer's ideas seem to run counter to this because of the key idea in his thinking that it is God's commands that should be followed, not the trends of the day.

Bonhoeffer's account of obedience to God also raises difficult questions at a time when religion is seen as a threat to countries and when state loyalty and national values are sought to be encouraged. Bonhoeffer would be sceptical of the idea that national values are Christian values, particularly in the light of his experience of National Socialism, where a state took control of a church. His words on setting aside the local law and being obedient to God's law could cause difficulties.

However, there is a great debate about the extent to which the world is becoming divided, with the super rich at one end of the divide and the very poor at the other. There seem to be many who are oppressed or held with suspicion, cast out from mainstream society. Bonhoeffer's message of solidarity seems relevant for Christians and all those who seek to work for the poor in the world.

Apply your knowledge

There are many issues which might benefit from Bonhoeffer's thinking. Look at the following starter suggestions and try to develop a few sentences for each to explore the possible relevance. You may need to do some research on the issues mentioned to help give enough detail to show how to apply Bonhoeffer's thinking. Look back at this chapter for the sections that dealt with those aspects of Bonhoeffer's thinking to be sure you understand them.

14. Try to link together Bonhoeffer's idea that Jesus is *for* the other and link it to issues such as:

    a. Migrants fleeing war and being stopped at Europe's borders or sent back.

    b. Poorly treated factory workers in developing countries.

    c. Victims of sexual abuse and domestic violence.

15. Try to link Bonhoeffer's idea that we need costly grace with the issue of religious freedom. Christians in countries such as the UK and the US benefit from the protection of religious freedom, but Christians in some other countries are oppressed for expressing their Christian faith.

Learning support

Points to remember

» Bonhoeffer lived at a time when the Nazi State was oppressing many groups in society and when German Christians had adopted many features of the National Socialist ideology. Bonhoeffer rejected this idea of the Church.

» Bonhoeffer called for obedience to God, not the State. This was what discipleship meant. No other ideology can be adhered to. No other authority should be followed and this could result in disobeying the State, resisting its attempt to control the Church and even working with those who sought to bring the State down, and challenging Christians who worked with the State.

» Bonhoeffer saw the Church as the salt and light for the community, and as a spiritual nourishment, for a people at a time of totalitarian ideology. He led an illegal seminary, forming a Christian community based on fellowship, Bible study and prayer.

» The true cost of discipleship was in rejecting the cheap grace which was to accept the living redemption message, without realising this required obedience to God and a change of heart. Costly grace means giving up other comforts and obeying God's call with actions.

» Bonhoeffer saw suffering, sacrifice and the cross as inevitable. Being a disciple meant bearing the cross with Jesus and this means being for and being with those who are oppressed. It is not about being religious, but being for others.

Enhance your learning

» Dietrich Bonhoeffer's book, *The Cost of Discipleship* (1959), is quite readable. It outlines in direct terms his thinking. Chapter 1 explores costly grace, Chapter 3 explores obedience and Chapters 7 and 30 explore the roles of the community of the Church. He begins his chapters with an extract from the New Testament and then follows with a discussion.

» To go further into Bonhoeffer's thought, read Part 2 of *The Cost of Discipleship*, which explores many moral questions through a study of the Sermon on the Mount.

» Martin Doblmeier's dramatised documentary, *Bonhoeffer* (2003), is a study of the life and works of Bonhoeffer.

Practice for exams

AS questions and A level questions look identical; the difference between AS and A level assessment is seen in the different proportions of marks awarded for two different skills: the skill of demonstrating knowledge and understanding (Assessment Objective 1, or AO1), and the skill of constructing a critical argument (AO2).

At AS, half the marks (15 marks) are available for knowledge and understanding, and the other half (15 marks) for the quality of your analytical and evaluative argument. You should aim to use your knowledge in order to support the argument you are making throughout the essay, rather than presenting descriptive knowledge in the first half and then an opinion in the second.

At A level, your demonstration of knowledge and understanding is awarded a maximum of 16 marks, and your analytic and evaluative skills are awarded a maximum of 24 marks. You should aim to concentrate on constructing a lucid argument, making use of your knowledge to add weight to the conclusions you draw.

'Using the will of God as a guide for moral behaviour is impractical, as in most circumstances it is impossible to know what God wants us to do.' Discuss.

This question invites critical consideration of the idea of using the will of God to guide moral action. The question suggests that this cannot work in practice because of the difficulties of working out what God wants.

Practise your skills for AS level

If you are answering this question for AS level, you could demonstrate knowledge and understanding by explaining how Christians seek to follow the will of God, for example through following church teaching, the Bible, prayer and the conscience. You should consider whether attempts to follow the will of God are impractical or whether the statement in the question is unfair.

Practise your skills for A level

If you are answering this question for A level, you need to consider whether the claim is fair, looking at possible Christian responses, such as that the will of God can be found through prayer, in the Bible and in the teachings of the Church, and assessing whether these give sufficient guidance for people to know what to do in their personal circumstances. Aim to decide what you plan to argue before you start, rather than as you write, so that you can structure your essay in a way that is most persuasive.

To what extent, if at all, does the theology of Bonhoeffer have relevance for Christians today?

For this essay, you need to be able to demonstrate a good knowledge and understanding of the key features of Bonhoeffer's theology, and the context within which he was writing. Where the question refers to 'Christians today', remember that not all Christians today live in your own country and social context.

Practise your skills for AS level

If you are answering this question for AS level, you should explain the key elements of Bonhoeffer's theology as well as the context within which he was writing, in order to show your skills in knowledge and understanding. You should also think about whether his ideas address issues that were distinctive of his era or whether they also could be significant for Christians today.

Practise your skills for A level

If you are answering this question for A level, it is particularly important that you do not spend all of your essay simply describing Bonhoeffer's thinking, but also consider whether his ideas about the Christian life can be useful for Christians in the twenty-first century or whether they are very specific to Bonhoeffer's own social context. You might want to argue that some aspects of his thought are more relevant to the present day than others. Aim to have a line of argument throughout your essay rather than just turning to evaluation as your essay draws to a close.

Glossary

act utilitarian: weighs up what to do at each individual occasion

active euthanasia: a deliberate action performed by a third party to kill a person, for example by lethal injection. Active euthanasia is illegal in the UK

aetion: an explanatory factor, a reason or cause for something

agape love: unconditional love, the only ethical norm in situationism

analogy: a comparison between one thing and another in an attempt to clarify meaning

Antinomian ethics: antinomian ethics do not recognise the role of law in morality ('nomos' is Greek for 'law')

a posteriori arguments: arguments which draw conclusions based on observation through experience

a priori arguments: arguments which draw conclusions through the use of reason

autonomy and the right to die: the idea that human freedom should extend to decide the time and manner of death

beatific vision: a face-to-face encounter with God

Bible/Scripture: the collection or canon of books in the Bible which contain the revelation of God

capitalism: an economic system based on the private ownership of how things are made and sold, in which businesses compete freely with each other to make profits

caritas: 'generous love', a love of others and of the virtues; the Latin equivalent of the Greek word agape

categorical imperative: an unconditional moral obligation that is always binding irrespective of a person's inclination or purpose

category error: a problem of language that arises when things are talked about as if they belong to one category when in fact they belong to another

cheap grace: grace that is offered freely, but is received without any change in the recipient, and ultimately is false as it does not save

Church tradition: the traditions of how Christian life in community works, in worship, practical moral life and prayer, and the teaching and reflection of the Church handed down across time

concordia: human friendship

concupiscience: uncontrollable desire for physical pleasures and material things

conscience: the term 'conscience' may variously be used to refer to a faculty within us, a process of moral reasoning, insights from God or it may be understood in psychological terms. Fletcher described it as function rather than a faculty

consciousness: awareness or perception

consequentialism: ethical theories that see morality as driven by the consequences, rather than actions or character of those concerned

consumerism: a set of social beliefs that put a high value on acquiring material things

contingent: depending on other things

conversion experience: an experience which produces a radical change in someone's belief system

corporate religious experience: religious experiences which happen to a group of people 'as a body'

corporate social responsibility: a sense that businesses have wider responsibilities than simply to their shareholders, including the communities they live and work in and to the environment

cosmological: to do with the universe

costly grace: grace followed by obedience to God's command and discipleship

cupiditas: 'selfish love', a love of worldly things and of selfish desires

deontological: from the Latin for 'duty', ethics focused on the intrinsic rightness and wrongness of actions

dignity: the worth or quality of life, which can be linked to sanctity or freedom

discipleship: following the life, example and teaching of Jesus

disembodied existence: existing without a physical body

dualism: the belief that reality can be divided into two distinct parts, such as good and evil, or physical and non-physical

duty: duties are created by the moral law, to follow it is our duty. The word deontological means duty-based

ecclesia: heavenly society, in contrast with earthly society

election (in a theological sense): predestination, chosen by God for heaven or hell

empiricism: a way of knowing that depends on the five senses

empiricist: someone who thinks that the primary source of knowledge is experience gained through the five senses

epistemic distance: a distance in knowledge and understanding

eudaimonia: living well, as an ultimate end in life which all other actions should lead towards

extrinsically good: good defined with reference to the end rather than good in and of itself. Fletcher argued only love was intrinsically good

faith: voluntary commitment to a belief without the need for complete evidence to support it

The Fall: the biblical event in which Adam and Eve disobeyed God's command and ate the fruit from the forbidden tree in the Garden of Eden; also used to refer to the imperfect state of humanity

forms: a name Plato gave to ideal concepts

free will: the ability to make independent choices between real options

good will: a person of good will is a person who makes decisions according to the moral law

globalisation: the integration of economies, industries, markets, cultures and policymaking around the world

grace: in theological terms, God's free and undeserved love for humanity, epitomised in the sacrifice of Jesus on the cross

grace of God: God's unconditional and undeserved gifts

hedonic calculus: the system for calculating the amount of pain or pleasure generated

hedonistic: pleasure-driven

Homoousios: of the same substance or of the same being

hypostatic union: the belief that Christ is both fully God and fully human, indivisible, two natures united in one person

hypothetical imperative: a moral obligation that applies only if one desires the implied goal

immediate revelation: where someone is given direct knowledge of God

incarnation: God born as a human being, in Jesus Christ

inconsistent triad: the omnibenevolence and omnipotence of God, and the existence of evil in the world, are said to be mutually incompatible

involuntary euthanasia: where a person is killed against their wishes, for example when disabled people were killed by Nazi doctors

justice: justice ordinarily refers to notions of fair distribution of benefits for all. Fletcher specifically sees justice as a kind of tough love; love applied to the world

kingdom of ends: an imagined future in which all people act in accordance to the moral law, the categorical imperative

legalistic ethics: law-based moral decision-making

liberator: a general term for someone who frees a people or group

limited election: the view that God chooses only a small number of people for heaven

logical fallacy: reasoning that has a flaw in its structure

materialism: the belief that only physical matter exists, and that the mind can be explained in physical terms as chemical activity in the brain

maxims: another word for moral rules, determined by reason

mediate revelation: where someone gains knowledge of God in a secondary, non-direct way

Messiah: in Christianity the word is associated with Jesus Christ, who is believed to be the Son of God and the Saviour. In Judaism the word is associated with individuals who rose up against oppression, the people of Israel

moral evil: the evil done and the suffering caused by deliberate misuse of human free will

moral law: binding moral obligations

mystical experience: experiences of God or of the supernatural which go beyond everyday sense experience

natural evil: evil and suffering caused by non-human agencies

natural law: a deontological theory based on behaviour that accords with given laws or moral rules (e.g. given by God) that exist independently of human societies and systems

natural theology: drawing conclusions about the nature and activity of God by using reason and observing the world

naturalistic explanation: an explanation referring to natural rather than supernatural causes

necessary existence: existence which does not depend on anything else

neoplatonism: philosophical thinking arising from the ideas of Plato

neurophysiology: an area of science which studies the brain and the nervous system

non-voluntary euthanasia: this applies when a person is unable to express their wish to die but there are reasonable grounds for ending their life painlessly, for example if a person cannot communicate but is in extreme pain

Non Treatment Decision: the decision medical professionals make to withhold or withdraw medical treatment or life support that is keeping a person alive because they are not going to get better, or because the person asks them to. Controversially it is also sometimes called passive euthanasia

numinous experience: an indescribable experience which invokes feelings of awe, worship and fascination

omnibenevolent: all-good and all-loving

omnipotent: all-powerful

omniscient: all-knowing

ontological: to do with the nature of existence

Original Sin: a state of wrongdoing in which people are born (according to some Christians) because of the sin of Adam and Eve

palliative care: end-of-life care to make the person's remaining moments of life as comfortable as possible

parable: a story told to highlight a moral message

Parousia: used in Christianity to refer to the Second Coming of Christ

particular judgement: judgement for each person at the point of death

Passion: Jesus' sufferings at the end of his life

personalism: ethics centred on people, rather than laws or objects

personhood: the quality of human life that makes it worthy – usually linked to certain higher capacities

positivism: proposes something as true or good without demonstrating it. Fletcher posits love as good

practical reason: the tool which makes moral decisions

pragmatism: acting, in moral situations, in a way that is practical, rather than purely ideologically

predicate: a term which describes a distinctive characteristic of something

primary precepts: the most important rules in life: to protect life, to reproduce, to live in community, to teach the young and to believe in God

Glossary

Prime Mover: Aristotle's concept of the ultimate cause of movement and change in the universe

principle of credulity: Swinburne's principle that we should usually believe what our senses tell us we are perceiving

Principle of Sufficient Reason: the principle that everything must have a reason to explain it

principle of testimony: Swinburne's principle that we should usually trust that other people are telling us the truth

principle of utility/greatest happiness: the idea that the choice that brings about the greatest good for the greatest number is the right choice

privatio boni: a phrase used by Augustine to mean an absence of goodness

Protestantism: a form of Christianity which rejects the authority of the Catholic Church and places greater emphasis on the Bible and on personal faith

Purgatory: a place where people go, temporarily, after death to be cleansed of sin before they are fit to live with God

qualitative: focused on quality (what kind of thing)

quality of life: a way of weighing the extrinsic experience of life, that affects or justifies whether or not it is worth continuing life

quantitative: focused on quantity (how many, how big, etc.)

rabbi: a Jewish teacher, often associated with having followers

rationalist: someone who thinks that the primary source of knowledge is reason

reason: using logical steps and thought processes in order to reach conclusions

redeemed: in theological terms, 'saved' from sin by the sacrifice of Christ

redemption: the action of saving or being saved from sin, error, or evil

reductive materialism: otherwise known as identity theory – the view that mental events are identical with physical occurrences in the brain

relativism: the rejection of absolute moral standards, such as laws or rights. Good and bad are relative to an individual or a community or, in Fletcher's case, to love

resurrection: living on after death in a glorified physical form in a new realm

revelation: 'uncovering'. In theological terms, this is when God chooses to let himself be known

rule utilitarian: weighs up what to in principle in all occasions of a certain kind

Sacred Tradition: the idea that the revelation of Jesus Christ is communicated in two ways. In addition to Scripture, it is communicated through the apostolic and authoritative teaching of Church councils and the Pope

sanctity of life: the idea that life is intrinsically sacred or has such worth that it is not considered within the power of a human being

sceptic: someone who will not accept what others say without questioning and challenging

scepticism: a questioning approach which does not take assumptions for granted

secondary precepts: the laws which follow from primary precepts

shareholder: a person who has invested money in a business in return for a share of the profits

sin: disobeying the will and commands of God

situational ethics: another term for situation ethics, ethics focused on the situation, rather than fixed rules

Socratic method: the method of philosophical reasoning which involves critical questioning

solidarity: an altruistic commitment to stand alongside and be with those less fortunate, the oppressed, those who suffer

Son of God: a term for Jesus that emphasises he is God incarnate, one of the three persons of the Trinity

soul: often, but not always, understood to be the non-physical essence of a person

stakeholder: a person who is affected by or involved in some form of relationship with a business

substance: a subject which has different properties attributed to it

substance dualism: the belief that the mind and the body both exist as two distinct and separate realities

summum bonum: the highest, most supreme good

synderesis: to follow the good and avoid the evil, the rule which all precepts follow

teleological: looking to the end results (telos) in order to draw a conclusion about what is right or wrong

teleological ethics: moral goodness is determined by the end or result

telos: the end, or purpose, of something

theist: someone who believes in a God or gods

theodicy: an attempt to justify God in the face of evil in the world

transcendent: being beyond this world and outside the realms of ordinary experience

universalism: the view that all people will be saved

unlimited election: the view that all people are called to salvation but only a few will be saved

voluntary euthanasia: this applies when a person's life is ended painlessly at their own request

whistle-blowing: when an employee discloses wrongdoing to the employer or the public

will: the part of human nature that makes free choices

wisdom literature: a genre of writing from the ancient world, teaching about wisdom and virtue. In the Bible, books such as Proverbs and Job are classified as wisdom literature

Word: from the Greek logos, another name for the second person of the Trinity, used at the beginning of John's Gospel to describe the incarnation which existed from the beginning, of one substance with and equal to God the Father

zealot: a member of the Jewish political/military movement that fought against Rome in the first century AD

Index